Native American Art at Dartmouth

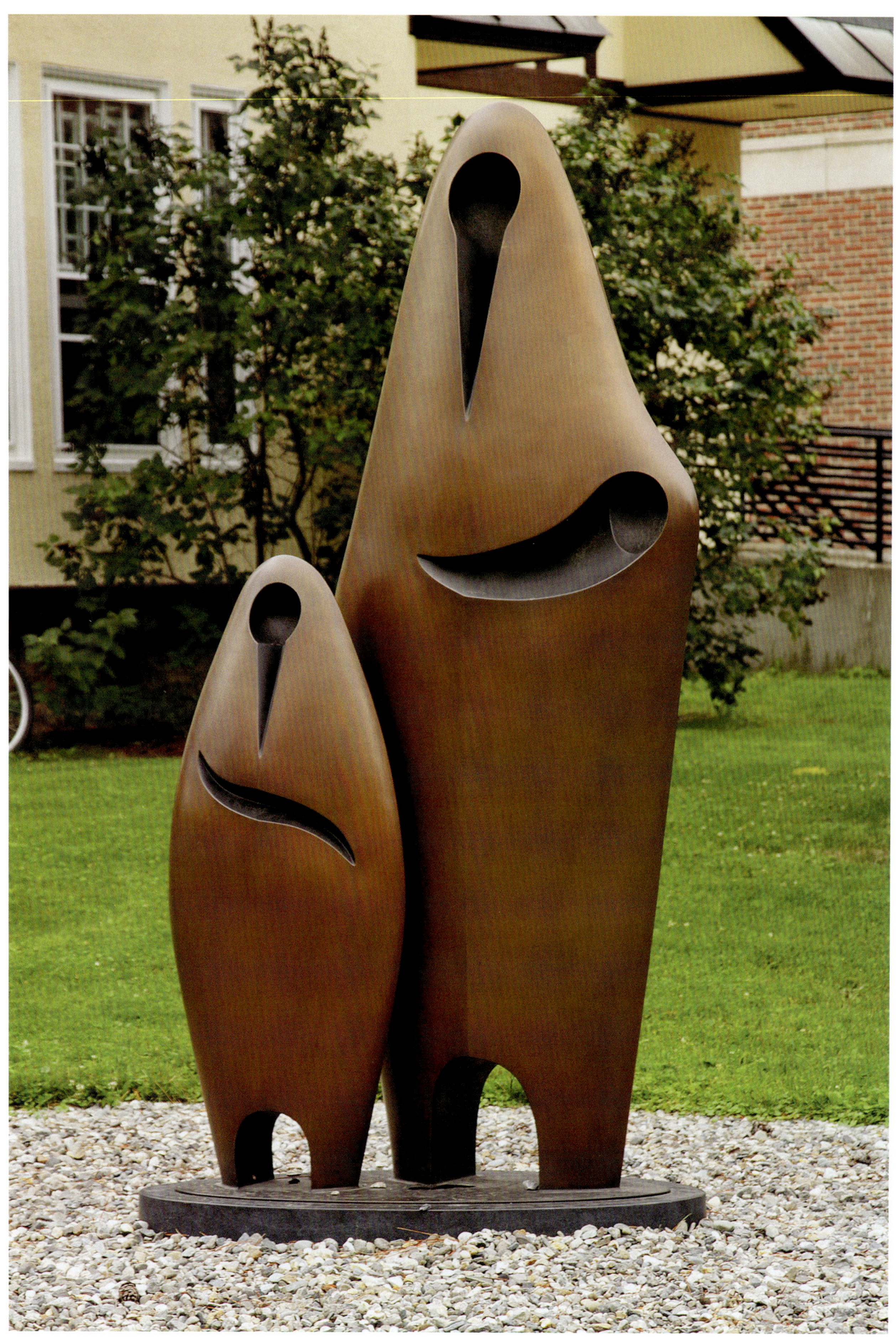

Native American Art at Dartmouth: Highlights from the Hood Museum of Art

With contributions by

George P. Horse Capture Sr.
Joe D. Horse Capture
Joseph M. Sanchez
Colin G. Calloway
Karen S. Miller

and

Leah Bowe
Sherry Brydon
Heather Igloliorte
Miles R. Miller
Jennifer Neptune
Megan A. Smetzer
Joyce M. Szabo
Jenny Tone-Pah-Hote

Hood Museum of Art, Dartmouth College
Hanover, New Hampshire

University Press of New England
Hanover and London

Published by
Hood Museum of Art, Dartmouth College
Hanover, NH 03755
www.hoodmuseum.dartmouth.edu
and
University Press of New England
1 Court Street, Suite 250
Lebanon, NH 03766
www.upne.com

Native American Art at Dartmouth: Highlights from the Hood Museum of Art was published to coincide with an exhibition of the same title held at the Hood Museum of Art from October 8, 2011, through March 12, 2012. Some of the objects in this publication did not appear in the exhibition.

This publication and its related exhibition were organized by the Hood Museum of Art, Dartmouth College, and generously supported by Mary Alice Kean Raynolds and David R. W. Raynolds, Class of 1949, Susan Ferris, the William B. Jaffe and Evelyn A. Hall Fund, and the Eleanor Smith Fund.

Edited by Nils Nadeau
Designed by Dean Bornstein

All object photography by Jeffrey Nintzel

Color separations by Professional Graphics, Rockford, Illinois
Printed and bound by Tien Wah Press (PTE) Limited, Singapore

Front cover: Mateo Romero, Cochiti Pueblo, *"Night" (Daryl Concha)*, from *The Dartmouth Pow-Wow Suite*, 2009, photo transfer and acrylic paint on panel. Purchased through the Mrs. Harvey P. Hood W'18 Fund; 2010.53.10.

Frontispiece: Allan C. Houser, Chiricahua Apache, *Peaceful Serenity*, 1992, bronze-plated steel. Purchased through a gift from Mary Alice Kean Raynolds and David R. W. Raynolds, Class of 1949; 2007.56. © 1992 Chiinde LLC.

Back cover: Artist unknown, Mi'kmaq (Micmac); Wabanaki or Haudenosaunee (Iroquois), Nova Scotia, New Brunswick, or New York, man's cap, about 1860, velvet, cotton cloth, glass beads, sequins, ivory, and thread. Purchased in memory of Stacey Coverdale, Class of 1988, made possible by an anonymous gift; 988.29.26943 (cat. 155).

Library of Congress Cataloging-in-Publication Data

Hood Museum of Art.
Native American art at Dartmouth : highlights from the Hood Museum of Art / with contributions by George P. Horse Capture . . . [et al.]. — 1st ed.
p. cm.
Published to coincide with an exhibition held at the Hood Museum of Art, Hanover, N.H., Oct. 8, 2011–Mar.12, 2012.
Includes bibliographical references and index.
ISBN 978-1-61168-033-1 (pbk. : alk. paper)
1. Indian art—North America—Exhibitions. 2. Art, American—20th century—Exhibitions.
3. Art, American—21st century—Exhibitions. 4. Indian art—Collectors and collecting—North America—Exhibitions. 5. Art—New Hampshire—Hanover—Exhibitions. 6. Hood Museum of Art—Exhibitions. I. Horse Capture, George P. II. Title.
III. Title: Highlights from the Hood Museum of Art.
E59.A7H76 2011
709.01'1—dc22

2011008142

Contents

Preface and Acknowledgments

In its first incarnation, Dartmouth College was dedicated primarily to educating "Indian" youth. Although the college's student body did not reflect this original mission until the 1970s, its complicated connection to the incredibly diverse and rich heritage of the original North Americans has been a constant throughout its history.[1] It has taken a long time for the history of domination of American Indians and their forced removal from their homelands to become an acknowledged part of the story of the formation of the United States of America. The country has been myopic on this subject, preferring to celebrate an idea or mythology of "Indian-ness," one often frozen in the past, while remaining ignorant of actual history and also the living traditions practiced by Native peoples today across this country. There has been a preference for thinking of "Indians" as being part of a homogenized cultural ideal with very little recognition of the vast cultural differences from one end of the country to the other, or of the fact that the trajectory of these cultures reflects change as well as continuity.

This catalogue and the related exhibition at the Hood Museum of Art were organized with these issues in mind—geographical and cultural diversity is emphasized by both the layout of the show and the sections of the book. The guest curators of the exhibition, George Horse Capture, Joe Horse Capture, and Joseph Sanchez, visited the museum for the first time in 2008 to review the collections and make an initial selection of objects. They were first contacted by Barbara Thompson, former curator of the Native American collections at the Hood, who invited them to Dartmouth to discuss the future exhibition. Barbara left the museum in 2007 and is now a curator at the Cantor Center for the Visual Arts at Stanford University, and we acknowledge the important role she played during her tenure in acquiring both traditional and contemporary Native American art for the collection. She was particularly instrumental in the acquisition of a large collection of Native American ledger drawings, as purchase and partial gift, from Mark Lansburgh, Class of 1949. The Horse Captures and Sanchez suggested that the collections should be augmented, if possible, before the exhibition was finalized and prior to sending this catalogue to press. While Brian Kennedy was director of this museum (July 2005 through August 2010), Joe Horse Capture, with the assistance of Karen Miller, Assistant Curator for Special Projects at the Hood, acquired works for the exhibition, including a painting by a former Dartmouth artist-in-residence, the late T. C. Cannon. The catalogue reflects these additions. The curators made subsequent visits as well, and the museum and the college thanks them for their dedication to this project and their meaningful interactions with students during their time here.

This book features a foreword by George Horse Capture, a brief history of Native Americans at Dartmouth College by Professor Colin Calloway, an interview with Joe Horse Capture by Karen Miller on his thoughts and process in selecting works of art for the show, and an essay by Joseph Sanchez about contemporary art and activism by Native artists. The catalogue sections present short essays by a diverse group of scholars about the Hood collections of Native American art that are represented in this exhibition. This catalogue also presents a history of the formation of the Native American art collection, which was created primarily through the donations of collectors, many of them alumni, whose relationships to the objects and the people who created them were distinctly varied. The story of how these objects arrived at this institution is told in turn by Karen Miller and Deborah Haynes, in the introduction and chronology, respectively.

This history, as Karen Miller shows, was in part related to Dartmouth's unique history with regard to Native Americans. The exhibition itself came out of a planned program of exhibitions and is the fourth in a series on the Hood Museum of Art's collections. It is intended to highlight the holdings of the college as well as delineate the history of collecting at an academic institution. After all, the bulk collections themselves do not reflect the eye of a curator but rather the collecting histories of their donors and, as such, reflect different types of contact and interaction between whites and Native people. While there were a few donors who were themselves Native Americans, most were not. Some of these objects were obtained during whaling trips in the nineteenth century, while others were collected during the reservation period at the beginning of the twentieth century by an inspector of schools for the U.S. Bureau of Indian Affairs. Still others passed down from a U.S. Army officer who participated in the Indian Wars in the late nineteenth century, a few were collected by a participant in a government biological survey, and over two hundred were amassed by twentieth-century American collectors who were interested in Plains and Woodlands art. Such a collection evidently supplies an absorbing history in and of itself, one that this exhibition and publication will only begin to tell.

The Hood Museum of Art would like to thank the many people who have made this exhibition and catalogue a reality. First, our thanks go to the original makers and artists of the art presented here. We would also like to thank the donors and collectors who have given generously to Dartmouth so that these objects could be studied at an institution of higher education. Mark Lansburgh, the collector of the Native American ledger drawings (the subject of a separate exhibition in fall 2010 and a forthcoming book), has indicated that he feels that the college and its students have much to learn from Native Americans, and that the Native American Studies Program and these collections at the Hood are important steps forward in that regard. He arranged for his collection to be acquired by Dartmouth precisely because he wished it to be at a college where Native students would have access to it.

Mary Alice Kean and David R. W. Raynolds, Class of 1949, have given a substantial and generous gift to the museum to present this exhibition and publish its catalogue. They have also not only made it possible to acquire a major work by the late artist Allen Houser—it now stands outside Sherman House on campus—but also championed the display of Native American art at the Hood. Without their great generosity, we would not have been able to accomplish this undertaking. In addition, we thank Susan Ferris for a generous gift toward this exhibition, as well as a number of Dartmouth alumni who have made significant contributions, including Harry Lewis, Class of 1955; Joe Obering, Class of 1956, and the foundation that bears his name; Stephen Lister, Class of 1963; Charles Nearburg, Class of 1972; and David Rettig, Class of 1975. We would also like to acknowledge the assistance of Henry Monahan. We are particularly indebted as well to the curators, George Horse Capture, Joe Horse Capture, and Joseph Sanchez, for their insight and dedication, as well as to Karen Miller, who was the curatorial coordinator for the exhibition and oversaw every aspect of the show. Her dedication to the project, as well as to acquiring additional works for it, is greatly appreciated. Additionally, Dartmouth Professors Bruce Duthu, Colin Calloway, and Vera Palmer provided their advice to the Hood staff, and we are particularly privileged to have them as colleagues.

We would like to thank independent scholar Sherry Brydon for her cataloguing of the objects selected for the exhibition and also for her work on the Native American ledger art collection, in consultation with the curators. Database Manager Deborah Haynes provided her invaluable knowledge of the history of the collections through the chronology printed here. Kathleen O'Malley, Acting Collections Manager and Assistant Registrar, oversaw the care of the objects and further arranged for Alison McCloskey of the Williamstown Art Conservation Center to evaluate and conserve a great many of the objects in the show; Kathleen herself cleaned and prepared others for photography and exhibition. Kathleen and Registrarial Assistant Rebecca Fawcett arranged for the photography of the objects by Jeffrey Nintzel. Juliette Bianco, Acting Associate Director, oversaw the organization and mounting of the exhibition with Karen Miller. Essi Rönkkö, Assistant Curator for Special Projects, and Nicole Gilbert, Exhibitions Coordinator, were instrumental in the production of the checklist and the permissions to publish these images. Patrick Dunfey, Exhibitions Designer, worked collaboratively with the curators to produce the design of the show, while Preparators John Reynolds and Matt Zayatz provided the mounts and Art Handler Sue Achenbach provided the framing. Lesley Wellman, Assistant Director and Curator of Education, and the education staff—Amy Driscoll, Neely McNulty, Vivian Ladd, and Adrienne Kermond—contributed educational materials and planned programs in collaboration with Sharon Reed, Programs and Events Coordinator. Nancy McLain, Business Manager, and Christine MacDonald, Business Assistant, have helped with all aspects of the financial support for the project. Former Collections Manager and Registrar Kellen Haak provided the history of the museum's participation in the Native American Graves Protection and Repatriation Act (NAGPRA), included here. The museum would like to acknowledge the work of Kellen in this regard; during his tenure at the museum, he guided the repatriation process and met with numerous Native American visiting delegations to show them the objects under consideration. Nils Nadeau, Communications and Publications Manager, edited the volume and steered it toward publication. His care and attention to detail is evident on every page. We would like to thank Michael Burton and Eric Brooks of the University Press of New England for their oversight of the publication of the book, which was beautifully designed by Dean Bornstein. We also thank, for their always helpful and informed assistance, Sarah I. Hartwell and Andrea Bartelstein, Reading Room Supervisors at Rauner Special Collections Library, Dartmouth College. Lastly, we would like to thank former curators Tamara Northern, who mentored many Native American students during her tenure as well as acquired significant works for the collection, including the signature work of Bob Haozous, *Apache Pull-Toy,* and Barbara Thompson, and former director Brian Kennedy, for their efforts on behalf of these collections. We are also grateful to Provost Carol Folt, who provided oversight of the museum during the last phase of the exhibition's planning and implementation.

This book is dedicated to the past and current Native American students at Dartmouth College. We hope all future Dartmouth students will continue to learn from these collections and absorb what they have to tell us about these great cultures of North America, as well as the living and vital art that continues to be made today by Native American artists.

KATHERINE W. HART
Interim Director and *Barbara C. and Harvey P. Hood 1918*
Curator of Academic Programming

NOTE

1. See Colin G. Calloway's recent publication *The Indian History of an American Institution: Native Americans and Dartmouth* (Hanover, N.H.: University Press of New England, 2010).

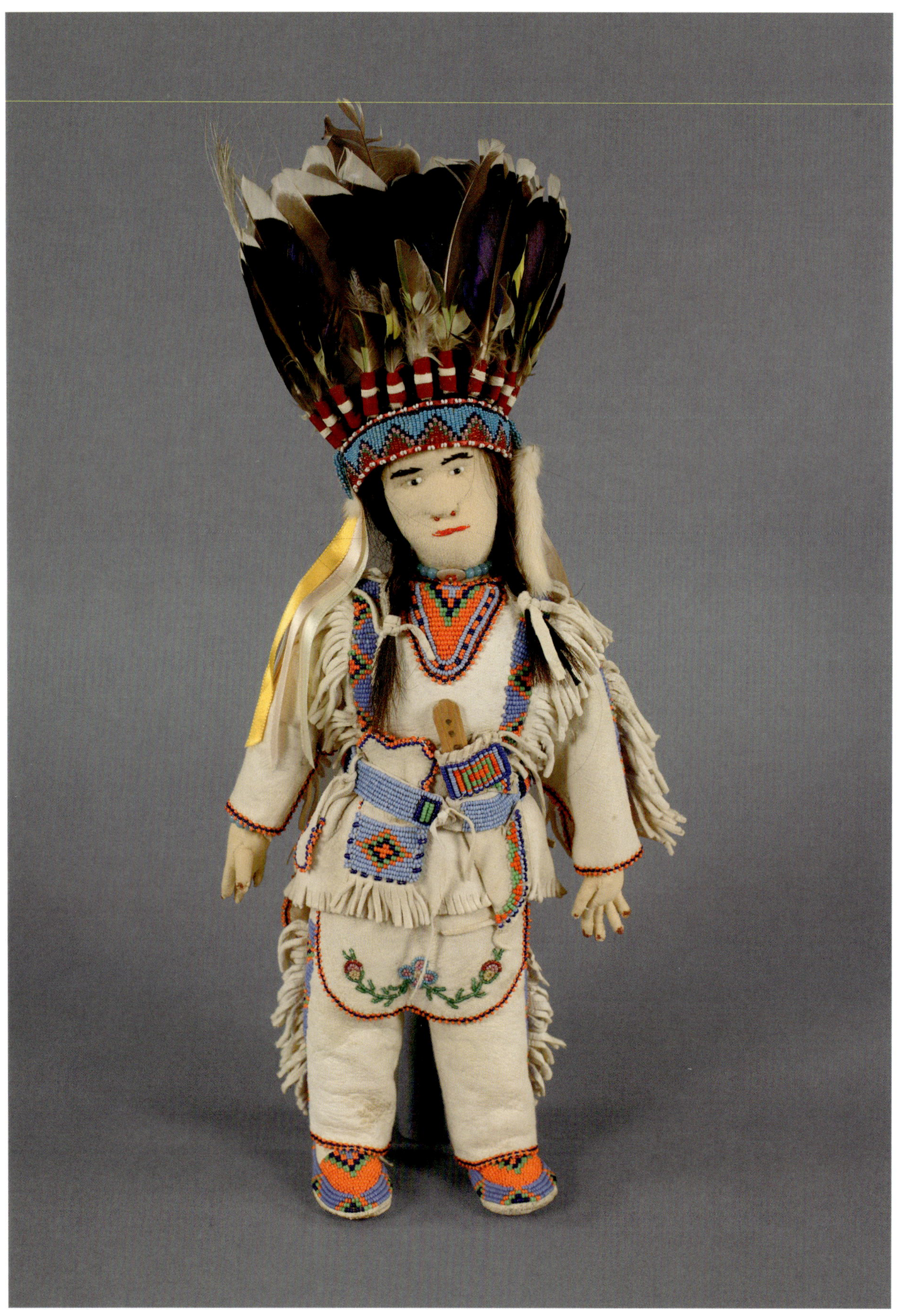

CAT. 86. Julia Ereaux Schultz, A'aninin (Gros Ventre), Fort Belknap Reservation, Harlem, Montana, Gros Ventre chief, 1948, hide, glass beads, mallard feathers, parrot feathers, human hair, horse hair, ribbon, cotton cloth, ermine tails, plastic beads, button, nylon fishing line, tape, felt cloth, wood, embroidery thread, paint, graphite, thread. The Wellington Indian Doll Collection: Gift of Barbara Wellington Wells; 987.35.26841.

Foreword: Living at Sunrise

It is difficult to believe that a mere five hundred years ago some Algonquian-speaking tribal people were catching their supper from the beautiful Connecticut or Ottauquechee Rivers at their favorite fishing hole not too far from where Dartmouth College is now. These were the *Alnôbak* or Abenaki and other divisions of their large related families, who found this idyllic region with the waterways filled with fish and the thick forests teeming with game.

During the Abenaki peoples' long life here, a balance emerged with the land and the environment and they become one. The tribes had their own names for themselves, but of the many tribes who lived in this area some Abenaki were known as "People of the Dawn Land" because of their eastern homeland. In the traditional Native world a tribe is often identified by location, so in honor of those early people who lived here for thousands of years, we recognize this distinction. This is and will always be their place.

Early Dartmouth History

One day a giant foreign ship appeared on their eastern shores and too soon the white-skinned newcomers, soldiers, settlers, and preachers alike, began to "remove" the Indian people from their homes, one way or another. There were earlier foreigners, but between the seventeenth and early eighteenth centuries the English incorporated Indian land into the thirteen English colonies as their own; others as well took part in the Indian removal, including the new "Americans." The small eastern tribes caught the brunt of the surge from Europe. For example, in Newfoundland, on the eastern seaboard, the Beothuk tribal people lived for a long time. Their numbers were small and they painted their bodies in the sacred color red, perhaps giving rise to the term "red man." In 1829, Nancy Shanawdithit, a Beothuk mother, died near St. Johns; she was thought to be the last member of her tribe on earth. Meanwhile, the tidal wave of Europeans rushed relentlessly westward, paying little heed to the Native people and their ancient residence.

Once the region was "cleared," the foreigners inexorably continued their expansion, and to build their "city upon a hill" and public institutions, churches, houses, farms, and roads began to cover the countryside. One way they figured to manage the "Indian problem" was through European education, so in 1754 the minister Eleazar Wheelock, for example, founded Moor's Indian Charity School in Lebanon, Connecticut, to educate and convert the Indian children, who would then return to their tribes to carry the word of the newcomers. Wheelock moved the school to Hanover, New Hampshire, in 1769 with the help of Samson Occom, a former pupil and Mohegan minister. Wheelock had dispatched Occom to Europe in 1766 to raise critical funding that in turn allowed for the establishment of Dartmouth College. Reverend Occom is believed to be a direct descendant of the famous Mohegan chief Uncas. John Wentworth, royal governor of the province of New Hampshire, acting for King George III of England, granted Wheelock a royal charter on December 13, 1769, establishing the college and naming it for his English friend, William Legge, 2nd Earl of Dartmouth, for the "youth of the Indian tribes in this land . . . and also of English youth and any others."

Reverend Occom experienced great disappointment and probably betrayal when he discovered that Eleazar Wheelock had used the funds he raised for enrolling primarily Englishmen and very few Indian students, as stated and promised in the royal charter. He quit his association with Dartmouth and helped to found Brothertown and lived among the tribal people there (Colin Calloway's essay in this catalogue explores the history of Native Americans at Dartmouth in detail).

Twenty-fifth Anniversary

Over the years of academic achievement, with the growth of a distinguished body of alumni of international prominence, Dartmouth College has earned an enviable and respected reputation in many fields of study. Its record speaks for itself, and it continues to refine those achievements today. In honor of the twenty-fifth anniversary of the Hood Museum of Art and 242 years since the college's founding, Dartmouth is presenting an exhibition of its own impressive collection of Native American art, both traditional and contemporary. By recognizing and expressing the college's historic relationship to the First Americans, this exhibition is another commitment to that bond. The Indian students have long attended these "Halls of Ivy" to learn, with the hope that the education will be reciprocal.

Discerning people have a tendency to want to learn more about the world of the American Indian, especially the traditional art, because art is universal and contains the essence of a people. This interest extends not only to the peoples and the tribes but also to their ethnographic and artistic creations as well. For some students an entrée to this world can be made easier by becoming familiar with the traditional art of the American Indian people, because all things are connected.

American Indian Art

As the Europeans poured into this country and began to "remove" the Indian people, they brought their goods and customs from the old country and viewed them as "classic." This Eurocentric attitude extended to most things and constrained mutual understanding between the two peoples. The Europeans usually ignored the aesthetic expressions of the Indian people, viewing them as "quaint" or "curiosities" or "crafts" instead of true art. This perception is a carryover from the Europe of the eighteenth and nineteenth centuries, where "art" just hangs on the wall or sits on a pedestal.

In the dynamic world of the migratory Indian people, life was difficult and everyone and everything performed more than one duty. For example, footwear not only protected the feet, but also became a venue for art when decorated with attractive and meaningful designs and colors; lodging not only meant protection from the elements but could be designed with the family's history, beliefs, and recorded great deeds or visions. That early European parochial definition of art has finally faded during the past two decades as an increasing number of aficionados have come to appreciate the many complex forms and contents of Native American art. The artwork in this exhibition is usually safely stored in the vaults of the Hood Museum of Art; it made its way there over many years through many Indian people and donors from across the country and beyond (see Karen Miller's essay and Deborah Haynes's chronology in this volume). Each tribal group proudly claims certain styles and skills in creating their unique masterpieces, but we cannot address them all at this time. The art is at least as important as the Indian people who created it, and this essay attempts to address not only some general aspects of the art but also the conditions of the people responsible for it. Other section essays in this catalogue go into specific detail, adding greater depth to this preliminary discussion.

Economics

Art follows from a culture group's relative economic security. When an adequate food supply exists, and the population is sufficient to enable some of its members to enjoy free time, a people can develop aspects of their culture such as art. For example, the domestication of corn in central Mexico demanded relatively little labor and time in exchange for an abundant food supply, thereby allowing the Native people to build pyramids and develop complex religious societies. The sea's bounty and the rich forests along the Northwest Coast gave the Tlingit Indian people and other tribes the opportunity to carve their magnificent art. The "Big Dog," as the Plains Indian people called the horse, allowed them to obtain their main source of food—the buffalo—almost at will. With the necessity of procuring food not dominating their every waking hour, other things became possible, such as some of the artistic traditions we see in this exhibition. On the other hand, the barrenness of Nevada shackled the Paiute people to a life of endlessly seeking sustenance, leaving little time for anything else; hence their artwork is made primarily in the form of baskets, created from available natural materials and the ancient petroglyphs that decorate their homeland.

Environment

A prime Native American identification factor is environment. Indian people live in areas that can be further grouped into environmental or cultural zones based upon shared traits. For example, the tribes that occupy the land stretching from the home of the Assiniboine people of central Saskatchewan, Canada, south to the home of the Kiowa people of mid-Oklahoma share the same general climatic conditions, terrain, vegetation, and animals, stretching over one thousand miles from north to south. Because of this, they have developed, with some minor exceptions, common traits and a spirituality that allows them to be further grouped together as Plains Indians. The Salish or Flathead people now reside in a zone called "Plateau"—an area located between the Plains and the Pacific Coast. As one becomes familiar with the flora and fauna of a given zone, the artwork of that zone's tribes becomes more explicable as well. For example, pottery and woven wool blankets and rugs usually come from the Southwest, where the Indian tribes such as the Navajo are sedentary and so can live with fragile items and exploit their sheep more than in most other zones. On the other hand, carved bone and tusk artwork generally comes from the far north, in Eskimo or Inuit country, where the large sea animals live. In the north and central United States, where the porcupine lives, the Indian people use their tiny quills for colorful and delicate embroidery on everyday items such as clothing, pipe stems, and staffs.

Although there are exceptions to this rule—prehistoric traded materials from other zones might include pipestone pipes, dentalia shells, gourds for rattles, and so on—the people in a specific zone generally utilize only materials that are native to that zone. If one recognizes the material of or placed on a given item, one may be able to determine which cultural zone produced it, though individual tribal styles must then come into play.

Utilitarian Art

The American Indian people lived an ocean away from the rest of the world's peoples for thousands of years and developed their own unique art and music, and they are generally little understood by the non-Indian world of today. Our music is much too esoteric to explain and appreciate here, but art is universal and can relate to most peoples. Living with the whims of nature, most of the tribes followed the food source and had to move with it, thus restricting the components of their lifestyle. For the true migratory people, everything in their world had to be light in weight, easily transportable and hardy. It would not be possible or practical to carve a statue of stone and then drag it from campsite to campsite, so they combined their need for the beauty of art with their practical everyday requirements. For example, the people of the Plains would paint their homes (tipis) with attractive and meaningful colors and symbols, or apply colorful decorations on their shoes (moccasins). This combination of practical usage and pure aesthetics is called utilitarian art.

In the long ago days the decorations could be paint, carving, weaving, or forms of beads. These beads could be of stone, bone, vertebrae, seeds, porcupine quills, seashells, and other such things. In addition to introducing many new things that later caused great damage to the Native people, the Europeans brought many delightful ones as well, foremost being the wonderful horse that changed our lives and the glass beads that created great beauty.

It can be said that traditional Native American art is utilitarian and can be divided into at least two major extremes; both relate to survival. The most obvious are items made and used by the warriors that protect the tribe. They include the iconic eagle-feather war bonnets worn by great Indian men of the Plains and the leaders, painted hide shields often portraying visionary symbols and colors, and tipis highlighted with meaningful colors and drawings.

At the other end of the age spectrum, but just as important, are the items made for the children. Children are vital for survival and provide our only connection to a sense of immortality. They are dearly loved in the traditional Indian world, not only by the parents but by the "aunts," "uncles," grandparents, and others. In this social structure all brothers to the child's father are the child's father as well, and the sisters to the mother are the child's mother too. There are no such things as cousins; the children of the brothers and sisters of the child's parents are all brothers and sisters to each other. Many believe that we are all related. So, when a woman is with child, many relatives and friends prepare to welcome the newborn with many gifts. Warrior items and items for children are usually well represented in today's museum collections for the power, beauty, artwork, and love they still hold.

Another special item is the moccasin—every museum has many of them, as everyone wore moccasins and they are plentiful. Indian people still proudly wear them at special events today. They are relatively small, hardy, and brightly attractive. Most importantly, moccasins are concise reflections of other items in a tribe. They usually utilize the same beading stitch in the bead application, materials, bead patterns, and colors as the larger pieces of clothing worn by a tribal individual. If one can become proficient at identifying tribal moccasin styles, it is a short step to identifying the larger items.

Most tribes quickly favored the colorful glass beads initially made in Venice and traded around the world. One of the first types of bead to arrive in the Plains area was the "pony" bead because, it is said, they were packed in on the backs of small horses. (Horses from the southwest came north in the early 1700s.) These eighth-inch beads came mostly in limited colors—red, white, and blue, with the tribes favoring the latter. It can be said that most items fashioned with pony beads have a pre-1850 origin. Around the middle of the nineteenth century, the smaller "seed" beads quickly replaced the pony beads because they were more plentiful and offered a much wider range of colors. The early "thread" came from animal tendons, but cotton thread became much more popular as soon as it became available.

Dispersion

Many people believe that each tribe creates its own unique symbols, colors, and exclusive designs in its artwork. The reality is usually quite different.

Within each cultural zone are tribes of varying influences; population is the determining factor. The larger tribes have, of course, a larger population base that contains a greater ratio of inventors, spiritual leaders, military leaders, warriors, and artists. These human resources energize the tribe by fostering accomplishments, and the large groups wield a greater impact and influence than the smaller groups. Guided by available materials, tribal traditions, borrowing, current trends, creativity, and peer pressure, artists in a larger tribe will periodically develop, accept, and utilize artwork with a definite identifiable style. Recognition of an art style is the most obvious element of determining the tribal origins of an item. As the style becomes entrenched in the tribe, it may spread to adjacent tribes. Eventually trading, spoils of war, intertribal marriages, and other forces can expand the spread and usage of the style, perhaps with slight modifications, thus increasing the artistic repertoire of the more distant tribes.

Within the Northern Plains there seem to be at least three major centers of traditional tribal art influence—the Lakota, the Blackfeet, and the Crow people. Each is a large tribe that has distinctive, identifiable art styles that can influence the adjacent smaller tribes in many diverse ways. Their influence can be compared to stones simultaneously dropped into a calm pond of water. The waves from the stones radiate symmetrically in clearly defined circles but lose strength as they travel outward. When the circles meet spreading circles from other artistic influences, the intersection disrupts the more dominant circle. These intersections form a new area that is still connected to, but different from, the initial impact area. Revisions or different influences can form in these outer areas.

Smaller countries react to the influences of larger nearby countries in a similar manner. Consider Switzerland. Most Swiss people speak a form of German, adopt many elements of the Italian culture, but use francs as their form of currency. Yet in spite of all of these outside influences, the Swiss combine everything together to form their unique culture. Likewise, many smaller tribes form their own art styles under these forces, expanding the American Indian traditional art palette.

Manufacture

Once these forces of dispersion and "overlap" are known, the challenges of positive identification become clearer. Once the cultural zone of a Native-made article has been determined, additional identifying steps are required. In applying the small colored glass beads on an item, each tribe favors a specific sewing technique. For example, the Lakota (or Sioux) people of the Dakotas almost exclusively use the "lane stitch" (also known as the lazy stitch), where a string of threaded beads is attached to the base material at regular intervals, forming ridges; this can be more easily understood when compared to railroad ties attached crossways to the direction of travel. The Crow people of Montana use the "modified lane" or the "Crow stitch," which only periodically attaches the threaded beads. The Blackfeet of Montana employ the "appliqué/overlay" stitch, which attaches the string of beads every three or four beads, forming a smooth surface. Only rarely will these tribes vary from their preferred bead application techniques and one aspect of tribal art identification is being familiar with these techniques.

The smaller tribes that lie between and adjacent to the large groups, for various reasons, use one or more of these three basic beading methods. The Assiniboine people of Montana, who are close relatives of the Lakota but long-term allies of the Cree people in Canada, use the "appliqué" stitch but have practiced the lane stitch as well. The Arapaho people of Wyoming and the Cheyenne people of Montana, longtime friends of the Lakota, favor the lane while the A'aninin (Gros Ventre) of Montana, even though related to the Arapaho, generally are "appliqué" people. There is no constant discernible set pattern or rule of thumb to determine how the tribes select their beading stitch technique; but once one memorizes who uses what, this determination is another clue to tribal art identification.

Tribal traditional artists also prefer distinct colors and patterns in their work. Given the large number of artists in a tribe and the lack of a strict art union to establish specific immutable rules and reference guides governing the art, certain symbols, patterns, and colors at an early time probably held a particular and specific meaning to a number of the producers. However, as more people later accepted the symbols, patterns, or colors, many artists undoubtedly attached their own meaning to them, until there was no longer any one definitive meaning to any one of them. Beauty and tradition are the catalysts that maintain them.

The pyramid pattern is a good example of this dispersion. Most tribes in the Plains and Plateau incorporate this shape into their art. Others use it too. Whatever its final form, either a smooth-sided shape or one of stacked squares, in various colors, with or without internal design elements, it remains the same basic symbol. Many Lakota people call it a tipi, probably referring to "home." The Blackfeet say it is a mountain, while others say it represents the earth. Regardless of its many interpretations, it fills the space in a pleasing manner, somehow relates to that tribe, and is regarded as significant. Triangles, squares, crosses, parallel lines, and many other elements also fall into this category.

Although the pattern or cut of an item is usually the paramount factor in tribal identification, similarities in shape or construction occur in other tribes as well. However, this aspect is much too complex and lengthy to discuss here.

Styles

It must also be known that Indian art is not static. The energy, creativity, and individuality of the artists and the spread of time all play major roles in the evolution of the art. In addition, as trade items become available, many of them soon become incorporated into the works of art. Various weaves and colors of wools as well as other textiles, bells, coins, shells, and glass beads of different sizes, shapes, and colors must all be considered, as they can fine-tune the chronology and tribal identification of a given piece. It is tempting to assume that every design and color held great meaning to the Indian people, but because of their love of beauty, many elements were used strictly for their aesthetics. Like other peoples, the Indian people have styles that change over time. Even revolutionary conversions have occurred, such as the almost total change to floral patterns from the traditional geometric ones by some tribes. All of these elements play a role in the identification of Indian art.

Further Research

One structured approach to identifying Plains Indian pieces is to attempt to learn as much as possible about one time period, focusing on only one object from one tribe. It may be best to begin at 1890, because this era is considered the epitome of traditional creativity and production. Focus on one type of object, for instance, moccasins, as their usage forms an unbroken chain with the distant past, and their styles can be observed in many other items produced by that particular people. Once you become somewhat familiar with this period you can work backward in time to when styles were more general, or forward to today when they fade. When you are fairly comfortable with recognizing the work of one tribe, you can expand to another.

Considering the forces and factors mentioned here, it can be said that although each piece was made by a member of one tribe, it is still difficult to specify that tribe with absolute accuracy, for the styles were often very similar.

There are many compelling attractions to the traditional art of the American Indian. It is, of course, created over the centuries by my people, wherever they might reside. The art in its numerous forms from across the hemisphere is quite beautiful, well formed, balanced, useful, colorful, and intricately made, and it transcends from the physical to other places. Most of the items were actually created and used by our ancestors. When our people were natural and free, they were on intimate terms with the spiritual world, which is mostly gone today. But the items still exist, and on special rare occasions one can even touch them and feel the continuing connection to those special people and times. This may be the closest we can ever come to them as we contend with the present world around us. But here too is a balance, one with loss and great joy. These items come from a people from long ago, and there is no comprehensive encyclopedia of traditional art knowledge or art union. No two pieces are exact duplicates, so when they are studied they are first identified as to function, then (the fun part) their tribal origin. Who made them and when? Don't rely on the museum records—they are often incorrect. Considering the numerous variables, no one person or group can accurately identify the origin of every item, because the actual makers of these beautiful items are for the most part anonymous and timeless, so the field is open to participate in the identification game.

Conclusion

When a small unique group encounters the world of a ubiquitous, portentous foreign people, their special status fades as they begin to be overrun by the dominant culture. Their traditions can become faint memories as they strive to compete and achieve in the newer, ever-changing universe. The world should make an effort to learn from them and their culture as their ancient traditions and beliefs have much to offer, perhaps even alternatives.

George P. Horse Capture Sr.

Native American Art at Dartmouth

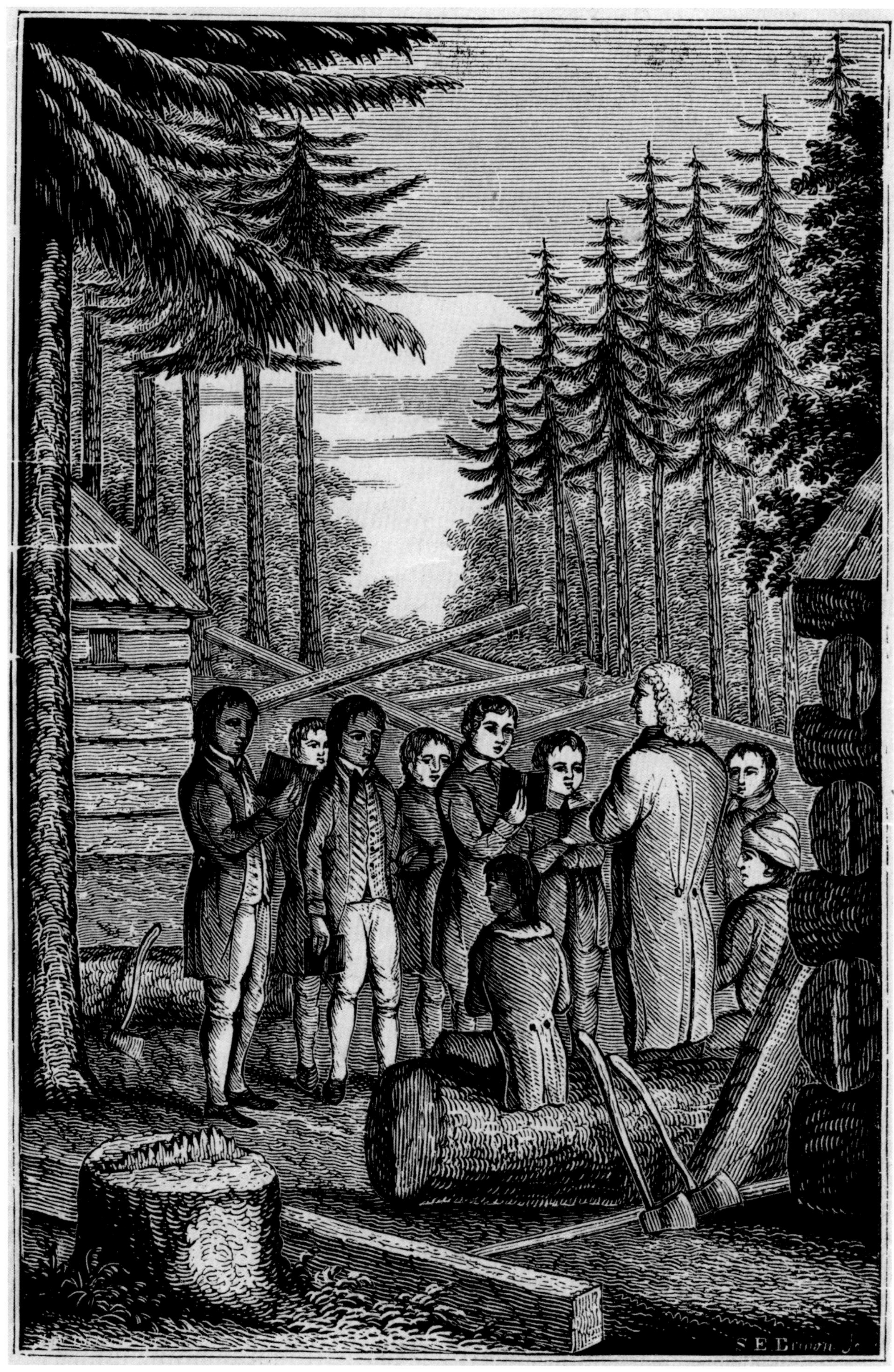

Samuel E. Brown (d. ca. 1860), *Founding of Dartmouth College in 1769,* 1839, engraving. Dartmouth College Library.

:: 1 ::

A School in the Heart of the Indian Country

Colin G. Calloway

Michael Dorris, the founding chair of the Native American Studies Program, once said that Dartmouth's Indian history really began in 1971, when the college finally committed itself to Native education in a meaningful way.[1] In many ways he was right. But Dartmouth has a much longer Native American history. Members of the Dartmouth community often invoke that history as part of an honorable or not-so-honorable tradition, but few people really know much about it beyond some words in the college charter, some knowledge of Samson Occom's fundraising efforts, and some awareness that the college failed for a long time to live up to its pledge and has since struggled to get things right. In fact, the bulk of Dartmouth's Indian history pertains to the period *before* 1971, and before most of its Native American students attended Dartmouth. It is a past that continues to shape Dartmouth's present.

Without Samson Occom, a Mohegan Indian from Connecticut, it is fair to say, there would have been no Dartmouth College. Occom never set foot on the Dartmouth campus, but he was, in effect, Dartmouth's first development officer. According to his autobiography (the first written by a Native American: he wrote a draft in 1765 and a longer version in 1768), Occom said he was raised as "a Heathen" but when he was sixteen, stirred by the emotional intensity of the Great Awakening, he put his trust in Christ and "found Serenity and Pleasure of Soul, in Serving God." He taught himself to read and write so he could better understand "the Word of God" and teach Mohegan children.[2] Occom also had more temporal reasons for advancing his literacy: he was a member of the Mohegan tribal council that was bringing a lawsuit to reclaim lost lands. In 1743, Occom sought out Eleazar Wheelock for instruction in reading.[3] Wheelock agreed to help, and Occom spent four years with him. Despite poor health and failing eyesight, he became fluent in English and proficient in Latin, Greek, and Hebrew, a remarkable achievement by any standards and particularly at a time when few people were literate even in their own language. On the basis of his success tutoring Occom, Eleazar Wheelock established Moor's Charity School in Lebanon, Connecticut.

As the school grew, Wheelock wanted to move it to a new location, "conveniently Situate in the Heart of the Indian Country." He sent Occom to England to raise money for the new school. The Mohegan preacher was a model of what Wheelock's schooling could accomplish, given the right level of funding. Large congregations gathered to hear Occom, and he raised £12,000 in England and Scotland, a huge amount for the time and nearly $2 million in current dollars. In December 1769, New Hampshire Governor John Wentworth signed a charter:

> That there be a college erected in our said province of New Hampshire by the name of Dartmouth College, for the education and instruction of youth of the Indian tribes in this land in reading, writing, and all parts of learning which shall appear necessary and expedient for civilizing and christianizing children of pagans, as well as in all liberal arts and sciences, and also of English youth and any others.

The phrase "and also of English youth and any others" looks like it was added as an afterthought to the mission of Indian education; in fact, it was the other way around. Wheelock's *first* draft of the charter said Dartmouth was being founded to educate "Youths of *the English* and also of the Indian Tribes," but then "he remembered that several thousand British benefactors had given thousands of pounds to a charity school primarily for Indians, not white colonists, and he scratched out the reference to English youth and added it at the end of the passage as if to indicate their subordinate position in his grand design."[4] But tinkering with the language did not alter the fact that Wheelock was already changing his mind about educating Indians, preferring to educate young Englishmen to carry out the missionary work. The college held its first, tiny, commencement in August 1771. Four students graduated, two of them "educated for missionaries among the remote Indians," and none of them Indians.

Occom saw what was happening. "I verily thought once that your Institution was Intended Purely for the poor Indians," he wrote his mentor; "with this thought I Cheerfully Ventur'd my Body & Soul, left my Country my poor young Family all my friends and Relations, to sail over the Boisterous Sea to England, to help forward your School." But now he found "that instead of your Semenary Becoming alma Mater, she will be too alba [white] mater to Suckle the Tawnees [Indians]." He feared that "the Poor Indians" would never have much benefit from it and warned, "We shall be Deem'd as Liars and Deceivers in Europe, unless you gather Indians quickly to your College, in great Numbers."[5]

Wheelock took umbrage at what he considered Occom's insubordination and ingratitude. He justified the shift to educating English boys for missionary work as the policy that would ultimately be of most benefit to the Indians: "Dartmouth College is and invariably has been and will be as long as any Indians are left primarily designed for them, and the presence of white students only serves to make the project more effective." Occom expressed interest in seeing the college Wheelock had built with the money he raised, but Wheelock did not encourage such a visit. Their correspondence eventually petered out, and "their 31-year relationship ended in mutual silence."[6]

The few Indians at the college were far from happy. Daniel Simon, a Narragansett, complained that he was required to do so much work on college upkeep that he had little time left for studying, which was not what he understood the purpose of the school to be. "What good will the Charity money do the Indians?" he asked; if they were expected to work to pay their way, they could just as well go somewhere else for their education. "Wo unto that poor Indian," said Daniel, "or white man that Should Ever Com to this School, without he is rich."[7] Daniel graduated in 1777, the first Native student to do so, but his was a common complaint. By the end of the eighteenth century, Dartmouth had graduated only three Indians in all.

However, Dartmouth's historic role in educating Indians was far greater than the rather paltry numbers of Natives who actually graduated would attest. Mohegan Joseph Johnson was educated at Moor's Charity School when it was located in Connecticut, received his preaching license at Dartmouth, and preached at the college on more than one occasion. He wrote (admittedly to Eleazar Wheelock): "I do ever retain in my mind with pleasure, and respects, DARTMOUTH AND HER SONS."[8] Wheelock brought Moor's Charity School with him when he moved to Hanover to start Dartmouth, and despite periodic interruptions in its operations, the school remained attached to Dartmouth and came under the responsibility of the Dartmouth president. Before it closed in the middle of the nineteenth century, many more Indians had attended Moor's Charity School than had attended the college. Some stayed at Moor's only for a short while. Some also made the transition from the school to the college, but most did not, and many never intended to do so—they came to complete a limited course of study and left. Some transferred to the college, only to stay a term or two. Most of the students at Moor's were teenagers or even children, and the college president supervised their care, instruction, and progress.

He also reported their expenses. By 1775, Wheelock had spent all the money Occom raised in England, mainly in building construction. But Scots had contributed £2,529, and the Society in Scotland for Propagating Christian Knowledge (the SSPCK), which managed the funds, kept a tighter grip on them than the English donors, refusing to allow Wheelock to divert money intended for Indians to broader educational purposes. Every Dartmouth president from the founding of the college to the twentieth century tried to wriggle out of the commitment, but the SSPCK would not budge. Rauner Library holds detailed ledger accounts and countless slips of paper recording just what was spent when and on whom for clothing, shoes, shoelaces, books, paper, food, lodging, laundry, mending, lamp oil, candles, firewood, trips home, and multiple other expenses. The accounts reveal names of some Indians who do not even appear on any of the official lists. The Scots, then, kept Dartmouth in the business of Indian education.

Although Wheelock began by educating Indians from southern New England—young women as well as young men—he became more interested in recruiting students from the Six Nations of the Iroquois of New York: the Mohawks, Oneidas, Onondagas, Cayugas, Senecas, and Tuscaroras. He considered them "a much better breed," less corrupted by contact with colonial society.[9] Mohawk Joseph Brant—who later gained fame, or notoriety, as a war chief during the Revolution and also translated the Christian gospel into Mohawk—attended Wheelock's school in Connecticut. After Wheelock relocated to Hanover, he tried to recruit Iroquois students for his new college. But the Iroquois rejected Wheelock's recruiting efforts, not out of ignorance concerning the education he was offering their children but because they already knew too much about it. Oneida parents had pulled their children out of his Connecticut school on rumors that they were being mistreated, and they had no intention of sending them to the new school: "English schools we do not approve of here, as serviceable to our spiritual interest," said the Oneida headmen, "& almost all those who have been instructed in English are a reproach to us." The Onondagas were even more forthright in expressing their views about Wheelock's schooling: "Learn yourself to understand the word of God, before you undertake to teach & govern others," they said; "learn of the French ministers if you would understand, & know how to treat Indians. They dont speak roughly; nor do they for every little mistake take up a club & flog them."[10] Few New York Iroquois came to Dartmouth.

But Wheelock needed Indians, thanks to the vigilance of the SSPCK. With no Indians students from the Iroquois in New York, or from west of the Appalachians, where his recruiters met a similar lack of interest, Wheelock turned to Canada, and the communities at Kahnawake, St. Francis (now Odanak), and Lorette. The Mohawk, Abenaki, and Huron Indians there had adopted so many English captives during the "French and Indian wars" that "English blood" ran through the children's veins; this, Wheelock believed, would make them better students. In the spring of 1772, Wheelock had only five Indian students, all of them from New England; by the end of 1774, he had "upwards of twenty," mostly from Canada.[11]

Abenakis continued to come to Hanover in the nineteenth century, but most of them were young and did not stay long. James Annance dropped out of Dartmouth after a year and became a guide in the White Mountains. He said Dartmouth "spoiled a great many good Indians and made very poor white men."[12] But Peter Paul Osunkerhine reputedly walked three hundred miles from Odanak to attend Moor's Charity School. When he returned to Odanak, he built a church and started a school himself.

While Indian students were few and far between until the late twentieth century, several of them made their mark. In the era of Indian removals, Maris Bryant Pierce, a Seneca (Class of 1840), worked to renegotiate the fraudulent Treaty of Buffalo Creek of

1838 even while he was still on campus. His staunchest non-Indian ally in the fight was the missionary Asher Wright, who attended Dartmouth in 1826–27. Joseph Pitchlynn Folsom (Class of 1854), a Choctaw, wrote a digest of his tribe's laws. Charles Eastman (Class of 1887), a Dakota, went on to medical school in Boston and became a physician on the Pine Ridge Reservation in South Dakota. He stood among the carnage at Wounded Knee in December 1890 after United States troops had massacred some three hundred people. As a lecturer and author, he became Dartmouth's most famous Native son. Jack Tortes Meyers, a Cahuilla from southern California, got into Dartmouth in 1905 under false pretences: Dartmouth alumni who saw him playing baseball in the Southwest recruited him, gave him train fare, and furnished him with a forged high school diploma. He did not last long at Dartmouth but went on to an impressive career in the major leagues. Ralph Walkingstick, a Cherokee, left Dartmouth to join the YMCA during World War I. He wound up in Mesopotamia and was not impressed—"Old Abraham used his best judgment when he left there for the Promised Land," he wrote. He was so happy to make it home to Muskogee, Oklahoma, that he never returned to Dartmouth after that.[13]

The presence of individual Native students did not reflect an institutional commitment to Indian education, however. "The whole business," wrote President Asa D. Smith in 1872, "has become a somewhat onerous one." He expressed "doubts whether the Indian business ought to be continued."[14] In the absence of real Indians, then, Dartmouth's "Indian traditions" developed around imaginary ones, expressed in war whoops and mascots, and the college's sports teams became the "Dartmouth Indians."

Dartmouth's Indian history involves not only the Indian students who came to campus but also the non-Indians associated with the college who went into Indian country and Indian affairs, sometimes with honorable intentions, sometimes not. Missionaries, Indian agents, and politicians from Dartmouth often participated in assaults on Indian cultures, lands, resources, and independence. In the eighteenth and nineteenth centuries, work in the "Indian business" often meant work in the land business. In the nineteenth and twentieth centuries, politics sometimes also implied involvement in Indian affairs. James Dean grew up with the Oneidas, and after he graduated from Dartmouth in 1775, he served as Indian agent and interpreter for them while growing prosperous on sales of Oneida land. Silas Dinsmoor (Class of 1791) served as Indian agent to the Cherokees and then to the Choctaws. He opposed Andrew Jackson and his Indian policy and was wounded "in a duel fought by gentlemen at table." Samuel Worcester (uncle of the more famous one in the Supreme Court case *Worcester v. Georgia*) and Alfred Finney dedicated their lives to missionary work with the Cherokees. Daniel Webster championed Indian rights in the South in the removal era, although he also invested in Indian lands in the North. Dartmouth men in Congress split on voting on the Indian Removal Bill, following party lines, not principle. Levi Woodbury, Class of 1809, was a reliable Jackson Democrat who voted for the Indian Removal Bill in the Senate; Jackson rewarded him by making him secretary of the treasury in 1834. Woodbury found himself with general supervision of the survey and sale of the Indian lands that flooded the market as a result of removals, and he exercised considerable political patronage in the appointment of district land officers. Appointees expected to make a profit as a reward for their party loyalty, after all, and Secretary Woodbury was notoriously lax about enforcing financial regulations. After Abraham Lincoln appointed John Goodwin (Class of 1844) as first governor of the Territory of Arizona, his first address to the territorial legislature called for a war of extermination against the Apaches.

In later years, Gordon Day, John C. Ewers, Bill Fenton, and Wilcomb Washburn all passed through Dartmouth on their path to becoming eminent scholars of Native American history and culture. Dartmouth hired the renowned Arctic explorer and anthropologist Vilhjalmur Stefansson as consultant to its museum in 1947. Stefansson donated his 25,000-volume library and extensive collection of papers to Dartmouth, and his work at the college in the 1950s and 1960s laid the groundwork for Dartmouth's continuing research in the Arctic. Vermonter Gordon M. Day took a position as research associate in the Anthropology Department at the college and devoted his energies to Abenaki research, particularly at St. Francis, where he recorded oral histories and material relating to Western Abenaki linguistics and ethnology. He prepared an Abenaki-English dictionary and deposited sixty reels of magnetic tape and 10,000 pages of manuscript on microfilm, plus notes, sketches, maps, and photographs, at Dartmouth. Day understood that the kind of work he did with Indian people was very different from the kind of work Eleazar Wheelock had in mind: "It seems fitting," he said, "that the Dartmouth College Library should become the repository of a collection pertaining to the original inhabitants of Vermont, New Hampshire, and western Maine. Perhaps it is also a little incongruous when we reflect on the probable reaction of Dr. Wheelock to a suggestion that his little Indian pupils from the bark houses of St. Francis were themselves the bearers of a culture which merited study."[15] Not all Dartmouth men made such positive contributions. Slade Gorton, Class of 1949, earned a reputation in later life as "the Custer of the Senate" and "Public Enemy No. 1" in Indian Country for his consistent opposition to Indian rights.

When Wheelock founded Dartmouth, it never occurred to him that he or his school had anything to learn from Indian people. Indian ways of knowing and learning were simply primitive superstitions that had to be eradicated if Indian students were to make any progress. In Wheelock's vision for Dartmouth, the few Indian students who attended were to be educated in English ways and Christianity, so they could serve as missionaries who would convert other Indians to English ways and Christianity. Not much changed as English colonial education for Indians gave way to American education for Indians. With the establishment of government-sponsored boarding schools later in the century, the United States waged a new war, this time on Indian children, as they sought to transform them from tribal members into individual citizens. School teachers and administrators tried to strip students of their Native languages, Native clothing, Native heritage, and Native identity and provided them instead with the minimal education and training necessary for them to function at the lower levels of American society. Indian education was "education for extinction"—cultural genocide waged with good intentions by people who sought to save the Indians from themselves.[16]

Two hundred years after its founding, however, Dartmouth finally made a sustained commitment to honor its original mission and moved, rather uncertainly at first, toward a different understanding of what constituted Indian education. President John Kemeny chose the college's bicentennial as the time to begin to make good on Dartmouth's promise. "Though the College he founded has prospered," said Kemeny, "only part of Eleazar's dream has come true." In two hundred years, only about a score of Native students had actually graduated from the institution. "Because I believe deeply in Eleazar's vision, I pledge my energies to the effort of translating the long-deferred promise of Dartmouth's charter into reality," he continued. For Kemeny and for Dartmouth, this was part of a larger commitment to equal opportunity and minority education. It was also a sign of changing times. The historically low numbers of Indian students at Dartmouth reflected "the deterioration of relations between whites and Indians," said Kemeny. "As the Indians were pushed farther West, it just didn't seem practical for them to attend." But after the social and political upheavals of the 1960s, the climate was very different. It was time for Dartmouth to do something.[17]

Kemeny announced in his inaugural address that Dartmouth hoped to enroll sixty Native students in the following four years. Fifteen Native students from thirteen tribes matriculated in the Class of 1974, bringing the number of Indian students on campus to twenty-three, the largest enrollment in Dartmouth's history. Dartmouth established the American Indian Program to provide cultural and academic support for its Native students. In the spring of 1972, on the recommendation of a committee co-chaired by Native American Program director Stuart Tonemah (a Kiowa-Comanche from Oklahoma) and a young assistant professor of history named James Wright, the Faculty of Arts and Sciences unanimously approved the adoption of a Native American Studies Program. Michael Dorris, a Modoc from Oregon, was hired, with a joint appointment in anthropology, to serve as chair. The new job was a challenge. "Nobody at Dartmouth knew what Native American Studies was supposed to be," Dorris recalled, "but the unpersuaded suspected that it somehow involved basket-weaving and mysticism, a sop to radical minority students."[18] In the fall of 1972, the Native American House opened at 18 North Park Street. It served as the residence and social/cultural space for Native students until a new Native American House, the former Occom Inn on North Main Street, was dedicated and opened in the fall of 1995. In 1973, the college formed the Native American Council, an organization of representatives from students, administration, and faculty with oversight of all activities relating to Native Americans at Dartmouth. That same year, Dartmouth held its first Pow-Wow. In 1975 a review committee strongly endorsed the Native American Studies Program. In its first two hundred years, only about sixty Native students attended Dartmouth College. Since the college recommitted itself to honoring its founding pledge, however, more than seven hundred Native students from more than 160 tribes, from Abenaki to Zuni, have attended. In the fall of 2009, Dartmouth matriculated more than fifty Native students—the first time in its history that Native American students comprised 5 percent of the entering class.

Dartmouth is now an institution that recognizes value in diversity—a place where far more students embrace their Native identity than set it aside. In Native American Studies, scholars explore issues of space, gender, artistic expression, representation, colonialism, indigenous sovereignty, and nationhood as essential lines of inquiry in attempting to better understand the Native American—and, therefore, the American—past and present. Students learn about Native American ways of living, organizing societies, and understanding the world; they study colonial power structures and the unique rights and political aspirations of Indian peoples in the United States and Canada; they explore the intersection of Indian and European histories and systems of knowledge, reading Locke, Rousseau, and Foucault alongside tribal origin stories, the epic of the founding of the Iroquois League, and the writings of Vine Deloria Jr. Living in a Native American community (albeit a rather transient and academic one), sharing experiences with Native students from all over North America, and having the opportunity to take classes that concentrate on Native issues can enhance Native students' appreciation of their culture and identity as well as increase their consciousness of Native rights and sovereignty. Like their grandparents and great-grandparents who grouped together and built their own communities to combat the homesickness, austerity, and racism they confronted in boarding schools, Native American students at Dartmouth have built a community here as well. Dartmouth began as an institution pledged to change Indians. Today's Native students are more likely to apply their education to ensure that Indians survive as Indians, and to change the world.

Dartmouth's Indian history is multifaceted: it has been an institution at the forefront of the English assault on Native American cultures; a colonial project physically located in Abenaki country; a college that lost sight of its founding mission, although it never relinquished its founding story; an "Indian school" without Indians; a place where young white men "played Indian" and established traditions associated with their own notions of what constituted "Indianness"; a college that recommitted itself to Native American education and achieved levels of success unmatched by other institutions, though largely by default; a place Native Americans have regarded with anger, bitterness, and affection. Dartmouth's Indian history is a troubled one, as is the history of Native Americans in this country. In all of its failings, contradictions, and attempts (sometimes misguided) to do the right thing, Dartmouth's story mirrors the larger story of English and American dealings with Native peoples, over time and across the continent. Through it all, the people Wheelock intended to change at Dartmouth have helped to change Dartmouth instead, and have ensured that, at least in some respects, Dartmouth is, after all, an Indian school.

Dartmouth is, therefore, better placed than ever before to appreciate the value of its Native American collections. Like Dartmouth, museums have had a troubled relationship with Native peoples. Too often in the past, museums served as repositories for colonial plunder, kept and displayed objects without concern for or sensitivity to the purpose, power, or proper care of them in Native communities, and adopted a resistive rather than collaborative stance in dealing with Native peoples. These days, hopefully, things have changed. The Native American Graves Protection and Repatriation Act (NAGPRA) in 1990 mandated that federally funded museums must work with Native communities to identify objects that should be returned home, and the Hood Museum of Art has been a willing and active collaborator in that process. In addition, attitudes towards the objects have changed. At a time when Dartmouth was admitting few if any Indian students, Dartmouth alumni were collecting Native artifacts. At a time when museums were interested in old Native things, not living Native people, artifacts were often displayed as examples of an exotic but dying culture, interesting but largely irrelevant to modern America. Such cultural arrogance and myopic self-satisfaction lingers, of course, but today at Dartmouth—an institution founded and predicated on the assumption that learning was a one-way street, with Indians on the receiving end—the collections at the Hood Museum of Art offer glimpses into the worlds and worldviews of peoples with a longer and deeper attachment experience on this continent, with their own philosophies of what constitutes an ordered universe and a human community, and with a different vision of what America was, is, and can be. These days, we ignore such understandings at our peril.

NOTES

1. This essay is excerpted and adapted from Colin G. Calloway, *The Indian History of an American Institution: Native Americans and Dartmouth* (Hanover, N.H.: University Press of New England, 2010).

2. Occom wrote the longer version of his narrative in response to questions raised about his identity as a recently converted Mohegan as he prepared to leave on his fundraising tour in England. Samson Occom, *A Short Narrative of My Life* (1768), manuscript and typescript in Rauner Special Collections Library, Dartmouth College; Joanna Brooks, ed., *The Collected Writings of Samson Occom, Mohegan: Leadership and Literature in Eighteenth-Century Native America* (New York: Oxford University Press, 2006), 32, 42–43, 51–54.

3. Brooks, ed., *Collected Writings of Samson Occom*, 13–14; W. DeLoss Love, *Samson Occom and the Christian Indians of New England* (1899; reprinted Syracuse: Syracuse University Press, 2000); Bernd Peyer, "The Betrayal of Samson Occom," *Dartmouth Alumni Magazine* 91 (Nov. 1998): 32.

4. Jere R. Daniell, "Eleazar Wheelock and the Dartmouth College Charter," *Historical New Hampshire* 24 (Winter 1969): 3–44; James Axtell, "Dr. Wheelock's Little Red School," in his *The European and the Indian: Essays in the Ethnohistory of Colonial North America* (New York: Oxford University Press, 1981), 108 ("then he remembered").

5. Rauner Library: Wheelock to Occom, Jan. 22, 1771, Ms. 771122; Occom to Wheelock, July 24, 1774, Ms. 771424; also in Brooks, *Collected Writings of Samson Occom*, 98–100.

6. Rauner Library: Occom to Wheelock, June 1, 1773, Ms. 773351; Wheelock to Occom, July 21, 1773, Ms. 773421; Peyer, "Betrayal of Samson Occom," 36.

7. James Dow McCallum, ed., *The Letters of Eleazar Wheelock's Indians* (Hanover, N.H.: Dartmouth College Publications, 1932), 221.

8. Laura J. Murray, ed., *To Do Good to My Indian Brethren: The Writings of Joseph Johnson, 1751–1776* (Amherst: University of Massachusetts Press, 1998), 247.

9. Ibid., 54.

10. The meetings with the Oneidas and Onondagas are recorded in Rauner Library, Ms. 772174.2 and Ms. 772331, and in McCallum, *Letters of Eleazar Wheelock's Indians*, 276–88.

11. Rauner Library: McClure to Rev. J. Caldwell, Dec. 1, 1774, McClure Ms. 774651.1.

12. Mason Wade, ed., *The Journals of Francis Parkman* (New York: Harper and Bros., 1947), 1: 21, 332, n. 20.

13. Walkingstick to Rugg, Apr. 5, 1918, and Apr. 8, 1919, Rauner Library, Alumni File.

14. Smith to Rev. J. B. Treat, Dec. 31, 1872, Rauner Library, SSPCK Records, folder 1-7.

15. Gordon M. Day, "The Dartmouth Algonkian Collection," in Misc. Material File. On Day and his work, see Michael K. Foster and William Cowan, eds., *In Search of New England's Native Past: Selected Essays by Gordon M. Day* (Amherst: University of Massachusetts Press, 1998); *Western Abenaki Dictionary*, two vols. (Ottawa: Canadian Museum of Civilization, Canadian Ethnology Service, 1994–95).

16. David Wallace Adams, *Education for Extinction: American Indians and the Boarding School Experience, 1875–1982* (Lawrence: University Press of Kansas, 1995).

17. Kemeny quotations from Charles Jay Kershner, "Eleazar Is Outdone," *Dartmouth Alumni Magazine* 63 (Oct. 1970): 32.

18. Michael Dorris, *The Broken Cord* (New York: Harper and Row, 1989), 31, 42.

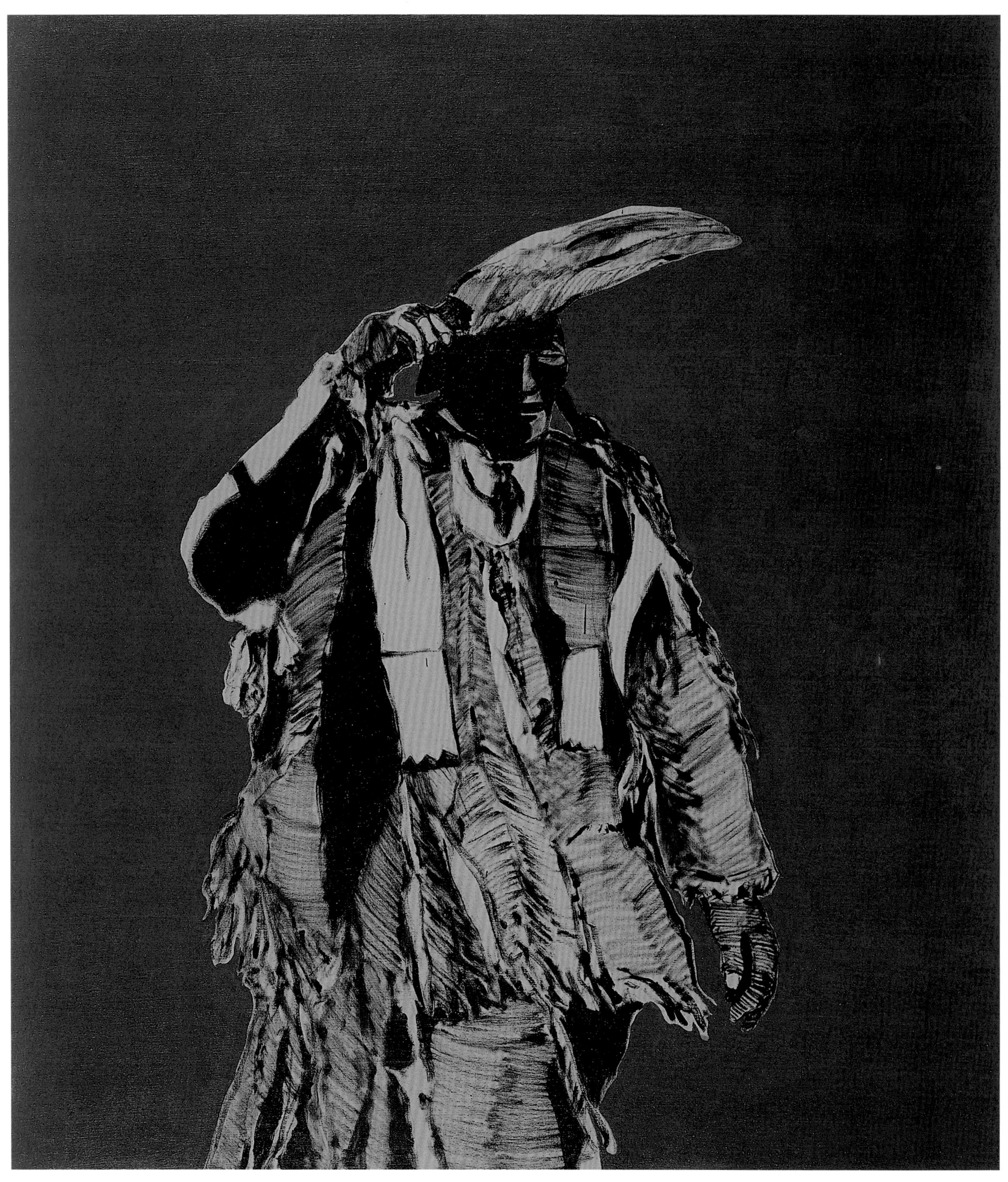

CAT. 52. Fritz Scholder, Luiseño (Luiseno), *Dartmouth Portrait #17*, 1973, oil on canvas, acrylic background. Purchased through the William B. Jaffe and Evelyn A. Jaffe Hall Fund; P.974.11.

:: 2 ::

Introduction: Native American Art at Dartmouth

Karen S. Miller

The Hood Museum of Art's Native North American holdings comprise a collection of approximately seven thousand objects that reveals a great depth of cultural complexity and artistic diversity. Almost half of the collection consists of archaeological materials such as stone artifacts, ceramic shards, and vessels, many of which were presented to the museum as gifts. The museum's collection of historic Native American art, much of which was also donated, is especially strong in basketry, beadwork, clothing, and others examples of the Plains pictorial tradition dating from around 1850 to the early 1900s. This area also includes the Mark Lansburgh Ledger Drawing Collection, comprising over 130 objects, which was featured in a fall 2010 exhibition at the Hood.

More recently, the Hood has begun to collect works by contemporary Native American artists, an effort largely spearheaded by former curator of African, Oceanic, and Native American collections Barbara Thompson (curator from 2002 through 2008). The Hood's growing collection of approximately four hundred works made by named Native American artists active from around 1900 to the present boasts a wide range of media, including ceramics, basketry, beadwork, glass, photography, canvas paintings, collages, and found objects. These works are crucial to the museum's mission of teaching with objects, and for presenting the continuity within Native American culture between the past and the present.

This exhibition and catalogue bring together for the first time the Hood's historic and contemporary collections of Native American art, demonstrating the diversity of these important holdings and testifying to the interest in Native cultures by Dartmouth faculty, students, and alumni, museum patrons, and community members. Though it is not encyclopedic, the exhibition is organized by region and includes many of the major art-producing cultures of Native North America. Where museum staff has been able to trace the provenance of objects, these narratives about a work's journey from its maker through the hands of its collectors to the Hood Museum of Art provide an alternate means of approaching and understanding the dynamic nature of the relationships between maker and collector that determine its fate.

The exhibition's contemporary works, including paintings Fritz Scholder created during his residency at Dartmouth in 1973, bronzes by Allen Houser as well as a large sculpture by his son Bob Haozous, ledger art by Dwayne Wilcox, and weavings by Sierra Teller Ornelas, reveal both the continuity and the perpetual evolution of long-held modes and conventions of cultural expression among Native peoples, whether through exchange among Native groups or between Natives and non-Natives. The contemporary work in particular also reveals artists' engagement with issues of Native self-identity, as it often builds upon or revisits historic forms of expression as a means of subverting stereotypes about Native art.

Native American Art at Dartmouth guest curators George Horse Capture, Joe Horse Capture, and Joseph Sanchez have each contributed a unique perspective and area of expertise to this exhibition. George Horse Capture and his son Joe are both members of the A'aninin (Gros Ventre) tribe from Fort Belknap Indian Reservation in Montana. George is an anthropologist/writer/lecturer/curator who has served as assistant professor of American Indian Studies at Montana State University (1977–79) and as curator of the Plains Indian Museum in Cody, Wyoming (1980–90). At the National Museum of the American Indian in Washington, D.C., between 1993 and 2005, he took an active role in most phases of the establishment of the museum, retiring in 2005 as the senior counselor to the director. He has both contributed to and edited numerous publications on Native American material culture. Joe Horse Capture is associate curator of Native American art at the Minneapolis Institute of Arts, where he has curated a number of exhibitions, including *From Our Ancestors: Art of the White Clay People* in 2010. Joseph Sanchez has served as museum deputy director as well as chief curator, exhibitions coordinator, and curator of exhibitions at the Institute of American Indian Arts (IAIA) in Santa Fe, New Mexico. An artist and museum professional who has been heavily engaged in promoting the contemporary Native American arts community, Sanchez received the Allan Houser Memorial Award for Excellence in the Arts in 2006.

This catalogue, with essays by the curators and a group of other independent scholars, as well as statements by the contemporary artists themselves, thus acknowledges the necessity of recognizing multiple voices and varied interpretations in coming to a fuller understanding of and appreciation for this work.

The Dartmouth College Museum and Native American Art

Dartmouth College's long association with Native Americans began with the school's founding in 1769 with a charter from George III for the "education and instruction of youth of the Indian tribes in this land . . . and also of English Youth and any others." Despite this, the college's first two hundred years were devoted mostly to educating non-Native students (only seventy-one Native Americans attended between 1770 and 1865, followed by just twenty-eight more in the succeeding hundred years). In 1970, Dartmouth's thirteenth president, John G. Kemeny, renewed the charter's original commitment and established Dartmouth's Native American Program and, shortly thereafter, the Native American Studies Department. Today 185 Native American students are enrolled, and a total of 834 students have graduated since 1970.

Certainly Dartmouth has long had a complicated relationship with Native America and Native Americans. Despite the fact that very few Native students were actually educated at Dartmouth until Kemeny's mandate in 1970, a sort of mythology nevertheless arose around Dartmouth's connection to Native America (see Colin Calloway's essay in this volume). In part because of this, a number of students, professors, and alumni took an interest in Native Americans over the years, particularly with regard to their material culture, and Dartmouth College began to actively collect works deemed worthy as ethnographic specimens in the late nineteenth and early twentieth centuries. These collections were eventually used mostly for teaching in the Anthropology Department, which was founded in 1967. In the earlier part of the twentieth century, these objects were viewed as traces of cultures that had been affected by relocation and assimilation—as artifacts of "vanishing" peoples. As a result, a type of "salvage mentality" characterized the earlier academic view of indigenous cultures at this time; it also formed the basis for much museum policy and practice into the 1970s. The Dartmouth College Museum had its own idiosyncratic history, in which donated objects considered to be duplicates were in some instances exchanged with other museums, such as the Reading Museum in England in 1939. Unlike some larger museums, such as the Smithsonian Institution, there were no collecting expeditions or large purchases at Dartmouth. However, it was thought to be desirable to have a collection that covered a wide range of indigenous groups. Interestingly, a number of Native American alumni gave works representing their own cultures: David H. Markham, Class of 1915 (Cherokee artifacts); Ronald B. Sundown, Class of 1932 (Seneca snow snake stick); and Henry G. Perley Jr., Class of 1943 (a collection of beadwork and clothing).

As Tamara Northern, curator of ethnographic art at Dartmouth from 1976 to 1999, wrote in 1985: "[The college's] collection was assembled during the period when traditional native cultures were changing rapidly and was formed with the intent of documenting the remaining spectrum of material culture."[1] The timeframe of the Dartmouth collection of traditional art ended at 1950, reflecting the dominant Western cultural mode of the nineteenth and twentieth centuries in which the material culture of the ethnic "other" in its "traditional" state is viewed as "pure" and therefore superior. American museum practice therefore adopted a collecting strategy focused on those objects produced before the time when cultural degradation or degeneration was thought to have begun.[2] It must be stated, however, that most of Dartmouth's collections in this area were not the result of a systematic policy of acquisition but rather gifts from a wide array of donors; there were not many actual purchases by the college itself. The few early pre-reservation objects in the collection were donated in the nineteenth century, while the bulk of the collections dates from the post-reservation period.

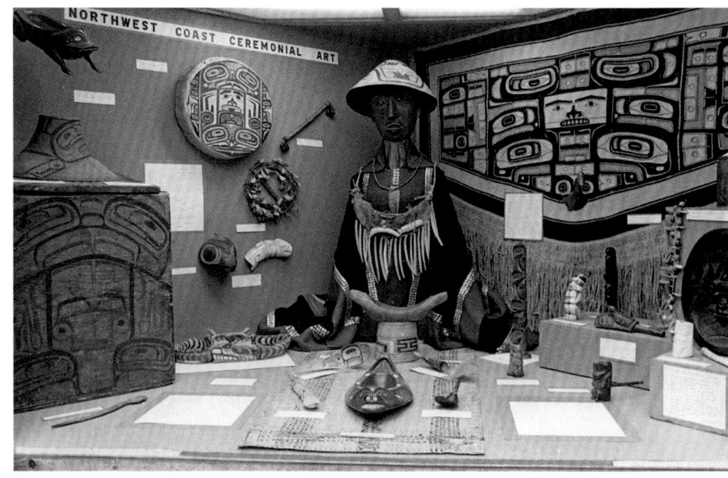

FIG. 2.1. "Northwest Coast Ceremonial Art," installation, Wilson Hall, Dartmouth College, ca. mid-1970s (indicated as "removed 1978").

The history of how the Dartmouth College Museum's Native American collections were assembled is addressed in W. Wedgwood Bowen's *A Pioneer Museum in the Wilderness* (1958). Many of the college's very earliest Native American artifacts did not survive the Dartmouth Hall fire of 1798 or the subsequent collection relocations of the following two centuries.[3] Its museum, nevertheless, went on to house "specimens" from a number of disciplines, tabulated in 1810, for example, as follows: anthropology, 101 specimens; zoology, 71 specimens; botany, 21 specimens; paleontology, 65 specimens; geology, 99 specimens; history, 3 specimens; unidentified, 23 specimens; and "freak," 15 specimens.[4] Some of the early Native American objects given to the collection and listed in the same 1810 ledger were a "Cherokee Pipe. Given by Mr. Fisk"; "A horn comb from Nootka Sound. Given by A. Holden"; and a "Squaw's fan. Given by Capt. Kendrick." The museum's unstated policy with regard to its ethnographic materials—"the encyclopedic documentation of world cultures"—remained fairly consistent through 1985, reflecting the cultural view of non-Western art as occupying a separate category from Western "fine art."[5] The separate fine art collections staff at the college, however, did acquire non-Western objects in the 1960s, 1970s, and early 1980s, but classified them as art, not ethnographic objects (fig. 2.1).

In general, of course, even "Native American art" itself is an essentialized classification heavily laden with centuries of stereotyping. Popular views of (as well as scholarship on) Native American art were for most of the twentieth century characterized by oversimplification and romanticization, mired as they were in the legacy of cultural evolutionary thinking that positions Western "civilized" people over indigenous "primitive" people, and in the link between

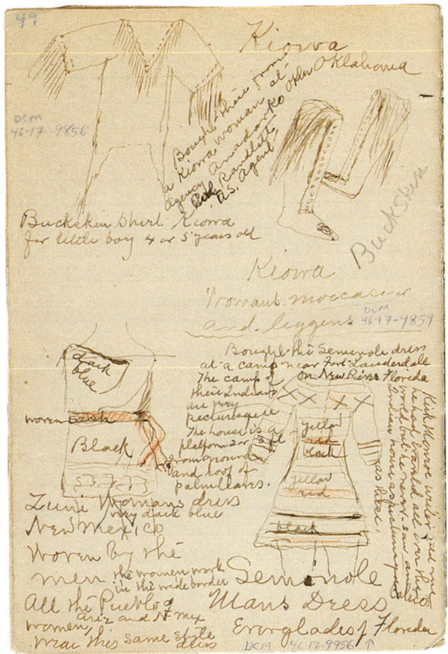

FIG. 2.2. From a notebook entitled "Indian Things. Churchill Museum. Catalogue. Mrs. Frank C. Churchill, Lebanon, NH," ca. 1909.

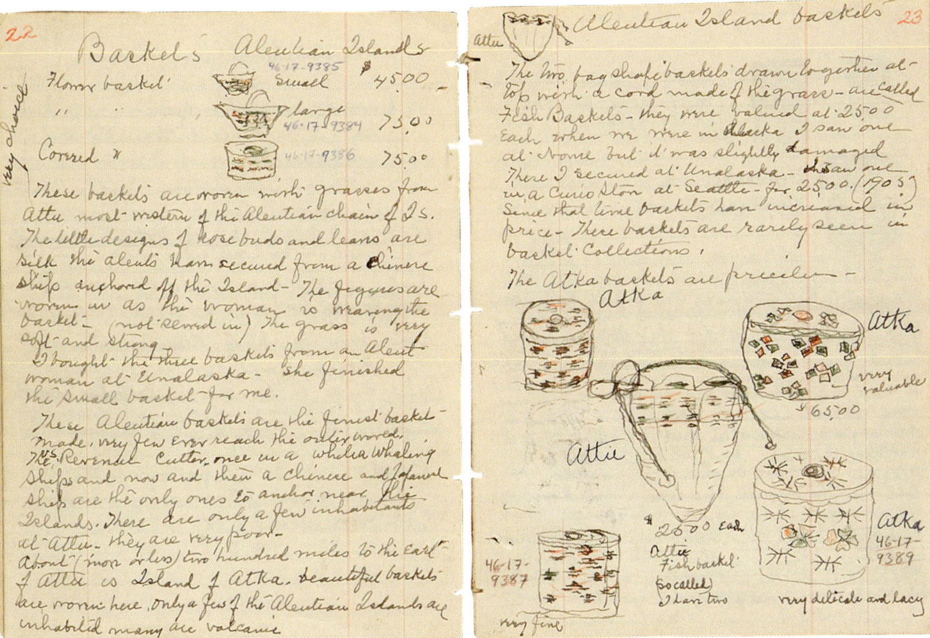

FIG. 2.3. From a notebook entitled "Indian Baskets. Alaska Curio's (*sic*)... Mrs. Frank C. Churchill. Churchill Museum," July–September 1905.

"authenticity" and "the traditional." Institutions held indigenous art to represent a pure culture in its ideal form, thus serving at once to "other" and to legitimize it. While Western art is largely defined by innovation, indigenous art has been largely defined (and constrained) by strict convention, in turn reflected by Western museum practice and especially its taxonomic focus on classification by type.

At Dartmouth, the Native American collection has a unique history characterized largely by a series of important donations. According to Bowen, the decade from 1935 to 1946 was very fruitful in terms of the amount of ethnological material donated to Dartmouth. Of particular note is the 1946 bequest of 1,400 objects by local residents Frank C. and Clara G. Churchill, representing culture areas across the continent. They collected the objects while Frank Churchill was a special federal inspector of Indian schools for the Bureau of Indian Affairs from 1899 to 1909.[6] Clara Churchill was the primary collector and kept a diary and took photographs during their travels. She recorded collection locations, forty-two of the objects' makers, and purchase prices. Though she did not record the maker of a Seminole men's shirt, she did record "Mrs. Adolf Rankin" as the maker of an Alutiiq basket (figs. 2.2 and 2.3), dated about 1905. After the Churchills retired to their home in Lebanon, New Hampshire, they opened the "Churchill Museum." Frank Churchill died in 1911, and the George Gustav Heye Foundation courted his widow, hoping to obtain the collection from her. She wanted the collection to remain near her home, however, and when she died in 1946, it was given to the Dartmouth College Museum. The collection is comprised largely of objects that were accessible to the public as part of the tourist trade around the turn of the century, including pottery, baskets, textiles, clothing, and other accessories, and more than half of the collection derives from the Southwest and Alaska. The Churchills also collected utilitarian objects that were not part of the typical tourist trade. While the collection does not include many objects of ritual significance, it did include two A:shiwi (Zuni) prayer sticks, which were repatriated in 1995 (see Kellen Haak's essay on the Hood's NAGPRA compliance later in this volume).

Other important early additions to the collection include the forty-four objects given by Mrs. William M. Leeds during the years 1879–88, including a Plains war bonnet, dated about 1870 (cat. 137); the gift of Southwest ceramics from Emily and George H. Browne, including a seed jar in Sikyatki Revival Style by the famous Hopi ceramist Nampeyo, dated to about 1900–1910 (cat. 70); the Kimberly collection of objects from Western Alaska and the Northwest Coast, bequeathed in 1922; the Wellington collection of 188 Indian dolls, which was gifted in 1987 (the Wellington doll collection was commissioned by "Duke" Wellington for his daughter in the 1940s and 1950s from well-known artisans with the understanding that the figures were to represent accurate depictions of traditional dress); the two hundred Northwest Coast, Arctic, and Subarctic objects collected by Axel Rasmussen and donated by Doris Meltzer between 1958 and 1966, including a Tlingit storage box (cat. 37); the eighty baskets donated by Mrs. Ida Farr Miller in 1944, including a Yokuts treasure basket, dated about 1890, from Kern County in northern California (cat. 50); and the Lt. Col. Alfred T. Clifton collection of Arctic material, given in 1942, including a Yup'ik *Nepcetat* mask, dated about 1930 (cat. 5).

Much later, in the fall of 1985, Mrs. Guido R. Rahr Sr. (parent of a member of the Class of 1951) donated her late husband's collection

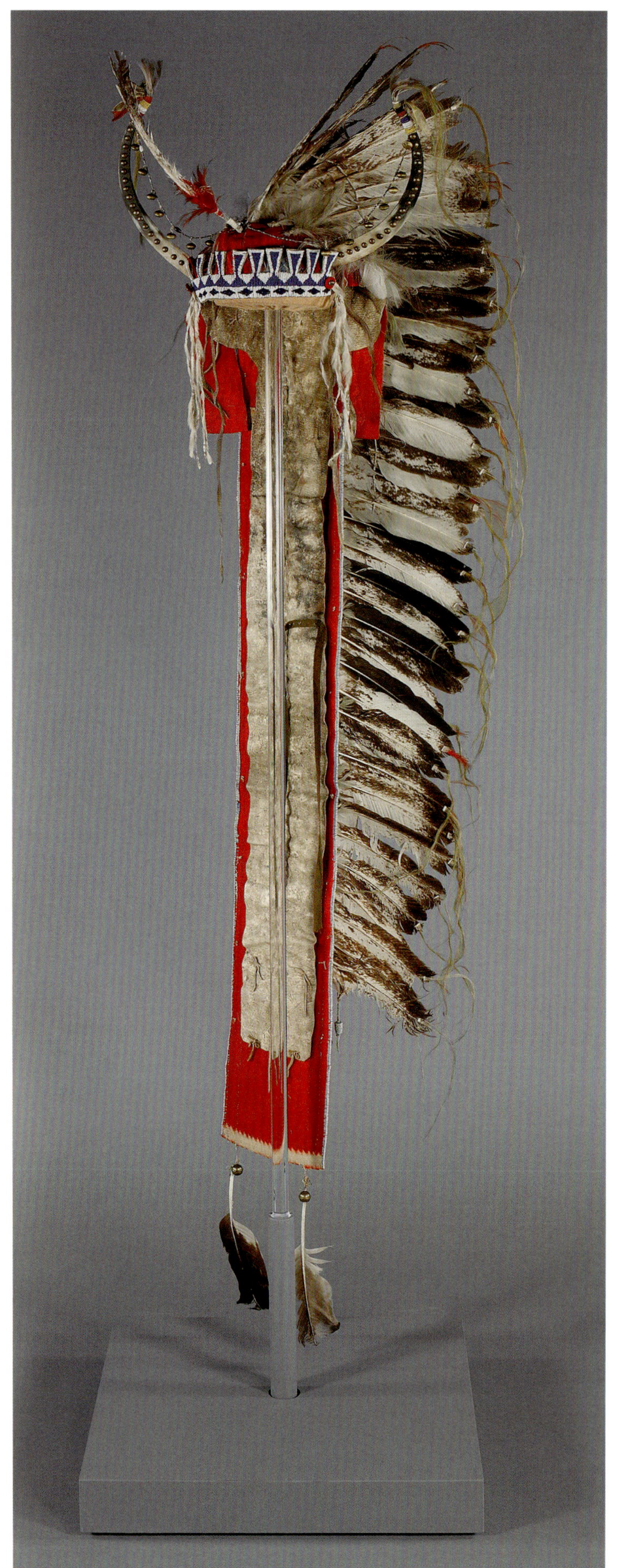

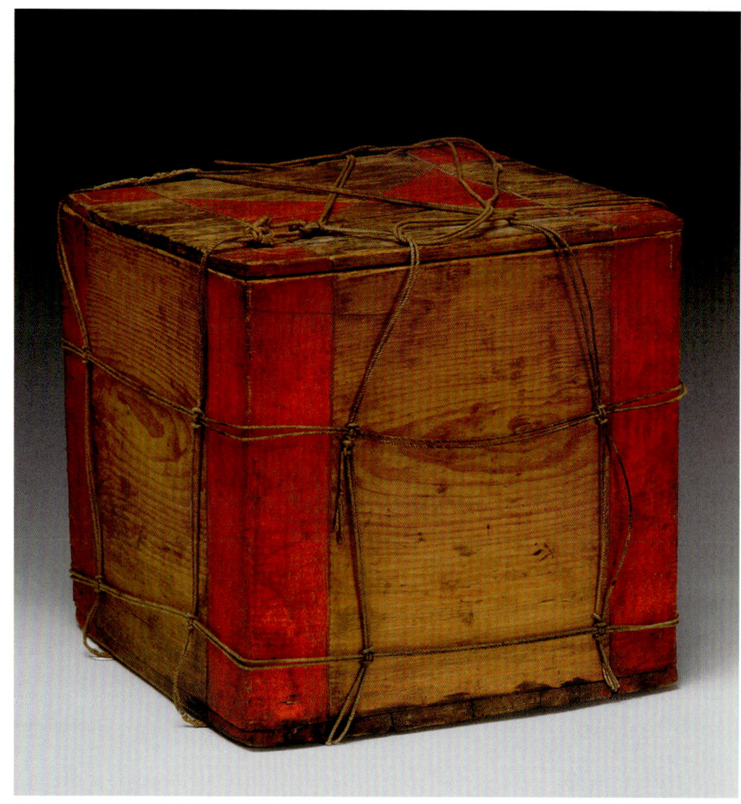

CAT. 37. Artist unknown, Tlingit, Hoonah, Alaska, storage box, after 1900, wood, paint, string, and spruce root. Gift of Doris Meltzer and the Meltzer Gallery; 159.1.14292.

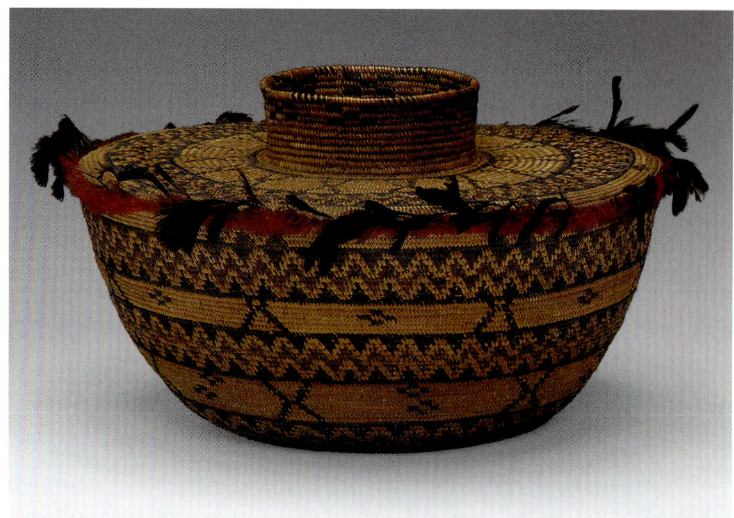

CAT. 50. Artist unknown, Yokuts, Kern County, California, treasure basket, about 1890, deer grass, bracken fern root, redbud, California valley quail crests, wool yarn. Gift of Mrs. Ida Farr Miller; 44.18.8755.

CAT. 137. Artist unknown, possibly Osage or Chaticks Si Chaticks (Pawnee), Oklahoma, split horn bonnet, about 1870, hide, rawhide, bald eagle feathers, downy feathers, toned turkey feathers, cow horn, glass beads, metal beads, brass hawk bells, brass tacks, wool cloth, ermine, thimbles, ribbon, horse hair, lead weight, dye, sinew, string, and thread. Gift of Mrs. William M. Leeds; 13.137.4094C.

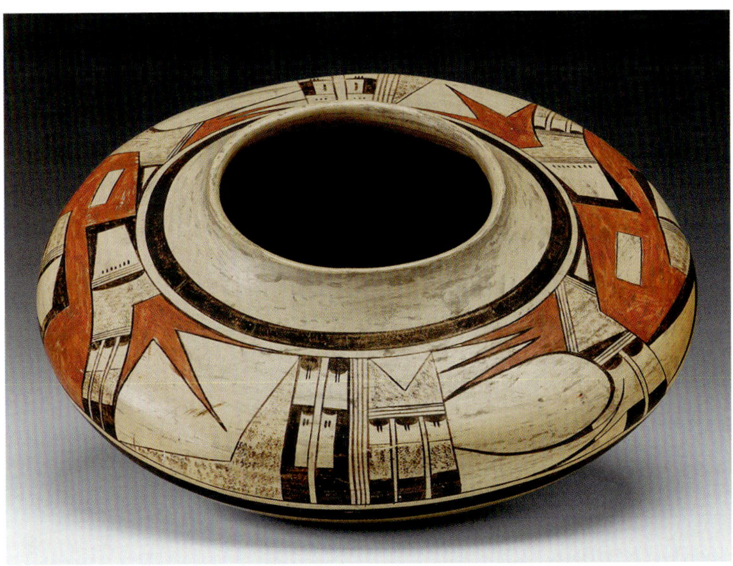

CAT. 70. Nampeyo, Hopi (Hano Pueblo), seed jar in Sikyatki Revival Style, about 1900–1910, earthenware, painted with colored slips and burnished. Gift of Mr. and Mrs. George H. Browne; 42.12.8107.

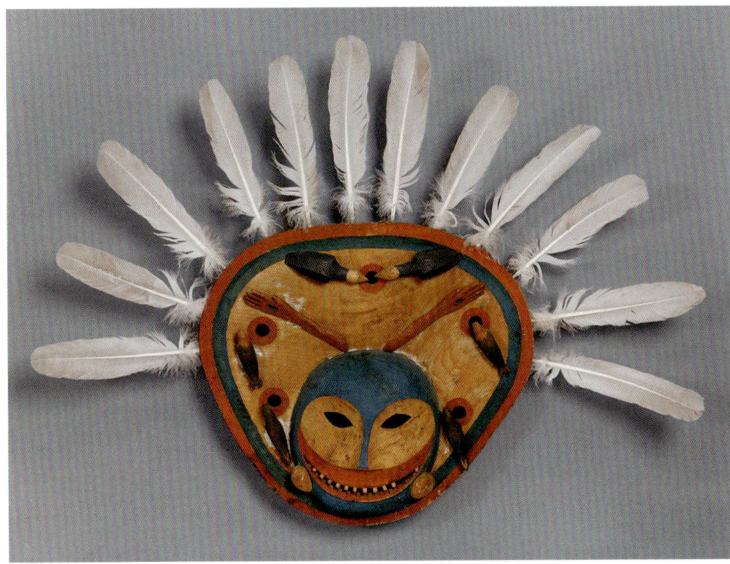

CAT. 5. Artist unknown, Central Yup'ik, St. Michael, Alaska, *Nepcetat* mask, about 1930, wood, paint, rawhide, nails, swan feathers, and seagull (replacement) feathers. Gift of Lt. Col. Alfred T. Clifton, Class of 1927P; 42.15.7803.

of Native American art to the Hood in his name. Primarily from the Plains and Woodlands regions, this group of 250 objects includes a Tsistsistas/Suhtai (Cheyenne) cradle, dated about 1870 (cat. 129).[7] A 1987 exhibition and publication of this collection titled *Patterns of Life, Patterns of Art: The Rahr Collection of Native American Art* highlighted this donation.

Other important donors of objects, who also provided information about the Native cultures they studied, were faculty members Vilhjalmur Stefansson, Elmer Harp Jr., and Alfred Whiting. Stefansson (1879–1962) and Harp (1913–2009) were Arctic explorers whose experiences and scholarship laid the groundwork for Dartmouth's Institute of Arctic Studies, while Professor Alfred F.

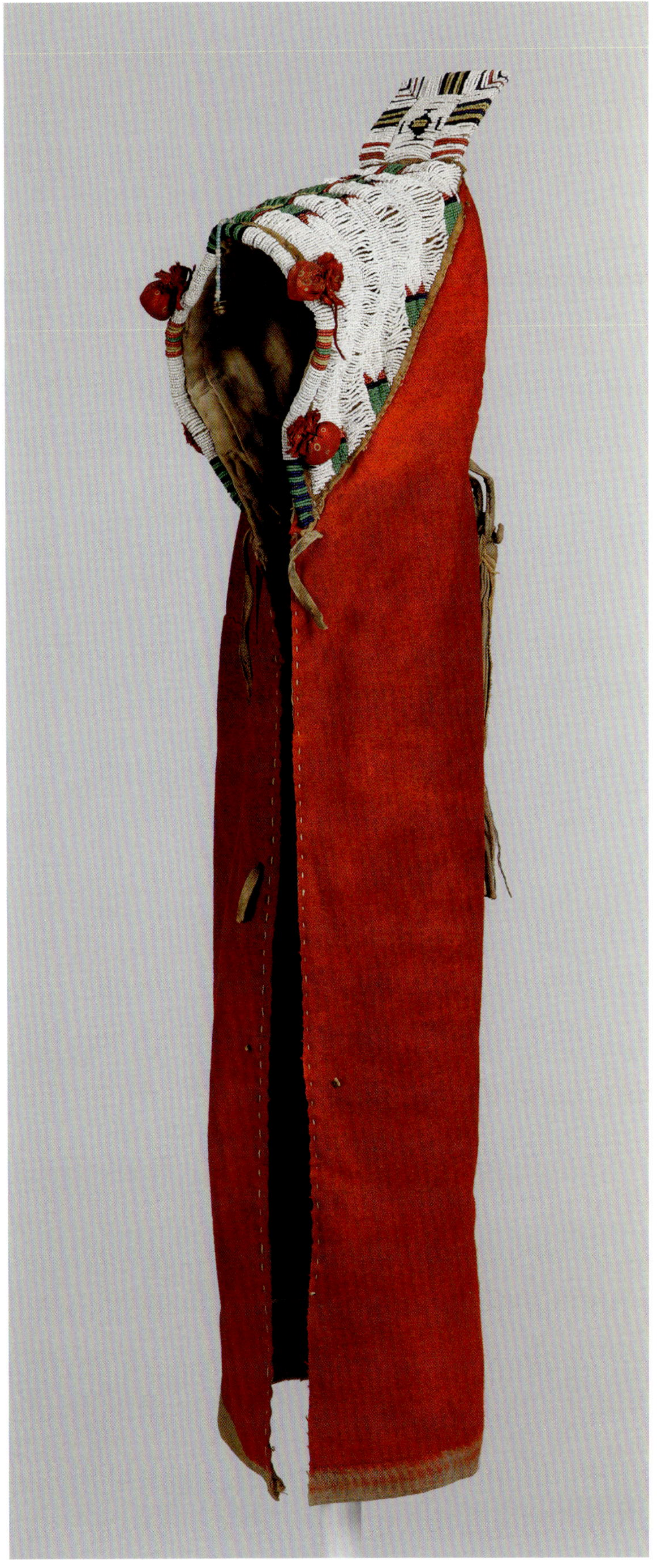

CAT. 129. Artist unknown, Tsistsistas/Suhtai (Cheyenne), cradle, about 1870, glass beads, stroud, Native-tanned bison hide, rawhide, wood, cotton cloth, brass bell, string, sinew, thread. Gift of Guido R. Rahr Sr., Class of 1951P; 985.47.26531.

Whiting (1912–1978; curator from 1955 to 1975) played an important role in the development of Dartmouth's Anthropology Department as well as its museum and collections.[8] Whiting was an ethnobotanist by training and collected about two hundred objects for the Dartmouth College Museum, including plant specimens and utilitarian objects from the Southwest. His teaching focused on contemporary material culture. In 1962 he invited Edmund Nequatewa (1880–1969), a Hopi teacher from Second Mesa, Arizona, to come to Dartmouth and demonstrate how to make digging sticks, drums, and prayer offerings.

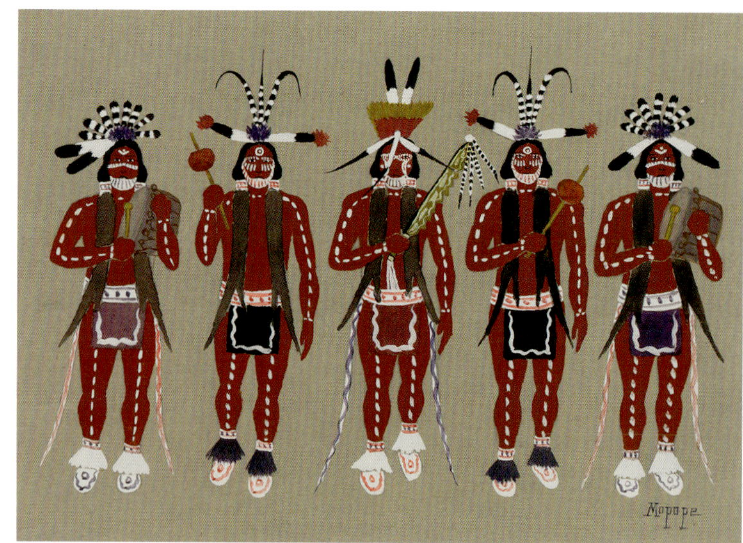

FIG. 2.4. Stephen Mopope, Gaigwa (Kiowa), *Gourd Dance*, before 1930, opaque and transparent watercolor over graphite on gray wove paper. Gift of Abby Aldrich Rockefeller; W.935.1.84.

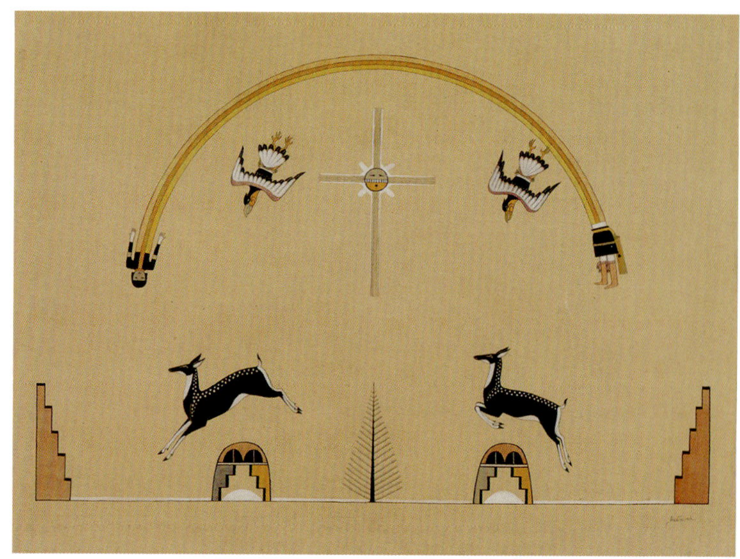

FIG. 2.5. Awa Tsireh (Alfonso Roybal), San Ildefonso Pueblo, *Rainbow and Deer Design*, before 1931, transparent and opaque watercolor over graphite on wove (Canson & Montgolfier) paper, mounted on board. Gift of Abby Aldrich Rockefeller; W.935.1.96.

Recent History

Late in the twentieth century, an ideological shift resulted in a change in Western art museum practice, setting the stage for the integration of Dartmouth College's museum collections under one roof. The Hood Museum of Art would join Dartmouth's ethnographic, archaeology, and history collections from Wilson Hall with the fine art collections, which had been housed in the Hopkins Center. Beginning earlier in the twentieth century, Western art museums had integrated indigenous objects into their collections; however, a further shift took place in the scholarship of the 1980s, reflective of the practice of "new art history," a subjective interpretive endeavor that privileges the positioning of the work of art in its historical and cultural context. When the Hood opened, the inaugural exhibition in its Gutman Gallery, named after generous donors Mary Bert and Alvin P. Gutman, Class of 1940, and dedicated to showing non-Western art, was devoted to the display of eighty Native American objects from the collection curated by Tamara Northern.

Though a comprehensive overview of Native American history is beyond the scope of this essay, it is important to bear in mind the profoundly traumatic and rapid cultural change that was forced upon Native Americans in the decades following first contact with European Americans. The transition from a subsistence lifestyle to a cash-based economy led to the development of a market for Native handicrafts, thus changing the way Native Americans viewed their own material culture. Western interest, to an extent, transformed the symbolic value of many art works (whether Inupiat ivory carving, Yup'ik mask, or Hopi kachina) from sacred objects to commodities. During the late nineteenth and early twentieth centuries, Native peoples also began producing items designed specifically for sale to non-Natives. Before long, then, collectors and museums likewise began to distinguish between this "tourist art" and objects made for Native use. While most of the objects collected and donated to Dartmouth by the Churchills were made for the tourist market, the distinction is less relevant today. Due to shifting notions about the work of indigenous cultures and a fundamental recognition that change and innovation are inherent to any aesthetically based cultural production, a work is not judged solely on notions of authenticity or "purity" but is, instead, viewed in context, whether commercial or ritual, as a product of its sociocultural milieu. In many respects this collection serves the Hood's teaching mission well, as both the functional objects and the more aesthetic works can be used in classes from a variety of disciplines and speak to historical, art historical, literary, religious, and societal issues.

Recent examples of work produced primarily for a non-Native audience includes the paintings of the Kiowa Five in Oklahoma and of the artists of the Santa Fe Studio School, both dating to the second quarter of the twentieth century. In each case, white teachers/mentors deliberately and purposefully shaped the artistic production of their Native students. The men from Anadarko, Oklahoma, who came to be known as the Kiowa Five—James Auchiah (1906–1974), Spencer Asah (1905–1954), Jack Hokeah (1902–1969),

Stephen Mopope (1898–1974), and Monroe Tsatoke (1904–1937)—began their studies with Susan Ryan Peters, the Indian Service Field Matron at the Kiowa Agency in Anadarko. She would introduce them to Professor Oscar Jacobson, director of the Art Department at the University of Oklahoma in Norman, in 1926, and he would help them lay the foundation for what would later become known as "Plains Indian painting." The men's representational, narrative style of depicting historical and ceremonial tribal events with single or grouped figures arranged in dramatic poses is reflected in the Hood's *Gourd Dance*, dated to before 1930, by Stephen Mopope (fig. 2.4).

Dorothy Dunn (1903–1992), an artist and art teacher, established the Studio School at the Santa Fe Indian School in 1932. *Rainbow and Deer Design*, dated before 1931, by Awa Tsireh (Alfonso Roybal, 1898–1955), San Ildefonso Pueblo, is representative of the work of this school, which is characterized by an illustrative style in which flat fields of color render scenes of ceremony, dance, and myth (fig. 2.5).[9] The Santa Fe Studio School ultimately spawned the Indian Fine Arts Movement, which "was predominately driven by non-Native tastes and ideas about what 'Indian art' and representations of 'Indians' should look like. Distanced as they were from pre-reservation Indian life, with only their lived experiences of the reservations to draw from, these new artists propelled themselves into the international art market by producing romantic depictions of pan-tribal lifestyle. These images soon evolved into the iconic stereotypes of the American Indian that continue to appear in American popular culture."[10] Characterized by simplified and romanticized depictions of ceremonial practices and of the mythologized relationship between indigenous peoples and nature, this style of painting is sometimes referred to as "Bambi art." Though it represents an important genre in twentieth-century Native American art (and is valued by collectors), this type of artistic production is controversial; contemporary Native artists in particular have opposed its apparent acquiescence to the notion that non-Natives can dictate to Natives what Native art is or is not.

Today, contemporary Native artists claim the right to determine what forms, materials, and ideas they will apply in their artistic expression. Beginning in the 1970s with Fritz Scholder and T. C. Cannon, and even dating back to Allan Houser in the 1960s—all of whom were involved with the Institute of American Indian Arts (IAIA), founded in 1962 in Santa Fe—there was a purposeful effort on the part of Native artists to reclaim their art and its cultural significance, both Native and non-Native. Their efforts (and those of their successors) are characterized by an innovative use of materials and an emphasis on free experimentation and personal expression, as well as a pointed engagement with identity politics. Through deliberate references to historical forms, they invoke their culture not in a nostalgic way but as a means of proclaiming its ongoing relevance. While their work is not bound aesthetically or formally to "traditional" material culture or modes of expression, they use these forms nevertheless as signifiers of culture, purposefully invoking ethnic signs as a means of affirming cultural identity.

With then Hood Director Derrick Cartwright's appointment of Barbara Thompson as curator of African, Oceanic, and Native American collections in 2002, the Hood Museum of Art undertook a purposeful effort to change the paradigms of collecting and

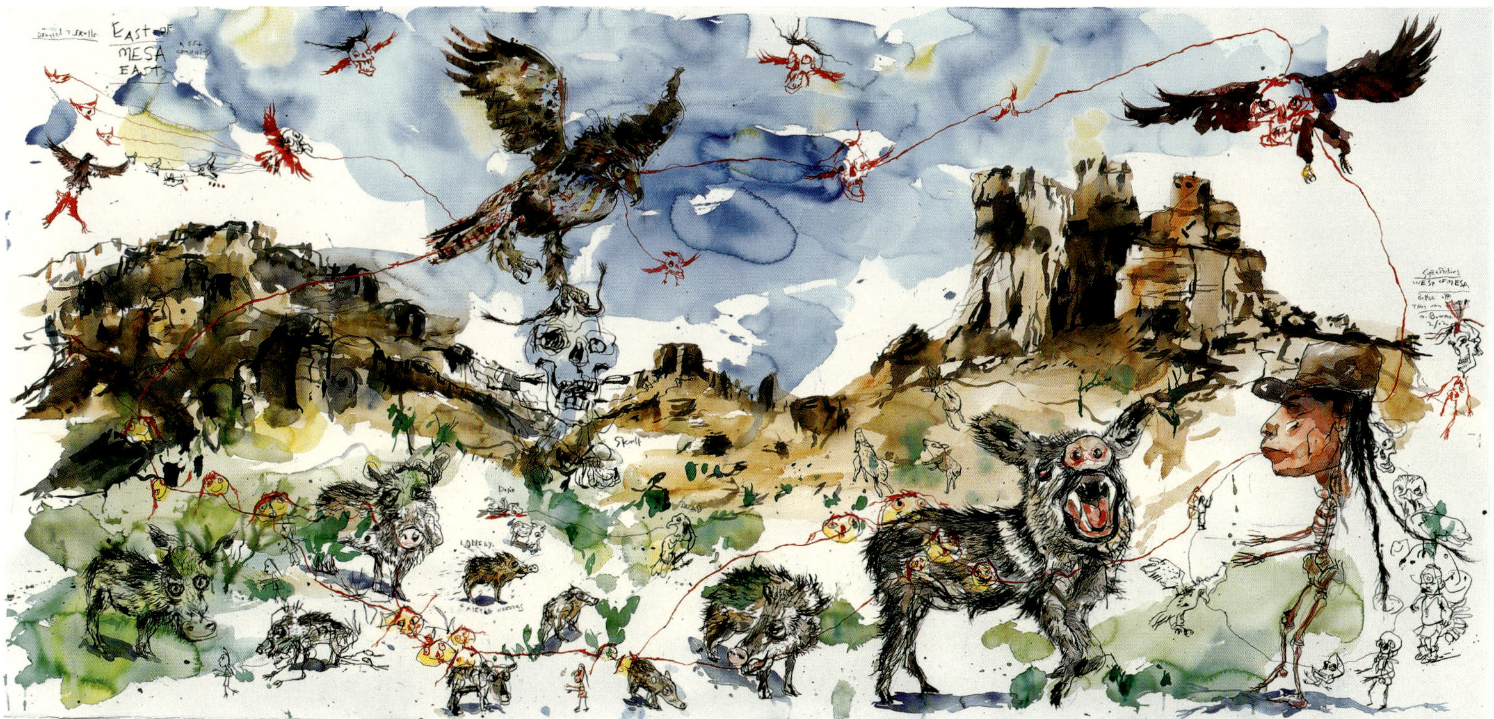

FIG. 2.6. Brad Kahlhamer, American, *East of Mesa East, A 55 Plus Community*, 2002, ink and watercolor on paper. Purchased through the Stephen and Constance Spahn '63 Acquisition Fund; W.2003.40.

exhibiting.[11] Toward this end, Thompson set out to expand the collection, particularly into categories of indigenous art that had been previously marginalized or excluded by art museums. Her stated aim was to "acquire objects that reflect the continuation *and* transformation of older cultural practices."[12] In both her acquisitions and her exhibitions, Thompson deliberately sought to link the present to the past:

> Although most museum practitioners and the public broadly think of these collections as comprising "traditional" objects from the precolonial/pre-settler and colonial/settler periods, museum curators of African, Oceanic, and Native American collections increasingly are recognizing the importance of acquiring works created after the 1950s as a reflection of the constant (re)negotiation and (re)definition of cultural, regional, national, and international artistic identities and boundaries. Not only can acquisitions of post-1950s art from these regions of the world help the public to reconnect with historic or traditional arts in new and challenging ways but they can more clearly communicate the complex and diverse nature of intercultural, multicultural, and transcultural relationships both in the past and the present.[13]

Among the acquisitions made during this time were Brad Kahlhamer's *East of Mesa East, A 55 Plus Community*, 2002 (fig. 2.6), Jaune Quick-to-See Smith's *The Rancher*, 2002 (cat. 84), and Hulleah J. Tsinhnahjinnie's *Photographic Memoirs of an Aboriginal Savant Living on Occupied Land,* 1994 (see pp. 74–75). The collection of contemporary Native American art continues to be part of the acquisition plan of the Hood Museum of Art going forward.

The Legacy of the Artist-in-Residence Program

Begun in 1929 largely through the efforts of Churchill (Jerry) Lathrop, professor of art and director of Dartmouth's art galleries (1928–69), Dartmouth's artist-in-residence program has represented an important contribution to campus life by what is now known as the Studio Art Department, bringing to Dartmouth figures as diverse as José Clement Orozco and Robert Rauschenberg. In writing about the program in his letters of invitation to prospective visiting artists, then director Matthew Wysocki summarized the program as follows: "The purpose of the Artist-in-Residence is two-fold: to afford students, faculty and the community the opportunity of witnessing a contemporary artist at work, exchanging ideas, opening new doors; and to offer the visitor a fresh environment in which to work—an academic environment where liberal humanistic studies at the undergraduate level are in the forefront, and in which the creative endeavor in the Arts and scholarship is encouraged."[14]

With Dartmouth's renewed commitment to the education of Native Americans and the implementation of initiatives in support of this effort, a number of Native artists were invited to campus for residencies, beginning with Fritz Scholder in fall 1973. David Rettig, Class of 1975, formerly a Santa Fe gallery owner and more recently curator of the Allan Houser Foundation, worked as a department assistant for Matthew Wysocki and recalled that Scholder was invited in response to the impetus created by Professor Michael Dorris and the fledgling Native American Studies Department at Dartmouth.[15] Scholder (1937–2005), Luiseno, was trained by Yanktonai Sioux artist Oscar Howe from 1950 to 1954 and then studied at California State University Sacramento under Wayne Thiebaud. He began an earnest exploration of Native-themed art when, in 1961, he became a graduate assistant in the Fine Arts Department of the University of Arizona. Upon receiving his MFA in 1964, Scholder began teaching at the Institute of American Indian Arts (IAIA) in Santa Fe, where he remained until 1969. In 1972, he was tapped by Adelyn Breeskin, curator of contemporary painting and sculpture at the Smithsonian Institution, for an exhibition in Washington, D.C., titled *Two American Painters*. Scholder was asked to name other Native American artists of note, and he chose a former student at the IAIA, T. C. Cannon. The two were promptly identified as the vanguard of the next generation of Native art.

While at Dartmouth, Scholder worked on a series of numbered portraits that includes *Dartmouth Portrait #17,* 1973 (cat. 52). The *Dartmouth Portraits,* comprised of over two dozen works, is "actually a series within a series—the larger series being that of the American Indian" that Scholder began painting in 1967.[16] In 1964, Scholder had promised never to paint an American Indian himself, so tired was he of stereotypical images of "traditional" Native life. Later, he said: "I broke my vow of 1964 because I saw my students trying to do something—trying to break out of the mold—and doing it badly. You can't teach painting, but you can set examples . . . so I painted an Indian."[17] *Dartmouth Portrait #17* makes direct reference to the controversy surrounding Dartmouth's Indian mascot that was very much in the public consciousness at the time, its use having been discouraged by the administration in the early 1970s. This painting, and *Drunken Indian in Car,* 1974 (cat. 53), capture Scholder's fundamental conviction: "In America Indian artists must step from the arena of curios and trinkets into the world of fine objects and expressive painting . . . Although I have painted what often appear to be ugly Indians, I have tried to paint the torture that it seems to me the Indians have had to go through . . . I have painted the Indian real, not red."[18] While at Dartmouth Scholder was extremely prolific, and his exhibition from September 28 to October 21, 1973, in the Jaffe-Friede Gallery of the Hopkins Center was comprised of eleven large canvases and nine lithographs. He also gave two slide lectures and made a lasting impression on both students and community members alike. Wysocki wrote: "Not only has he completed numerous canvases but he has had considerable contact with the students in terms of both lectures and painting demonstrations"[19] The Hood has in its collection three paintings and ten prints by Scholder, a concrete and lasting legacy of his time at Dartmouth.

The next Native American to be invited to Dartmouth as artist-in-residence was (fittingly, given his association with Scholder) T. C. Cannon, who came during summer 1975. His exhibition, held

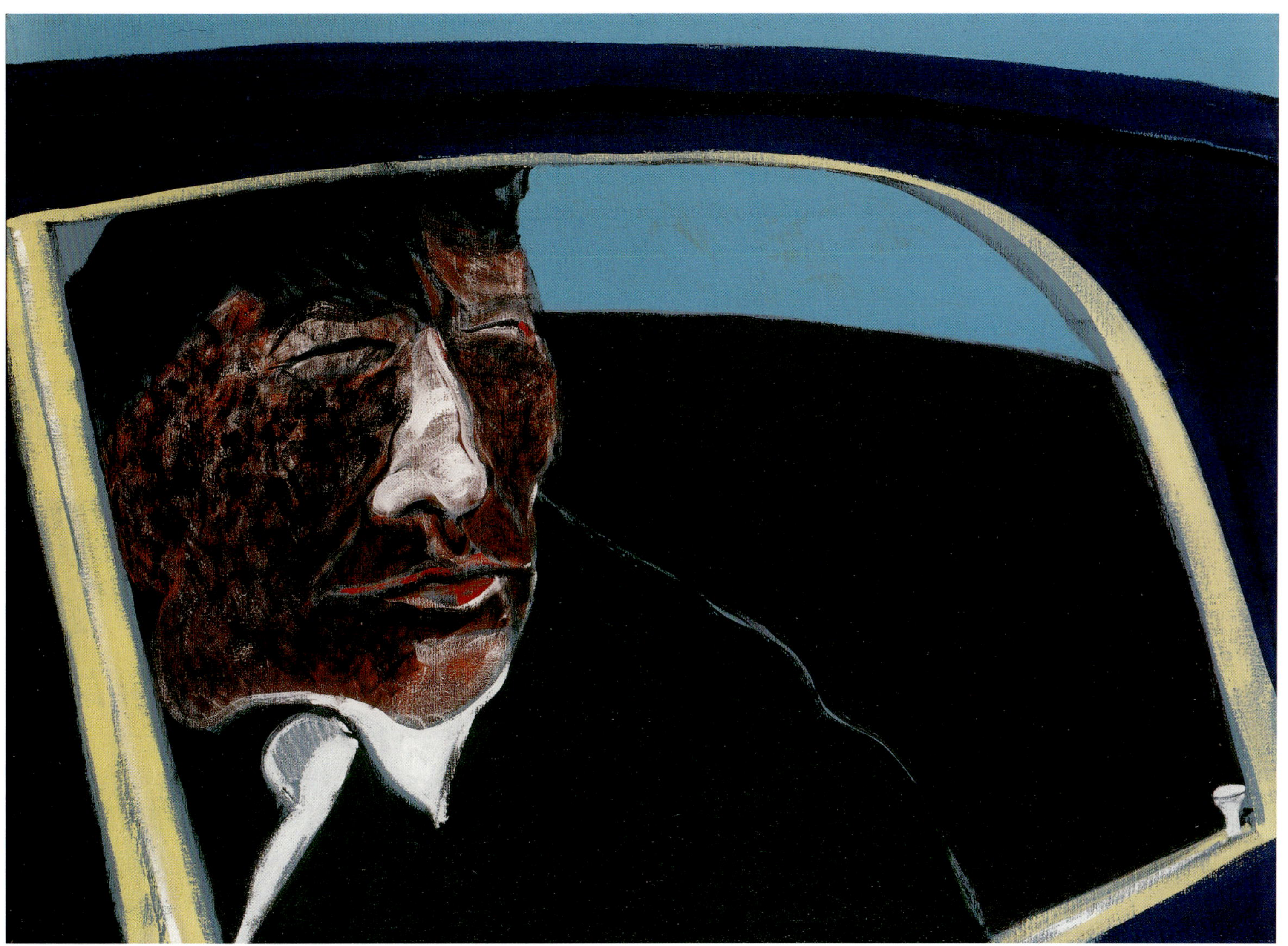

CAT. 53. Fritz Scholder, Luiseño (Luiseno), *Drunken Indian in Car*, 1974, acrylic on canvas. Gift of Jane and Raphael Bernstein; P.986.77.6.

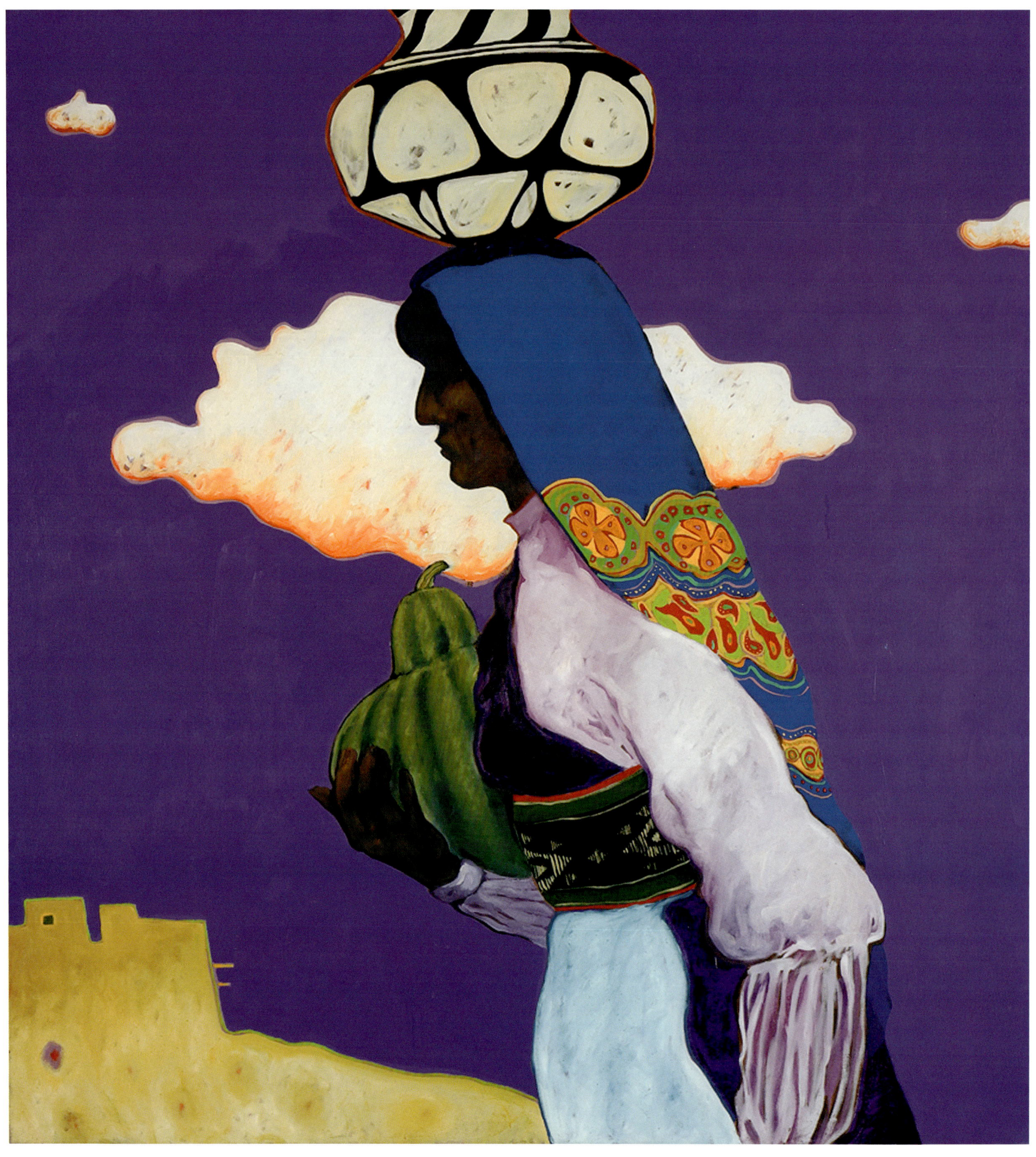

CAT. 119. T. C. Cannon, Gaigwa (Kiowa)/Caddo/Choctaw, *Cloud Madonna*, 1975, acrylic on canvas. Promised gift of Charles E. Nearburg, Class of 1972; EL.2010.86.

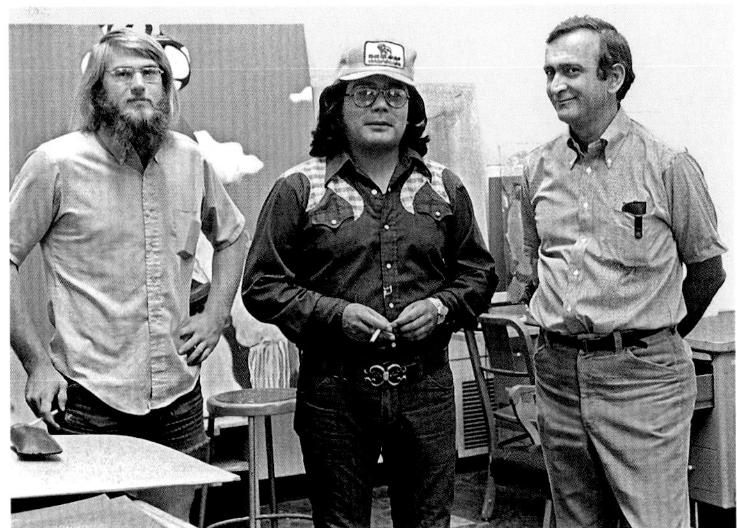

FIG. 2.7. David Rettig, T. C. Cannon, and Varujan Boghosian in front of *Cloud Madonna*, Hopkins Center, Dartmouth College, summer 1975. Photo by Matthew Wysocki.

in the Beaumont-May Gallery from July 18 to August 31, 1975, included eight large canvases, plus selected drawings and mixed-media works. While at Dartmouth, Cannon painted two of his most well known works, *Cloud Madonna* (cat. 119) and *Collector #5*. In December 2010, *Cloud Madonna* became a promised gift to Dartmouth from Charles Nearburg, Class of 1972; the Hood also has in its collection a print of *Collector #5* (cat. 120), one of a series of woodcuts authorized by Cannon in 1978 that were produced in Japan.[20] At the time of his 1972 two-man show with Fritz Scholder, Cannon entered into a contract with New York dealer Joaquin (Jean) Aberbach, allowing Aberbach exclusive rights to all of Cannon's work; as a result, no paintings remained at Dartmouth after his residency. Cannon was tragically killed in an automobile accident in 1978 at the age of thirty-one, cutting short his extremely promising career. Beyond the art he left behind is a legacy of mentorship that includes people he came to know during his time at Dartmouth. David Rettig, a senior at Dartmouth when he met Cannon, wrote: "T. C. became like a brother to me. I thought, 'This guy is a real artist. He's an important artist. He has a real message, something to say.' I came to idolize him. He treated me as an equal. The artwork I was doing he was always complimentary of, for the most part. He's really the reason I came to Santa Fe. It was he who encouraged me to move here" (fig. 2.7).[21]

David Rettig later nominated Allan Houser as artist-in-residence for spring 1979 and Houser's son Bob Haozous as artist-in-residence for summer 1989, both of whom Rettig initially came to know through T. C. Cannon. Houser's Dartmouth exhibition was held in the Beaumont-May Gallery from April 20 to May 20, 1979, and his residency coincided with a time of great interest in Native American issues in general and Native life at Dartmouth in particular. Bob Haozous arrived on campus in late June of 1989 and remained through August. David Rettig was Haozous's principal dealer at that time, and it was he who arranged the shipping of seventeen large steel sculptures to Dartmouth for Haozous's exhibition in the Jaffe-Friede and Strauss Galleries from July 15 to September 17, 1989. One of these works, titled *Apache Pull Toy*, 1988, was donated to the Hood with funds provided by Joe Obering, Class of 1956, and is today a centerpiece of the contemporary Native American collection.

With the Hood's conception in 1978 as a "laboratory for the study of works of art, from painting and sculpture to graphics and film; and man's artifacts, including a full spectrum of primitive and prehistoric cultures" and the museum building's completion in 1985, Dartmouth gained a new venue for the display and study of material acts of creative expression, including those of Native Americans.[22] While the Artist-in-Residence Program has remained under the auspices of the Studio Art Department in its home in the Hopkins Center, the Hood has also undertaken a number of projects involving Native artists since its opening, notably James Luna's residency in 1995 (initiated by then Associate Director Suzanne Gandell [now Hinman]) and three traveling exhibitions, including *Reservation X: The Power of Place; Seven Native Artists, Seven Installations* in 2001.

Two of the traveling exhibitions were hosted by the Hood in 1989—*Objects of Bright Pride: Northwest Coast Indian Art from the American Museum of Natural History* and *Plains Indian Art: Continuity and Change,* an exhibition from the American Indian Program, National Museum of Natural History, Smithsonian Institution—demonstrating the museum's commitment to bringing first-rate objects and contemporary scholarship to the Dartmouth community. JoAllyn Archambault, curator of the latter, celebrated the cultural moment represented by the exhibition: "Contemporary artists continue to embrace new influences and materials, reinterpreting objects according to their own creative vision. They remain vital contributors to Indian life, helping to shape the future of their traditions and their communities."[23]

In *Tribal Identity*, an installation in the Harrington Gallery that was open from October 11 through December 24, 1995, Luiseno/Diegueno artist James Luna confronted issues of contemporary Native identity (fig. 2.8). The brochure's introduction states that Luna's "installations have been described as transforming gallery spaces into battlefields where the audience is confronted with the nature of cultural identity, the tensions generated by cultural isolation, and the dangers of cultural misinterpretation—all from a Native perspective."[24] In the installation, Luna placed large photos of Native American Dartmouth students in their traditional dress and also in contemporary college attire. During his residency Luna also presented a performance piece with film in the Hopkins Center's Alumni Hall that derived from a manifesto of sorts: "We Indian people must have the voice in its deciding: who we are; what are our cultures; who are our tribal members. It has been too long that this has all been done for us."[25] Also in 1995, Associate Director Suzanne Gandell, a scholar of Southwest Native American pottery, co-

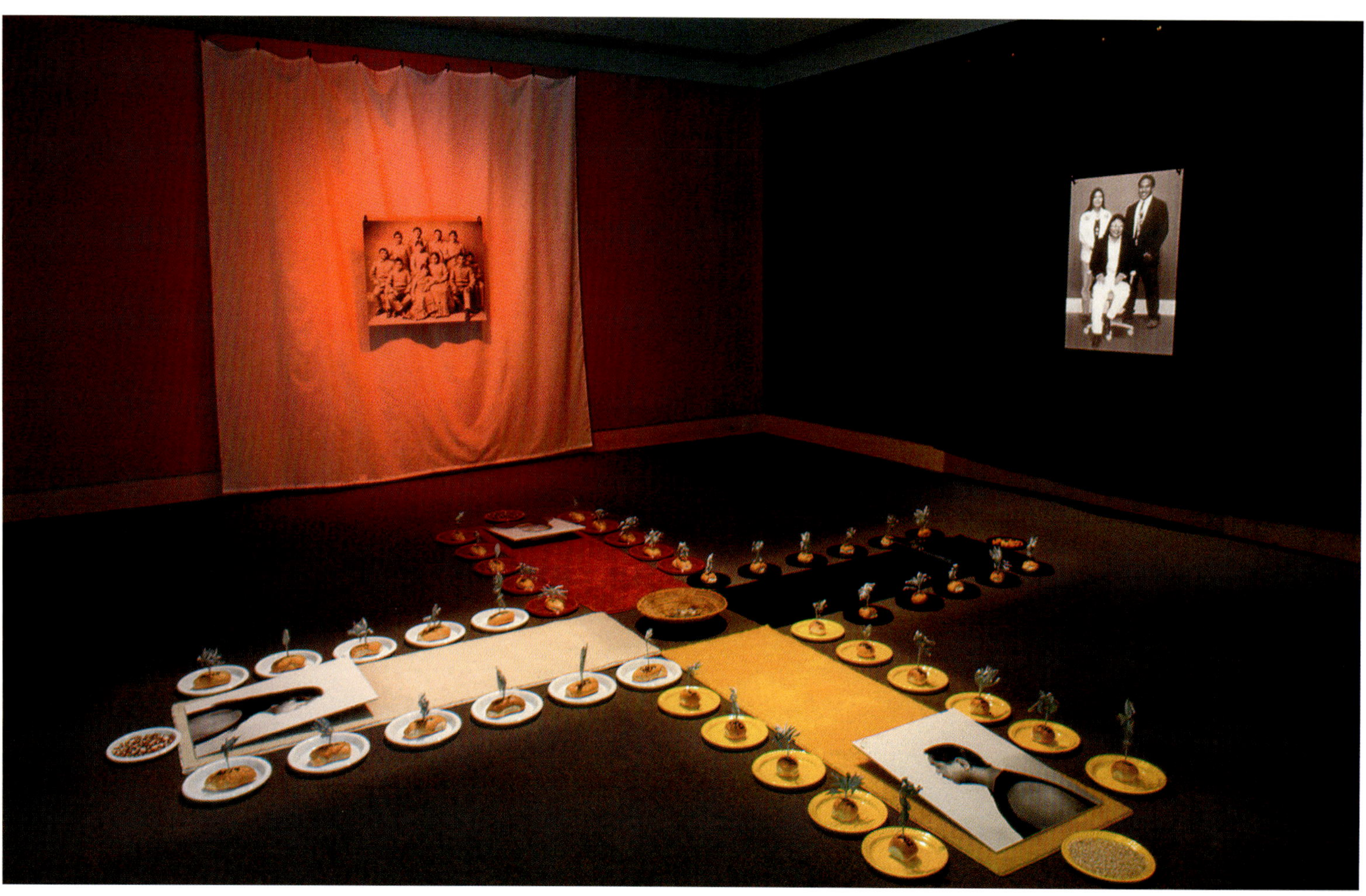

FIG. 2.8. James Luna's installation at the Hood Museum of Art, 1995.

curated, along with three Dartmouth students, an exhibition titled *Image and Self in Contemporary Native American Photoart: Works by Carm Little Turtle, Shelly Niro, Jolene Rickard, Hulleah Tsinhnahjinnie, and Richard Ray Whitman*. In 2001, the Hood invited Rayna Green, who had formerly taught at Dartmouth and who is now curator and director of the American Indian Program at the Smithsonian National Museum of American History, to curate an exhibition titled *Survival/Art/History: American Indian Collections at the Hood Museum of Art*. In this show, she stressed the survival of art, culture, and human beings through stories associated with the objects on display. She also pointed to humor and creative ingenuity as important strategies in bolstering the continuity of American Indian culture and art.

Since the 1990s the Hood Museum of Art has adopted an increasingly global and non-Western focus. In the spring of 2001, Lisa LeFlore, a member of the Class of 2001, organized a special Harrington Gallery exhibition based on her Dartmouth senior fellow project titled *Cultural Survival: Chiricahua–Fort Sill Apache Identity Explored through Wearable Sculpture and Traditional Art*. This exhibition grew out of LeFlore's research into her own people's late-nineteenth-century history and especially their failed but valiant resistance to the U.S. Army. She designed the installation and included copies of archival images, examples of the traditional dress of the Chiricahua–Fort Sill Apache, and pieces of her own wearable sculpture, which she had created in response to the imprisonment and forced removal of her people from their homeland.

Later in 2001, the exhibition *Reservation X: The Power of Place; Seven Native Artists, Seven Installations*, organized by the Canadian Museum of Civilization in Hull, Quebec, occupied the entire second floor of the museum. Curated by Gerald McMaster, *Reservation X* brought together seven up-and-coming Native artists from Canada and the United States: Mary Longman, Nora Naranjo-Morse, Marianne Nicolson, Shelley Niro, C. Maxx Stevens, Joline Rickard, and Dartmouth alumnus Mateo Romero, representing disparate tribal and geographical affiliations. Their show culminated the museum's focus in 2001 upon contemporary art within a global context.

In 2007, Hood staff created or coordinated three Arctic-themed projects. In April, Peter Irniq, first commissioner of the Inuit province of Nunavut in Canada, was invited to build an *inuksuk* in front of McNutt Hall on the Dartmouth campus, where it remains today. The first half of the year also saw the mounting of the exhibition *Thin Ice: Inuit Traditions within a Changing Environment*, organized by the Hood, which was joined in April by *Our Land: Contemporary Art from the Arctic*, a traveling show organized by the Peabody-Essex Museum in Salem, Massachusetts.

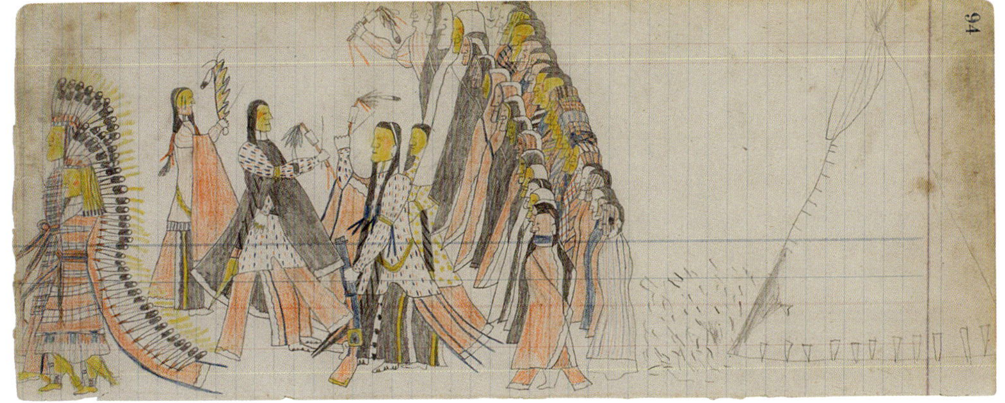

FIG. 2.9. Artist unknown (Arrow), Tsistsistas (Cheyenne), untitled (an honoree in the Tsistsistas [Cheyenne] Kit Fox Society social dance), page number 94, from the Arrow's Elk Society Ledger, about 1874–75, graphite and colored pencil on laid ledger paper. Gift of Mark Lansburgh, Class of 1949, in honor of Jim Yong Kim, 17th President of Dartmouth College; 2009.45.

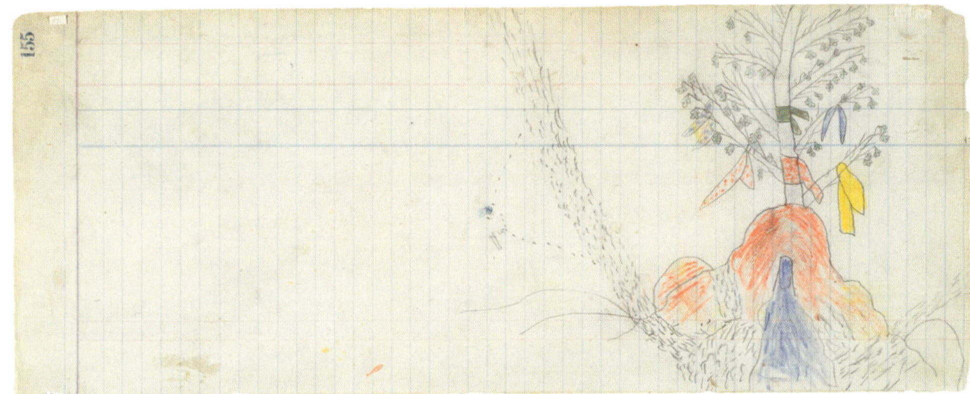

FIG. 2.10. Artist unknown (Arrow), Tsistsistas (Cheyenne), active late 19th century, untitled (sacred site, a spring and tree), page number 155, from the Arrow's Elk Society Ledger, about 1874–75, graphite and colored pencil on laid ledger paper. Mark Lansburgh Ledger Drawing Collection: Gift of Mark Lansburgh, Class of 1949, in honor of Brian P. Kennedy, Director, Hood Museum of Art; 2008.76.1.

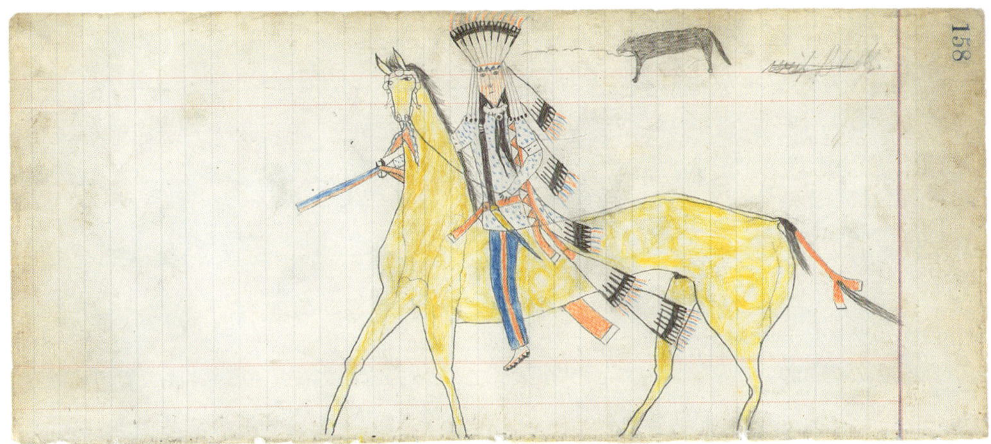

FIG. 2.11. Frank Henderson, Inunaina (Arapaho), untitled (equestrian portrait of an Inunaina [Arapaho] warrior), page number 158, from the Frank Henderson Ledger, about 1882, graphite, colored pencil, and watercolor on laid ledger paper. Mark Lansburgh Ledger Drawing Collection: Gift of Mark Lansburgh, Class of 1949, in honor of Barbara Thompson, Curator of African, Oceanic, and Native American Collections, Hood Museum of Art, 2002–2008; 2007.89.1.

Building the Collection

In December 2007, the Hood Museum of Art, the Office of the President, and the Office of the Provost collaboratively acquired the Mark Lansburgh Ledger Drawing Collection. Considered to have been the largest and most diverse collection of historic Native American drawings in private hands, this acquisition was a concrete demonstration of Dartmouth's continuing commitment to the field of Native American studies.

It had been the longtime desire of Mark Lansburgh, Class of 1949, that this collection would come to Dartmouth, and he worked closely with former curator Barbara Thompson toward this end. Then Director Brian Kennedy and Barbara Thompson met with then Dartmouth President James Wright, then Provost Barry Scherr, and former Librarian of the College Edward Connery Lathem to bring their attention to this important collection; they subsequently traveled to Santa Fe to visit Lansburgh and view the drawings. As a historian, James Wright understood the collection's historical relevance as well as its importance as a resource for Dartmouth students learning about the pivotal period in the nineteenth century from which these drawings date. It became clear that this was an opportunity not to be missed, and a deal was brokered to bring the collection to the Hood.

Subsequent to this, Lansburgh made a gift of several ledger

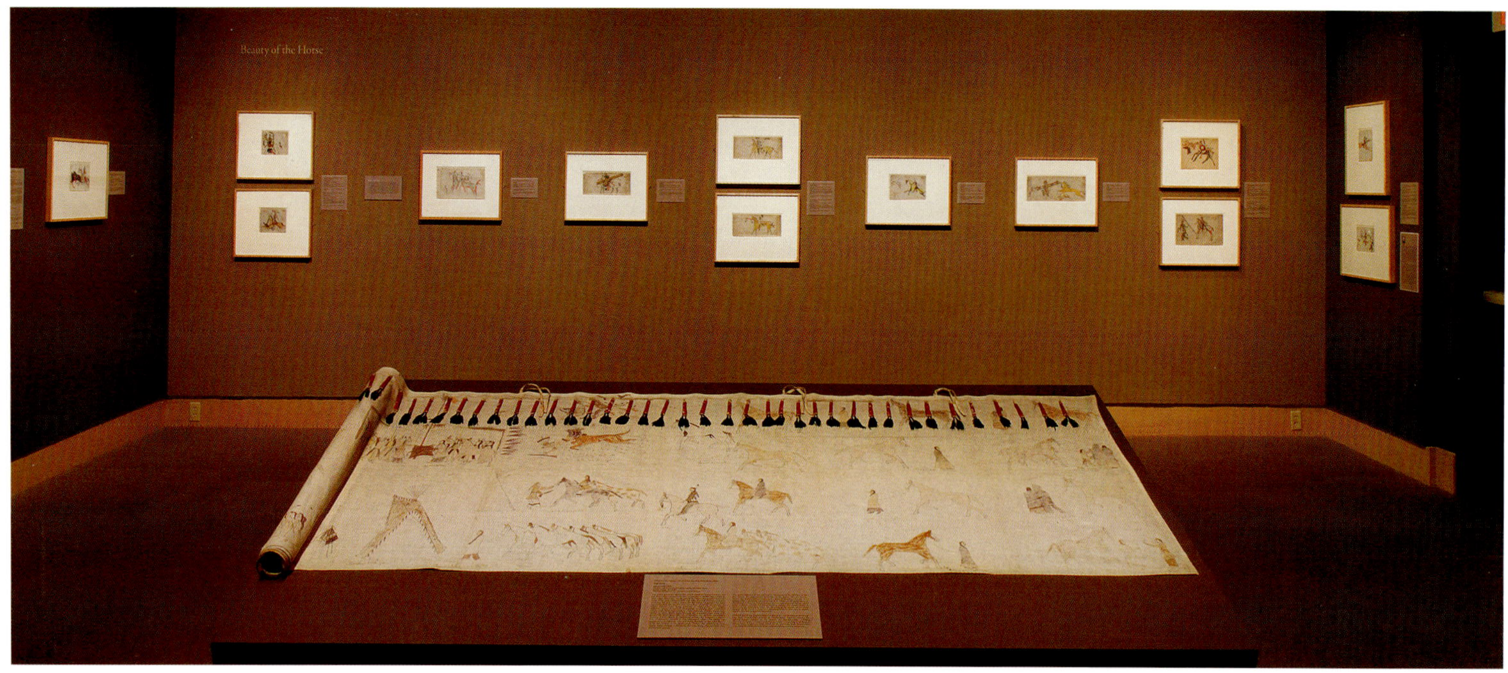

FIG. 2.12. *Native American Ledger Drawings from the Hood Museum of Art: The Mark Lansburgh Collection*, 2010. Photo by Jeffrey Nintzel.

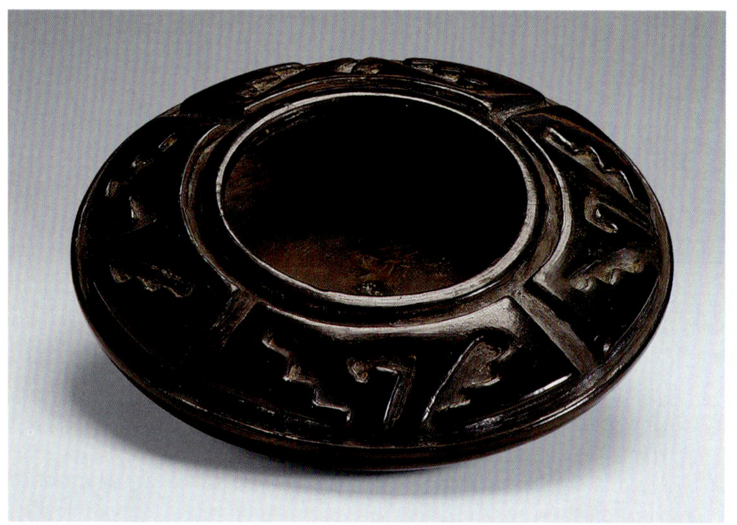

CAT. 72. Margaret Tafoya, K'apovi (Santa Clara Pueblo), bowl, mid-20th century, polished blackware. Gift of Marsha J. and Joel D. Ash, Class of 1956, Thayer 1958; 2009.94.

drawings, in honor of Dartmouth's seventeenth president, Jim Yong Kim (fig. 2.9); in honor of Brian Kennedy (fig. 2.10); and in honor of Barbara Thompson (fig. 2.11). During the fall of 2010, the Hood featured the exhibition *Native American Ledger Drawings from the Hood Museum of Art: The Mark Lansburgh Collection*, presenting sixty-six of these powerful drawings (fig 2.12).

Other Dartmouth alumni have also played an important role in the Hood's recent focus on its Native American collection. Stephen A. Lister, Class of 1963, a resident of Santa Fe and member of the Hood's board of overseers, donated an Eastern Sioux (Dakota) vest to the museum in 2008 (cat. 102). Dating to about 1880 and made of tanned hide and cotton fabric, it is profusely decorated with dyed

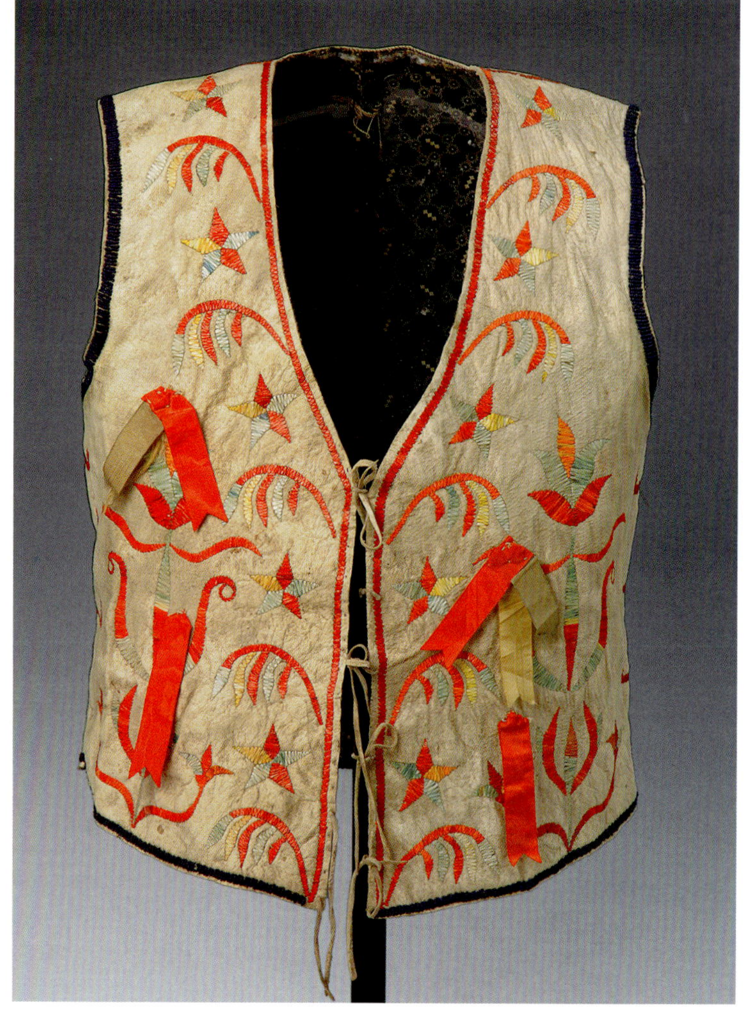

CAT. 102. Artist unknown, Dakota (Eastern Sioux), vest, about 1880, Native-tanned hide, cotton fabric, porcupine quills, ribbon, glass beads, aniline dye, ink, sinew, and thread. Gift of Stephen A. Lister, Class of 1963; 2008.82.

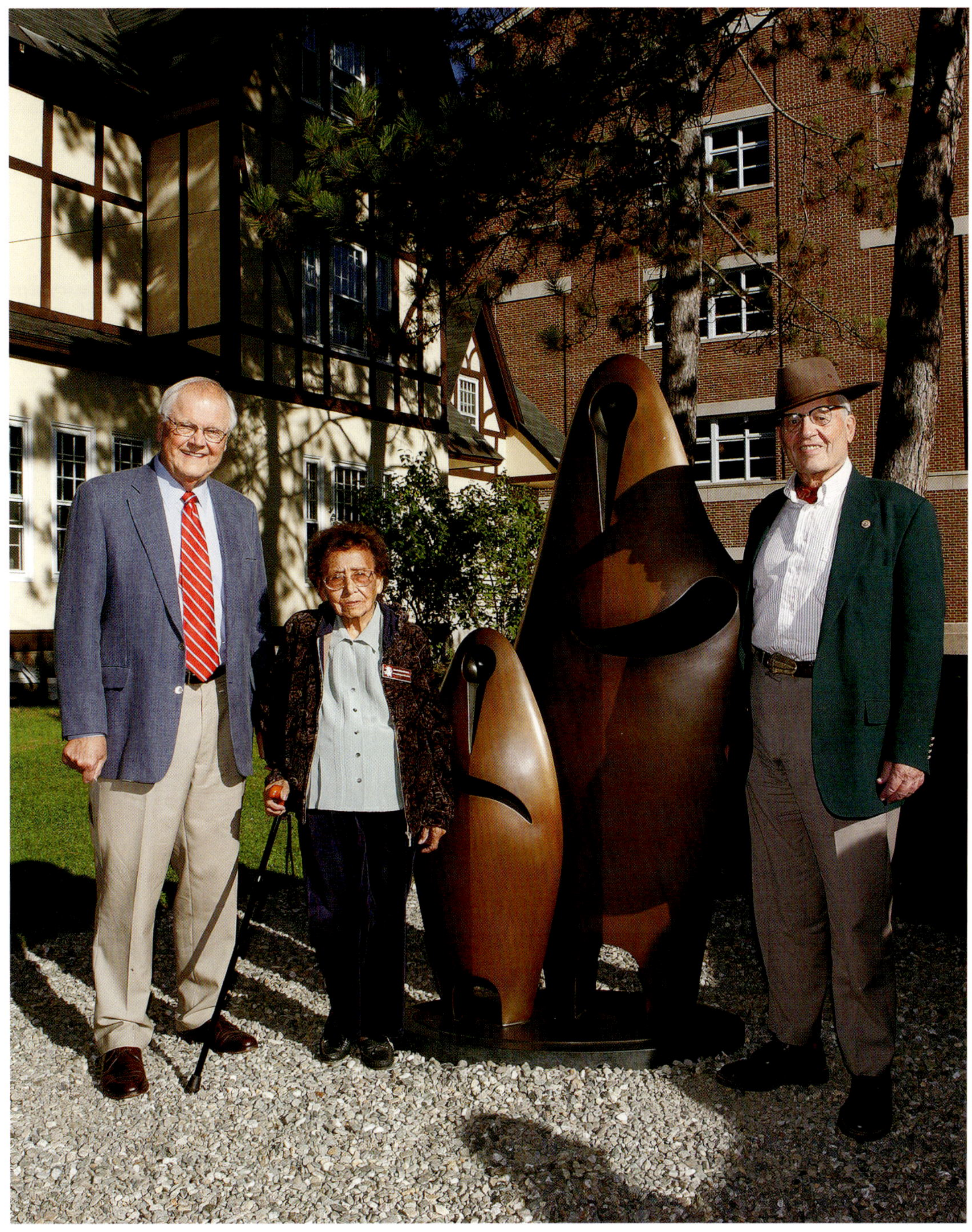

FIG. 2.13. Unveiling of Allen Houser's *Peaceful Serenity*, 1992 (Hood Museum of Art; 2007.56), October 7, 2007, in front of Sherman House on the Dartmouth campus. From left: President James Wright, Anna Maria Gallegos Houser (the sculptor's widow), and David R. Raynolds, Class of 1949. Photo by Joseph Mehling.

porcupine quills in an abstract floral pattern. A classic example of its type, it is related formally and culturally to both the Plains and Great Lakes/Woodlands regions, in that its dyed porcupine quill-work, typical of the Plains, is arrayed in the floral patterns that are more common to Woodlands tribes. The co-president of the campus student group Native Americans at Dartmouth, Chelsey Luger, Class of 2010, was filmed by Hood staff discussing this vest, which represents the convergence of her own heritage as both Lakota and Ojibwe.

Joel D. Ash, Class of 1956, Thayer 1958, donated a ceramic bowl by Margaret Tafoya (1904–2001) in 2009 (cat. 72). Descended from a long line of expert potters from Santa Clara Pueblo in New Mexico, Tafoya is known for her deeply carved and polished black-ware, and this bowl represents an important addition to the Hood's Southwest ceramics collection.

In recent years, David R. W. Raynolds, Class of 1949 (and class-mate of Mark Lansburgh), and his wife, Mary Alice Kean Raynolds, have become major supporters of the Hood in the area of Native

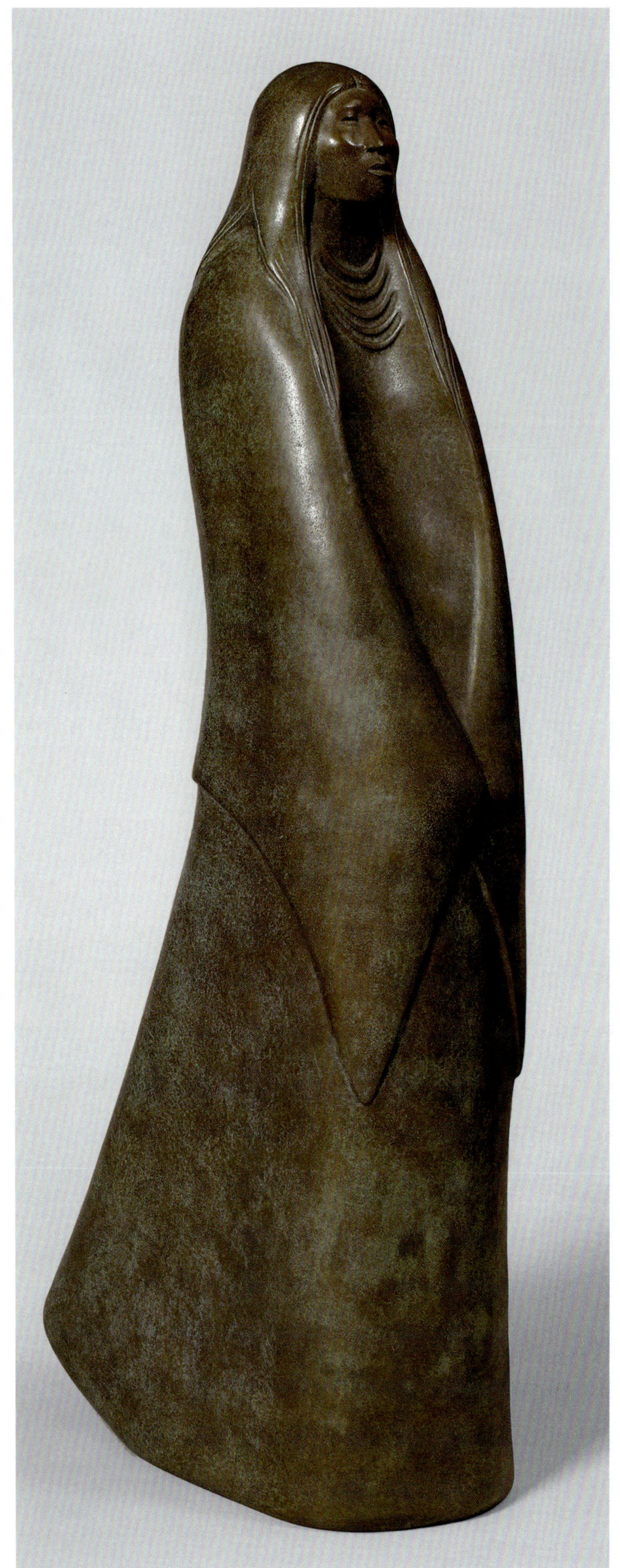

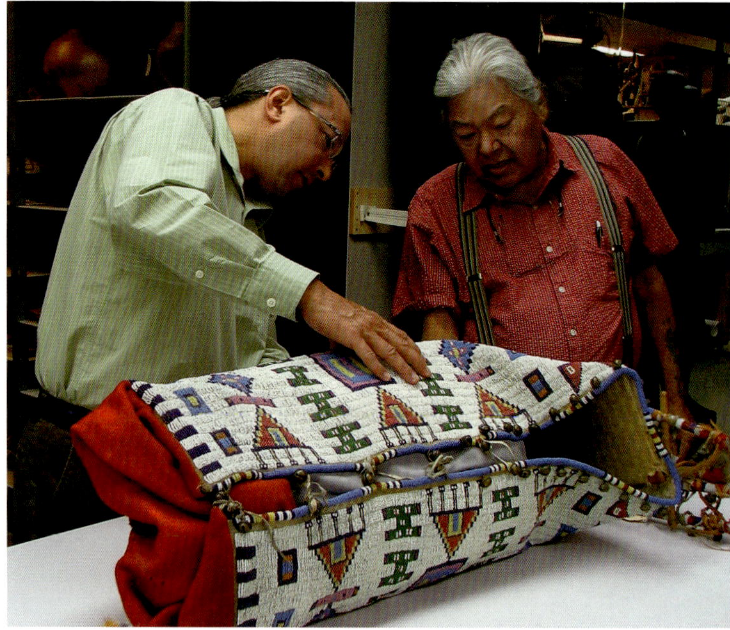

FIG. 2.14. Joe Horse Capture and George Horse Capture in the Hood Museum of Art's Bernstein Study-Storage Center reviewing the Native American collections, August 2008.

American art. In October 2007, the Raynoldses made possible the Hood Museum of Art's installation of Allan Houser's (1914–1994) sculpture *Peaceful Serenity,* 1992 (fig. 2.13), in front of Sherman House, the home of Dartmouth's Native American Studies Department. The Raynoldses also contributed vital support to the present exhibition.

In the fall of 2009, the Hood was given another work by Allan Houser, titled *Taza*, by Harry T. Lewis Jr., Class of 1955, Tuck 1956, 1981P (cat. 77). This stunningly beautiful major bronze sculpture, cast from a work originally carved in Indiana limestone in 1991, is an important addition to the Hood's collection of twentieth- and twenty-first-century Native American art. Houser, the first Chiricahua Apache child born out of captivity in the twentieth century (and twenty-seven years after Geronimo surrendered to the U.S. Army in 1886), is regarded as one of the century's most important Native American artists. He played a pivotal role in the development of Native American modern and contemporary art while teaching at the Institute of American Indian Arts in Santa Fe from 1962 until his retirement in 1975. He came to Dartmouth as an artist-in-residence in 1979. Later in his career, he emerged as a major international figure and had solo exhibitions around the world; between his retirement and his death, in fact, he produced almost one thousand realistic and abstract sculptures in stone, wood, and bronze. Houser is recognized for synthesizing the traditional Native American narrative traditions in which he had been trained as

CAT. 77. Allan C. Houser, Chiricahua Apache (Fort Still Apache), *Taza*, 1991, bronze. Gift of Harry T. Lewis Jr., Class of 1955, Tuck 1956, 1981P; 2009.70. © 1991 Chiinde LLC

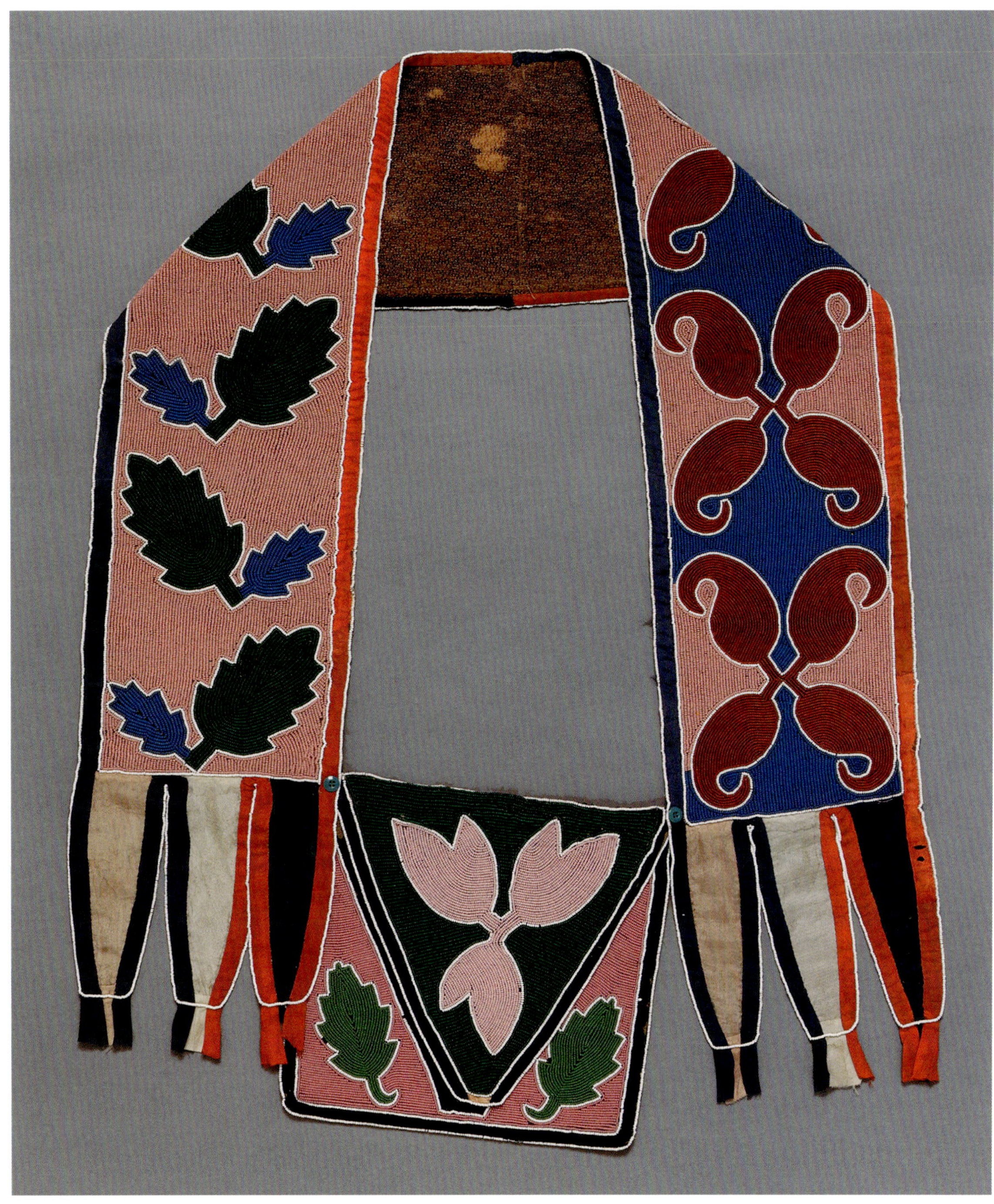

CAT. 149. Artist unknown, Lenape (Delaware), bandolier bag, about 1850, glass beads, cotton cloth, ribbon, wool cloth, buttons, and thread. Purchased through the Miriam and Sidney Stoneman Acquisitions Fund; 2008.93.

a painter (in both Oklahoma and Santa Fe) with a distinctly modernist aesthetic. His unique style activates both positive and negative space to evoke action, emotion, and relationship, as is evident in *Peaceful Serenity*, an abstract representation of a mother and her children (see the frontispiece of this volume).

In 2008, the planning for *Native American Art at Dartmouth* began in earnest. Then Director Brian Kennedy and then Curator of African, Oceanic, and Native American Collections Barbara Thompson made the decision to contract with three guest curators to plan and implement this exhibition, and George Horse Capture, Joe Horse Capture, and Joseph Sanchez were brought to the Hood during the summer of that year to review the collection and plot their strategies for exhibiting this large and diverse body of works (fig. 2.14). They arrived at a thematic organizing principle based on the geographic distribution of culture groups as a means of providing the best overarching narrative structure to the collection's disparate elements. Each thematic grouping would include both historic and contemporary objects, with the hope that the exhibition would communicate the equally viable poles of Native American artistic expression: cultural change/renewal and consistency/integrity.

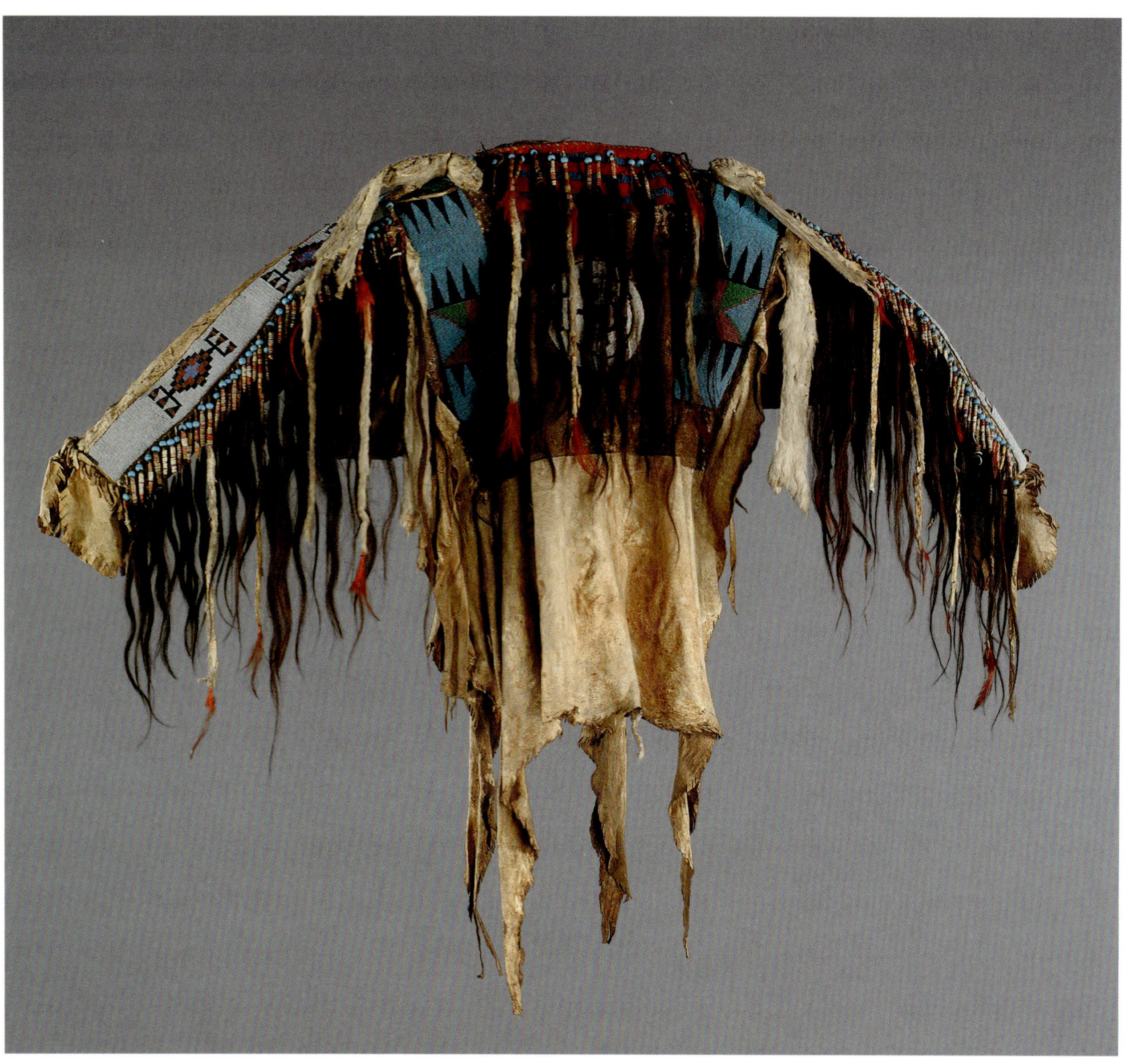

CAT. 93. Artist unknown, Siksika (Blackfeet), beaded and fringed hide man's shirt, about 1880, Native-tanned hide, glass beads, porcupine quills, human hair, wool cloth, cotton cloth, ermine, downy feathers, paint, dye. Purchased through the Mrs. Harvey P. Hood W'18 Fund; 2009.14.

George Horse Capture, with his years of experience at the National Museum of the American Indian, among a number of other important institutions, lent his particular expertise to the Plains materials. Joseph Sanchez, then acting director of the Institute of American Indian Art in Santa Fe and an artist in his own right, took responsibility for curating the contemporary works. Joe Horse Capture, currently an associate curator at the Minneapolis Institute of Arts, drew upon his established relationships with a number of institutions and contacts among curators and artists to advise the Hood on potential acquisitions to strengthen its historic collection. Among the twenty acquisitions made by the museum since are a Delaware bandolier bag, about 1860 (cat. 149), a beaded and fringed hide man's shirt, dated about 1880 (cat. 93), and a Nakota Winter Count, dated about 1917 (cat. 117).

An effort was also undertaken to acquire contemporary works by important Native artists in a number of media. In the spring of 2009, Brian Kennedy commissioned Mateo Romero, Class of 1989, to paint a series of ten portraits of current Native American Dartmouth students as they danced at Dartmouth's annual Pow-Wow. Romero, born in 1966, is Tewa, Cochiti Pueblo, and lives on the Pojoaque Reservation north of Santa Fe. In May 2009 he traveled to Dartmouth to photograph dancers at the Pow-Wow. He completed the almost life-sized portraits in 2010; they feature eight undergraduates, a sister of two Dartmouth students, and author Louise Erdrich, Class of 1976, whose daughter Aza, Class of 2011, is one of the undergraduates featured, all dressed in their tribal regalia. Created through Romero's signature technique of overpainting a photographic image, these works represent a continuation of the artist's series on the dance that includes *Deer Dancer at Daybreak* (cat. 66), which was acquired by the Hood in 2008. The brilliant

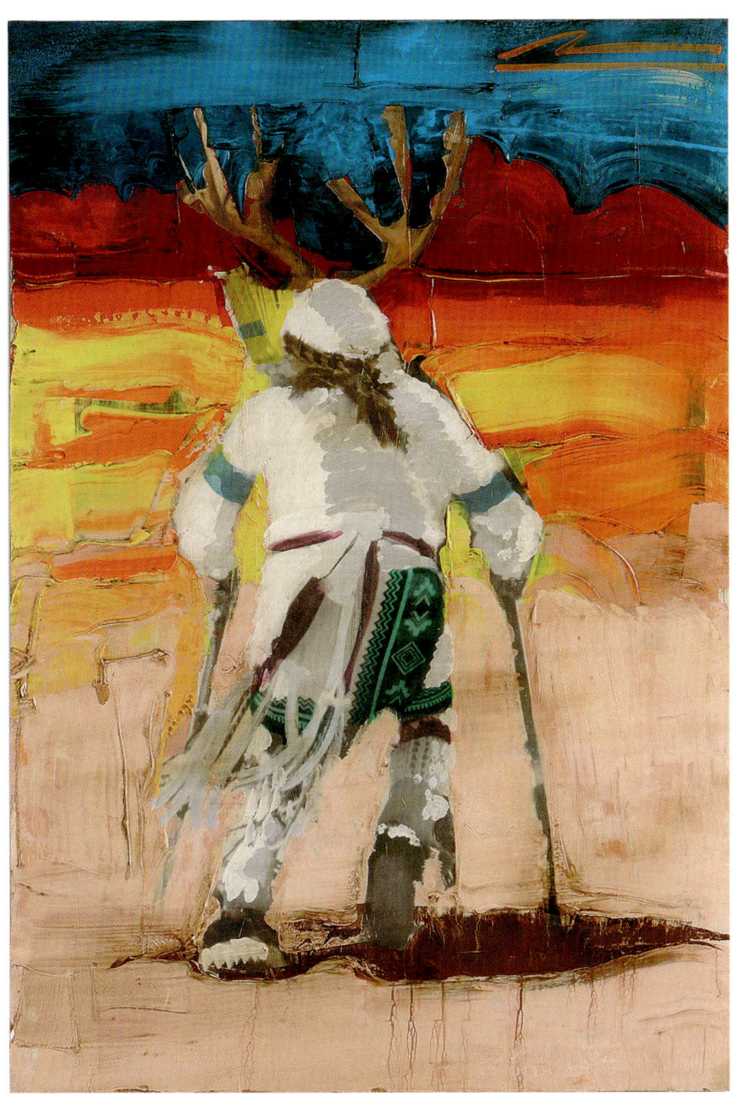

CAT. 66. Mateo Romero, Cochiti Pueblo, *Deer Dancer at Daybreak*, 2007, oil and mixed media on plywood. Purchased through the Olivia H. Parker and John O. Parker '58 Acquisition Fund; 2008.52.

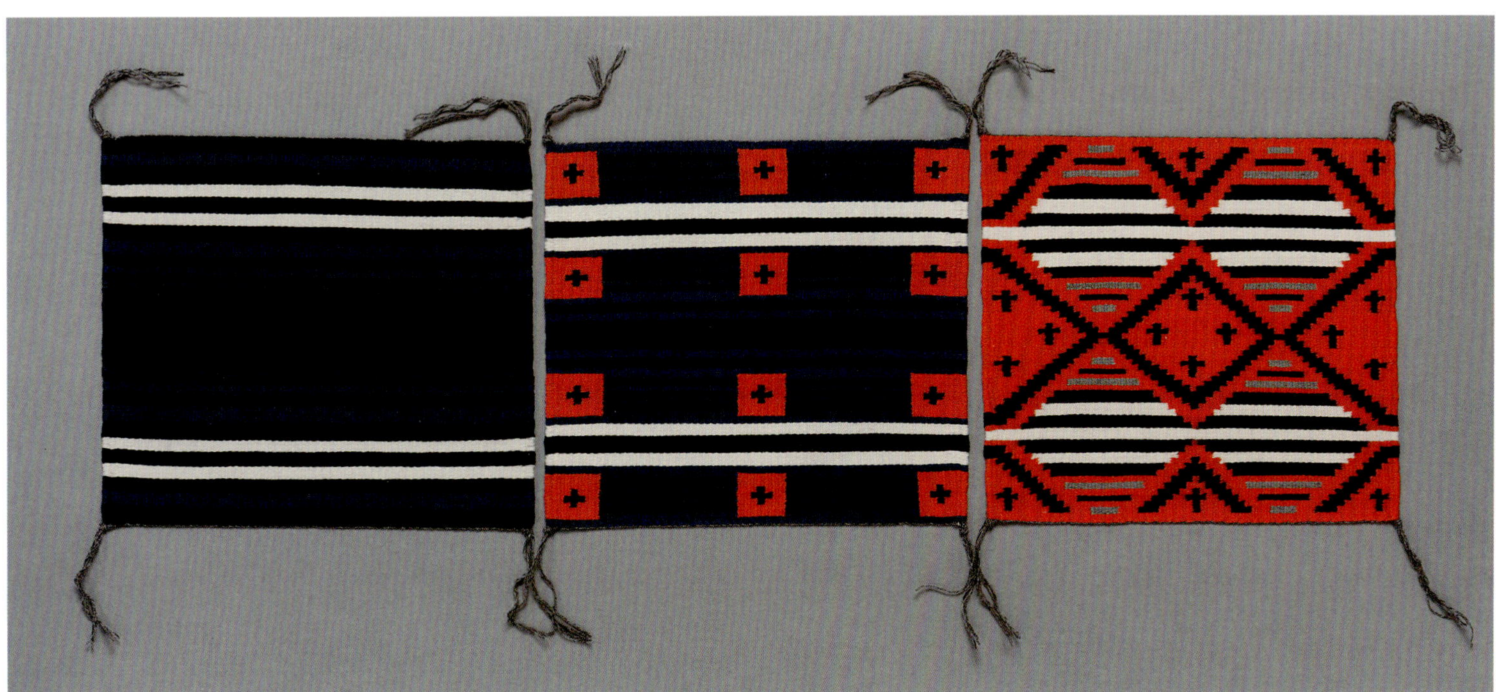

CAT. 81. Barbara Teller Ornelas, Diné (Navajo), *Chief Blankets: Phase One; Phase Two; Phase Three*, 2010, wool and vegetable dye. Purchased through the Alvin and Mary Bert Gutman '40 Acquisitions Fund and the Hood Museum of Art Acquisitions Fund; 2010.71.

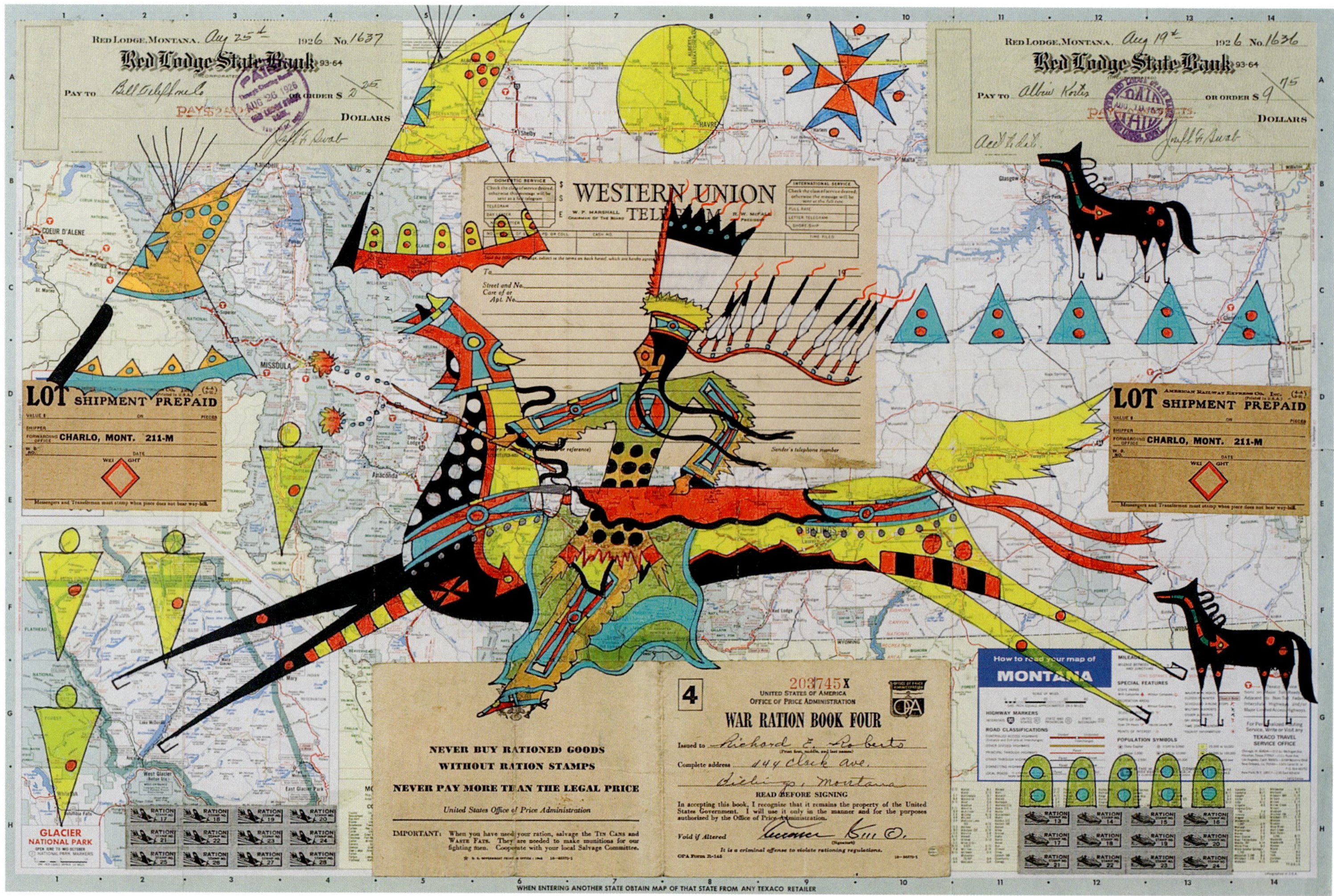

FIG. 2.15. Terrance Guardipee, Blackfeet, *Mountain, Chief, Blackfeet War Leader*, August 2008, mixed-media collage with colored pencil, felt-tipped pen, and Hi-Liter. Purchased through the Virginia and Preston T. Kelsey '58 Fund; 2008.60.

palette, powerful brushstrokes, and bold, sculptural drips create dynamic, expressionistic works that reveal the influence of Romero's distinguished Dartmouth professor Ben Frank Moss. In this series, the figures of the dancers appear to almost hover atop the painting's surface, achieving a dreamlike quality and evoking the power of ritual (see the cover of this volume).

Other recent acquisitions by contemporary artists include ledger art by Terrance Guardipee (fig. 2.15), Darryl Growing Thunder, Dwayne Wilcox (cat. 115), and Sheridan MacKnight; weavings by mother and daughter Barbara Teller Ornelas (cat. 81) and Sierra Teller Ornelas (cat. 82); duck decoys by Mike Williams (cat. 58); a carved, inlaid buffalo horn by Kevin Pourier (cat. 114); and a ceramic work by Diego Romero (cat. 65).

While Dartmouth College has always had a fascination with Native America, the lens through which Native people and cultures have been viewed has changed dramatically over time. The same is true for Native American art. In the twenty-first century, art historians and museum curators recognize the necessity of placing work in its historical and cultural context, and current scholarship and practices of collection and display reflect the importance of asking questions about the relationship between the artist's work and any relevant social, aesthetic, and political issues. An even more recent trend toward privileging aesthetics over historical context is also emerging, as fine art museums move away from heavily contextualized display practices (such as lengthy wall labels), which can divert attention from the works themselves. This catalogue and exhibition begin to tell the story of the makers, collectors, and exhibitors of these works of art, and of the ways in which perspectives about them have shifted over time.

NOTES

1. Tamara Northern, "Native American Art," in *Treasures of the Hood Museum of Art, Dartmouth College* (Hanover, N.H.: Hood Museum of Art, Dartmouth College, 1985), 51.

2. On the "salvage mentality" and other concepts related to the Western collecting of non-Western material culture, see James Clifford, *The Predicament of Culture: Twentieth-Century Ethnography, Literature, and Art* (Cambridge, Mass.: Harvard University Press, 1988); Douglas Cole, *Captured Heritage: The Scramble for Northwest Coast Artifacts* (Norman: University

of Oklahoma Press, 1985); Diane Fane et al., *Objects of Myth and Memory: American Indian Art at the Brooklyn Museum* (Brooklyn: Brooklyn Museum, 1991). On the history of Western museum practice, see *Exhibiting Cultures: The Poetics and Politics of Museum Display,* ed. Ivan Karp and Steven D. Lavine (Washington, D.C.: Smithsonian Institution Press, 1991).

3. The Dartmouth College Museum occupied a number of buildings on campus, including Dartmouth Hall, 1791–1840; Reed Hall, 1840–1871; Culver Hall, 1871–1896; Butterfield Hall, 1896–1928; Wilson Hall, 1928–1985; and presently, of course, the Hood Museum of Art (opened 1985).

4. W. Wedgwood Bowen, *A Pioneer in the Wilderness* (Hanover, N.H.: Dartmouth College Museum, 1958), 15.

5. Northern, "Native American Art," 51.

6. Clara and Frank Churchill lived in Lebanon, New Hampshire, where Mr. Churchill was president of the Free Press Company. They visited over one hundred tribes throughout the nation while he was in the employ of the U.S. Government. For three years the Churchills were stationed at Muskogee, Oklahoma, in the Indian territory of the "Five Civilized Tribes." They also traveled widely through the Southwest, augmenting their collections with almost four hundred objects representing a number of cultures in this area, including over forty Navajo blankets and several large ollas from Acoma, New Mexico. They also collected beaded work from the Sioux, Kiowa, Blackfeet, Cheyenne, and other Plains tribes. In the summer of 1905, President Teddy Roosevelt appointed Churchill as special emissary to Alaska to report on Eskimo schools and the progress of a government-sponsored program for the domestication of reindeer. For three months the Churchills voyaged more than ten thousand miles, mostly aboard the U.S. Revenue cutter *Bear*, traveling as far as Point Barrow, the northernmost settlement on this continent. On this trip they also collected almost two hundred Eskimo artifacts, along with numerous other Northwest Coast items.

7. For an overview of the life and collection of Guido Rahr, see *Patterns of Life, Patterns of Art: The Rahr Collection of Native American Art* (Hanover, N.H.: University Press of New England, 1987).

8. For a history of the Dartmouth College Museum that complements Bowen's, see the essay "A History of the Dartmouth College Museum Collections" by Jacquelynn Baas in *Treasures of the Hood Museum of Art* (Hanover, N.H.: Hood Museum of Art, Dartmouth College, and Hudson Hills Press, 1985). For an overview of the history of the Arctic and Northwest Coast collections, including those objects contributed by Vilhjalmur Stefansson and Elmer Harp, and a listing of all donors of Arctic materials to the Hood Museum of Art, see the essay "Arctic, Northwest Coast, and Polar Exploration Collections of Dartmouth College" by Kesler H. Woodward in Nicole Stuckenberger, *Thin Ice: Inuit Traditions within a Changing Environment* (Hanover, N.H.: Hood Museum of Art, Dartmouth College, 2007). Former Hood curator Barbara Thompson's essays "Collecting 'Africa' at the Hood Museum of Art, Dartmouth College," *Collections: A Journal for Museum and Archives Professionals* 3, no. 4, and 4, no. 1 (spring 2008), and "The African Collection at the Hood Museum of Art," *African Arts* 37, no. 2 (summer 2004), provide a comprehensive overview of the history of the non-Western collections at Dartmouth.

9. Both the Mopope and the Tsireh paintings were given to Dartmouth by Abby Aldrich Rockefeller in 1935 as part of a large gift of one hundred drawings, sculptures, and paintings.

10. Barbara Thompson, brochure for the exhibition *Picturing Change: The Impact of Ledger Drawing on Native American Art,* Hood Museum of Art, Dartmouth College, December 11, 2004–May 15, 2005, pp. 6–7.

11. Thompson, "Collecting 'Africa' at the Hood Museum of Art, Dartmouth College," 38.

12. Ibid., 39.

13. Ibid.

14. Matthew Wysocki, letters to Allan Houser, December 5, 1978, and Bob Haozous, December 9, 1987, respectively.

15. Personal communication, September 14, 2010.

16. From a Hopkins Center press release dated November 14, 1973.

17. From a Hopkins Center press release dated October 1, 1973.

18. Ibid.

19. From a Hopkins Center press release dated November 14, 1973.

20. "This series was to be a collaboration with master Japanese woodcutter Maeda and the honorable printer Uchikawa, two of Japan's national treasures. It also gratified Cannon that Native American art was finally receiving the attention it deserved, rather than being restricted to a craft or an anthropological 'stepchild' of fine art." Joan Frederick, *T. C. Cannon: He Stood in the Sun* (Flagstaff: Northland Publishing, 1995), 147–48.

21. Personal communication, September 14, 2010.

22. David McLaughlin, foreword, *Treasures of the Hood Museum of Art,* 6.

23. JoAllyn Archambault, *Plains Indian Art: Continuity and Change* (Washington, D.C.: National Museum of Natural History, Smithsonian Institution, 1989).

24. *Tribal Identity: An Installation by James Luna*, Hood Museum of Art, Dartmouth College, October 11–December 24, 1995, p. 2.

25. Ibid.

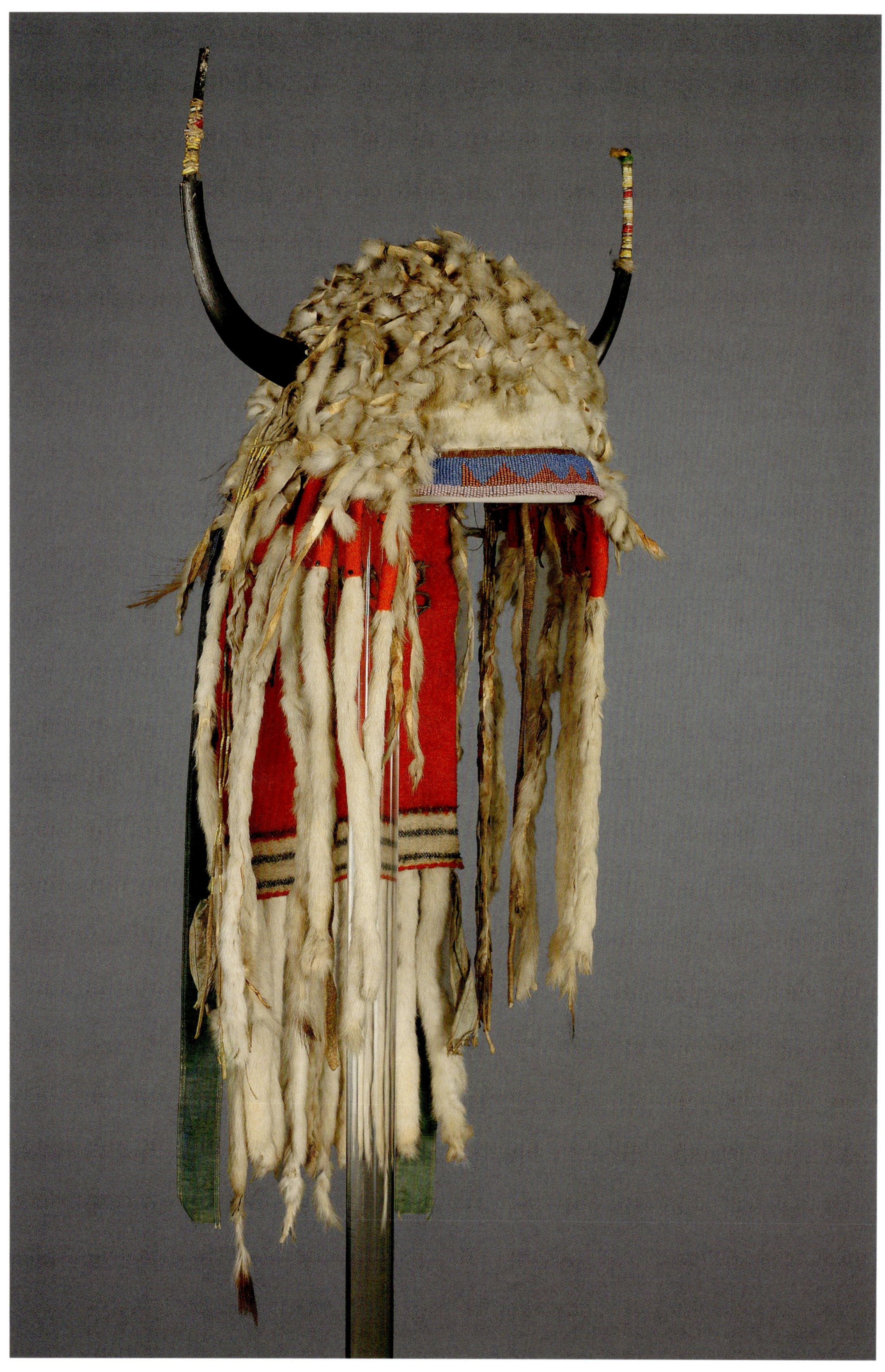

CAT. 94. Artist unknown, Northern Plains, split horn bonnet, late 19th–early 20th century, felt, commercial leather, Native-tanned hide, bison horn, weasel fur, wool cloth, glass beads, quills, feathers, sinew, thread, and lazy stitch beading. Gift of Guido R. Rahr Sr., Class of 1951P; 985.46.26647.

:: 3 ::

An Interview with Guest Curator Joe D. Horse Capture

Joe D. Horse Capture and Karen S. Miller

This interview with Joe D. Horse Capture, associate curator of Native American Art at the Minneapolis Institute of Arts and guest curator of *Native American Art at Dartmouth*, by Karen Miller, assistant curator for special projects at the Hood Museum of Art and coordinator of the exhibition, was recorded on November 4, 2010. As one of three guest curators, he gives his perspective on organizing an exhibition of Dartmouth's Native American collections, highlights some important works, and describes how he approached the project.

KAREN MILLER: How did you come to be involved with the exhibition?

JOE HORSE CAPTURE: I became involved through my father, George Horse Capture. I've worked on exhibitions with him before. We worked together on a show called *Beauty, Honor, and Tradition: The Legacy of Plains Indian Shirts* several years ago. He's been a curator for all of his life. He was a curator at the Plains Indian Museum in the late 1970s in Cody, Wyoming. Then from there he went to the National Museum of the American Indian. So he gave me a call, we came here and looked at the objects, and we partnered up on the show—it's a great opportunity and honor to work with him again.

KM: So in the summer of 2008, you and your father came to Hanover and you set out to review the entire Native American collection at the Hood. Can you tell me a little bit about that experience?

JHC: Well, whenever one goes to another place to review a collection, there's always a certain excitement, because you never know what you're going to find. So we went through shelf by shelf, aisle by aisle, through all of the objects. And it was great fun, because as we'd pull objects out, we'd talk about them together and determine quality as well as importance—sometimes they're two separate things. We realized that the Hood certainly has some nice objects. In order to make an encyclopedic collection, or add a little more depth, there was some work that needed to be done, which the Hood has done and hopefully will continue to do. But in my mind I could start to see how this exhibition would be organized.

Some people work in a traditional way, but I need to spend some time with the objects. I go into storage and look at them and put them in different categories, and see how these relate to this object, or how that grouping relates to the other. One way that people sometimes do these types of indigenous-culture exhibitions is chronologically. I think this is inherently wrong, because these cultures usually don't look at themselves chronologically. Oftentimes their lives are based on themes or on different types of concepts. When a museum approaches the material from a chronological point of view, it almost implies an evolution, which almost implies beginning and end, which almost implies primitive and contemporary, which I think is very, very wrong.

As you go through the exhibition at the Hood, you'll notice that in each of the different regions there are certain themes. Maybe with a contemporary work we'll talk about a traditional theme in a very contemporary way, but that theme or that idea will also come through in some of the much older objects. So as we started to talk through how the show would be organized, we thought, well, chronology won't work. Tribes won't work either, because with any limited collection, you don't have every tribe represented, so you can't do tribes. We preferred cultural region. Because when you have cultural region, the visitor is forced to look at these groups within it, at how these different tribal groups interrelate in the same area. I think it's an easier interface for an audience. I also think it's easier to collect that way.

KM: Could you talk more about the notion of an encyclopedic collection, compared to what we have at the Hood, particularly in relation to the history of the collection?

JHC: The Minneapolis Institute of Arts, for example, where I am a curator, is a huge institution. We have a certain amount of resources. We have over half a million visitors a year. So part of our goal is to have an encyclopedic museum, and in our Native American gallery, which is also divided by region, we tried to get a little bit of everything. The Hood is smaller, so instead of approaching the whole project from an encyclopedic point of view, we tried to find objects that are *representative* of each of the regions—representative of some of the finest work produced by Native Americans, both historic and contemporary. Certainly the collection can't be everything for everyone, and there isn't a permanent gallery of Native American art at the Hood. Of course I'm an advocate of having a permanent space.

There's a collector named Gene Thaw—he gave his collection to the Fenimore Art Museum in Cooperstown several years ago—and he has this traveling exhibition that we took in Minneapolis. His point of view is that he is not necessarily interested in the cultural importance of the object. He started his collection purely based on aesthetics. He has a prints and drawings background, and he's not interested in the cultural background of an object. If it's beautiful, that's enough. I don't remember the direct quote, but he said something to the effect that Native American art is equal to any art that's been produced by any culture in Europe or in Asia. Along those lines, I've always felt that museums that have Native American collections need to have a permanent space for them that should be treated like the others. If you have a permanent space for Western art, whether it is ancient Western art, or whether it is painting or general European art, you also have to have a gallery of non-Western art, particularly of Native America, on permanent display. Otherwise you're doing your visitors a disservice, because they're only seeing what they think they want to see in a museum, which is usually Western painting. As a multicultural institution, you have an obligation to represent all sides. Otherwise you're not giving these visitors, the majority of whom are non-Native, that other point of view. I think any museum has a duty to do that.

KM: Can you explain a little more about your distinction between the quality and the importance of the object in a museum collection?

JHC: I think you have to consider the mission of the museum. If you have a science/anthropology/history museum, they're more into collecting cultural material. So their priorities around importance are slightly different from those of an art museum. They want an object of high cultural importance, like, "Oh, this is an object that was used for such-and-such ceremony." Now the museum that I work at, the Minneapolis Institute of Arts, as well as here at the Hood Museum of Art, we aren't interested in cultural importance, or at least we shouldn't be, in my view. Instead, we're interested in the art aspect—we're interested in the aesthetics, in how beautiful the object is. To me, that should be the number-one priority as we form collections, either through purchase or through gift. We need to acquire objects that are beautiful because the idea, of course, is to show our audience the beautiful traditions of Native America from the ancient times to historic times to contemporary times. So it really depends on the mission of the museum. As an art museum, we look at artistic quality rather than cultural importance.

KM: At the same time, wouldn't you agree, we have to be sensitive to issues of culture and cultural symbolism and ceremony.

JHC: Absolutely. This is important, too, because Native America is very much a living culture. As these collections start to form, you have to be sensitive to the communities that the objects come from, and you have to ensure that the objects comply with NAGPRA, the Native American Graves Protection and Repatriation Act. Of course there are some things you can't collect. But in certain cultural regions, like for example where I'm from, the Plains, objects that are spiritually powerful, sacred objects, aren't necessarily beautiful. The beauty of this kind of object is not in its physical qualities but in its spiritual qualities. So cultural sensitivity and cultural importance are also very different from one region to another.

KM: So you can't divorce culture from quality or importance. You always have to have that cultural awareness when you're dealing with non-Western objects.

JHC: You need to have a sensitivity to these cultures, and a respect, and as museums form collections, they need to be for everybody. So if you have a Native or non-Native come into the museum and look at these objects, they need to feel comfortable and be able to learn about and appreciate these great and beautiful works. One has to be very sensitive, then, about what to collect and also sensitive with display as well.

KM: Your role with the Hood Museum of Art has grown in the past two years. You have been asked to be a consultant for acquisition and deaccession, and to be a guest curator of the Mark Lansburgh Ledger Drawing Collection.

JHC: As we started to look through the collection, myself and my father as well as the exhibition team at the Hood, it was easy to see holes in it. And what we'd do is we'd keep an eye out for objects that would appear on the market, and when museum staff found an object, they would ask me for my thoughts about it. So we did the best we could considering what was available, and what funds were available, and we tried to move the collection forward for the exhibition. Hopefully as time goes on, and this exhibition closes, that priority will still continue of building the collection, particularly because of the Hood's relationship with Dartmouth, which has a large Native American student population. I take the point of view that once you do a show, it never really closes. You've already developed this relationship with the Native American Studies Department, and with the students.

I think it's pretty obvious historically that there's always been some tension between museums and Native Americans—particularly anthropology museums. It's the way these collections were formed. Now, over the past ten to twenty years, there's been a resurgence of Native Americans involved in museums. My father is evidence of that. The National Museum of the American Indian, which has a staff that is almost all Native American, is evidence of that. I am evidence of that as well, as a second-generation Native curator. There is certainly a movement, and a very strong movement, toward having Native people themselves interpret their culture within a museum setting, and have control over or significant input on how these collections are formed and how they are displayed and how they are treated.

So considering the history of Dartmouth College, and considering that the graduates of Dartmouth are very accomplished, I think it is more important than ever for the college and the museum to come together and make a new program that really promotes Native American students' involvement in the Hood Museum of Art, by assisting them with the work of interpretation. Maybe through a new internship program, or through museum studies classes. I think Dartmouth could design a program so that Native students could come here and not only get a great education but also work in a museum and really have input and learn about these objects and hopefully create the third generation of Native American curators. And, of course, part of that would be having a permanent collection on view at the museum so it can be a working collection as well.

KM: During your time at Dartmouth, you have had some contact with Native American Studies faculty and students, and you've been part of the effort to increase that involvement in the exhibition of the Lansburgh Collection and in *Native American Art at Dartmouth*.

JHC: I felt as though there was a lot of enthusiasm in the department and its students, as well as at the museum, to build a better relationship. I think a lot of Native students maybe hadn't even come to the museum before, and this was an opportunity to open the door, to make them feel welcome and involve them in the program in one way or another, whether it's in the interpretation of cultural importance or the expression of their own personal view of a particular object in an exhibition, or whether it's through an internship involved with the show. I think working with students is critically important, and hopefully this exhibition will be the first step down a long road of continuing development of this relationship.

KM: You are known as someone who is an authority particularly on Plains Indian attire. So that would be the focus of your scholarship. Earlier you touched on the fact that it is virtually impossible to be an expert in every area.

JHC: Because of the expanse of Native North American cultures, it is difficult to find somebody who's an expert on everything, so most museum people, and most scholars, have their own expertise. Because I am from the Plains, and because I learned a lot from my father, my expertise is the Plains, and particularly the northern Plains. That's just sort of the way it worked out. And obviously this is true of my father as well.

KM: I would now like to get your take on some of the objects in the exhibition.

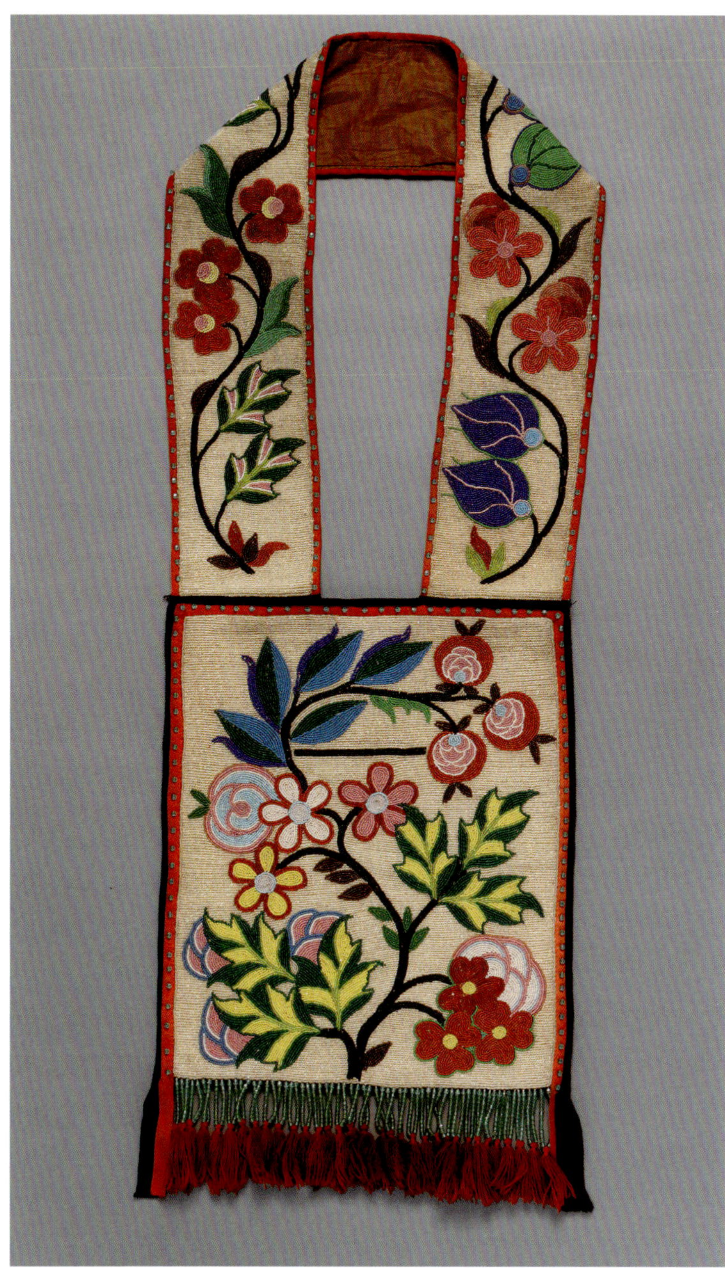

CAT. 141. Artist unknown, Anishinaabeg (Chippewa/Ojibwa), White Earth Reservation, Minnesota, bandolier bag, about 1900, glass beads, cotton cloth, wool yarn, wool binding, and thread. Bequest of Frank C. and Clara G. Churchill; 46.17.9874.

JHC: There are several object types in the exhibition from different regions, and maybe I will go over a few of my favorites, if I may, and the reason why I think they're important. For example, we have a classic Anishinaabe bandolier bag from the White Earth Reservation, Minnesota—it has a white background and dates probably right around the turn of the twentieth century (cat. 141). As with many bandolier bags, it's done in a spot-stitch technique; others are done on a loom. The spot stitch, which involves two threads, really brings the beads flat to the surface: you have one thread of beads that you place down on the surface, and you use a second thread to stitch the first one down every few beads or so. You can also make nice curves in your beaded line this way, as you see with this

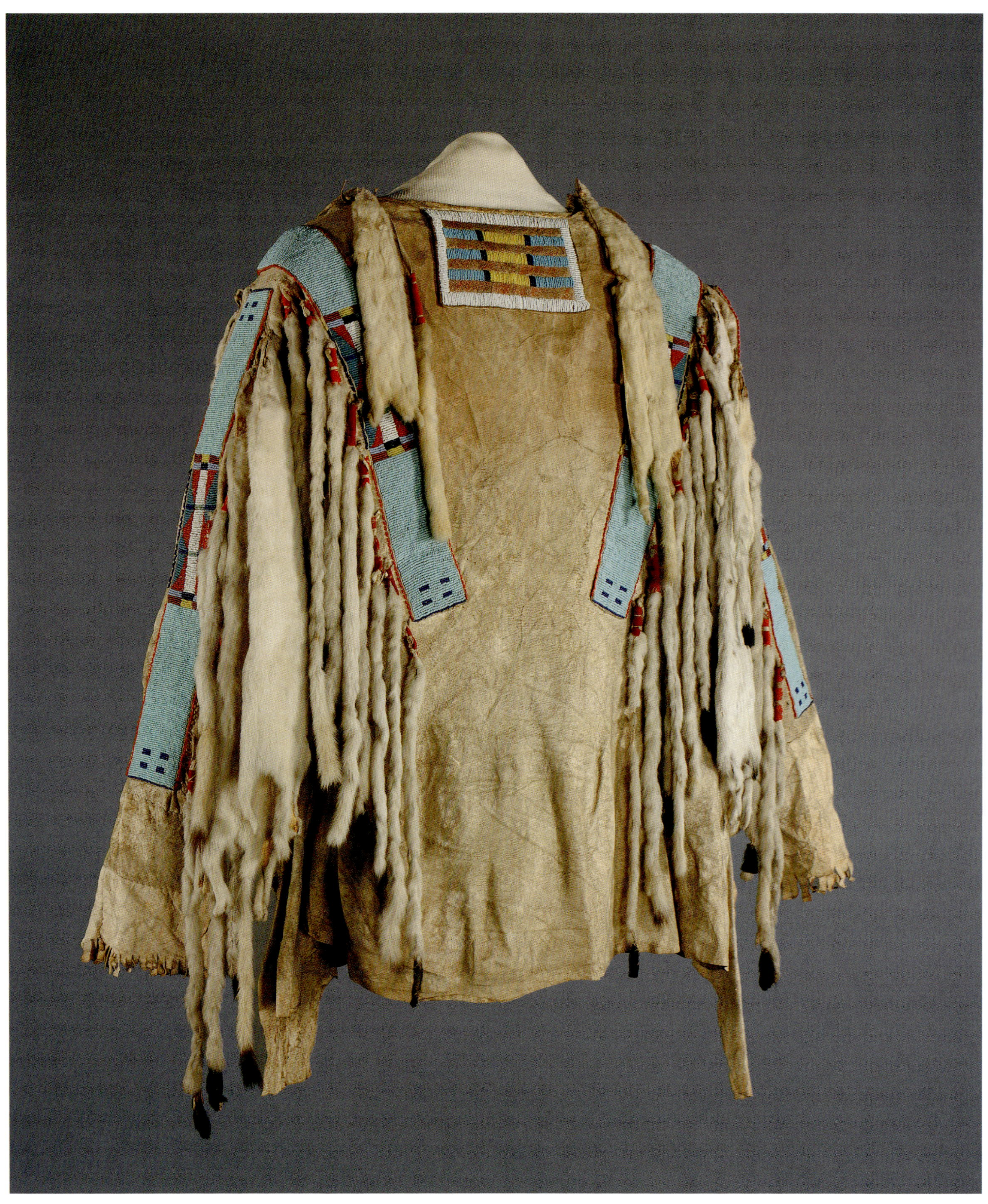

CAT. 89. Artist unknown, Apsáalooke (Crow/Absaroke), man's war shirt, about 1915–20, Native-tanned deer hide, glass beads, ermine fur, buffalo fur, canvas, wool cloth, ochre, string, and thread. Gift of Guido R. Rahr Sr., Class of 1951P; 985.47.26601.

bandolier bag, its flowers and so on. This is a later bag as well, because it doesn't really have a bag function anymore. It has a horizontal line on it where the bag slit used to be, but that's all.

What makes this object really interesting is the articulation of those flowers. They're two-toned, which I think is really nice. With many bandolier bags, you almost find consistent elements among them. There's a plant that grows up the center. Sometimes on each of the straps you'll see a plant that goes along the side too. On this plant you'll have flowers, you'll have berries, and you'll have leaves. So in order to think about this object in a bigger context and understand its symbolism, we have to think about the nature of plants. When the plant starts to grow in the springtime, little leaves form. And when the leaves form, it is able to absorb more power from the sun, and it forms the flowers, then it grows some more, then it forms the berries. Then after summer and into fall, the leaves start to fall off and the berries fall onto the ground and the plant starts to wither to go to sleep. Then as the winter comes along, the plant dies and goes back down into the earth, but those seeds come back up in the spring. So within one object you have represented the elements of regeneration. You have the plant that goes up, the seeds that go down, then next year it happens again. And I think that is a basic philosophical way of looking at how Native American cultures see themselves. I think of it as a continuum, and I think that this object, although it was done over a hundred years ago, really speaks to how Native cultures, historically but also with traditional people today, really look at themselves, and to their worldview. It's a continuum. For many people, you grow up, you start a family, you have kids, you die, your kids grow up. It goes on and on, much like the plant, which is reflected on the bandolier bag. So the object is beautiful, the colors are stunning, but also I think there's another story behind it.

Another of my favorite objects is the Crow or Apsaalooka men's shirt (cat. 89). Shirts were made by women for men, and men of high regard or honor within their culture had these type of shirts in particular. The beadwork was done by women. This is a classic Apsaalooka style, with the pink, the light blue, and the ermine. Ermine are sort of like little weasels, and in the summertime they are grey or brown, but in wintertime they're white. That's when they are harvested to put on shirts. Now this particular one has several full ermines on it, as well as the ermine tails. Again, as with many objects, there are multiple interpretations here, because the ermine is sort of a cranky little animal—it's sort of vicious. They put it on the shirt to incorporate that power, plus the ermine on the shirt just looks great.

The pipe bag, which would be used to hold a man's smoking implements, is another object type we see from the Plains (cat. 134). These objects all have to be mobile, so you either wear them or you carry them. This particular one, which is southern Cheyenne, is a really fine example. The beadwork is exquisite, it has little tabs along the bottom, and it has a really fine fringe on it. But the reason I really like it—you can particularly see it on the flaps that come down

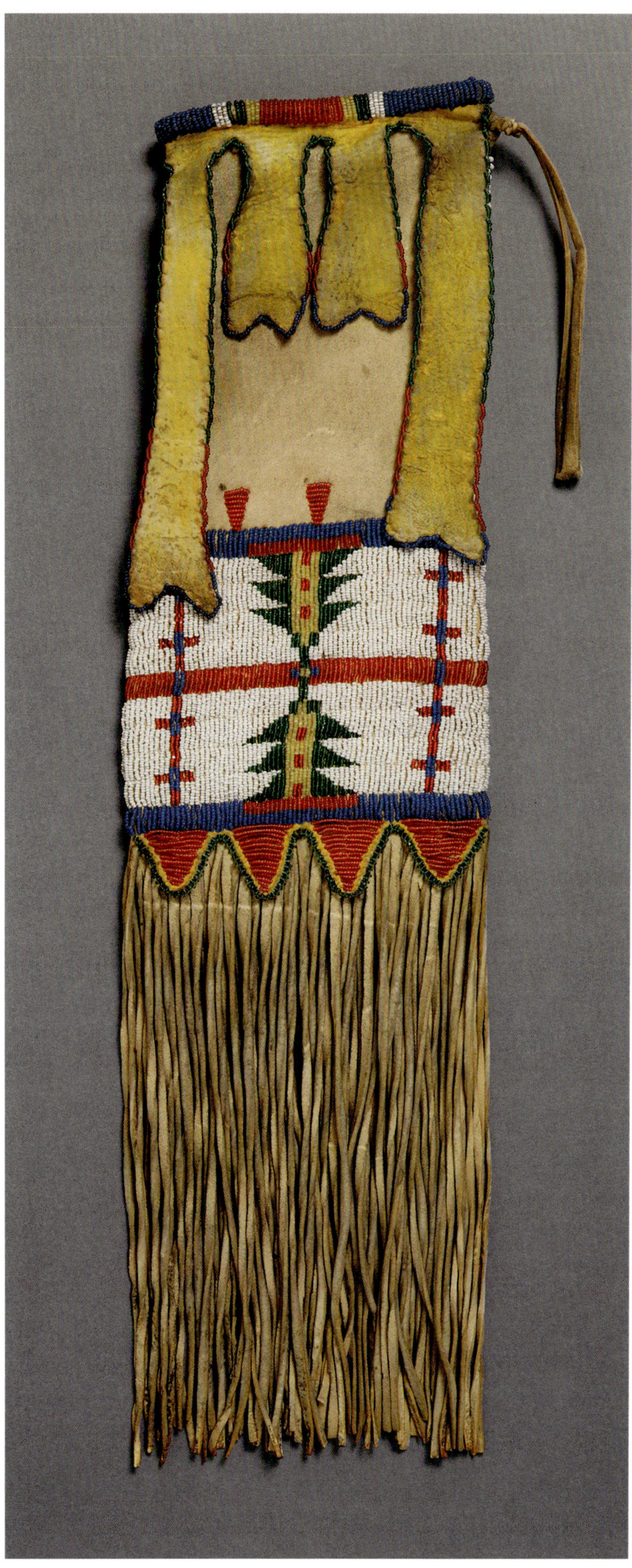

CAT. 134. Artist unknown, Tsistsistas/Suhtai (Cheyenne), pipe bag, about 1890, Native-tanned hide, glass beads, sinew, and ochre. Gift of Guido R. Rahr Sr., Class of 1951P; 985.47.26556.

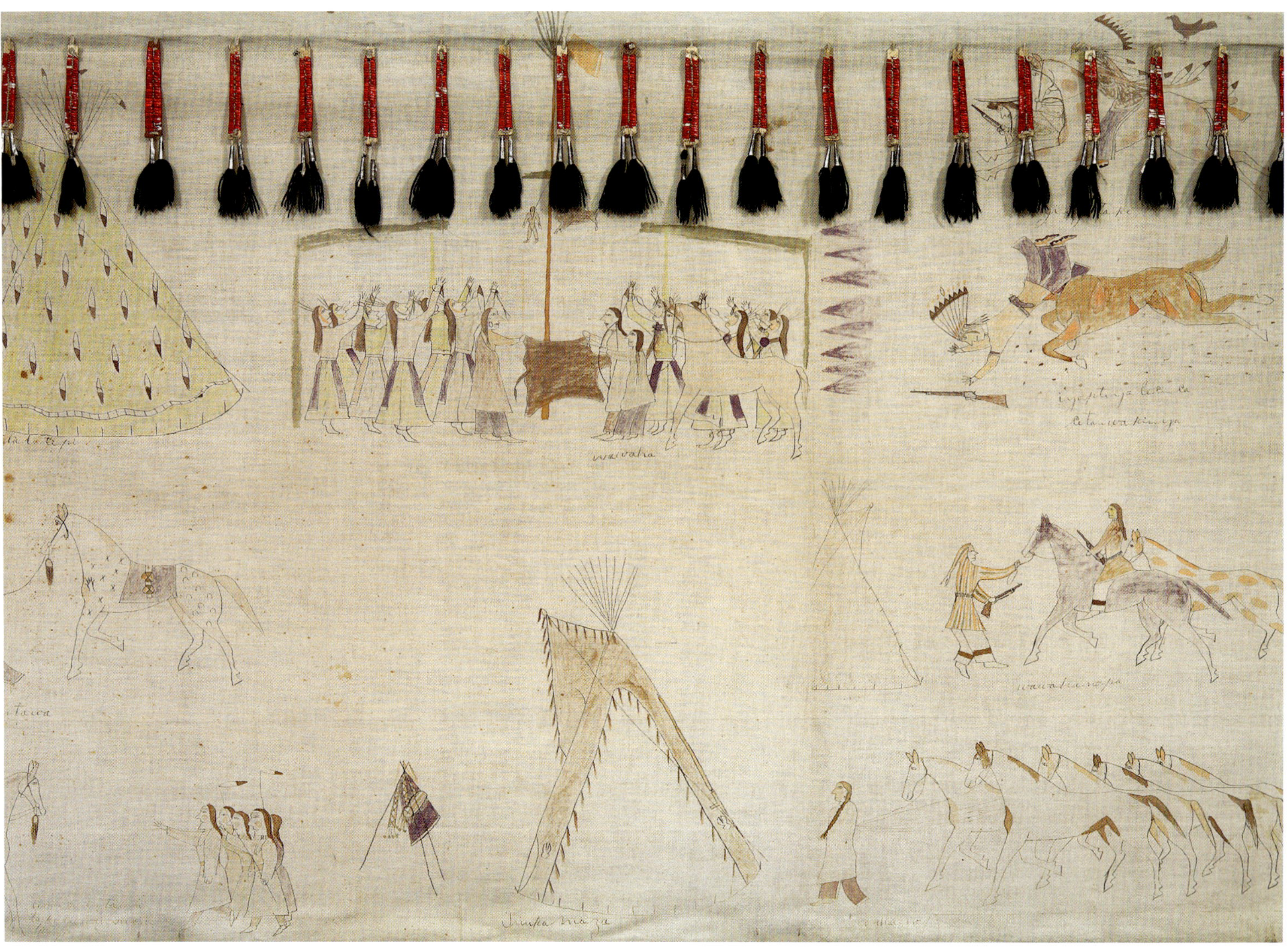

CAT. 113. Artist unknown, Lakota (Teton/Western Sioux) (Standing Rock), tipi liner (detail), about 1910, muslin, paint, porcupine quills, rawhide, Native-tanned hide, cotton cloth, tin cones, dye, wool yarn, ink, string, and thread. Purchased through the Mrs. Harvey P. Hood W'18 Fund; 2009.10.

from the top—is because they added a little bit of yellow color to the hide, so it has a really nice warm feeling. The color scheme is just perfect, with the yellow, the warmth of the hide, the red on the bottom. It's really a stunning object.

In one of my expeditions with the staff of the Hood, we were in a well-known dealer's adobe house. When a house is adobe, it's really hard to make two levels. So the house just went on and on and on. I got completely lost, but eventually I came upon this large bookshelf and up on top the dealer had this huge piece of painted canvas. It was a Plains Indian pictographic muslin (cat. 113). In historic times, men would draw their exploits on buffalo hides and wear them. Another thing they would do, once they were given cotton and muslin cloth, is they would make these liners that go inside the teepee, and they would paint their battle exploits inside of there. And that's essentially what this was. I recognized the style. It was probably made from Standing Rock Reservation, which is the Hunkpapa Lakota. They had these lights on it, which was hurting the object. So I suggested to the Hood team that they should really consider this object. You know with dealers it's always a sort of back-and-forth thing, but finally they acquired it and I got to see the object firsthand on one of my visits out here. It's an outstanding object because it shows many aspects of traditional culture. It shows some of the sacred ceremonies, it shows hunting, it shows courting, and considering how much light they had on it, it's still in reasonably good shape. What makes it particularly unique is that when it was collected, the names of the people were written on it in Lakota. It's this really loose cursive, so it's kind of hard to read it. I think a great project would be to try to identify the people who are actually depicted here. Which is very unusual. With many pictographic pieces, you never really know who's on there.

And there is the Native American Church peyote collection (cats. 128 and 132). The Native American Church, which I am not a member of, is a very interesting movement that started in the 1800s. Essentially they combine traditional Native American beliefs with

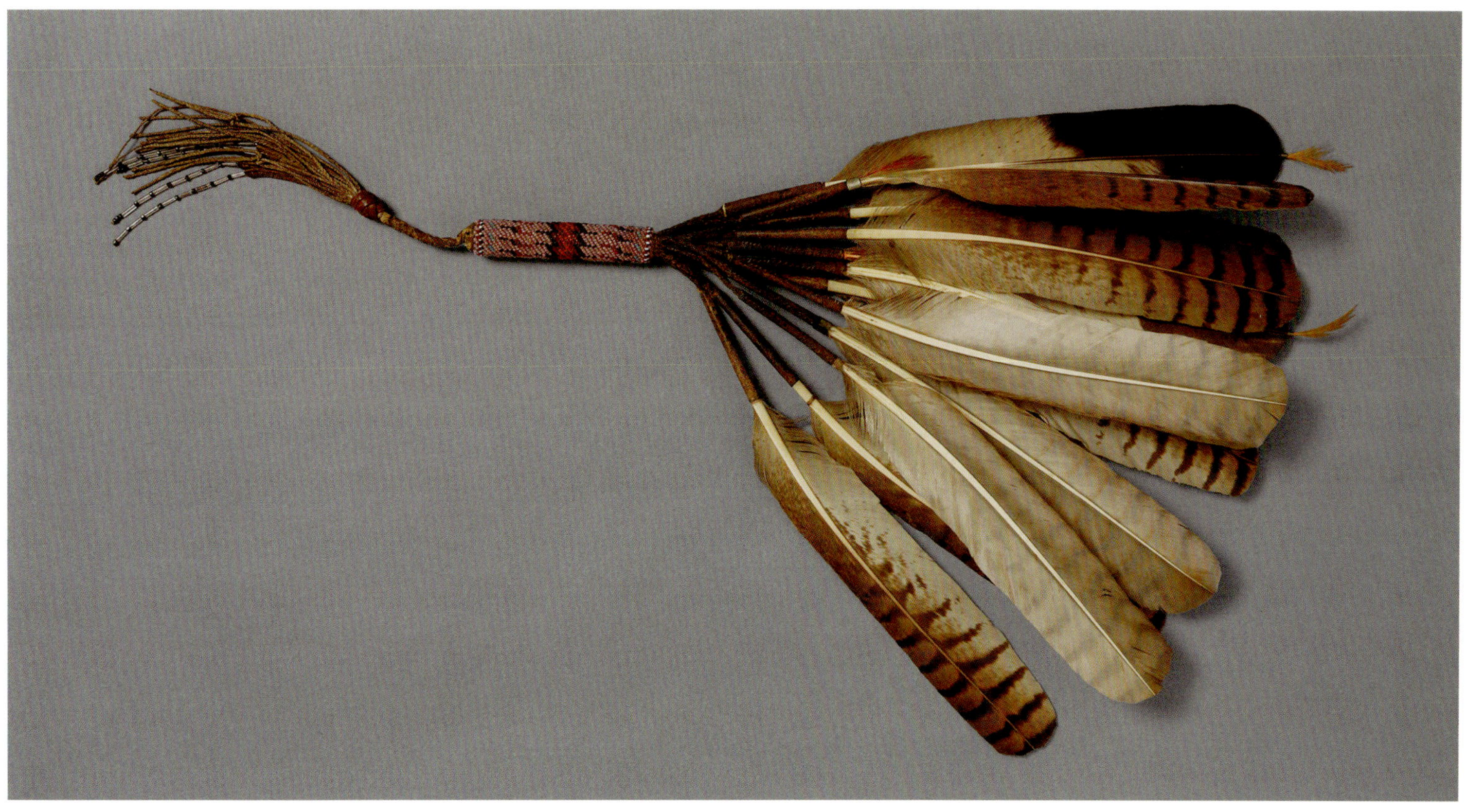

CAT. 128. Artist unknown, Southern Plains, peyote fan, about 1900, hawk feathers, eagle feathers, downy feathers, Native-tanned hide, rawhide, commercial leather, glass beads, metal, dye, and thread. Gift of Guido R. Rahr Sr., Class of 1951P; 985.47.26474.

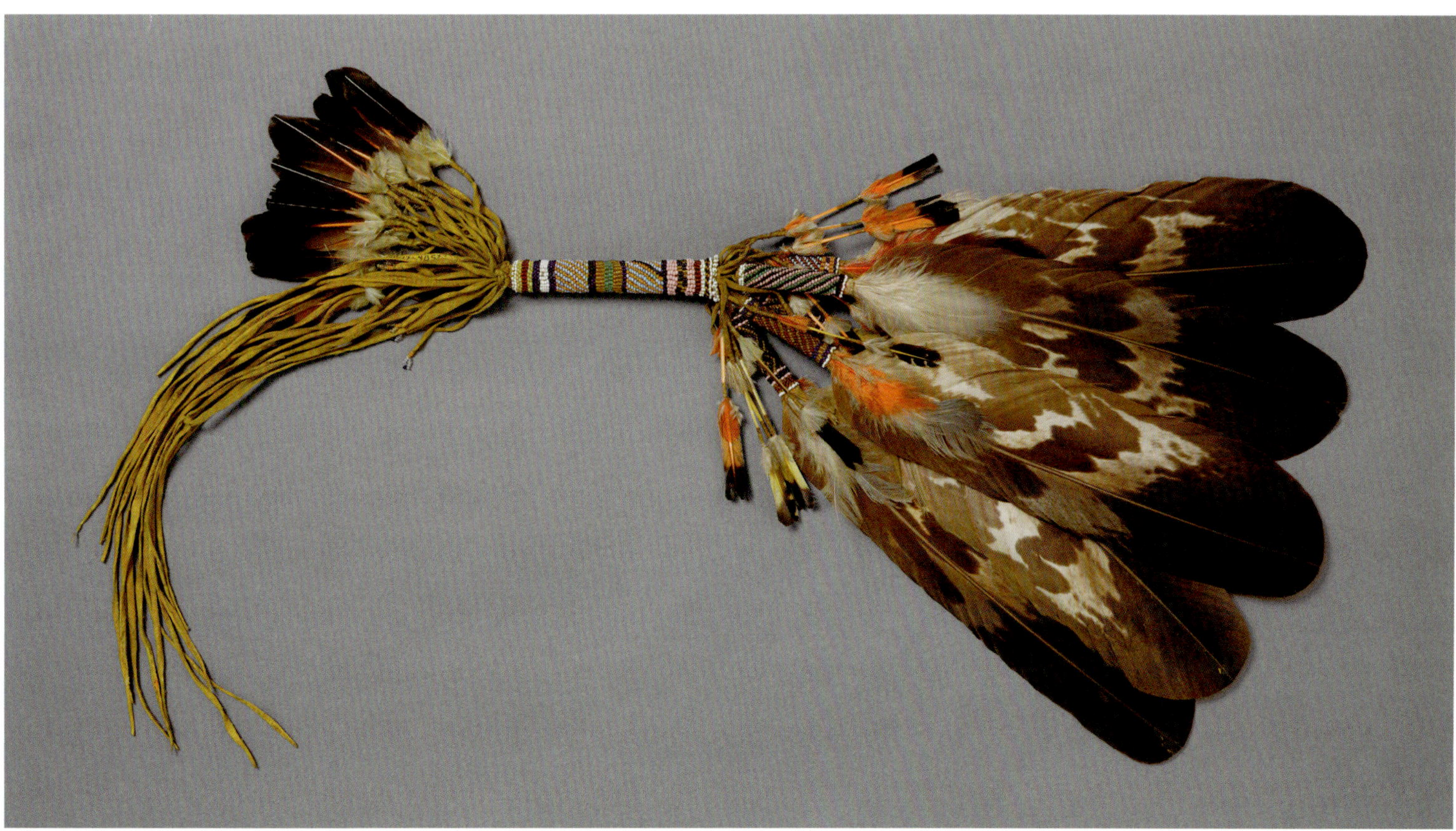

CAT. 132. Artist unknown, Tsistsistas/Suhtai (Cheyenne), peyote fan, about 1900, eagle feathers, flicker feathers, downy feathers, hide, glass beads, ochre, sinew, dye, and thread. Bequest of Frank C. and Clara G. Churchill; 46.17.9852.

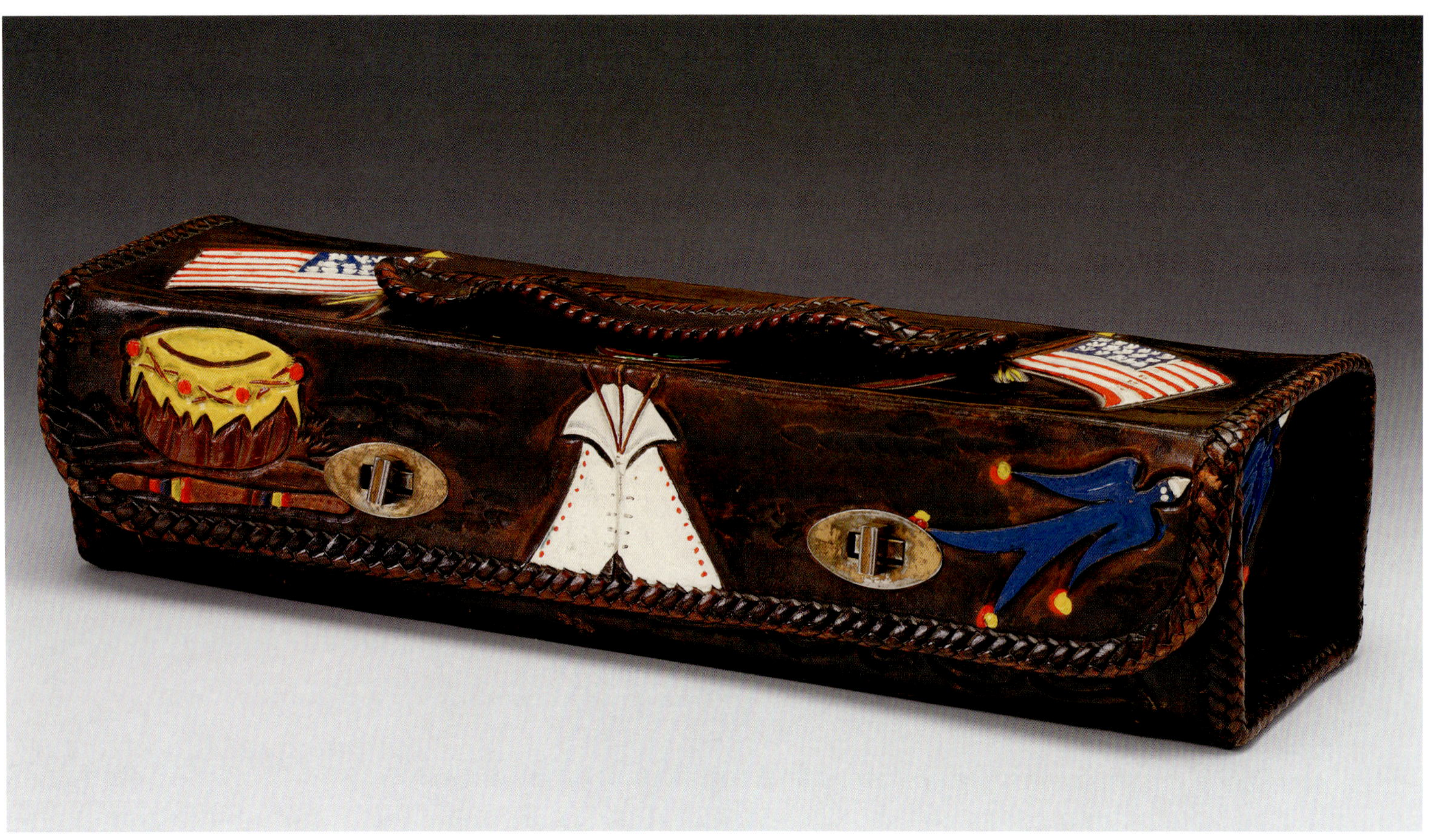

CAT. 122. Artist unknown, Gaigwa (Kiowa) or Niuam (Comanche), peyote box, about 1940, leather, paint, brass, metal, and thread. Purchased through the Endowment Fund for the Acquisition and Preservation of Native American Art and the Hood Museum of Art Acquisitions Fund; 2009.32.

Christianity, and they conduct these ceremonies. It's a very historic movement but there are many people who still practice this way as well. And they use these particular implements for their ceremonies, which run all night long. They have a teepee where they have their ceremony—you go in as the sun goes down and they conduct the ceremony all night long, then you come out in the daylight again. So if you think about it in a Christian sense, there's an idea of transformation, of being baptized or rebirthed. Native American Church objects are interesting because there's a certain stitch that is used. It's called a peyote stitch and it's often done on the handle of the object. Before this movement came along, you didn't really find that stitch. They have their own style. And also in the Native American Church, both men and women did beadwork. Whereas historically, apart from this movement, the men never really did that at all.

They'd have a little box that they would put their ceremonial objects in, and then the outside of this box would have imagery of elements from the church (cat. 122). They have the sacred teepee where they would have their ceremony; they would have the water drum; and they also would have this bird on there who really sort of acts as a messenger. Now the water drum has its own interesting story to it (cat. 127). When they would put the hide on, they left a little bit of water inside it, and they would use little rocks around the edges and then tie it with a rope. And on the bottom of the drum, the design of the rope is in the shape of a star, which is a morning star. With many Plains tribes, a morning star plays a very important role. It's of course the beginning of the day, but in the traditional stories, Morning Star is actually also a character. Also the drum with the ropes and the rocks around the edge, as you look at it, is reminiscent of the crown of thorns that Jesus wore. So it sort of has a double effect as well. And with the water in the center of it, as they're performing their ceremony and hitting the drum and singing, they can manipulate the water inside as they move the drum to get different tones.

KM: Given your obvious interest in these objects, how do you think they could or should be used for teaching?

JHC: I think the Hood Museum of Art has a very unique responsibility to what is a very ambitious and well-regarded Native American student population at Dartmouth. You're building a collection and having a major exhibition. This is a great opportunity to forge a long-term relationship with the Native American Studies Department and the students, because there are many, many layers to these objects. They are not static. And many of their stories and different

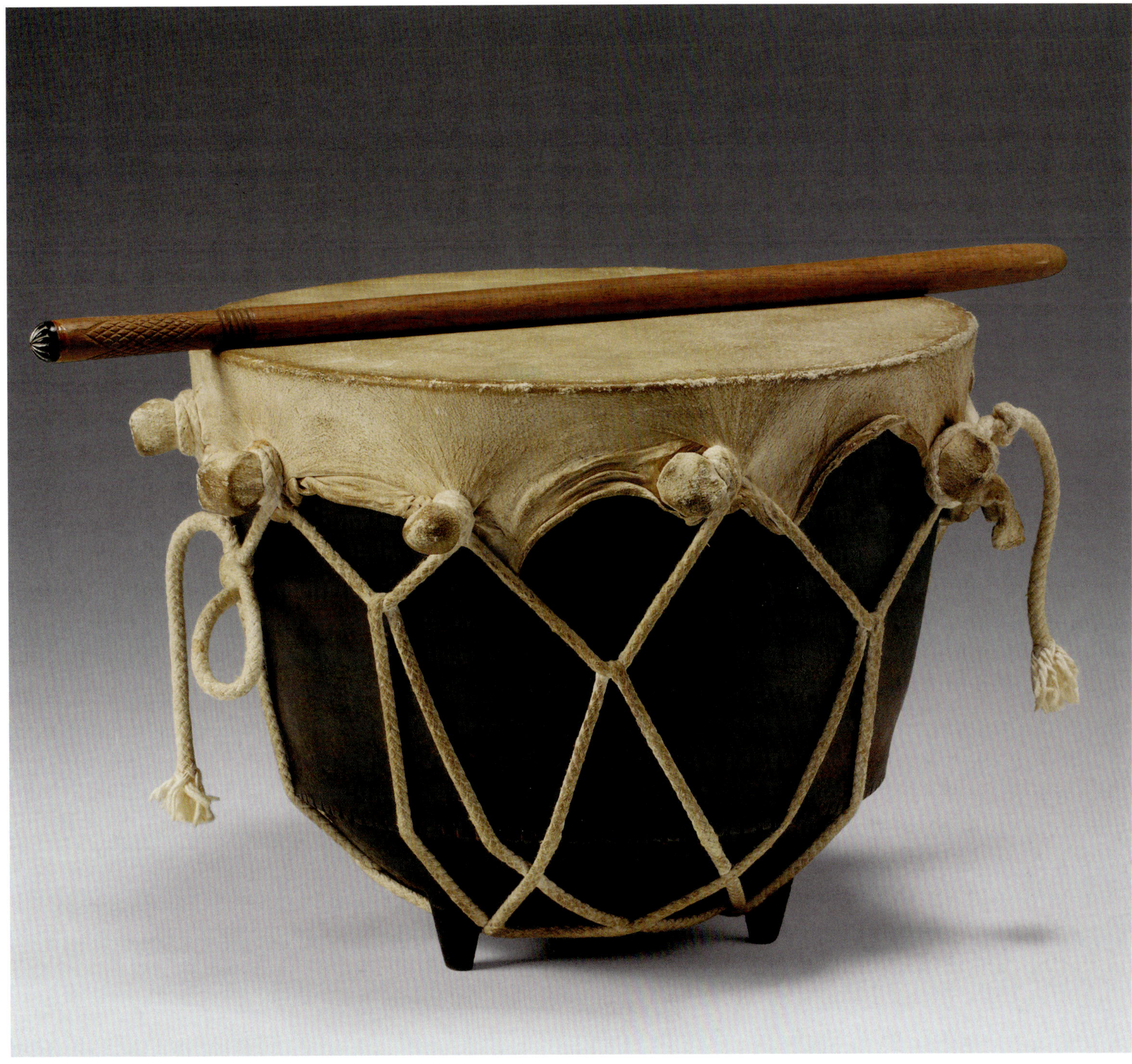

CAT. 127. Artist unknown, Southern Plains, drum and drum beater, about 1930, drum: iron, Native-tanned hide, cord, and stones; drum beater: wood and paint. Museum purchase; 158.28.14245.

interpretations come from people like myself but also students who might be familiar with them and know their culture. So this is an opportunity for a great relationship that really needs to continue to move forward for the long term, because Dartmouth and the Hood could be real leaders in forging a relationship between the college's Native American collection and its Native American students. They need to—it's their obligation.

Don't leave the Rez Without It!

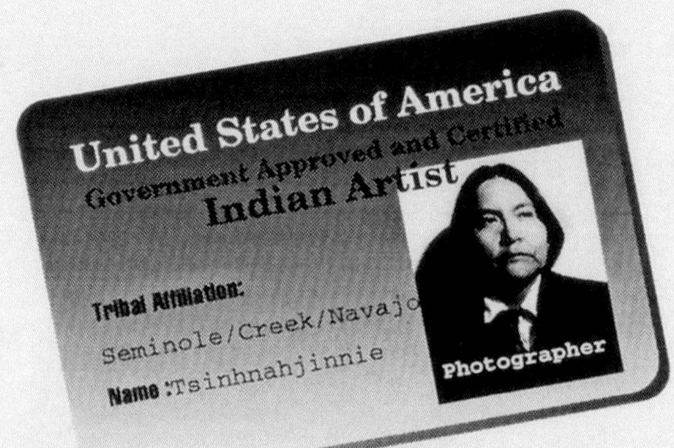

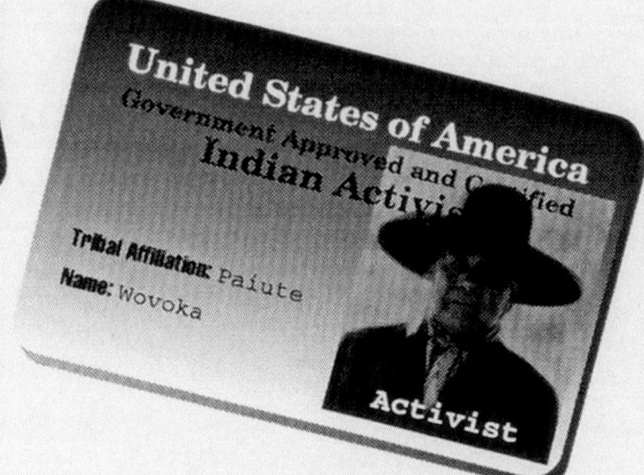

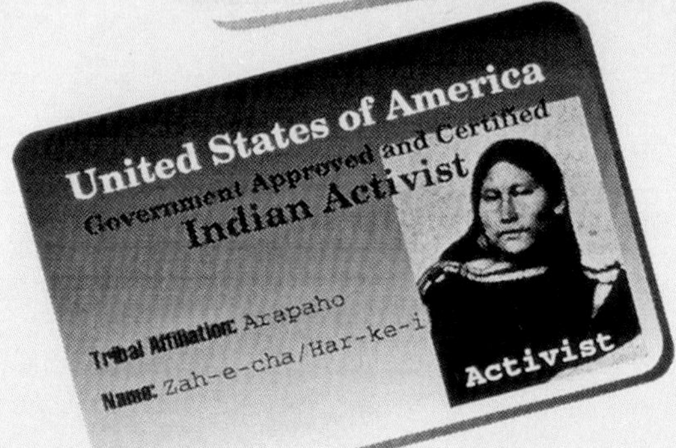

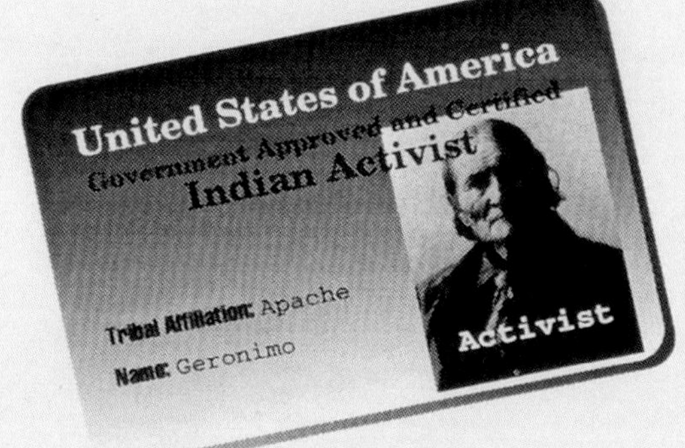

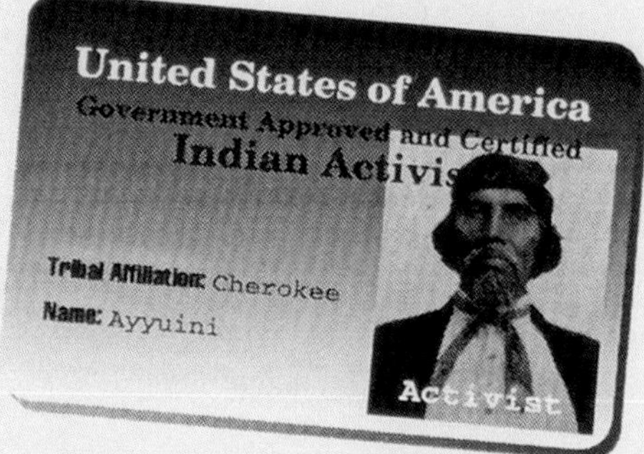

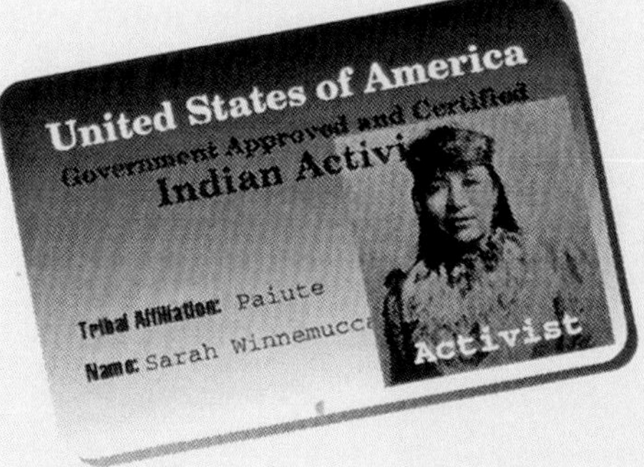

NEVER!

:: 4 ::

The Continuity of Tradition: A Native Aesthetic

Joseph M. Sanchez

Art has long been used in native traditions, including those of the Native Americans, to incorporate visual and tactile representations of religion and cosmology into everyday life. Traditional native art served as a daily, practical reminder of tribal values. While this sacred function continues today, contemporary native art faces the challenge of appropriation by a contemporary art market whose function is profane—that is, focused on individual and commercial success. This is dangerous path for the native artist: if art ceases to reinforce culture, the culture itself will likely perish.

Native American art in particular, whether contemporary or traditional, is inspired by ceremony, influenced by community, and evocative of our relationship to the earth. It also reminds us of the recent history of cultural and physical genocide of Native people. Contemporary Native American art continues to realize a unique aesthetic tradition that is not bound by any European art aesthetic. Critics sometimes mistake it for being "primitive," demonstrating their lack of access to the culture and ceremony that informs it. In addition, some of the meanings of this art are not meant to be analyzed as such but only experienced. Native artists and Native critics alike can fall prey to the pressures of a system that would engage this work only in the context of European art history. It is obvious that the masterworks of Native people are at the very same level of aesthetic excellence and creative vision as any masterwork of the European or American canon, but it must be recognized that this work is functional as well as aesthetic. Though many people know this to be the case, it bears reiteration as we consider our own definitions of art. Along these lines, I curated a retrospective of work by Bob Haozous in 2004 called *Indian Art for Indian People* at the Institute of American Indian Arts Museum in Santa Fe, New Mexico. Natives and non-Natives alike both admired and questioned this effort to inspire Native artists to create work that was both meaningful and culturally responsible. This exhibition implied that by carefully considering the purpose of their work, contemporary Native artists could regain some control over the commercial and scholarly dialogue about Native art and perhaps even reinstate and reemphasize Native art as an expression of functional cultural beliefs within the Native community.

FRONTISPIECE: Hulleah J. Tsinhnahjinnie, Seminole/Diné (Navajo)/Creek, *Don't leave the Rez Without It!* (detail), from *Photographic Memoirs of an Aboriginal Savant (Living on Occupied Land)*, 1994, 15 prints with text and photographic and cartoon reproductions. Purchased through the Contemporary Art Fund; 2007.55.

The Western European concept of duality, which sets humans apart from Nature, constitutes another major difference between Native and non-Native perspectives on art and life. The idea that all things on this earth have equitable significance, and that humanity is just one small part of creation, is contrary to the Western European worldview. This difference, among others, contributes to the theoretical positioning of the work by the "conquered and colonized" Native artist as a cultural artifact or memento of a vanishing race and ethos, and the physical positioning of the work in the curiosity cabinets of the Euro-American museum. In the act of simply creating their culturally invested work, Native artists find themselves misunderstood by and ultimately separated from the practitioners of mainstream American contemporary art.

Native artists also must contend with a commercially driven perception of the self that is mired in the romantic—a Hollywood version of Native history that seeks to keep Native artists in the Kemo Sabe mode of always being the sidekick with the quaint and simple outlook on life. In a 1987 article in *American Indian Art Magazine*, Phoenix-based writer Ron McCoy quotes H. Malcolm Grimmer, owner of Morning Star Gallery in Santa Fe:

> I think the basic desire to collect Indian art comes from childhood. We've all been exposed to the Indian of TV, movies, books, and scouting jamborees. Once the little boy or girl grows into a self-confident individual, there's a feeling of wanting to own what they once only read about. What's important is American Indian art is still accessible. In what other culture can you acquire an example of its basic artistic heritage for what are, all things considered, reasonable prices?[1]

For the art collector, the fantasy of a vanishing "Noble" race and genocidal guilt came into play in contributing to Native art becoming collectible and, therefore, salable "art" in the general Western sense. The marketing of Native art as the remains of once Rousseau-like cultures that were wiped out genocidally inspired great interest in the material remains of Native ancestors and their traditions throughout North and South America. This continuing morbid interest in Native American cultural remains, especially art, has encouraged self-described archaeologists and anthropologists and art collectors to become "pot diggers" to supply today's Native art markets without thought for or acknowledgment of related living cultures or the Native ancestors that are being dug up. Given the success of groups such as the Cowboy Artists of America, who make "nostalgic" art about Native people in the galleries of Santa Fe and around the world, this romantic fantasy of lost and raped cultures remains powerful in the minds of today's collectors of Native art, both traditional and contemporary.

Those Native artists who would both recognize and reinstate the original role of their work—the expression of cosmological and religious priorities in the context of everyday life—must first of all find a way to make a living in today's society and then deal with the lack of Native languages, the loss of the wisdom of the elders, and the isolation of urban life without access to an integrated community. In a larger society where art functions as a symbol of success and status, and even as proof of cultural superiority, Native artists must not succumb to the rewards of compensation or individual recognition and instead commit themselves to work that reinforces and sustains their tribal values and cultural beliefs.

In her 1984 book *Has Modernism Failed?* Suzi Gablick states, "One of the chief functions of a cultural tradition is the creation of exemplary models for a whole society, life histories which may be held up as paradigms or archetypes, and which give meaning and create value."[2] In their work, then, Native artists today must further recognize a history of continued colonization—the anguish of cultural and physical genocide and the fact that citizenship as Americans or Canadians is, in fact, only a recent occurrence. One might even say that we Native artists are in the fight of our lives to retain *our* history—not the one prescribed by academia but the legends and oral histories of our ancestors, which, like the art that depicts them, remind us of our truth and cultural continuity. The "research" that has resulted from the exhumation of over 300,000 of our ancestors over the past several hundred years serves as a constant reminder of the objectification of Native peoples by Western "institutions" of higher learning. The repatriation of our ancestors and sacred objects comprises an ongoing battle cry for the Native people as well as meaningful subject matter in the work of contemporary Native art.

That the boarding school experience has become the subject of many of the paintings and performances of contemporary Native artists is not surprising, as the removal and forced assimilation of the children of Native cultures continues to be a lasting cultural trauma. The success of this operation in breaking the continuity of our tradition cannot be understated, and its effects are insidious, manifested in those Native people who attempt to claim some part of the American dream of individual success by repeating the mistreatment, selfishness, and egocentric behavior of the colonizer. Our loss of Native languages and the erosion of ceremonial practices over the past one hundred years amounts to cultural genocide that can be countered best by a renewed devotion to a Native art that evokes our cultural values and not the individualism that modern society rewards, usually to everyone's detriment. In today's art world, the elevation of "art heroes" (through the complicity of curators, museums, and collectors) and private financial supporters greatly limit the selection of available art presented in our public institutions.

I speak from the heart for Native people and do not take our current situation lightly. I humbly act as a voice, whenever I can, for all Native people as they watch a way of life be sacrificed to the meager rewards of a lifestyle that does not respect nature as equal to humanity. Our elders have often said to me, "You will not survive if you have only money to eat." Yet Native society continues to foot the bill for America's greed. One cannot ignore the mining of Black Mesa in Arizona or Serpent River in Ontario, Canada, when you feel the uranium tailings on your face as they blow across the land, filling your lungs and the lungs of your children, dusting all living things with death. The dumping and storage of nuclear waste on Native lands continues to occur; oil spills take place in northern reserves without any concern for the Natives affected; the waters continue to be polluted and animal and plant life destroyed without remorse. It is more and more evident each day that this taking without thinking has consequences that we have yet to understand. Is it coincidental that a new term, "environmental racism," has recently been coined by the activist community that recognizes that the lower your socioeconomic status, the more likely you are to physically suffer from environmental degradation. Native art can speak to these ongoing violations against all that lives: "A society that consumes a third of the world's resources requires more land and makes bigger handprints each year in succession. Those handprints have caused a great loss of life—human, four-legged, winged, finned, and those with roots."[3]

Native people represent less than 2 percent of the American population but in fact control considerable natural resources in the land left to them through the creation of the reservation system. This is a potentially powerful basis for economic self-sufficiency that could allow Native to support a renaissance of Native value systems and cultural history; however, Natives must be wary of continued assimilation and perhaps the dissolution of the reservation system, which would make these lands completely accessible and finally put an end to the "problem" of Native resistance. The cultural viewpoint of caring for the land is of paramount importance.

Do Native artists have a responsibility to speak to this issue of originally imposed and, now, self-imposed loss of cultural identity? Should we continue to question the appropriation of Native ceremony and symbol by non-Native artists, sports teams, military complexes, and Hollywood in an act of continued stereotyping of the Native American? Or should we ignore oppression and marginalization in favor of assimilation and acceptance, value money over life, and cease to speak out against the ongoing pressure to conform to ideals that are not ours? Native artists can help all of humanity remember its connections to the natural world—the plant and animal life, the rocks, the trees, the air we breathe, the water—not as remnants of our ancient past or resources there for the taking but as equal occupants of an amazing planet we call home.

The Native American's presence on this continent is described in the Western historical record as the legacy of stone age "primitives" who crossed the Bering Strait, which of course reinforces this idea that there are no living Native cultures, since they "vanished" with the last ice age. This theory still informs discussions presented to American schoolchildren, as addressed by Hachivi Edgar Heap of Birds in his sign painting in this exhibition, titled *Who Owns History?* Here is another opportunity for Native artists to set the record straight. While contemporary art in American museums has not included work by Native Americans until recently, it has featured work by contemporary artists whose appropriation of Native culture is both obvious and endorsed—for example, Max Ernst owes a considerable artistic debt in his appropriation of Northwest coast cultural symbols; Marsden Hartley made many renowned paintings following his Native-inspired trip to the Southwest; and Picasso himself had no problem borrowing from "primitive" culture as he fashioned his own revolution in modern art. Artists today continue to look to the art of indigenous people for a sense of spirit and design in an effort to re-energize a Western art that has lost much of its "magic."

In his 1991 book *Towards a Political History of Native Art*, Alfred Youngman states, "Native art's rightful place in Canadian and Western art history has gone largely unrecognized, and the debt which modernism owes Native art and the depths to which modern and post-modern art have been influenced by Native art may never be known."[4] He then asks Native artists a question that is deliberately challenging, especially in an elite art world full of "isms": "Is your art work Indian art?" Daphne Odjig responds (in another context): "What can be more Indian than the spirituality as defined in my paintings?"[5] Jimmy Durham goes further still: "The implication is that the work of an Indian artist is more restricted, narrow and perhaps even less serious, while that of an artist is more universal, more sophisticated, and conceivably of lasting importance. Oddly, it is only the art of white men that ever achieves such cultureless, cosmic universality."[6]

Which then begs the question: indigenous artists or artists in a global community? This very issue loomed large in Venice during the symposium titled *Vision, Space, Desire,* the purpose of which was to review and discuss the roles and participation of indigenous people in international biennales worldwide. In his foreword to the symposium's publication, W. Richard West, founding director of the National Museum of the American Indian, states, "These artists, curators and scholars—from many nations and states of mind—have kicked the tires and looked under the hood of the old apparatus of Western-dominated art, and they are not buying it."[7] Though little was ultimately accomplished in the symposium regarding the international biennale process, indigenous artists, curators, and scholars brought to light many issues, especially appropriation, exclusion, and the racist "elite factor" that dominates the history of this international art practice.

Suzi Gablik speaks to the commercial aspect of art in *Has Modernism Failed?*: "A work of art is a gift, not a commodity . . . Every modern artist who has chosen to labor with a gift must sooner or later wonder how he or she is to survive in a society dominated by market exchange. And if the fruits of a gift are gifts themselves, how is the artist to nourish himself, spiritually as well as materially, in an age whose values are market values and whose commerce consists almost exclusively in the purchase and sale of commodities?"[8] The fact that Native art is now also an investment commodity is evident in the sensational prices brought by cultural objects in the "traditional" art market. Contemporary Native artists find themselves deeply conflicted about the monetary encouragement of collectors who want to perpetuate the creation of traditional masterworks in a market that has more buyers than objects. Thankfully, the watchful eye of Native America as a whole, and the threat of legitimate federal prosecution, has now limited the quantity of our cultural history that is for sale.

While it is indeed hard to fault contemporary Native artists who make work for the market, they are complicit in the backward stories this work perpetuates about Native culture. While work that replicates the "isms" of the artistic canon, whether historical or contemporary, is certainly more commercially viable and easier to position historically, new directions in creative thought and a deeper understanding of the art process possess value too. The historically narrow view of Native art that informs markets like the Santa Fe Indian Art Market does painfully little to educate the larger American population about the current state of these living cultures. Though progress has been made, especially in the media arts, in communicating a reality beyond the romanticism of the Santa Fe Market, the burden for real change must fall on artists willing to risk the success of their careers by creating work not for money but to express our cultural beliefs.

The separation of art by Native Americans from other American artists in America's art museums continues to this day. Recently Native artists whose work fits in the categories of modernism, postmodernism, and so on, have been included in exhibitions of American art, but other artists whose work does not fit as neatly continue to escape recognition, including, prominently, Allan Houser[9] and his son Bob Haozous.[10] We must also consider the impact on America's contemporary art scene by the likes of Kiowa/Caddo artist T. C. Cannon, whose work remains mostly unnoticed and undocumented.[11] Certainly many contemporary Native artists have struggled to find a voice amid the admonitions of Native elders and the exclusionary practices regarding "Indian" art in mainstream contemporary art. The selling of cultural practice and oral history meant for only the community can find the Native artist at odds with the elders and limit the expression of self in today's world. Norval Morrisseau, or "Copper Thunderbird," is known as the first artist of First Nations ancestry to break the white-art barrier with his exhibition at Pollock Gallery in Toronto in 1962; by the 1970s, he had inspired enough followers in his Native art style to be dubbed the grandfather of the Woodlands school.[12] Daphne Odjig's more personal style of exploration of Native themes and stylistic innovation attracted the attention of international greats such as Picasso and Chagall. Alex Janvier's work compares to

Kandinsky and Klee in the eyes of many curators and critics in their writings, and his murals are of such beauty and scale that they cannot be ignored.[13] The Canadian press dubbed him "Alexangelo" after the creation of *Morning Star*, his 450-square-meter mural in the Museum of Civilization in Hull, Quebec. Unlike the United States, Canada has recently taken steps to recognize these artistic giants of the Native world with one-person exhibitions in the National Gallery of Canada and lifetime achievement honors such as the Order of Canada[14] and the Governor General Laureate.[15]

In the United States, Native artist George Morrison, of Chippewa and Ojibway descent, included among his friends Jackson Pollock, Willem de Kooning, and Franz Kline; he was awarded a Fulbright scholarship and the John Hay Whitney fellowship.[16] Practicing avant-garde art in New York allowed Morrison to escape the racism that was prevalent in his home; by his own account, in fact, there were no Native artists to study in the art curriculum of those early years, so he became well versed instead in the many forms of European modernism. He later returned to his native Minnesota in the 1970s to learn and teach about Native art history. His mature work was then collected by museums and champions of Native art who had once ignored him for not being "Indian enough." The life and art of George Morrison, whose mixed blood and education allowed him access to both Native and non-Native worlds, demonstrate the contradictions that are involved in the effort to create work that is culturally relevant.

Fritz Scholder,[17] who is one-quarter Mission Luiseno, studied with Oscar Howe[18] in high school, then with Wayne Thiebauld[19] at California State University. He ultimately got his MFA from the University of Arizona and become the painting and art history instructor at the newly formed Institute of American Indian Arts in Santa Fe, New Mexico.[20] Scholder describes his move to Santa Fe: "Upon my arrival in Santa Fe in 1964, I vowed that I would not paint the Indian. The non-Indian had painted the subject as a noble savage and the Indian painter had been caught in a tourist-pleasing cliché. I retracted my vow of 1964 for several reasons, one of those being a teacher's frustration upon seeing a student with a good idea fall short of the solution. After class the immature struggles with paint and concept haunted me. One winter evening early in 1967 I decided to paint *an Indian*."[21] Scholder's statement indicates that he finally decided to paint the Indian that was real, not the stereotype.

The 1970s proved to be a key decade in the development of contemporary Native art; it also saw the beginning of the American Indian Movement, irrefutable land claims from many individual tribes, and a return to ceremonial life on the reservation. It was during 1970 and 1971 that Fritz Scholder created his famous series of lithographs at the University of New Mexico's Tamarind Institute. *Indian at the Circus* and the notorious *Indian at the Bar* created a much-needed stir among Natives and non-Natives alike at this monstrous but "real" depiction of Native America.

The innovative artist-in-residence program at Dartmouth College invited Fritz Scholder in the fall of 1973, followed by T. C. Cannon in the summer of 1975 and Allan Houser in 1979. (Houser's son, Bob Haozous, would later become an artist-in-residence at Dartmouth in summer of 1989. The Hood Museum of Art now has major works by all four artists in its collection.) In 1974, across the border in Canada, a group of seven Native artists that included Canadians as well as an American expatriate created the first contemporary Native artist corporation, Professional Native Indian Artists, Inc.[22] In northern Arizona, the year 1973 saw Michael Kabotie, with Terrance Talaswaima, Delbridge Honanie, Neil David Sr., and Milland Lomakena, explore fresh interpretations of traditional Hopi art forms as part of the group Artist Hopid.[23] Further south, in Phoenix, I participated in the formation of Moviemento Artistico Del Rio Salado (MARS), founded in 1978 as a response to the exclusion of Arizona Chicano artists in the *2nd Southwest Chicano Art Invitational* at the Heard Museum. As coordinator of that exhibition, I met with artists Jim Covarrubias and Manuel Acuna (Yaqui), and we decided that the best response was to have our own exhibition, featuring a more inclusive view of Chicano and Indian arts in Arizona, at the Encanto Park Pavilion in downtown Phoenix. This event led to the official creation of MARS as a nonprofit arts organization with its own gallery in the Phoenix *barrio*. Ariztlan was also founded in 1978 to join the visual artists of MARS with writers, poets, dancers, musicians, actors, filmmakers, educators, and community organizers from around the state of Arizona in an effort to again pressure Arizona's art-funding agencies to recognize Chicano and Native art and artists. This organization would meet in different cities in Arizona, bringing art, dance, and theater to a different town every month during its early years. The group went on to create art exchanges with universities in Mexico, film workshops involving Hollywood's most promising Chicano film directors and actors, dance workshops with national dance companies, and other means of support for Chicano musicians.

At the same time, on a national level, the formation of the National Association of Artist Organizations (NAAO)[24] pulled together groups of artists and artist-run spaces from around the country to petition the National Endowment for the Arts to fund art and artists who create beyond the narrow window of approval and acceptance of major museums in this country. The true success of this organization was the inclusion of Native artists and other artists of color in the big picture of American art. Forty-plus years have passed with little change in the attitudes of the museum world, but in the Native world, the emergence of Native artists whose art strives to reinstate our ceremony and cultural tradition speaks to the currents of change flowing there.

Today the contemporary Native artist is faced with monetary interests that seek to control the content and vision of his or her work. In addition, Native artists still have to contend with the misconception that their work does not fit into the contemporary art world and would be better suited to archaeology and anthropology museums, not museums of fine art. They are even told that their artwork does not have enough cultural context to be collected by the Native collector! One answer to this quandary would be the creation of art that succeeds on both fronts—in terms of Native traditionalism and in terms of the art world—and this would surely be a new movement in the history of American art.

NOTES

1. Ron McCoy, in *American Indian Art* (1987): 56.

2. Suzi Gablik, *Has Modernism Failed?* (New York: Thames and Hudson, 1984).

3. Winona LaDuke (Anishinaabeg), foreword to Lyuba Zarsky's *Is Nothing Sacred? Corporate Responsibility for the Protection of Native American Sacred Sites,* Sacred Land Film Project, 2006.

4. Alfred Youngman, *Towards a Political History of Native Art from Visions of Power: Contemporary Art by First Nations, Inuit and Japanese Canadians* (Centre for Contemporary Canadian Art, 1997, 2008).

5. *Daphne Odjig: Making History,* 13. Odjig was born on the Wikwemikong Reserve on Manitoulin Island in 1919. "The artist's stylistic and thematic developments have been pivotal to the creation of a First Nations art history that parallels—and at times intersects with—developments in the history of contemporary Canadian art. Moreover, Odjig's position as an important cultural spokesperson during a particularly vibrant and challenging period in Aboriginal-white relations in Canada has resulted in a changed cultural landscape for contemporary practicing visual artists of Native ancestry . . . Daphne Odjig is a self-taught artist. Nevertheless, she began exhibiting professionally in the late 1960s." Carol Podedworny, *Odjig: The Art of Daphne Odjig, 1960–2000* (Toronto: Key Porter Books, 2001), 13.

6. Youngman, *Towards a Political History of Native Art.* Jimmie Durham (Cherokee) was born in Arkansas in 1940. He is a visual artist, a political activist for the American Indian Movement, and an essayist. In the 1960s and 1970s he dedicated his time to theatre and performances, and since the 1980s he has been creating strange objects—assemblages and installations that derive principally from his Native culture and in turn deconstruct the stereotypes and prejudices of Western culture. See http://www.arteallarte.org/aap/english/2003/durham/.

7. W. Richard West Jr., foreword, *Vision, Space, Desire, Global Perspectives and Cultural Hybridity* (Washington, D.C.: National Museum of the American Indian, Smithsonian Institution, 2006), 10.

8. Gablik, *Has Modernism Failed?.*

9. Allan Houser was born on June 30, 1914, as Allan C. Haozous. His parents, Sam and Blossom Haozous, were members of the Chiricahua Apache tribe who were held as prisoners of war for twenty-three years. Allan's father was with the small band of Warm Springs Chiricahuas when their leader, Geronimo, surrendered to the U.S. Army in 1886 in the northern Mexican state of Chihuahua. Allan was the first child born free in Oklahoma, where his family stayed after many of the other Apaches traveled to New Mexico to join the newly created Mescalero Reservation. Raised on a farm, he began carving and drawing and eventually joined the painting school at the Santa Fe Indian School, referred to as the "Dorothy Dunn school." By 1939, his work was being exhibited around the country. Allan married Anna Marie Gallegos in 1939 and moved his family to Los Angeles in 1941. Commissioned to create a memorial for Native students from Haskell who died in World War II, he completed his first major marble sculpture in 1948. He then moved to Brigham City, Utah, and taught at the Intermountain Indian School for the next eleven years. In 1962, Allan was asked to join the faculty of the newly created Institute of American Indian Arts in Santa Fe. There he started the Sculpture Department and began focusing his own artistic output on three-dimensional work. As he taught and created sculpture, he began integrating the aesthetics of the modernists with his narrative ideas. By the late 1960s, he had begun exhibiting this sculpture, and the influence of his unique style grew. In 1975, Allan retired from teaching to devote himself fulltime to his own work. In the two following decades, he produced close to one thousand sculptures in stone, wood, and bronze while emerging as a major figure on an international scale. He had nearly fifty solo exhibitions in museums and galleries in the United States, Europe, and Asia, and he continued working tirelessly until his death on August 22, 1994. See www.allanhouser.com/tribute.php.

10. Bob Haozous was born in Los Angeles in 1943 to Allan Houser and Anna Marie Gallegos (Navajo/Spanish). He grew up in Apache, Oklahoma, and northern Utah and attended Utah State University before serving four years in the U.S. Navy. Following military service, he attended the California College of Arts and Crafts in Oakland, receiving a BFA in 1971. Three years later, Haozous won the Grand Prize at the Heard Museum's *Sculpture II* exhibition. In 1999 and 2001 he helped organize the first Native American Pavilions at the Venice Biennale—a groundbreaking effort to inspire Native artist to create a more meaningful contemporary statement of identity. See the biographical notes in *Relations Indigenous Dialogue,* ed. John R. Grimes and Joseph M. Sanchez (Santa Fe: Institute of American Indian Arts Museum, 2006).

11. Influential contemporary Kiowa painter T. C. Cannon is widely considered to be the Van Gogh of Native American art. Cannon is unquestionably the star of the young artists who left the Institute of American Indian Arts in Santa Fe, New Mexico, in the 1960s and went on to change Indian art into the contemporary scene we recognize today in galleries across the country. Cannon's untimely death at the age of thirty-one in a 1978 car accident catapulted him to cult status among Indian artists of the time. His sophisticated use of color and style, coupled with unflinching political content, gave voice to a new generation of socially aware modern Native American artists and writers. See http://www.joanfrederick.net/cannon.html.

12. Norval Morrisseau was born at Sand Point Reserve, near Beardmore, Ontario, on March 14, 1932. He is a self-taught artist of Ojibwa ancestry. See the gallery guide created by the Institute of American Indian Arts Museum in Santa Fe on the occasion of the premiere of *Norval Morriseau Shaman Artist,* June 15–September 3, 2007, an exhibition organized and circulated by the National Gallery of Canada.

13. Alexandre Simeon Janvier was born on Le Goff Reserve, Cold Lake First Nations, Alberta, on February 28, 1935. His father, Harry, was one of the last hereditary chiefs, until he was deposed by the electoral system in 1947. The Janvier children were raised in the Chipewyan tradition, speaking the Dene language, until they attend the Blue Quill Residential Indian School near St. Paul, Alberta. Janvier recalled, "By today's terms, it was a Rhodesian situation. The whites were whites and the natives knew their place . . . We were told to accept the best of both worlds, but they didn't know anything about ours; what it meant was accepting the white world" (Helen Melnyk, "Janvier—Name, not a Number," *Edmonton Journal,* March 18, 1978). In his various roles as artist, educator, government consultant, and political activist, Janvier has made numerous and significant contributions to the developing field of aboriginal art and art history in Canada. His dedication in his work with artists' organizations and federal agencies and his vision in demanding a serious framework for the study and presentation of Native art have inspired a new generation of contemporary Native artists. Alex Janvier's history as an artist parallels the politics and history of Native art in Canada since the early 1960s. See Lee Ann Martin, *The Art of Alex Janvier: His First Thirty Years, 1960–1990* (Thunder Bay, Ontario: Thunder Bay Art Gallery, 1993).

14. Established in 1967 by Queen Elizabeth II, the Order of Canada is the centerpiece of Canada's honors system and recognizes a lifetime of

outstanding achievement, dedication to the community, and service to the nation. The Order recognizes people in all sectors of Canadian society.

15. The annual awards of the Governor General Laureate, funded and administered by the Canada Council for the Arts, were created in June 1999 and presented for the first time in March 2000 by Her Excellency the Right Honourable Adrienne Clarkson, Governor General of Canada. The awards recognize distinguished career achievement in the visual and media arts by Canadian artists, as well as outstanding contributions to the visual and media arts through voluntarism, philanthropy, board governance, community outreach, and professional activities. See www.canadacouncil.ca.

16. George Morrison, as told to Margot Fortunato Galt, *Turning the Feather Around: My Life in Art* (St. Paul: Minnesota Historical Press, 1998).

17. Fritz Scholder, born in Breckinridge, Minnesota, in 1937, grew up in North and South Dakota. He received his first art training from the Sioux painter Oscar Howe in South Dakota. See *Fritz Scholder: Paintings and Monotypes* (Santa Fe: Twin Palm Publishers, 1988), and John Wilmerding, *The Mystery and History of Fritz Scholder's Art* (Santa Fe: Twin Palm Publishers, 1988).

18. Oscar Howe was born on May 13, 1915, at Joe Creek on the Crow Creek Indian Reservation of South Dakota. His great-grandfathers, Bone Necklace and White Bear, were hereditary chiefs of the Yankonai and noted orators. He is seen as a model of cultural vitality, one who bridged the Indian and non-Indian worlds and achieved a continuity between an ancient tradition and the twentieth century.

19. Wayne Thiebaud (born November 15, 1920) is an American painter whose most famous works are of cakes, pastries, boots, toilets, toys, and lipsticks. He is associated with the pop art movement because of his interest in objects of mass culture, although his works, executed during the 1950s and 1960s, slightly predate the works of the classic pop artists. Thiebaud uses heavy pigment and exaggerated colors to depict his subjects, and the well-defined shadows characteristic of advertisements are almost always included in his work.

20. The Institute of American Indian Arts (IAIA) is located in one of the most diverse concentrations of Native peoples in North America, in the heart of the nation's oldest multicultural community and in one of the largest art markets in the country. The City of Santa Fe's population is 63,203. See http://www.iaia.edu/about.php.

21. *Fritz Scholder: Recent Work*, exhibition catalogue (Norman: University of Oklahoma, School of Art, 2002).

22. In November 1973, with the assistance of John Dennehy of the Department of the Secretary of State, the seven artists (Daphne Odjig, Norval Morrisseau, Alex Janvier, Jackson Beardy, Carl Ray, Eddy Cobiness, and myself) developed a proposal to formalize their organization into the Professional Native Indian Artists, Inc. (PNIA), to be funded by the Department of Indian Affairs. The "Indian Group of Seven," as they were frequently called, pursued the following objectives: to develop a fund to enable artists to paint; to develop a marketing strategy involving prestigious commercial galleries in order to exhibit their works; to travel to aboriginal communities to encourage young artists; and to establish a trust fund, using a portion of the sales of artworks, for a scholarship program for emerging artists. See Martin, *The Art of Alex Janvier*.

23. Artist Hopid, *Native Peoples Heard Fair Guide* (Phoenix: Heard Museum, 2010), 14.

24. National Association of Artist Organizations (NAAO) is a national nonprofit created to advocate for artists and art organizations outside of the mainstream of America's museum and music hierarchy. Founded in the late 1970s during a conference in Los Angeles that included no representation of people of color except for the black director of the WATTS Tower museum and myself, NAAO became an inclusive supporter of the diversity of the arts in America. Its conferences around the country introduced a wide variety of arts created in rural and urban America to the major cities and mainstream American art world. I was one of the first board members representing MARS and Ariztlan and the first Minority Board Member at Large, representing all people of color. I was also the curator of the Performance Rodeo at the Diversity/Unity Conference in Houston, Texas.

:: 5 ::

A Selection of Contemporary Native American Art in the Hood Museum of Art's Collection

Artist statements taken from conversations or correspondence with Karen S. Miller in 2010, unless otherwise noted.

Rick Bartow, Wiyot (Mad River Wiyot), born 1946

The Tale That the Crow Told
No Dogs at the Ceremony
The Dancers Arrive
Acquiring a Taste for Crow

From the series of four paintings titled
The Ceremony That Never Was, 2006
Acrylic on panel
Purchased through the Hood Museum of Art Acquisition Fund; 2008.6.1–4

FROM THE ARTIST:

What is ceremony? What comprises ceremony? Where does the ceremony start and where does it stop?

I am involved in ceremony as much as I can. I love ceremony. It gives shape to my life. As far as I know, it keeps me going . . . that spiritual feeling that we seek in ceremony . . . that makes you unequivocally correct in what you're doing . . .

The Ceremony That Never Was is a bit facetious. Sometimes people think that ceremony is something that I don't think it is personally.

I think ceremony is simply living in a good manner.

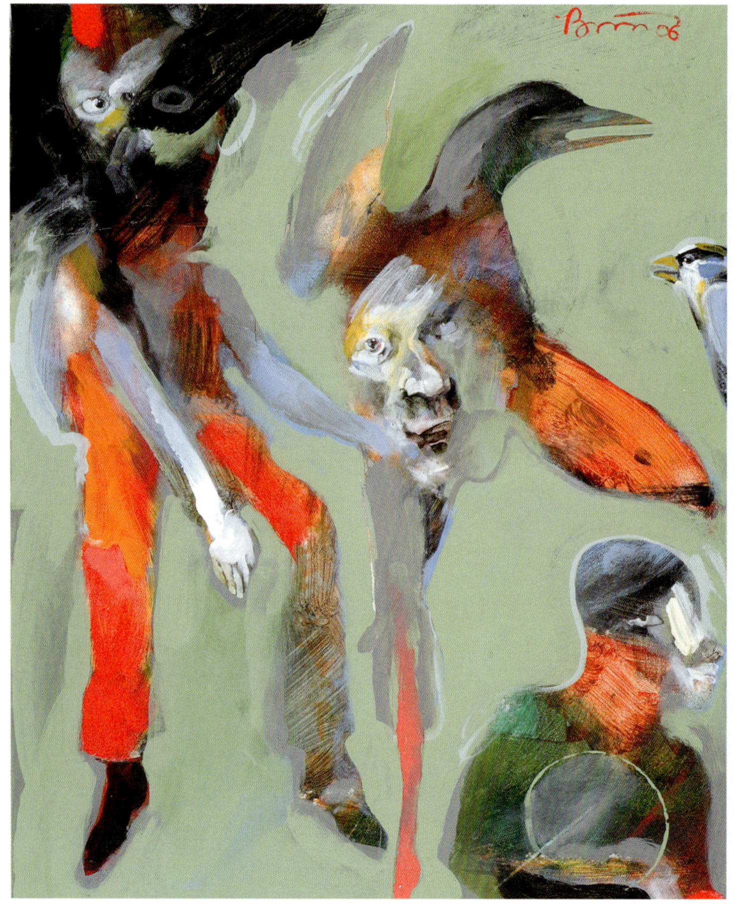

1

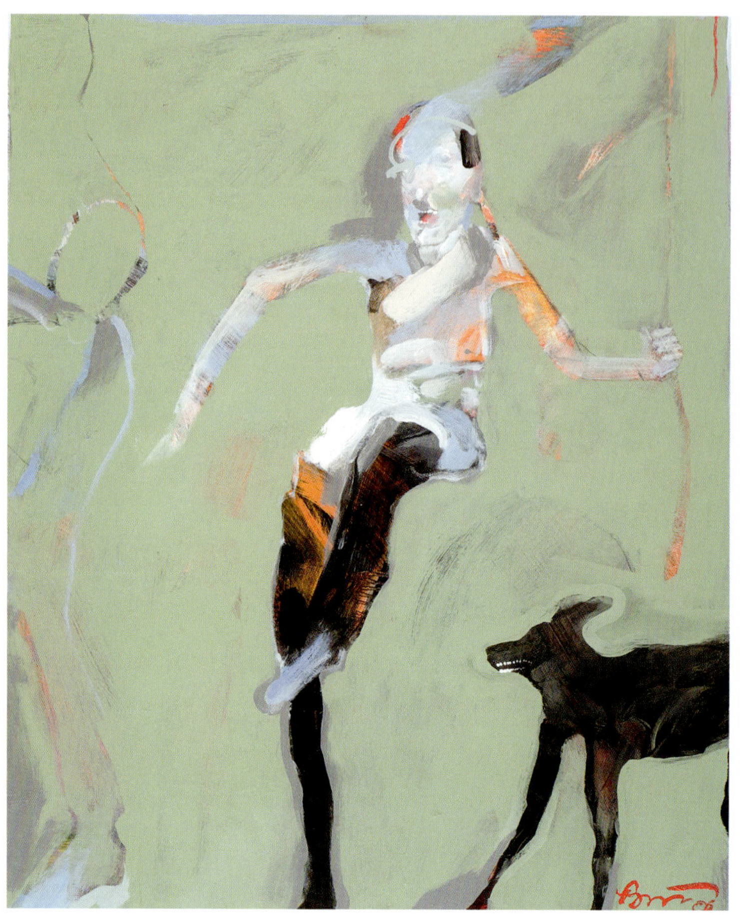

2

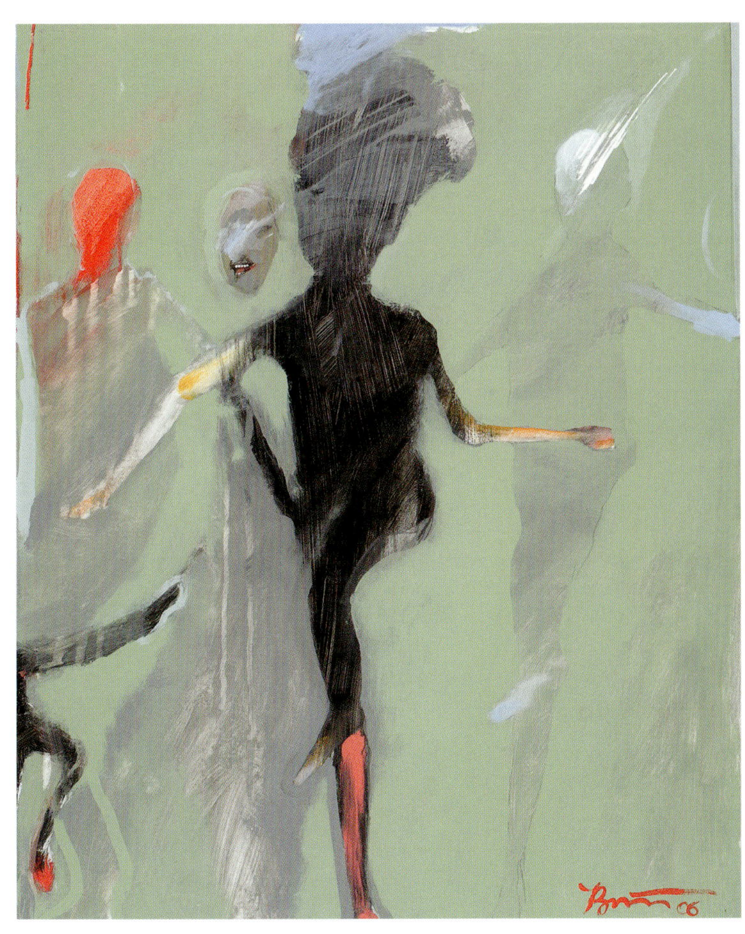

3

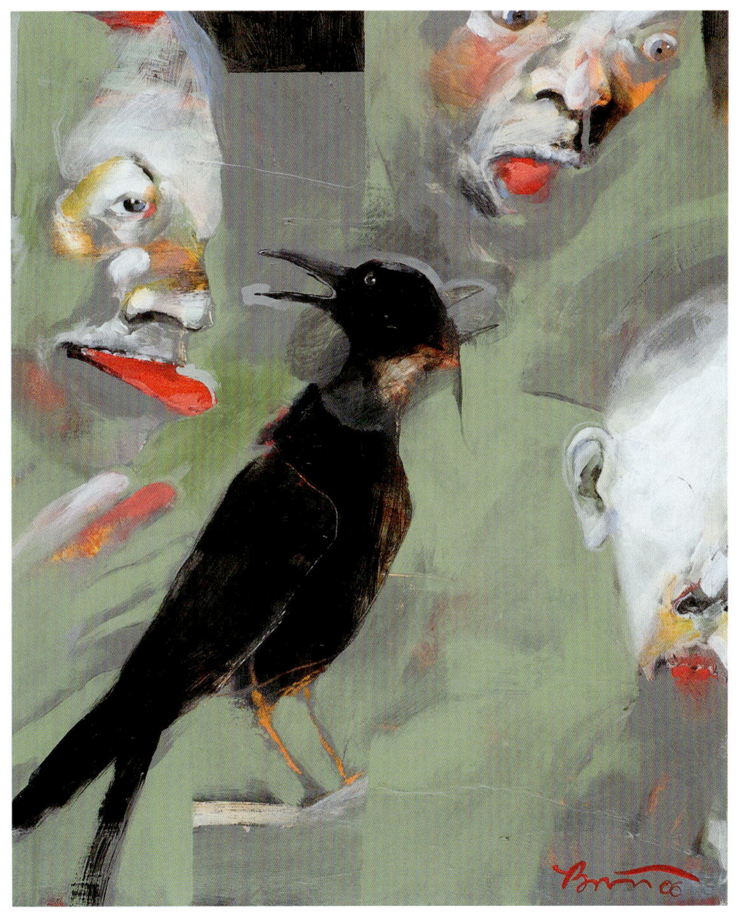

4

Rebecca Belmore, Anishinaabe (Chippewa / Ojibwa), born 1960

Fringe, 2007

Digital photograph
Purchased through the Elizabeth and David C. Lowenstein '67 Fund and the Olivia H. Parker and John O. Parker '58 Acquisition Fund; 2010.65

FROM THE ARTIST:

Some people look at this reclining figure and think that it is a cadaver, but I look at it and I don't see that. I see it as a wound that is on the mend. It wasn't self-inflicted, but nonetheless, it is bearable. She can sustain it. So it is a very simple scenario. She will get up and go on, but she will carry that mark with her.

(Rebecca Belmore in conversation with Kathleen Ritter, Vancouver, April 19, 2008, as quoted in "The Reclining Figure and Other Provocations," *Rebecca Belmore: Rising to the Occasion* [Vancouver: Vancouver Art Gallery, 2008]; reproduced with the permission of the author)

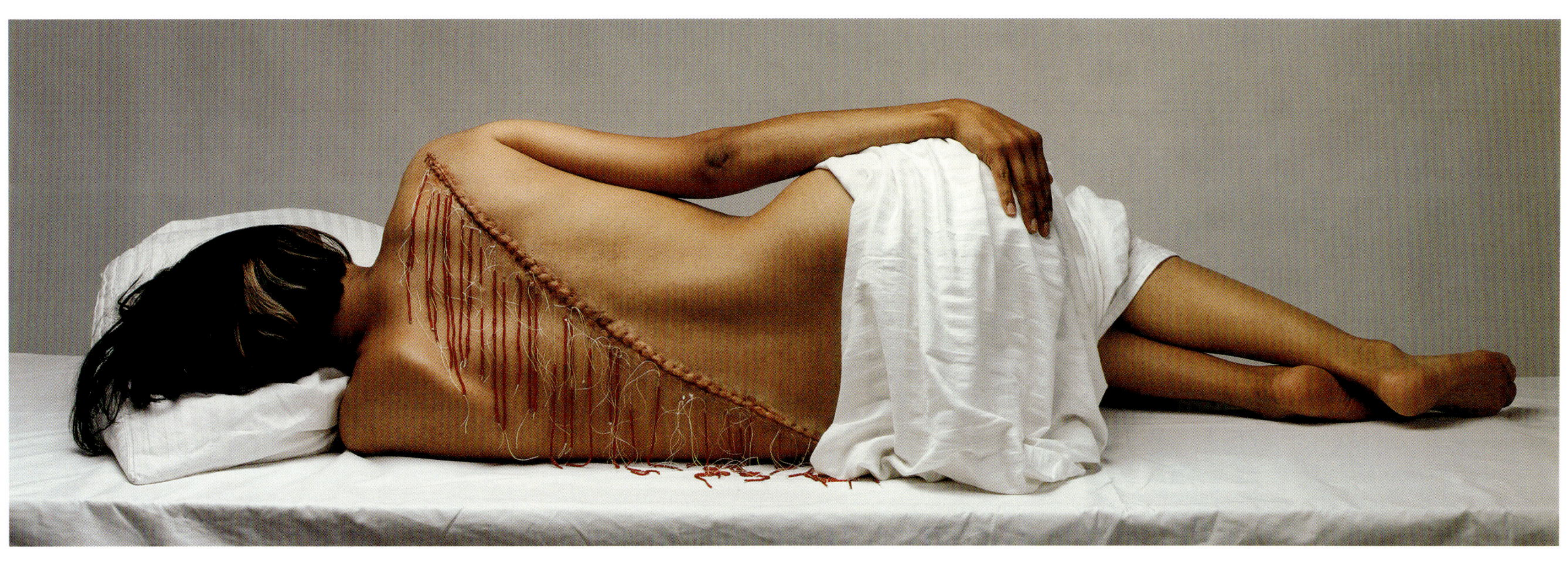

Nicholas Galanin, Tlingit / Unangant (Aleut), born 1979

What Have We Become? Vol. 3, 2007

Book made of blank white pages with face of the artist cut out of it
Purchased through the Virginia and Preston T. Kelsey 1958 Fund; 2007.36.1

What Have We Become? Vol. 5a, 2007

Cut pages from the book *Under Mount Saint Elias*
Purchased through the Virginia and Preston T. Kelsey 1958 Fund; 2007.36.2

FROM THE ARTIST:

The blank book is one without any cultural context . . . a form of liberating myself as an artist. There's so much room for growth, especially in the indigenous art world, and that's what I'm exploring through the diversity of medium . . . so many layers and meanings . . .

This was a series of concept-based work, looking at how my culture had been influenced by text and the world of museums and academia, and how my culture was transformed through that [text] medium. A lot of the text is written from this foreign perspective.

As I read about our history it becomes a vehicle . . .

I did a lot of traditional apprenticeships in the Northwest Coast area. That was a form of learning about my history and culture.

Not everyone questions where the information in these books comes from. That was the inspiration for this series.

There's a lot of conservatism in Northwest Coast artwork and the artwork that comes from the romanticization of our culture, which is tied to these texts. There wasn't a lot of interest in the real portrayal of today's culture.

I have a history. I have an understanding of traditional forms. That foundation might ease people's judgment of my new ideas and new work. I've got a little experience in that side of the culture.

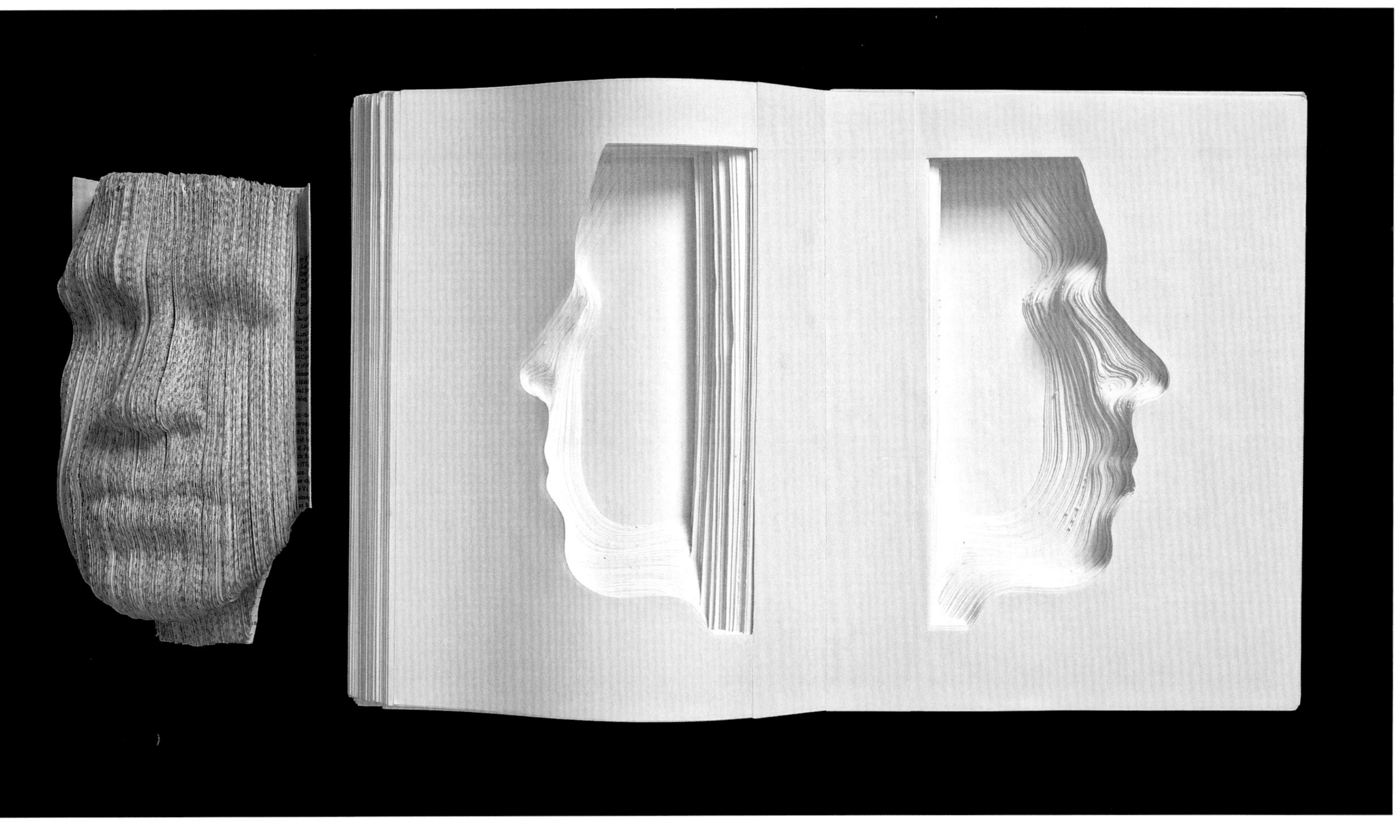

Bob Haozous, Chiricahua Apache / Diné (Navajo), born 1943

Apache Pull-Toy, 1988

Painted steel
Purchased through the Joseph B. Obering '56 Fund; S.989.17

FROM THE ARTIST:

Indian humor and ridicule serve various functions. In Indigenous society the most biting form of humor for serious social misbehavior is ridicule. Harmony is maintained by using humor for serious and non-serious occurrences in daily life. Humor is ever prevalent and can encompass all issues, from minor to culturally threatening situations. The most extreme solution would have included banishment. This punishment would be insignificant in the Western world, whereas in the Indigenous world this would be akin to a death sentence. Cultural exclusion would jeopardize a person's self-perception as an integral part of the whole society. An essence of tribalism is the holistic sense of oneself, not only with those people within your personal communal relationship but all of the animate and inanimate things of life that make you who you are. Consequently, when a person is banished from a Native society, that person quite literally loses the right to exist in his previous cultural and physical universe. In Western civilization, where individualism is extolled as the finite value of politics, religion, economics, and society in general, expulsion carries little threat.

The sculpture *Apache Pull-Toy* is a play on role reversal. Davie Crockett, celebrated frontiersman and Indian fighter, made the comment "just like shooting dogs" when questioned about his killing of Indian people. This dehumanized attitude toward the Indigenous inhabitants of this country was common throughout America's history. During the Westernization of many countries, the killing of the natives was high sport. With this sculpture I've placed the viewer into the frame of mind of the victim and target of this sport. This stereotyped blond, blue-eyed example of racial dominance with the "good guy" white hat serves as a reminder of our past insensitivities. The message isn't intended to challenge or threaten, but to remind and re-remind us of our common humanity. *Apache Pull-Toy* is a reversal of sensitivities that places the "white" man as a target for his own past and current misbehaviors.

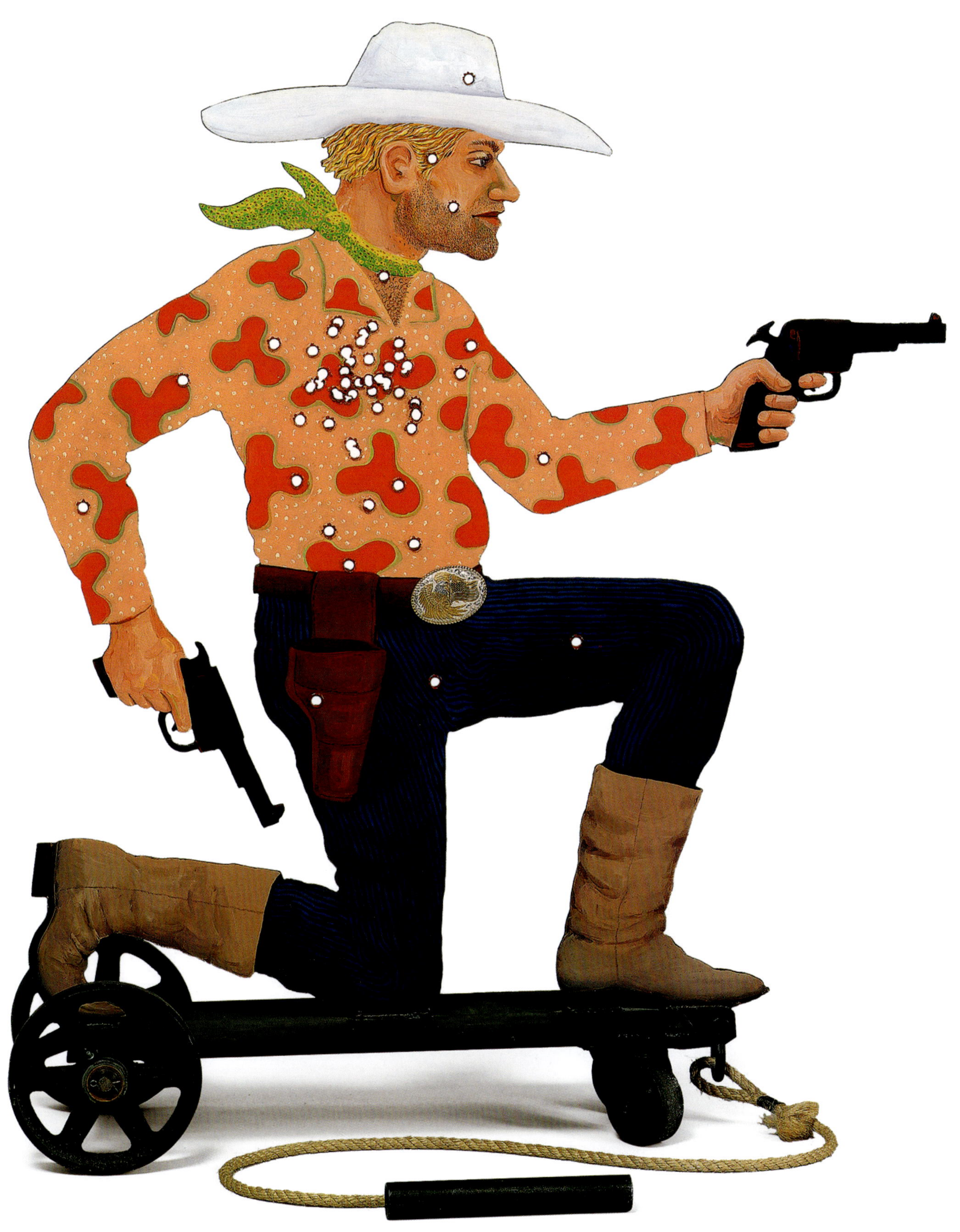

Hachivi Edgar Heap of Birds, Tsistsistas / Suhtai (Cheyenne) / Inunaina (Arapaho), born 1954

. . . *Who Owns History?*, 1992

Metal sign
Gift of Monroe A. Denton Jr., Class of 1968; Mis.2003.25.1

FROM THE ARTIST:

This series of text panels was inspired by a monument sponsored by the D.A.R. in Point State Park and in front of the state museum. The words on my public art panels were quoted from the D.A.R. monument [stating] that there has been "Anglo Saxon supremacy established in the U.S.A." . . . The D.A.R. was also deeded land within Point State Park. This land was [denoted] by metal plaques in the cement walkways. This seemed to also be an odd practice to give state park land to a social group, within a state park. Of course I take exception to the D.A.R. quote about Anglo Saxon supremacy. From my research I found that the D.A.R. was actually talking about the large population of eastern Europeans who were brought into Pennsylvania to work the mines. The racial slur was directed at that non-Anglo population yet also affects Native Americans and other people of color in the U.S.A. . . . The monument and my panels bring forth the question as to who does "own" history as it is written, recorded, and transmitted.

Because the state museum would allow my panels only to be as close as forty feet to the D.A.R. monument, there was confusion as to the referent of the panels. My art works were bent up, torn, and defaced because of this confusion and not being able to properly implicate the D.A.R. monument. We then placed stickers on each panel explaining the reference, and the vandalism halted.

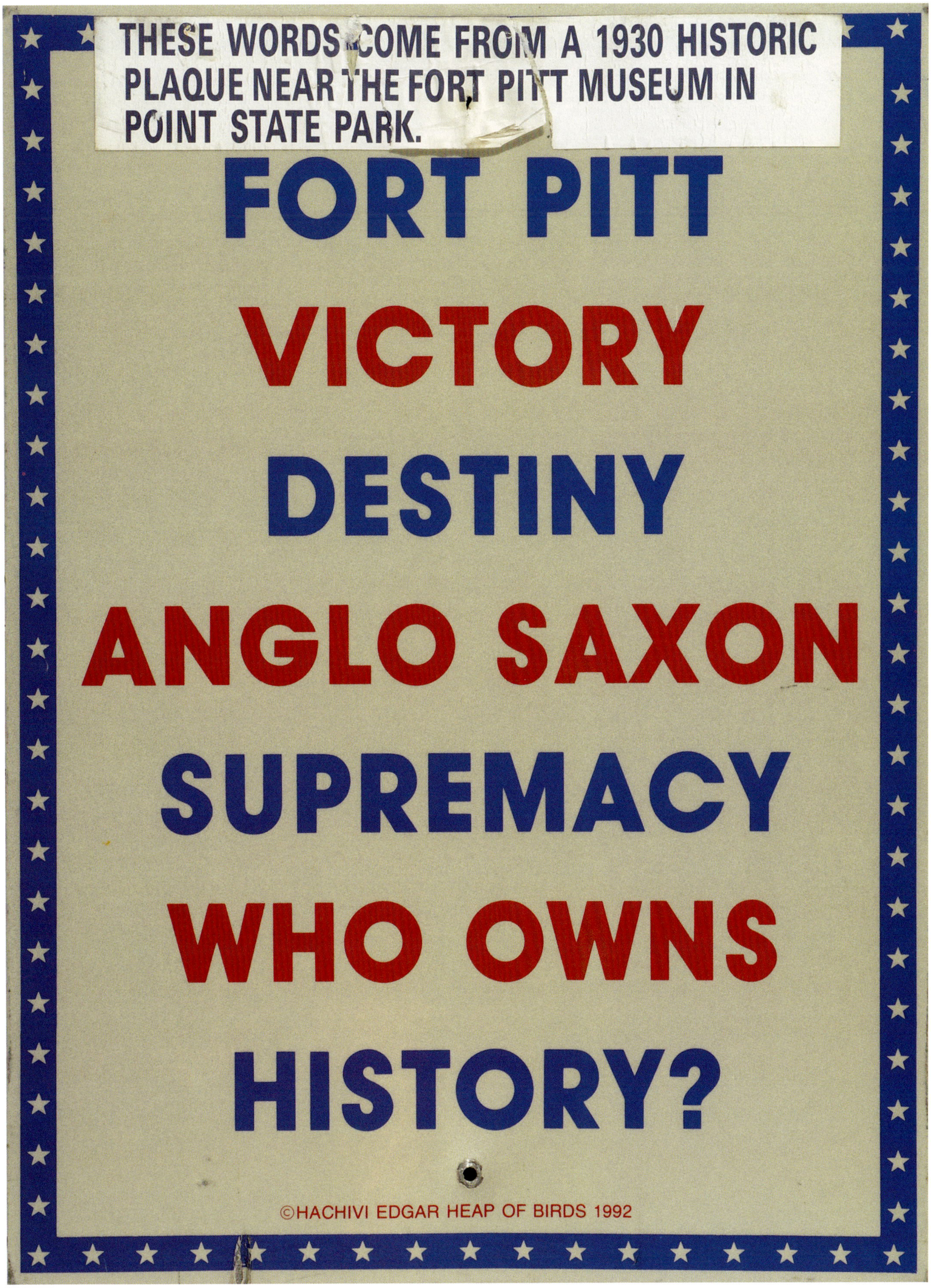

THESE WORDS COME FROM A 1930 HISTORIC PLAQUE NEAR THE FORT PITT MUSEUM IN POINT STATE PARK.

FORT PITT
VICTORY
DESTINY
ANGLO SAXON
SUPREMACY
WHO OWNS
HISTORY?

©HACHIVI EDGAR HEAP OF BIRDS 1992

Zig Jackson, Numakiki (Mandan) / Minitari (Hidatsa) / Sahnish (Arikara), born 1957

China Basin District, number 2 of 4 from the series *Entering Zig's Indian Reservation*, negative: 1997, print: 1997–98

Gelatin silver print
Purchased through the Harry Shafer Fisher 1966 Memorial Fund; 2007.37.1

FROM THE ARTIST:

Why do I have to go and photograph Indians on a reservation? Why can't I be my own Indian on my own reservation? So I came up with the idea of Zig's Reservation. I would occupy different areas, for example, Golden Gate Park. They were going to build a ballpark in China Basin, which was an area with a lot of homeless people, and they were going to make them move. So I took my sign and put it up there . . . and the cops gave me fifteen minutes to move, so I went to City Hall and I occupied the grounds of City Hall with my sign.

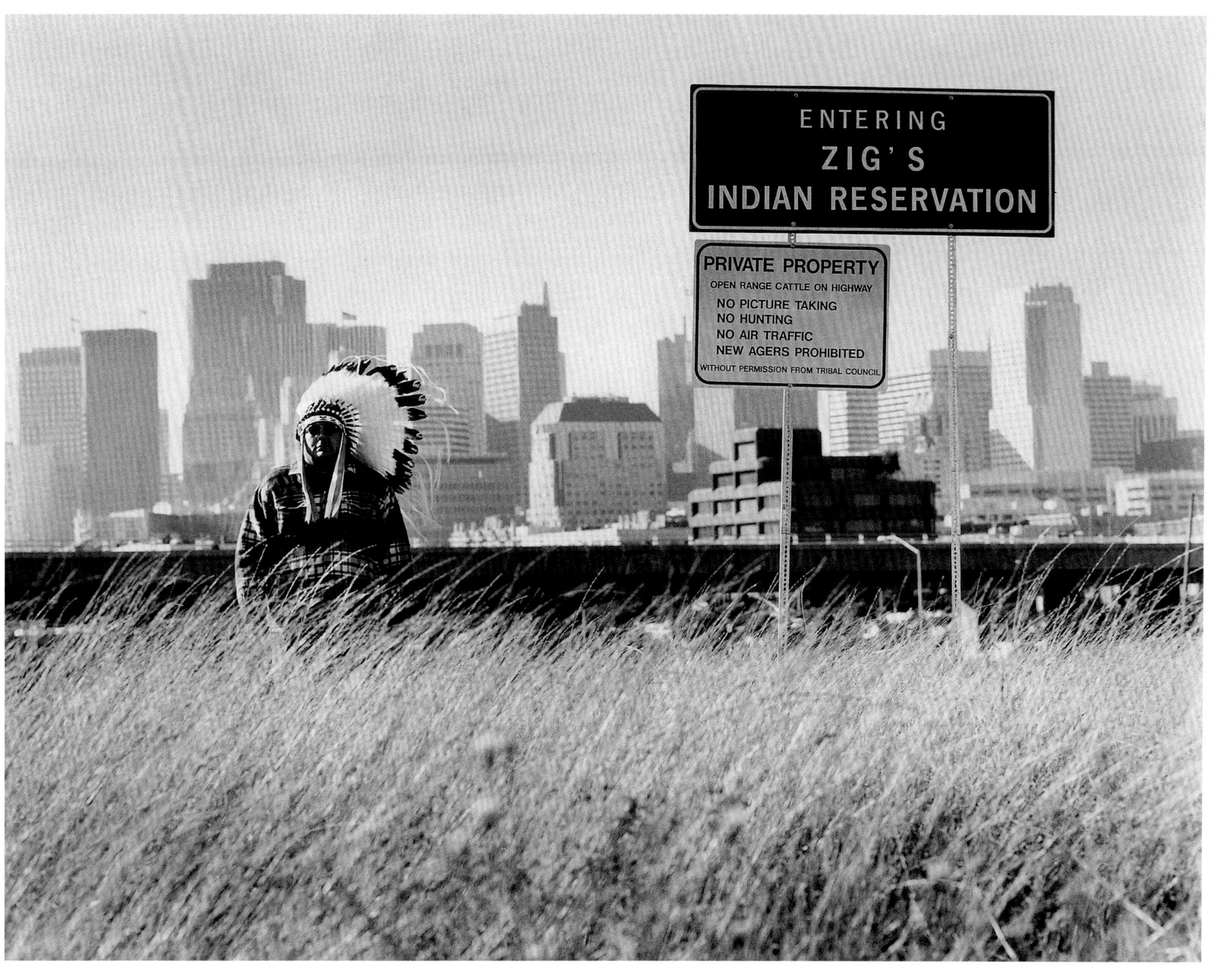
ENTERING
ZIG'S
INDIAN RESERVATION
PRIVATE PROPERTY
OPEN RANGE CATTLE ON HIGHWAY
NO PICTURE TAKING
NO HUNTING
NO AIR TRAFFIC
NEW AGERS PROHIBITED
WITHOUT PERMISSION FROM TRIBAL COUNCIL

James Lavadour, Walla Walla (Wallawalla), born 1951

Untitled (panels 1–9), 1995

Color lithographs with chine collé collage on tan, white, and green papers
Purchased through the Virginia and Preston T. Kelsey 1958 Fund; PR.995.44.1–9

FROM THE ARTIST:

I'm a painter and I live on the land, and the two things just went together. There's no difference between the land and paint . . . erosion and sedimentation, and layers . . . How that kind of energy is transformed from one thing to another as you move on the land . . .

I've been exploring various aspects of this my whole life. Making a landscape is a flow of material, it's a flow . . .

The same thing that's happening in the painting is happening in the land.

It's a structure for me. It's essentially an architectural abstraction because it creates a space.

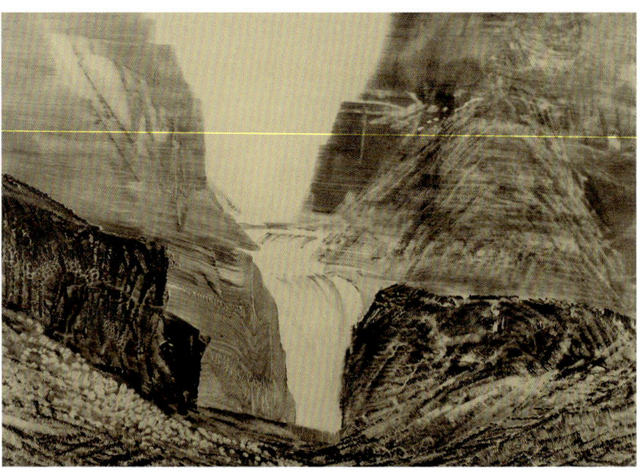

1

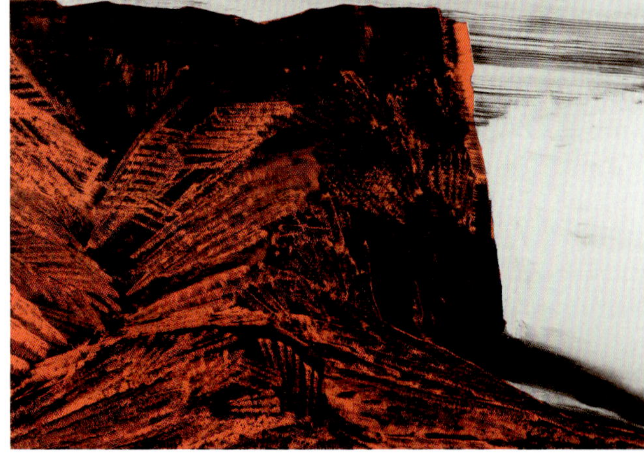

4

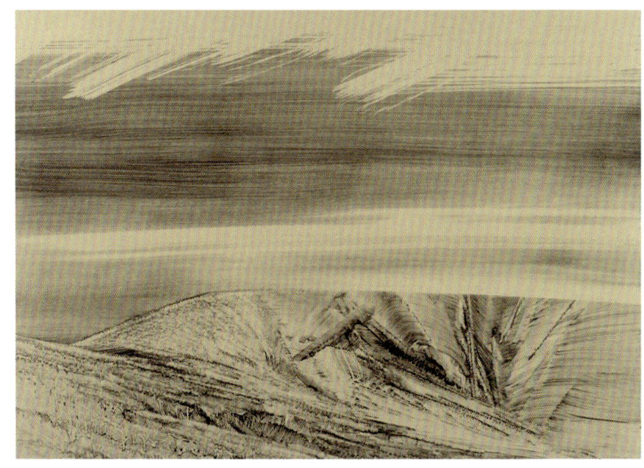

7

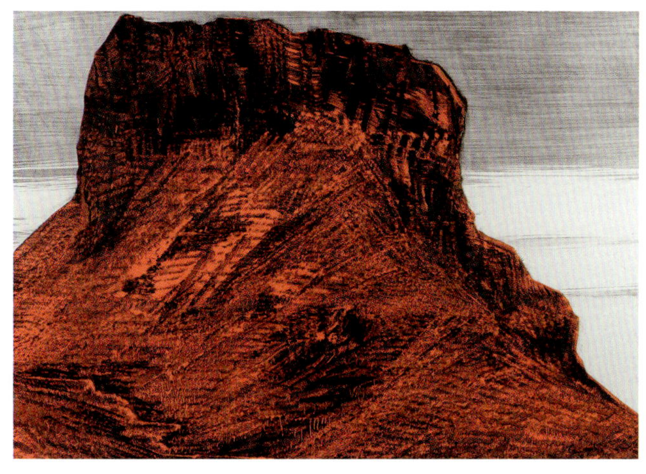

2

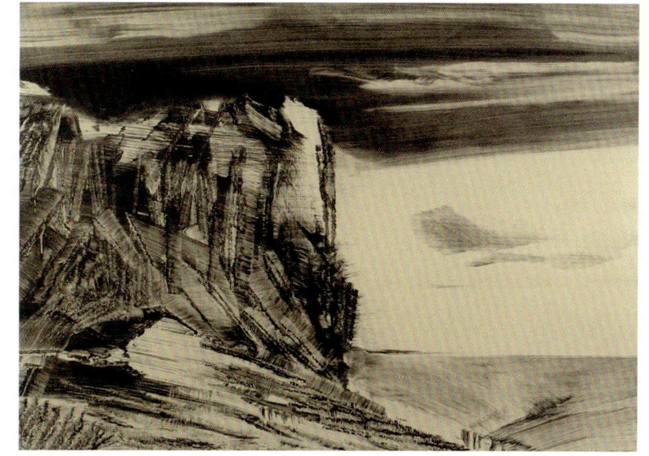

3

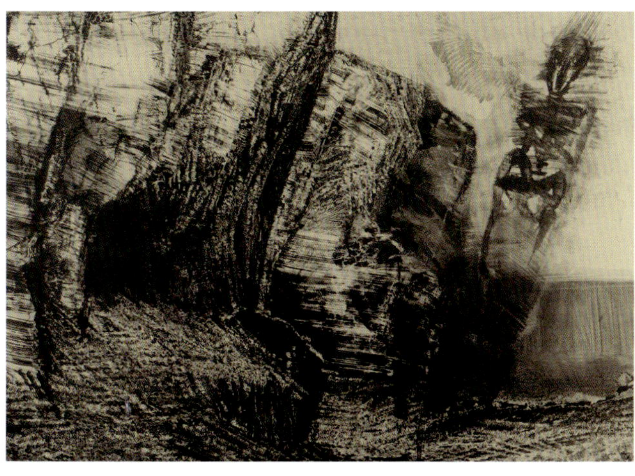

5

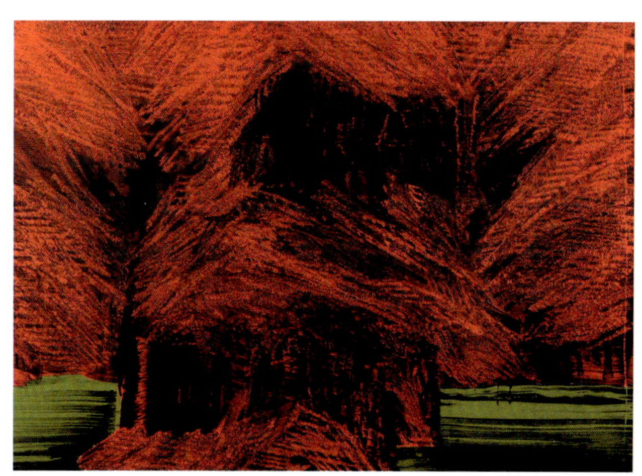

6

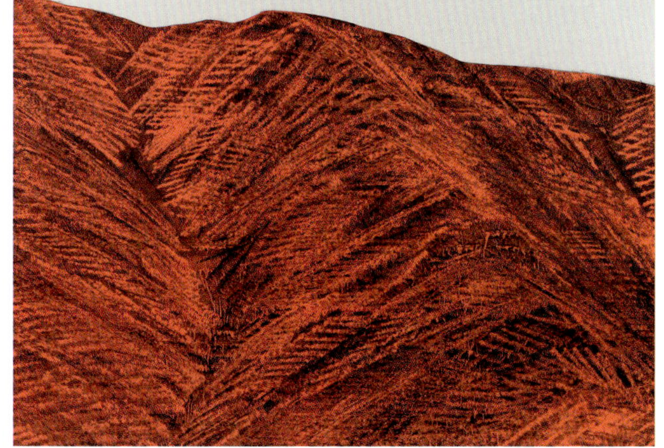

8

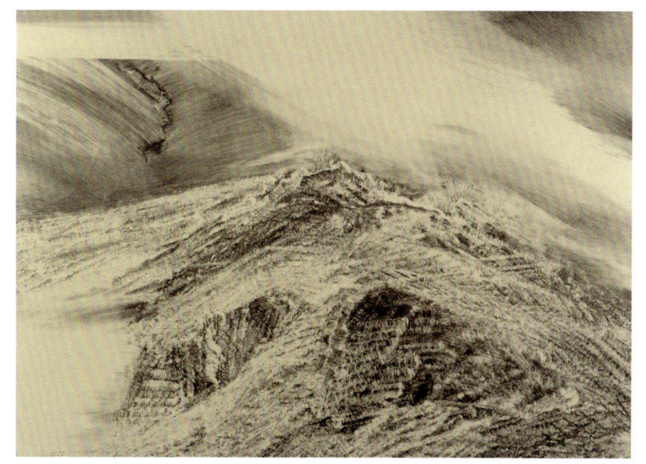

9

Truman Lowe, Ho-Chunk (Winnebago), born 1944

Wing, 1995

Corkscrew willow branch, handmade paper with watermarks, cotton fiber abaca, sisal, flax
Purchased through the Class of 1935 Memorial Fund; 2008.41.3

FROM THE ARTIST:

My work is an aesthetic examination of my immediate environment, and of earlier people who lived in this region and created objects and stories reflective of their time. It involves patterns taken from nature, and forms built from materials taken from the environment. *Wing* is a cast paper piece. All of the materials used are taken from wood. I felt that using cast paper as a medium was justified in that I was staying with tradition but using fiber in its present-day form.

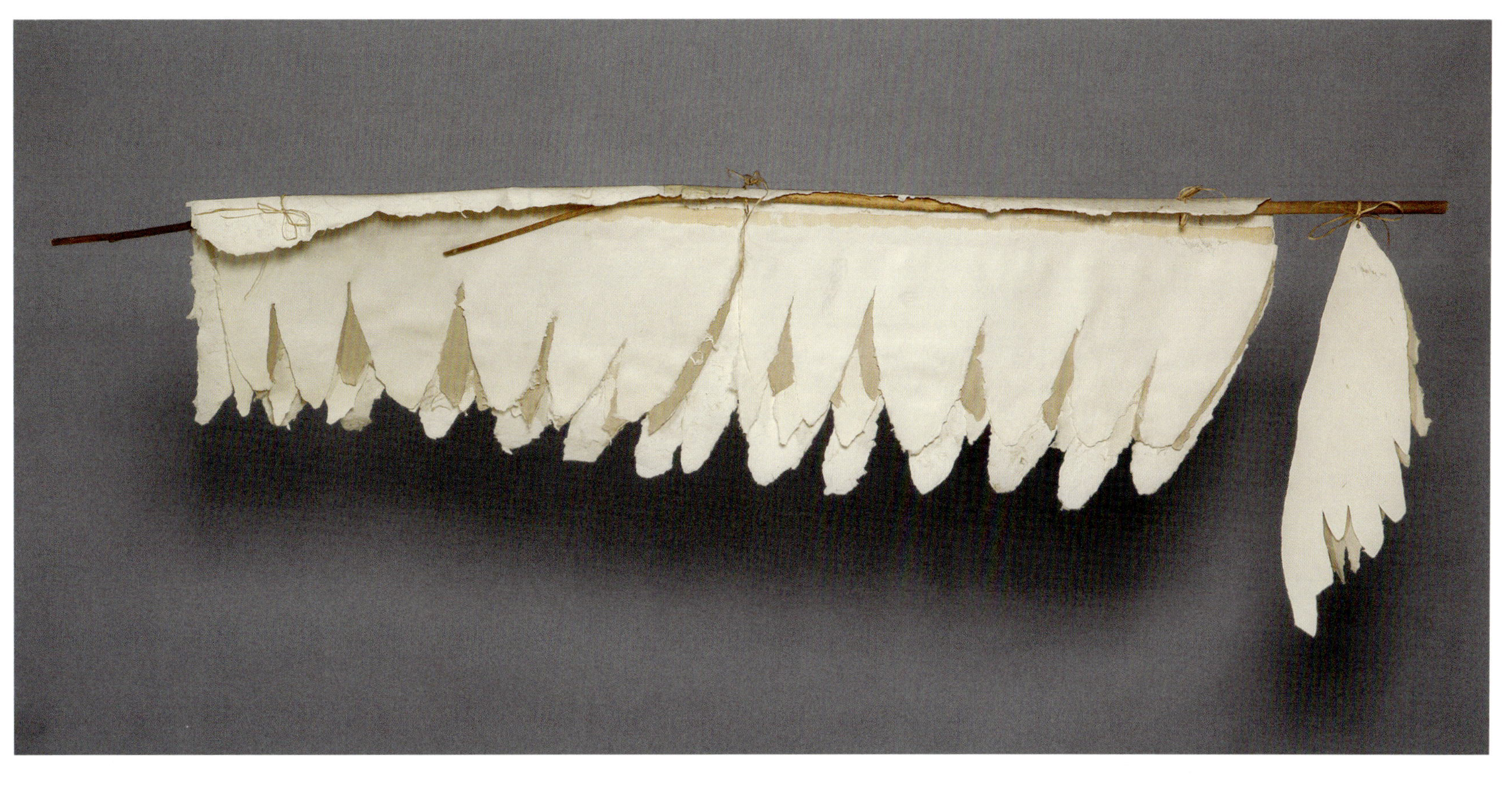

Kevin Pourier, Oglala Lakota, born 1959

Monarch Buffalo Horn Cup, 2009

Buffalo horn, sandstone, mother of pearl
Purchased through gifts from the Lathrop Fellows; 2009.59

FROM THE ARTIST:

There is a very famous photograph of the great leader Sitting Bull with a monarch butterfly wing in his hatband. That photo alone shows me that he knew of the power and the beauty of the butterfly. Looking at the time that the photo was taken, a time when we were having everything taken from us—our way of life, our land, our buffalo, spirituality—and our people were being killed, one has to understand what kind of turmoil a leader would be going through, but yet he had the awareness and understanding of all things, even the little things like butterflies. Who can we name today who would do something like that under the same circumstances?

The monarch also has a special meaning to me, and this is the reason I have incorporated the image into my work. I was participating in one of our most sacred ceremonies, the Hunblechea, where we go alone to a hill and seek guidance from our creator. It was the next morning after the first night and there was the biggest monarch that I had ever seen coming through the woods toward me. He looked like he was just floating on the wind. It seemed as if he circled me for an unusually long time and then flew away. His presence took away the loneliness, the cold and hunger I was feeling. When we were brought down from the hill, everyone else had beautiful stories of the visions that they had seen—ancestors visiting them and talking to them, buffalo spirits and eagle spirits coming and telling them things—and all I had was a little butterfly.

I finally told the medicine man six months later about my butterfly story, and he told me that it was a great experience and that from that time on I would be reminded of our lifeways whenever I would see a butterfly. Today, we see butterflies when no one else seems to notice. It makes me smile and remember whenever one comes to us.

The monarch butterflies that are carved on this horn cup represent love and respect to the Lakotas. The very idea that they fly thousands of miles to go back to their home and be with their own shows a great love and commitment. They have been carved into what the Lakota People consider to be one of the most sacred of items, the buffalo horn. The Spirit of the Buffalo lives in the horn cap. During our ceremonies the buffalo skull is the center of our altars.

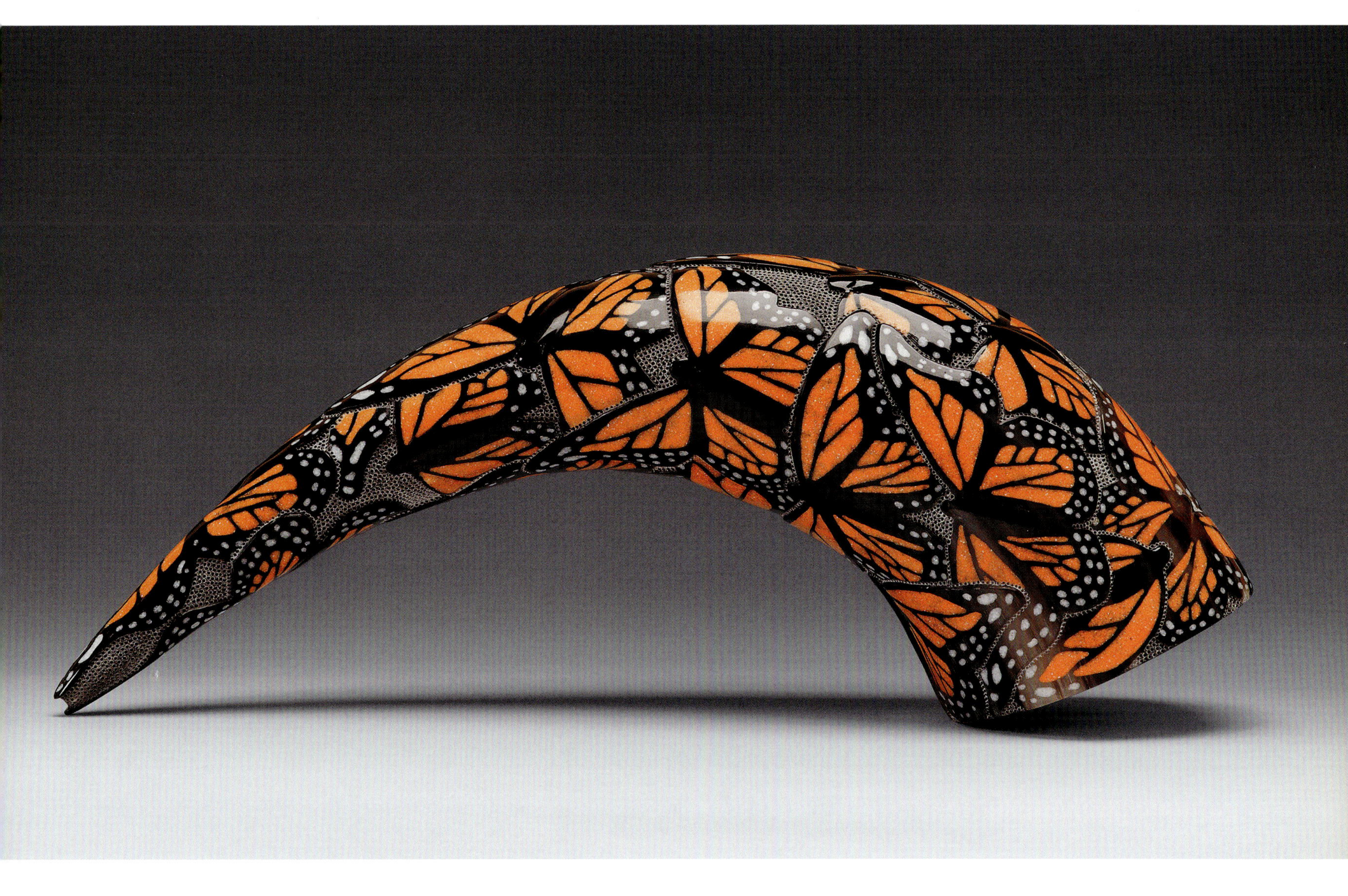

Jaune Quick-to-See Smith, Salish (Flathead) / French Cree / Shoshone, born 1940

The Rancher, 2002

Acrylic on canvas
Purchased through the William S. Rubin Fund; 2005.13

FROM THE ARTIST:

I call myself a cultural art worker. I use humor and satire to examine myths, stereotypes, and the paradox of American Indian life in contrast to the consumerism of American society. My work is philosophically centered by my strong traditional beliefs and political activism.

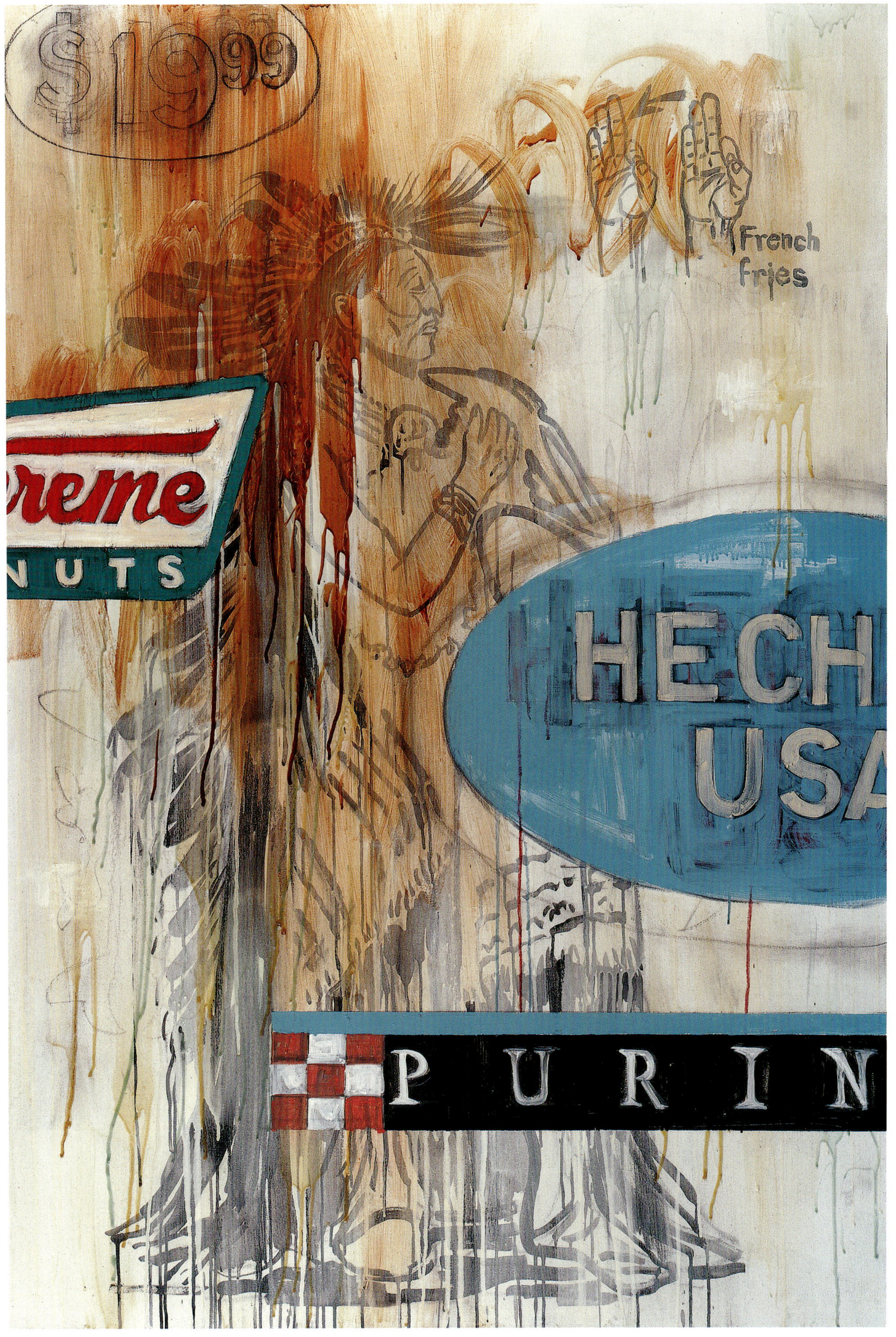
$19.99
French fries
reme
NUTS
HECH
USA
PURIN

Diego Romero, Cochiti Pueblo, born 1964

Pod Mound, 2010

Ceramic, Native clay and Native slip, kiln fired
Purchased through the Kira Fournier and Benjamin Schore Contemporary Sculpture Fund and the Hood Museum of Art Acquisition Fund; 2010.54

FROM THE ARTIST:

Through dance and art . . . is my connection to my Indian self, something I'm constantly reexamining and redefining. I think it's a situation that constantly needs to be reexamined, redefined. At what point do I consider myself an Indian? At what point do I consider myself this kid that grew up in a comic book store in Berkeley . . .

I do think humor is medicine. When we look at art and laugh or chuckle, in a sense, we heal. It's part of a healing process: being able to laugh at oneself or the absurdity of a situation is a way of healing. That's where the healing begins.

I'm trying to break down those stereotypes of the Noble Savage . . . that have been ingrained in us as a society since childhood, which, I have to say, was my experience growing up in a non-Native community in Berkeley.

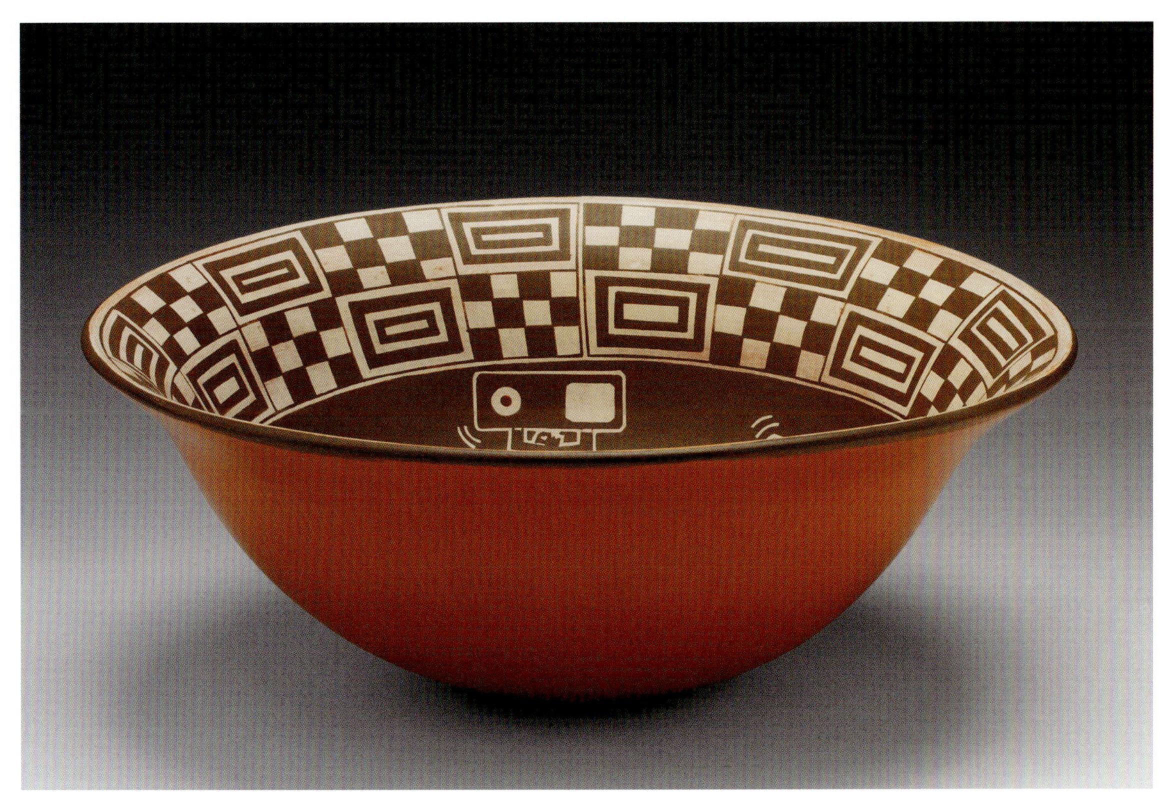

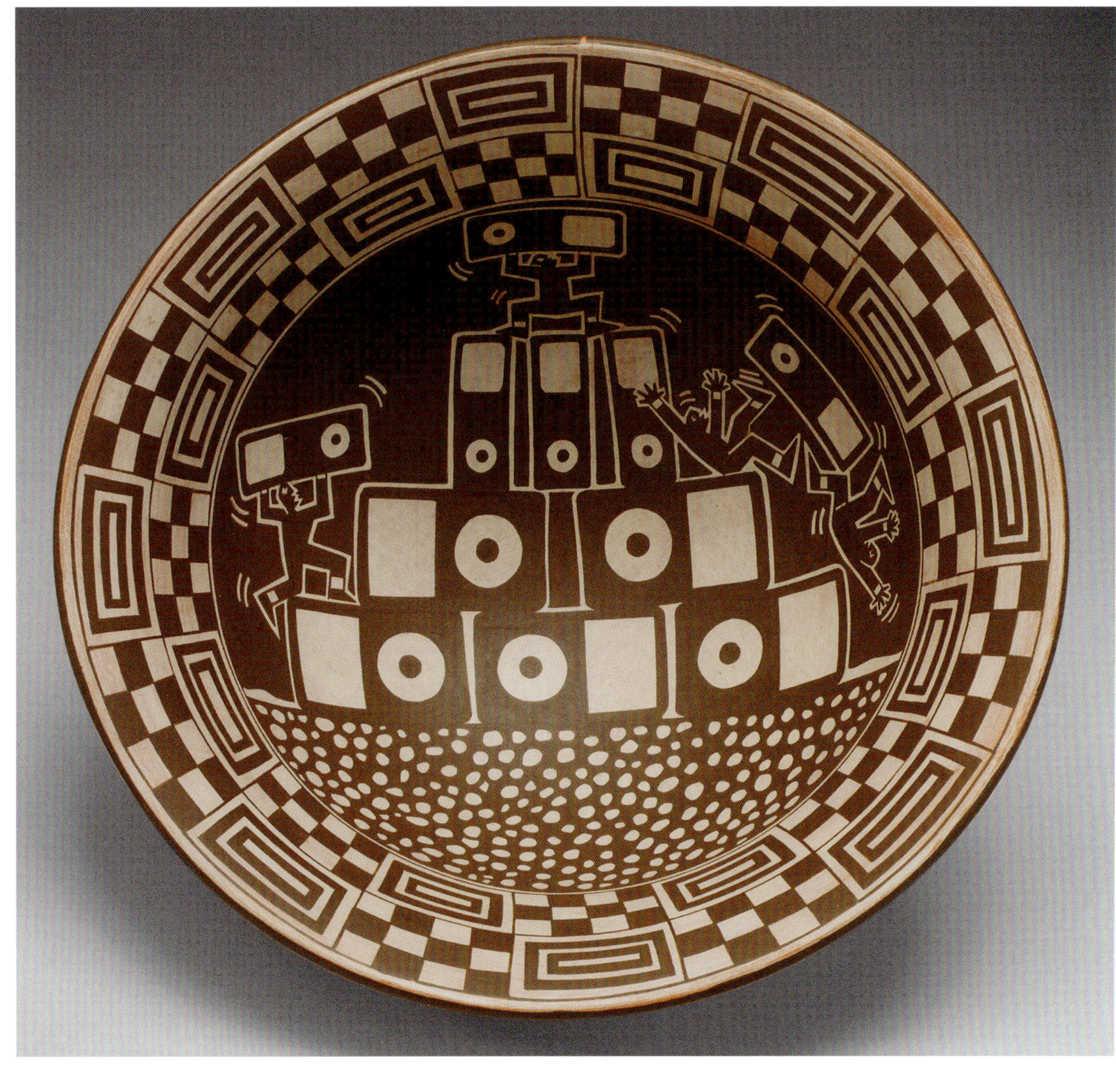

Mateo Romero, Cochiti Pueblo, born 1966

The Dartmouth Pow-Wow Suite, 2009

1. "Celestial #2" (Shannon Prince); 2. "Celestial #1" (Taiyin Snowflower); 3. "Fire" (Eliza Doreen Yellow Bird); 4. "Air" (Jiles Pourier); 5. "Bloom" (Kayla Gebeck); 6. "Big Green" (Lindsay Borrows); 7. "Louise Erdrich"; 8. "Day" (Hannah Watah); 9. "Aza Erdrich Dorris"; 10. "Night" (Daryl Concha)

Photo transfer and acrylic paint on panel
Purchased through the Mrs. Harvey P. Hood W'18 Fund; 2010.53.1–10

FROM THE ARTIST:

Dartmouth College has been a part of my life for as long as I can remember. Although I graduated in 1989 and have since been part of numerous academic programs, being a part of the Dartmouth family has been a tangible and real aspect of my life as a mature artist. As my first art dealer in Santa Fe, David Rettig, Class of 1975, once commented, we are part of the Dartmouth Tribe now.

As an undergraduate, two iconic artist/teachers stood out in my mind. The first was Varujan Boghosian. Varujan showed me by his example how an artist carried himself in the world as he wrestled with his act of creation. Witty, humorous, generous, he encompassed the essence for me of the lyrical, aesthetic side of the art paradigm.

Of equal importance was Ben Frank Moss. Ben showed me in his own work how to build paintings—line, color, edge, texture, movement, temperature of color, local color, abstraction. This is the formal vocabulary of the easel painter. Ben showed me what it took to become a painter, both in the exuberance of his work and in the austerity of his life as a devoted artist.

The *Dartmouth Pow-Wow Suite* has given me the opportunity to come full circle in my artistic life as an active participant in the vibrancy of the Dartmouth community. It is with tremendous joy and energy that we created these portraits of current Dartmouth students and alumni.

We began by photographing the Dartmouth Pow-Wow in 2009. Photographic images are selected, enlarged, transferred to panel, and painted on with acrylic. Tar glaze is applied at the end for surface luminosity and atmosphere. The end result is a collision between photographic portraiture and abstract expressionist paint handling. There is a palpable tension between figure and ground, literal and abstract, portraiture and the nostalgic quality of action painting.

In many Native communities the dance holds a powerful, central place in the structure of the worldview. Dances are, at different times, social, amorous, honoring, ceremonial, spiritual. In the Tewa Pueblos in northern New Mexico, dancers entering the houses of their relatives say, "We Dance for Life." It is in this spirit that I offer these paintings to the audience. My hope is that the works transcend the limits of ethnic culture and address the audience on a human level.

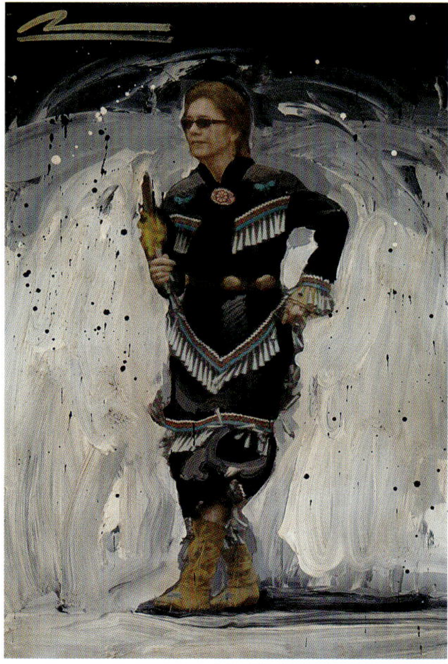

7

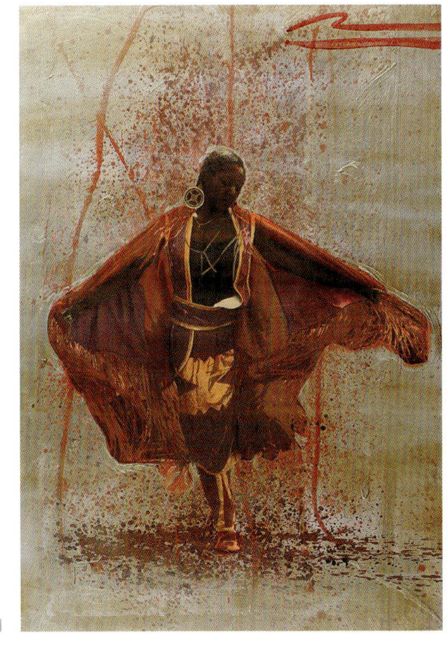
1

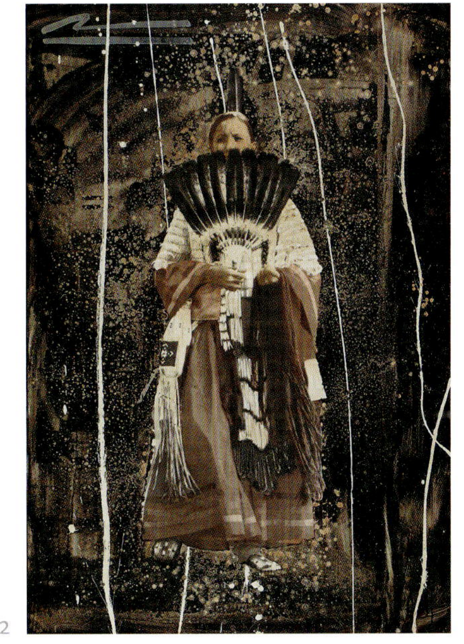
2

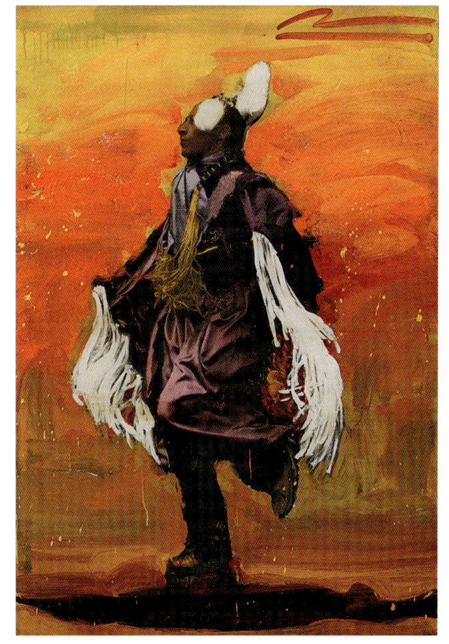
3

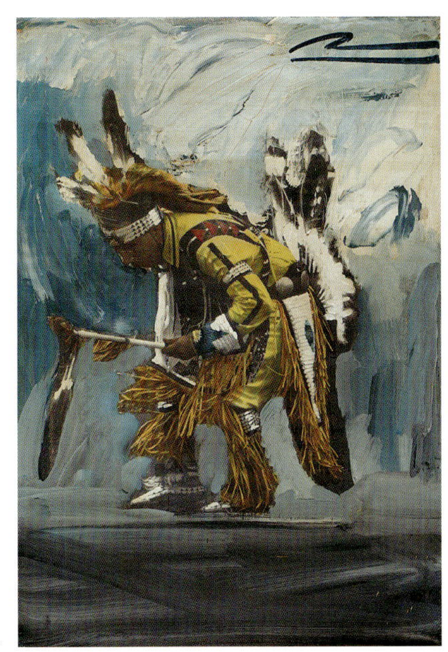
4

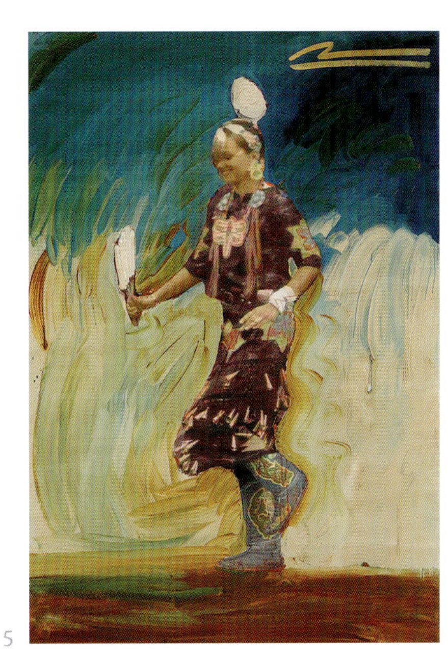
5

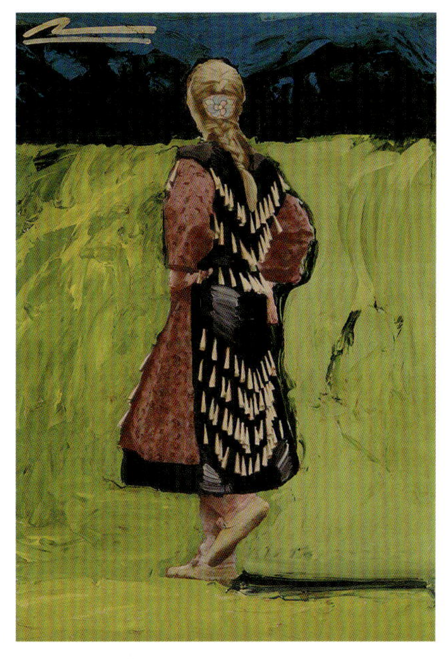
6

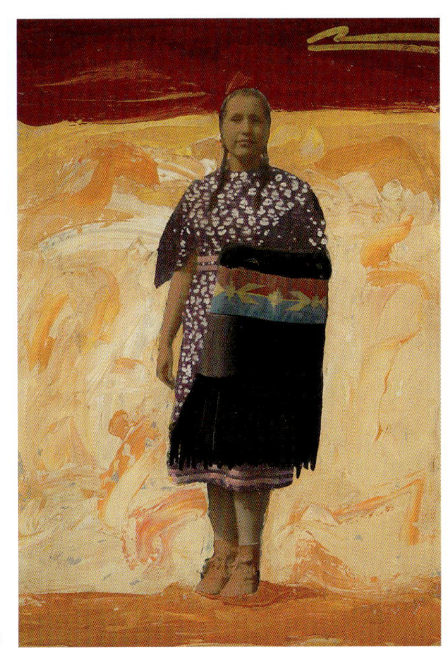
8

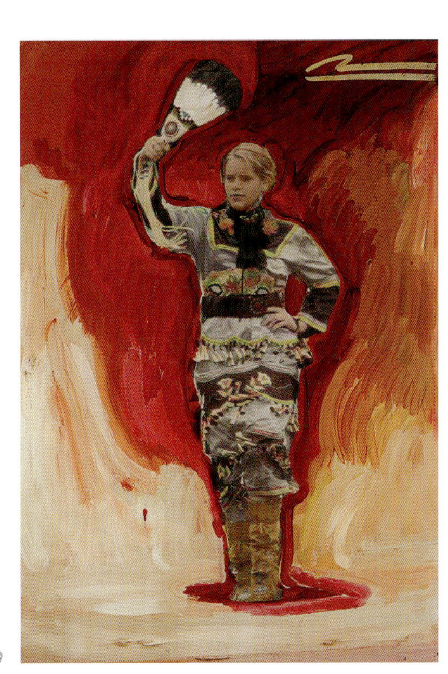
9

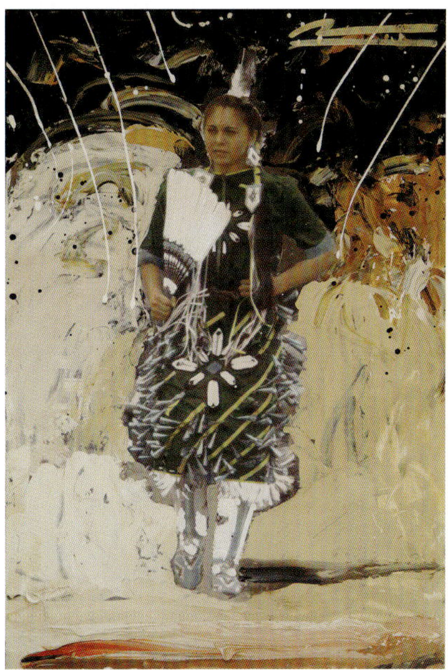
10

Preston Singletary, Tlingit, born 1963

Tlingit Crest Hat, 2006

Etched blue glass
Purchased through the Claire and Richard P. Morse 1953 Fund, the William S. Rubin Fund, the Alvin and Mary Bert Gutman '40 Acquisition Fund, and the Charles F. Venrick 1936 Fund; 2007.12

FROM THE ARTIST:

I've been working with hot glass since 1982. After learning the basics, I attended the Pilchuck glass school and learned how artists work with glass. That first year in 1984 I met two Native artists, Larry Ahvakahna and Tony Jojola. They encouraged me to look to my cultural roots for inspiration.

A couple of years later, I was ready to try it. In 1988 at Pilchuck I met David Svenson, who had lived up in Haines, Alaska, and learned the tradition of carving and Tlingit culture. He too encouraged me on my path. I dabbled with it while trying to develop a career in music, but it wasn't until 1995 when I decided to place myself on the path that I am on today. The hat forms are the first pieces I developed for design work. Learning the formline design was a tough process but over time a personal style tends to emerge.

This crest hat is a testament to the fluidity of the design style of the Tlingit. The design is distributed across the entire area and is filled methodically with the design elements of ovoids and u-forms. Designs like this would be worn by noble people within the community and denote a high status.

Today I am firmly connected to the tribal community of the Northwest coast and have worked with Native Americans from around the country. In addition, I have worked with the Maori of New Zealand and Native Hawaiians. I advocate the material because I feel that there is much to discover with glass and its translucency and shadow effect. Given that some of the materials that are traditionally used for Indigenous art are becoming scarce, I think that new materials will be adapted to tell the stories of the people.

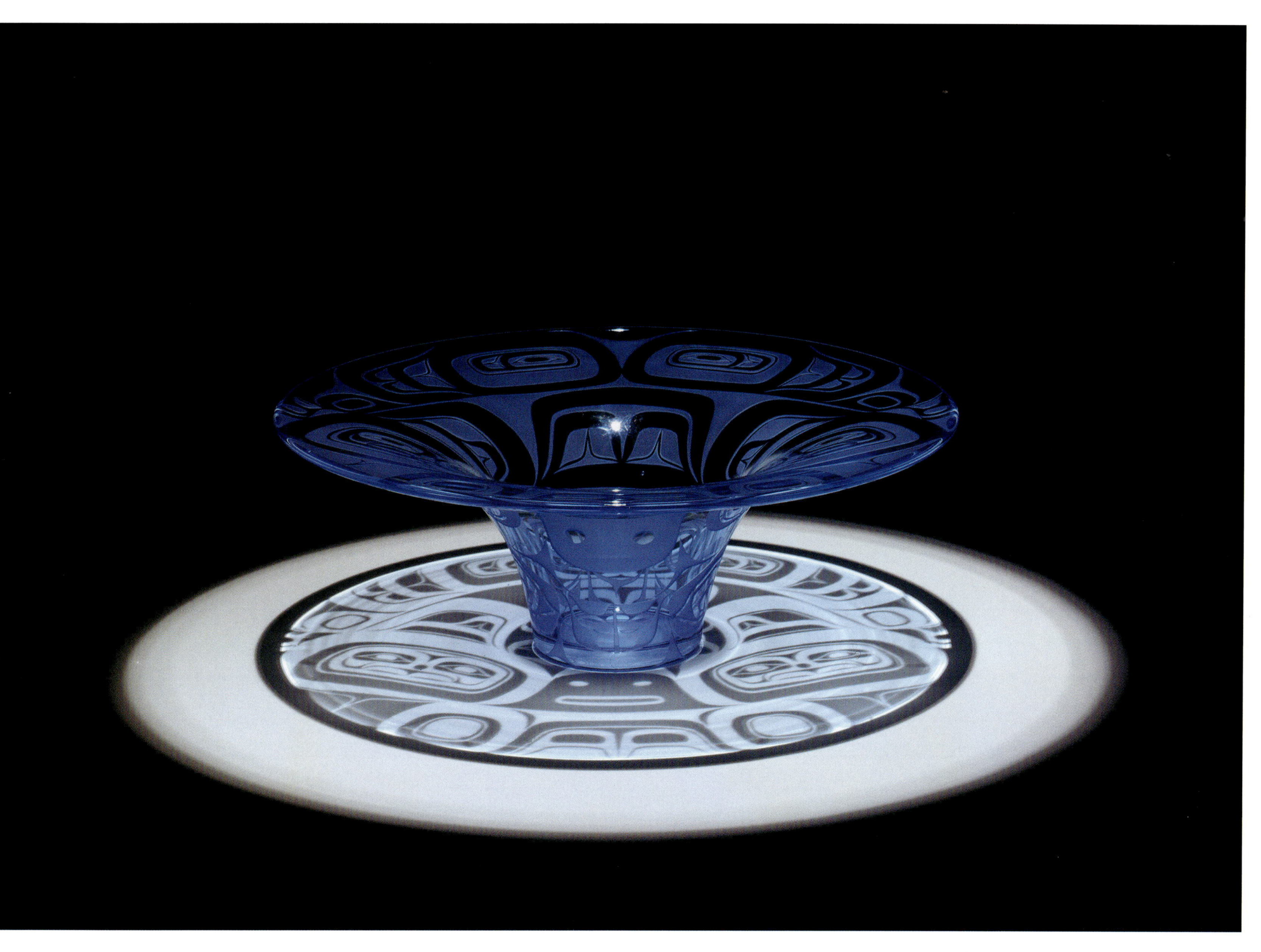

Sierra Teller Ornelas, Diné (Navajo), born 1981

Forbidden Love, two-weaving set, 2009

Wool, vegetable dye
Purchased through the Alvin and Mary Bert Gutman '40
Acquisition Fund; 2009.54

FROM THE ARTIST:

I call it *Forbidden Love* [because] it was inspired by my then boyfriend . . . I was feeling pretty whimsical and high school about our relationship and wanted to make something that was like the doodles you draw on your notebook when you really like someone. It's also a nod to interracial dating (he is white, I am not) and the trepidation that that brings, hence them being in those little boxes that resemble the one in the video game . . . One ghost is green and the other is purple. They are thinking about each other but they don't know that. Only you as the viewer can see what they are thinking about.

I assume most would classify it as a pictorial, but I would not. I would call it a contemporary Navajo tapestry . . . I am weaving a traditional way because I'm weaving something that's a reflection of the time I live in. In that way, it's traditional. This is my landscape, my pop culture landscape, the one I interact with every day.

The thing that I would like to impart is that I hope my work and the work of a lot of new weavers motivates the general public to see Navajo weaving as an art form. Many people have a postcard picture of who weavers are—women sitting in front of a Hogan weaving under a tree—but more often than not we're weaving in an air-conditioned house, hopped up on coffee and listening to cable TV while we weave into the night. But I hope that whether you're looking at a rug made one hundred years ago or last month, know that it was made by someone with a sense of style and artistic vision and in many cases someone with a sense of humor and a strong opinion about the world around them.

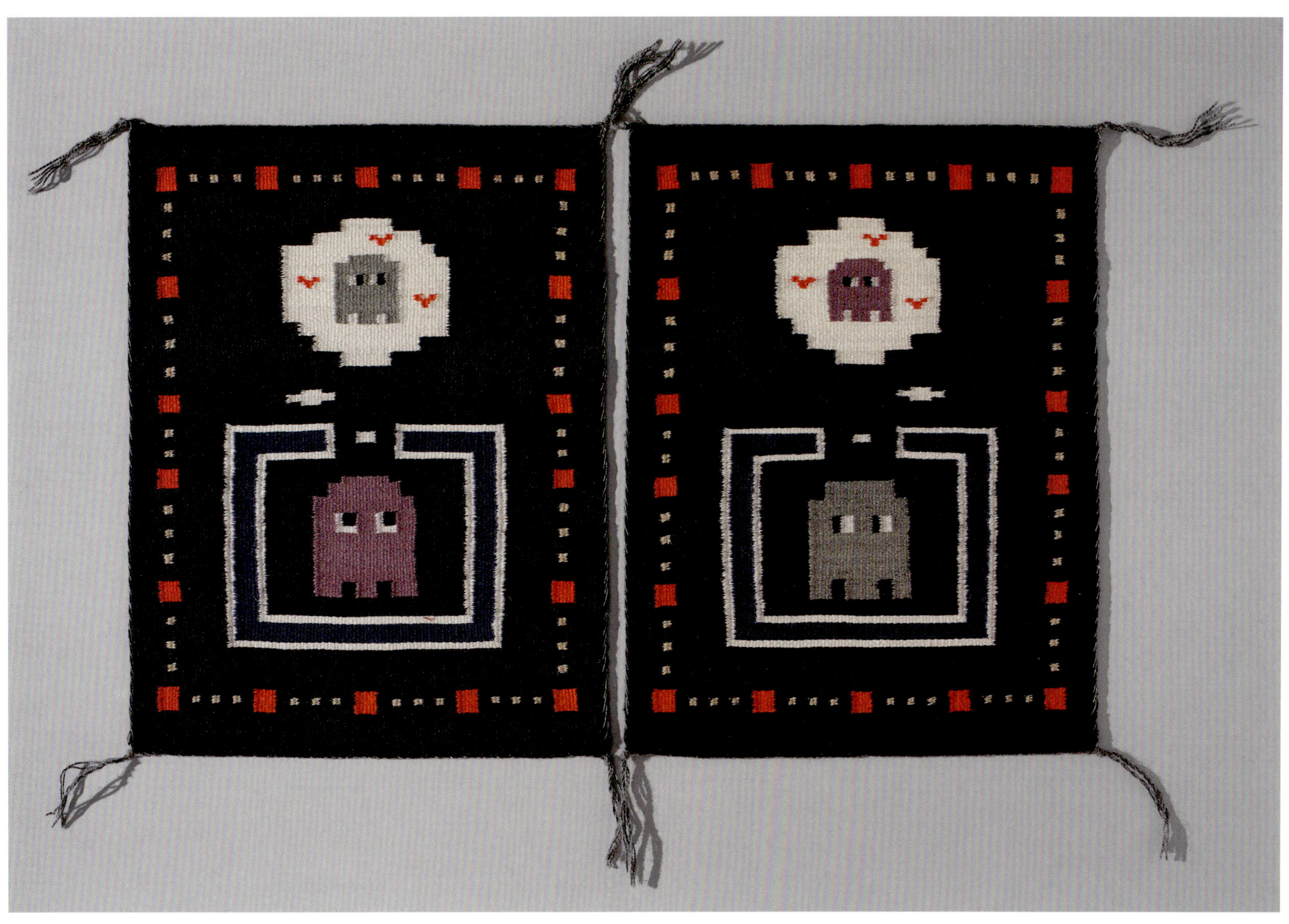

Hulleah Tsinhnahjinnie, Seminole / Diné (Navajo) / Muscogee (Creek), born 1954

Photographic Memoirs of an Aboriginal Savant (Living on Occupied Land), 1994

Fifteen prints with text and photographic and cartoon reproductions
Purchased through the Contemporary Art Fund; 2007.55

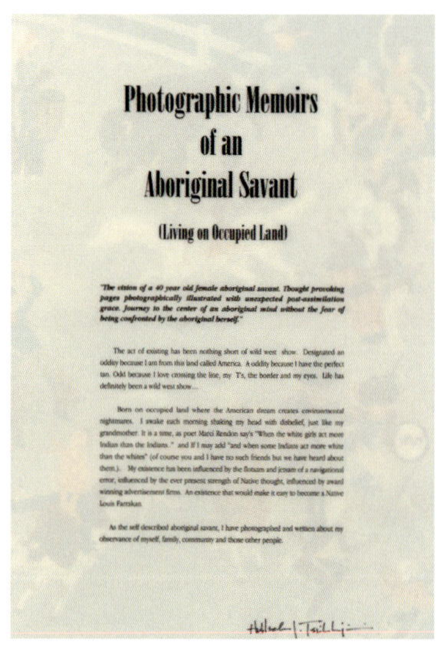

FROM THE ARTIST:

In these "memoirs" I present myself the way I see myself rather than being interpreted by others. In creating this sovereign space, I am able to regain control over this narrative, enabling the viewer to journey to the center of an aboriginal mind without the fear of being confronted by the aboriginal herself.

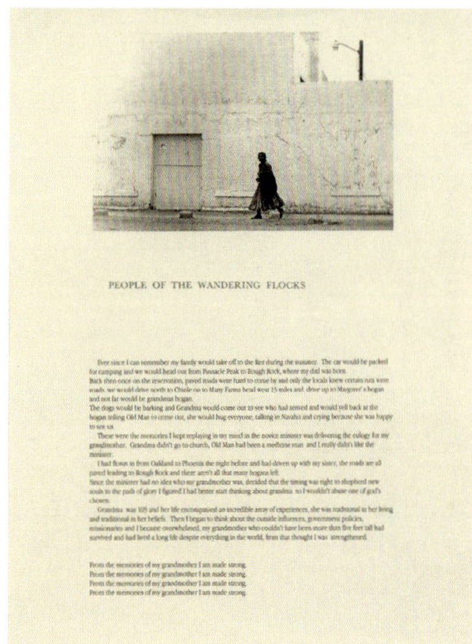

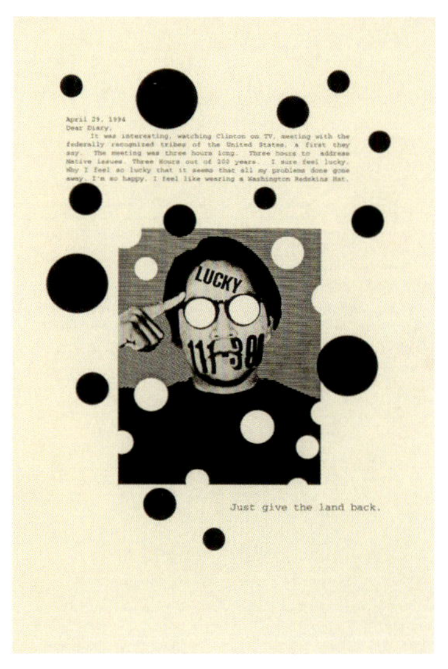

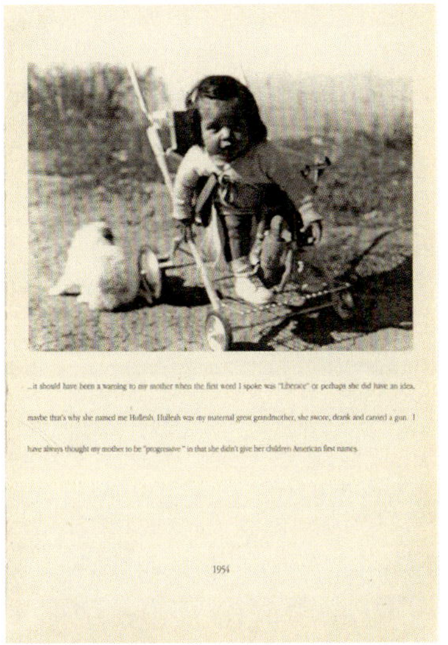

...it should have been a warning to my mother when the first word I spoke was "Electric" (or perhaps she did have an idea, maybe that's why she named me Hulleah). Hulleah was my maternal great grandmother, she swore, drank and carried a gun. I have always thought my mother to be "progressive" so that she didn't give her children American first names.

1954

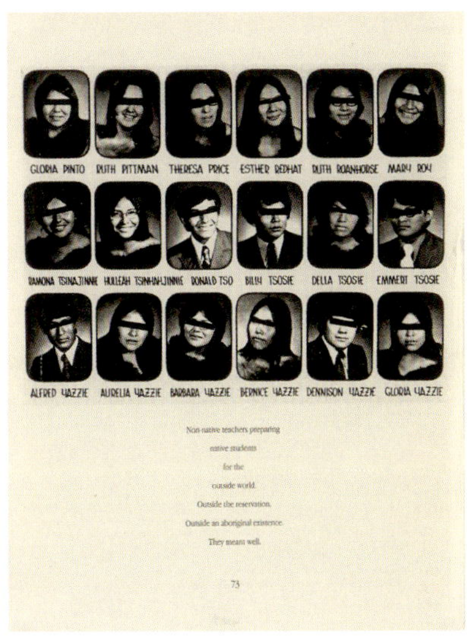

Non-native teachers preparing
native students
for the
outside world.
Outside the reservation.
Outside an aboriginal existence.
They meant well.

73

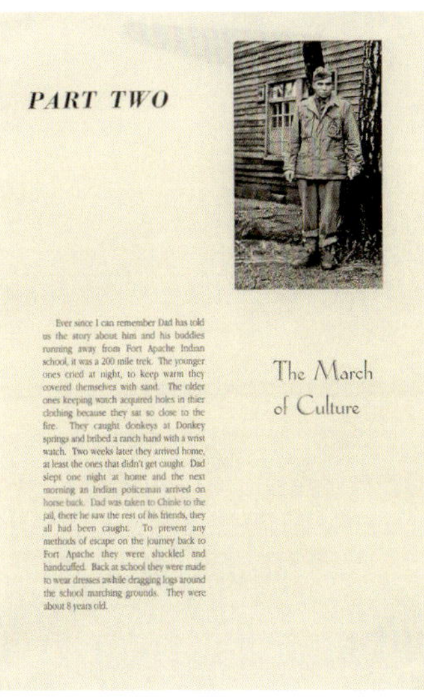

PART TWO

The March of Culture

Ever since I can remember Dad has told us the story about him and his buddies running away from Fort Apache Indian school, it was a 200 mile trek. The younger ones cried at night, to keep warm they covered themselves with sand. The older ones keeping watch acquired holes in thier clothing because they sat so close to the fire. They caught donkeys at Donkey springs and bribed a ranch hand with a wrist watch. Two weeks later they arrived home, at least the ones that didn't get caught. Dad slept one night at home and the next morning an Indian policeman arrived on horse back. Dad was taken to Chinle to the jail, there he saw the rest of his friends, they all had been caught. To prevent any methods of escape on the journey back to Fort Apache they were shackled and handcuffed. Back at school they were made to wear dresses awhile dragging logs around the school marching grounds. They were about 8 years old.

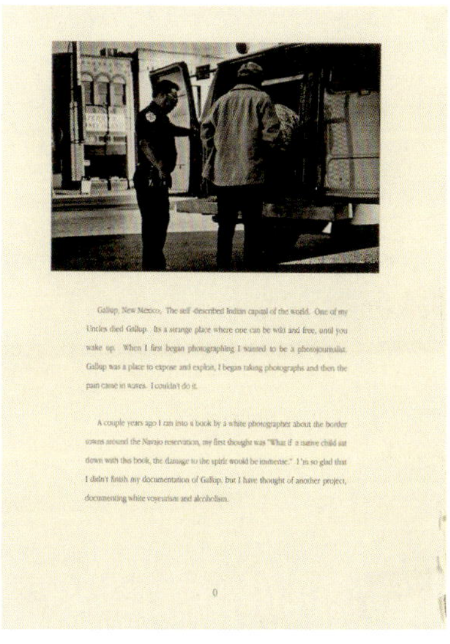

Gallup, New Mexico. The self described Indian capital of the world. One of my Uncles died Gallup. Its a strange place where one can be wild and free, until you wake up. When I first began photographing I wanted to be a photojournalist. Gallup was a place to expose and exploit, I began taking photographs and then the pain came to surface. I couldn't do it.

A couple years ago I ran into a book by a white photographer about the border towns around the Navajo reservation, my first thought was "What if a native child sat down with this book, the damage to the spirit would be immense." I'm so glad that I didn't finish my documentation of Gallup, but I have thought of another project, documenting white veneration and alcoholism.

0

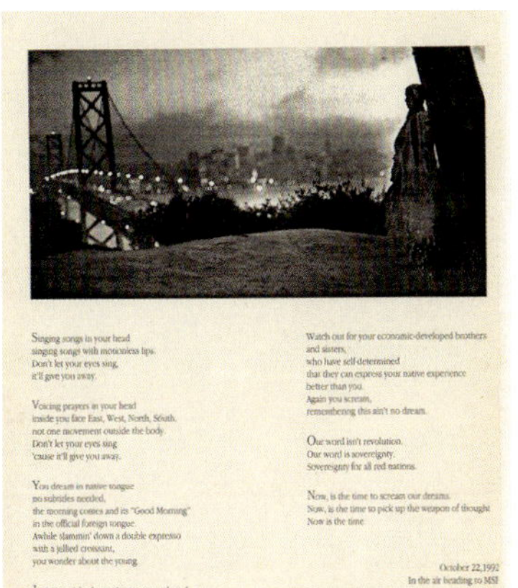

October 22,1992
In the air heading to NYC

4

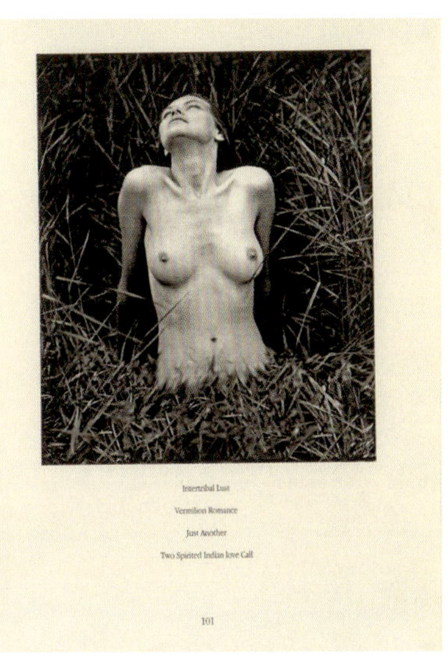

Interracial Lust
Vermilion Romance
Just Another
Two Spirited Indian love Call

101

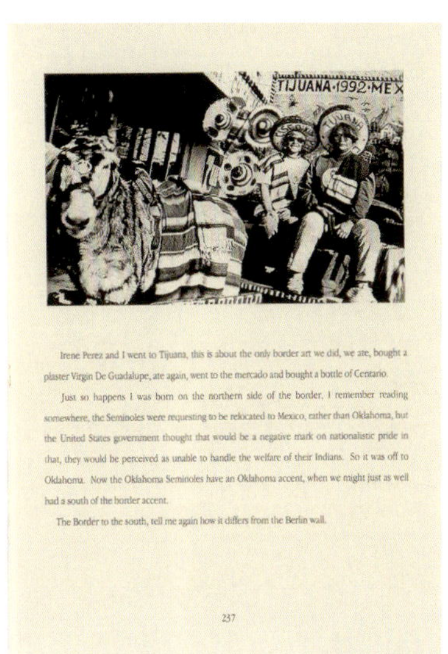

Irene Perez and I went to Tijuana, this is about the only border art we did, we ate, bought a plaster Virgin De Guadalupe, ate again, went to the mercado and bought a bottle of Centario.

Just so happens I was born on the northern side of the border. I remember reading somewhere, the Seminoles were requesting to be relocated to Mexico, either than Oklahoma, but the United States government thought that would be a negative mark on nationalistic pride in that, they would be perceived as unable to handle the welfare of their Indians. So it was off to Oklahoma. Now the Oklahoma Seminoles have an Oklahoma accent, when we might just as well had a south of the border accent.

The Border to the south, tell me again how it differs from the Berlin wall.

237

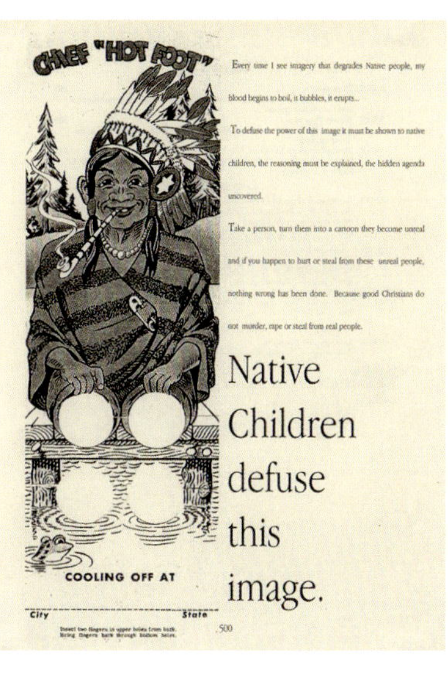

Every time I see imagery that degrades Native people, my blood begins to boil, it bubbles, it erupts...

To defuse the power of this image it must be shown to native children, the reasoning must be explained, the hidden agenda uncovered.

Take a person, turn them into a cartoon they become unreal and if you happen to hurt or steal from these unreal people, nothing wrong has been done. Because good Christians do not murder, rape or steal from real people.

Native Children defuse this image.

500

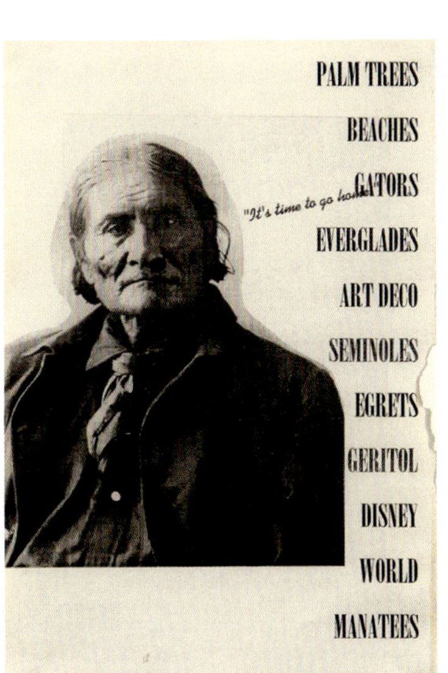

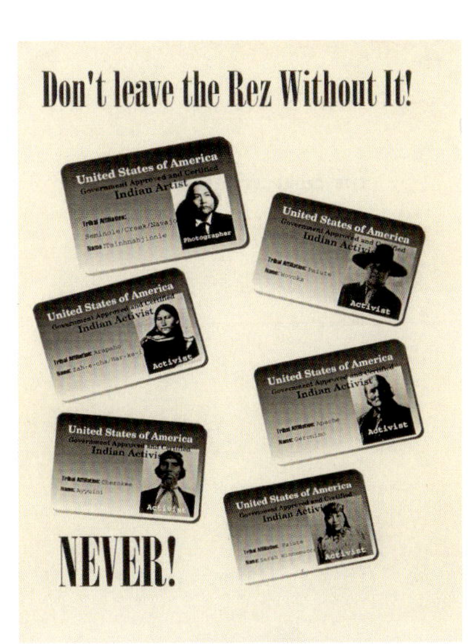

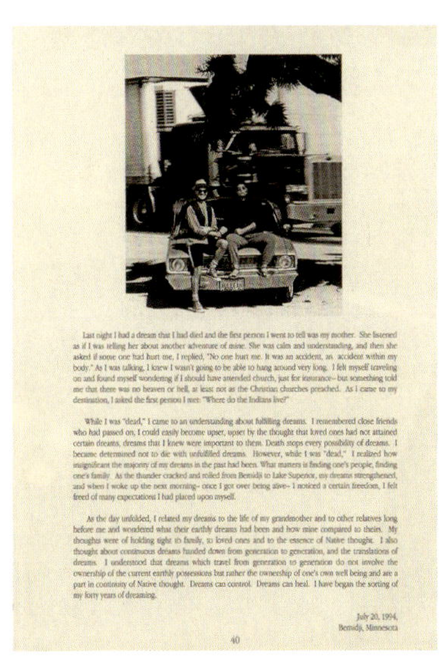

Last night I had a dream that I had died and the first person I went to tell was my mother. She listened as if I was telling her about another adventure of mine. She was calm and understanding, and then she asked if some one had hurt me, I replied, "No one hurt me. It was an accident, an accident within my body." As I was talking, I knew I wasn't going to be able to hang around very long. I felt myself traveling on and found myself wondering if I should have attended church, just for insurance-- but something told me that there was no heaven or hell, at least not as the Christian churches preached. As I came to my destination, I asked the first person I met: "Where do the Indians live?"

While I was "dead," I came to an understanding about fulfilling dreams. I remembered close friends who had passed on, I could easily become upset, upset by the thought that loved ones had not attained certain dreams, dreams that I knew were important to them. Death stops every possibility of dreams. I became determined not to die with unfulfilled dreams. However, while I was "dead," I realized how insignificant the majority of my dreams in the past had been. What matters is finding one's people, finding one's family. As the thunder cracked and rolled from Bemidji to Lake Superior, my dreams strengthened, and when I woke up the next morning-- once I got over being alive-- I noticed a certain freedom, I felt freed of many expectations I had placed upon myself.

As the day unfolded, I related my dreams to the life of my grandmother and to other relatives long before me and wondered what their earthly dreams had been and how mine compared to theirs. My thoughts were of holding tight to family, to loved ones and to the essence of Native thought. I also thought about continuous dreams handed down from generation to generation, and the translations of dreams. I understood that dreams which travel from generation to generation do not involve the ownership of the current earthly possessions but rather the ownership of one's own well being and are a part in continuity of Native thought. Dreams can control. Dreams can heal. I have began the sorting of my forty years of dreaming.

July 20, 1994,
Bemidji, Minnesota

40

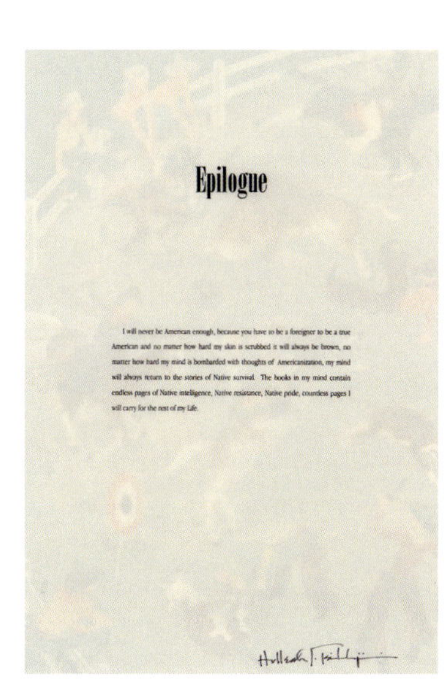

Epilogue

I will never be American enough, because you have to be a foreigner to be a true American and no matter how hard my skin is scrubbed it will always be brown, no matter how hard my mind is bombarded with thoughts of Americanization, my mind will always return to the stories of Native survival. The books in my mind contain endless pages of Native intelligence, Native resistance, Native pride, countless pages I will carry for the rest of my Life.

Dwayne Wilcox, Oglala Lakota, born 1957

Best Two Outa Three, 2008

Crayon, graphite, colored pencil, and felt-tipped pen on ledger paper
Purchased through the Guernsey Center Moore 1904 Fund; 2008.59.7

FROM THE ARTIST:

Best Two Outa Three is from a series of pictures that I'm not sure I'm done with, 'cause I think there's plenty of room for more . . . If we had a do-over, what kind of game could we play so we could have an equal shot at the deal. If our leaders and their leaders had an equal shot, level the playing field . . . without anyone getting hurt other than just being a sore loser at a game.

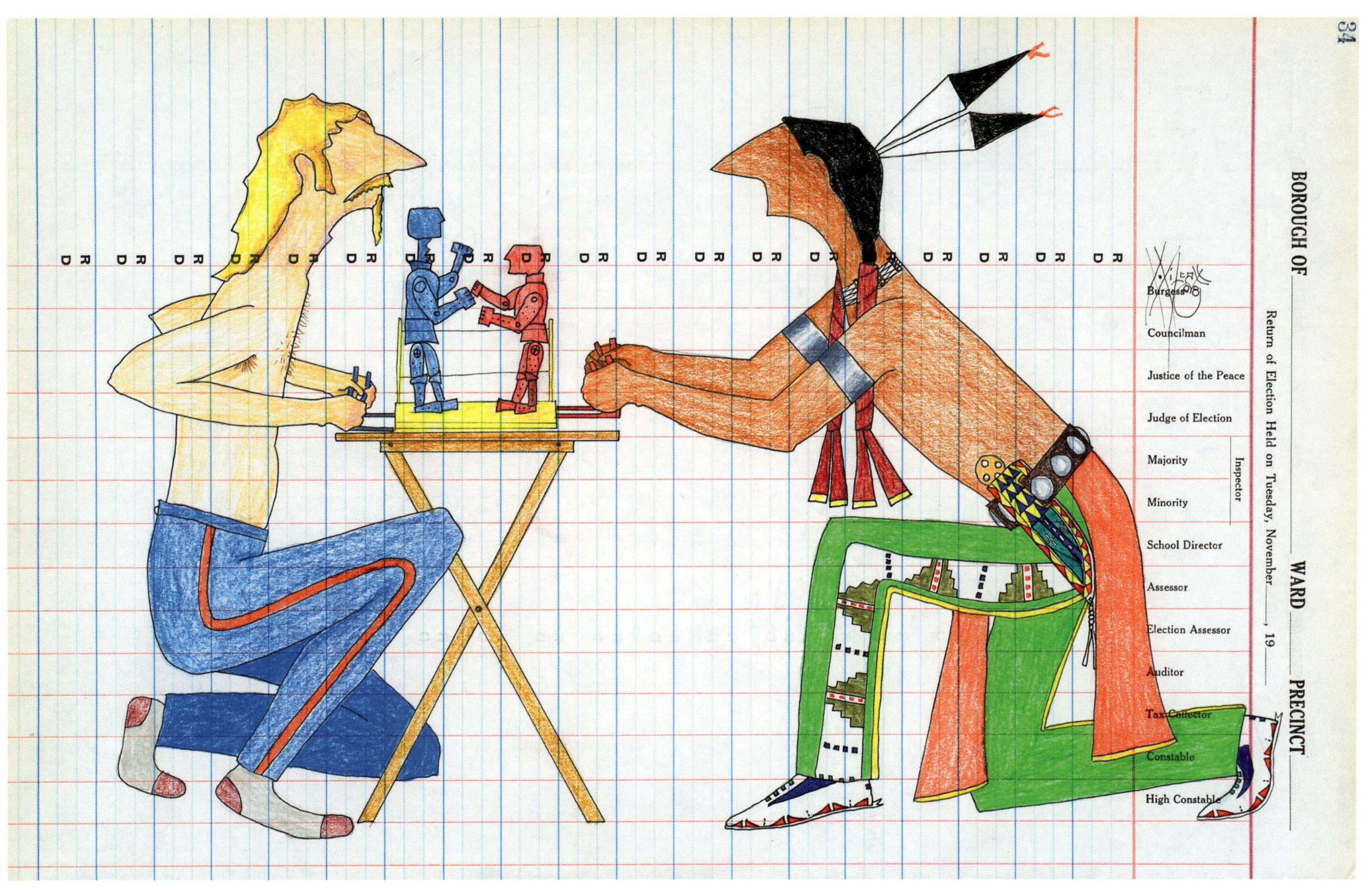
34
BOROUGH OF
WARD
PRECINCT
Return of Election Held on Tuesday, November , 19
Burgess
Councilman
Justice of the Peace
Judge of Election
Majority
Minority
Inspector
School Director
Assessor
Election Assessor
Auditor
Tax Collector
Constable
High Constable

Catalogue

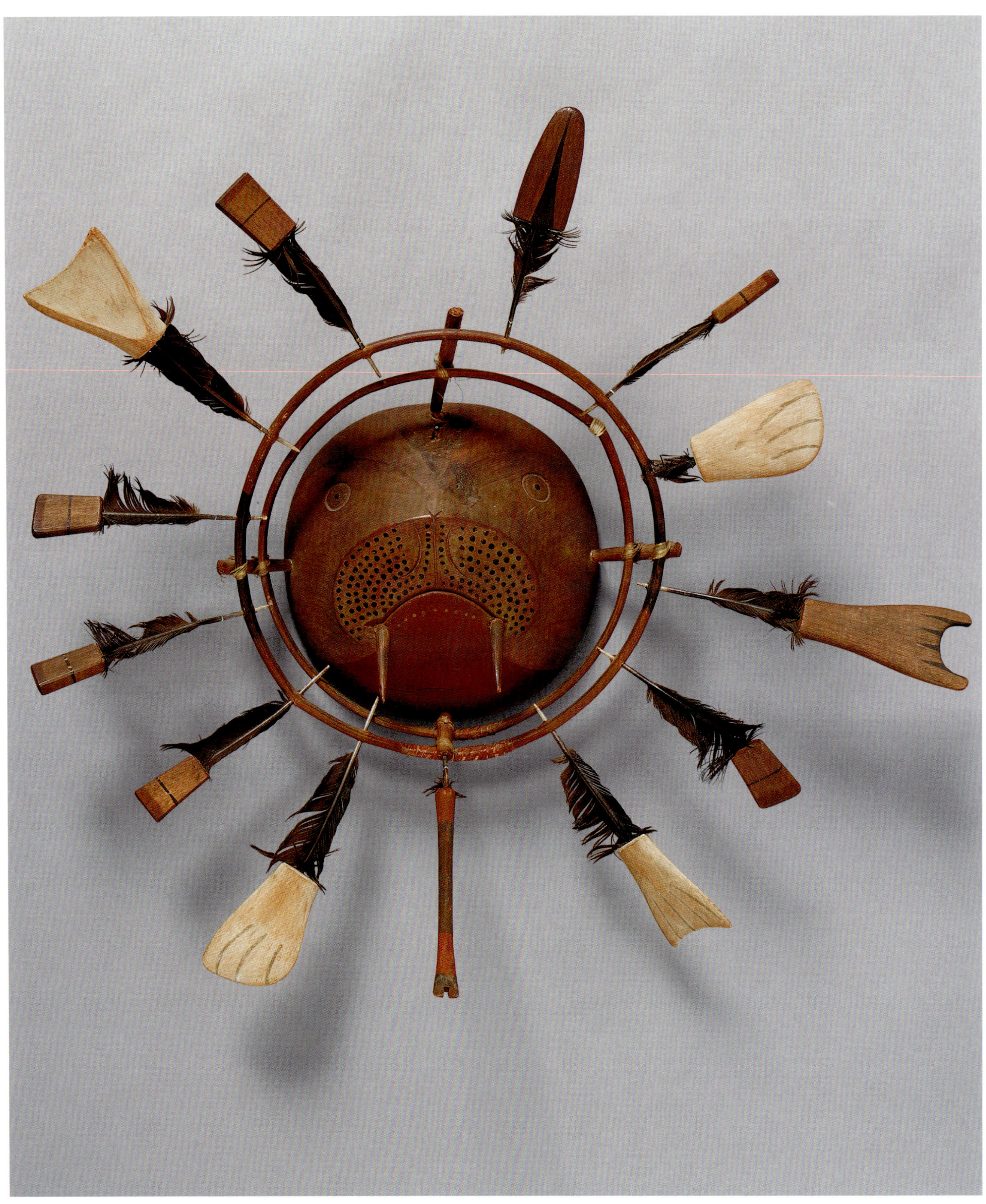

CAT. 4. Artist unknown, Central Yup'ik, Nunivak Island, Alaska, mask, about 1930, wood, paint, feathers, sinew, string, and nails. Gift of the Estate of Corey Ford, Class of 1921H; 169.75.24910.

:: 6.1 ::

Arctic and Subarctic: Innovation and Ingenuity

Heather Igloliorte

The Hood Museum of Art's collections from the Arctic and Subarctic, spanning well over a century of artistic production, reveal a fascinating history of innovation and resourcefulness among the coastal and interior Native peoples. Comprised primarily of objects made for personal use and trade from the mid-nineteenth to the late twentieth centuries, these collections evidence both the ingenious use of natural materials available throughout the Arctic and Subarctic territories and the enterprising incorporation of *new* European media and technologies as contact with outsiders increased over many decades of intercultural encounter. Important exchanges and communications between European and Aboriginal cultures as early as the turn of the nineteenth century are also highlighted in the Hood's collections, as are the significant continuities between early contact works and artistic traditions still practiced throughout the Arctic and Subarctic regions today.

For all of the cultural groups featured in these collections—from the western Arctic in Alaska and the Canadian Northwest Territories and Nunavut to Greenland, and throughout the western and central Subarctic as well—life changed with the influx of new technologies and resources that contact with European, Russian, Canadian, and American traders, whalers, and explorers brought about. Some of the earliest trading of artistic productions was instigated by commercial whaling, sealing, and walrus hunting vessels along the circumpolar coastline; in the Western Arctic collection, for example, the small Inupiaq (Alaskan Inupiat Eskimo) scrimshaw, c. 1900 (cat. 11), was created using a technique believed to have been introduced by Russian traders coming from Siberia as early as the seventeenth century. Scrimshaw is the practice of engraving ivory or bone surfaces with a pointed metal object and filling those lines with ink or other forms of black pigment. This technique has been practiced in western Alaska for over fifteen hundred years, beginning with simple geometric and dot-pattern formations and leading up to the complex scenes of daily life that were popular at the turn of the twentieth century. Realistic depictions of landscapes or hunting and whaling scenes on ivory or bone may be centuries old, but this early-twentieth-century piece is a particularly intriguing example of the detail and accuracy that are possible even on such small scale.

Alaskan Native artists in the late nineteenth and early twentieth centuries also applied their skills in scrimshaw and carving to the creation of other souvenir goods, such as pipes, matchstick holders, and cribbage boards. The Hood's western Arctic collection features two such objects made specifically for trade: a pipe bowl, c. 1920 (cat. 10), of walrus ivory with fine relief sculpture encircling its base, and an exquisitely carved cribbage board, c. 1920 (cat. 8), also made of ivory. The cribbage board ranks among the most intricately carved and detailed boards in any Canadian or American museum collection—its intertwined sea mammals are skillfully overlapped within the shape of the original tusk, and the faces of

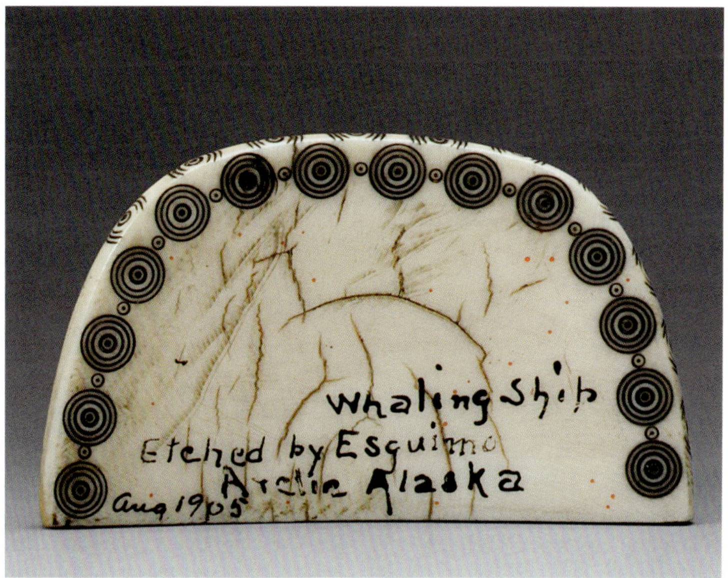

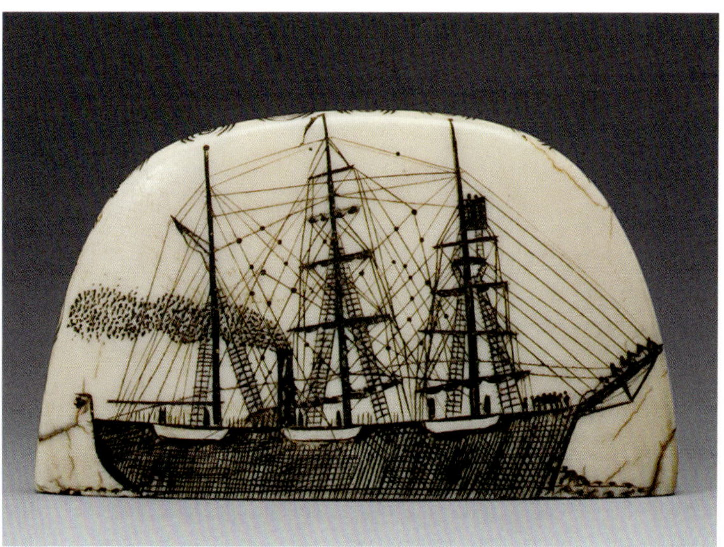

CAT. 11. Artist unknown, Inupiat, scrimshaw, about 1900, bone, graphite. Bequest of Frank C. and Clara G. Churchill; 46.17.14737.

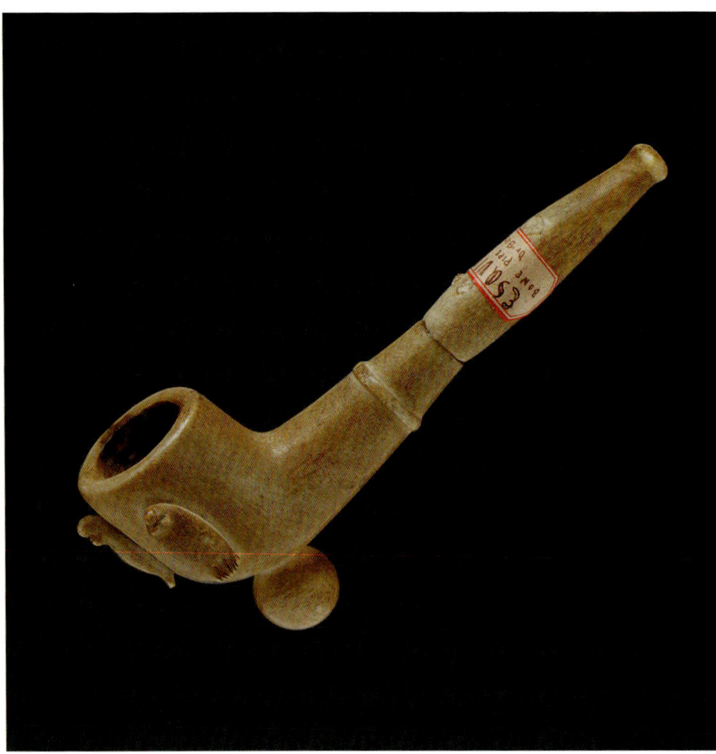

CAT. 10. Artist unknown, Inupiat, pipe bowl, about 1920, walrus ivory. Gift of Glover Street Hastings III; 181.2.26112.

the seals and walruses flanking the small cribbage board in the center are delicately engraved and tinted black. Frequently, these cribbage boards contained hidden compartments or sliding doors for storing custom-made wood or ivory pegs, a feature that would have surely appealed to the whalers and traders for whom the games were intended.

Hudson Bay Company post managers and trappers from the interior who moved west from Hudson's Bay through Chipewyan territory in the early eighteenth century to establish contact with Aboriginal populations living along the Mackenzie River (and later in the northwestern interior) were another source of cultural contact that impacted artistic production. In exchange for furs and pelts, the Aboriginal people received axes, knives, files, guns and ammunition, needles, thread, man-made dyes and glass beads, commercial embroidery fabrics, wool cloth, and warm duffel. While the skill sets required to hunt, trap, and sew remained unchanged, the range of available tools shifted radically, and some of these new implements and materials had a profound impact on the production of items for trade, use, and personal adornment. In the early contact period, Northern Athapaskan clothing, particularly "dress" clothing, was adorned with delicate, naturally dyed porcupine quillwork that was fringed with hide and elaborated with dentalium shells, silver-willow seeds, or other natural accoutrements. Because of the preexisting emphasis on personal adornment, Aboriginal women welcomed the new tools and began to supplement indigenous materials with brightly colored accessories and dyes acquired through trade. For example, compared to the painstaking process of extracting sinew for sewing, the sheer convenience of simple items such as metal needles and thread, provided in an array of bright colors at relatively little expense, propelled the intricate silk thread embroidery and beadwork traditions that continue to flourish in these regions today. A stunning example of this art is the Hood's gun case, c. 1920 (cat. 18), from the western Subarctic collection, which features many of the techniques of ornamentation favored by the Slavey Dene (Athapaskan) peoples in their formal attire: Native-tanned, contrasting smoked and unsmoked caribou hide with hide fringe, embellished with embroidered wool detailing and complex glass beading in a floral design.

Of course, in many instances, newly introduced European imports were no match for Aboriginal technologies. For example,

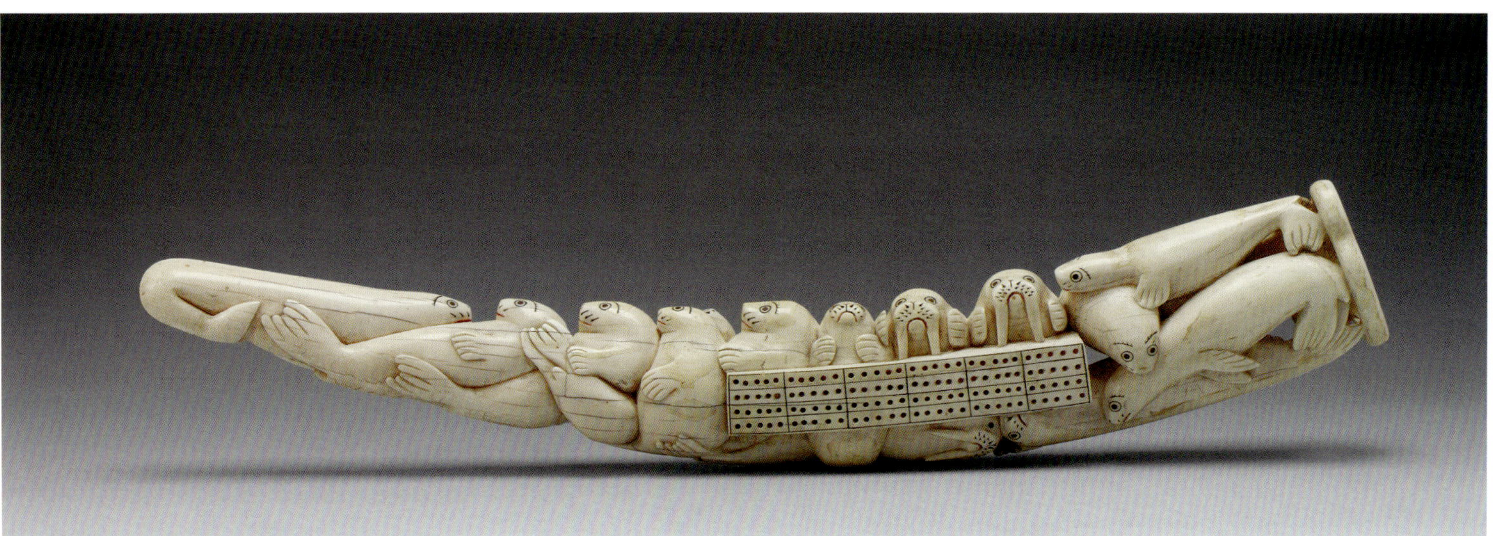

CAT. 8. Artist unknown, Inupiat, cribbage board, about 1920, ivory, wood, graphite, and pigment. Gift of the Estate of Corey Ford, Class of 1921H; 169.75.24892.

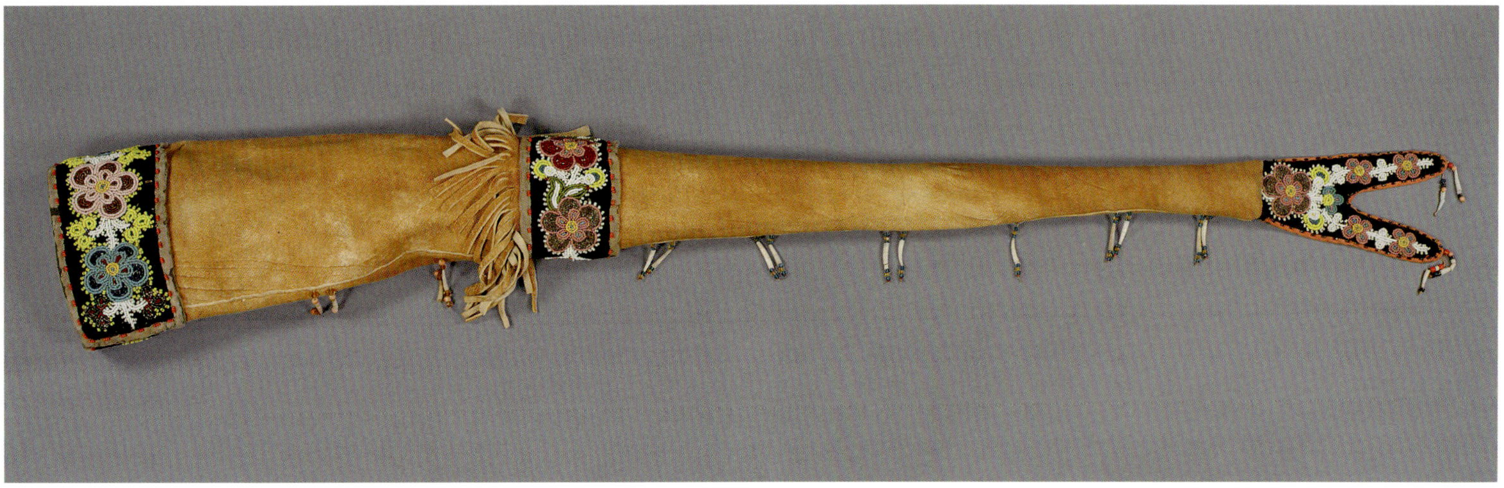

CAT. 18. Artist unknown, Northern Athapaskan (Slavey Dene), Northwest Territories, gun case, about 1920, Native-tanned smoked and unsmoked caribou hide, cotton, wool cloth, glass beads, dentalium shells, thread, and ribbon. Gift of Guido R. Rahr Sr., Class of 1951P; 985.47.26571.

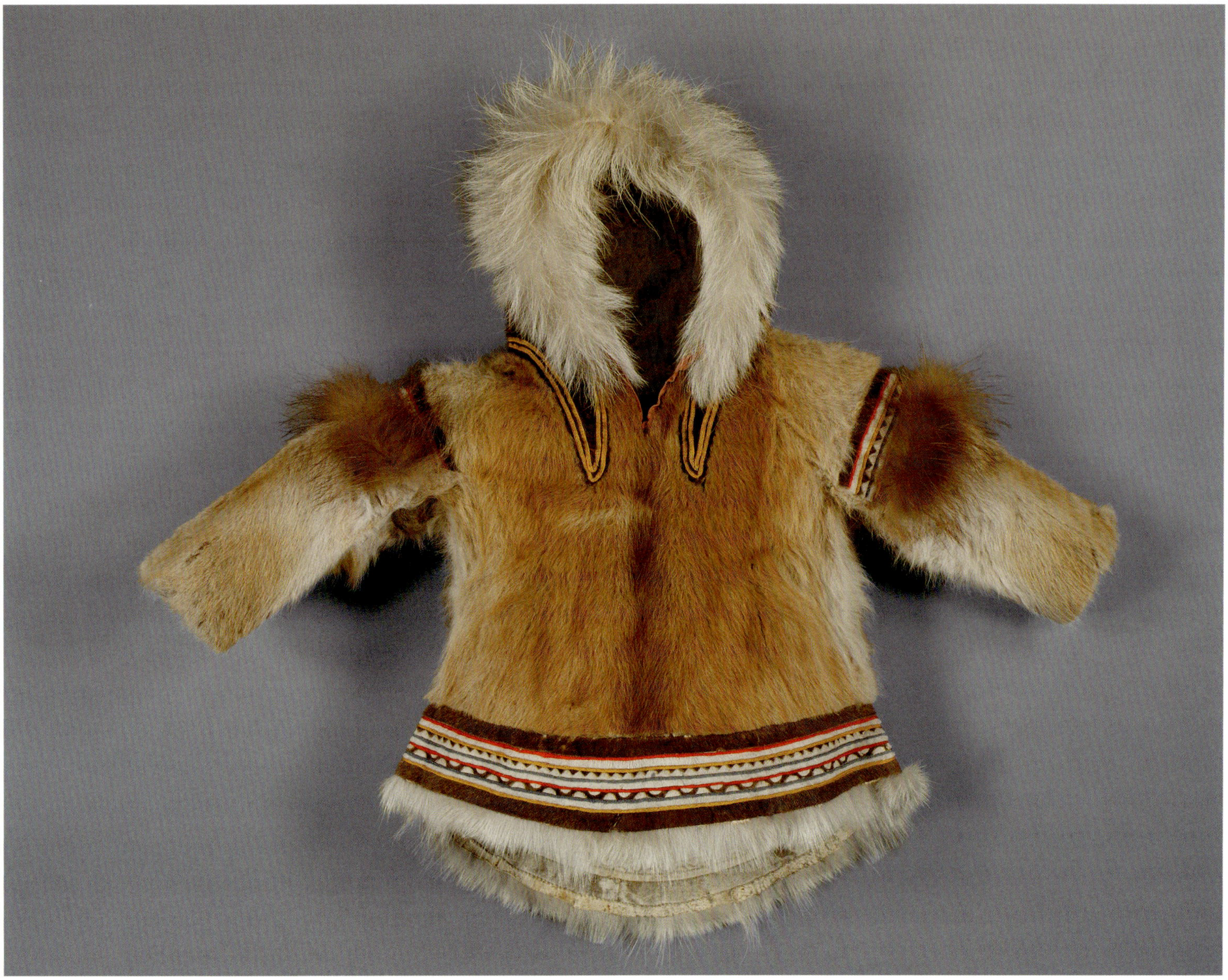

CAT. 1. Artist unknown, Inuit, Northwest Territories, MacKenzie region, boy's parka, about 1920, caribou hide, seal fur, wolf fur, rabbit fur, cotton, cotton trim, sinew, and thread. Gift of Mrs. A. Lincoln Washburn, Class of 1935W; 174.2.25532.

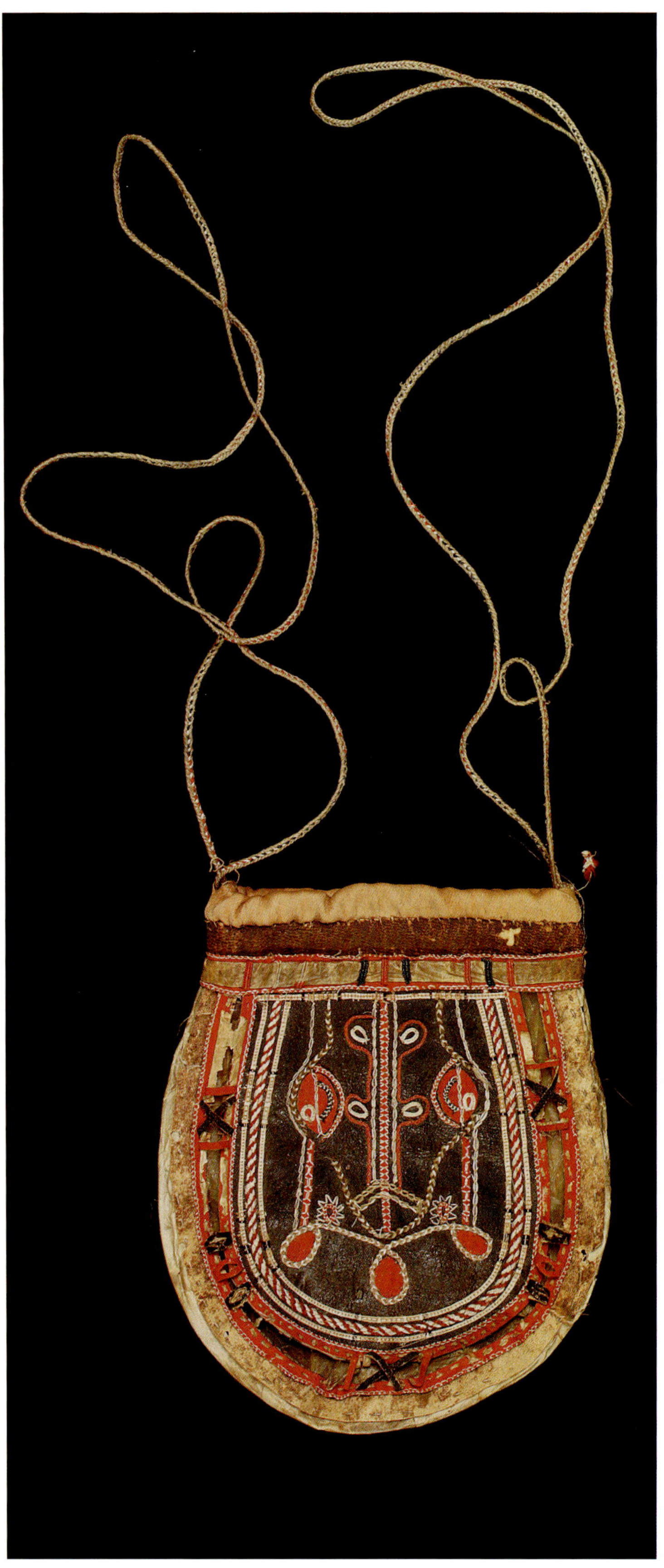

CAT. 2. Artist unknown, Alutiiq (Koniag), Kodiak Island, Alaska, tobacco bag, about 1850, hide, seal intestines, cotton cloth, sinew, wild rye grass, wool thread, vermilion, graphite, dye, and thread. Source unknown, possibly gift of Mary E. Hall Hubbard; 13.1.581.

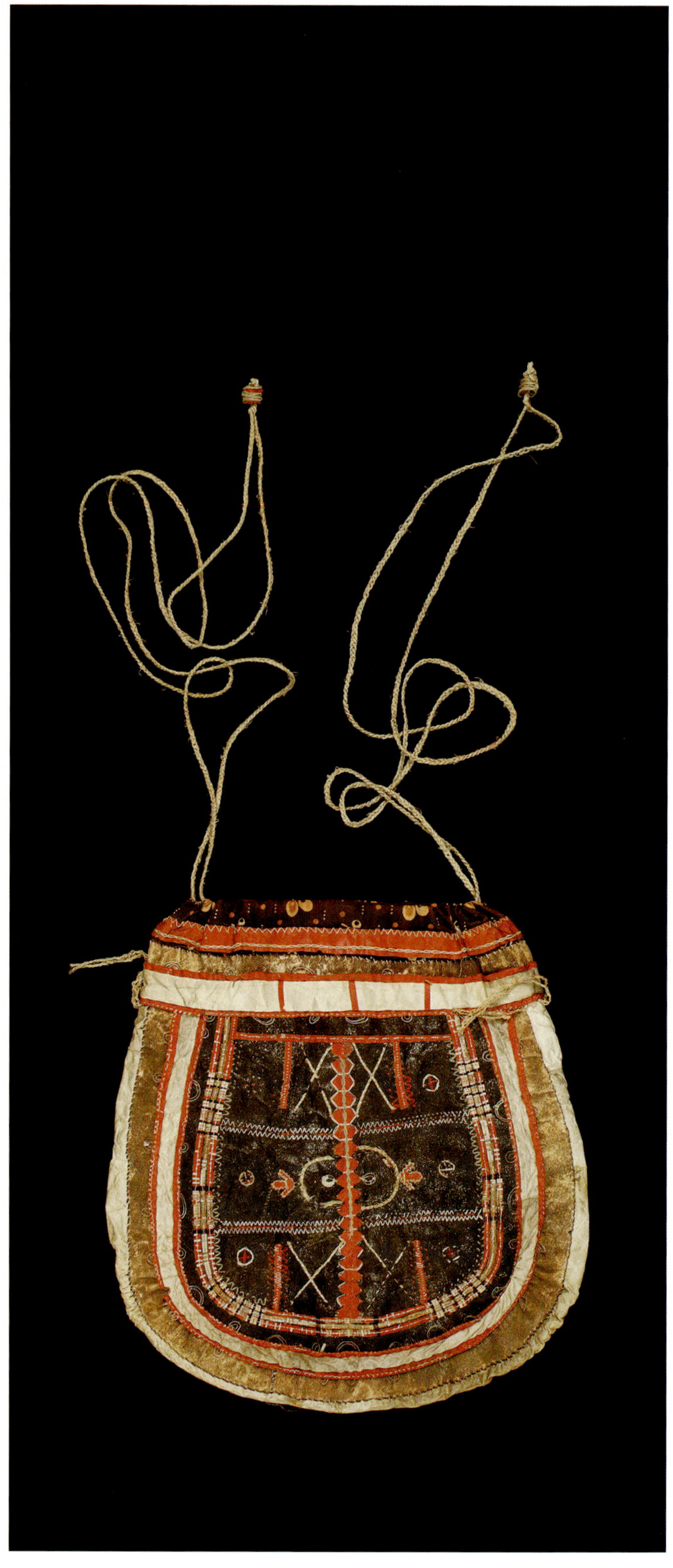

CAT. 3. Artist unknown, Alutiiq (Koniag), Kodiak Island, Alaska, tobacco bag, about 1850, hide, seal intestines, cotton cloth, sinew, wild rye grass, wool thread, vermilion, graphite, dye, and thread. Source unknown, possibly gift of Mary E. Hall Hubbard; 13.1.582.

European winter clothing could not rival the established use of tanned hide and fur garments, which were specifically created to be wind and waterproof as well as impervious to the cold. The boy's parka, c. 1920 (cat. 1), from the western Canadian Arctic and the tobacco bags, c. 1850 (cats. 2 and 3), from the western Arctic both integrate non-Native materials for decoration but rely on early contact and pre-contact materials and methods for maximum functionality: the pouches were made waterproof by their fabrication in seal intestine and sinew, and, while the small parka may be embellished in European-style cotton trim, its construction of thick fur provides protection from the winter elements.

Other objects featured in the Hood Museum of Art's Arctic and Subarctic collections exemplify different ways in which Aboriginal communities have chosen to rely on indigenous materials and methods of artistic production throughout the pre- and post-contact periods. Items such as the wooden Yup'ik mask, c. 1930 (cat. 4, see p. 80), from the western Arctic collection were created originally for personal, ceremonial, or religious purposes in the pre- and early-contact eras. Among the many groups of circumpolar Inuit and Eskimo, those in Alaska were the only ones to create wooden masks; in Alaska, Dorothy Ray explains in *Eskimo Masks: Art and Ceremony*, "ceremonialism reached its highest development." When used by the community, masks are but one element in a complex assemblage of song, dance, personal ornamentation, gesture, and story in both religious and secular ceremonies honoring animals sought in the hunt, the spirits of significant beings, or the past, via the performance of a narrative history. Like many Alaskan Native masks, the Yup'ik mask has elements designed to create movement during a performance. The feathers, which are supported by concentric wooden rings, would have shivered along the radiating appendages of flippers, tails, and hunting implements as a performer wore it. The survival of the feathers in this piece is a testament to the skill of its creator, the care of its original collector, and the custodianship of the current conservator; many perishable items such as these have not fared so well over such a long period of time. While many Arctic and Subarctic artists continue to make masks from indigenous materials for use in community-based ceremonies and performances, these striking pieces have also caught the attention of the contemporary art world, making them highly sought after by collectors of Aboriginal art around the world.

Among the other highlights of the Hood's Arctic and Subarctic collections are two exquisite wild rye grass baskets that were also created using indigenous materials and techniques. The basket, c. 1905 (cat. 12), and the basket and lid, c. 1870 (cat. 13), were likely made for personal and domestic use; basketry created for trade generally incorporated techniques taught by traders, which these do not. The Hood's exceptional early pieces are notable for their demonstrated ingenuity in the use of color and patterns of ornamentation, and for the perfect symmetry of the form and designs created in the coiled grass patterns. It is possible that the design that adorns the brightly colored bowl and cover of the basket and lid—which

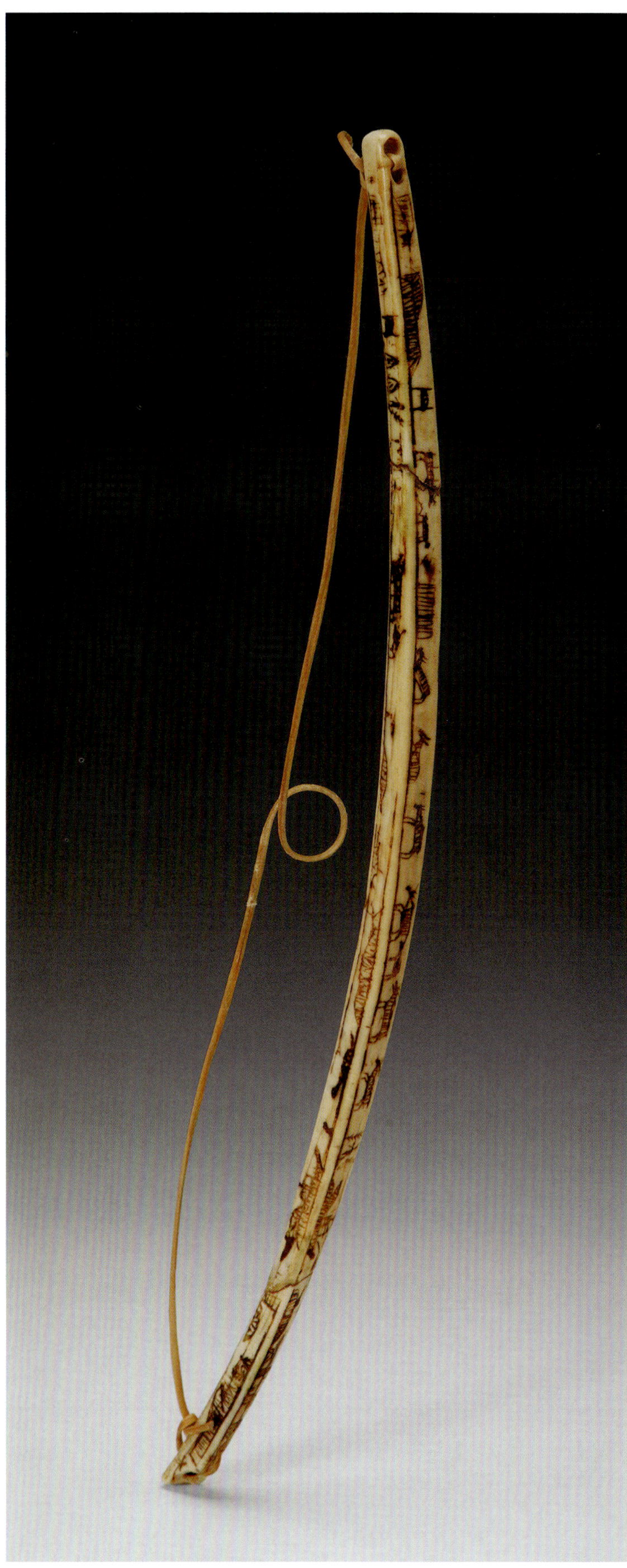

CAT. 7. Artist unknown, Inupiat, Cape Prince of Wales, Alaska, ivory bowl drill, about 1900, ivory and rawhide. Gift of Frank C. and Clara G. Churchill; 46.17.9597.

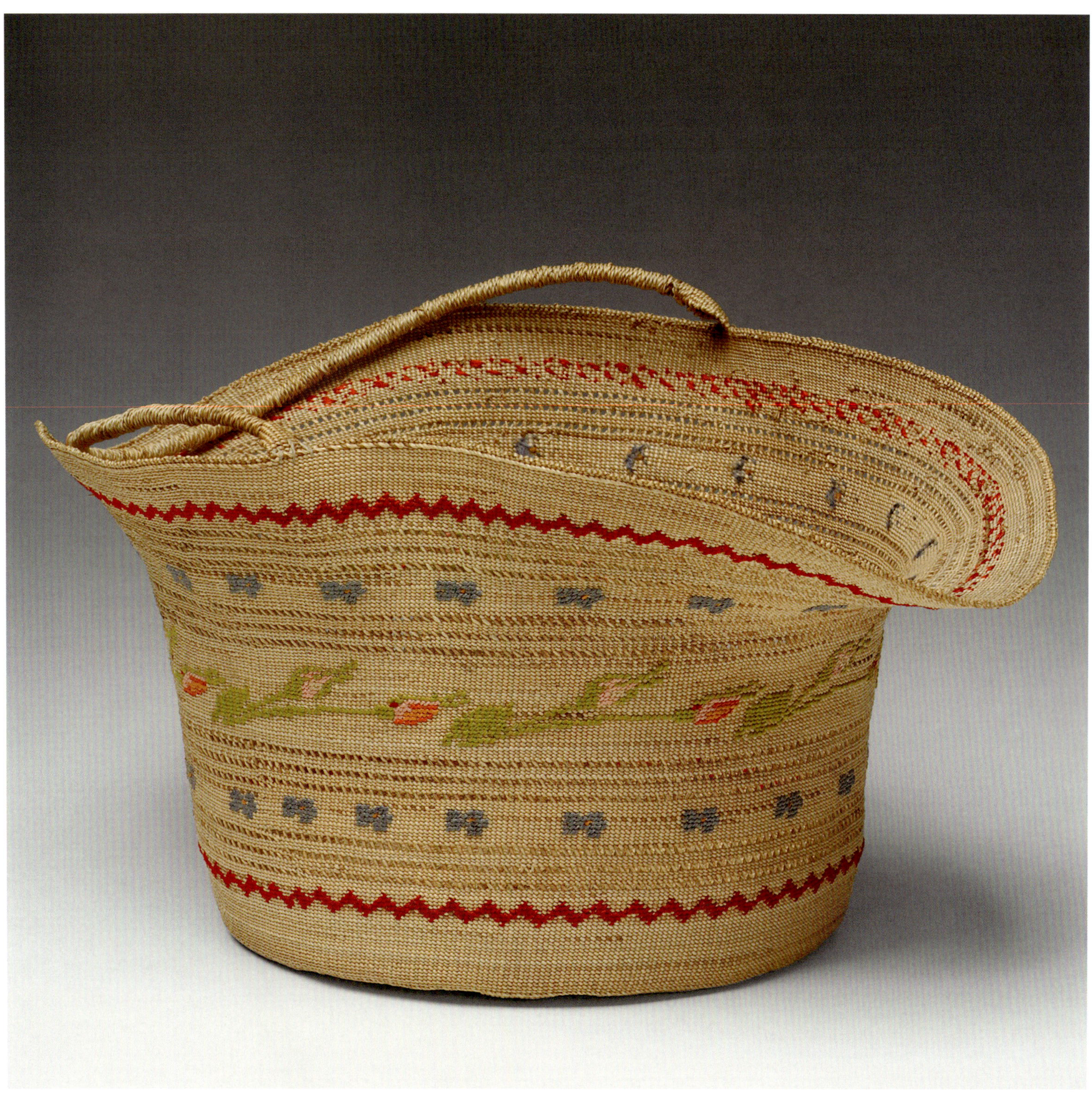

CAT. 12. Mrs. Adolf Rankin, Unangan (Aleut), active early 20th century, Unalaska, Aleutian Islands, Alaska, basket, about 1905, wild rye grass. Bequest of Frank C. and Clara G. Churchill; 46.17.9384.

alternates green with red and green with blue—was inspired by summer berries, while the open basket with its handle appears to be encircled by a garland of flowers. The original purpose of these baskets may have been to store sewing supplies and household items, but today, the practice of basketry continues to thrive in a market that values fine craftsmanship, and artistic production has grown to include not just traditional baskets, trays, and hot plates but models, teapots, and whimsical human and animal figurines.

As the objects in the Hood Museum of Art's Arctic and Subarctic collections reveal, the history of artistic production across these vast and varied regions is both dynamic and continuous, inventive and traditional. In some instances, European products replaced old-

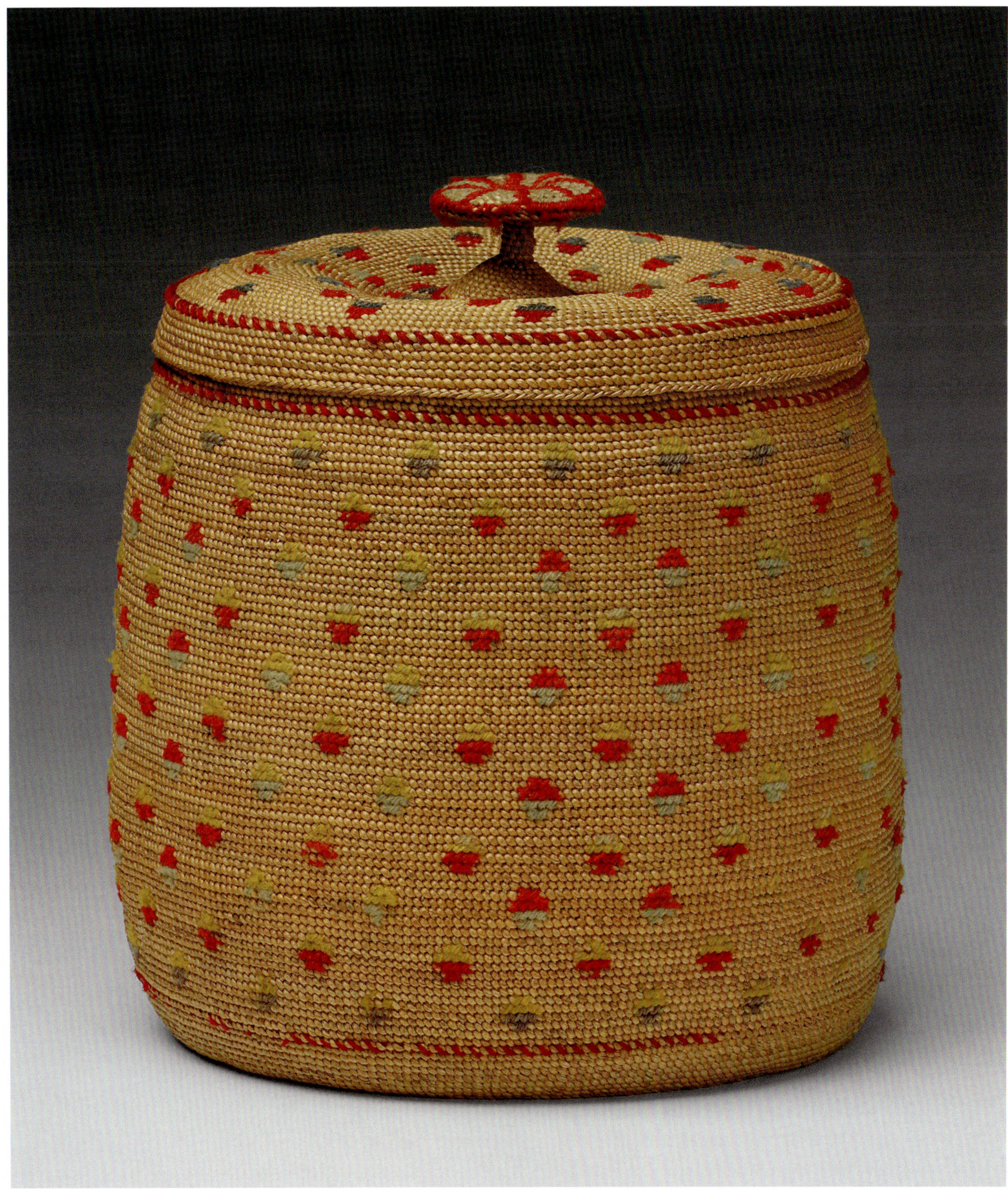

CAT. 13. Artist unknown, Unangan (Aleut), Aleutian Islands, Alaska, basket and lid, about 1870, wild rye grass and woolen yarn. Gift of Warren Prosser Smith, Class of 1913; 168.95.24525.

er materials or inspired fresh modes of production; in others, new technologies and techniques were adapted into existing traditions, so that novel materials and practices were aligned with centuries-old Aboriginal methods. At the same time, communities have frequently chosen to maintain their use of indigenous materials and forms, or they have reinvented them in ways that reveal little or no European influence. All of these scenarios have been borne out in different ways, at different times, and to different degrees among the many cultures that inhabit the Arctic and Subarctic regions. Although there is a great deal of variety in the regional, temporal, and cultural composition of the works represented here, the innovation and creativity of these artists resonates through them all.

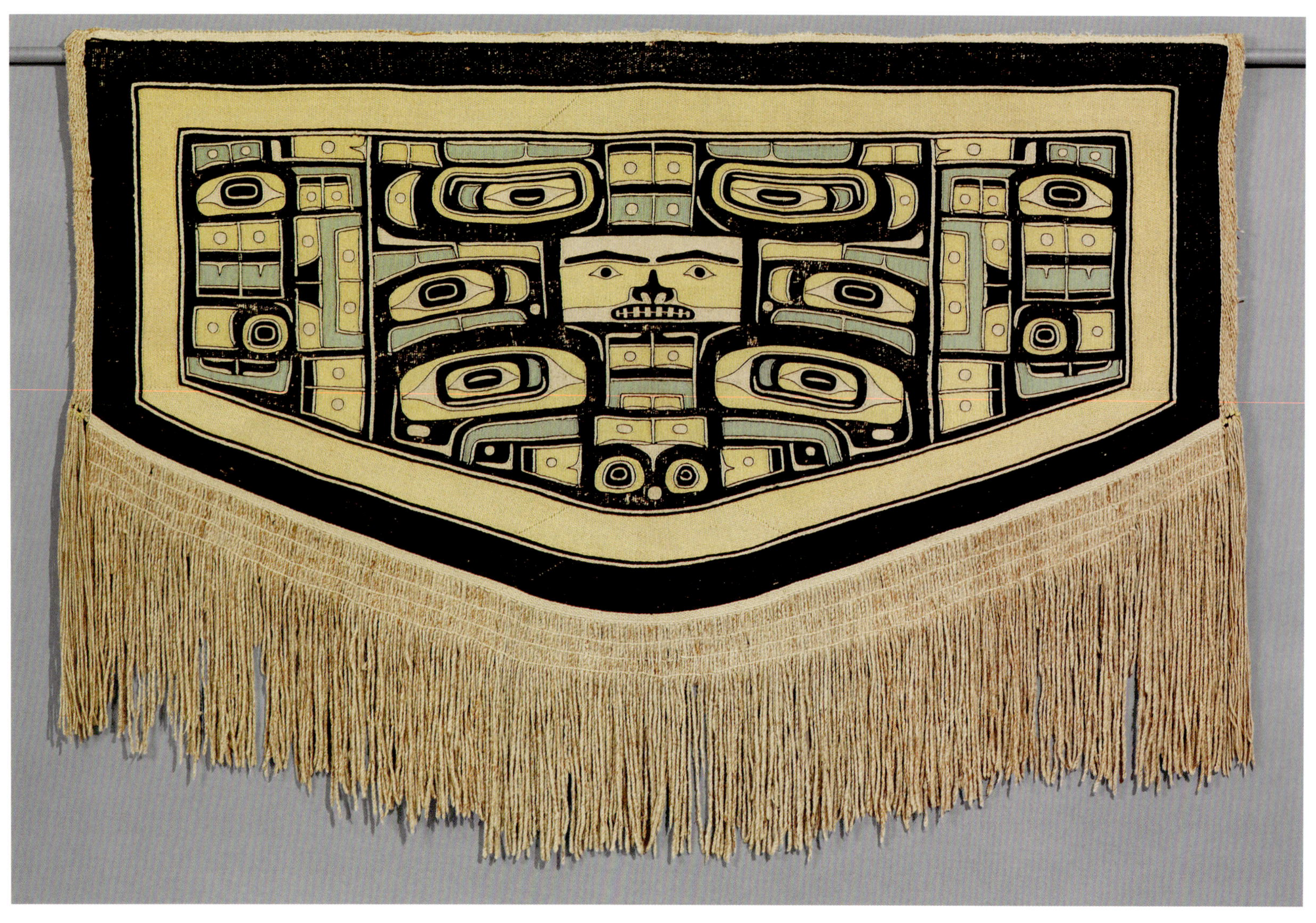

CAT. 33. Artist unknown, Chilkat Tlingit, Chilkat robe (*naaxein*), about 1850–1880, mountain goat wool, cedar bark, native dyes. Gift of Robert L. Ripley, Class of 1939H; 40.15.12586.

:: 6.2 ::

Northwest Coast: Expressing Identity in an Intercultural World

Megan A. Smetzer

Nicholas Galanin, a contemporary artist of Tlingit descent, utilizes humor and irony to critique the devastating legacy of colonialism on the Northwest Coast of North America. Like his ancestors before him, Galanin lives and works in an intercultural world, and the art he produces engages with global issues that resonate locally. Literally hand-cut from the pages of Frederica de Laguna's long out of print, three-volume work on the Yakutat Tlingit of southeast Alaska, *What Have We Become? Vol. 5a* (cat. 28) is a self-portrait that confronts the often-fraught relationship between indigenous peoples and the anthropologists who "create" them.[1] Although Galanin and other indigenous people acquire knowledge from long-standing oral traditions and historic visual artistic practices, they also read the ethnographies written about them and visit museums that contain the objects of their ancestors. For better or worse, these writings and exhibitions, usually produced by cultural outsiders, contribute to the shape of contemporary indigenous identity. In his evocative piece, Galanin argues that he is a re-shaper of knowledge and the producer of his own identity.

Many of the objects created by indigenous artists in the mid- to late nineteenth century also speak directly to the working-out of identity within the increasingly difficult circumstances of colonialism and, later, settler culture. Beginning in the eighteenth century with the onset of the fur trade, waves of smallpox and other diseases decimated indigenous communities; colonial governments criminalized cultural practices through unjust laws upheld using "gunboat diplomacy"; and pressure upon community members increased to assimilate as second-class citizens into the cash economy and Christianity. It is important to note, however, that each community endured and survived this period in a different way, due in part to the duration and intensity of its contact. Some communities, positioned to control the land-based fur trade, maintained the balance of power well into the nineteenth century, while others were more radically transformed at an earlier date. Despite the dramatic changes brought to bear, indigenous people along the coast worked hard to maintain important cultural connections while also incorporating new ideas and modes of being introduced during this era.

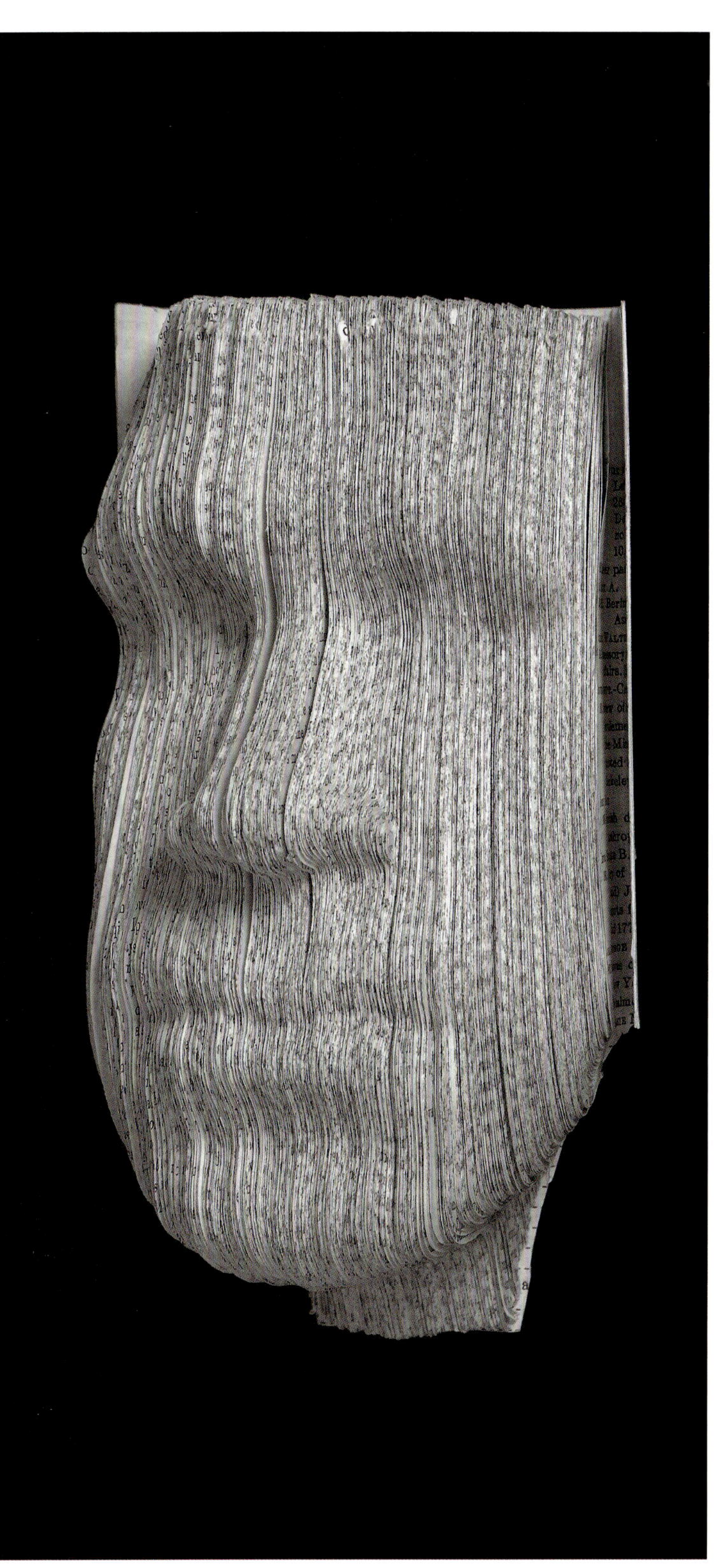

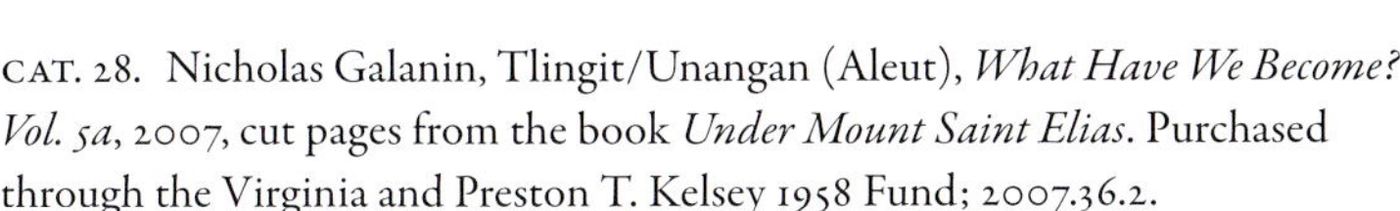

CAT. 28. Nicholas Galanin, Tlingit/Unangan (Aleut), *What Have We Become? Vol. 5a*, 2007, cut pages from the book *Under Mount Saint Elias*. Purchased through the Virginia and Preston T. Kelsey 1958 Fund; 2007.36.2.

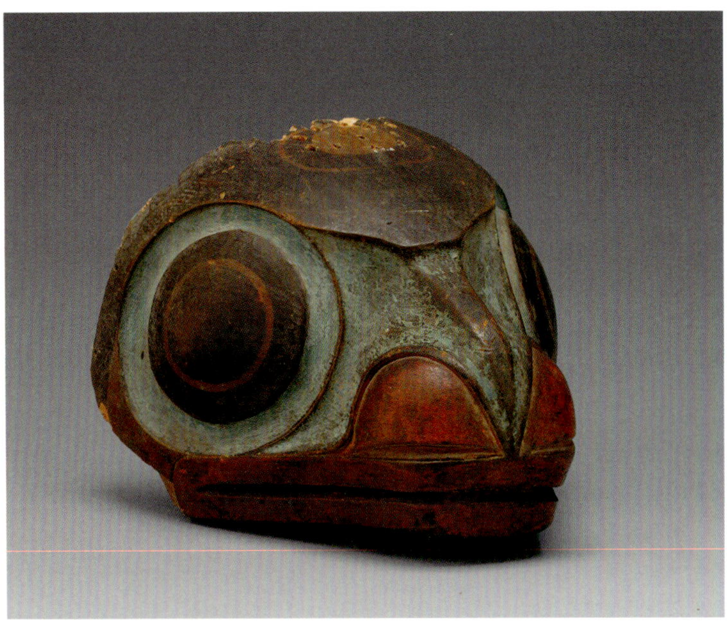

CAT. 34. Artist unknown, Tlingit, frontlet or headdress ornament, about 1860, wood, paint, twine, and sea lion bristle fragments (possibly). Gift of Mrs. Margaret Kimberly; 22.3.1891.

One of the most important ceremonial events for Northwest Coast people was, and continues to be, the potlatch. Central to coastal indigenous epistemologies, the potlatch was targeted by missionaries and government officials as the main impediment to assimilation. As a result, the Canadian government outlawed the potlatch in 1884 through the Indian Act, and in 1904, it was banned in Alaska. Despite colonial opposition, potlatching continued, often in secret. Eventually, through the hard work of the Alaska Native Brotherhood and Sisterhood and similar groups in Canada, which were established in the early twentieth century, perceptions and laws were slowly changed to end discrimination and the potlatch came out into the open once again.[2]

Though the sequence and type of events that occur within a potlatch vary from community to community, there are underlying similarities that are foundational, and they are based on complex status hierarchies and relationships. Among the Tlingit, for example, individuals are born into the moiety of their mother, either Raven or Eagle/Wolf. Hereditary rights and privileges are also obtained matrilineally. Within each moiety are clans, represented by specific crests derived from encounters with supernatural

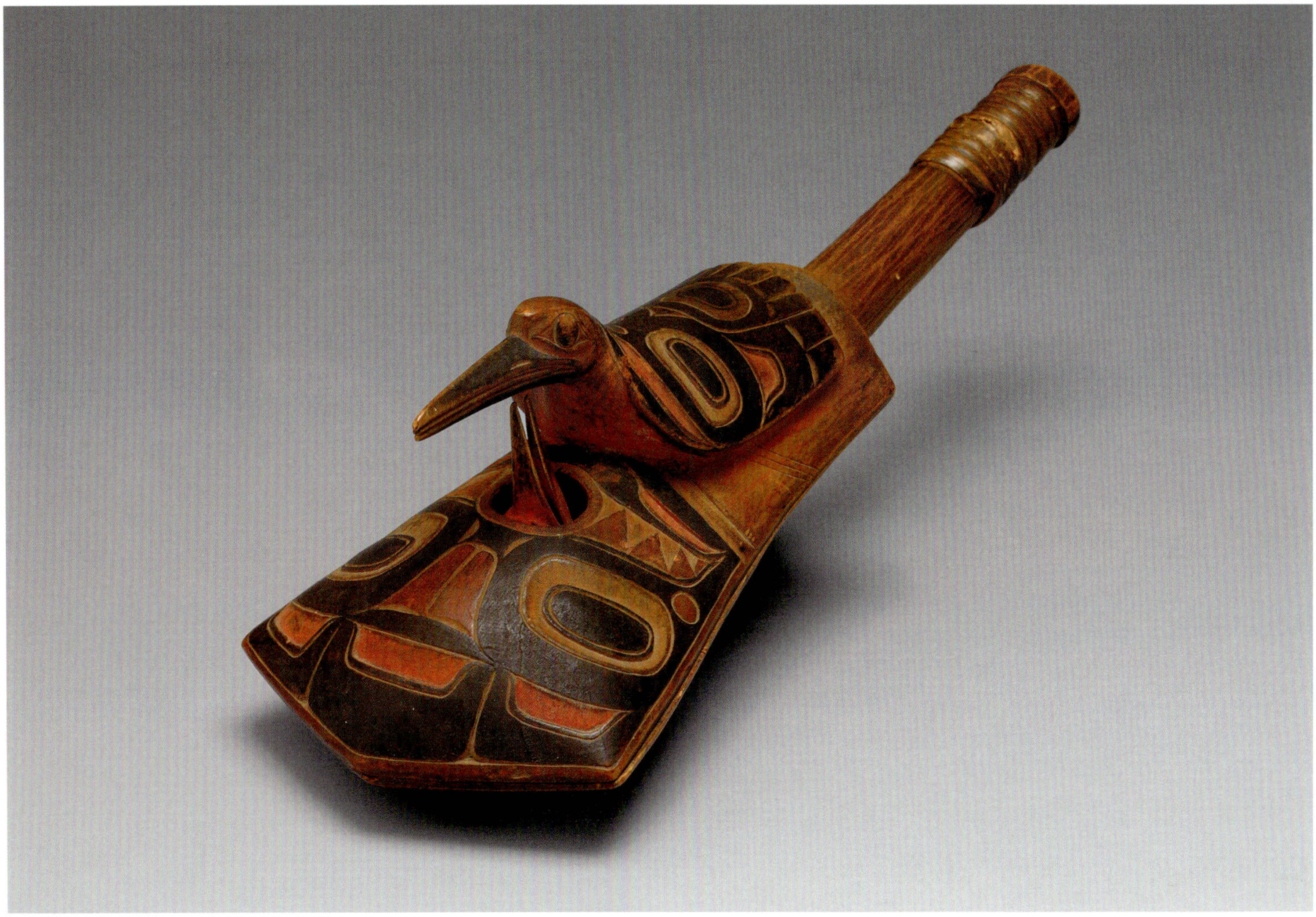

CAT. 35. Artist unknown, Tlingit, rattle, about 1850, wood, spruce root, pigment. Gift of Mrs. Margaret Kimberly; 22.3.1892.

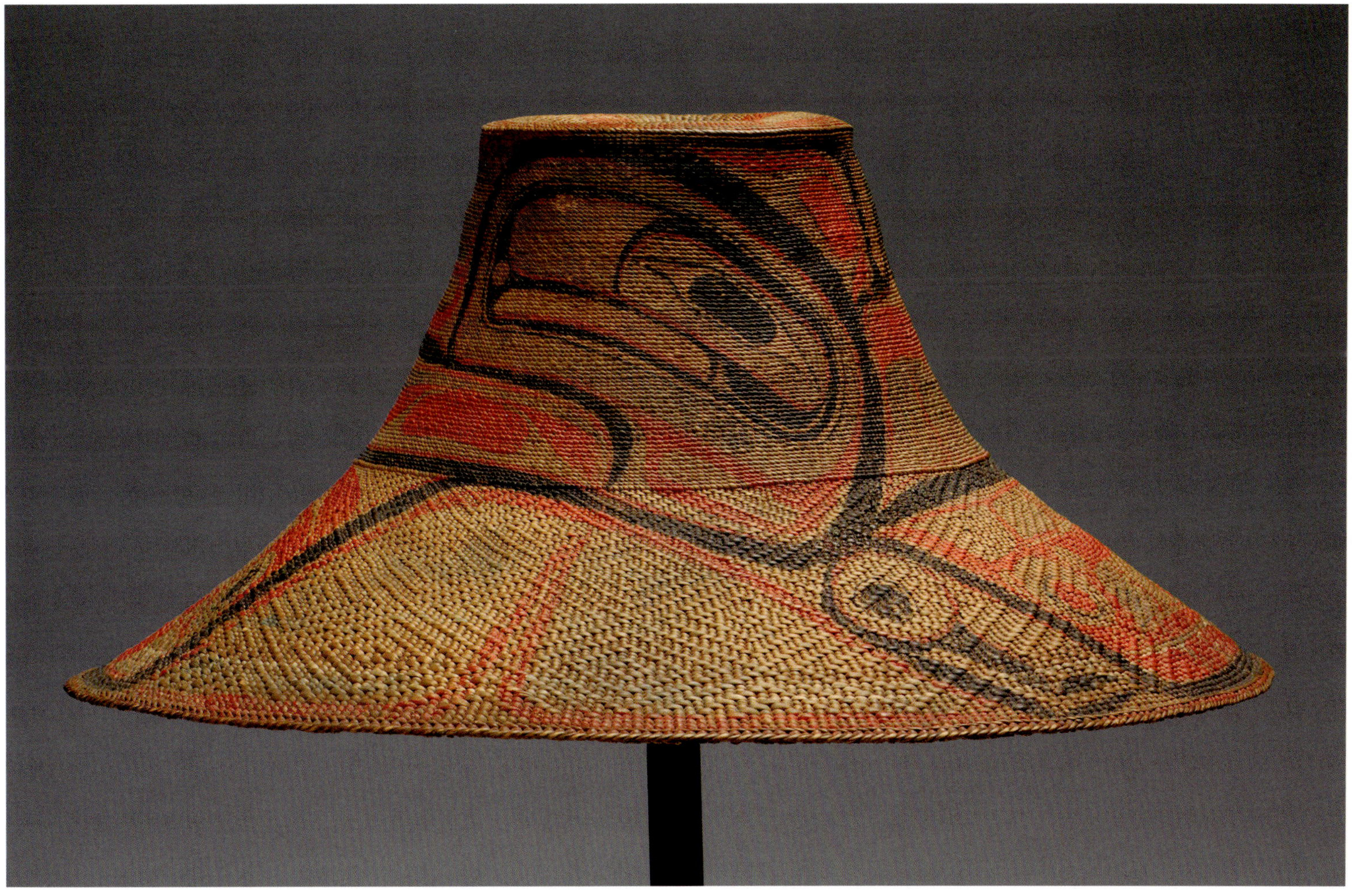

CAT. 22. Artist unknown, Haida, Haida Gwaii (Queen Charlotte Islands), British Columbia, hat, about 1860, spruce root, paint, cotton cloth, and thread. Gift of Mrs. Margaret Kimberly; 22.3.1927.

beings, often in the shape of an animal. Clans are further divided into house groups or lineages. Ceremonial duties, such as the hosting and witnessing of a potlatch, are split along moiety lines to ensure balance and reciprocity.

Potlatches are held to commemorate significant events, such as the memorialization of an important clan leader, the assumption of new leadership roles, the naming of children, the payment of debt, the raising of a totem pole, or the building of a clan house. The oration, feasting, dance and song performances, and distribution of wealth at a potlatch reinforce relationships between clans, articulate clan histories and ties to the land, and establish hierarchies of wealth and prestige. Within this context, both the hosts and the guests from the opposite moiety, who are paid to witness these events, wear specific items of clothing and jewelry that embody clan identity and rank. Some of the earliest pieces in the Hood Museum of Art's exhibition are visual representations of these epistemologies. A Tlingit *shakee.at* (frontlet or headdress) appears to depict a sea lion and likely references the crest of the wearer as well as specific clan histories and territorial and ceremonial rights (cat. 34). A circa 1850 Tlingit rattle in the shape of a *tináa* (copper shield representing wealth), which would be used during the performance of the songs and dances shared at a potlatch, suggests the prestige of its owner (cat. 35). It may also reveal a connection to the recently revitalized *Tináa Hít* (Copper Shield House) of Sitka, Alaska.[3] A Haida *Xaad dajaangaa* (painted and woven hat) indicates for other potlatch attendees the crest of the wearer, which appears to be an eagle or raven (cat. 22). This hat also illustrates the collaborative skills of the female weaver and male painter on this and other regalia.

In addition to creating items to be worn or given away within the context of the potlatch, indigenous artists took advantage of the financial opportunities that arose from producing works for the outsiders who began traveling to the coast in the late eighteenth century. Fur traders, followed by missionaries, government officials, settlers, and eventually tourists, by the end of the nineteenth century, desired souvenirs of their travels. As early as the 1820s, Haida carvers began shaping argillite, a dense, black carbonaceous shale, into small, portable objects that could be easily transported by the rapidly increasing number of Russian, American, and British fur traders seeking sea otter pelts. Some carvings depicted important

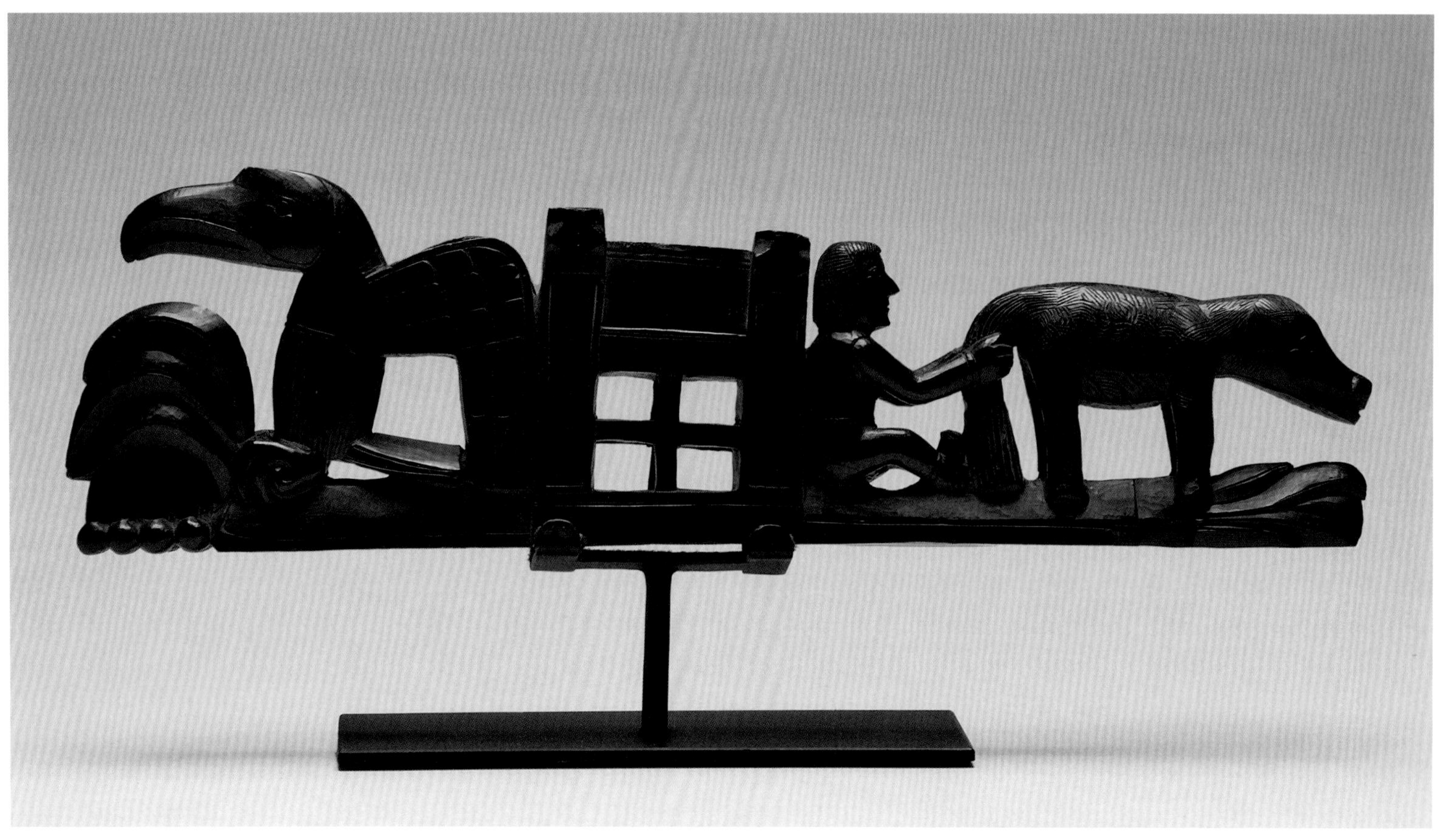

CAT. 24. Artist unknown, Haida, Haida Gwaii (Queen Charlotte Islands), British Columbia, pipe, about 1840–60, argillite. Purchased through the Mrs. Harvey P. Hood W'18 Fund and the Hood Museum of Art Acquisitions Fund; 2009.3.

supernatural beings and significant origin stories, while others, such as the circa 1840–60 pipe embellished with a steamship cabin flanked by an eagle in the stern and a man and dog in the bow (cat. 24), illustrate an interpretation of the new arrivals to the territory.

By the 1880s, the Northwest Coast, and Alaska in particular, became an increasingly popular tourist destination. Thousands of people traveled by steamship each summer to see the dramatic landscape of steep mountains and icy glaciers, and to interact with its indigenous people, whom they believed were untouched by civilization and soon to disappear. Victorian-era notions of indigenous people as "vanishing" arose partially in response to the increasing industrialization of the United States and elsewhere, as well as the anthropological notions of cultural evolutionism that suggested that all people had to pass through a series of stages to become truly civilized. Those of European descent were considered to have reached the pinnacle of civilization, whereas everyone else filled the lower ranks. Tourists, espousing these ideals and at the same time looking for alternatives, sought out those handmade objects that they felt represented the antithesis of modernization.

Baskets, woven out of red or yellow cedar or spruce roots, fulfilled this requirement and rapidly became one of the most desired souvenirs. Visitors coveted spruce root baskets embellished with false embroidery patterns made from dyed grass, especially those made in Yakutat, Alaska. One typical example is a circa 1900 berry basket with three pattern fields (cat. 31). The design of the upper and lower fields is known as "shaman's hat," and the central field is called "leaves of the fireweed." The fields are separated by an open eye-hole weave, which was quick to execute and appealed to the intended audience.[4] Tourists, primarily women, collected baskets in the thousands, many of which ended up in Victorian "Indian corners." These small collections, usually located in a public space within the home, not only highlighted the travel experiences of the collector for her friends but also served as a means for educating children about the wider world within the domestic sphere.

The craze for baskets and other objects such as beaded moccasins, miniature paddles and totem poles, and silver bracelets and spoons also worked in favor of the women who made these items or sold them on behalf of their male relatives. Missionaries supported participation in the curio trade as a means for indigenous people to enter the cash economy, as this was seen as more "civilized" than the redistribution of wealth through the potlatch. In turn, by participating in the souvenir trade, indigenous women were able to support their families financially and pass along their knowledge and skills to future generations. In some cases, these women also raised money for the continuation of long-standing cultural practices, such as the potlatch.

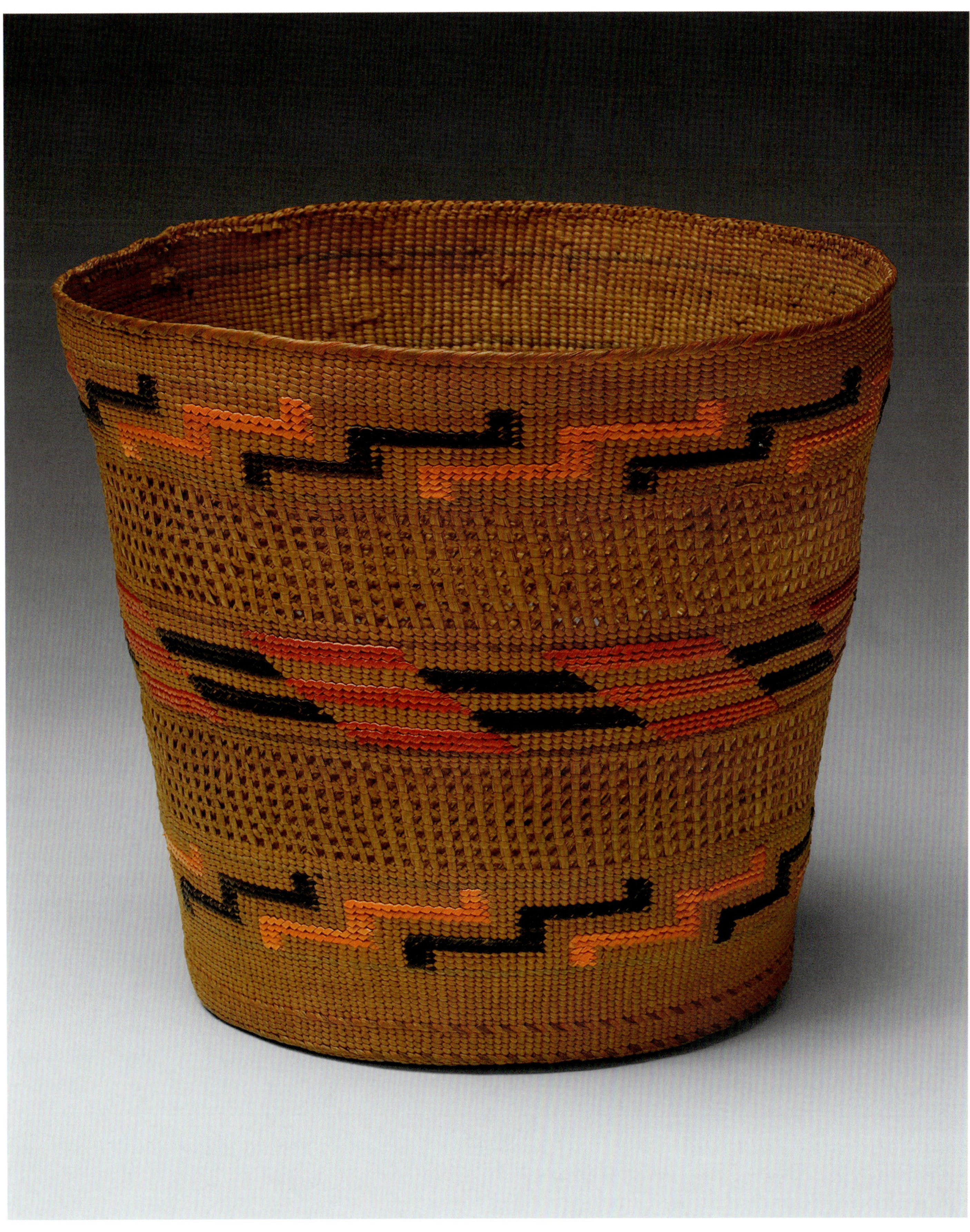

CAT. 31. Artist unknown, Tlingit, Yakutat, Alaska, berry basket, about 1900, spruce root, grass, and dyes. Bequest of Frank C. and Clara G. Churchill; 46.17.9391.

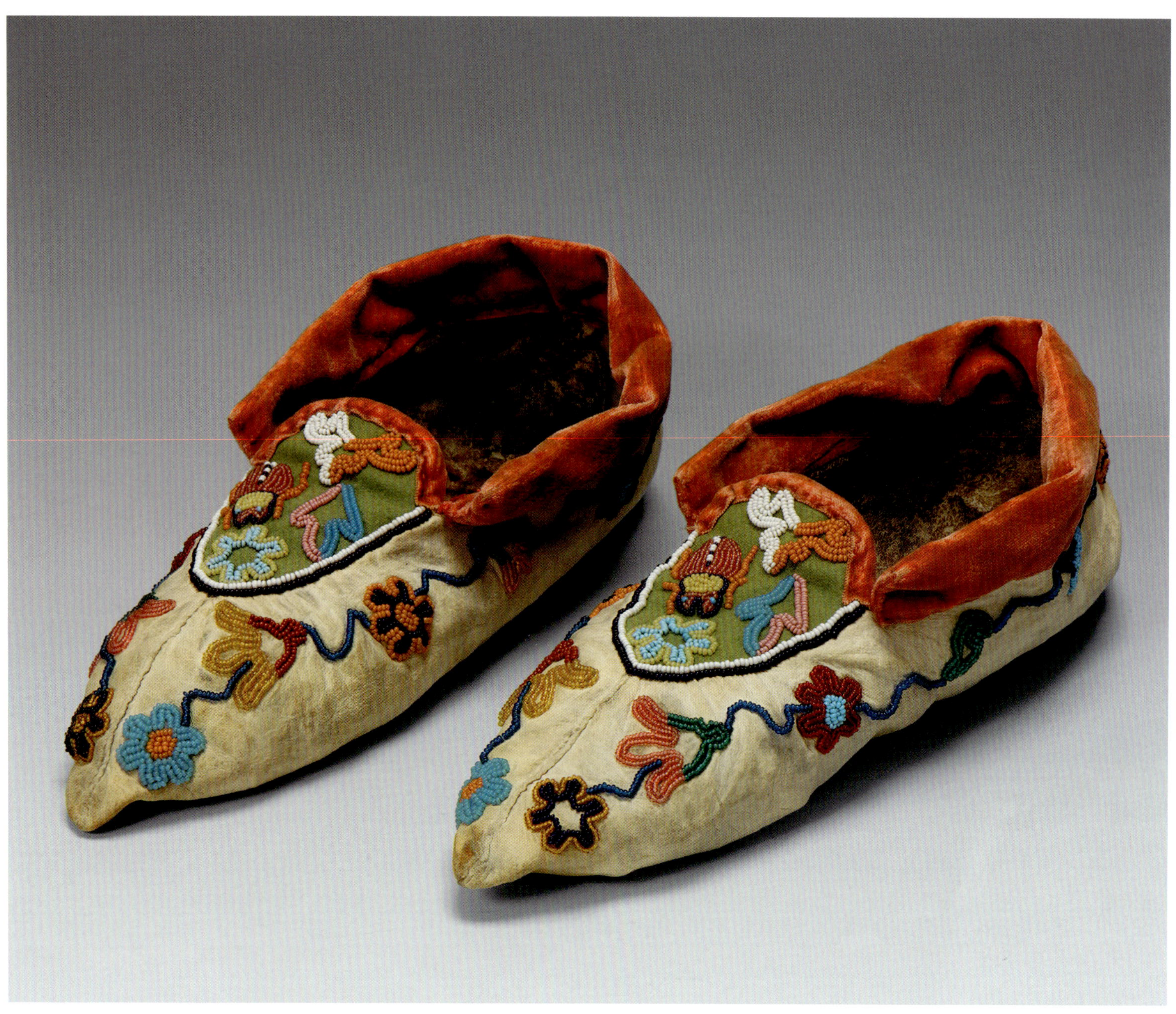

FIG. 6.2.1. Artist unknown, Tlingit, woman's moccasins, about 1890–1900, Native-tanned hide, glass beads, wool cloth, velvet, thread. Gift of Guido R. Rahr Sr., Class of 1951P; 985.47.26640.

As Galanin's self-portrait emphasizes, and as can be seen in the other objects presented in this essay, indigenous artists on the Northwest Coast have a long history of working out their identity within a complex transcultural context. Their ongoing engagement with the striking aesthetic qualities of Northwest Coast art is also rooted in long-standing cultural practices, as illustrated by the work of contemporary Tlingit artist Preston Singletary, whose medium of choice is blown and sand-carved glass. Though Singletary's technique is relatively new within Tlingit cultural contexts, the use of glass on the Northwest Coast is not. Tlingit women began working with glass beads in the early years of contact, acquiring large beads through trade with the Russians, which they then used to embellish the edges of regalia. With the introduction of seed beads in the second half of the nineteenth century and the acquisition of beading techniques from interior Athapaskan-speaking people, Tlingit women experimented with color and design, developing the foliate and seaweed motifs found on a pair of moccasins made for sale (fig. 6.2.1). They also began beading crest designs, which were located front and center on ceremonial tunics and dance collars, a practice that continues to this day.

Like his female ancestors, Singletary expands on the visual expression of clan and crest identity by incorporating new techniques.

In his 2006 piece *Tlingit Crest Hat* (cat. 29; see also p. 71), Singletary explores the reflective and transparent qualities of glass in relation to Tlingit design. Singletary's glass hat rests on its crown, allowing light to pass through and cast elaborate shadows. Singletary chooses not to represent an identifiable crest figure; instead, he creates an elaborate pattern around the brim that illustrates the complexity and elegance of Tlingit design as it has been developed by generations of artists.

Though separated by more than a century, the works in this exhibition are multilayered expressions of deep cultural knowledge and the engagement with shifting intercultural realities. As their ancestors did before them, Nicholas Galanin and Preston Singletary utilize new strategies to engage with contemporary global processes in ways that resonate locally. Although the materials, techniques, and audiences have expanded, each piece attests to the strength and creativity of indigenous people along the Northwest Coast from the past and into the future.[5]

NOTES

1. Frederica De Laguna, *Under Mount Saint Elias: The History and Culture of the Yakutat Tlingit* (Washington, D.C.: Smithsonian Institution Press, 1972).
2. In 1951 the law against the potlatch was dropped from the Indian Act.
3. For the history of this house, see *Anóoshi Lingít Aaní Ká: Russians in Tlingit America*, ed. Nora Marks Dauenhauer, Richard Dauenhauer, and Lydia T. Black (Seattle: University of Washington Press, 2008), 105.
4. See Frances Paul, *Spruce Root Basketry of the Alaska Tlingit*, 2nd ed. (Sitka: Sheldon Jackson Museum, 1991).
5. I would like to thank Mique'l Askren for her comments on early drafts of this essay.

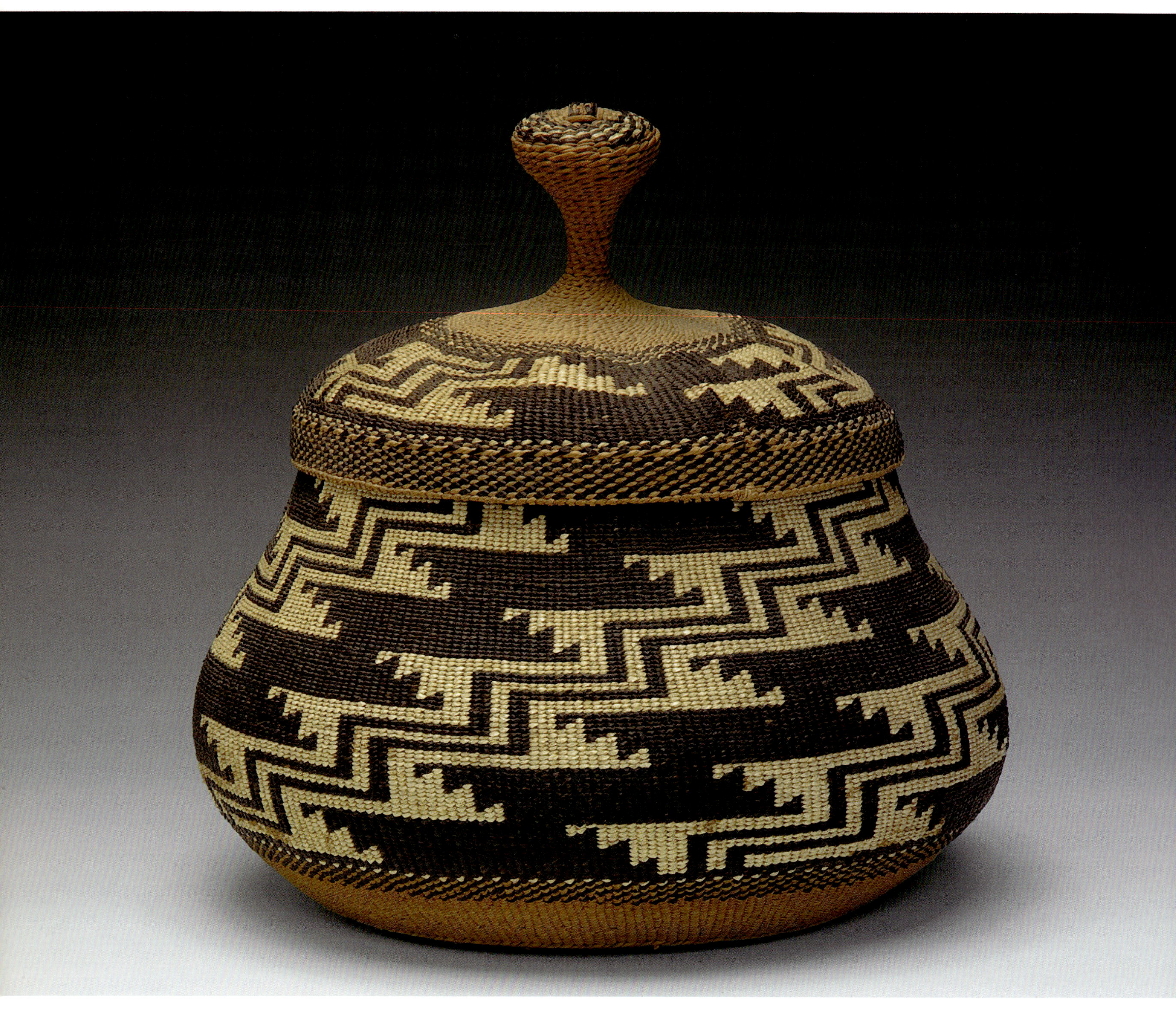

CAT. 42. Elizabeth Conrad Hickox, Karuk (Karok)/Wiyot, or Louise Hickox, Karuk (Karok), basket, about 1925, wild grape root, myrtle sticks, hazel, maidenhair fern, yellow-dyed porcupine quills, and stag horn lichen. Gift of Mrs. James Foster Scott, in memory of her late husband, Victor J. Evans; 157.9.1389.

:: 6.3 ::

Plateau and California: Nature and Rebellion Inspire Visual Stories

Miles R. Miller

Although rock art—petroglyphs and pictographs—is outside the scope of the Hood Museum of Art's collection, its influence upon the artists who created this collection's objects is strong. Perhaps, long, long ago, a child listening to an elder tell stories wondered what *T'at'aliya* (Witch Woman),[1] *Wawayay* (Cannibal Mosquito),[2] or the man-eating water monster[3] would look like, then later left his vision of these figures on the rock walls. Regrettably, we have lost the ability to interpret this rock art today. Nevertheless, these distinct and recognizable patterns represent powerful symbols of place that connect us to our culture, history, environment, knowledge, and values. Today the rock art images are identified as deer, elk, mountain goat, fish, and people, left behind to describe a hunting party story, village site, or location for good fishing. Contemporary Plateau and California regional artists gain inspiration from these ancient art forms, using these designs on baskets, in jewelry, or in paintings.[4]

While nature might be said to inspire the traditional artist, rebellion stirs the modern artist, particularly in reaction to the economic, social, and psychological problems facing Indian youth in the United States.[5] The California and Plateau baskets, beadwork, and fine art selections in this exhibition date from 1875 to 2009, a period of continuity in guiding principles but also considerable evolution and groundbreaking experiments in Native American art. Basketry traditions in particular represent a steadfast commitment from generation to generation based upon a shared dedication to creative designs and techniques. Traditional artists listen to the legends, explore the rugged landscape, and experience the beauty of wildlife, then render their reactions as visual stories. Modern artists also draw from that history, and that heritage, from the perspective of contemporary Native American experience, creating frequently comical, disturbing, or nonrepresentational interpretations of current sociopolitical events that have a profound impact on Native American lives. Individually, these works reflect tribal and familial histories; together, both old and new art forms comprise an "ancestry of experience"[6]—that is, expressions of how we see, understand, and represent our families, our homes, and the world around us.

Although there are distinct cultural differences between the various tribes of the two regions in question here, the coiled and twined basket techniques and geometric designs reflect their surroundings in similar ways (cat. 42). The basket makers do not look at their work as art but as a "reminder of home."[7] To the Yakama people, in fact, the "Origin of Basket Weaving"[8] is a time-honored tale about the occasion when Cedar Tree taught a young Klickitat girl to weave coiled cedar root baskets; as time went on, nature would also provide the designs woven into those baskets. Alone, these austere geometric images comprise abstractions of mountains, the diamonds on a rattlesnake's back, stars, animal tracks, and the human figure. Taken together, they tell multifaceted stories of significant familial and tribal events.

The coiled and feathered baskets signify the importance (and graceful beauty) of birds but also serve as complex narratives concerning the lives of the Yokut and Pomo tribes of California. The intricate weaving technique of these baskets tells a story about special ceremonies, presentation objects, and our relationships with each other and with neighboring communities. These baskets were also buried with departed loved ones. Wasco basket weaver Patricia Gold says, "All of our baskets tell a story."[9] While viewing the treasure basket (cat. 50), imagine what might have been happening 120 years ago as a Yokut elder gathered the materials and with gentle, meticulous finger movements incorporated quail feathers and wool yarn into the basket. What story does this basket tell? How is this basket design a reminder of home? What is the Yokut peoples' origin of basket weaving? These and other questions may never be answered—due to unknown circumstances, the artists had to part with their work, and over time the story that accompanied this particular piece was lost.

The earliest influences of the beadwork artist were the traditional designs of the basket weaver, though these were soon enough subjected to introduced materials, media, and patterns. By 1805, the Plateau people had acquired a wide variety of materials through trade routes, including glass beads, cotton thread and needles, wool, cotton, and velvet fabrics, and silk and velvet ribbon.[10] In time, beads of varying colors and sizes arrived, allowing for more creative and intricate floral and figural designs. The floral beadwork design of the Plateau moccasins (fig. 6.7.1) suggests central Washington wildflowers growing on the far-reaching sagebrush that covers the foothills lying east of the Cascade Mountain range. A number of stories surround Plateau moccasins, including the "Origin of Plateau Moccasins,"[11] which explains the deep significance of their unique heel tab, or fringe. It is a salute to the Ants, the legendary characters that saved a young Plateau woman from a water monster. Plateau artists continue to make moccasins with the heel tab as a time-honored tradition. And as the years pass, the next person will learn the legend while watching and learning from an elder the fine art of moccasin making:

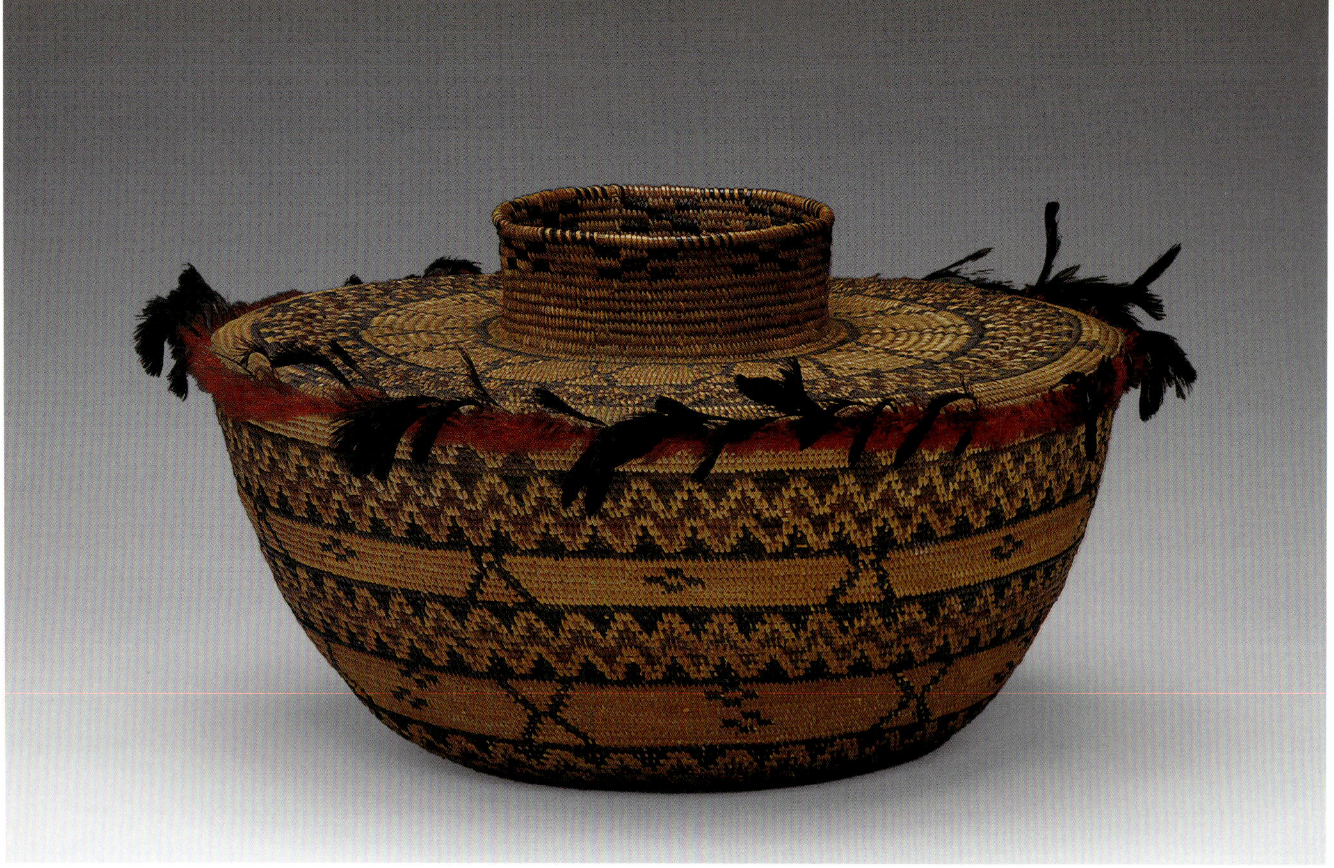

CAT. 50. Artist unknown, Yokuts, Kern County, California, treasure basket, about 1890, deer grass, bracken fern root, redbud, California valley quail crests, wool yarn. Gift of Mrs. Ida Farr Miller; 44.18.8755.

> Traditional artists learn their skills by observation; they learned to take pride in their heritage through the creation of their own story from extended family members. The baskets, beadwork, pottery, etc., all major forces in their world view surround them; hold them close to their heritage. Knowing how to make these things was just a part of life, comparable to a rite of passage, but after being exposed [through a Western education] to historical and political issues our peoples have faced, they became symbolic of our lives and the continuation of a belief system, a living tradition that persisted despite the fact that these things could be expressed through very modern media today.[12]

If modern Native American artists cannot rewrite history with the stroke of a paintbrush, they can certainly influence the minds of the viewing audience. Artists such as Fritz Scholder and Harry Fonseca were moved by legendary characters and falsely romanticized Native American figures, which they transformed into modern Native American icons of a sort, populating anecdotes of generational trauma.

In 1965, as an Institute of American Indian Arts faculty member, Fritz Scholder purposefully turned his attention to the Indian subject. His now iconic portraits were intended to be disturbing or comical renderings derived from the past and from current events. He writes:

> When I first came to Santa Fe, I vowed to myself that I would not paint Indians. Then I saw the numerous over-romanticized paintings of the "noble savage" looking into the sunset and decided that someone should paint the Indian in a different context. My concern therefore includes depicting the strange paradox created in the transition to the 20th century; the quiet humor of the nature-oriented person; the faces that show the imposition of the non-Indian and the tenacity for holding onto an identity; the monstrous metamorphosis that at times makes the Indian his own worst enemy; the contemporary Indian/cowboy with a can of beer in his hand . . . In the final analysis, however, the Indian Series is an optimistic reaction to a new era of the emerging American Indian.[13]

Scholder's devotion to the situation of real Native Americans, not the already clichéd themes of other Native artists—"we are still here," identity, genocide, broken treaties—constitutes an inspiring reuse of tradition as a springboard for personal creative action.[14] His screenprint *Untitled (Screaming Indian)* (cat. 55) represents an eerie, poignant counterstatement to the nineteenth-century American belief that Native American people were a "vanishing race." This Indian does not vanish, whatever his struggle may be with the massive field of light brown that surrounds him.

While the specific Native stories informing the designs (and functions) of the twined bags, hats, and coiled cedar root baskets of the Yakama, Nez Perce, Warm Springs, and Okanagan plateau artists remain shrouded, their presence is still strong. Among the objects in the Hood's collection is a finely woven twined bag with intact design elements, though a frayed edge kept it from the exhibition itself. Their beauty aside, these large twined bags of hemp and grass or cornhusk were the gunny sacks, the Mason jars, and the freezer bags of long ago.[15] People used these lightweight, easily transportable bags to store dried foods and personal belongings from season to season and when moving from one camp to another. They were also highly prized trade items among families and neighboring tribes. Today, Joe Feddersen and Patricia Gold, contemporary Plateau artists, find inspiration in the graceful beauty of these bags and their evidence of traditional Plateau designs. Feddersen's prints, weavings, and glass pieces represent modern reinterpretations (but not a revival, exactly) of Plateau culture. Gold's weavings are more of a visual record of old and nearly lost designs and weaving techniques of the Wasco people. Their bags represent a tribute to the beauty of the region's culture, the ties with the past, and the artistic talents of the first residents along this great river—the ancestors of the people of the mid-Columbia.[16]

All of us were taught the histories of Columbus, Lewis and Clark, and countless other early American discoverers, but the history of the Native people they encountered faded to nothing. To most modern Native American people, historic museum collections are carefully preserved but ultimately misinterpreted symbols of a disappearing culture. Despite the truth and aesthetic presence still obvious in these many objects, Native Americans themselves are still visualized only in a past or romanticized context. My intention with this essay has been to suggest an alternative, one found both in the products of tradition and the voice of the living artist today. Other aspects fill out this multidimensional interdependent link. In the evocative words of W. Richard West, "Place determines who we are in that it establishes our relationship to everything around us. Our cultures, including our aesthetic productions, grow out of that relationship to place. I say relationship rather than 'connection,' because the latter's meaning seems too mechanical to express the rich intermesh between person and place in Native life. It is not simply a 'connection to the land' but a multidimensional interdependence between place and community that shapes the way we live and think."[17] There is the deep spiritual relationship to the land, expressed through the act of gathering and sharing traditional Native foods. There is the deep spiritual interaction between grandparents and grandchildren who listen intently to legends about how landmarks were formed and explanations of how animals received their markings. For Native American artists in particular, there are the oral legends and sacred songs that represent the heart knowledge and blood memory of a time even before people. From this link comes art, itself linked, as it in turn links again in a deep spiritual connection among the generations and even centuries of hands that made it.

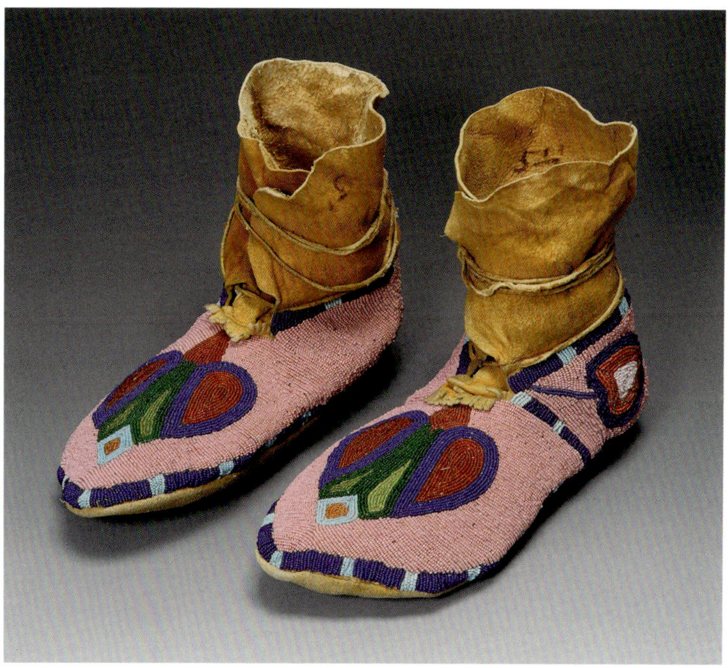

FIG. 6.3.1 Artist unknown, Nimi'ipuu (Nez Perce), moccasins, about 1920, Native-tanned hide, glass beads, thread. Bequest of Frank C. and Clara G. Churchill; 46.17.9857.

NOTES

1. Deward E. Walker Jr. and Virginia Beavert, *"T'at'aliya": The Way It Was (Anaku Iwacha Yakima Indian Legends)* (The Consortium of Johnson O'Malley Committees, Region IV, State of Washington, 1974), 78.

2. Walker and Beavert, *"T'at'aliya,"* 96.

3. Yakama Nation oral history.

4. Miles R. Miller, "*This Place Called Home:* A Columbia Plateau Arts & Culture Exhibit & Study Guide," master's thesis, University of Washington, Seattle, 2008, p. 23.

5. Bill Anthes, "Postscript: Making Modern Native American Artists," in *Native Moderns: American Indian Painting, 1940–1960* (Durham: Duke University Press, 2006), 179.

6. Leilani Holmes describes an ancestry of experience in three parts: heart knowledge, blood memory, and the voice of the land. Heart knowledge is passed on to others in the context of relationships and deep feelings of connection. Blood memory is knowledge that passes through generations, so Hawaiians are united with the *kupuna* (elders) of generations past. And the voice of the land is knowledge embedded in a grounded cosmology, existing not for its own sake but rather as a continuing reminder of the subjectivity of *'aina* (land). See Leilani Holmes, "Heart Knowledge, Blood Memory, and the Voice of the Land: Implications of Research among Hawaiian Elders," in *Indigenous Knowledges in Global Contexts: Multiple Readings of Our World*, ed. George J. Sefa Dei, Budd L Hall, and Dorothy Goldin Rosenberg, OISE/UT, 37–53 (Toronto: University of Toronto Press, 2000).

7. Delia Velasco, personal communication, August 2010.

8. Walker and Beavert, *"T'at'aliya,"* p. 61

9. Jill R. Chancey, ed., *By Native Hands: Woven Treasures from the Lauren Rogers Museum of Art* (Laurel, Missouri: Lauren Rogers Museum of Art, 2005).

10. Miller, "*This Place Called Home*," 23.

11. Yakama Nation oral history.

12. Velasco, personal communication.

13. Anthes, "Postscript," 181.

14. Ibid., 180.

15. Mary D. Schlick, *Columbia River Basketry: Gift of the Ancestors, Gift of the Earth* (Seattle: University of Washington Press, 1994), 134.

16. Ibid., 145.

17. W. Richard West, *The Changing Presentation of the American Indian: Museums and Native Cultures* (Seattle: University of Washington Press, 1999).

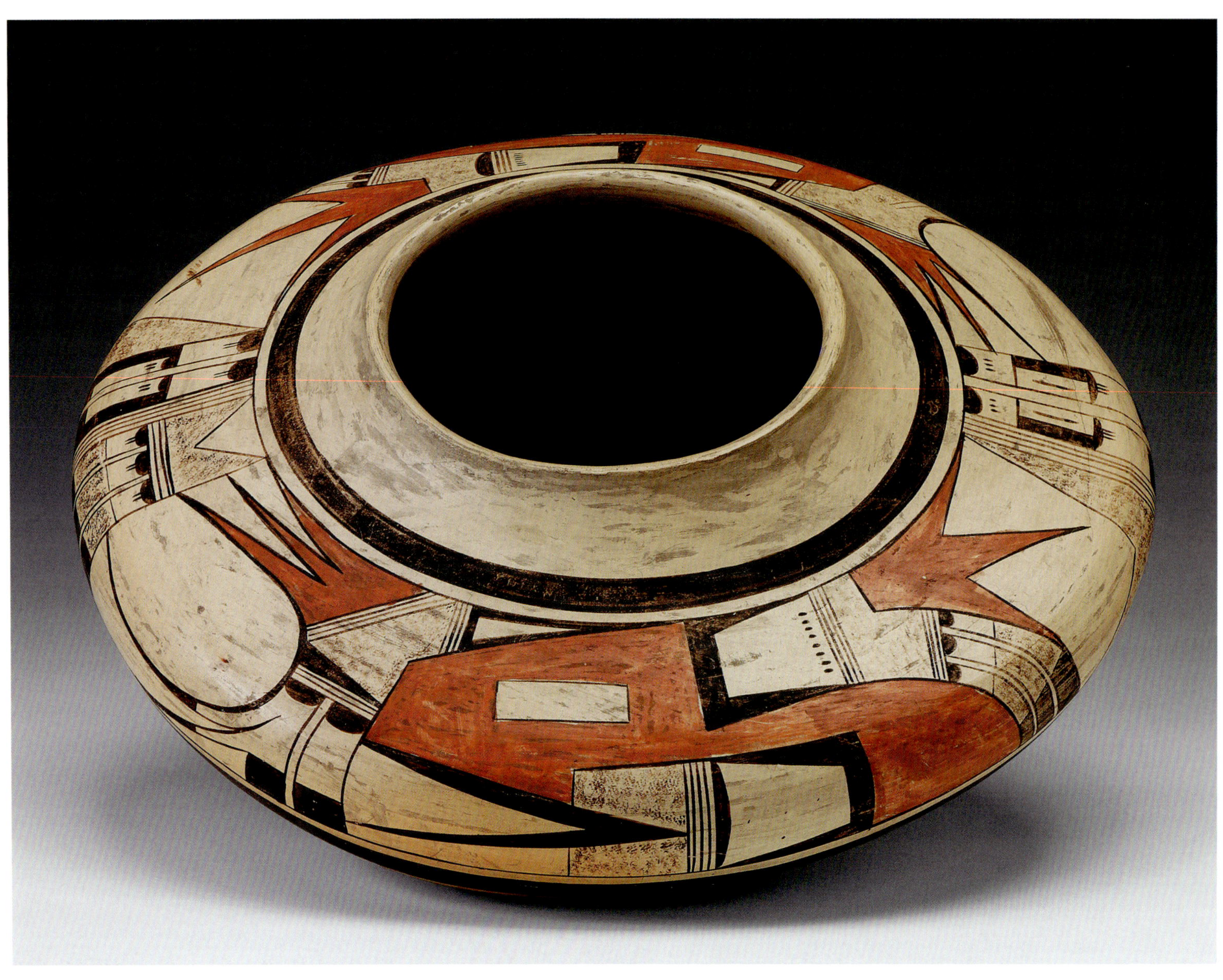

CAT. 70. Nampeyo, Hopi, seed jar in Sikyatki Revival Style, about 1900–1910, earthenware, painted with colored slips and burnished. Gift of Mr. and Mrs. George H. Browne; 42.12.8107.

:: 6.4 ::

Southwest: Diversity in a Land of Dramatic Contrasts

Joyce M. Szabo

Rich in the dramatic beauty of mountains and desert, the American Southwest has been home to Native people for at least fifteen thousand years. As in many other parts of Native North America, big-game hunters and foragers were followed by hunters of smaller game, who supplemented their diets by gathering widely dispersed nuts and grains. After approximately 300 BCE—the actual time varying in different parts of the Southwest—agricultural societies developed more sedentary lifestyles. The Southwest offered a land in which complex archaeological cultures subsequently developed, built large-scale, sophisticated communities, engaged in cultural exchange with Mesoamerica, and created spectacular works of art in a staggering range of materials. The descendants of those cultures, together with other Native people who have entered the Southwest at various times, continue to live in the region and to create a diversity of art forms that speak strongly to the connection to the land, to belief systems, and to contemporary life interwoven with long-held tradition.

Ancestral Pueblo people lived in the Four Corners area where the states of New Mexico, Colorado, Utah, and Arizona meet. However, an extreme drought that extended from 1276 to 1299 forced most people to move further east, closer to the Rio Grande and more reliable water sources.

Baskets were prominent in early settlements, but, by approximately 700, coiled, hand-built ceramics became more apparent. Ancestral Pueblo ceramics are most often painted black on a white or grey background, at least until late in the archaeological sequence. Geometric designs predominate. The Hood Museum of Art's ladle, probably dating from 1250 to 1300 or so, has a bowl with a square unpainted center (cat. 64). Heavy applications of black pigment in the offset quartered subdivisions that surround the white center carry geometric patterns of zigzags and angular interlocking scrolls that suggest some of the complexity of ancient Pueblo ceramic patterns. Unpainted or reserved centers inside bowls or ladles may represent the place of emergence for the Pueblo people from the underworld into this world. That place of emergence is also given form in ceremonial structures within Pueblo communities.

As farmers in a land that often has too little rainfall, the people who inhabit the nineteen pueblos of New Mexico, who speak five distinct languages, and the twelve Hopi villages in northeastern Arizona, which have their own language as well, continue the rich ceremonial life of their ancestors, calling upon deities and messengers to those deities to bring agricultural fertility. Ancestors join those intermediaries who live in the mountains of the Southwest and watch over their descendants. The Pueblo worldview is built

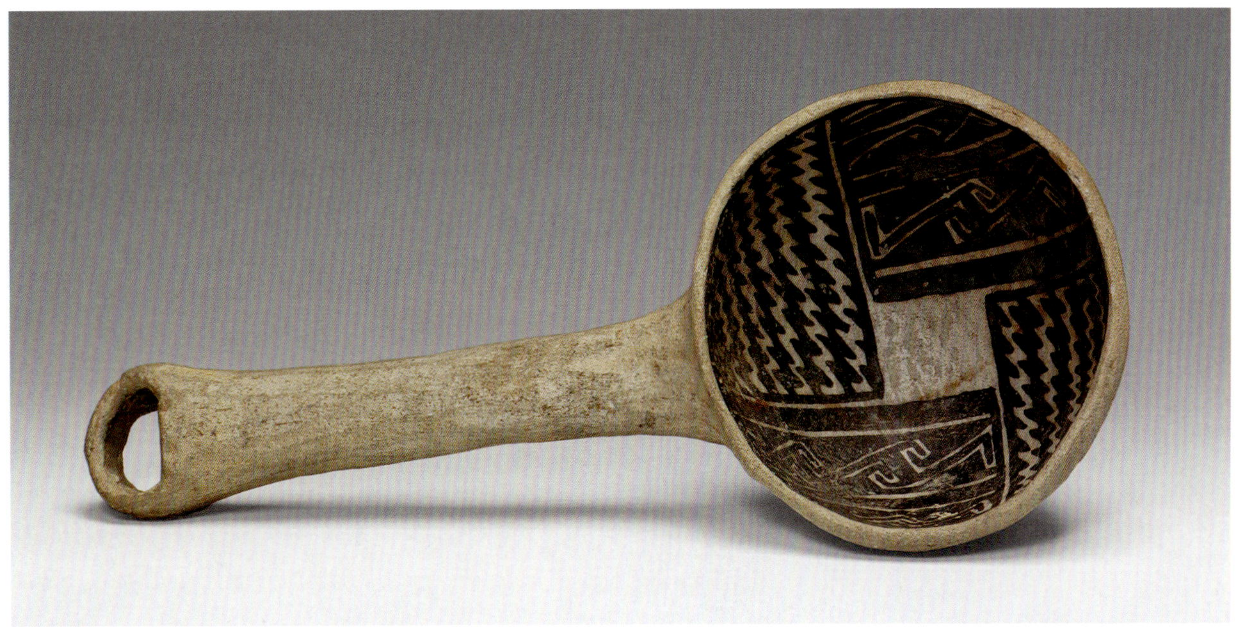

CAT. 64. Artist unknown, Ancestral Puebloan, ladle, Late Pueblo III Phase, 1250–1300, earthenware, painted with colored slips. Bequest of Frank C. and Clara G. Churchill; 46.17.10686.

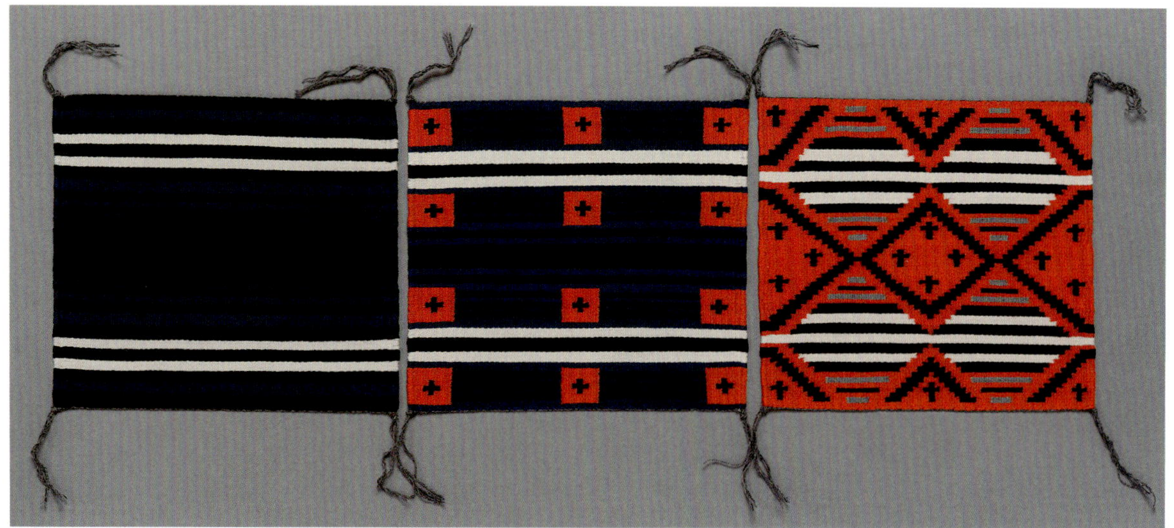

CAT. 81. Barbara Teller Ornelas, Diné (Navajo), *Chief Blankets: Phase One; Phase Two; Phase Three,* 2010, wool, vegetable dye. Purchased through the Alvin and Mary Bert Gutman '40 Acquisitions Fund, 2010.71.

around these needs and a deep respect for ancestors, land, animals, and each other.

In 1540 the Spanish arrived in the Southwest, and with them came disease and war, in addition to new crops and new ways of life. Imposing their belief structures on the indigenous people of the Southwest, the Spanish in effect forced Native people to begin practicing their ritual observances in secret. Even though Native people ultimately found ways to continue their own beliefs while also adopting some of the ways of the Spanish, the first several centuries of contact were disastrous on many levels. Ultimately, the Pueblo people joined together in a revolt in 1680 and successfully drove the Spanish from what is now New Mexico. The Spanish, however, returned some twelve years later to reestablish their hold on the region.

Descendants of the ancient archaeological cultures of the Southwest were joined during the late pre-contact years by people who entered the region from the north. These new people, now known as the Navajo or Diné and various Apache groups, were Athapaskan speakers closely related to the many Athapaskan groups still found in the Subarctic area of Native North America. The Athapaskans brought with them their own worldviews and lifestyles but adjusted those to the new environment of the Southwest as well as to their Pueblo neighbors. While it is not known for certain when these newcomers first entered the Southwest, general consensus suggests that they arrived between the fourteenth and the beginning of the sixteenth centuries, many locating near the Four Corners region, while other Apache groups moved further east and south into New Mexico. Initially more reliant on hunting, the newcomers remained far more nomadic than the Pueblo people. For various Apache groups, mountain spirits not only offered assistance in locating game and enabling healing but also had (and continue to have) important roles in bringing blessings to bear during young women's coming of age celebrations. The Diné worldview focuses on vital connections to healing powers and the necessity of keeping all aspects of life in balance, particularly through a complex ritual system.

With their entrance into the Southwest, the Spanish brought horses that would, with rapid speed, change the character of much of Native North America. They also brought sheep, cattle, and wheat. Sheep were of particular importance to some of the Athapaskan-speaking people, and the Diné, unlike their farming Pueblo neighbors, turned to sheep herding as a major occupation. They grazed their flocks over large areas of the region, and Diné women rapidly became expert weavers of wool blankets. In fact, Diné wearing blankets were held in higher esteem by most people than the blankets long woven by Mexican and New Mexican Hispanic weavers, so much so that in 1807 two master weavers were brought from Mexico to Santa Fe in present-day New Mexico to improve the quality of New Mexican Hispanic textile arts.

Diné wearing blankets, extant from at least the late seventeenth century, were often striped, the bands of color running vertically along the wearer's spine. Such wearing blankets were highly prized; it was said that they were so tightly woven that they were waterproof. The natural white, black, brown, and grey colors from the sheep were augmented by various dyes; initially, indigo blue, imported from Mexico, was extremely important. Also frequently added was red, either achieved through dying with cochineal, a color processed from the crushed bodies of a small beetle native to Mexico, or, by the nineteenth century, obtained from commercially woven red trade cloth that was unraveled and then the yarn reused by Diné weavers. Gradually these weavers achieved a rich diversity of color through vegetal dyes and, ultimately, through the use of commercial aniline dyes that became available in the second half of the nineteenth century.

A variant of the wearing blanket, known as a Chief Blanket, became an important part of the Diné weaver's repertoire by the first few decades of the nineteenth century. This blanket pattern, while still striped, varied dramatically from the vertically striped wearing blankets. The First Phase Chief Blanket, dating from approximately 1800 to 1850, had broad stripes in dark colors, often black with narrow stripes of indigo within the bands, running horizontally around the body when the blanket was worn. These evenly

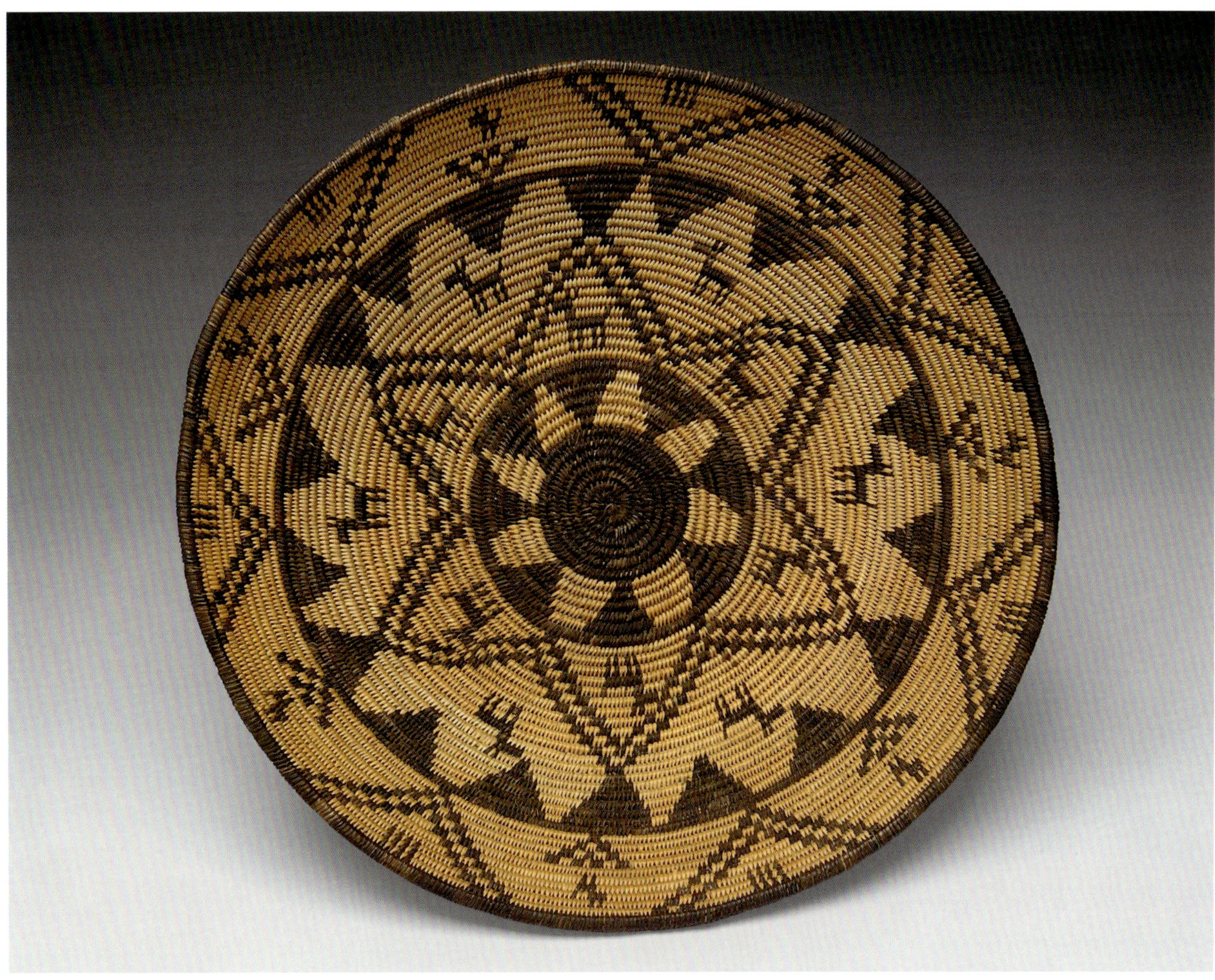

CAT. 78. Artist unknown, Western Apache, basket, about 1900, willow, cottonwood, devil's claw. Museum purchase; 51.27.12829.

spaced bands at the top and bottom of the blanket were offset by a broader, double-wide band in the midsection of the blanket, appearing at what would have been the wearer's waistline. First Phase Chief Blankets have this simple bold-striped pattern. Second Phase Chief Blankets, made prominently between the early years of the nineteenth century and 1870, maintained the basic patterning of the First Phase but added twelve blocks or areas of color to the blanket, one at each corner, four at the middle edges of the blanket, and four more running in an evenly spaced line down the wearer's back. These spots of color were most often red, their vibrancy contrasting with the natural white and black bold stripes of the rest of the blanket. A Third Phase design, prominent between 1860 and 1880, reduced the number of color areas from twelve to nine by combining the central band's color sections into three larger blocks. Sometimes the color areas became diamonds, with whole, half, and quarter diamonds appearing in various parts of the pattern. These boldly patterned blankets still maintained the tightly woven character of the vertically striped blankets and became particularly popular with Plains and Great Basin tribes to the north and east of the Diné homeland. Barbara Teller Ornelas's (b. 1954) 2010 *Chief Blankets: Phase One; Phase Two; Phase Three* are, at ten by nine and one-half inches each, miniature, finely woven versions of their nineteenth-century predecessors, the play of patterns and colors reflecting the long-established aesthetic of these famous wearing blankets (cat. 81).

Apache cultures are well known for their woven baskets. After entering the Southwest, the Apache peoples remained more hunters and gatherers than farmers and sheepherders like their Pueblo and Diné neighbors, and baskets were particularly important in their lives. When outside markets developed in the later nineteenth century, Apache weavers created many elaborate baskets for sale as well. The Western Apache peoples, particularly the San Carlos and White Mountain Apache, have created coiled baskets in a wide range of shapes and sizes, from *ollas* over three feet tall to contemporary miniatures of an inch or less in height. Western Apache weavers are best known for the inclusion of human and animal forms as part of many designs—this combination of tiny figurative elements and bold geometric patterns represents a distinctive aesthetic, as evidenced by the Hood Museum of Art's large basketry bowl (cat. 78). Willow provides the lighter visible color and devil's claw, the darker brown, both intersecting in a complex radiating pattern of petals, geometric forms, and small quadrupeds. At more than thirty-six inches in diameter, the Hood's basket is a masterful example of Apache weaving.

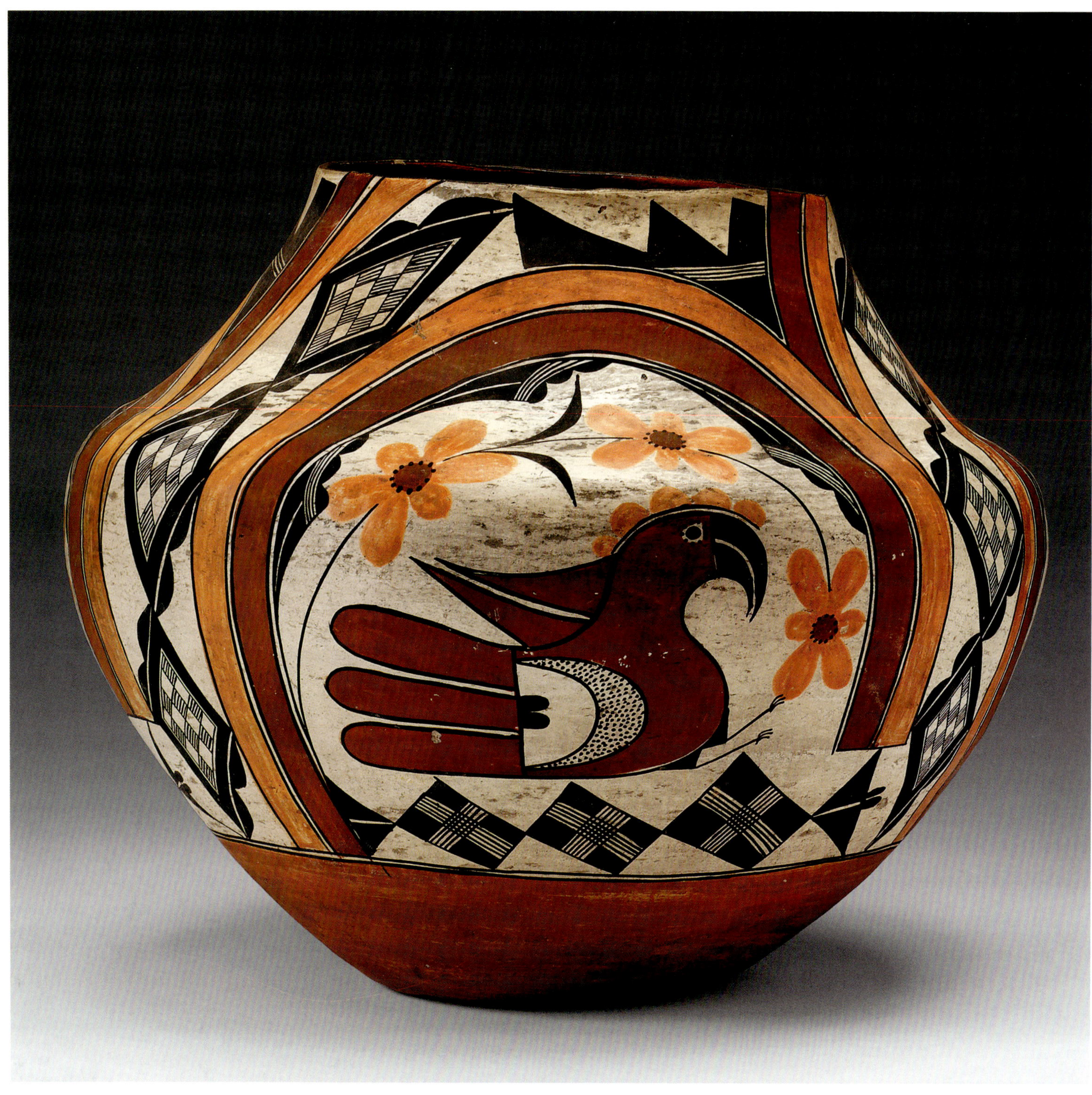

CAT. 62. Artist unknown, Acoma Pueblo, water jar (*olla*) depicting macaw or parrot with overarching flowers and double rainbow, about 1900, earthenware, painted with colored slips and burnished. Bequest of Frank C. and Clara G. Churchill; 46.17.10077.

While the Athapaskan-speaking people of the Southwest are not well known for a long history of ceramic arts, their Pueblo neighbors excelled at this art form, just as their ancestors had done. Designs changed after European contact, and floral patterns and animals, particularly a diversity of birds, were frequent additions by the second half of the nineteenth century. Each pueblo developed its own strong aesthetic. Acoma became well known for particular hard, thin-walled ceramics with complex, finely drawn linear patterns as well as rainbow and parrot forms that carry messages concerning water and agricultural fertility. Acoma potters have a close connection to a strong black-and-white aesthetic but also explore a wide range of earth colors, especially in late-nineteenth- and early-twentieth-century examples such as that found in the Hood's collection (cat. 62).

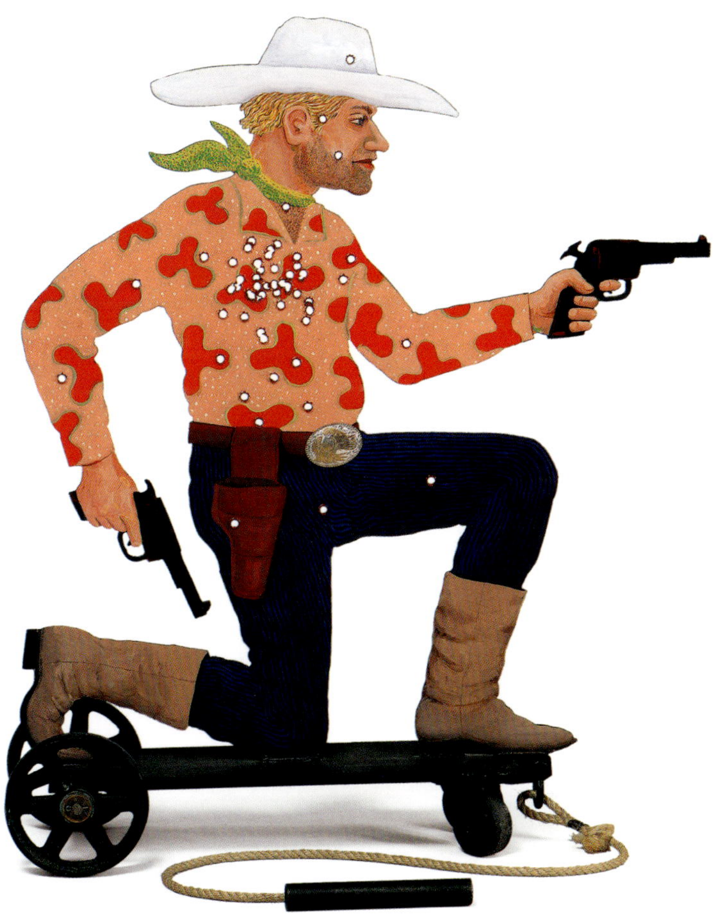

CAT. 76. Bob Haozous, Chiricahua Apache/Diné (Navajo), *Apache Pull-Toy,* 1988, painted steel. Purchased through the Joseph B. Obering '56 Fund; S.989.17.

At the First Mesa village of Hano at Hopi, an important ceramic development occurred during the late nineteenth and early twentieth centuries. Hano is a village that was settled by Tewa-speaking Pueblo people from the Rio Grande area who fled there after the Pueblo Revolt of the late seventeenth century. According to both Hopi and Tewa memories, the Tewa people were allowed to settle at Hano, a location at the beginning of the mesa where a first attack from enemies might occur, if the Tewa agreed to guard the mesa. The Tewa, well respected as warriors, accepted these terms, and thus First Mesa has villages of Hopi people as well as Hopi-Tewa.

It was in the village of Hano that a revival of an archaeological type of ceramics occurred, a revival that was not simply a copying of earlier work but a new creative inspiration based upon recently excavated ceramics. Nampeyo (1860–1942), a Hopi-Tewa woman, was recognized as an expert potter by her early adulthood. Her husband, Lessou, worked as an assistant on academically sponsored excavations underway near First Mesa, and Nampeyo would eagerly examine the pottery fragments that were unearthed. It was from these fragments that she began to reconstruct the design system and color aesthetics of Sikyatki Polychrome, which dates to the fifteenth and sixteenth centuries. Frequently asymmetrical in design and often covered with bird wings or beaks in abstracted form, Sikyatki vessels came in a variety of forms, but the seed jar or squat, wide-shouldered vessel with a narrow opening appealed most to Nampeyo. It was on vessels of this shape that the dynamic quality of Sikyatki designs could sweep over the surface in her finest work. The Hood Museum of Art is extremely fortunate to have one of these jars dating from the early years of the twentieth century (cat. 70; see p. 100). Sikyatki Revival Polychrome remains a major Hopi-Tewa style today, with many potters, including Nampeyo's descendants, expanding the original type in diverse ways.

While some Native artists in the Southwest continue to work in and experiment with materials and forms long used in their cultures, many other artists express their creativity and concerns in distinctly different ways. Bob Haozous (b. 1943), an artist of Chiricahua Apache and Diné heritage, often inverts stereotypical images in a humorous yet simultaneously serious manner. His preferred medium is welded steel, and he frequently works on a large scale. The Hood's *Apache Pull Toy* of 1989 turns the tables on generally expected views of the past (cat. 76). Riddled with bullet holes, Haozous's blond cowboy appears with guns drawn as if fighting his unseen but understood enemies. However, in this reconfiguration of power now employed by the artist, it is the Apache, and by extension all Native people, who not only prevail in this battle but who can also pull the cowboy around, not the reverse. Artists like Haozous use their art to offer social commentary, often with irony, to make themselves heard and seen as twenty-first-century forces.

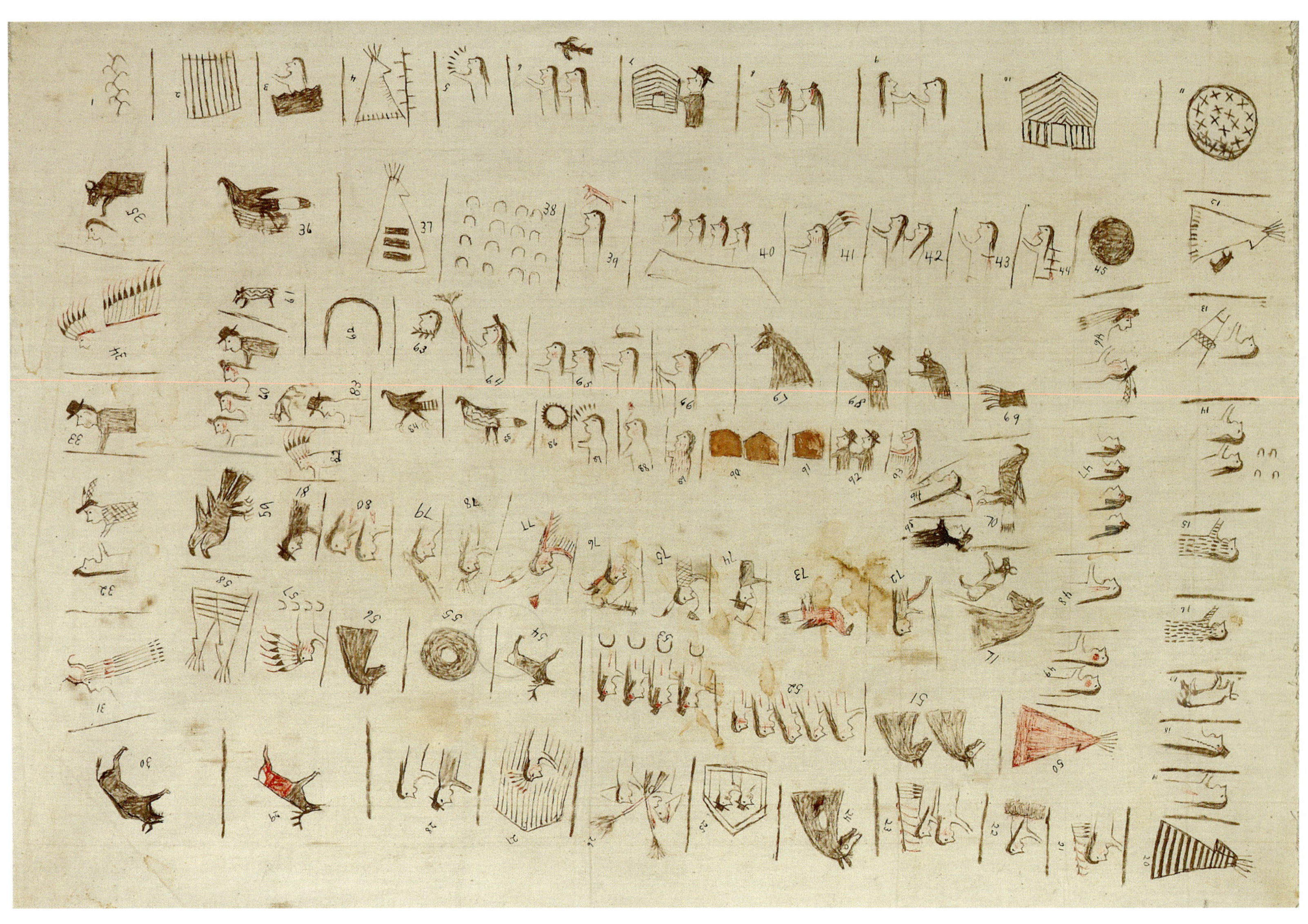

CAT. 117. Artist unknown, Nakota (Yankton Sioux), winter count, recording the years 1823–1917, about 1917, colored pencil and crayon on muslin. Purchased through the William S. Rubin Fund, the Guernsey Center Moore 1904 Memorial Fund, the William B. and Evelyn F. Jaffe (58, 60, & 63) Fund, the William B. and Evelyn A. Jaffe Hall Fund; 2009.65.

:: 6.5 ::

Plains: Recalling the Past and Illustrating the Present

Jenny Tone-Pah-Hote

> I dream of a great breadth of Indian art to develop that ranges through the whole region of our past, present, and future.
>
> —T. C. Cannon[1]

T. C. Cannon, a well-known painter, wrote the above for a brochure that accompanied an exhibition of his art at the Southern Plains Museum in Anadarko, Oklahoma, in 1971. His quotation, and paintings such as *Collector No. 5,* provokes questions about the interplay among the past, present, and future in Plains art. Objects in the Hood Museum of Art's collection span both historic and contemporary art forms that are all part of the individual and collective histories of Native peoples across the Plains. They demonstrate the multiple ways in which art serves as a bridge between the past and the present, and the ways artists create objects that illustrate bonds within families and communities and across broad audiences. In this essay, I will provide a brief overview of Hood objects from the Plains and discuss three of them in particular in relation to the above themes. I will examine the means through which T. C. Cannon engaged Native history as a site of commentary in the woodblock print of *Collector No. 5,* one of his most familiar paintings (cat. 120).

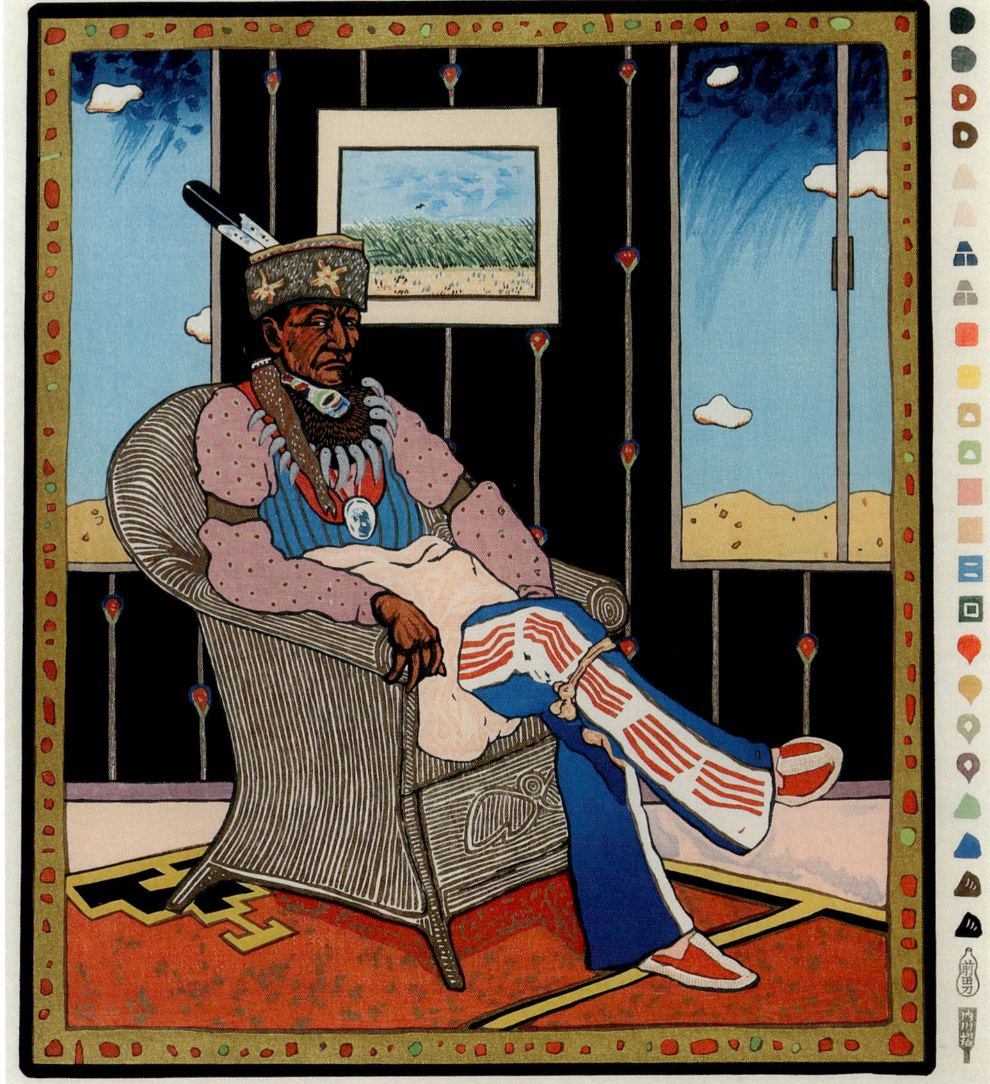

CAT. 120. T. C. Cannon, Gaigwa (Kiowa)/Caddo/Choctaw, Kentaro Maeda (woodblock carver) and Matashiro Uchikawa (printer), *Collector No. 5*, about 1977, color woodblock print. Purchased through the Stephen and Constance Spahn '63 Acquisition Fund and the Hood Museum of Art Acquisition Fund in honor of Barbara Thompson, Curator of African, Oceanic, and Native American Collections, Hood Museum of Art, 2002–2008; 2008.57.

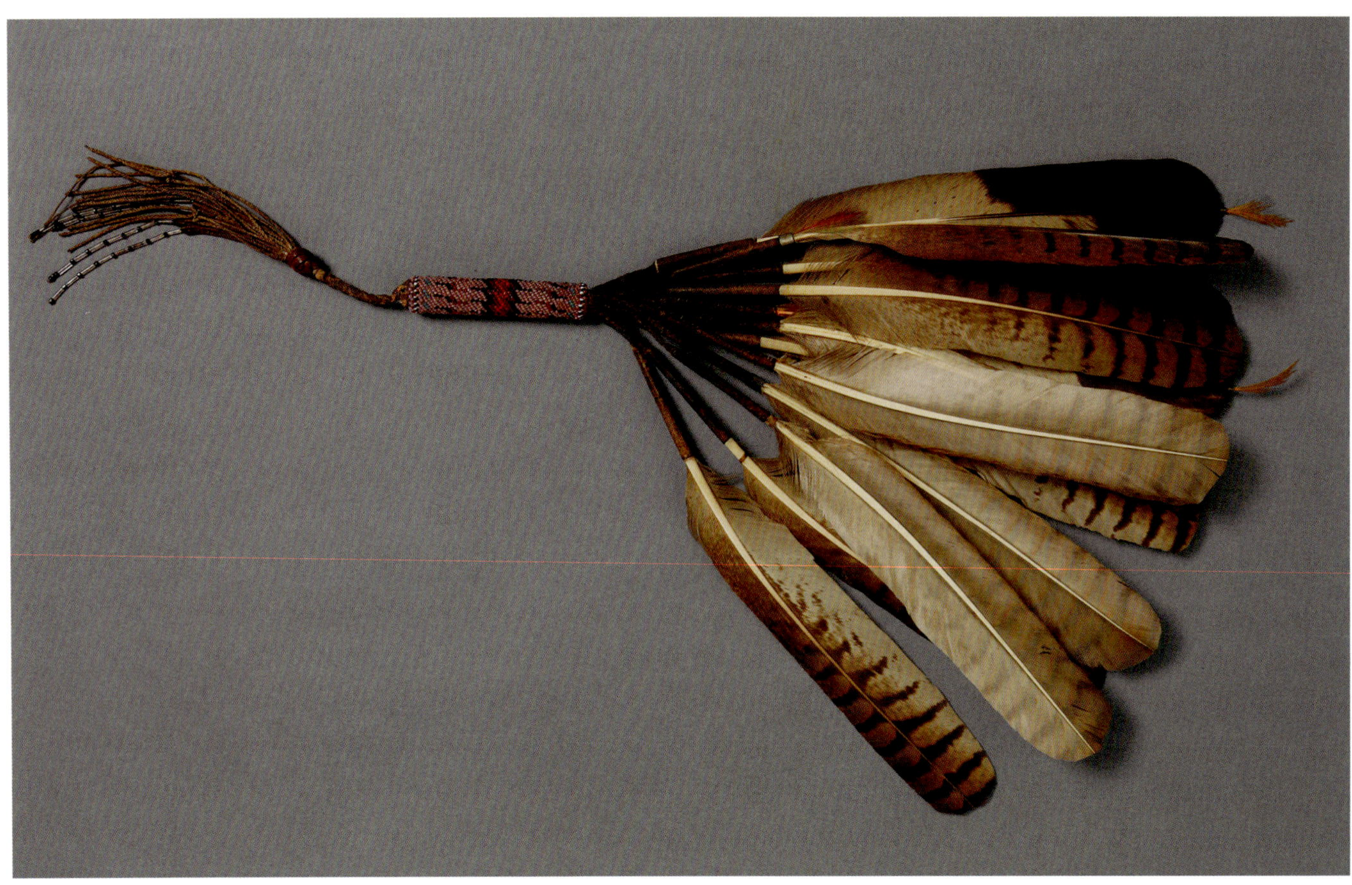

CAT. 128. Artist unknown, Southern Plains, peyote fan, about 1900, hawk feathers, eagle feathers, downy feathers, Native-tanned hide, rawhide, commercial leather, glass beads, metal, dye, and thread. Gift of Guido R. Rahr Sr., Class of 1951P; 985.47.26474.

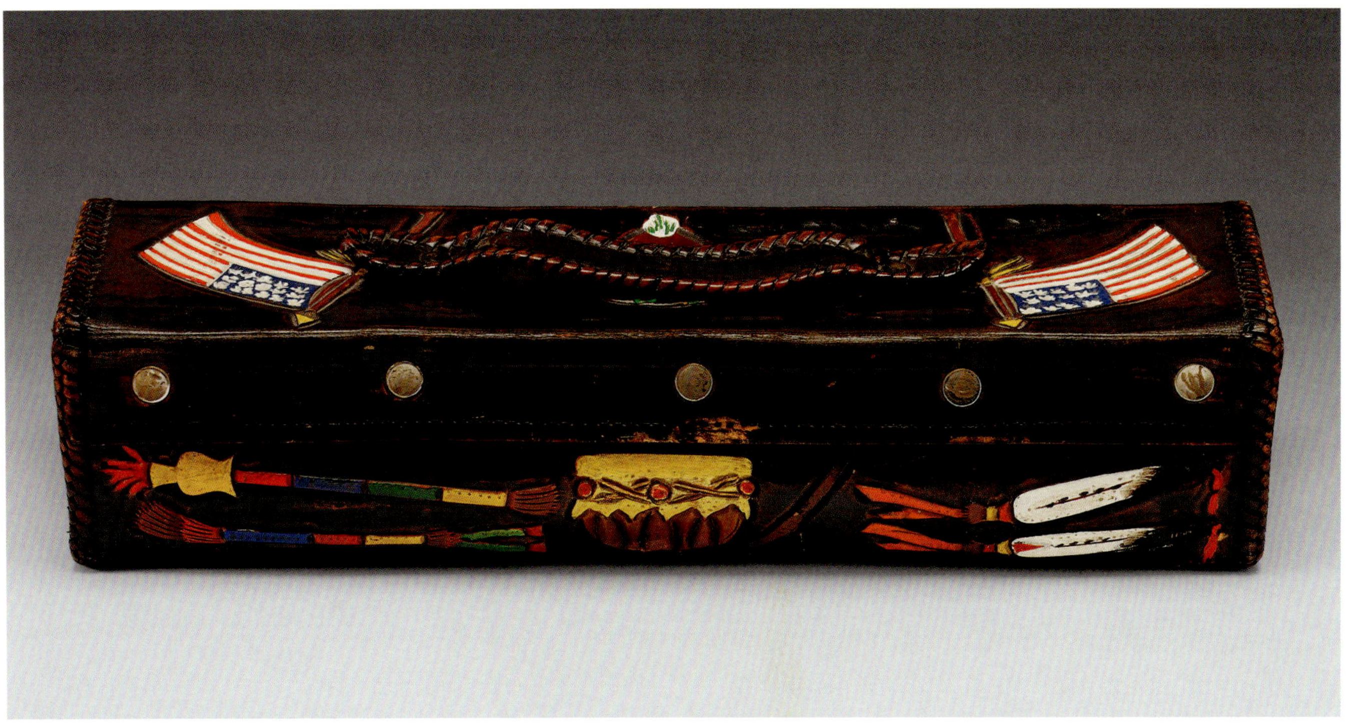

CAT. 122. Artist unknown, Gaigwa (Kiowa) or Niuam (Comanche), peyote box, about 1940, leather, paint, brass, metal, and thread. Purchased through the Endowment Fund for the Acquisition and Preservation of Native American Art and the Hood Museum of Art Acquisitions Fund; 2009.32.

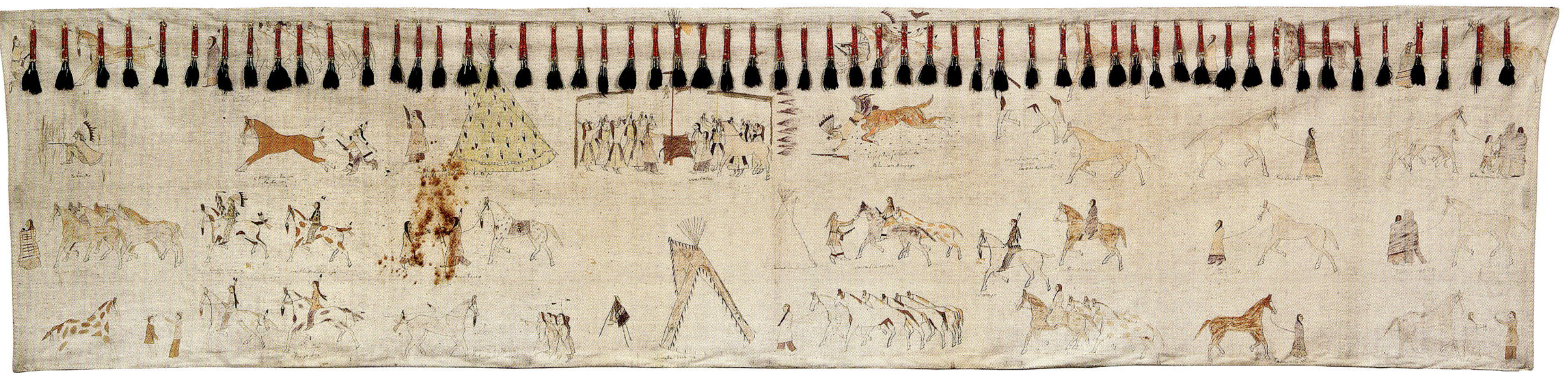

CAT. 113. Artist unknown, Lakota (Teton/Western Sioux) (Standing Rock), tipi liner, about 1910, muslin, paint, porcupine quills, rawhide, Native-tanned hide, cotton cloth, tin cones, dye, wool yarn, ink, string, and thread. Purchased through the Mrs. Harvey P. Hood W'18 Fund; 2009.10.

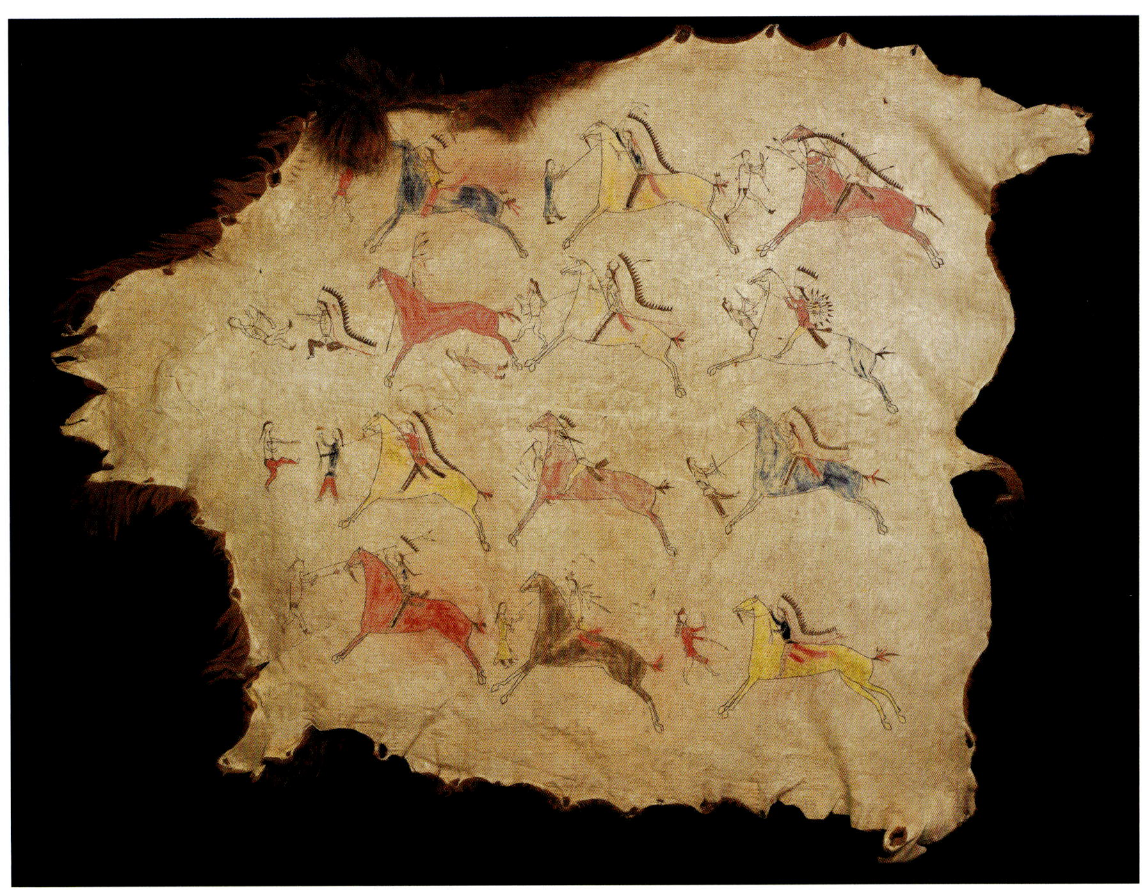

CAT. 111. Artist unknown, Lakota (Teton/Western Sioux), pictorial buffalo robe, about 1870, buffalo hide, paint, ink, and sinew. Purchased through the Florence and Lansing Porter Moore 1937 Fund; 2009.13.

As a whole, this collection represents the talents of nineteenth-, twentieth-, and twenty-first-century artists from Native nations across the Plains. It underscores the artistic accomplishments of unique men and women while also demonstrating how they have drawn inspiration from multiple sources. For example, the twentieth-century Southern Plains peyote fan and peyote box adorned with religious symbolism reflect the influence of the Native American Church upon art forms from this area and elsewhere (cats. 128 and 122). The collection also highlights the significance of gender in shaping Plains art. Historic pieces, such as the pictorial Lakota tipi liner and painted robe (cats. 113 and 111), highlight representational arts that emerged as men depicted their own deeds in battle. While men made many (though not all) of the paintings and drawings in this collection, women completed most of the objects, which illustrates their importance as artists in media such as beadwork, quillwork, and abstract painting on parflesche. Items of dress from the Northern Plains, such as the men's shirts and beaded pipe bags, demonstrate women's artistic skills and men's achievements as warriors. They also honor the individuals who wore and used them.

The Crow cradleboard (cat. 87), created in roughly 1880, is an excellent example of the ways in which women embraced new materials and incorporated them into their already rich arts of

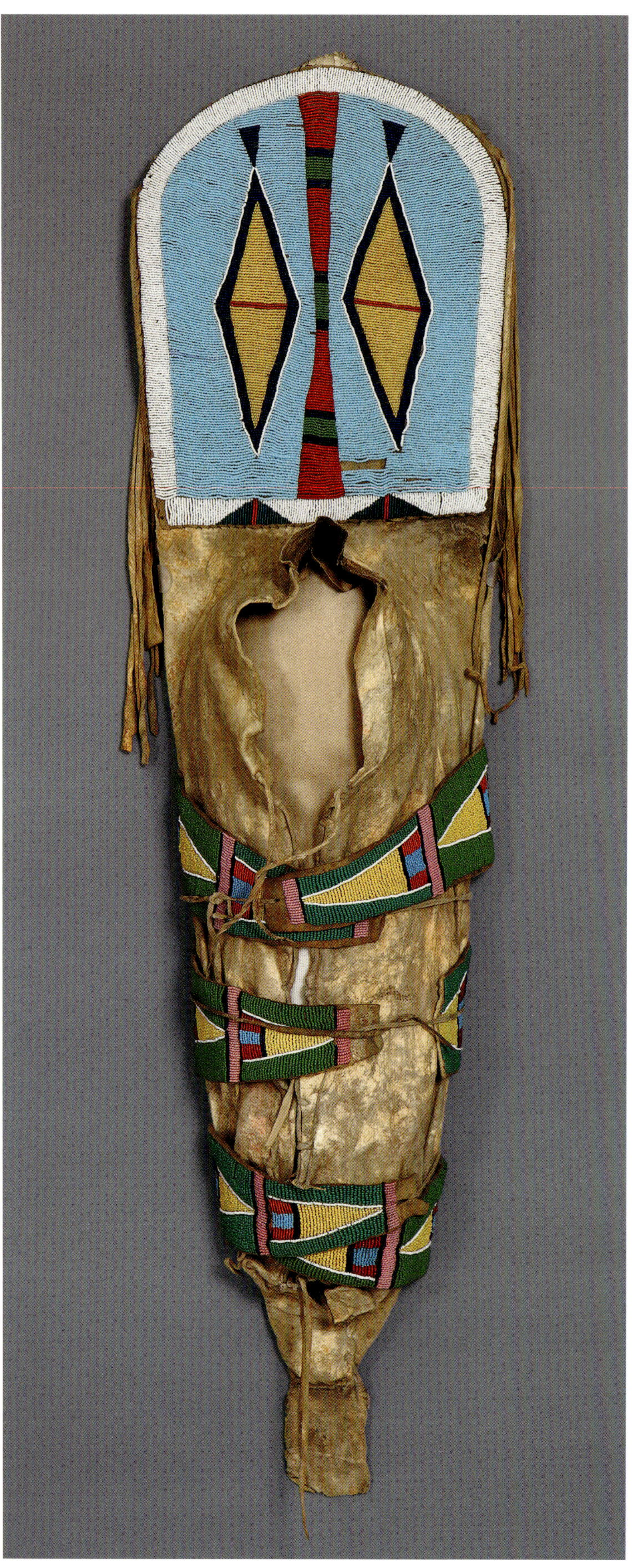

CAT. 87. Artist unknown, Apsáalooke (Crow/Absaroke), cradle, about 1880, Native-tanned deer or bison hide, wood, glass beads, sinew, paint, and thread. Gift of Guido R. Rahr Sr., Class of 1951P; 985.47.26532.

adornment during the nineteenth century. Though the Crow probably acquired beads through trade during the late 1700s, François Larocque, a trader, observed their use only in 1805, when beadwork served as a complement to quillwork. Women did not engage in beadwork as a major Crow art form until after 1850.[2] The designs in the beadwork of this cradleboard reveal links to older art forms such as abstract parflesche painting and quillwork. The top of the cradleboard features two yellow diamonds outlined in black and white on a light blue background, while the triangular straps feature another set of designs that mirrors their shape in long, multicolored triangles outlined in white beads. The long triangles and outlines of the beadwork recall the triangles and outlining seen on painted items made of parflesche. The smaller blocks of line designs featured at the base of the beaded flaps, used to hold the child in place, echo older quilled line and block motifs as well.[3]

Despite these clear influences, the artist has introduced her own vision into the beadwork of this piece through her skillful execution and composition of its designs, and through her use of color on the top and bottom portions of the cradleboard. Though the artist has incorporated some light blue, a color that many Crow women favor, she prefers yellow in the design and green as a background, thereby illustrating her own individual style and taste. Her evident skill would have earned her a great deal of respect and recognition within her community, and perhaps would have allowed her to influence the beadwork of others as well.[4]

In contrast, the Nakota "winter count" underscores the continuities of pictorial art over time (cat. 117; see p. 106), particularly in relation to maintaining unfolding tribal histories. Russell Thornton has explained that the term derives from the Lakota names for these records: *waniyetu wówapi* (literally, "winters they draw") and *waniyetu yawapi* ("winters they count").[5] This winter count, painted in 1917 on muslin, illustrates the history of a *tiospaye*, a larger family group that composed a band, and would have aided in the recollection of events that occurred in a year. These pictographic works, mnemonic devices for the winter count keeper and others, recorded events that entire bands would recognize and individuals could use to calculate their ages and to tell stories depicted in the winter count.[6]

Individual winter count keepers drew images of events that included particular battles, epidemics of disease, and ceremonial events. The late Vine Deloria Jr. describes winter counts as follows: "They indicated the psychic life of the community—what was important to that group of people as a group."[7] The winter count keeper was well versed in the narratives presented by the pictographic images.[8] Nakota and Lakota people have continued to tell their own family and local histories though winter counts even today.[9]

Like the cradleboard, this muslin winter count also demonstrates the ways in which artists elaborated upon their artistic traditions utilizing new media. Winter counts drawn on cloth are part of a larger spectrum of counts maintained on animal hides and on paper. Some later winter counts even added words to the pictographs, as Lakota people began using the written form of their language alongside pictographs to further describe important events.[10]

Contemporary artists, both men and women, have continued to build upon these various visual arts and the histories that they embody. The woodcut print of T. C. Cannon's *Collector No. 5* represents an important work by an artist who used elements and images from Native histories as he created pieces for late-twentieth-century audiences. Cannon was also attuned to the political changes that Native people sought during his own lifetime.[11] Cannon (Kiowa, Caddo, and Choctaw) was born in 1946 in Lawton, Oklahoma, and passed away in 1978. He was a Vietnam veteran who became part of the Kiowa Black Legs Society, an important military organization. He was also a writer and musician whose musical influences included Woody Guthrie and Bob Dylan.[12]

By the time Cannon taught at Dartmouth College in 1975, he had become an established artist. He attended the Institute of American Indian Arts, the San Francisco Art Institute, the College of Santa Fe, and the Central State University in Edmond, Oklahoma.[13] While serving in Vietnam, he prepared works for a prestigious exhibition hosted by the National Collection of Fine Art in 1972 called *Two American Painters*. The exhibition, which featured Cannon and his onetime teacher Fritz Scholder, traveled across Europe as well.[14]

The Hood Museum of Art's woodcut print from one of Cannon's most famous paintings is striking. It highlights his evident skill with the medium. It also expresses Cannon's philosophy about Native American art (see the quotation at the beginning of this essay). Basing his work on a historical photograph, Cannon creates an image of a collector, dressed in finery, comfortably sitting in front of Van Gogh's *Wheat Field*, possibly a recent acquisition of his. *Collector No. 5* conveys the conviction that Native peoples continue to craft contemporary, fluid identities that allow for multiple possibilities. In addition, his work synthesizes the influences of both early-twentieth-century American Indian painters and European artists like Van Gogh.[15] Cannon's use of lush, saturated colors in particular recalls Van Gogh but also the Kiowa Five and other Native artists who painted a generation before him. Cannon's interest in Native pasts that are rich in ideas and images as well as his present moment gave him a clear and unique voice and style that resonated with the intensified Native political activism of the 1960s and 1970s, through which Native people across the county sought their autonomy and the ability to present their own cultural and political visions. Cannon's *Collector No. 5* expresses those ideas as well.

Native artists from the past through the present have long made pieces that are deeply relevant to their families, communities, and the wider world, and the Plains works represented in the Hood Museum of Art's collections are no exception to this rule, incorporating "new" means and methods of art as diverse as colored beads and the painting of Van Gogh. Beautiful in their own right, these objects also demonstrate the relevance of art in the lives and histories of Native peoples.

NOTES

1. Quoted in Joan Frederick, *T. C. Cannon: He Stood in the Sun* (Flagstaff: Northland Publishing, 1995), 113.

2. William Wildschut and John Ewers, *Crow Indian Beadwork: A Descriptive and Historical Study* (New York: Museum of the American Indian, Heye Foundation, 1959), 48–50. I base my analysis of the cradleboard's beadwork on Wildschut and Ewers's discussion.

3. Ibid.

4. Robert H. Lowie, "Crow Indian Art," *Anthropological Papers of the American Museum of Natural History* 21 (New York: American Museum Press, 1924), 290.

5. Russell Thornton, "A Rosebud Reservation Winter Count, Circa 1751–1752 to 1886–1887," *Ethnohistory* 49, no. 4 (2002): 723.

6. Christina E. Burke, "Wani Yetu Wówapi: An Introduction to Lakota Winter Counts," in *Year the Stars Fell: Lakota Winter Counts at the Smithsonian* (Washington, D.C.: Smithsonian National Museum of Natural History, Smithsonian National Museum of the American Indian, in association with University of Nebraska Press, 2007), 3.

7. Vine Deloria Jr., *God Is Red: A Native View of Religion*, 2nd ed. (Golden: Fulcrum Publishing, 1992), 99.

8. Burke, "Wani Yetu Wówapi," 2.

9. For an example of a contemporary winter count, see Emil Her Many Horses, "Afterward: Tasunka Ota Win Waniyetu Wówapi (Her Many Horses Winter Count)," in *Year the Stars Fell: Lakota Winter Counts at the Smithsonian*.

10. Ibid., 4.

11. Frederick, *T. C. Cannon,* 112–13.

12. William Wallo and John Pickard, *T. C. Native American: A New View of the West* (Oklahoma City: Persimmon Hill Publication, 1990), 35–36.

13. Adelyn D. Breeskin, *Two American Painters: Fritz Scholder and T. C. Cannon* (Washington, D.C.: Smithsonian Institution Press, 1972), 18; Wallo and Pickard, *T. C. Native American,* 58.

14. Wallo and Pickard, *T. C. Native American,* 59–60.

15. Ibid., 76; Frederick, *T. C. Cannon,* 103.

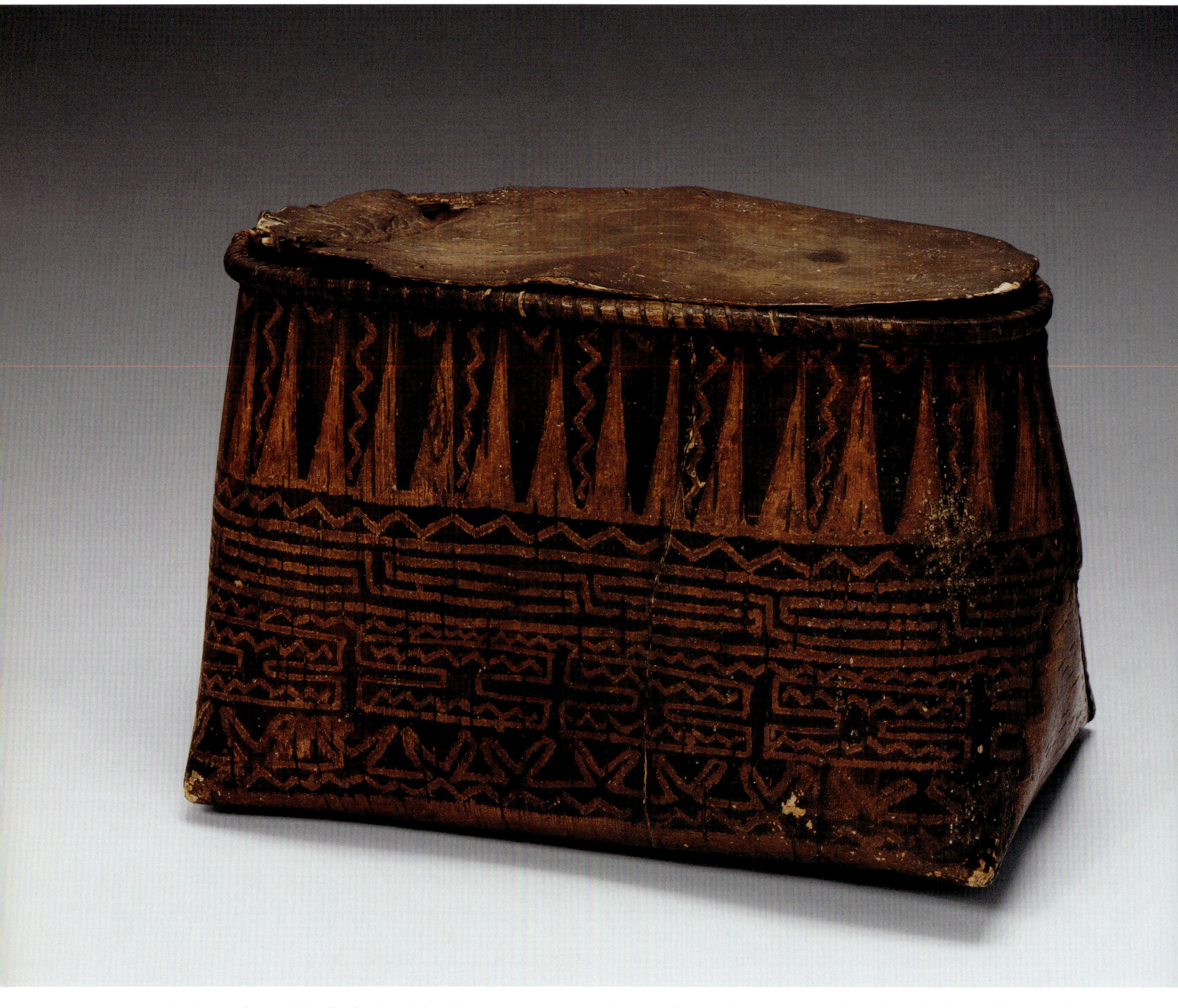

CAT. 148. Artist unknown, Woodlands, Great Lakes, Wisconsin area, container depicting the cosmological universe and, on the underside, two Thunderbirds, about 1800, birch bark, wood, spruce root, and twine (added later). Museum purchase; 163.66.15194.

:: 6.6 ::

Woodlands: Symbolism and Cosmology

Sherry Brydon

The Woodlands collection of the Hood Museum of Art features examples of many of the fine contributions made by northeastern Native American artists to the world of art. These works fulfilled a variety of personal purposes and reveal a great depth of creative expression and cultural meaning. The majority of the pieces, including bandolier bags (cat. 142), which are particularly well represented in the collection, cradles (cat. 144), and clothing (cats. 154 and 155), were made for the family and affirmed the values of the community. Particularly intriguing are those objects made primarily for sale, because they betray no loss of quality or care; while the Anishinaabeg basket (cat. 143) and Haudenosaunee beaded bag (cat. 152) and clothing (cats. 154 and 155) were intended for the market, for example, they display an uncompromising aesthetic, excellence of execution, and a sense of history and cultural ideals.

Some of these works also refer to Native American spirituality.[1] The geometric motifs around the outside of the Anishinaabeg basket likely allude to ancient Great Lakes aesthetic and religious traditions. The lid is quilled in a delicate floral pattern, while its rim is largely decorated with natural, undyed quills, except for red and green dyed quills acknowledging the four sacred cardinal directions. In this context, then, the floral element at the center possibly represents the Middle World, or land, amid the symbolism of the cosmological universe. The beadworker who made the Haudenosaunee bag included a central heart motif that dominates the design, likely drawing her inspiration from the heart imagery incorporated into Haudenosaunee cradles, clubs, pipes, knives, and silverwork, as well as another equally powerful influence: for more than four hundred years, many Haudenosaunee have found faith in Roman Catholic teachings, and Catholic devotional images of the Sacred Heart of Jesus and Immaculate Heart of Mary treat the physical heart as a symbol of spirituality and reverence. Two sun symbols bracket the heart motif, asserting and celebrating Native American expressions of spirituality and belief in tandem with it.[2] Artists often included their spirituality in their work, whether it was intended for personal use or for trade; it could be part of the ephemeral act of creating the object itself, or subject to restrained and sometimes elusive representations, or the inspiration for richly symbolic designs.

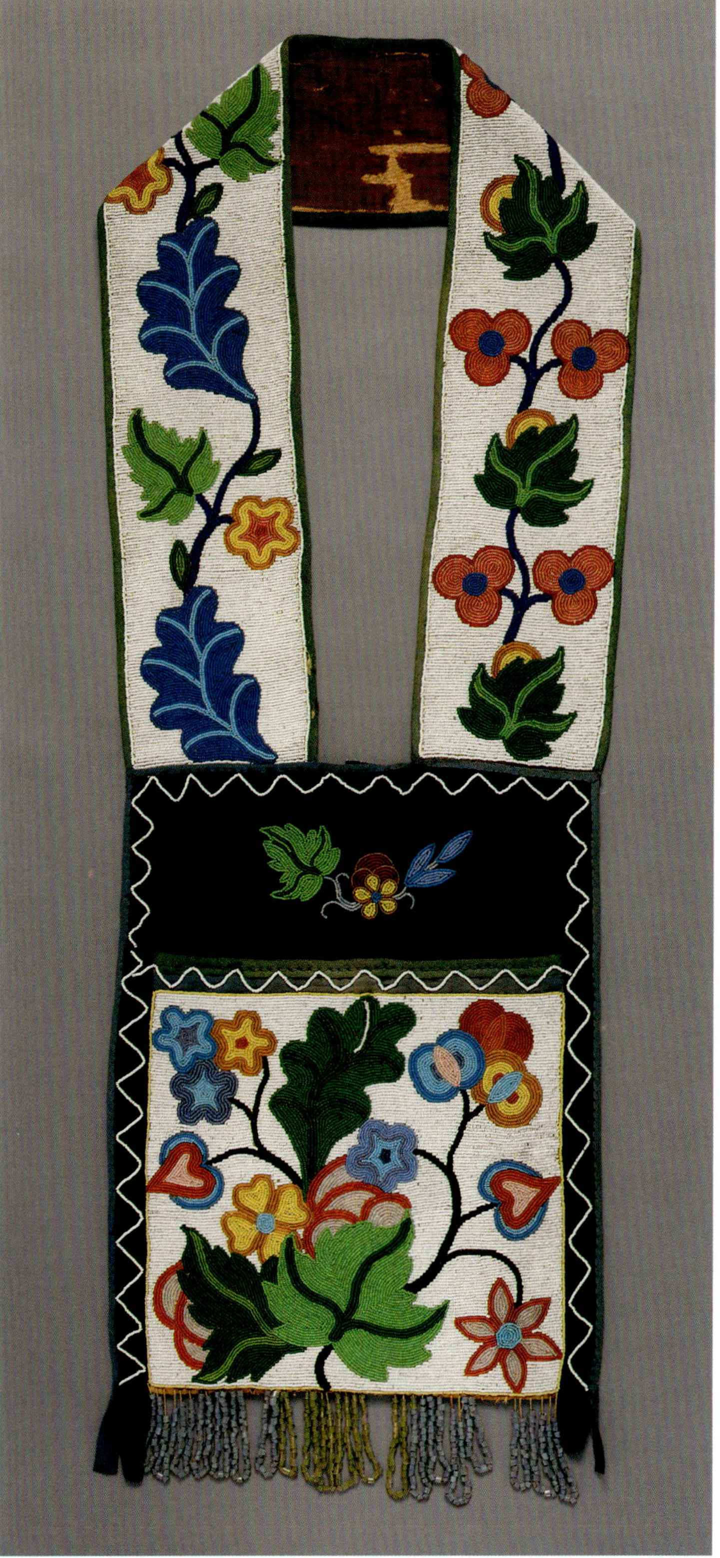

CAT. 142. Artist unknown, Anishinaabeg (Chippewa/Ojibwa), White Earth Reservation, Minnesota, bandolier bag, about 1890, glass beads, cotton cloth, velveteen, wool binding tape, string, and thread. Gift of Glover Street Hastings III; 181.2.26046.

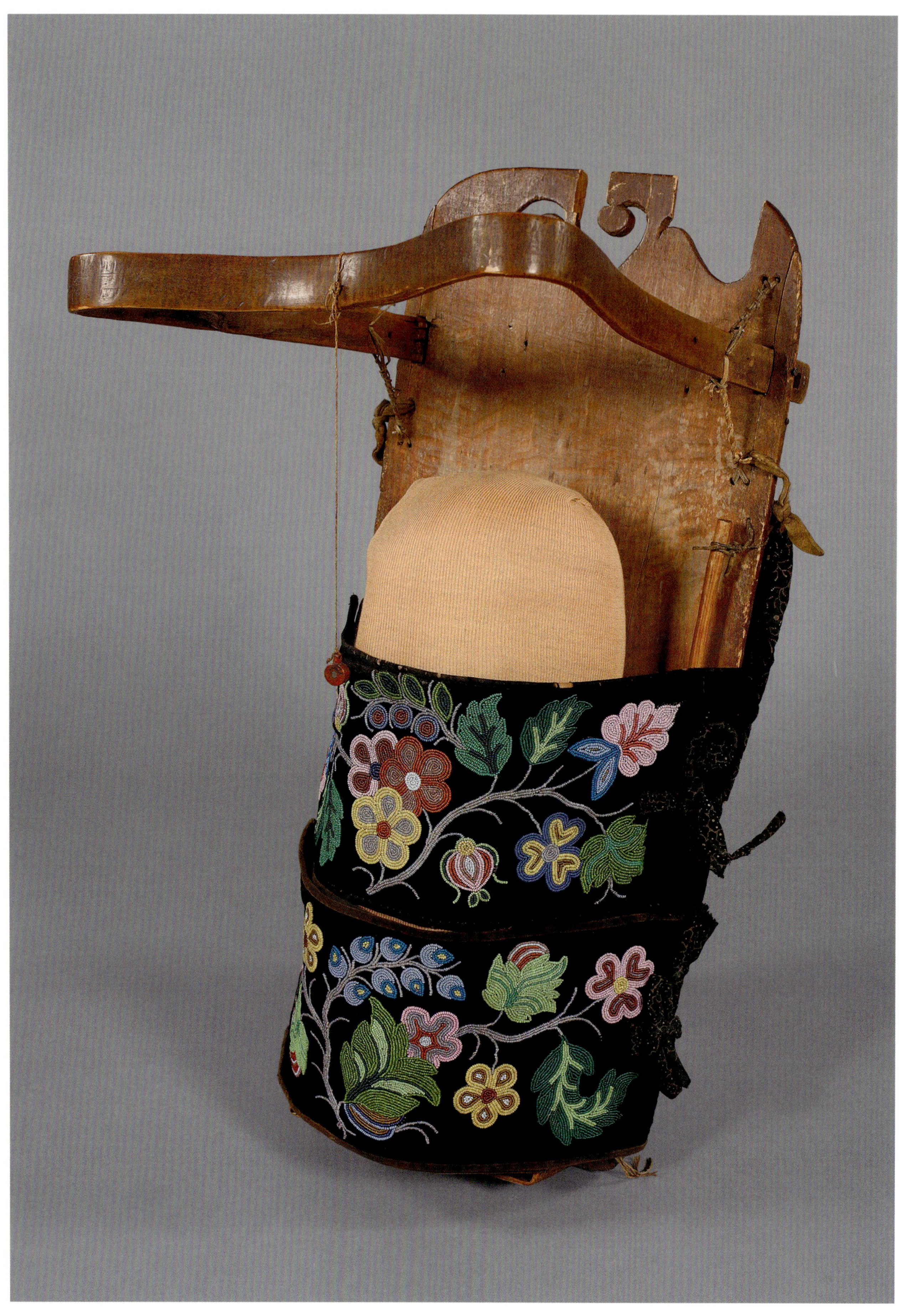

CAT. 144. Artist unknown, Anishinaabeg (Chippewa/Ojibwa), cradle, about 1890, wood, birch bark, velveteen, cotton cloth, glass beads, hide, rawhide, metal, catlinite, lead, twine, and thread. Gift of Guido R. Rahr Sr., Class of 1951P; 985.47.26533.

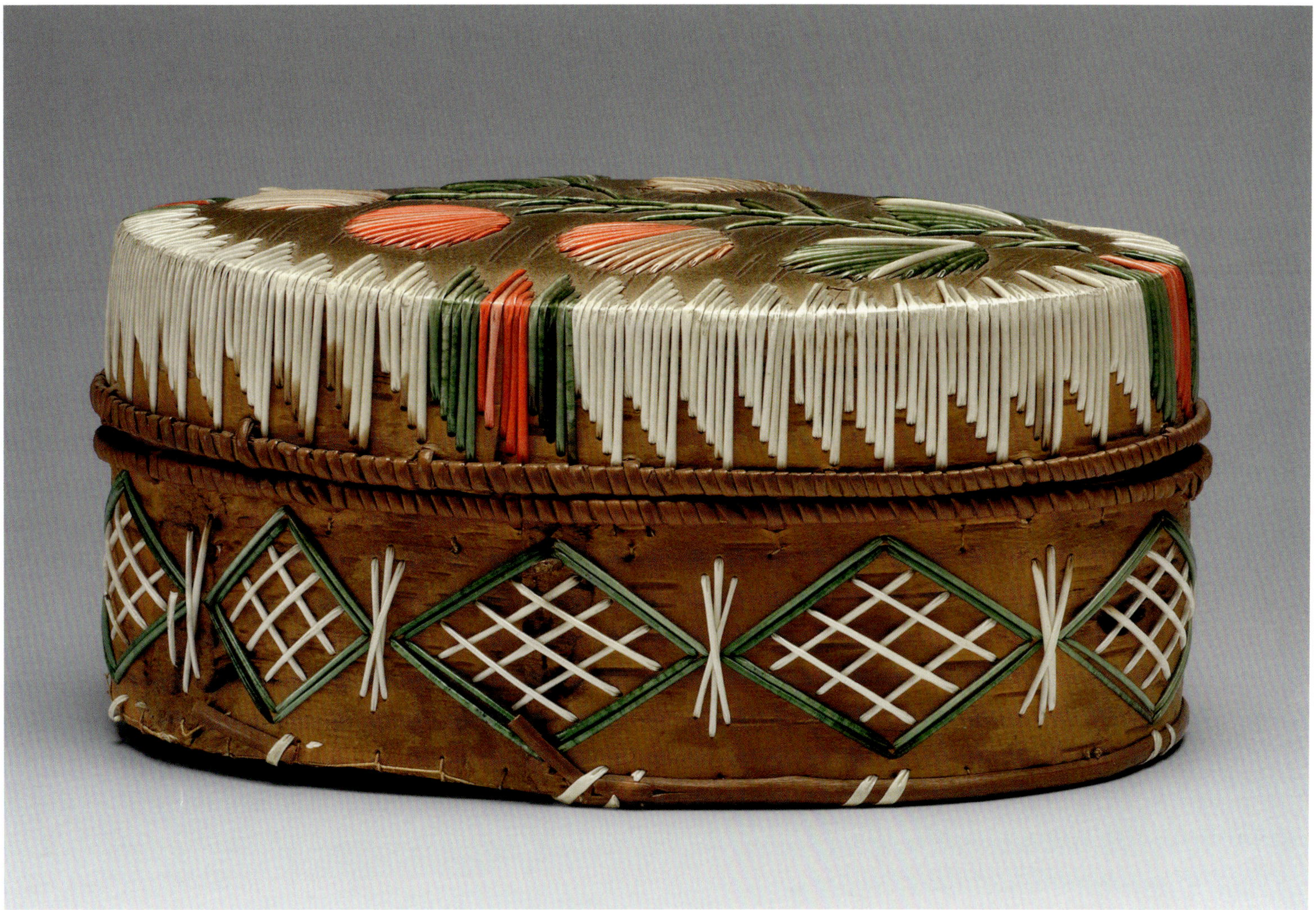

CAT. 143. Artist unknown, Anishinaabeg (Chippewa/Ojibwa), basket, about 1900, birch bark, spruce root, wood, porcupine quills, thread, and dye. Bequest of Frank C. and Clara G. Churchill; 46.17.9562.

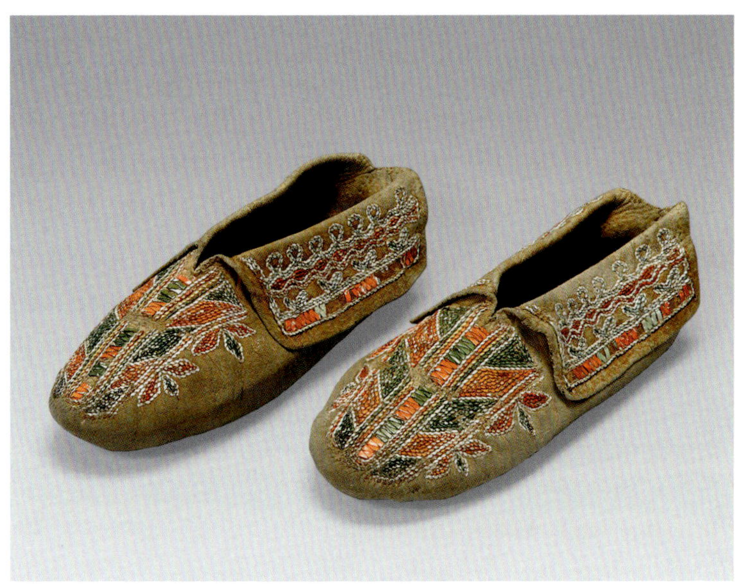

CAT. 154. Artist unknown, Seneca; Haudenosaunee (Iroquois), New York, moccasins, about 1820, deer hide, porcupine quills, dye, sinew, ribbon, thread. Gift of Robert G. Chaffee, Class of 1936; 159.14.14400.

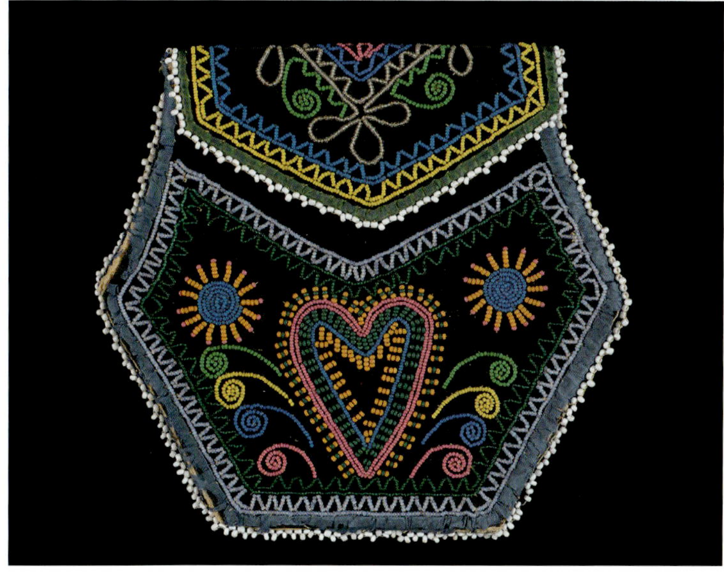

CAT. 152. Artist unknown, Seneca; Haudenosaunee (Iroquois), New York, bag, about 1830, glass beads, velvet, cotton cloth, ribbon, and thread. Purchased through the Mrs. Harvey P. Hood W'18 Fund and the Hood Museum of Art Acquisitions Fund; 2009.4.

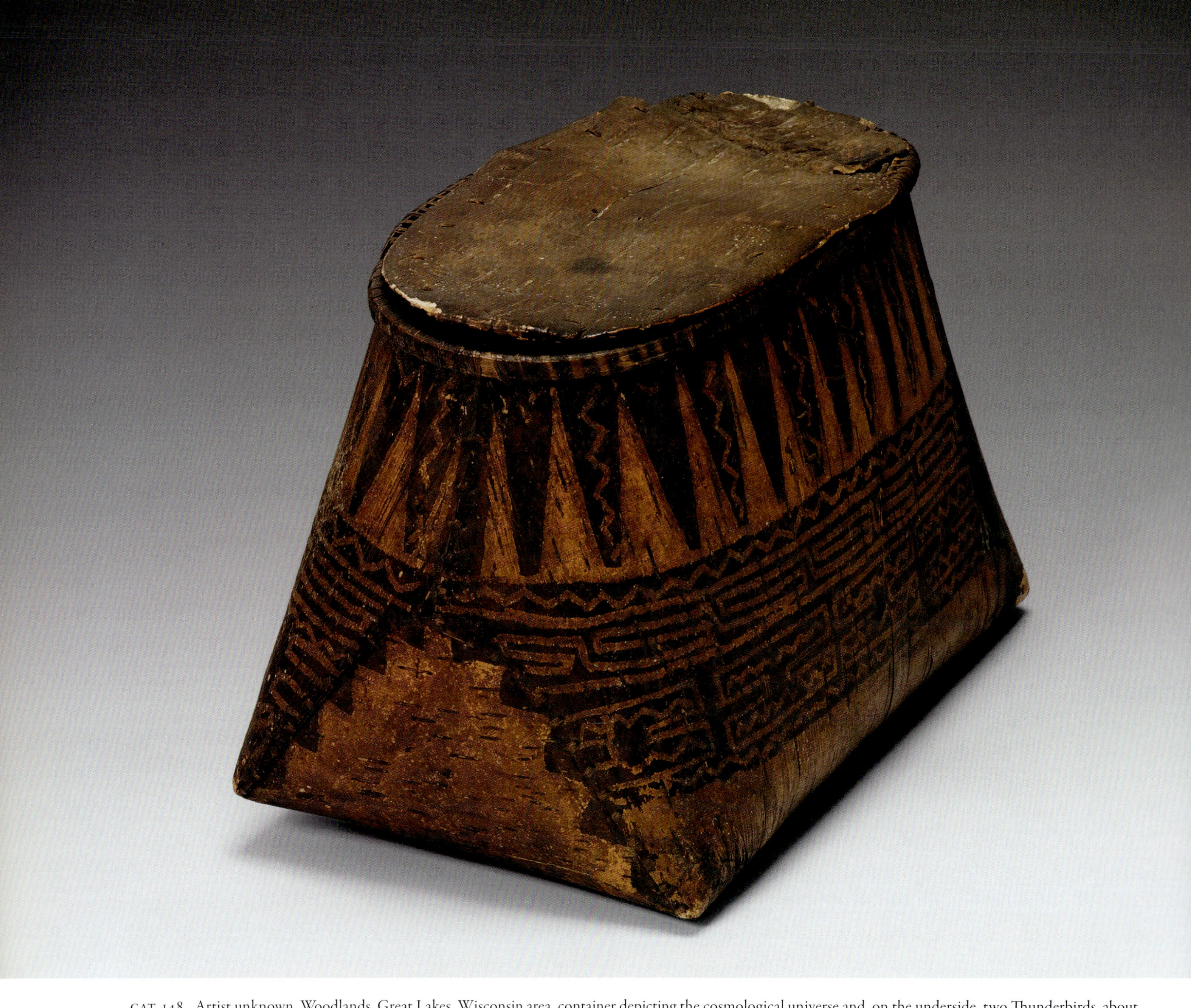

CAT. 148. Artist unknown, Woodlands, Great Lakes, Wisconsin area, container depicting the cosmological universe and, on the underside, two Thunderbirds, about 1800, birch bark, wood, spruce root, and twine (added later). Museum purchase; 163.66.15194.

The Hood Museum of Art has a work in its collection that is particularly distinguished for its considerable depth of symbolism, and I will describe it here at some length. Approximately two hundred years ago, an Anishnaabe artist living in the Western Great Lakes area incised this birchbark container (cat. 148; see also p. 112) with powerful symbols that evoke the cosmological universe and their rulers. This abstract and stylized imagery has an extensive symbolic vocabulary, a network of layered meanings that envisions a great and ordered cosmos. These symbols reach back to the peoples of the Mississippian era (1000–1600 CE), the ancestors of the Woodlands and Plains Indians. Some of the most fundamental aspects of the cultural and spiritual experiences of the Woodlands and Plains cultures are symbolized in this exceptional container.

The imagery focuses upon the two realms of the Native American cosmos: the Above World and the Underwater World. The Middle World is generally not represented as such but is understood to be the space between the Above World and the Underwater World—an island that floats on a great body of water. The realm of the Middle World, however, may be referenced in the materiality of this object. The tough bark of the birch tree forms the container, wooden splints reinforce the rim, and spruce roots secure the splints to the outer edge of the rim. Nourishment from the Middle World also provided life for trees in general, and, consequently, for the objects made from them. The inner bark of the birch tree is dark, and the artist here has incised its soft surface to expose the lighter color underneath, using a technique known as *sgraffito* to create the imagery that expresses the most essential qualities of the Above World and the Underwater World. On the top half of the container, a row of vertical triangles represents the Above World; on the bottom half, a horizontal band of linear designs represents the Underwater World. The background of the Above World zone is light, and the massing of the composition is fairly open. The tapering triangles circle the opening of the container, and their apex points downward at the Underwater World. In contrast to the Above World, the background of the Underwater World is dark. The composition is deep and the symbols are densely massed, evoking the fathomless waters of this realm.

The two realms portrayed on this container represent a cosmic universe of immeasurable consequence in which two powerful supernaturals, or manitous—the Thunderbird of the Above World and the Great Horned Underwater Panther of the Underwater World—hold power. The Thunderbird and the Underwater Panther are forever engaged in a cosmic clash for dominance, a war of no retreat and no advance in a place of eternal time, space, and energy. The Thunderbird and the Underwater Panther rule over environments that are beyond the perception and immediate access of humans. As such, both manitous are sources of power for hunters, warriors, and healers, who seek their assistance through fasting and prayer. A revelatory dream or vision reveals the blessing of a manitou for an individual, who then receives it as a guardian spirit. Hunters, warriors, and healers honored this guardian spirit through dedicated spiritual practices and symbolic references on both ritual and personal objects.

Below the container's rim here, a row of elongated triangles, each of which represents a stylized feather, symbolizes the Thunderbird. Every second triangle has a light-toned zigzagged line down the center to evoke the lightning bolts that Thunderbirds shoot from their eyes and their flapping wings. Thunderbirds are closely associated with raptorial birds and share the power of flight, allowing them access to the Above World and the Middle World as well. In addition, both Thunderbirds and raptorial birds are formidable and aggressive predators, exemplifying the traits that warriors and hunters honored. In Mississippian times, objects such as copper poussé plates, ceramic vessels, effigy pipes, and shell masks and gorgets portrayed warrior chiefs with raptorial markings around their eyes, some of which were also detailed with lightning bolts.[3] By the early 1800s, Thunderbirds with lightning symbols appear on Great Lakes twined bags, quill-embroidered black-dyed pouches, and beaded bandolier bags.[4] These highly valued pouches and bags were worn by hunters and healers. Thunderbirds with jagged lightning-bolt imagery were also painted on the vision-inspired designs of Plains drums and war shields and incised on Woodlands and Plains war clubs.[5]

The encircling tapered triangles on the Hood's container also refer to the life-giving rays of the sun. Between 1000 and 1400 CE sun ray motifs appear in the center of Mississippian shell gorgets that were worn by warriors and spiritual leaders.[6] Such sun symbolism also appears on nineteenth-century Plains warriors' clothing, specifically in the painted "sunburst" or "feathered-circle" designs of buffalo robes, as concentric circles of radiating triangles or mirror-image triangles.[7] Sun symbolism is also represented in Plains war shields. The circular shape of the shield is the sun's disc, and the eagle feathers around the circumference are its radiating rays.[8] Similarly, sun ray and feather symbolism are evident in the circular arrangement of eagle feathers in the headdresses worn by Plains warriors. Each triangle on this Great Lakes birchbark container is both a feather plume and a ray of the sun.

The Underwater World symbols on this container, as noted above, are emphasized through the darkness of the dense patterning, which alludes to watery depths. A band of wavy lines frames the top and bottom of the Underwater World and appears internally in the H-shaped elements.[9] Underwater World and wave symbolism often appear together. A finely carved heddle in the Thaw Collection at Fenimore Art Museum embodies these elements as well, with two stylized Underwater Panthers poised atop it with their long tails dropping along the sides into waves depicted along the bottom.[10] This common association arises from the belief that waves and whirlpools came about as a result of the Underwater Panther whipping its powerful, long tail around in the water. Some Woodlands and Plains ball-headed war clubs have long-tailed animals carved at the top to aid the warrior spiritually; other war clubs and pipes portray associated Underwater beings with various waveform symbols.[11] These symbols in effect double as waves of moving water and as the ridged back of the Underwater Panther, and versions of them ranging from stylized to quite abstract also often appeared on twined bags, quill-embroidered black-dyed bags, and small beaded pouches.[12] Medicines, amulets, and vision-inspired objects were commonly stored and protected in these bags. The density of symbols on the lower half of the birchbark container may also relate to abundance in general or to the wealth associated with the Underwater World in particular. Precious metals such as copper contributed to one's prestige and power, and this source of wealth came from the scaly covering of the Underwater Panther's body. Although the Underwater Panthers bestowed certain gifts upon warriors and others, they were also associated with the inherent danger of the open water, wind, and weather. Offerings, especially from travelers making their way by canoe over large bodies of water, were therefore made to the Underwater World's manitou.

The axis mundi, or central tree, is the spiritual and metaphysical connector of the Above World, Middle World, and Underwater World. It is the sacred center of the universe—the meeting place of the four cardinal directions—and it represents the means by which a shaman travels through the realms. Perhaps the act of inserting important objects through the opening of the birchbark container

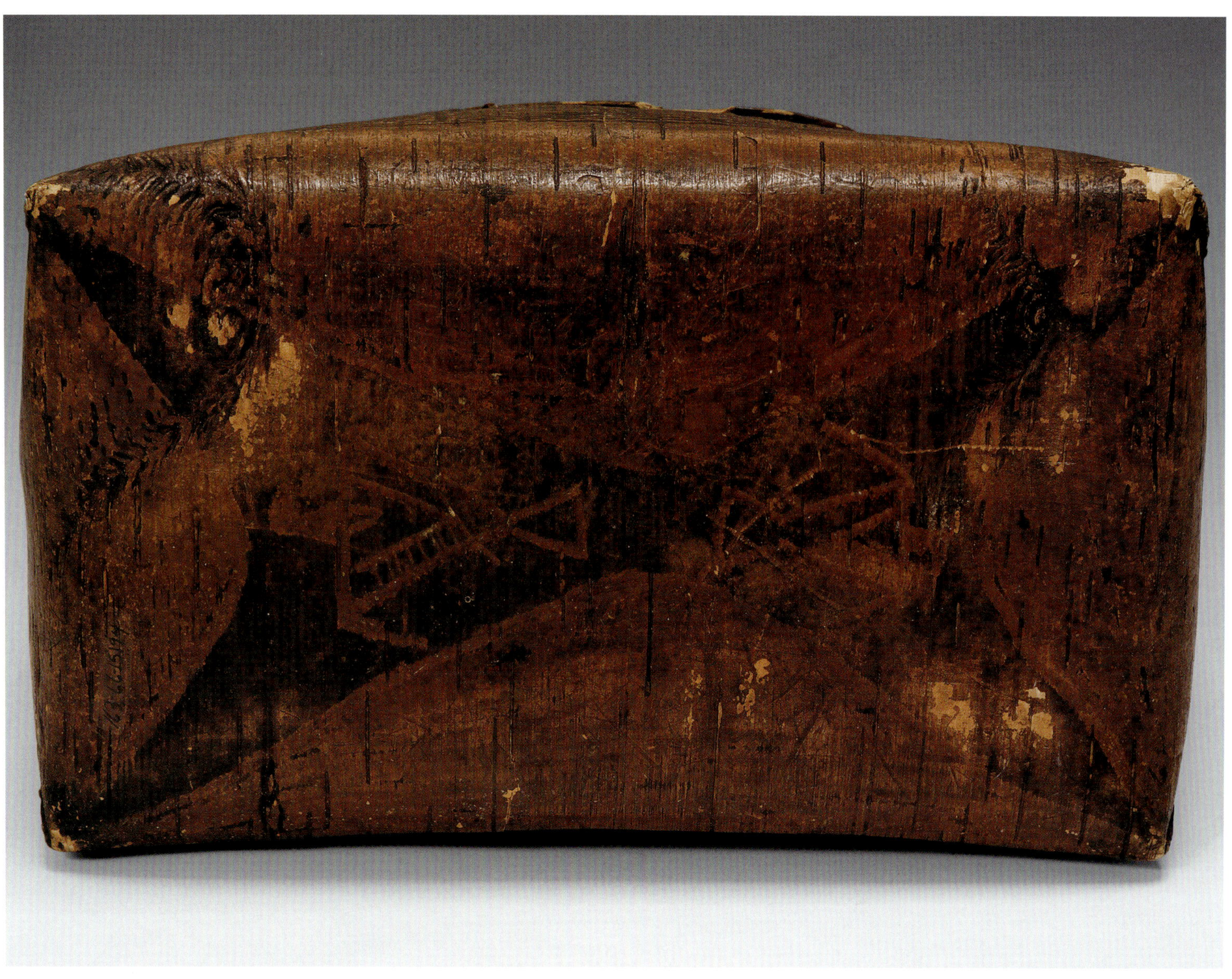

FIG. 6.6.1. Detail of two Thunderbirds from cat. 148, Artist unknown, Woodlands, Great Lakes, Wisconsin area, container depicting the cosmological universe and, on the underside, two Thunderbirds, about 1800, birch bark, wood, spruce root, and twine (added later). Museum purchase; 163.66.15194.

(and symbolically through the three realms of the cosmos) was meant to evoke the axis mundi as a metaphorical safeguard for them within a cosmological universe.[13]

Finally, two stylized representations of Thunderbirds appear on the bottom of this extraordinary container (fig. 6.6.1). They are perfect mirror images except for the orientation of the heads, which oppose one another, facing eastward and westward, respectively. The outlined bodies of the Thunderbirds are angular, with an hourglass shape, and executed in bold lines, while their heads are completely and emphatically incised. Two different hands appear to be at work in their creation—one Thunderbird is more sharply angled, has broader but shorter wings and a more prominent head, and has a body and tail that meet at a distinct point, while the other does not.

Both Thunderbirds display heartlines, a reference to the life force. These heartlines are symbolized by a single triangle or V-shape on the chest on one Thunderbird and a double V-shape on the other one.[14] As noted earlier, twined bags, black-dyed bags, small beaded pouches, war clubs, and pipes also typically portrayed Thunderbirds, many with similar heartline representations. The bottom of the container has a reddish appearance that is most obvious in the incised lines of the Thunderbirds, especially on their heads, where ochre, a pigment with ancient significance and spiritual associations, was applied to the surface after it was worked. Ochre, and the color red in general, signified life force, vitality, and general wellbeing.[15] The skeletal markings at the ribcage of one of the Thunderbirds refer to shamanic power, likely alluding to the shaman's ability to die and be reborn. In this act of transcendence and transformation, shamans discard their flesh, leaving only their skeleton, as they cross the boundary from life to death to perform healing and receive visions and finally journey back to the living. The shaman's ability to communicate with animal spirits and change between human and animal form also inspires this powerful imagery.

The Anishinaabeg used birchbark containers of this type and construction extensively to store food. Birchbark possesses a natural preservative, betulin, that helps prolong foodstuffs by resisting spoiling and fungal outbreaks. This unique container may have held medicines or other important items as well, much like the aforementioned bags and pouches; it is one of only three known from the western Great Lakes that date to the early nineteenth century. There are two birchbark containers presently in Italy that can be compared to this exceptional container. Collected in 1823 west of Lake Superior by G. Costantino Beltrami, the containers feature *sgraffito* imagery like the Hood's that includes symbols of the Underwater World and the four cardinal directions.[16] A small vertical split on one side of the Hood container has been repaired with three spruce root stitches, likely by the original owner, and the top stitch appears to have broken shortly after repair, given the even tone of the surface area. (Large splits have since caused damage to both sides). A book dealer purchased the container in the Midwest, and Dartmouth College acquired it in 1963. Although very little is known of its precise background, a partial history of this container appears in its rich symbolism, a testament to the cosmic landscape of the many Native Americans whose ancestors came from the Great Lakes region, and earlier from the ancient Midwest and South.

NOTES

1. Ruth B. Phillips, *Trading Identities: The Souvenir in Native North American Art from the Northeast, 1700–1900* (Seattle: University of Washington Press, 1998), 195–96.

2. This juxtaposition of a heart motif with two sun symbols sometimes reads as a face as well; see Gerry and Jo-Anne Biron, *Made of Thunder, Made of Glass: American Indian Beadwork of the Northeast* (published by Gerry Biron, 2006), p. 9, fig. 7, a circa 1822 example (see also p. 21, fig. 16); see also Gilbert Vincent, et al., *Art of the North American Indians: The Thaw Collection* (Cooperstown: New York State Historical Association, in association with the University of Washington Press, 2000), 43, T689. Sun symbols also appear on the Potawatomi bandolier bag (cat. 147) and the top of the man's cap (cat. 155) in this publication.

3. David H. Dye, "Art, Ritual, and Chiefly Warfare in the Mississippian," in *Hero, Hawk, and Open Hand: American Indian Art of the Ancient Midwest and South,* ed. Richard F. Townsend (Chicago: Art Institute of Chicago, in association with Yale University Press, 2004), p. 190, fig. 1; F. Kent Reilly III, "People of Earth, People of Sky: Visualizing the Sacred in Native American Art of the Mississippian Period," in Townsend, *Hero, Hawk, and Open Hand,* p. 130, fig. 10. Some Underwater Panthers from the Mississippian period also had raptorial markings around their eyes.

4. Ruth B. Phillips, "Dreams and Designs: Iconographic Problems in Great Lakes Twined Bags," in *Great Lakes Indian Art,* ed. David W. Penney (Detroit: Wayne State University Press, 1989), p. 55, fig. 3; Jonathan King, *Thunderbird and Lightning: Indian Life in Northeastern North America* (London: Trustees of the British Museum by British Museum Publications, 1982), p. 65, fig. 71; *Art of the Great Lakes Indians* (Flint, Mich.: Flint Institute of Arts, 1973), p. 58, fig. 225.

5. Vincent, *Art of the North American Indians*, p. 123, T86; p. 107, T53a,b.

6. George E. Lankford, "World on a String: Some Cosmological Components of the Southeastern Ceremonial Complex," in Townsend, *Hero, Hawk, and Open Hand*, p. 208, fig. 2.

7. Evan Maurer, *Visions of the People: A Pictorial History of Plains Indian Life* (Minneapolis: Minneapolis Institute of Art, 1992), pp. 190–91, fig. 148; Vincent, *Art of the North American Indians*, p. 156, T50.

8. Ted J. Brasser, "By the Power of their Dreams," in *The Spirit Sings: Artistic Traditions of Canada's First Peoples,* ed. Julia D. Harrison (Toronto: McClelland and Stewart, 1987), 117.

9. On one side of this container, there is an additional wavy line that appears in the middle of the composition; above the bottom wavy line, there is a running line of small V-shaped elements. This symbol also appears on Iroquois moccasins from the same period (see this publication, p. 115).

10. Vincent, *Art of the North American Indians*, p. 63, T310.

11. Ruth B. Phillips, "Northern Woodlands," in *The Spirit Sings: Artistic Traditions of Canada's First Peoples: A Catalogue of the Exhibition,* ed. Julia D. Harrison (Toronto: McClelland and Stewart, 1987), p. 59, W98; Douglas Ewing, *Pleasing the Spirits: A Catalogue of a Collection of American Indian Art* (New York: Ghylen Press, 1982), p. 125, fig. 77; Vincent, *Art of the North American Indians*, p. 106, T54.

12. Phillips, "Dreams and Designs," p. 57, fig. 8; Ted J. Brasser, *"Bo'jou, Neejee!": Profiles of Canadian Indian Art* (Ottawa: National Museum of Man, 1976), p. 53, fig. 60, p. 97; American Museum of Natural History 50/9742.

13. The Hood's yarn bag, cat. 146, likely symbolizes the cosmological universe—the feather-like motif represents the Above World, the diamond is associated with the Middle World, and, on the bottom panel, the otter tail motif refers to the Underwater World. Phillips, "Dream and Designs," pp. 63–67.

14. These triangle or V-shaped heartlines, either outlined or infilled, were often seen in other media as well, especially twined bags.

15. Ruth B. Phillips, *Patterns of Power: The Jasper Grant Collection and Great Lakes Indian Art of the Early Nineteenth Century* (Kleinburg, Ontario: McMichael Canadian Collection, 1984), p. 89, fig. 89, pp. 51–52; Richard Conn, *Native American Art in the Denver Art Museum* (Seattle: University of Washington Press, 1979), p. 88, fig. 93.

16. Ruth B. Phillips, "Like a Star I Shine: Northern Woodlands Artistic Traditions," in Harrison, *The Spirit Sings,* p. 90, fig. 84; Leonardo Vigorelli, *Gli Oggetti Indiani Raccolti Da G. Constantino Beltrami* (Bergamo, Italy: Civico Museo E. Caffi, 1987), p. 83, fig. 31, p. 53 and p. 13, fig. 32, p. 54. The Beltrami containers also have diamond motifs, equal-armed crosses, and small circles linked at regular intervals in a line incised on the exterior surfaces.

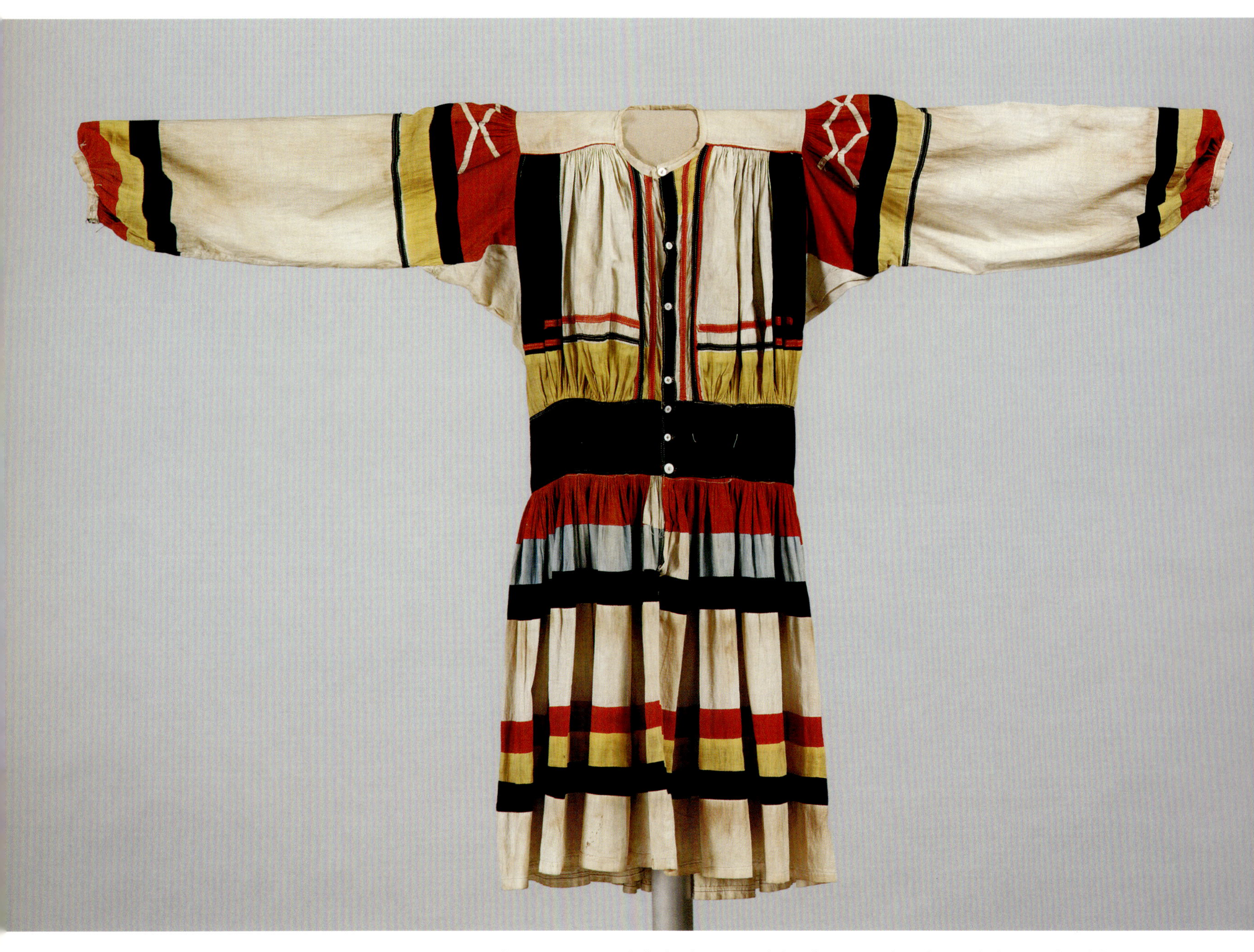

CAT. 161. Artist unknown, Seminole, man's shirt tunic, about 1900, cotton cloth, dye, buttons, and thread. Bequest of Frank C. and Clara G. Churchill; 46.17.9956.

:: 6.7 ::

Southeast: Ancient Concepts, Modern Arts

Leah Bowe

The Southeast as an indigenous culture region is an enormous and varied area. In historic times, it included the states of Florida, Georgia, the Carolinas, Tennessee, Kentucky, Alabama, Mississippi, and Louisiana, as well as parts of Illinois, Ohio, West Virginia, Virginia, and Arkansas; since Removal in 1840, it could be said to incorporate much of eastern Oklahoma as well. Prior to Removal, there were at least six completely distinct language groups, making "linguistic diversity in the Southeast . . . comparable to that in the California-Oregon and Northwest Coast area, the most linguistically diverse area in North America."[1]

The many different Native nationalities indigenous to the Southeast were linked by their cultural and religious beliefs, due in part to the rise of the Southeastern Ceremonial Complex (1200–1650 CE) during the latter part of the cosmopolitan Mississippian period (approximately 800–1500 CE). The people who lived within this society are frequently referred to as "Moundbuilders" because of the huge earthen mounds, used as the foundations of temples and royal homes, that occupy the centers of their cities, or *talwas*;[2] the modern Native Americans of the Southeast are their descendants. Within Moundbuilder civilization, different *talwas* acted as discrete vortices of power, leading to the development of separate but related art styles. Because of the immense influence of this prehistoric civilization, the cultural power of the Southeast was felt well beyond its geographic borders.[3]

The Hood Museum of Art has a small but compelling collection of Southeastern objects that exemplify the cultural and artistic diversity of the region. Ranging from a Mississippian-era bottle from Eastern Arkansas to a Chitimacha double-woven basket from the Gulf Coast of Louisiana, and Cherokee baskets from North Carolina to a Florida Seminole man's "big shirt" (c. 1910), the collection represents a kind of "Four Directions" of the Native American Southeast.

The earliest Southeastern object in the Hood's collection is a Mississippian-era owl effigy bottle from Crittenden County, eastern Arkansas (cat. 163). This piece dates to approximately 1450, the time of the collapse of Mississippian chiefdoms (perhaps due to political upheaval) just before contact with Europeans. Because the jar was found in the region of Arkansas just adjacent to Tennessee, it is very likely ancestral Quapaw material.[4] This jar is quintessentially Southeastern and Mississippian in form, manufacture, and intended use. The shape of the vessel is a typical unpainted hooded bottle form, with a bulbous body and a wide neck terminating in a naturalistically modeled owl head with the vessel's opening at the back of it.[5] In this period, ceramists display an evident interest in reproducing real animals, and this particular owl appears to be a barred owl.

An extremely wide variety of vessel types was combined with effigy animal forms during the late Mississippian period in the Arkansas/Tennessee region, from bowls with simple animal legs to closed vessels whose entire bodies are animals. Ceramic vessels made during the Mississippian period benefited from the new technological advance of shell-tempered clay, which makes a fired pot extremely strong. The large flared opening at the back of the owl effigy's head indicates this vessel would have been filled with offerings of liquid or food, perhaps for a house altar or a grave. What is certain is that it was made for indigenous use, and that it had a religious function.

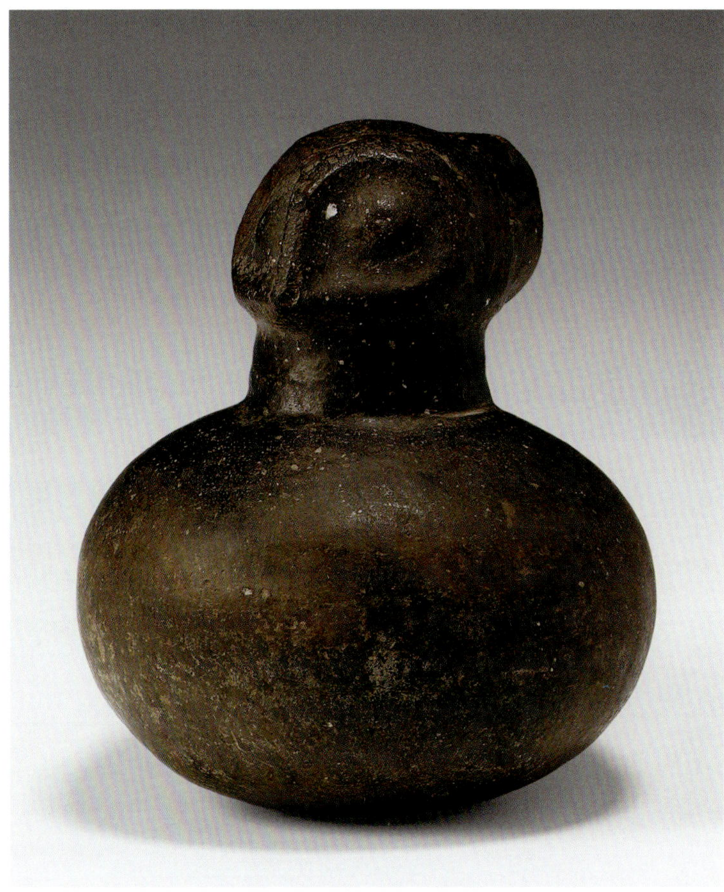

CAT. 163. Artist unknown, Mississippian Tradition, owl effigy bottle, Mississippian Period, about 1450 CE, grey earthenware. Gift of Alexis Chapman Proctor, Class of 1918; 167.38.24228.

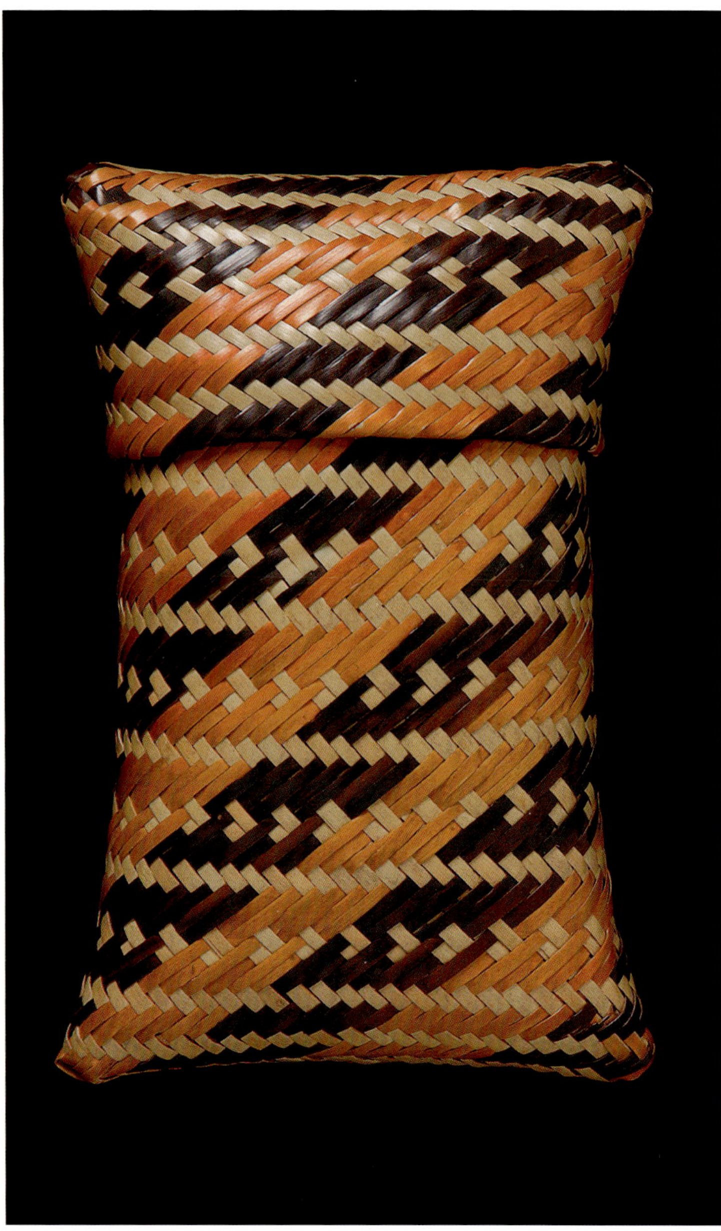

CAT. 162. Artist unknown, Chitimacha, cigar case or wallet, about 1900, river cane, butternut root dye, and bloodroot dye. Bequest of Frank C. and Clara G. Churchill; 46.17.9533.

By the time this bottle was produced, the people who made it had long been part of the aforementioned Southeastern Ceremonial Complex, a religion that described the realm of the cosmos as three-layered, with a variety of animals and mythic beings acting as intercessors between those layers.[6] Birds were regarded as messengers for humanity to the world above,[7] which is one explanation for the inclusion of an avian form on a jar intended to carry ritual offerings.

The Chitimacha people, a contemporary Native American nation in southern Louisiana,[8] are famed for the rivercane plaited basketry that has been produced in the Southeast since prehistoric times.[9] Designs found in historic and contemporary basketry can also be found in the fingerwoven wool garters and belts used by Southeasterners during both Mississippian and historic times. Using the tough, waterproof fibers of the rivercane plant (sp. *Arundinaria*), Chitimacha women create household items of exceptional beauty and strength.

The Chitimacha basket in the Hood Museum of Art's collection is a small rectangular lidded piece called a *kak't*, the style of which is usually referred to as a "cigar case" (cat. 162). Baskets of this type have many uses, including the storage of small personal items such as tobacco, sacred medicines, or jewelry. They are also well suited for sale outside the indigenous community, because their small size makes them an easily portable souvenir. The Hood's *kak't* exhibits the typical traits of a Chitimacha basket, including a squared base with rounded sides, extremely thin cane splints, and a banded construction against which both geometric and curvilinear designs appear. This piece is made from plaited rivercane colored with butternut root (black) and bloodroot (red) as a bold background for the traditional "mouse tracks" pattern in the cane's natural color. The basket demonstrates the doublewoven technique in which Chitimacha weavers excel: the interior is woven first and the exterior woven over it, like an extremely complicated, two-sided braid. The cane is always woven so that the shiny side faces out, which is both aesthetic and utilitarian, in that it makes the basket waterproof.

The Cherokee, an Iroquoian-speaking people in North Carolina and Oklahoma, are one of the largest Native American groups in the United States, and like the Chitimacha and other Southeastern groups, they are famed for the creation of plaited rivercane baskets. The Cherokee object (*talutsa* or *talutsa ihya*) in the Hood's collection is a large plaited storage basket (cat. 165). In prehistoric and early historic times, baskets of this type stored perishable goods like dried food or clothing. For this reason, they are single-weave plaited, with a loosely plaited design at the neck of the basket that acts as a vent, allowing the stored grains or cloth within to remain dry. These baskets also typically feature a square base with bulging walls and a reinforced round mouth, as well as cane fibers dyed with walnut (black), walnut leaves (brown), and bloodroot (red) designs that avoid the Chitimacha's inclination toward curvilinear patterns.

As characteristic of traditional Cherokee basketry as this piece may be, however, it is also startlingly modern in some regards. The name of the pattern woven into it is "peace pipe," a phrase borrowed from the well-known Plains religious implement. While this pattern in fact predates contact with either European Americans or Plains Indian tradition, it has been renamed in order to enhance the basket's appeal to non-Cherokee buyers, a major shift that took place at one time in the Cherokee economy. Though originally intended solely for indigenous use, Cherokee cane baskets (and, later, those made of oak splints) also became viable trade goods between Cherokee women and colonists or the newly minted Americans.

CAT. 165. Artist unknown, Cherokee, storage basket, about 1915, river cane, butternut root dye, and bloodroot dye. Gift of Mary Louis Warden Stewart; 996.42.30331.

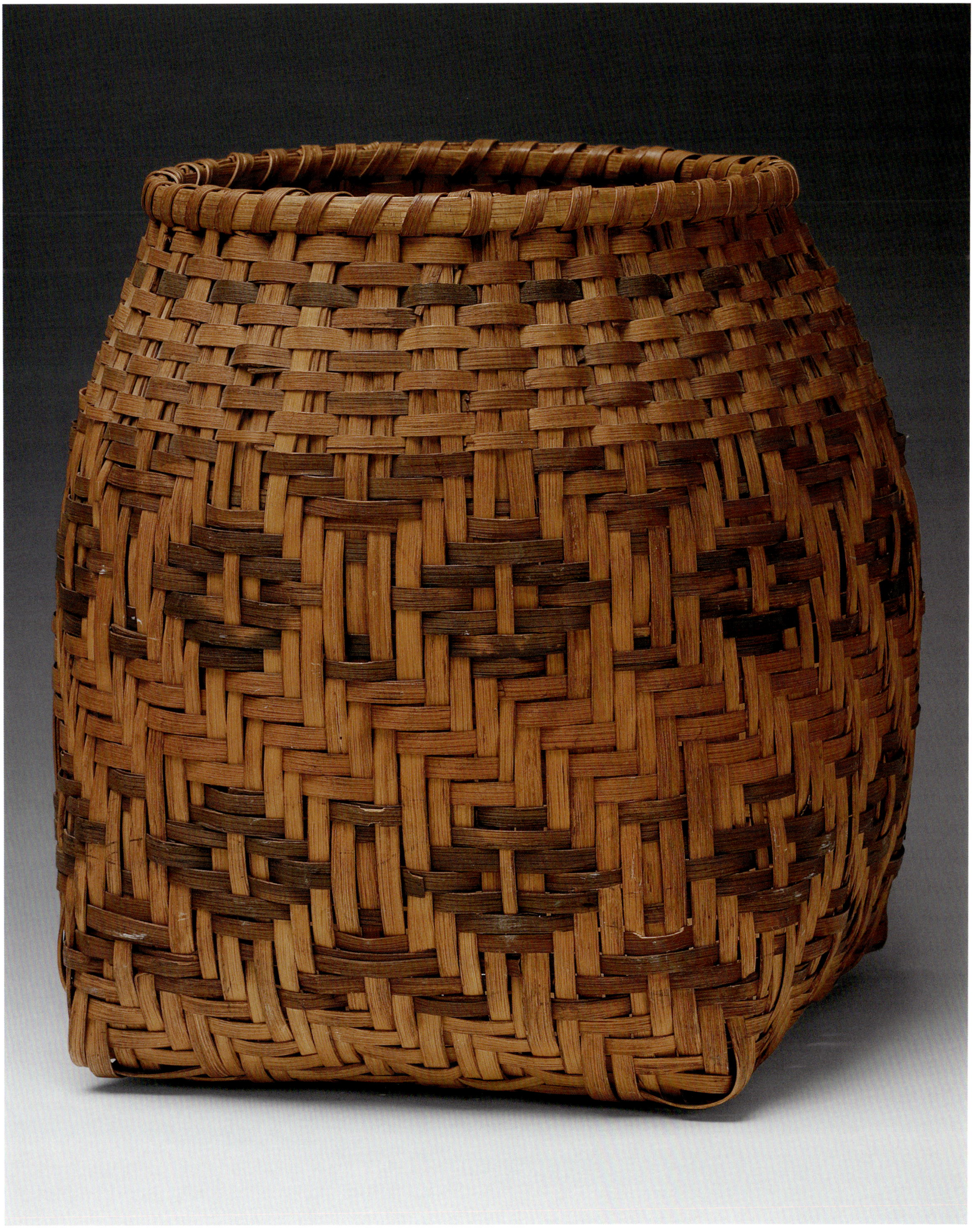

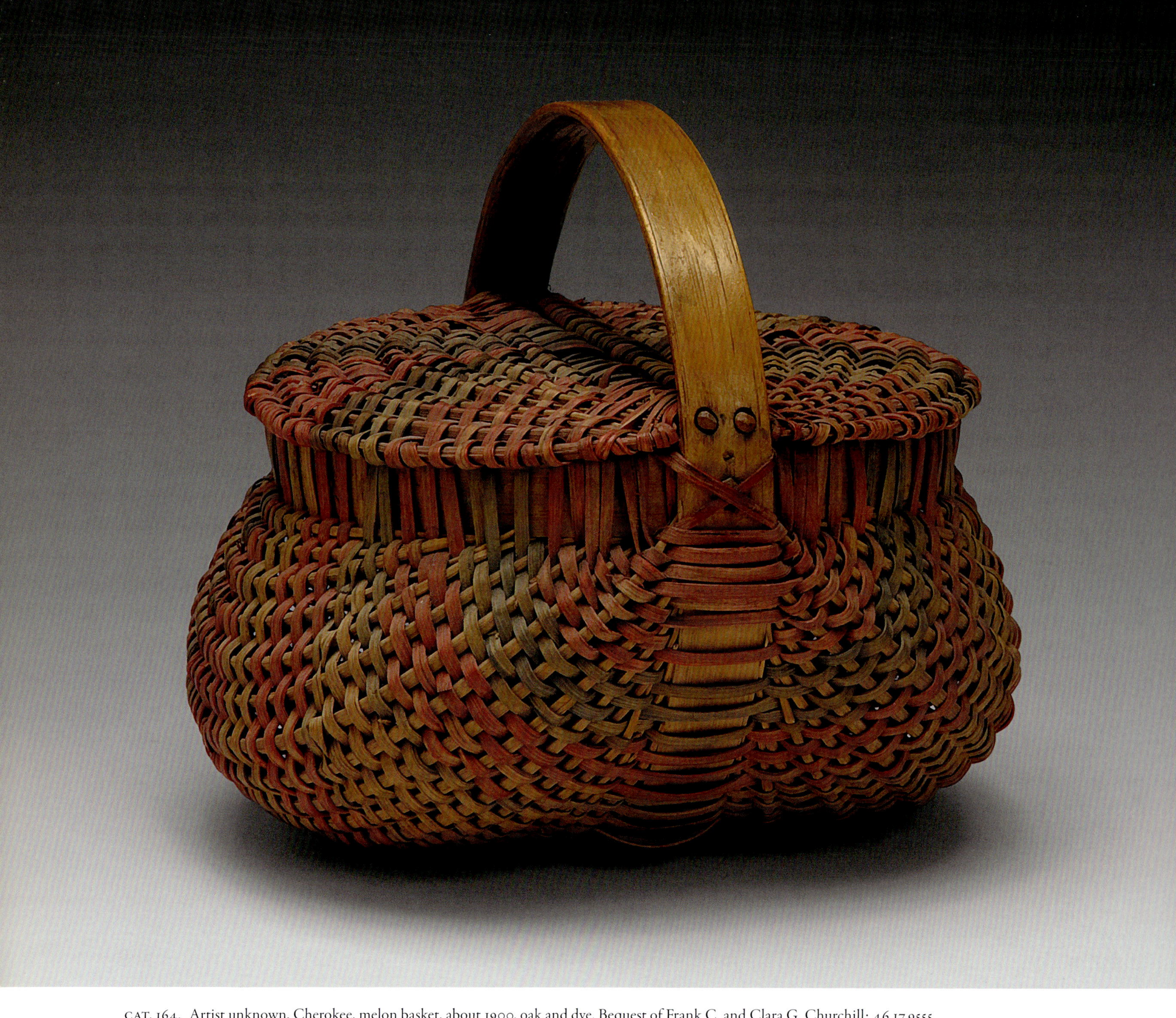

CAT. 164. Artist unknown, Cherokee, melon basket, about 1900, oak and dye. Bequest of Frank C. and Clara G. Churchill; 46.17.9555.

In contrast to the *talutsa ihya*, the Cherokee *talutsa kohinusti* ("carrying basket") or *talutsa deganulitsiyi* ("rib basket")—or what the non-Cherokee usually calls a "melon basket"—represents a new form that was acquired from Euro-American missionaries to the Cherokee around 1800 or so (cat. 164).[10] The *talutsa deganulitsiyi* is consistently made of white oak, a fiber considered by the Cherokee to be too rough for a presentable basket previous to the Removal period. These baskets are woven in the indigenous local plaited technique, but always in single-woven wicker, not the double-woven flat plaiting used with rivercane. The bodies of the baskets are lobed or bi-lobed, as in this example (sometimes referred to as a "buttocks" basket); they feature a handle, a carved foundation, and attached hinged lids. White oak baskets by Cherokee women previous to the incorporation of the melon basket style were exclusively used as rough utility baskets to store dried fish and meat. The melon basket in particular, however, has been a trade object between Europeans and Cherokees since its very inception. Perhaps in deference to Euro-American tastes, the dyes used on melon baskets are always aniline, which allows weavers to experiment with new color combinations; the Hood's basket, for example, is striped in pink and green. The small woven pedestal is a uniquely Cherokee innovation for this type of basket.

Melon baskets represent more than just a stylistic change in Cherokee weaving, of course; they are also a byproduct of the destruction of the traditional Cherokee economy brought on by the encroachment of white settlers on Indian lands. The popularity of white oak as a basketry material only increased when access to rivercane became limited, due to that encroachment and, later, Removal to Oklahoma. In another subtler but still poignant change to their traditional lifeways, Cherokee men also wove oak splint baskets, while the weaving of rivercane had always been limited to women.

The Seminole are a Muskogean-speaking people in Florida and Oklahoma, a historical offshoot of the Creek Confederacy that began to break away due to political differences in the 1770s. Because the Creek Confederacy's lands were in what is now Georgia and Alabama, Creek and Seminole ancestors have been in contact with Europeans since De Soto's expedition in 1540. This long history of almost five hundred years of mutual observation and cultural borrowing radically changed regalia, among other things, in the Southeast. Before contact with Europeans, clothing in the region was generally made of deerskin, but from the moment of contact, Southeastern Indians began to trade their deerskins for European-made wool and cotton cloth and clothing. These textiles had the advantage of being ready-made and available in abundant colors and patterns, so that they instantly broadcast one's status as a trader. Native women in the Southeast also began to pick and choose stylistic elements of European-made clothes to blend with Native styles in profoundly unique ways. The *focsikchobee,* or "big shirt," of the Florida Seminole originally developed out of European-style calico hunting shirts and jackets in the late 1700s, modified to adapt to the tropical weather of the deep south. By the start of the First Seminole War in 1817, most Southeastern Indians were wearing clothing made entirely of trade fabric.

The Hood Museum of Art's collection contains a rare and early Florida Seminole man's big shirt (cat. 161; see p. 120). The style of Florida Seminole clothing typically changed briskly and obviously, making their textiles easily datable by style to within ten years of their manufacture. The absence of the patchwork that the Florida Seminole are famous for marks this big shirt's manufacture at sometime between 1900 and 1910. This pre-patchwork shirt does, however, have a diamond-shaped pattern in appliquéd cloth on the shoulders, which might be related to the Mississippian-era symbol for rattlesnakes.

A man would have worn a shirt like this with a bandana at the neck, shoes, and leather leggings when going into town, even adding a Western-style vest and cloth turban on dress occasions. Generally made of light cotton or gauze, and usually mainly white, big shirts are breathable garments that protect one's skin from sun and insects. By the 1940s, the big shirt had changed drastically to include short tails intended to fit inside slacks, reflecting the fact that Seminole men had joined the workforce as either entertainers in tourist villages or tomato pickers in nearby agricultural fields.

Though perhaps presented as both static and falsely unique within a museum context, all of the Native objects from the Southeast in the Hood Museum of Art's collection can be related to present Native American cultures, as they are all representative of current practices. The persistence and evolution of these art forms in the face of adversity is rather extraordinary. For example, numerous contemporary Oklahoma and North Carolina Cherokee weavers continue to produce and teach the traditions of both rivercane and white oak basketry, even expanding that tradition to include baskets woven of honeysuckle vine (among the Oklahoma Cherokee).[11] Rivercane weaving is still alive and well among the Chitimacha.[12] The patchwork technique that evolved from earlier appliquéd textiles among the Florida Seminole now represents their national fabric and has furthermore spread to the Oklahoma Seminole and Muscogee Creek. Finally, several ceramists from different Native nations within the Southeast have begun to delve into their ancestral artistic past and have recently revived some forms of Mississippian-era pottery and jewelry.[13]

NOTES

1. Charles Hudson, *The Southeastern Indians* (Knoxville: University of Tennessee Press, 1976), 22.

2. *Talwa* is a Muscogee Creek word that means "town with a ceremonial ground." The word for a village that does not act as a ceremonial center is *talofa.*

3. In the Hood Museum of Art's collection, see, for example, the Delaware bandolier bag, Dene rifle bag, and White Earth Ojibwe shoes, all of which exhibit "floral" designs that are in fact ancient motifs of state power propagated during the late Mississippian period.

4. The modern Quapaw Nation, a Siouan-speaking Southeastern group, has been headquartered in the extreme northeastern corner of Oklahoma since Removal in 1840.

5. Vessels of this type are commonly referred to as "Bell-Plain."

6. In extremely brief, simplified terms, those layers can be described as the Underworld (populated by fish, snakes, and mythic beings like Underwater Panther who were associated with malevolent power); the Human World; and the Upper World (populated by avian beings and mythic creatures like Thunderbird).

7. Richard Townsend (ed.), *Hero, Hawk, and Open Hand: American Indian Art of the Ancient Midwest and South* (Chicago: Art Institute of Chicago, in association with Yale University Press, 2004), 144.

8. The Chitimacha are speakers of a language isolate that is unrelated to other languages in the Southeast.

9. Fragments of plaited rivercane basketry have been recovered from archaeological sites in the Southeast as early as the late Woodland Period (600–900 CE).

10. The Moravians in particular established a mission at Springplace, Georgia, in 1801.

11. See the work of Thelma Forrest (Oklahoma), Charlotte Coates (Oklahoma), Lucille Lossiah (North Carolina), Martha Ross (North Carolina), and many others.

12. Descendents of the famous early-twentieth-century weaver Clara Darden are particularly active.

13. See the work of Jerri Red Corn, Bill Glass, Dan Townsend, Knokovtee Scott, Charley Johnson, and Kenneth Johnson, among others.

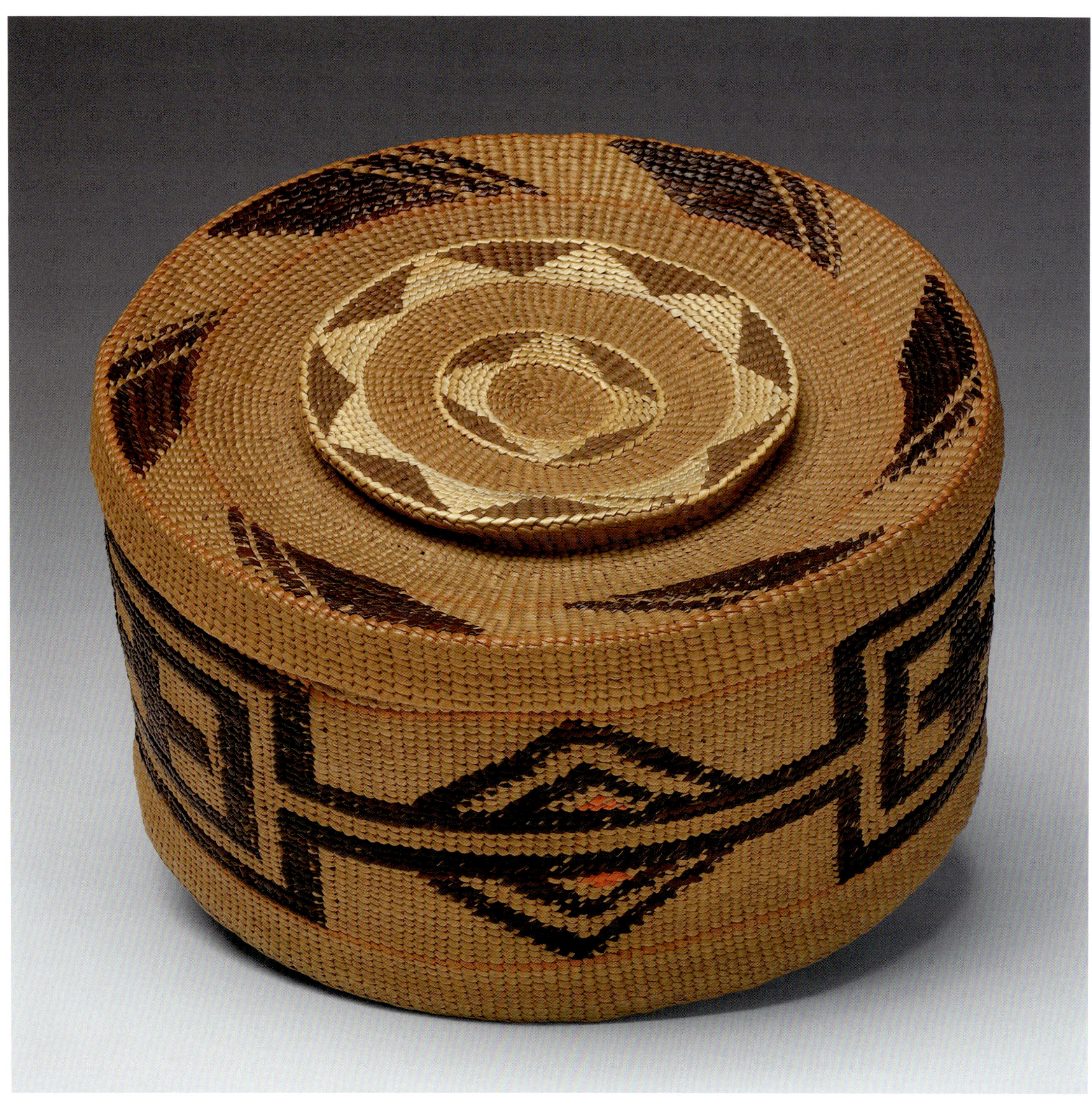

CAT. 36. Artist unknown, Tlingit, Hoonah, Alaska, rattle-lit basket, about 1900, spruce root, maidenhair fern, bear grass, dyes, pebbles. Bequest of Frank C. and Clara G. Churchill; 46.17.9398.

:: 6.8 ::

Baskets: Weaving Beauty into the World

Jennifer Neptune

The Hood Museum of Art's collection of Native American basketry includes examples from all across the North American continent. These baskets all have stories to tell—about the land and culture that they come from, and about their weavers and their connections to their ancestors and commitment to the continuation of their culture's traditions for the generations yet to come. Throughout the ages, baskets and related woven objects have held an important place in the survival of tribal people. Utility baskets are used to gather, prepare, cook, and store food; other baskets and cradleboards keep babies comforted and safe; woven clothing, hats, and mats provide protection from the elements; and certain kinds of baskets continue to play an important part in ceremony and the passing of traditions from one generation to the next.

Of all the art forms of the indigenous peoples of North America, none is more connected to traditions and to landscape than basketry. The humblest of utility baskets and the most complex and beautiful of ceremonial baskets are both the result of hundreds and often thousands of years of a culture's intimate connections to the plants, trees, spirits, topography, and climate of the land they inhabit.

In the northeast, where the first rays of sunlight warm the rocky shores, the weavers of the Maliseet, Micmac, Passamaquoddy, and Penobscot tribes utilize the trees of their vast forests for their weaving materials. While birchbark, spruce root, and the inner barks of basswood and eastern white cedar were common choices, black or brown ash is recognized as the primary "basket-tree" of this region. In some northeast creation stories, the people are born from the brown ash tree. They perfected strong and sturdy pack baskets that could be carried on the back with woven basswood tumplines or stored in the curves of a birchbark canoe, as well as finer and more intricate baskets of ash splints and sweetgrass that would later come to be known as "fancy baskets" (cat. 157).

Further inland, along the Saint Lawrence River to the Great

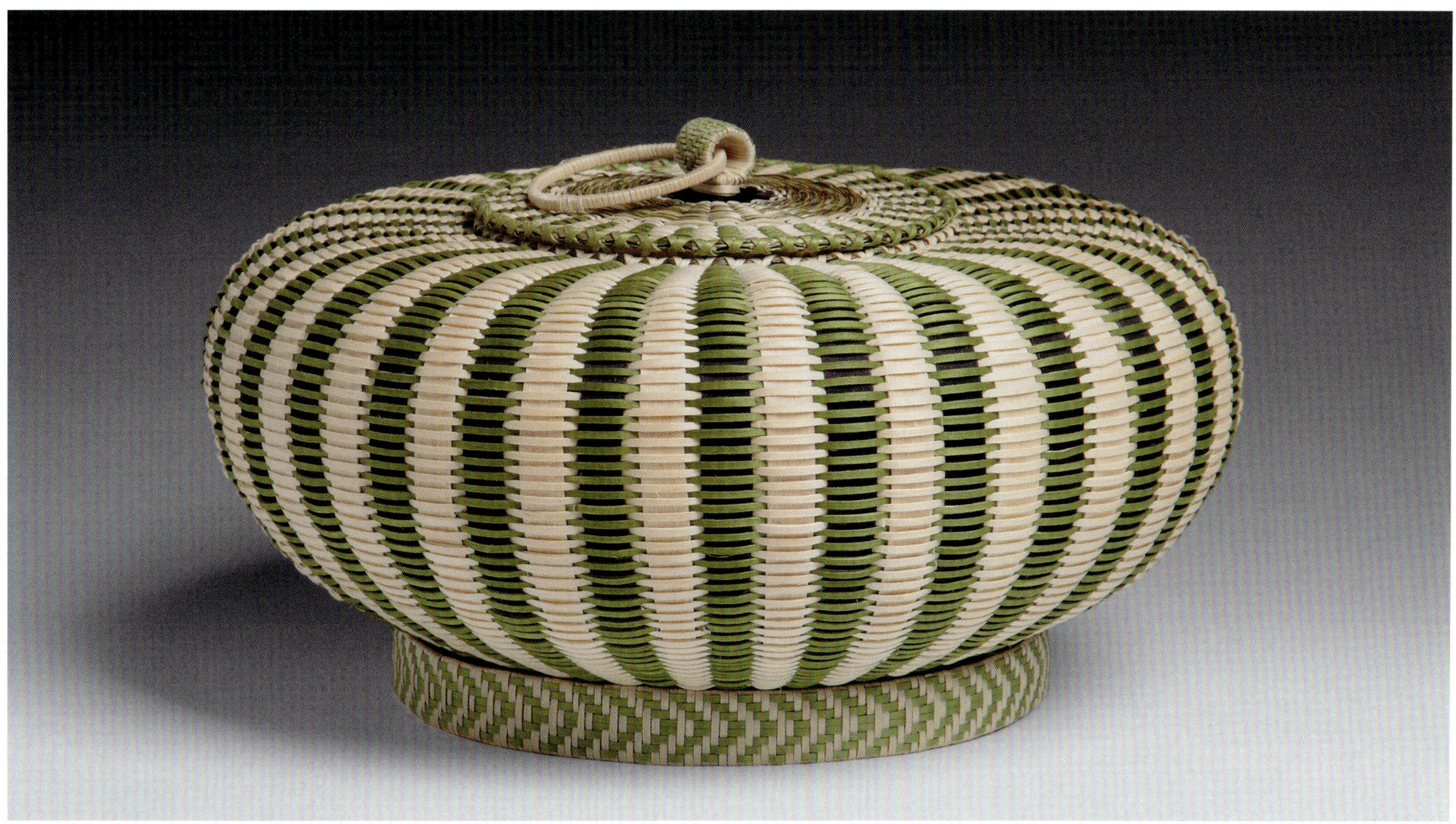

CAT. 157. Jeremy Frey, Passamaquoddy; Wabanaki, green urchin basket, 2008, brown ash, sweetgrass, dye. Purchased through the Phyllis and Bertram Geller 1937 Memorial Fund; 2008.51.

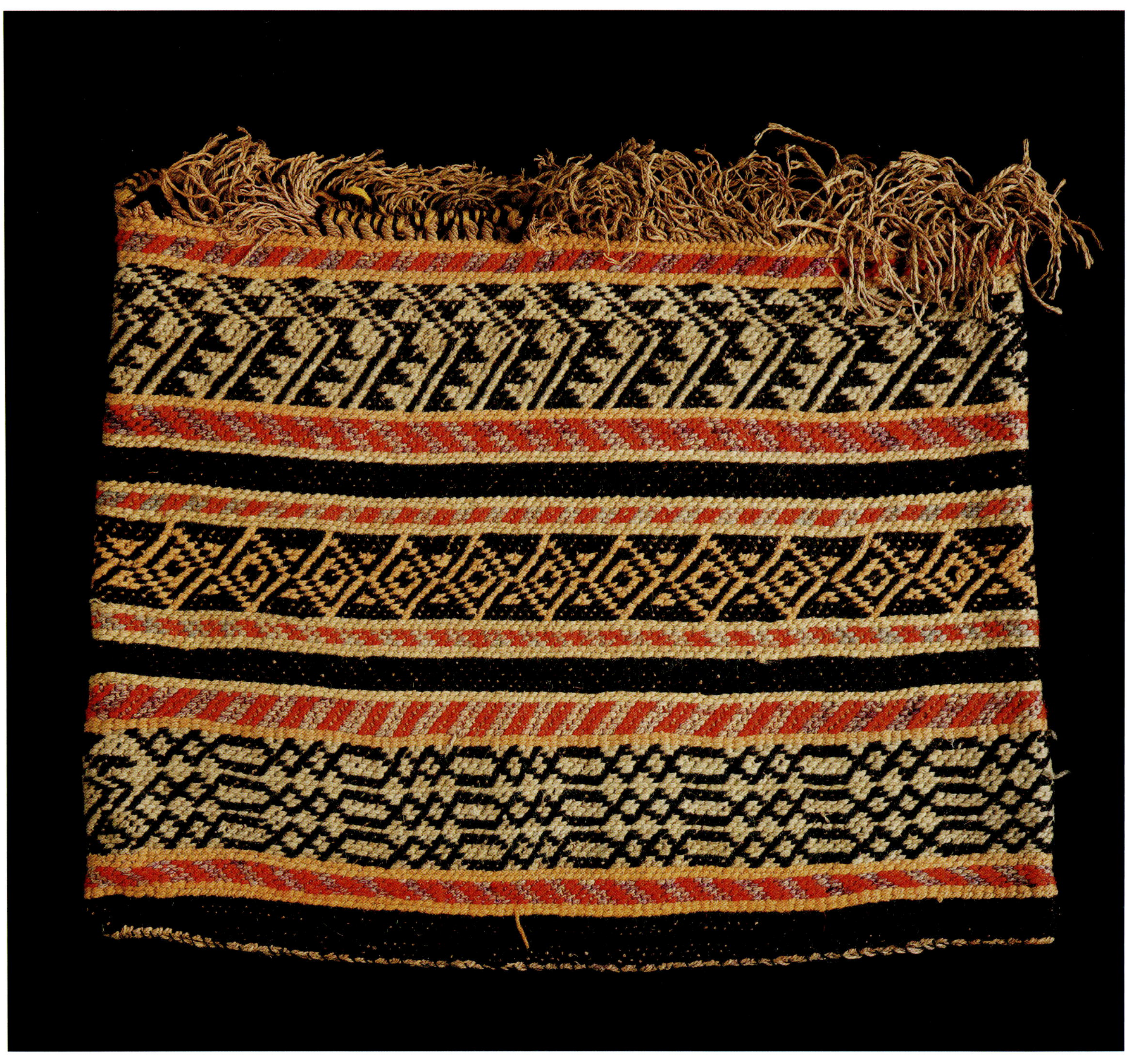

CAT. 146. Artist unknown, Putawatomi or Menominee (Menomini), Wittenburg, Wisconsin, bag, about 1890, yarn, fiber, aniline dye, thread. Museum purchase; 55.4.13245.

Lakes, the weavers of the Abenaki, Mohawk, Ojibwa, and Potawatomi nations also made use of the forest trees of their homelands. Black ash splints were heavily utilized for basket material throughout this region. The Mohawk are well known for their functional as well as beautiful corn washing and sifting baskets made of black ash, and for their intricate fancy basket work. In the Great Lakes area, birchbark containers and tightly woven basswood bags played an important role in the processing and storage of wild rice (cat. 146).

Traveling south along the backbone of the Appalachians into the warm and humid southeastern forests, we find that the Cherokee, Choctaw, Chickasaw, and Chitimacha tribes excelled at plaited rivercane basketry. This area is especially well known for double-woven rivercane storage baskets, as well as corn-processing baskets—that is, sifters, sieves, and winnowing baskets. Other basketry materials from this area include white oak, hickory, dogwood, honeysuckle, and pine needles (cat. 165).

Following the sun as it journeys to the southwest mountains,

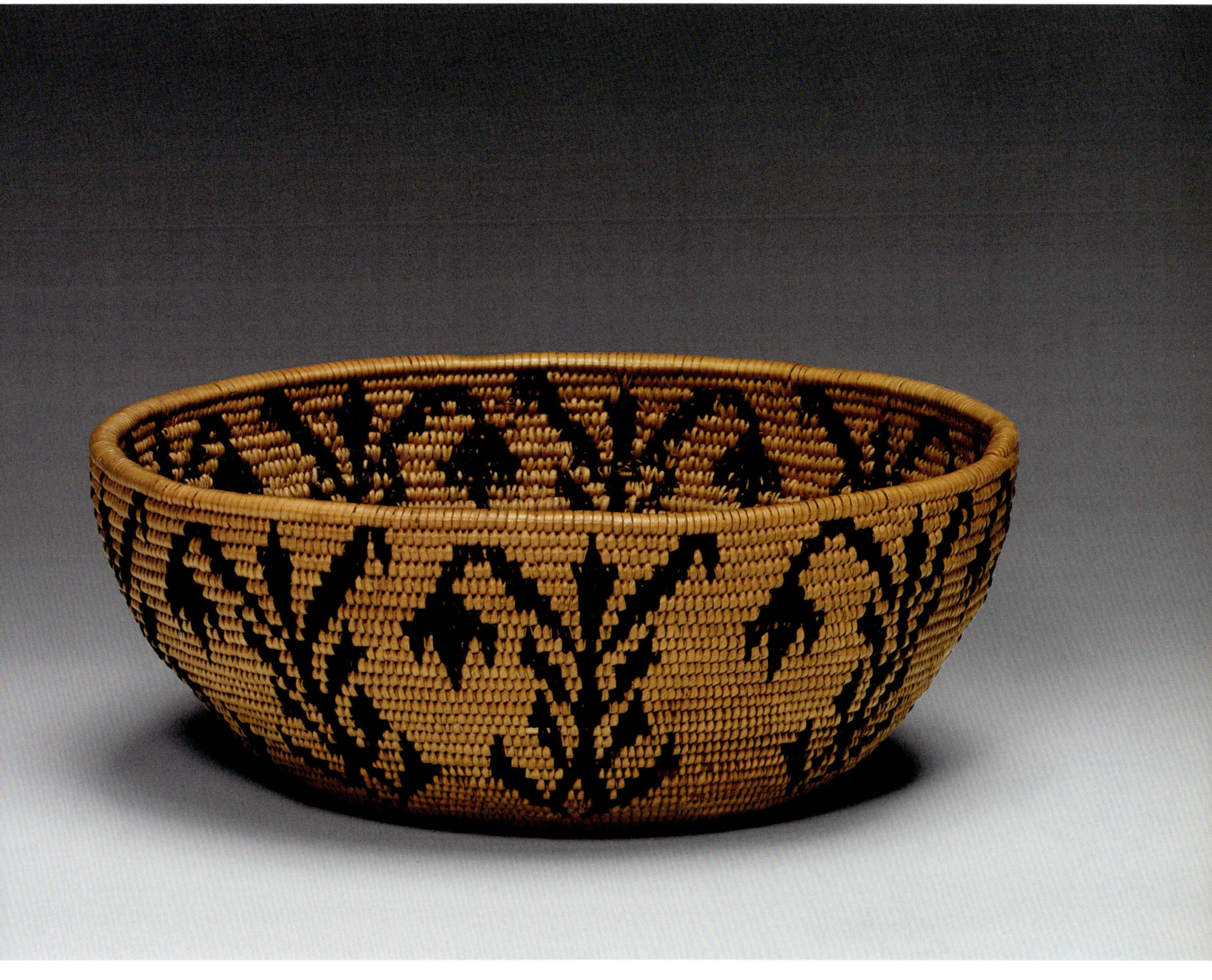

CAT. 59. Artist unknown, Washoe (Washo), basket, about 1905, willow, bracken fern root, and grass. Bequest of Frank C. and Clara G. Churchill; 46.17.9356.

mesas, and deserts, the Pueblo tribes, as well as Hopi, Navajo, Apache, Yavapai, and Tohono O'odham, depend on the plants of their varied homelands to provide weaving materials. Using unique wicker and coiling techniques, the Hopi produce renowned colorful plaques and open baskets of sumac, yucca, and rabbitbrush. The Apache use willow and sumac to weave trays and burden baskets. Farther south, the Tohono O'odham use beargrass, willow, and devil's claw to weave their baskets.

North of Arizona, between the Rocky and the Sierra Nevada mountain ranges, are the Great Basin and Plateau culture areas. In the southern parts of this vast region, the Washoe, Paiute, and Shoshone used primarily willow in their basketry. Jar-shaped baskets were woven and sometimes covered with pitch from conifer trees so they could be used for cooking or storing water. In the northern parts, the Wasco and Nez Perce used beargrass to create finely woven twined bags for gathering edible roots, such as camas (cat. 59).

On the shores of the west coast, where the last rays of sunlight kiss long sandy beaches before sinking into the Pacific, we come to

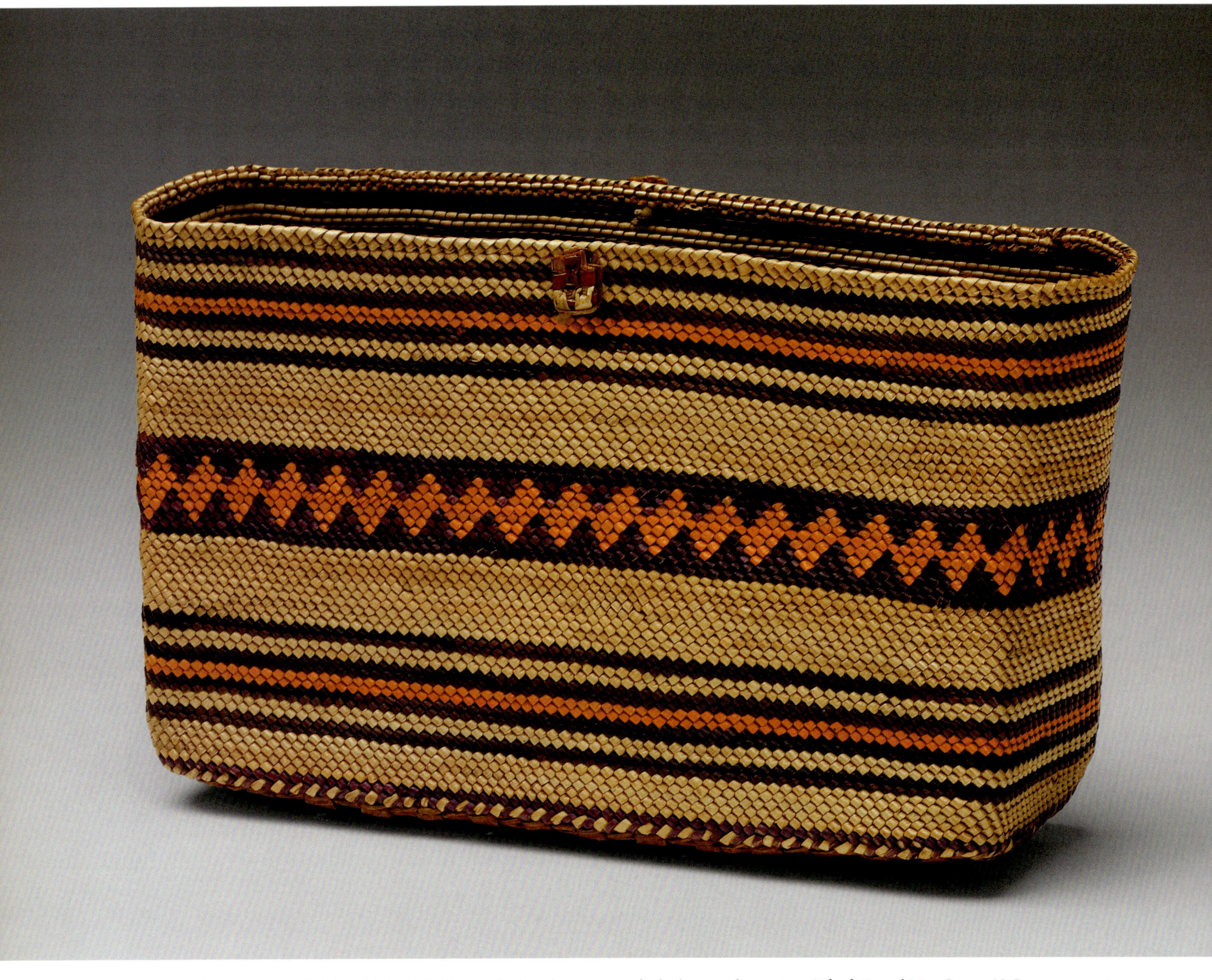

CAT. 40. Artist unknown, Salish or Makah, Washington, basket, about 1900, cedar bark, grass, dyes, string. Gift of Mr. and Mrs. George H. Brown; 42.12.8510.

the diverse cultures and landscapes that make up California. Instead of corn, acorns are one of the most important food resources. Throughout this area, then, specialized baskets for processing, cooking, and eating acorns are made. In the more arid south, the Luiseno and Cahuilla weave with deer grass, juncas, and sumac (cat. 56). In central California, Pomo, Miwok, and Yukut weavers use sedge root, willow, and bracken fern; some weavers also specialize in coiled baskets decorated with feathers and shell beads. Farther up the coast, in the land of the giant redwood forests, the Hupa, Karuk, and Yurok use spruce roots, beargrass, maidenhair fern, wild grape root, myrtle sticks, and hazel to weave a variety of basket styles ranging from food storage and preparation containers to intricate hats to cradleboards (cats. 41 and 49).

In the temperate rainforest of the Northwest Coast, the weavers of the Salish, Haida, Tshimshian, Tlingit, and Makah specialize in baskets for harvesting fish, shellfish, and berries (cat. 40). They are also recognized for their finely woven rattle-top baskets and woven hats (cat. 36 [see p. 126] and cat. 30). The weaving materials of this area include red and yellow cedar bark, spruce roots, beargrass, cattails, and maidenhair fern. The Hood Museum of Art collection

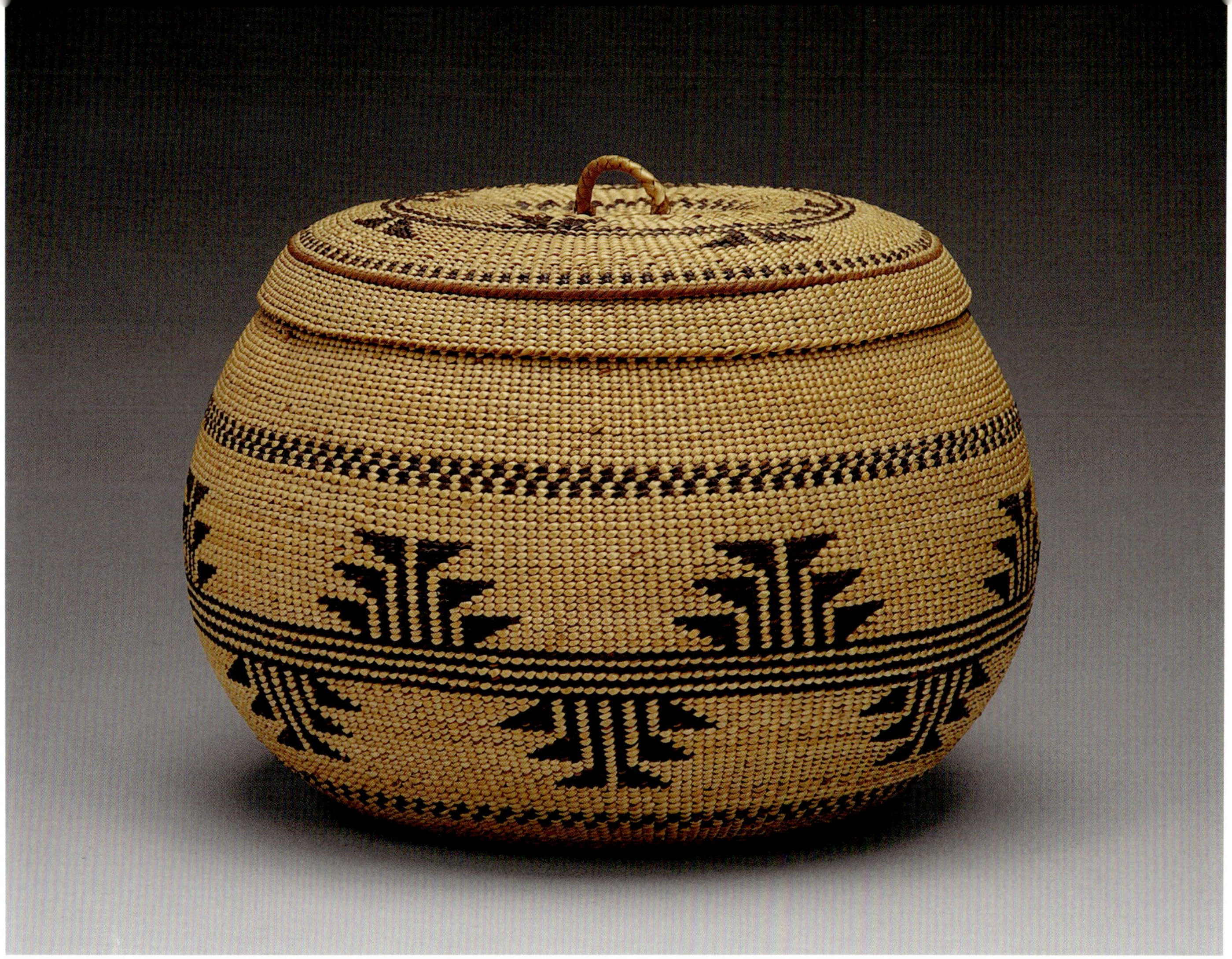

CAT. 41. Artist unknown, Hupa, Karuk (Karok) or Yurok, basket, early 20th century, conifer root, bear grass, hazel, maidenhair fern, and twine. Gift of Donald C. McIntire, Class of 1906; 54.18.12950.

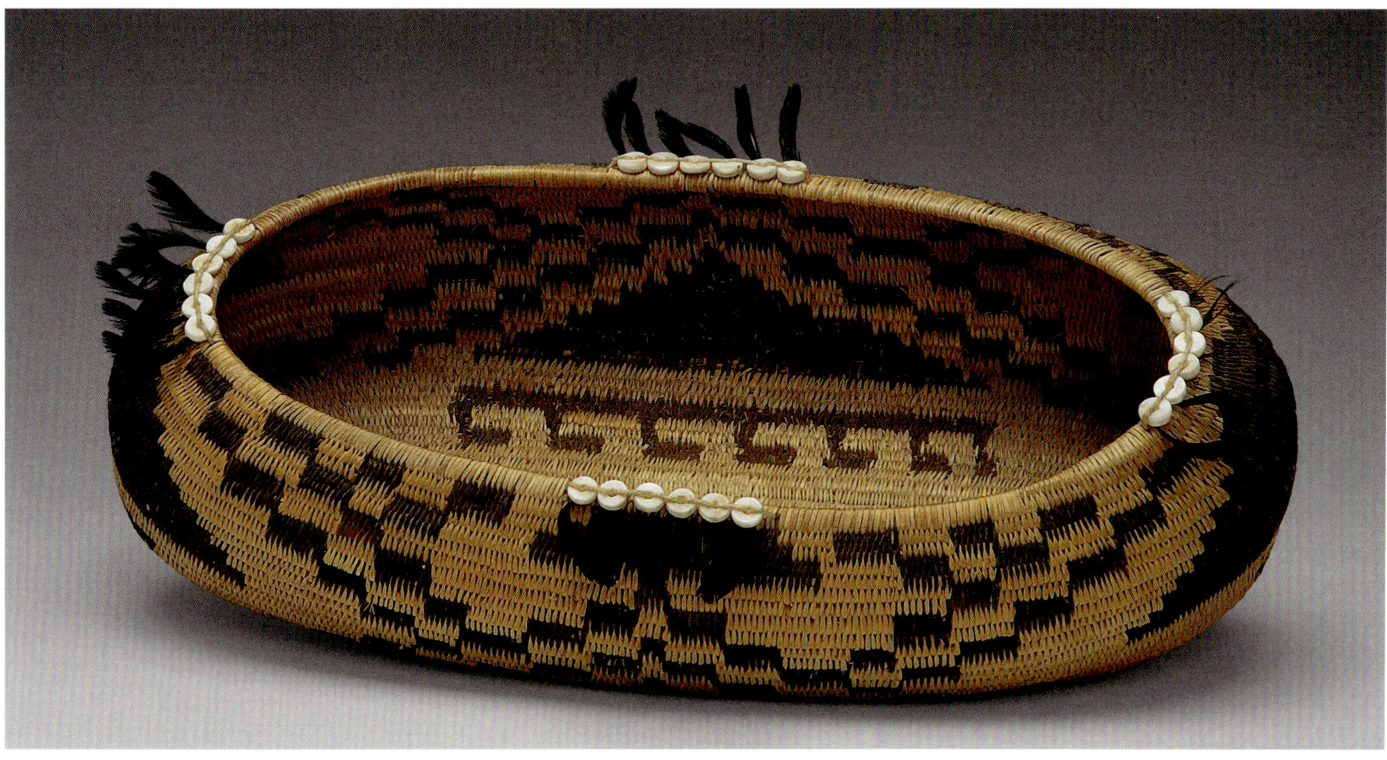

CAT. 49. Artist unknown, Pomo, basket, about 1905, sedge root, willow, bracken fern root, California valley quail crests, clamshell disc beads, and string. Bequest of Frank C. and Clara G. Churchill; 46.17.9333.

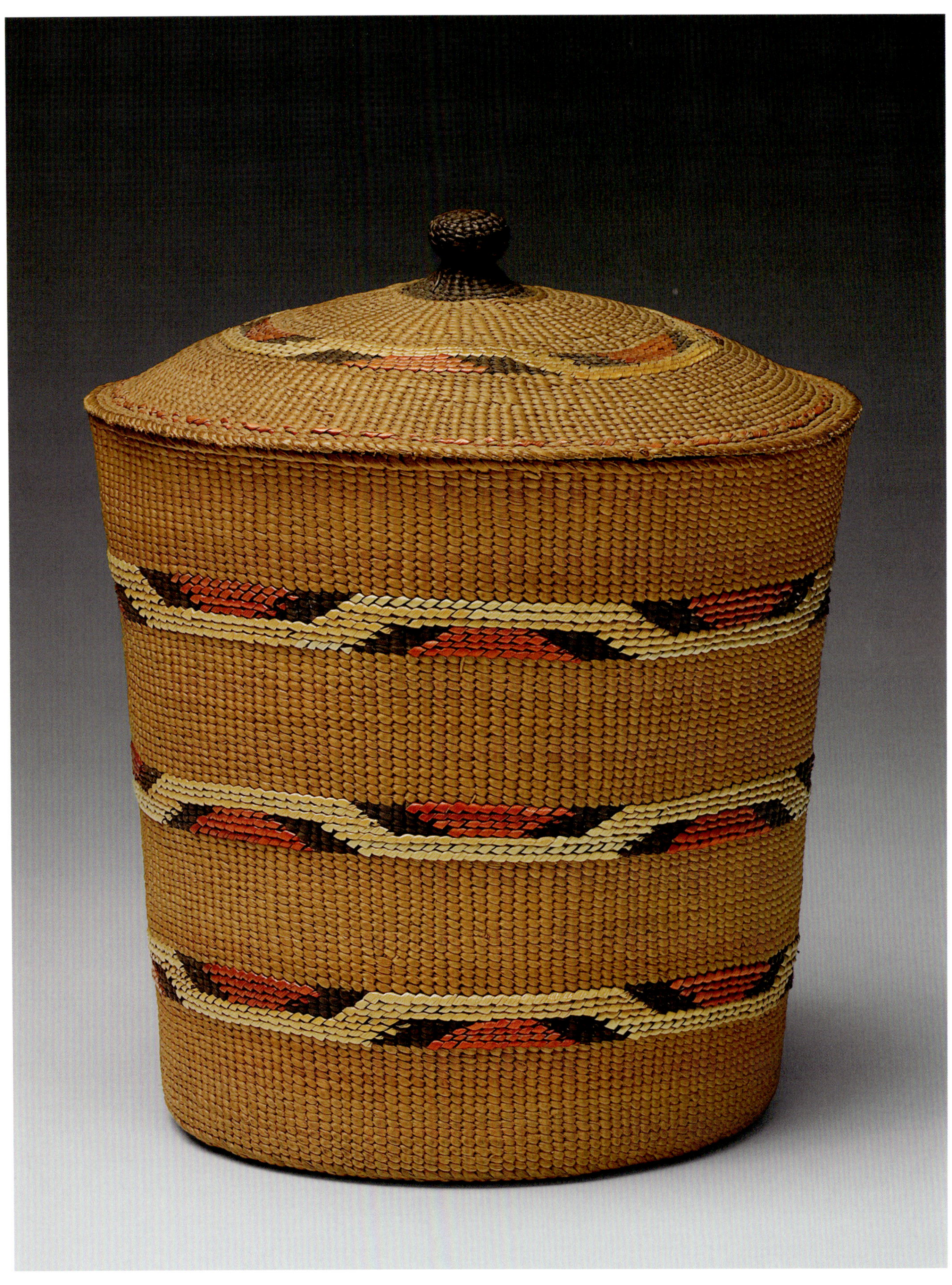

CAT. 30. Artist unknown, Tlingit, Yakutat, Alaska, basket, about 1905, spruce root, grass, dyes. Bequest of Frank C. and Clara G. Churchill; 46.17.9392.

includes a beautiful example of a traditional Haida hat woven of spruce root and painted with Northwest Coast designs (cat. 22).

Moving north to the lands of spruce forests, tundra, and snow is the culture area of the Arctic and Subarctic, an enormous territory stretching from the Pacific Ocean in Alaska across northern Canada to the Atlantic shores of Labrador. In the southern regions of this area, the Athabaskan, Cree, Naskapi, and Montagnais use birchbark to create containers for storage and cooking. The Aleut and Yup'ik are known for their very finely woven rye grass baskets and bags, and the Inupiaq for woven baleen baskets. The Inuit use grasses to make coiled baskets.

While the materials and techniques that weavers use vary by tribe and geographical region, they face many of the same challenges, including habitat destruction caused by development and urban sprawl; changes in land management practices; international border issues between the United States, Canada, and Mexico that divide tribes and disrupt traditional gathering practices; and the impact of invasive species, diseases, and climate change. In response, weavers have formed regional organizations to ensure that Native weaving materials and traditions will continue into the future. The largest of these organizations are the California Indian Basketweavers Association, the Northwest Native American Basketweavers Association, Tohono O'odham Community Action, and the Maine Indian Basketmakers Alliance. As you contemplate each basket in the Hood Museum of Art's collection, you might see it not just as an exquisite object but as a beautiful paragraph in the life story of the individual weaver, a reflection of the strength of his or her people, and a testament to his or her relationship with the forces of the nature to weave beauty into the world.

Illustrated Checklist of the Exhibition

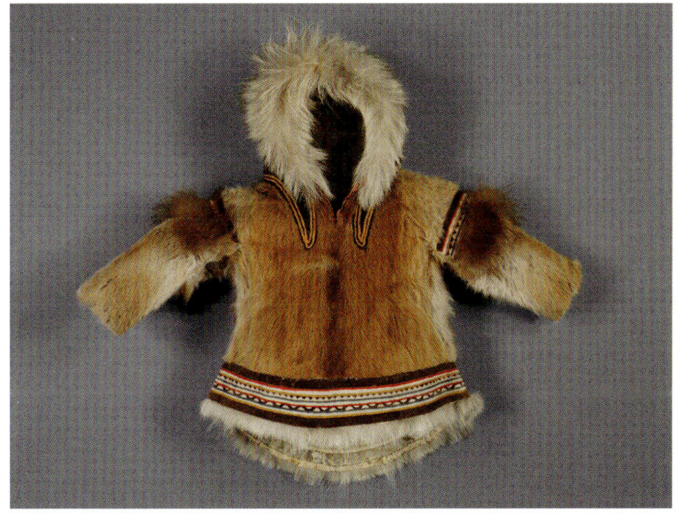

1

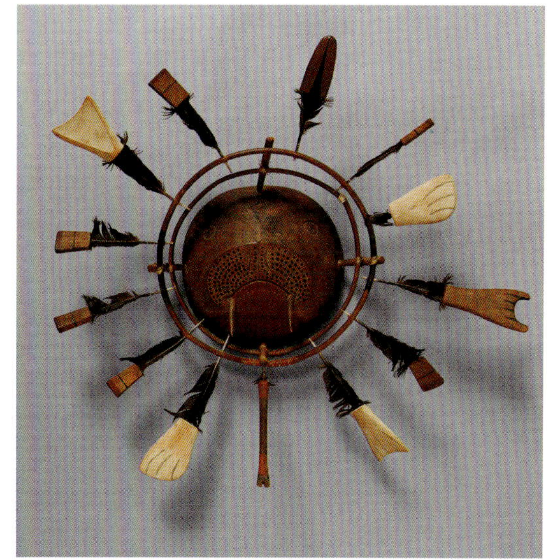

4

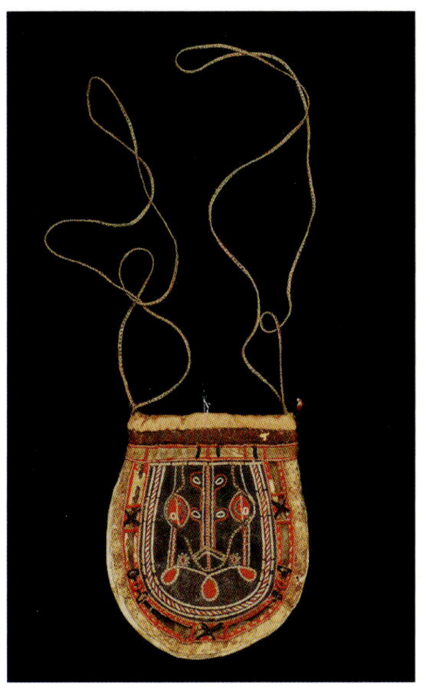

2

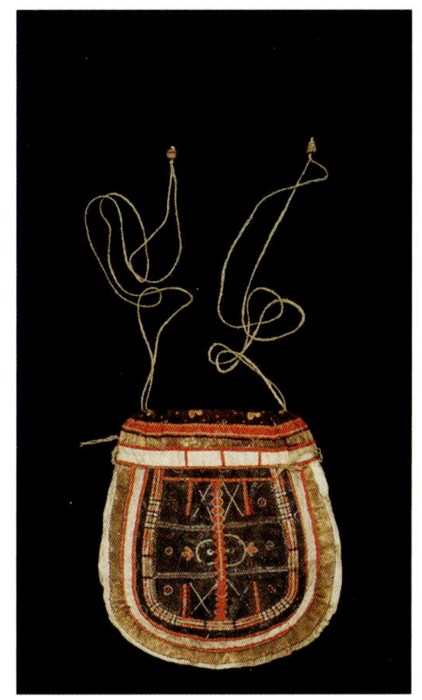

3

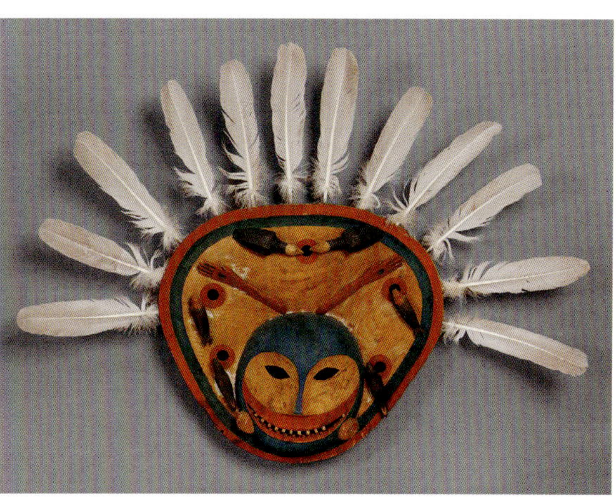

5

Arctic

Central Arctic

1. Artist unknown, Inuit, MacKenzie region, Northwest Territories

Boy's parka, about 1920

Caribou hide, seal fur, wolf fur, rabbit fur, cotton, cotton trim, sinew, and thread
59.5 x 68 cm (cuff to cuff across chest); 38 cm (widest garment hem); 30 cm (left proper arm length); 28 cm (right proper arm length)
Gift of Mrs. A. Lincoln Washburn, Class of 1935W; 174.2.25532

Western Arctic

2. Artist unknown, Alutiiq (Koniag), Kodiak Island, Alaska

Tobacco bag, about 1850

Hide, seal intestines, cotton cloth, sinew, wild rye grass, wool thread, vermilion, graphite, dye, and thread
17.5 x 14.2 cm (bag only); 57.5 cm (overall)
Source unknown, possibly gift of Mary E. Hall Hubbard; 13.1.581

3. Artist unknown, Alutiiq (Koniag), Kodiak Island, Alaska

Tobacco bag, about 1850

Hide, seal intestines, cotton cloth, sinew, wild rye grass, wool thread, vermilion, graphite, dye, and thread
24.4 cm (bag); 53 x 22.7 cm (with drawstring extended)
Source unknown, possibly gift of Mary E. Hall Hubbard; 13.1.582

4. Artist unknown, Central Yup'ik, Nunivak Island, Alaska

Mask, about 1930

Wood, paint, feathers, sinew, string, and nails
8 x 57.2 cm
Gift of the Estate of Corey Ford, Class of 1921H; 169.75.24910

5. Artist unknown, Central Yup'ik, St. Michael, Alaska

Nepcetat mask, about 1930

Wood, paint, rawhide, nails, swan feathers, and seagull (replacement) feathers
48.5 x 52.5 cm
Gift of Lt. Col. Alfred T. Clifton, Class of 1927P; 42.15.7803

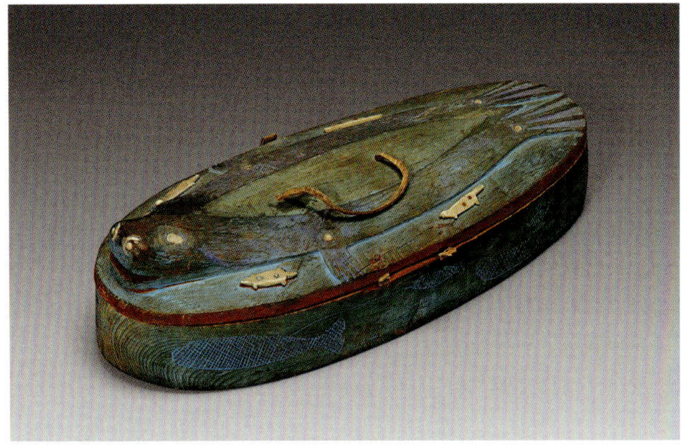

6

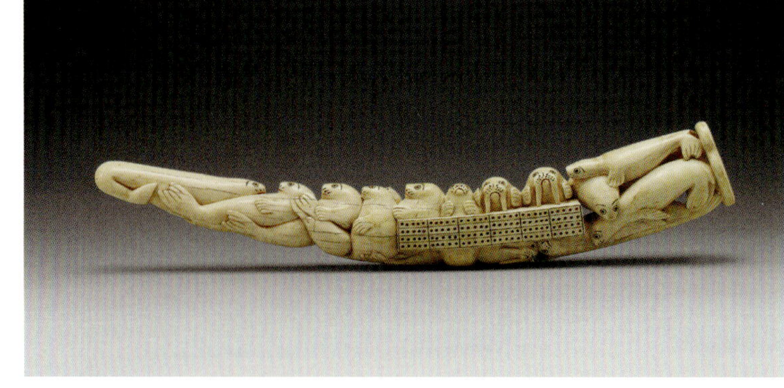

8

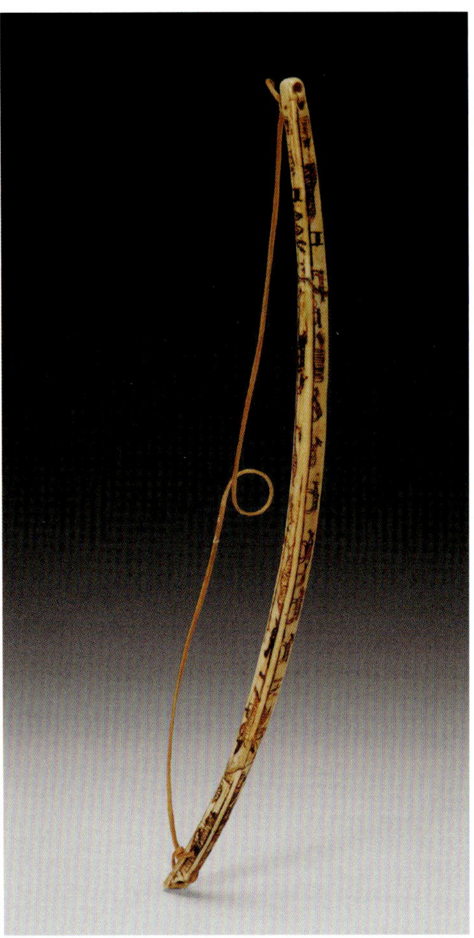

7

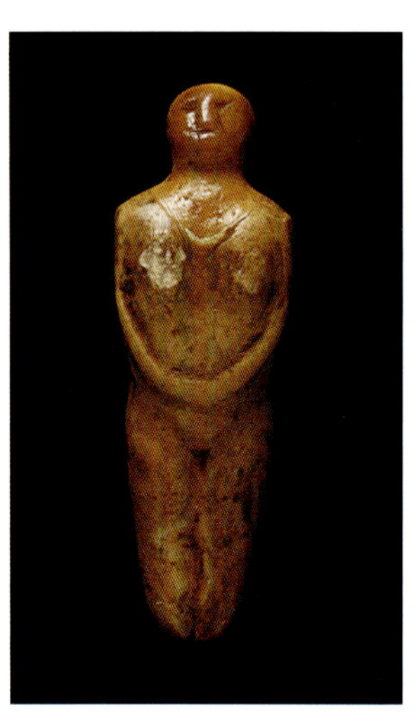

9

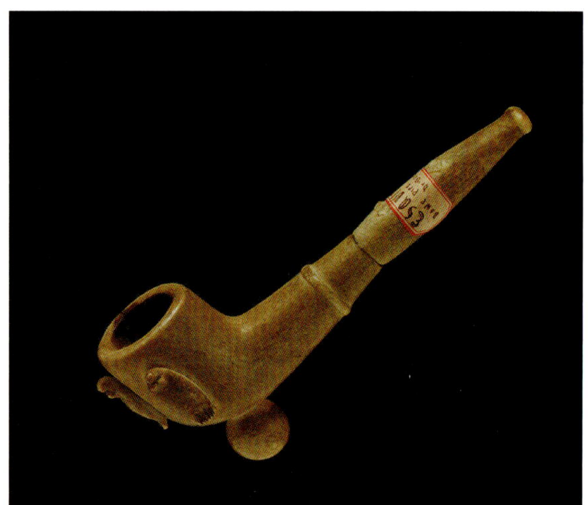

10

8. Artist unknown, Inupiat

Cribbage board, about 1920

Ivory, wood, graphite, and pigment
53 x 7.5 x 5 cm
Gift of the Estate of Corey Ford, Class of 1921H; 169.75.24892

6. Artist unknown, Central Yup'ik, St. Michael, Alaska

Woman's work box, about 1900

Wood, paint, ivory, rawhide, and metal
32.5 x 12.5 x 8.3 cm
Gift of Lt. Col. Alfred T. Clifton, Class of 1927P; 42.15.7804

7. Artist unknown, Inupiat, Cape Prince of Wales, Alaska

Bow drill, about 1900

Ivory and rawhide
41.5 cm
Gift of Frank C. and Clara G. Churchill; 46.17.9597

9. Artist unknown, Inupiat, Point Barrow, Alaska

Female figure, about 1905

Ivory
4.1 x 1.4 cm
Bequest of Frank C. and Clara G. Churchill; 46.17.9736

10. Artist unknown, Inupiat

Pipe bowl, about 1920

Walrus ivory
12 x 5 x 3.7 cm
Gift of Glover Street Hastings III; 181.2.26112

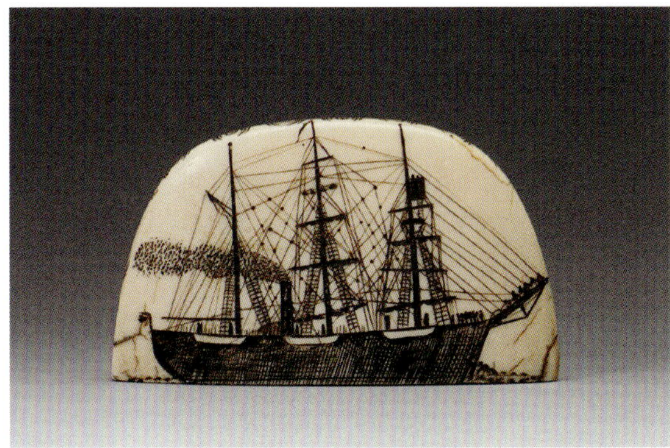

11

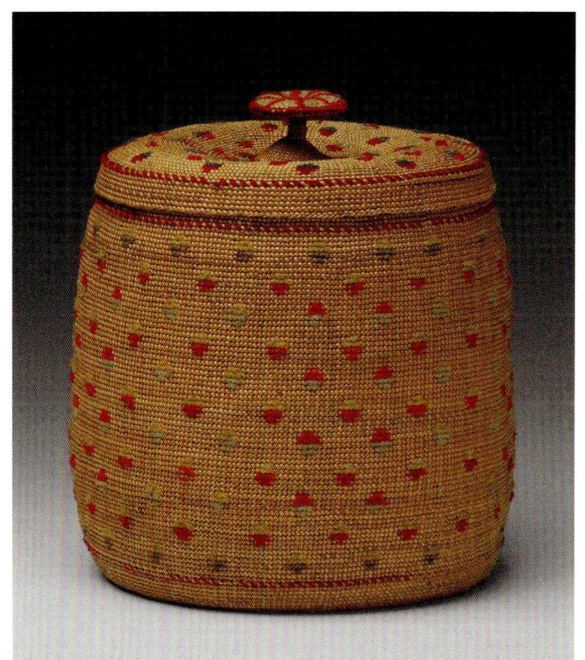

13

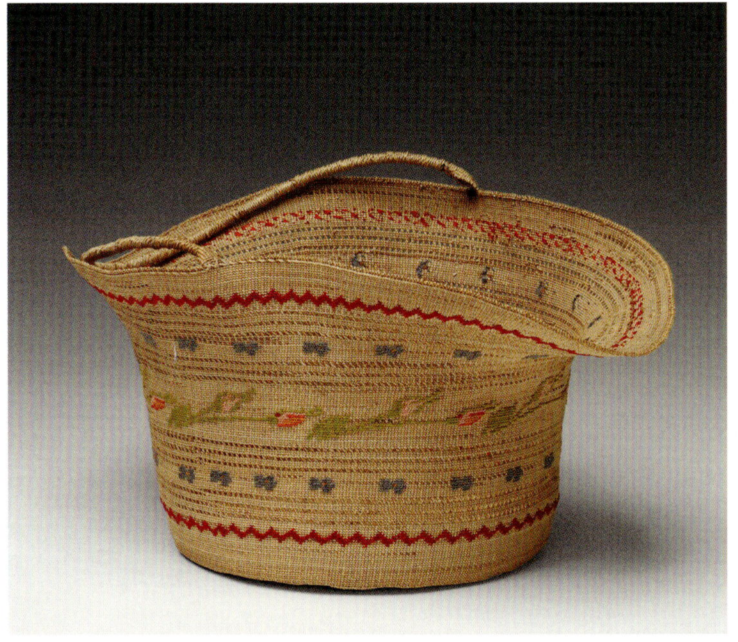

12

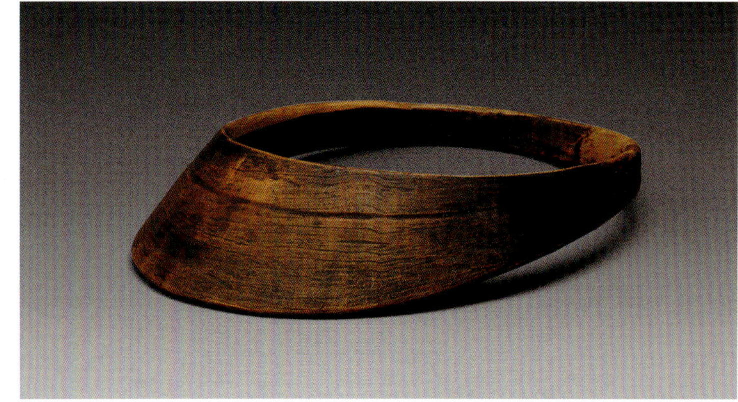

14

11. Artist unknown, Inupiat

Scrimshaw, about 1900

Bone, graphite
4.2 x 7.5 x 5 cm
Bequest of Frank C. and Clara G. Churchill; 46.17.14737

12. Mrs. Adolf Rankin, Unangan (Aleut), active early 20th century, Unalaska, Aleutian Islands, Alaska

Basket, about 1905

Wild rye grass
11 x 24.3 cm; 21 cm (including handle)
Bequest of Frank C. and Clara G. Churchill; 46.17.9384

13. Artist unknown, Unangan (Aleut), Aleutian Islands, Alaska

Basket and lid, about 1870

Wild rye grass and woolen yarn
18 x 14.5 x 3 cm (lid only); 14 cm (basket without lid)
Gift of Warren Prosser Smith, Class of 1913; 168.95.24525

14. Artist unknown, Unangan (Aleut), Aleutian Islands, Alaska

Visor, about 1900

Wood and metal
5 x 18 x 25 cm
Museum purchase; 54.67.13226

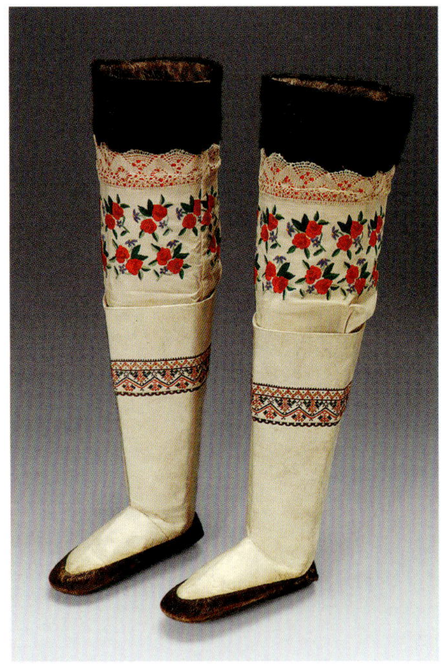

15

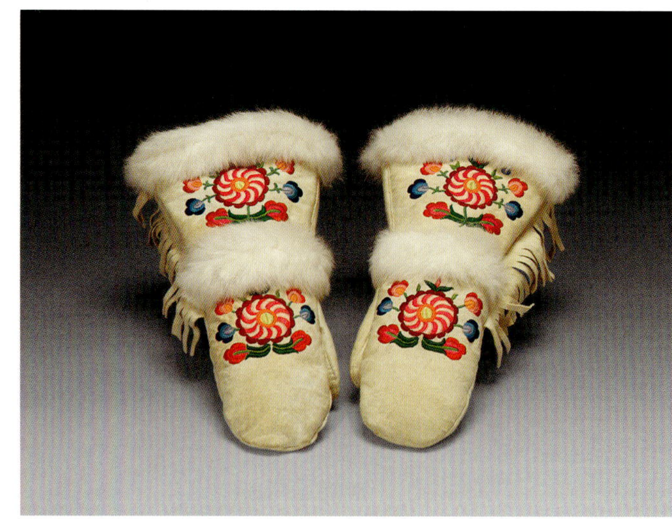

17

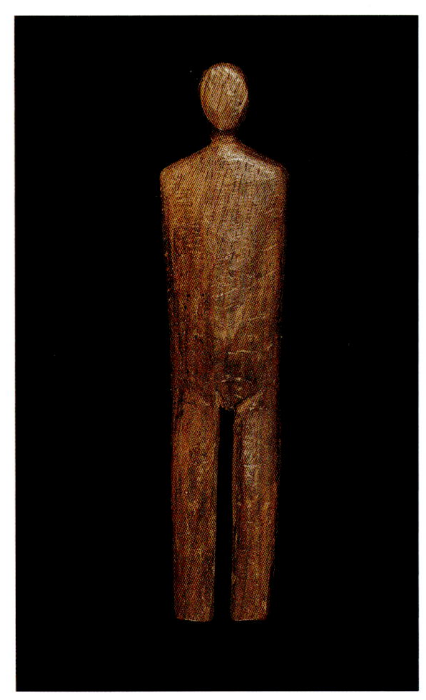

16

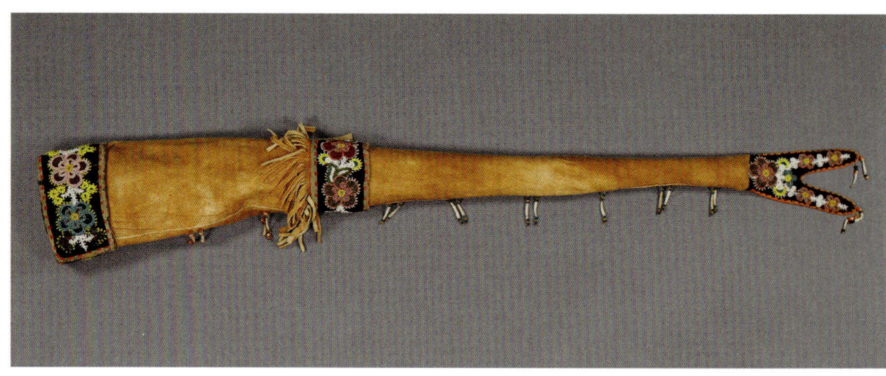

18

Greenland

15. Artist unknown, Kalaallitt, Nuuk, Greenland

Formal girl's boots, 1945

Sealskin, hide, cotton cloth, silk, lace, dye, embroidery thread, and thread
59.5 x 23 cm; 21.5 cm (heel to toe)
Gift of Mona Lloyd; *157.14.13901*

16. Artist unknown, Kalaallitt, West Greenland

Doll, about 1895

Wood
15.5 x 3.6 cm
Gift of Mrs. William Stickney, Class of 1900W; 164.21.15449

Subarctic

Central Subarctic

17. Artist unknown, Cree (Norway House Cree), The Pas, Manitoba

Mitt, 1985

Hand-tanned bleached deer hide, rabbit fur, silk embroidery thread, silk, cotton lining, and thread
37 x 21 x 4.4 cm
Purchased through the Phyllis and Bertram Geller 1937 Memorial Fund; 2006.44.4

Western Subarctic

18. Artist unknown, Northern Athapaskan (Slavey Dene), Northwest Territories

Gun case, about 1920

Native-tanned smoked and unsmoked caribou hide, cotton, wool cloth, glass beads, dentalium shells, thread, and ribbon
124.5 (130 cm including bead pendants on forked tab) x 20.7 cm
Gift of Guido R. Rahr Sr., Class of 1951P; 985.47.26571

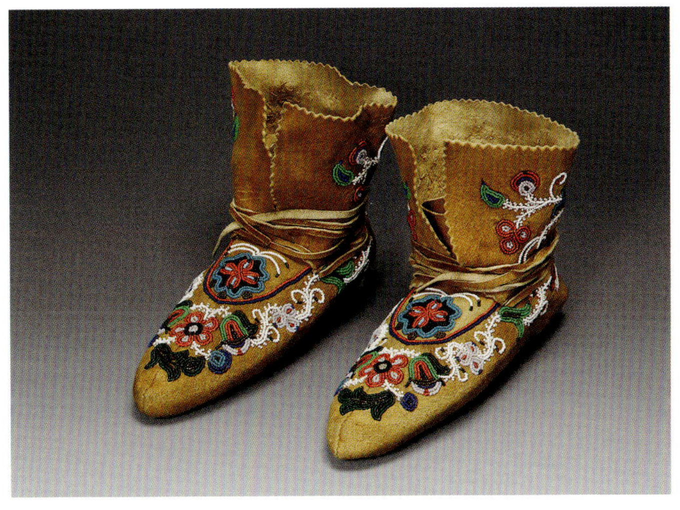

19

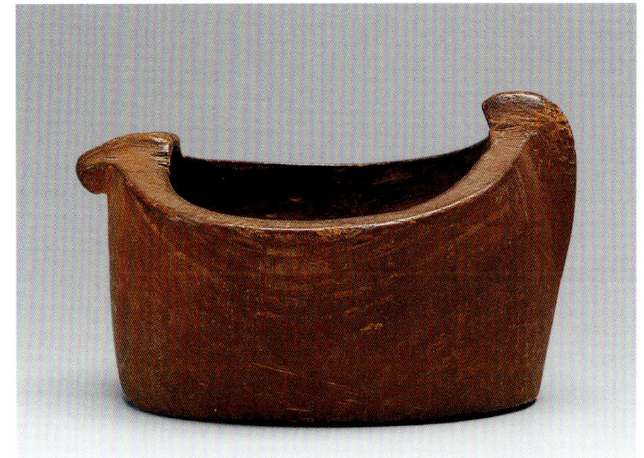

21

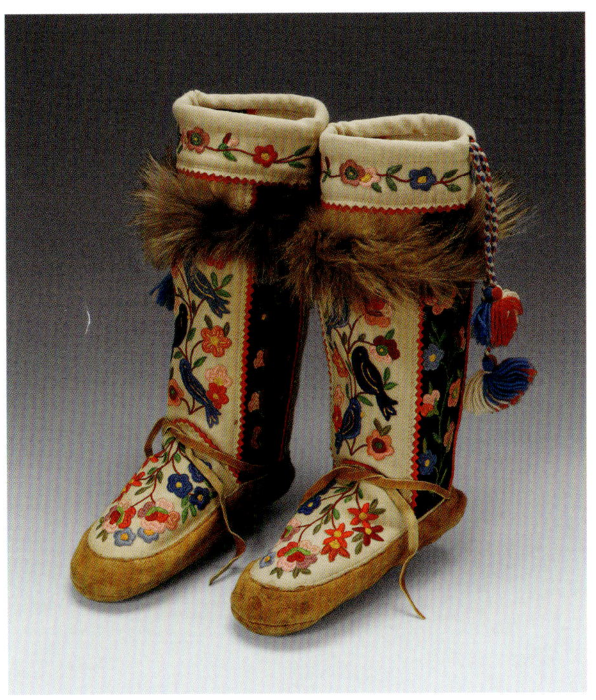

20

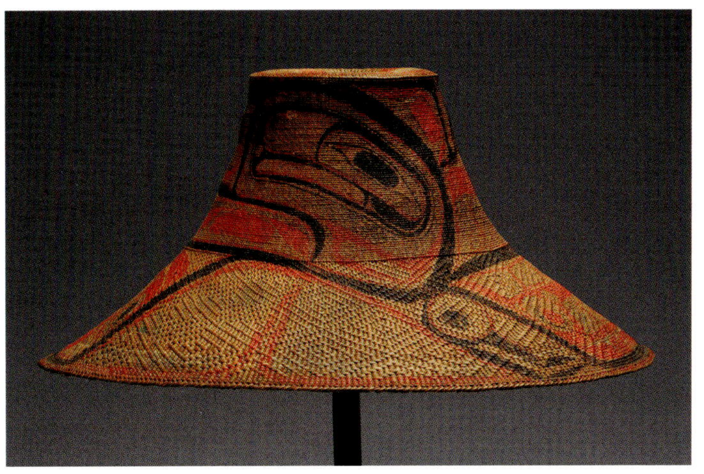

22

19. Artist unknown, Northern Athapaskan (Slavey Dene)

Moccasins, about 1910–20

Native tanned and smoked hide, glass beads, metal beads, and thread
16.5 x 25 x 10.7 cm
Gift of Lt. Col. Alfred T. Clifton, Class of 1927P; 42.15.7813

20. Artist unknown, Northern Athapaskan (Slavey Dene), Hay River, Northwest Territories

Mukluks, about 1940

Tanned and smoked moose hide, duffle, embroidery thread, wolf fur (added at a later date), yarn, and thread
32 x 20.5 cm; 22 x 14 cm
Gift of Professor and Mrs. Trevor Lloyd; 159.45.14678

Northwest Coast

Northern Northwest Coast

21. Artist unknown, possibly Eyak

Bowl, about 1890

Wood and pigment
9.5 x 8.5 x 5.5 cm
Gift of Mrs. Charles Sheldon; 50.42.12482

22. Artist unknown, Haida, Haida Gwaii (Queen Charlotte Islands), British Columbia

Hat, about 1860

Spruce root, paint, cotton cloth, and thread
16 x 37 cm
Gift of Mrs. Margaret Kimberly; 22.3.1927

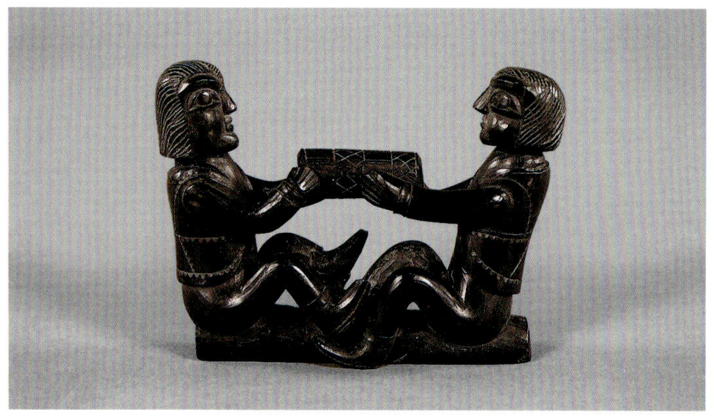

23

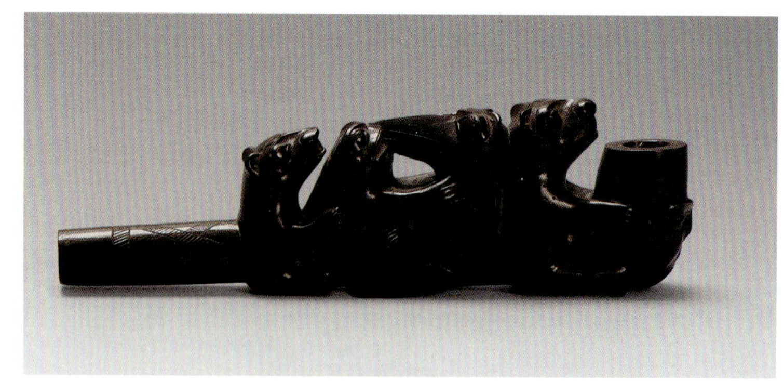

25

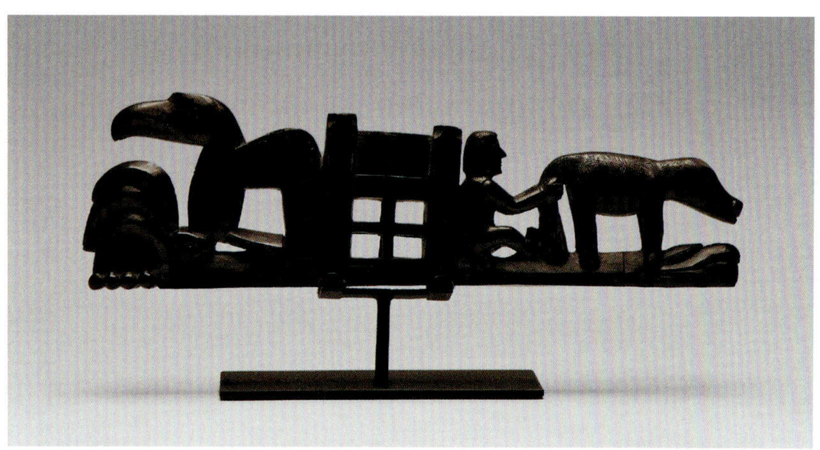

24

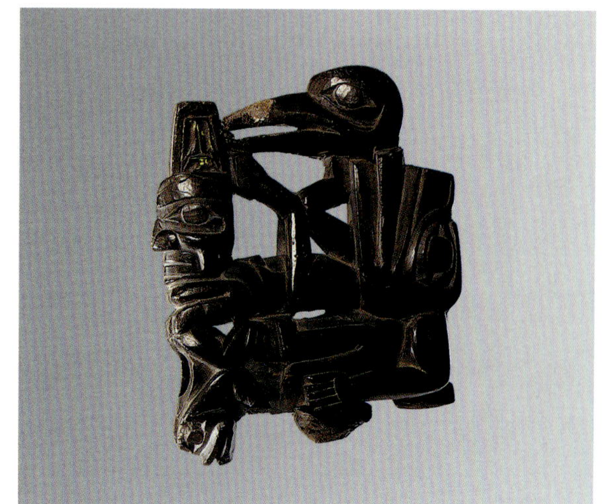

26

23. Artist unknown, Haida, Haida Gwaii (Queen Charlotte Islands), British Columbia

Male figures, about 1850

Argillite
7.2 x 9.5 x 2.3 cm
Gift of Mrs. James Foster Scott, in memory of her late husband, Victor J. Evans; 157.9.13876

24. Artist unknown, Haida, Haida Gwaii (Queen Charlotte Islands), British Columbia

Pipe, about 1840–60

Argillite
9.5 x 31.7 x 2.3 cm
Purchased through the Mrs. Harvey P. Hood W'18 Fund and the Hood Museum of Art Acquisitions Fund; 2009.3

25. Artist unknown, Haida, Haida Gwaii (Queen Charlotte Islands), British Columbia

Pipe, 1860

Argillite
7.5 x 24.5 x 4 cm
Gift of Mrs. James Foster Scott, in memory of her late husband, Victor J. Evans; 157.9.13875

26. Artist unknown, Haida, Haida Gwaii (Queen Charlotte Islands), British Columbia

Pipe bowl, 1860

Argillite
8.5 x 10.2 x 2.4 cm
Gift of Glover Street Hastings III; 181.2.26119

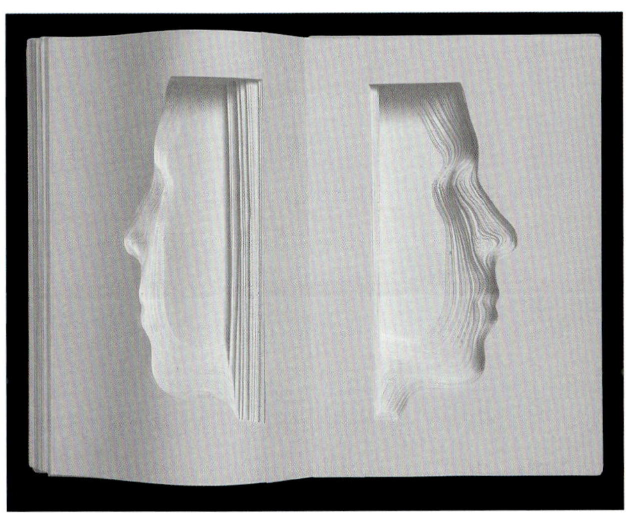

27

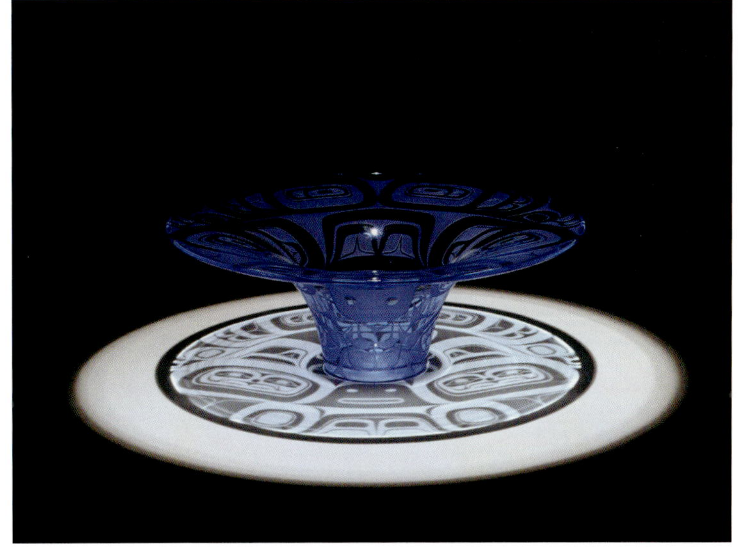

29

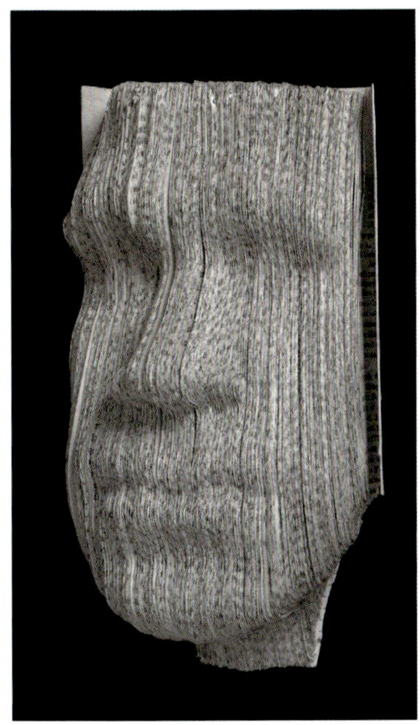

28

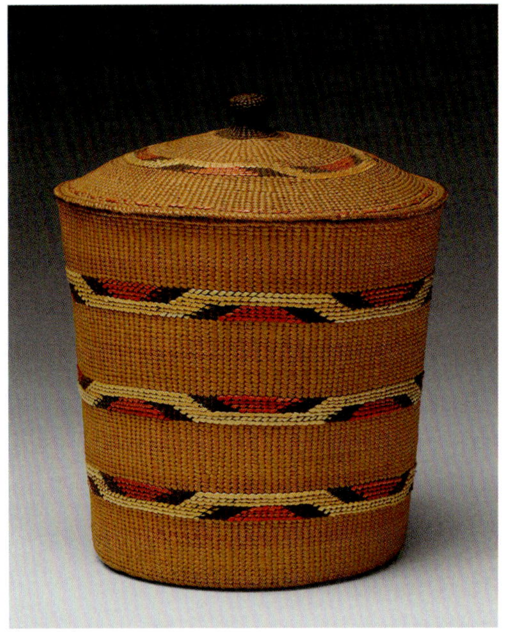

30

27. Nicholas Galanin, Tlingit / Unangan (Aleut), born 1979

What Have We Become? Vol. 3, 2007

Book made of blank white pages with face of the artist cut out of it
7.7 x 44.3 x 28.7 cm
Purchased through the Virginia and Preston T. Kelsey 1958 Fund; 2007.36.1

28. Nicholas Galanin, Tlingit / Unangan (Aleut), born 1979

What Have We Become? Vol. 5a, 2007

Cut pages from the book *Under Mount Saint Elias*
22 x 13 x 11.5 cm
Purchased through the Virginia and Preston T. Kelsey 1958 Fund; 2007.36.2

29. Preston Singletary, Tlingit, born 1963

Tlingit Crest Hat, 2006

Etched blue glass
17.8 x 48.3 cm
Purchased through the Claire and Richard P. Morse 1953 Fund, the William S. Rubin Fund, the Alvin and Mary Bert Gutman '40 Acquisitions Fund, and the Charles Venrick 1936 Fund; 2007.12

30. Artist unknown, Tlingit, Yakutat, Alaska

Basket, about 1905

Spruce root, grass, and dyes
15 (including lid) x 12.6 cm; 12 cm (basket only)
Bequest of Frank C. and Clara G. Churchill; 46.17.9392

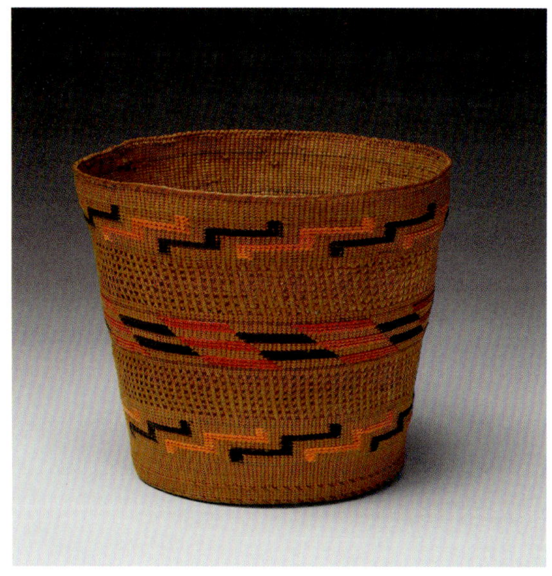

31

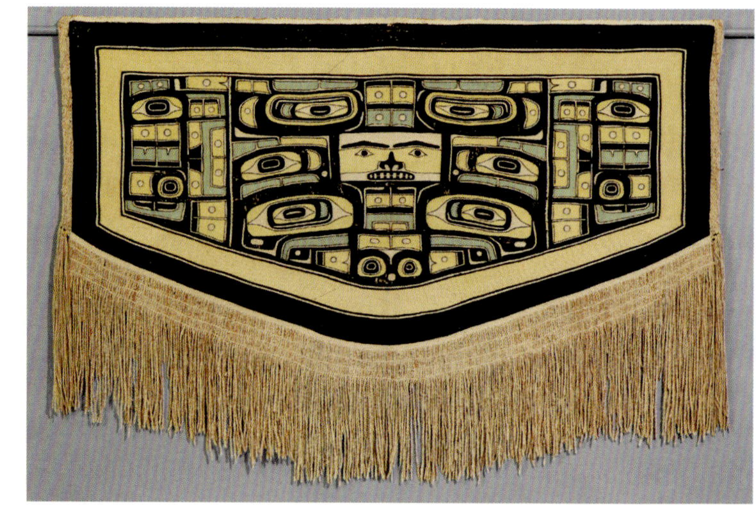

33

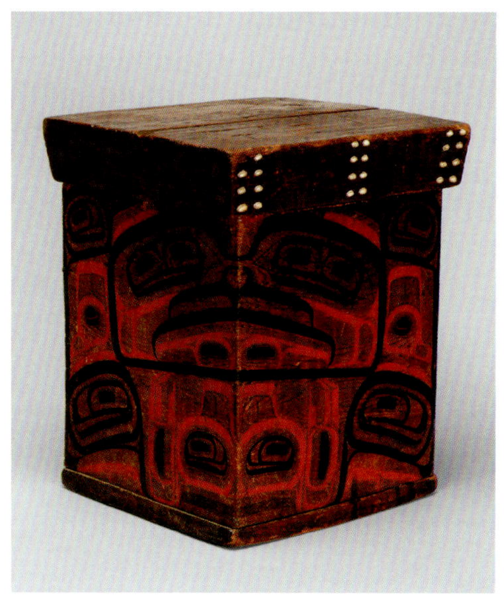

32

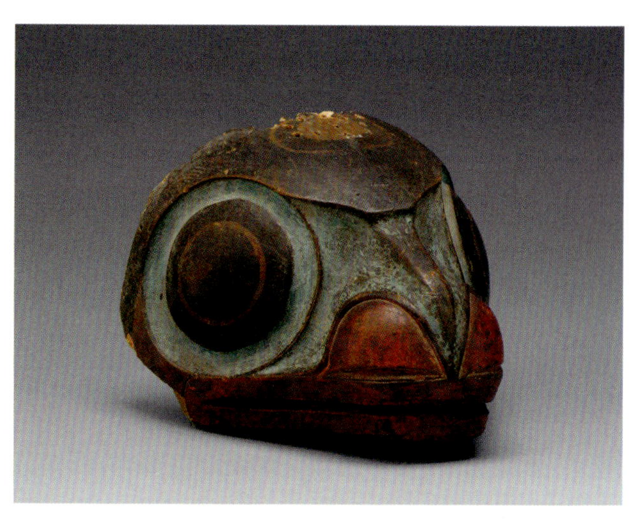

34

31. Artist unknown, Tlingit, Yakutat, Alaska

Berry basket, about 1900

Spruce root, grass, and dyes
14.6 x 17.3 cm
Bequest of Frank C. and Clara G. Churchill; 46.17.9391

32. Artist unknown, possibly Tlingit

Box, about 1880

Cedar, red turban snail opercula, paint, and metal
Box: 40 x 34 x 33 cm; lid: 8 x 39.4 x 36.3 cm; box and lid: 47.5 cm
Purchased through the William B. Jaffe and Evelyn A. Jaffe Hall Fund and the Hood Museum of Art Acquisitions Fund; 989.24.27037

33. Artist unknown, Chilkat Tlingit

Chilkat robe (*naaxein*), about 1850–80

Mountain goat wool, cedar bark, and native dyes
87 x 175 cm
Gift of Robert L. Ripley, Class of 1939H; 40.15.12586

34. Artist unknown, Tlingit

Frontlet or headdress ornament, about 1860

Wood, paint, twine, and sea lion bristle fragments (possibly)
11 x 14 x 11.5 cm
Gift of Mrs. Margaret Kimberly; 22.3.1891

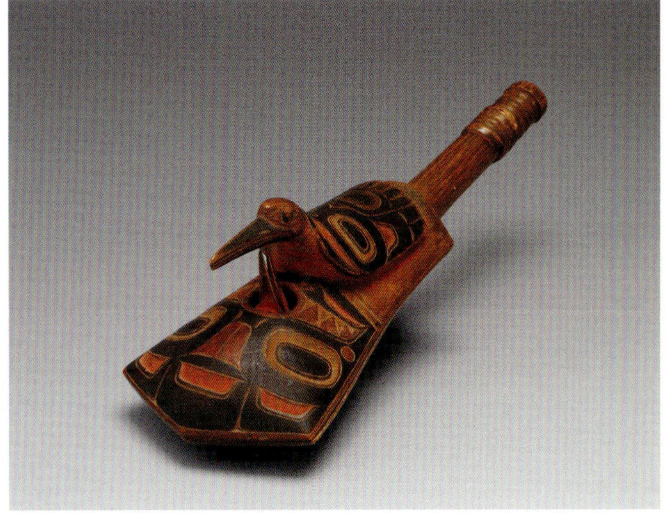

35

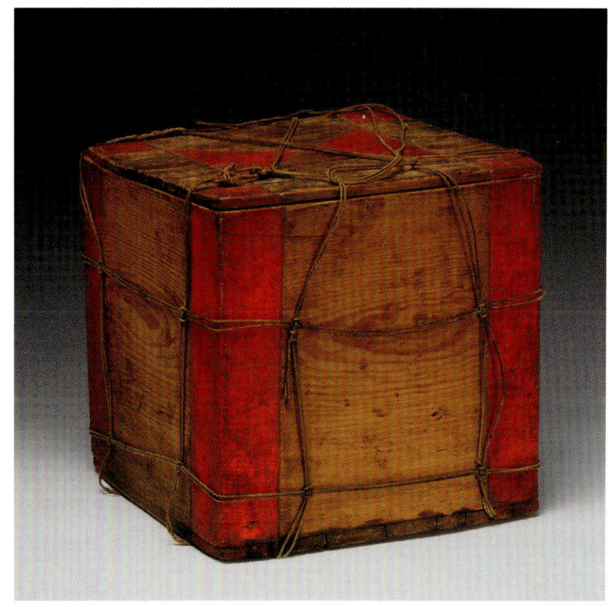

37

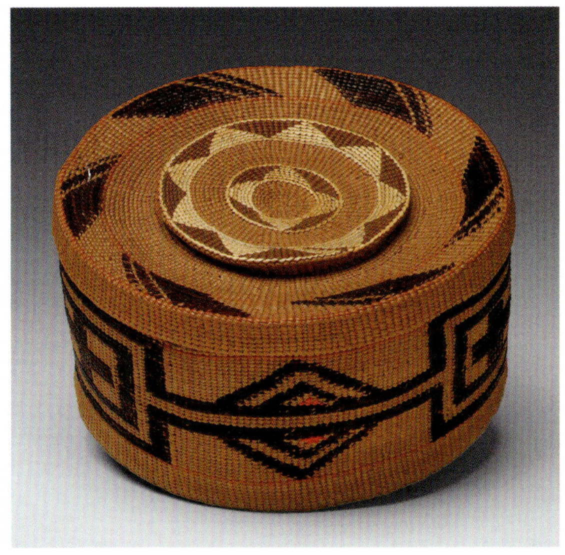

36

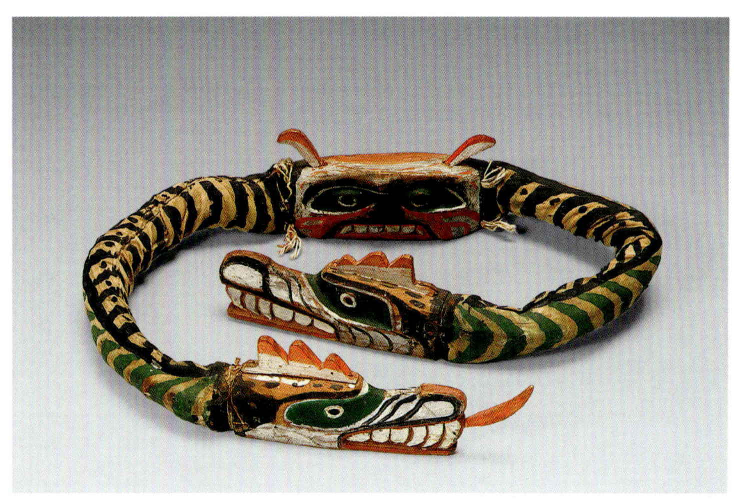

38

35. Artist unknown, Tlingit

Rattle, about 1850

Wood, spruce root, pigment
24.5 x 8 x 8 cm
Gift of Mrs. Margaret Kimberly; 22.3.1892

36. Artist unknown, Tlingit, Hoonah, Alaska

Rattle-lid basket, about 1900

Spruce root, maidenhair fern, bear grass, dyes, and pebbles
9 x 18.5 cm (basket and lid)
Bequest of Frank C. and Clara G. Churchill; 46.17.9398

37. Artist unknown, Tlingit, Hoonah, Alaska

Storage box, after 1900

Wood, paint, string, and spruce root
32 x 32 x 32 cm
Gift of Doris Meltzer and the Meltzer Gallery; 159.1.14292

Central Northwest Coast

38. Artist unknown, Kwakwaka'wakw (Kwakiutl)

Ceremonial ornament, about 1900

Belt, cedar, cotton cloth, wool cloth, paint, metal, cord, and string
9.2 x 125.5 x 4 cm
Acquired by exchange from Ralph C. Altman; 55.27.13321

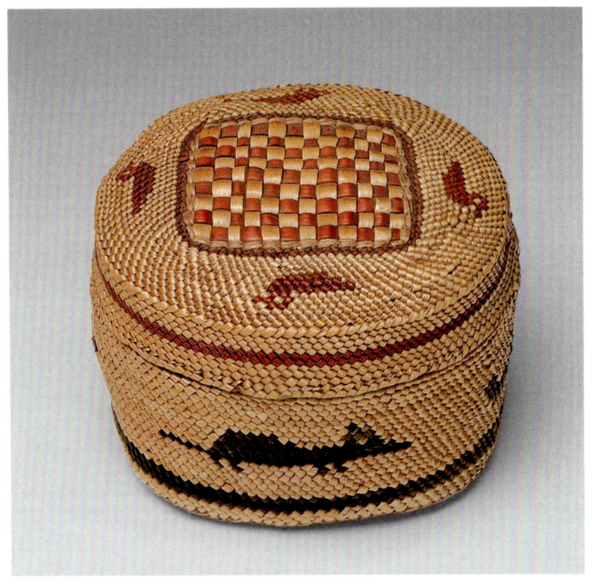

39

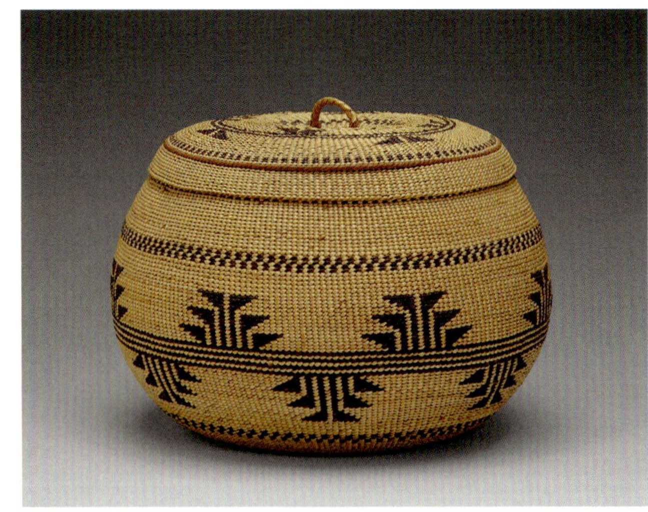

41

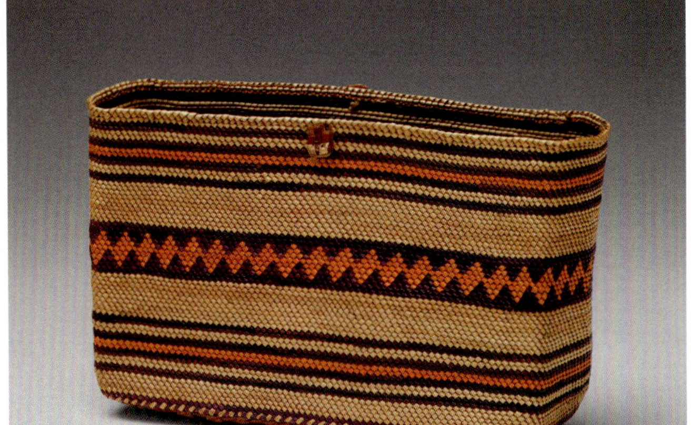

40

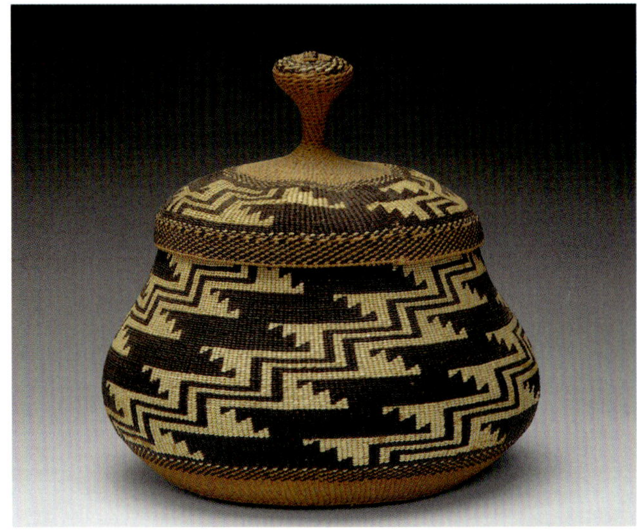

42

Southern Northwest Coast

39. Artist unknown, Makah, Cape Flattery, Washington

Basket, about 1930

Cedar bark, grass, and dye
7 x 10.5 cm (including lid)
Gift of Mr. and Mrs. George H. Browne; 42.12.7958

40. Artist unknown, Salish or Makah

Basket, about 1900

Cedar bark, grass, dyes, and string
11 x 18 x 4.5 cm
Gift of Mr. and Mrs. George H. Browne; 42.12.8510

California

Northern California

41. Artist unknown, Hupa, Karuk (Karok) or Yurok

Basket, early 20th century

Conifer root, bear grass, hazel, maidenhair fern, and twine
10 x 12.5 cm (basket only); 1.3 x 11.8 cm (lid only); 11.5 cm (lid and basket including loop)
Gift of Donald C. McIntire, Class of 1906; 54.18.12950

42. Elizabeth Conrad Hickox, Karuk (Karok) / Wiyot, 1872–1947, or Louise Hickox, Karuk (Karok), 1896–1967

Basket, about 1925

Wild grape root, myrtle sticks, hazel, maidenhair fern, yellow-dyed porcupine quills, and stag horn lichen
12.2 x 15 cm (basket only); 8.5 x 11.3 cm (lid only); 19.5 cm (basket and lid together)
Gift of Mrs. James Foster Scott, in memory of her late husband, Victor J. Evans; 157.9.13894

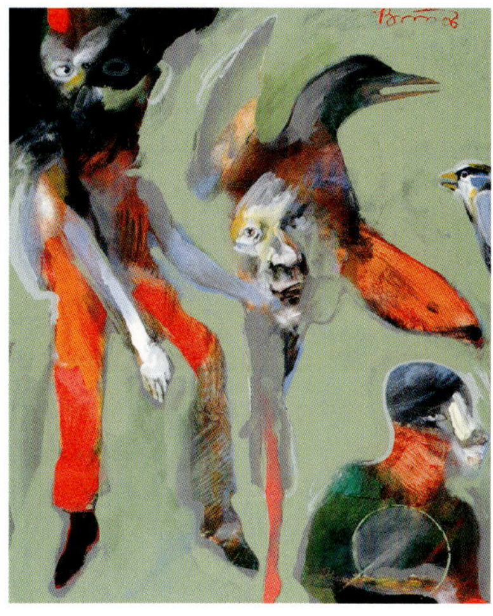

43

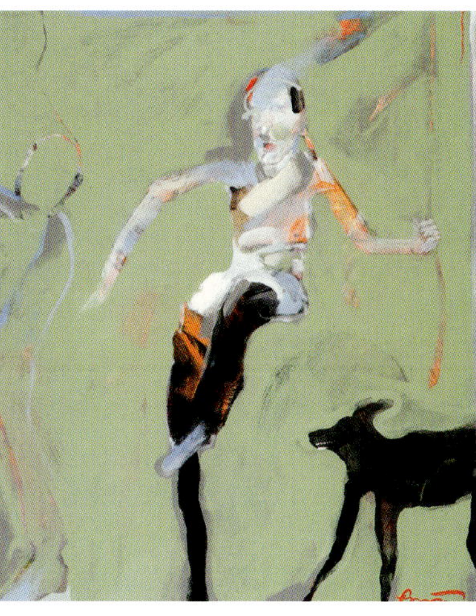

44

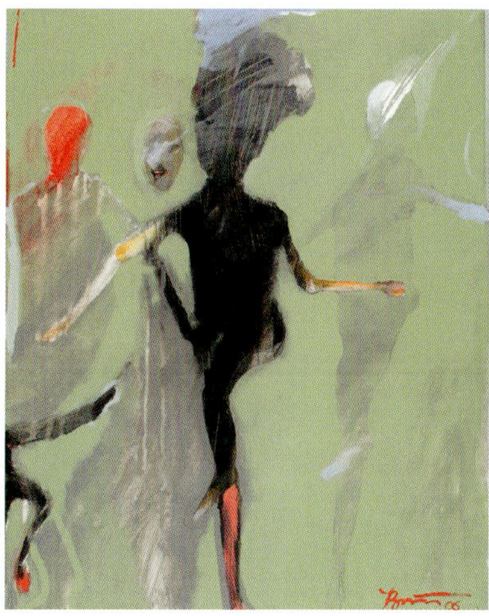

45

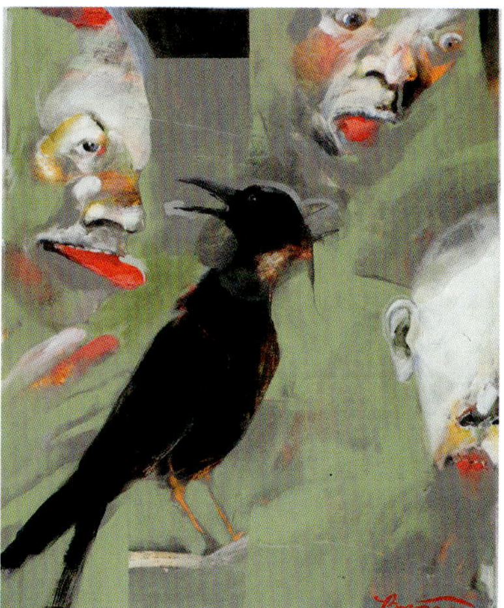

46

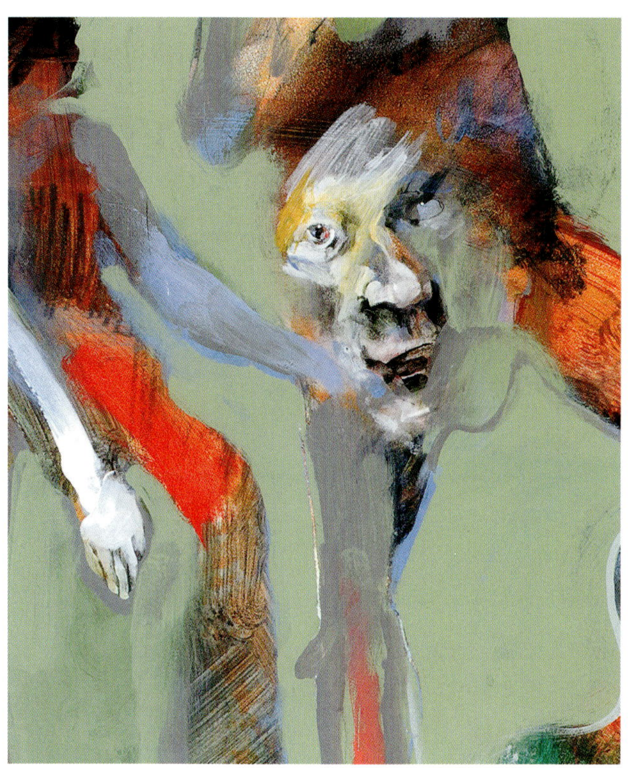

43 (detail)

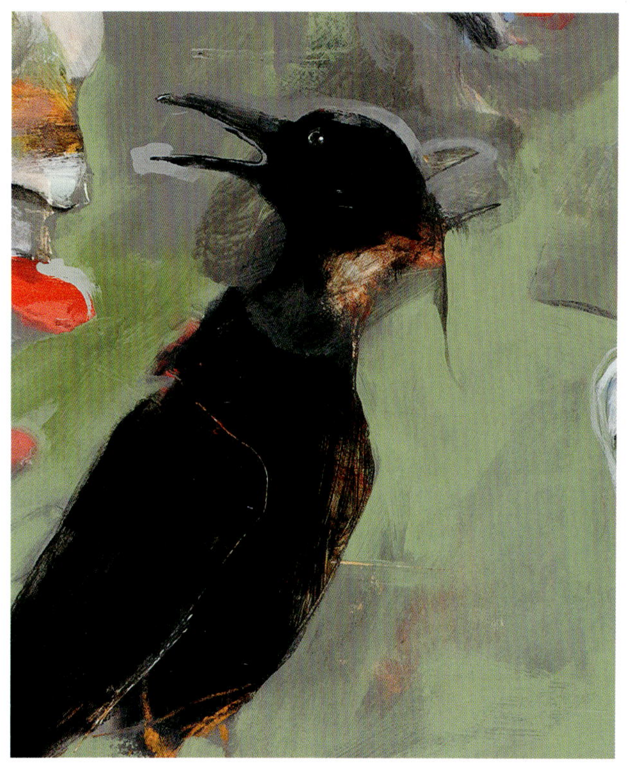

46 (detail)

43–46. Rick Bartow, Wiyot (Mad River Wiyot), born 1946

The Tale That the Crow Told, 2006
No Dogs at the Ceremony, 2006
The Dancers Arrive, 2006
Acquiring a Taste for Crow, 2006

From the series *The Ceremony That Never Was*
Acrylic on panel
Each: 51 x 40.8 x 2.3 cm
Purchased through the Hood Museum of Art Acquisitions Fund; 2008.6.1–4

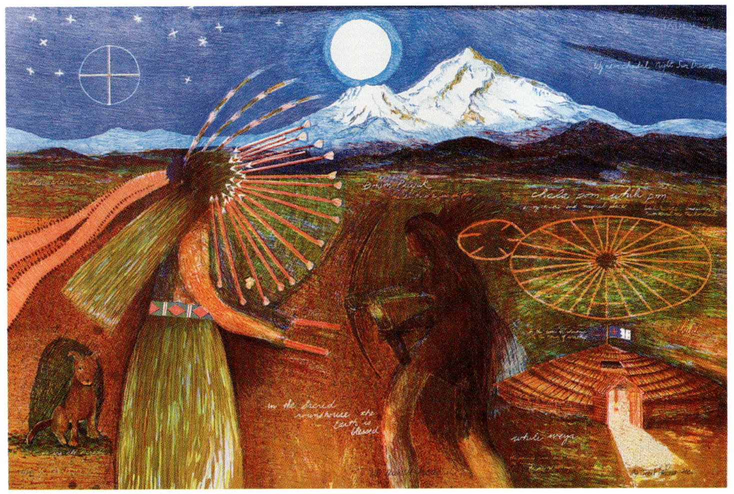

47

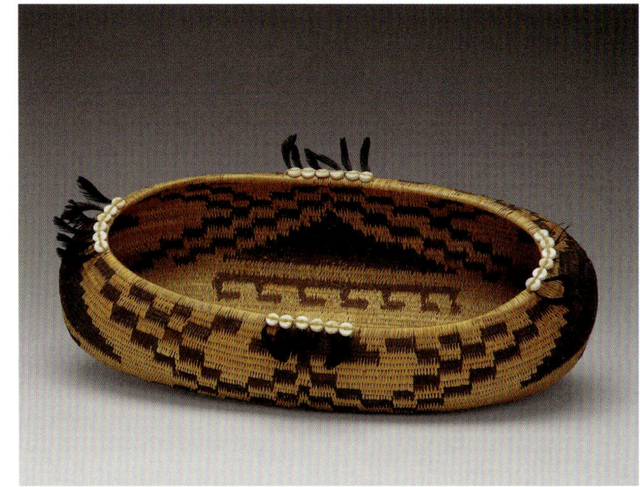

49

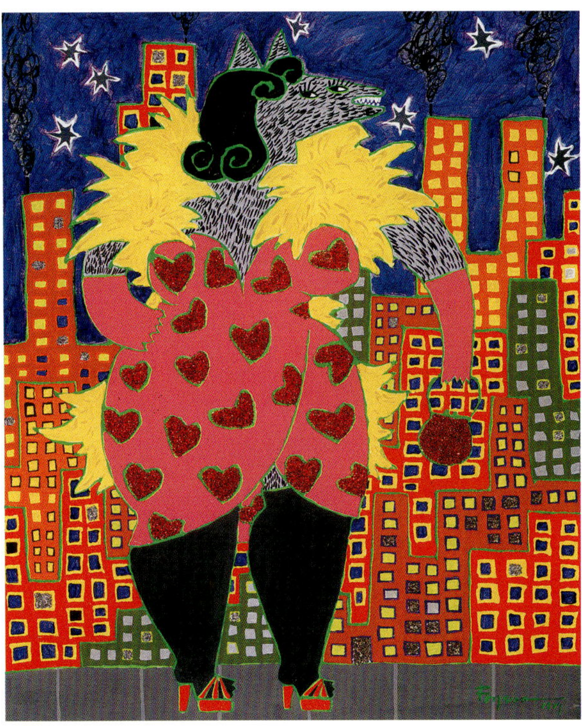

48

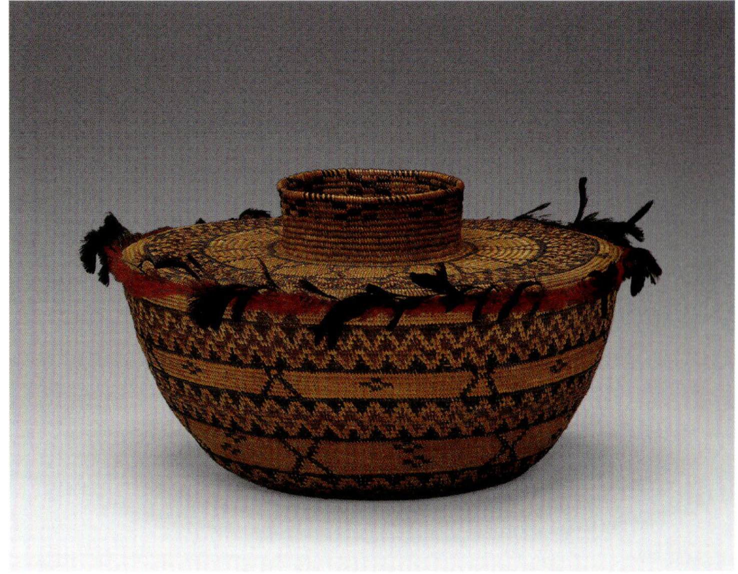

50

Central California

47. Frank LaPena, Maidu / Wintun (Nomtipom Wintu), born 1937

We Are All Sacred, 2001

Hand-colored lithograph on paper
76.2 x 101.6 cm
Purchased through the Class of 1935 Memorial Fund; 2008.41.1

48. Harry Fonseca, Southern Maidu (Nisenan) / Hawaiian / Portuguese, 1946–2006

Coyote Woman in the City, 1979

Acrylic, glitter, and foil on canvas
76.2 x 61 cm
Gift of the Class of 1962, P.989.10

49. Artist unknown, Pomo

Basket, about 1905

Sedge root, willow, bracken fern root, California valley quail crests, clamshell disc beads, and string
26 x 13 x 6 cm
Bequest of Frank C. and Clara G. Churchill; 46.17.9333

50. Artist unknown, Yokuts, Kern County, California

Treasure basket, about 1890

Deer grass, bracken fern root, redbud, California valley quail crests, and wool yarn
12.5 cm h. x 22 cm dia. (26 cm dia. including quail crests)
Gift of Mrs. Ida Farr Miller; 44.18.8755

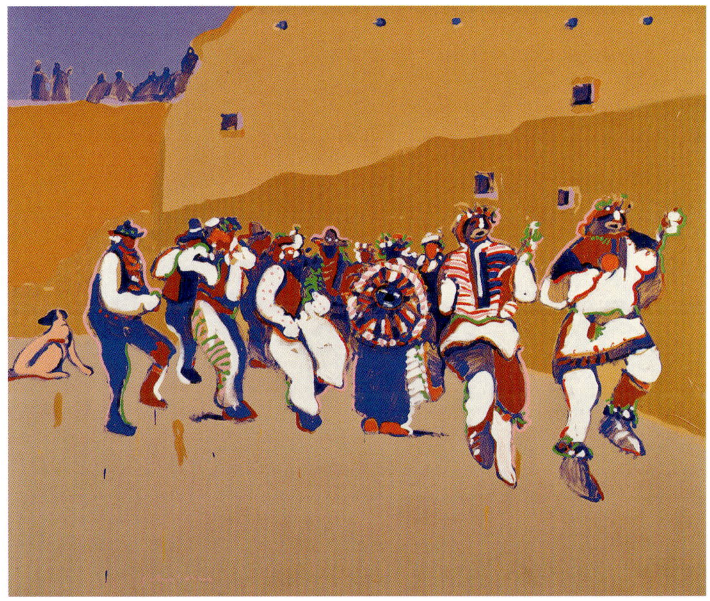

51

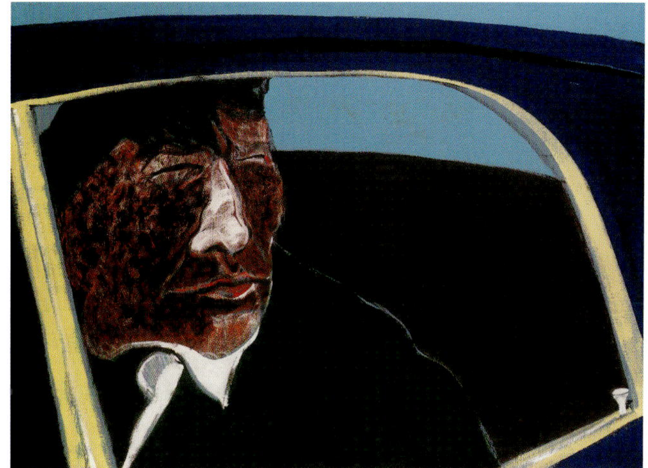

53

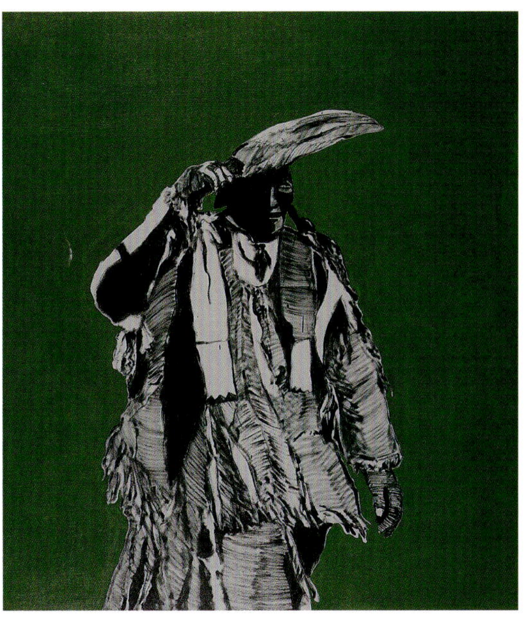

52

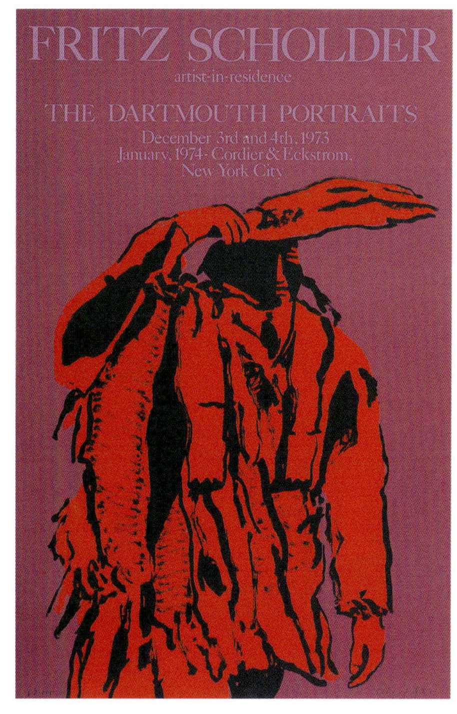

54

Southern California

51. Fritz Scholder, Luiseño (Luiseno), 1937–2005

Dancers and Dog, 1972

Acrylic on canvas
172.7 x 203.2 cm
Gift of Mr. and Mrs. Varujan Boghosian; P.980.16

52. Fritz Scholder, Luiseño (Luiseno), 1937–2005

Dartmouth Portrait #17, 1973

Oil on canvas, acrylic background
203.2 x 172.7 cm
Purchased through the William B. Jaffe and Evelyn A. Jaffe Hall Fund; P.974.11

53. Fritz Scholder, Luiseño (Luiseno), 1937–2005

Drunken Indian in Car, 1974

Acrylic on canvas
76.6 x 102 cm
Gift of Jane and Raphael Bernstein; P.986.77.6

54. Fritz Scholder, Luiseño (Luiseno), 1937–2005

Fritz Scholder: The Dartmouth Portraits, 1973

Screenprint on wove paper
84.9 x 54 cm
Gift of Varujan Boghosian; PR.993.56.4

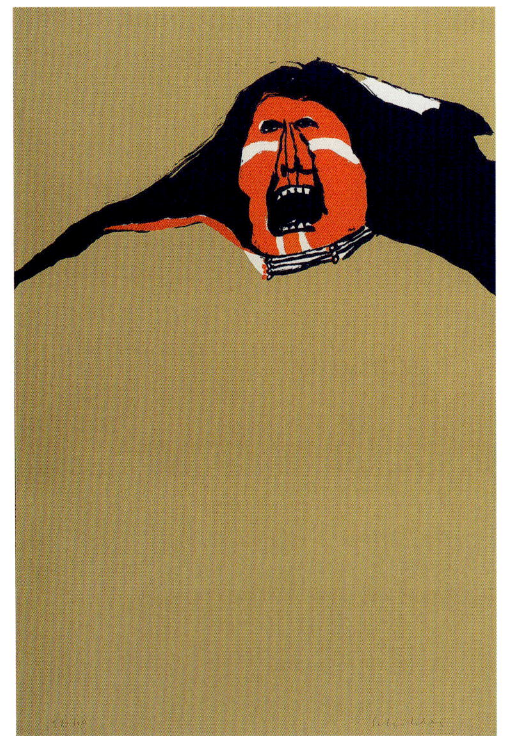

55

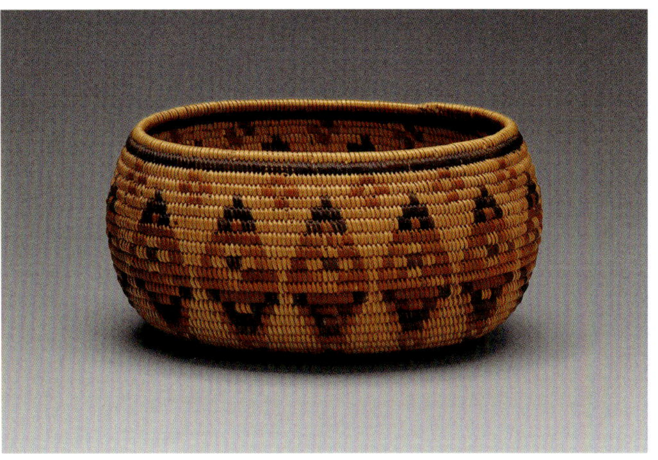

56

57

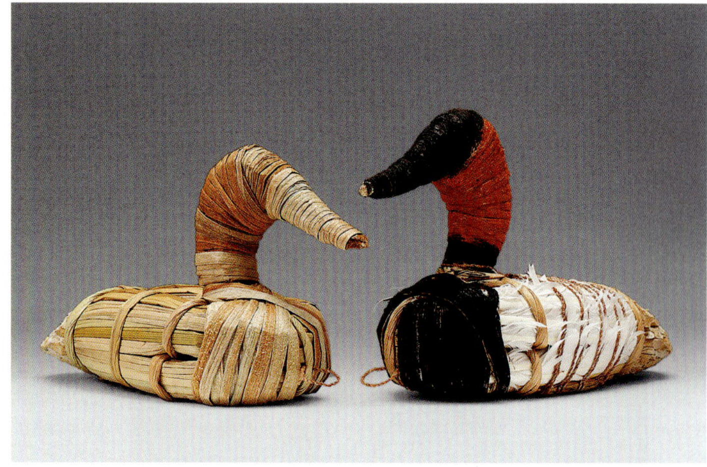

58

55. Fritz Scholder, Luiseño (Luiseno), 1937–2005

Untitled (Screaming Indian), 1973

Screenprint on wove paper
85.8 x 56.4 cm
Gift of Varujan Boghosian, PR.993.56.5

56. Artist unknown, Luiseño (Luiseno)

Basket, about 1900

Deergrass, juncas, sumac, black-dyed juncas rush, and grass
10.5 x 8.6 x 5.6 cm
Bequest of Frank C. and Clara G. Churchill; 46.17.9304

57. Artist unknown, Luiseño (Luiseno)

Basket, about 1900

Juncas, sumac, black-dyed juncas rush, and grass
7.2 x 15 cm
Bequest of Frank C. and Clara G. Churchill; 46.17.9306

Great Basin

Paiute

58. Mike Williams, Walker River Paiute; Northern Pauite (Paviotso), born about 1956

Male and Female Canvasback Duck Decoys, 2009

Tule, cattails, natural pigments, and feathers
Each decoy: 20.3 x 27.9 x 11.4 cm
Purchased through the Alvin and Mary Bert Gutman '40 Acquisitions Fund; 2009.55.1–2

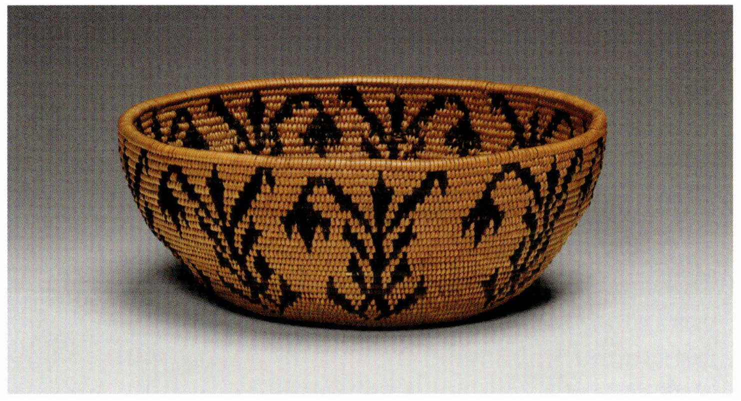

59

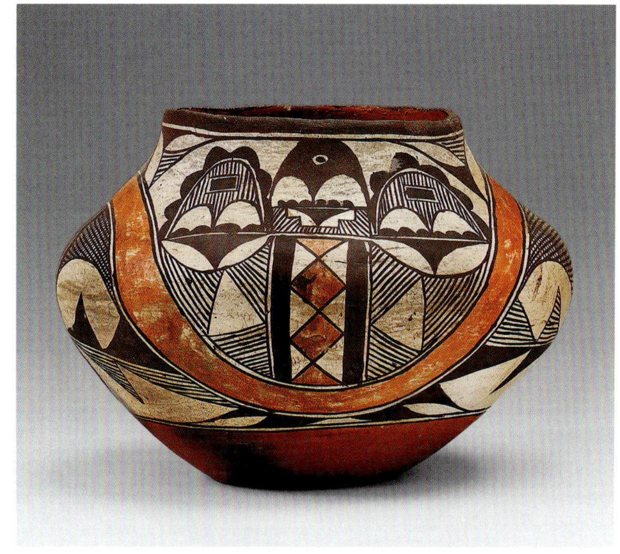

61

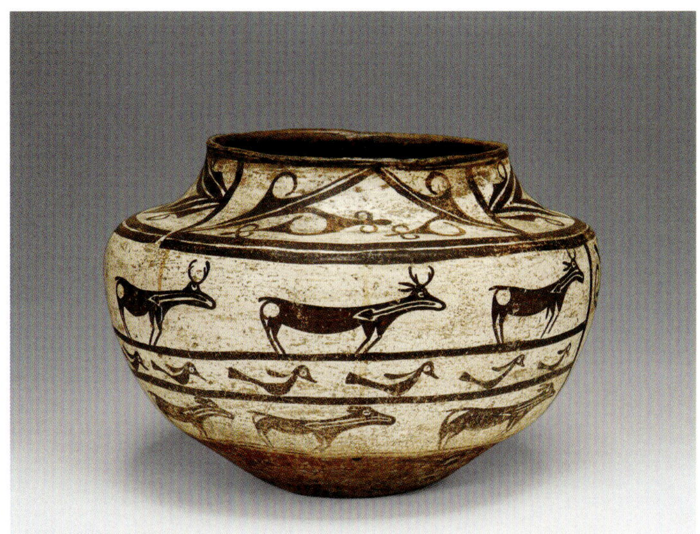

60

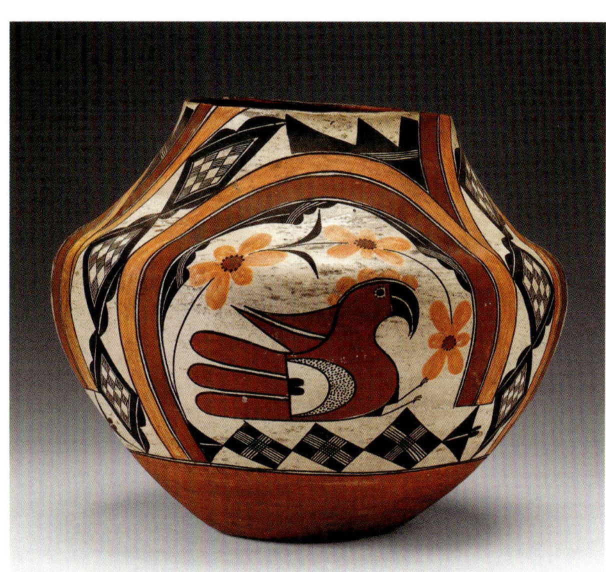

62

Washoe

59. Artist unknown, Washoe (Washo)

Basket, about 1905

Willow, bracken fern root, and grass
7 x 18 cm
Bequest of Frank C. and Clara G. Churchill; 46.17.9356

Southwest

Pueblo

60. Artist unknown, A:shiwi (Zuni Pueblo)

Storage jar (*olla*), about 1870–1910

Earthenware with colored slips and burnished
24.5 x 34 cm
Gift of Heidi and Arthur Lewis Wood, Class of 1934; 987.61.26901

61. Artist unknown, Acoma Pueblo

Water jar (*olla*) depicting rainbow arching over crosshatched elements, about 1900

Earthenware, painted with colored slips and burnished
15.5 x 19.3 cm
Bequest of Frank C. and Clara G. Churchill; 46.17.10066

62. Artist unknown, Acoma Pueblo

Water jar (*olla*) depicting macaw or parrot with overarching flowers and double rainbow, about 1900

Earthenware, painted with colored slips and burnished
27.6 x 27.8 cm
Bequest of Frank C. and Clara G. Churchill; 46.17.10077

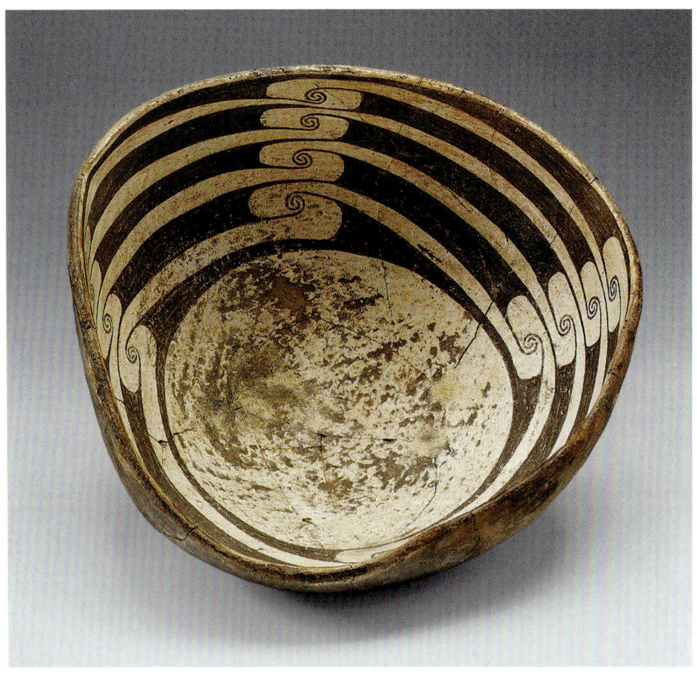

63

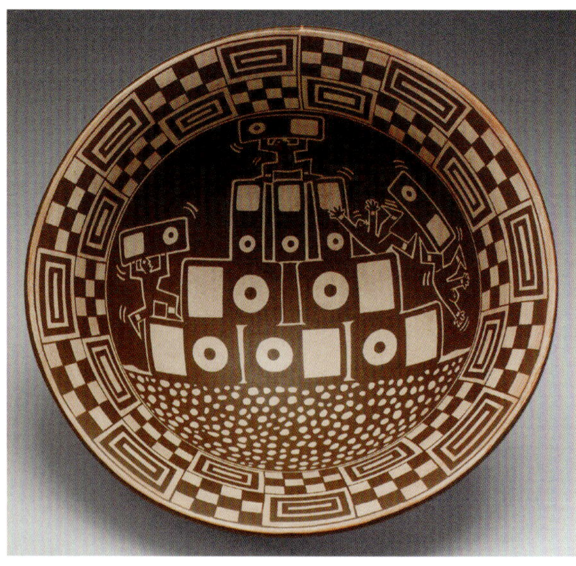

65

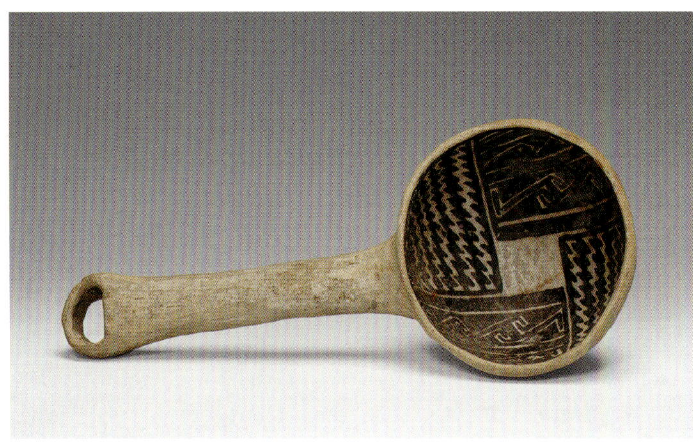

64

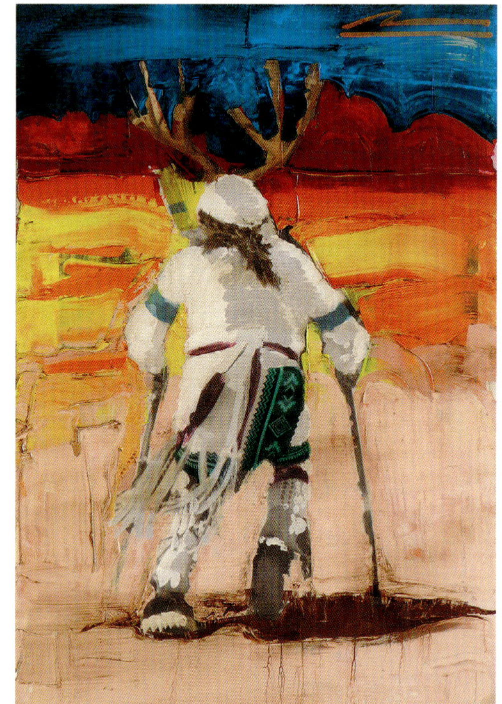

66

63. Artist unknown, Ancestral Puebloan, Mimbres, Mogollon Tradition

Bowl depicting concentric circles with interlocking scrolls in a quartered pattern, Classic Mimbres Phase, 1050–1250

Earthenware, painted with colored slips
15.5 cm h. x 31.5 cm dia.
Museum purchase; 183.1.26375

64. Artist unknown, Ancestral Puebloan, Little Colorado River, Tuba City, Arizona

Ladle, Late Pueblo III Phase, 1250–1300

Earthenware, painted with colored slips
6.5 x 27 x 12 cm
Bequest of Frank C. and Clara G. Churchill; 46.17.10686

65. Diego Romero, Cochiti Pueblo, born 1964

Pod Mound, 2010

Native clay and slip, kiln fired
Diameter: 38.1 cm
Purchased through the Kira Fournier and Benjamin Schore Contemporary Sculpture Fund and the Hood Museum of Art Acquisitions Fund; 2010.54

66. Mateo Romero, Cochiti Pueblo, born 1966

Deer Dancer at Daybreak, 2007

Oil and mixed media on plywood
152.4 x 101.6 cm
Purchased through the Olivia H. Parker and John O. Parker '58 Acquisition Fund; 2008.52

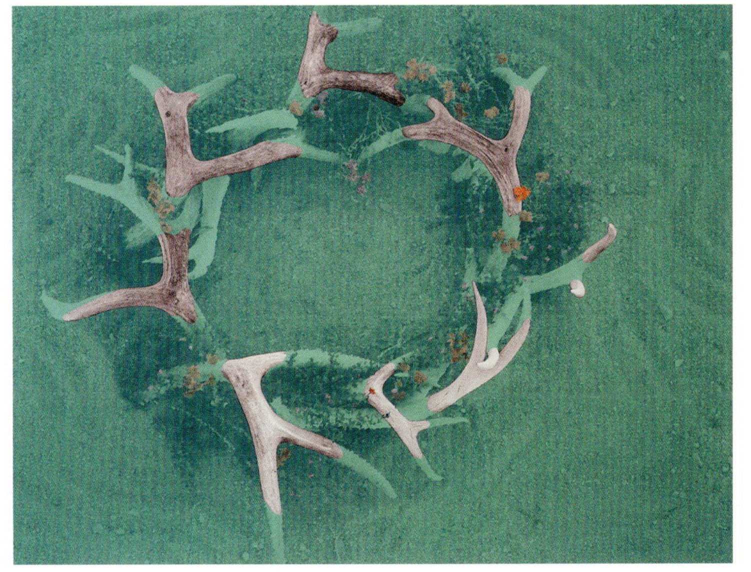

67

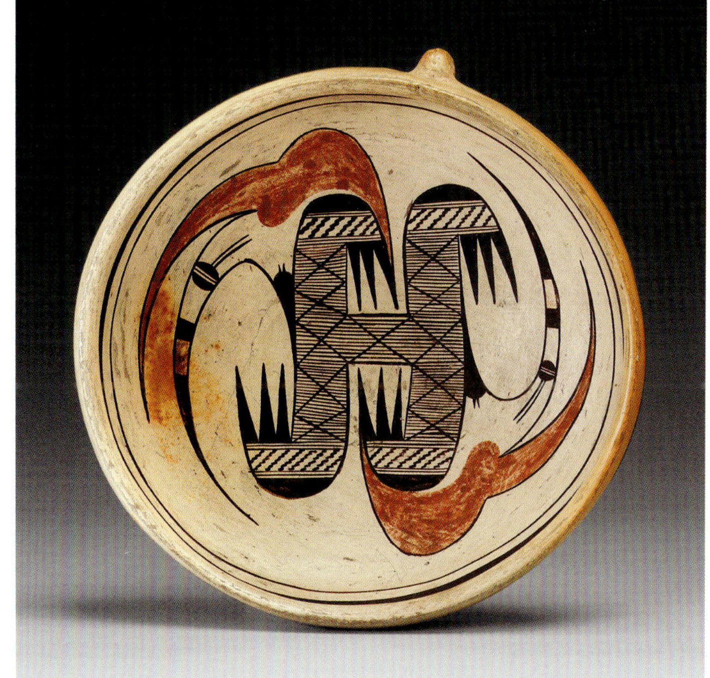

69

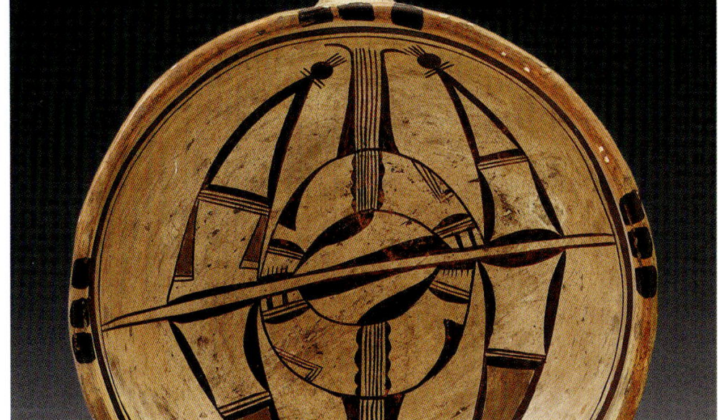

68

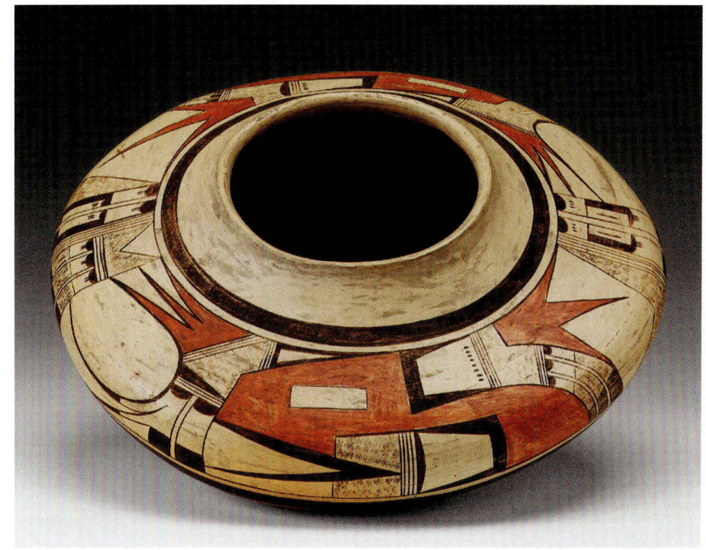

70

67. Victor Masayesva Jr., Hopi, born 1951

Ground Zero, negative: 1998, print: 2007

Epson pigment print
Image: 43.3 x 55.7 cm; sheet: 61 x 50.8 cm
Purchased through the Harry Shafer Fisher 1966 Memorial Fund; 2007.37.2

68. Nampeyo, Hopi; Hano Pueblo, about 1860–1942

Bowl, early 1890s

Earthenware, painted with colored slips and burnished
8.9 x 24 cm
Gift of Bradley M. Patten; 34.37.6004

69. Nampeyo, Hopi; Hano Pueblo, about 1860–1942

Bowl, depicting migration design, about 1900–1907

Earthenware, painted with colored slips and burnished
6 x 18.5 cm
Bequest of Frank C. and Clara G. Churchill; 46.17.10111

70. Nampeyo, Hopi; Hano Pueblo, about 1860–1942

Seed jar in Sikyatki Revival Style, about 1900–1910

Earthenware, painted with colored slips and burnished
14.5 x 3 cm
Gift of Mr. and Mrs. George H. Browne; 42.12.8107

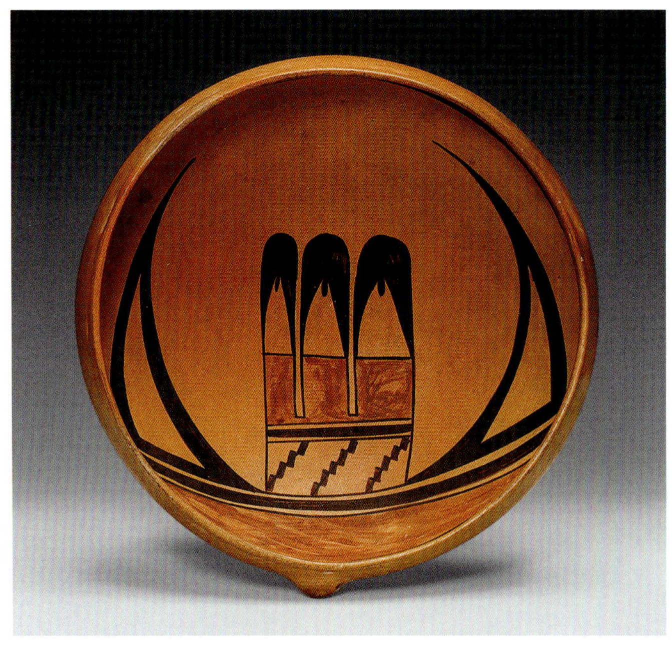

71

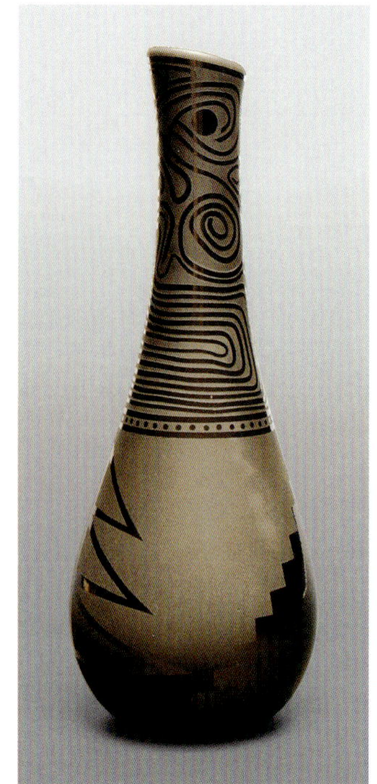

73

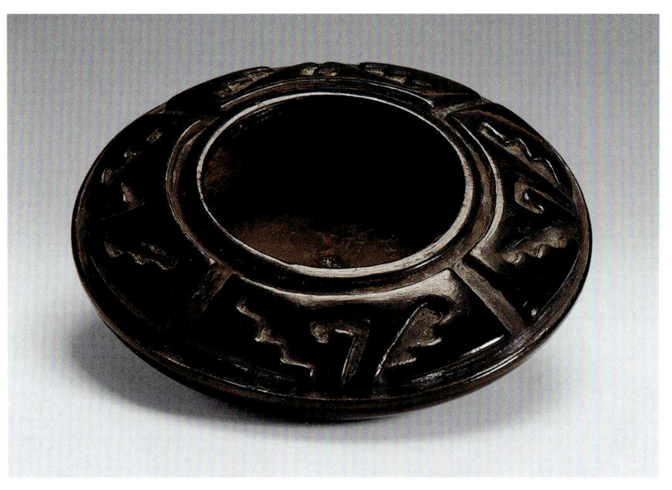

72

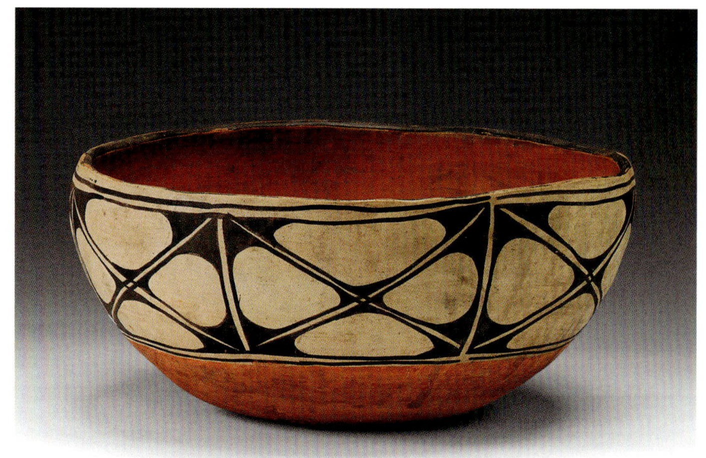

74

71. Artist unknown, Hopi

Bowl, about 1920

Earthenware with colored slips and burnished
19 x 24 cm
Gift of Glover Street Hastings III; 181.2.26069

72. Margaret Tafoya, K'apovi (Santa Clara Pueblo), 1904–2001

Bowl, mid-20th century

Polished blackware
6.4 x 23.8 cm
Gift of Marsha J. and Joel D. Ash, Class of 1956, Thayer 1958; 2009.94

73. Robert "Spooner" Marcus, Ohkay Owingeh Pueblo (San Juan Pueblo), born 1975

Evergreen, 2007

Blown glass
37.7 x 13 x 13 cm
Purchased through the Contemporary Art Fund; 2007.31

74. Artist unknown, Santo Domingo Pueblo

Dough bowl depicting diagonally quartered paneled design with ovoids, about 1890

Earthenware, painted with colored slips and burnished
17.8 x 37.8 cm
Gift of Mrs. Charles Sheldon; 50.42.12473

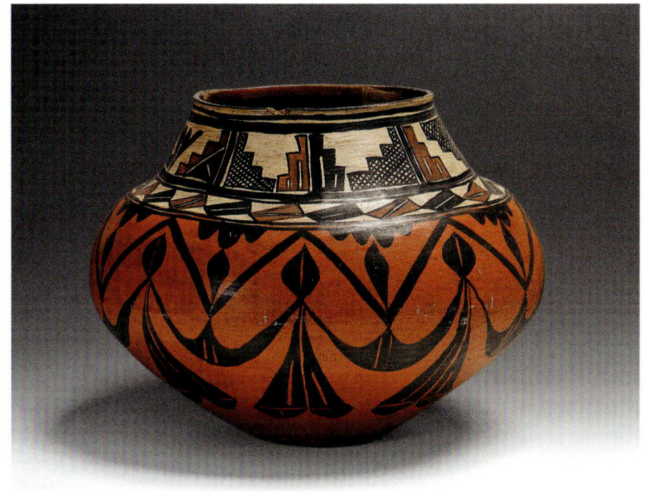

75

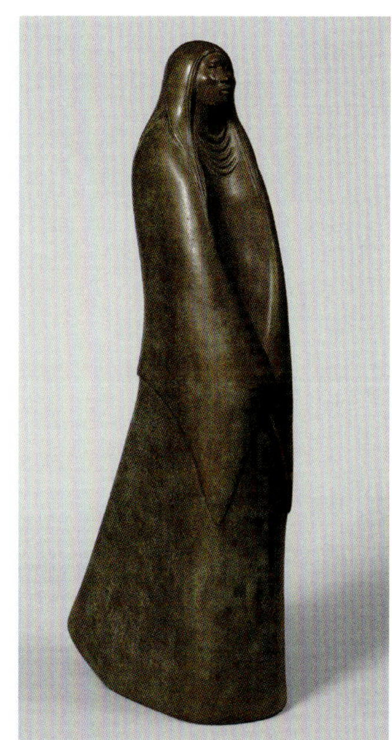

77

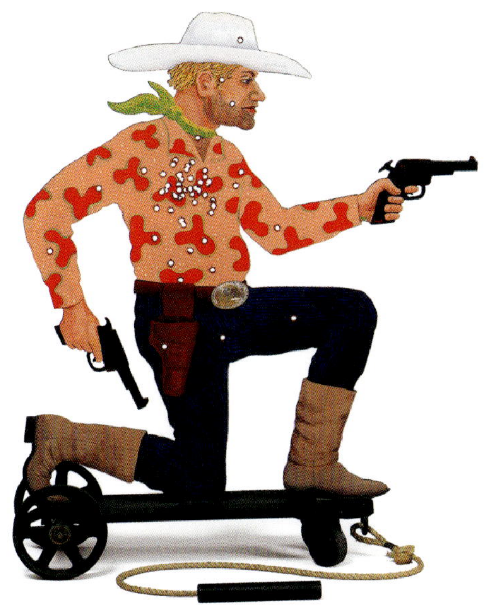

76

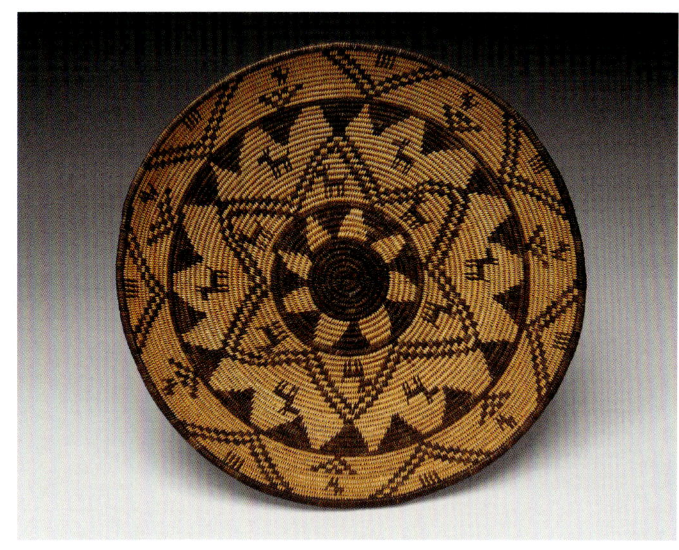

78

75. Artist unknown, San Ildefonso Pueblo

Water jar (*olla*), about 1890–1905

Earthenware, painted with colored slips and burnished
27.3 x 18 cm
Bequest of Frank C. and Clara G. Churchill; 46.17.10032

Southern Athapaskan

76. Bob Haozous, Chiricahua Apache / Diné (Navajo), born 1943

Apache Pull-Toy, 1988

Painted steel
137.2 x 121.9 x 40.6 cm
Purchased through the Joseph B. Obering '56 Fund; S.989.17

77. Allan C. Houser, Chiricahua Apache (Fort Still Apache), 1914–1994

Taza, 1991

Bronze
160 x 55.9 x 30.5 cm
Gift of Harry T. Lewis Jr., Class of 1955, Tuck 1956, 1981P; 2009.70
© 1991 Chiinde LLC

78. Artist unknown, Western Apache

Basket, about 1900

Willow, cottonwood, and devil's claw
7 x 36.3 cm
Museum purchase; 51.27.12829

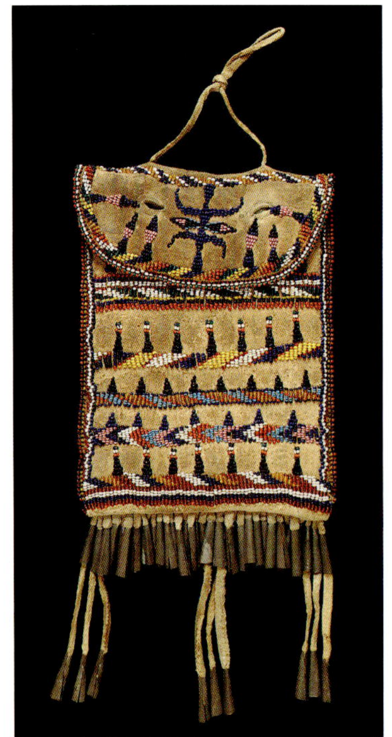

79

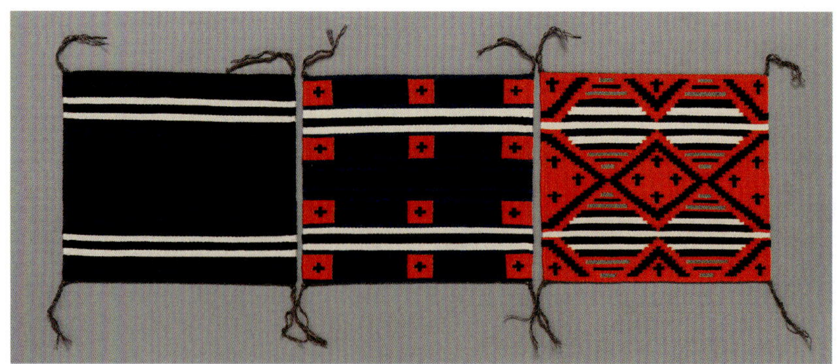

81

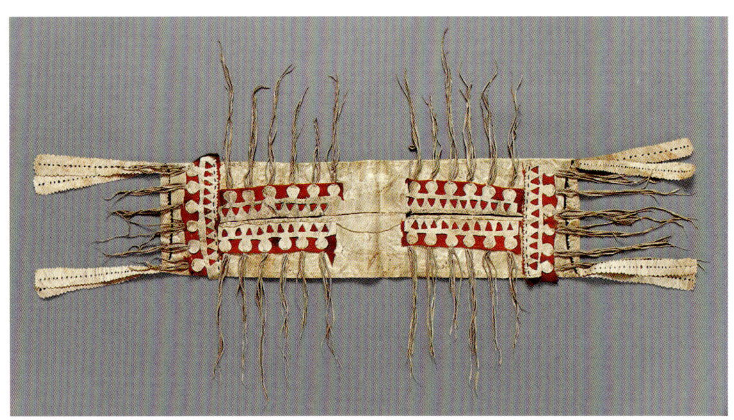

80

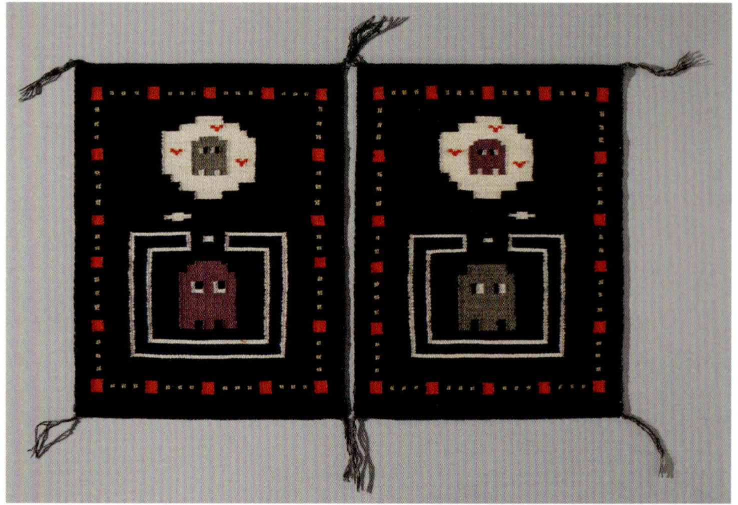

82

79. Artist unknown, Apache

Pouch, about 1890

Native-tanned hide, glass beads, tin cones, tin button, and thread
30 x 14 cm (includes long fringe); 40 cm (includes suspension loop and long fringe);
22 cm (pouch with short fringe only)
Gift of Capt. Herbert L. Shuttleworth II, Class of 1935; 43.25.8600

80. Artist unknown, Mescalero Apache

Saddle bag, about 1900

Rawhide, Native-tanned hide, wool cloth, glass beads, sinew, and ink
82.5 x 23 cm; 132 cm (including rawhide fringe)
Bequest of Frank C. and Clara G. Churchill; 46.17.9959

81. Barbara Teller Ornelas, Diné (Navajo), born 1954

Chief Blankets: Phase One; Phase Two; Phase Three, 2010

Wool and vegetable dye
Three textiles: each 25.4 x 24.1 cm
Purchased through the Alvin and Mary Bert Gutman '40 Acquisitions Fund and the Hood Museum of Art Acquisitions Fund, 2010.71

82. Sierra Teller Ornelas, Diné (Navajo), born 1981

Forbidden Love (two-weaving set), January–July 2009

Wool and vegetable dye
Each textile: 38.1 x 28.3 cm
Purchased through the Alvin and Mary Bert Gutman '40 Acquisition Fund; 2009.54

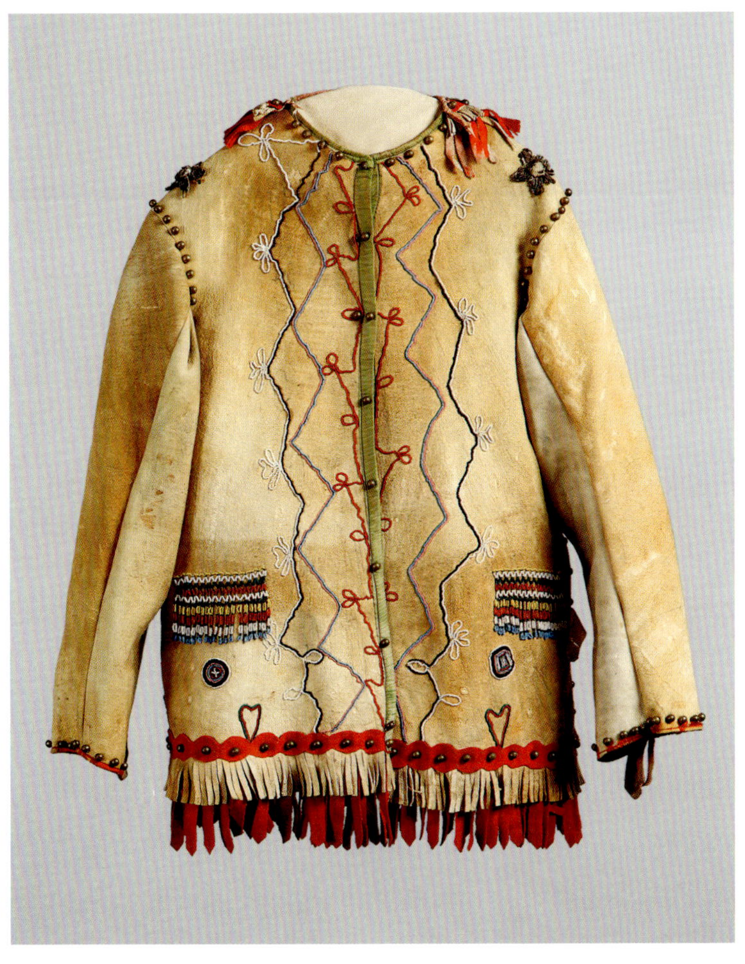

83

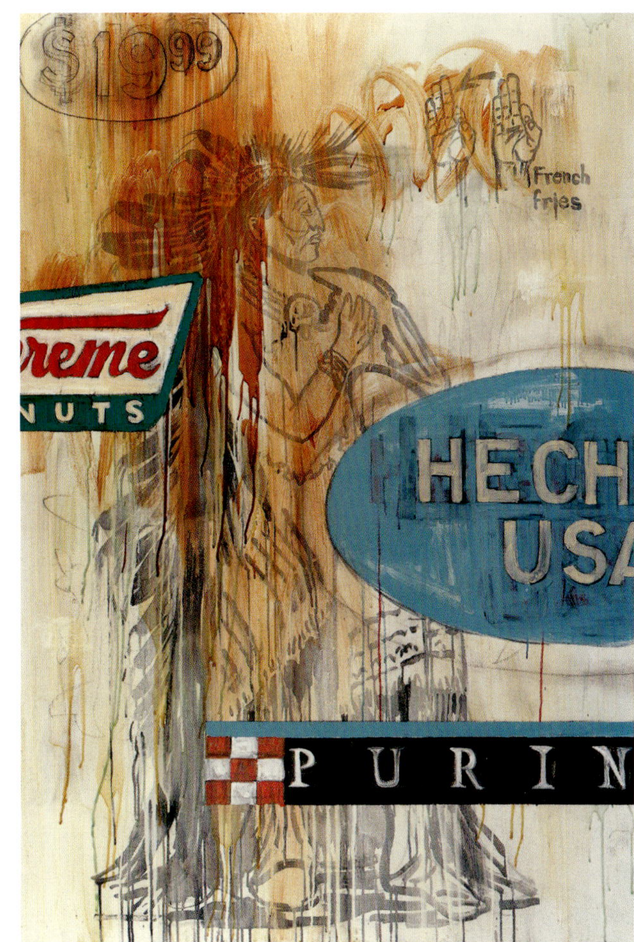

84

Plateau

83. Artist unknown, Nimi'ipuu (Nez Perce)

Jacket, about 1875

Native-tanned and smoked hide, wool cloth, ribbon, cotton binding tape, glass beads, brass buttons, metal sequins, metal thread, and thread
79 x 54 x 157 cm (cuff to cuff along the shoulders)
Gift of Mrs. William M. Leeds; 13.137.4094A

84. Jaune Quick-to-See Smith, Salish (Flathead) / French Cree / Shoshone, born 1940

The Rancher, 2002

Acrylic on canvas
183.5 x 122.2 cm
Purchased through the William S. Rubin Fund; 2005.13

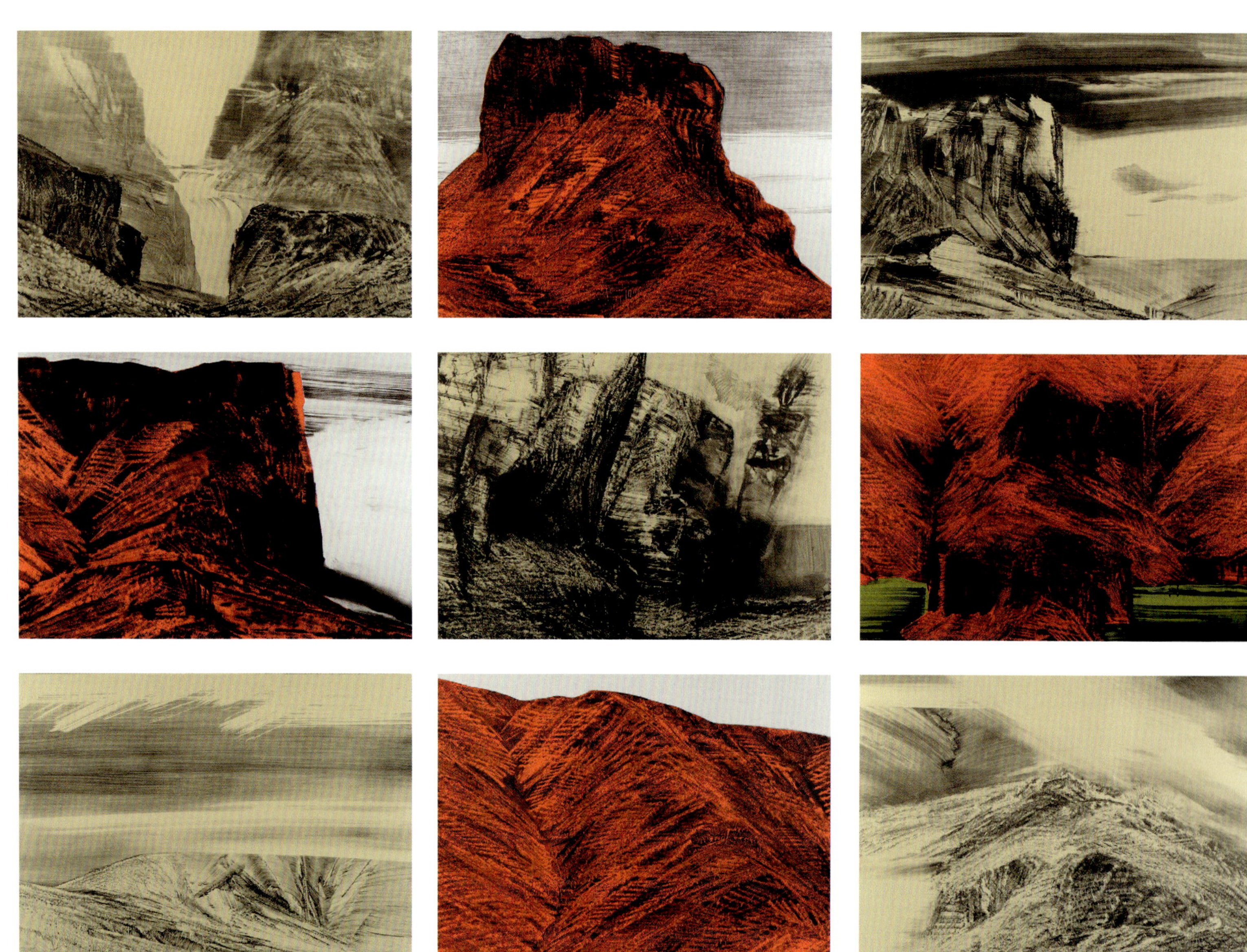

85

85. James Lavadour, Walla Walla (Wallawalla), born 1951

Untitled (panels 1–9), 1995

Color lithographs with chine collé collage on tan, white, and green papers
Each lithograph: 71.7 x 96.8 cm
Purchased through the Virginia and Preston T. Kelsey 1958 Fund; PR.995.44.1–9

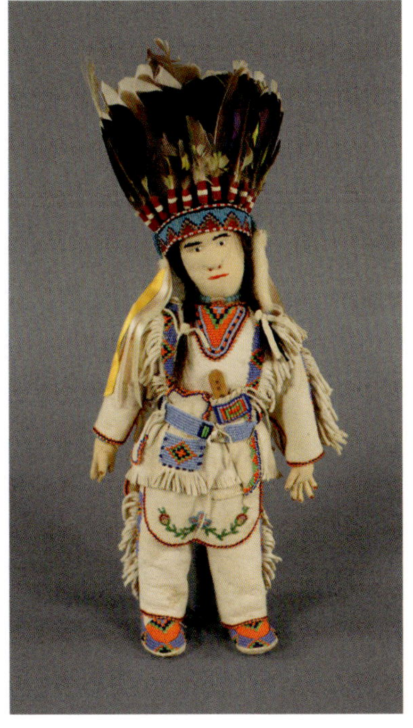

86

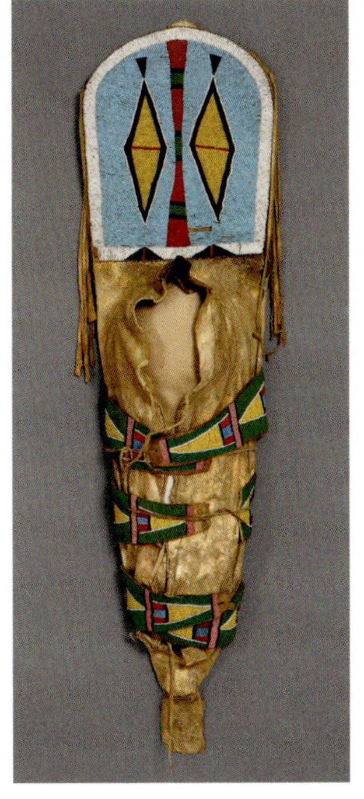

87

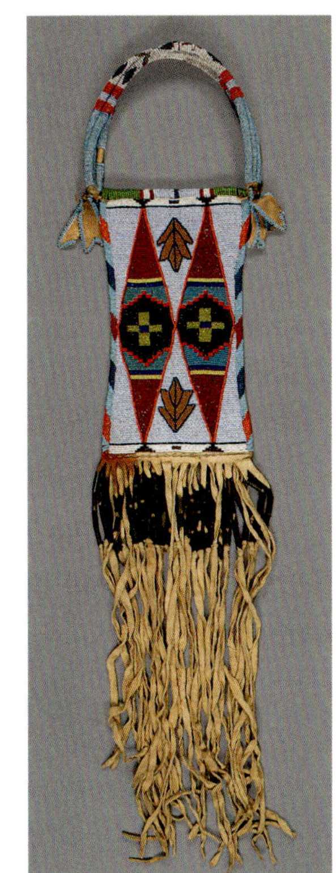

88

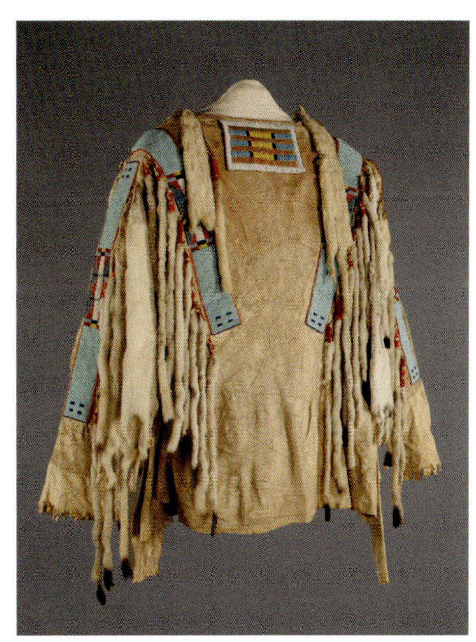

89

Plains

Northern Plains

86. Julia Ereaux Schultz, A'aninin (Gros Ventre), 1872–1973, Fort Belknap Reservation, Montana

A'aninin (Gros Ventre) chief, 1948

Hide, glass beads, mallard feathers, parrot feathers, human hair, horse hair, ribbon, cotton cloth, ermine tails, plastic beads, button, nylon fishing line, tape, felt cloth, wood, embroidery thread, paint, graphite, and thread
Warrior: 32.5 x 19.5 x 6.5 cm; headdress: 26 x 17 x 10 cm (with horse hair extensions and ribbon fringe); warrior and headdress: 44 cm
The Wellington Indian Doll Collection: Gift of Barbara Wellington Wells; 987.35.26841

87. Artist unknown, Apsáalooke (Crow / Absaroke)

Cradle, about 1880

Native-tanned deer or bison hide, wood, glass beads, sinew, paint, and thread
114 x 30.5 x 17 cm (includes bottom tab to top of cradle); 152.5 cm (with fringe)
Gift of Guido R. Rahr Sr., Class of 1951P; 985.47.26532

88. Artist unknown, attributed to Apsáalooke (Crow / Absaroke)

Man's handbag, about 1890

Native-tanned hide, glass beads, metal beads, brass buttons, canvas, wool, cord, and thread
60 x 15 cm (pouch including fringe); 74 cm (total height, strap including fringe)
Gift of Eleanor Clark French, Class of 1930W; 989.41.27056

89. Artist unknown, Apsáalooke (Crow / Absaroke)

Man's war shirt, about 1915–20

Native-tanned deer hide, glass beads, ermine fur, buffalo fur, canvas, wool cloth, ochre, string, and thread
70 x 165 cm (cuff to cuff); 87 cm (bottom edge)
Gift of Guido R. Rahr Sr., Class of 1951P; 985.47.26601

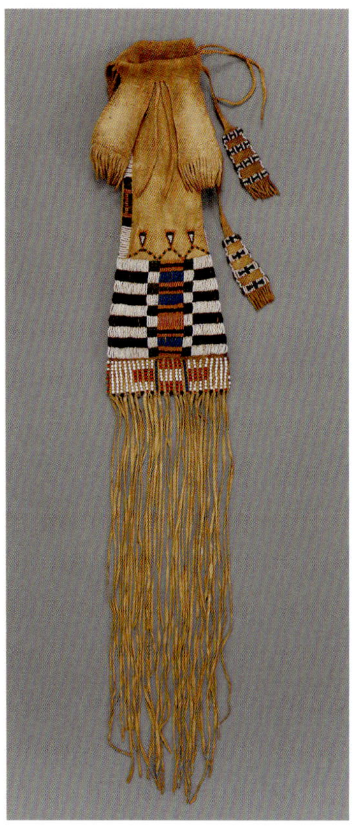

90

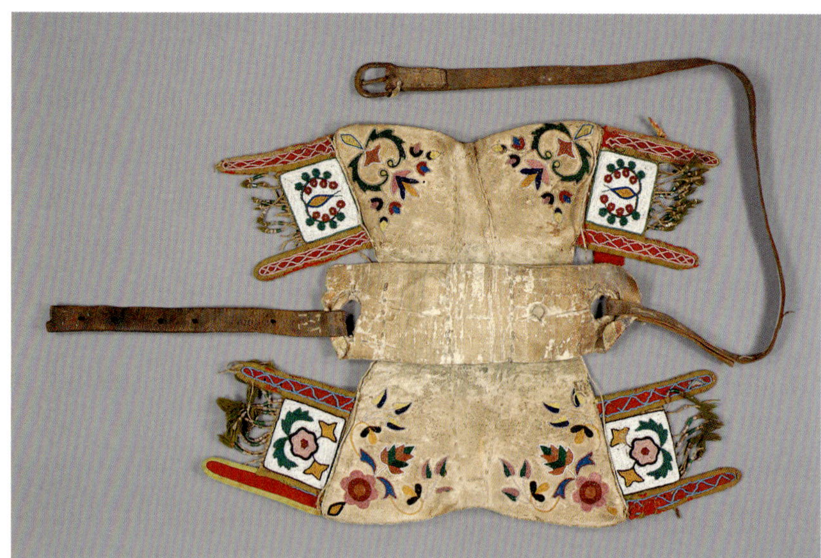

92

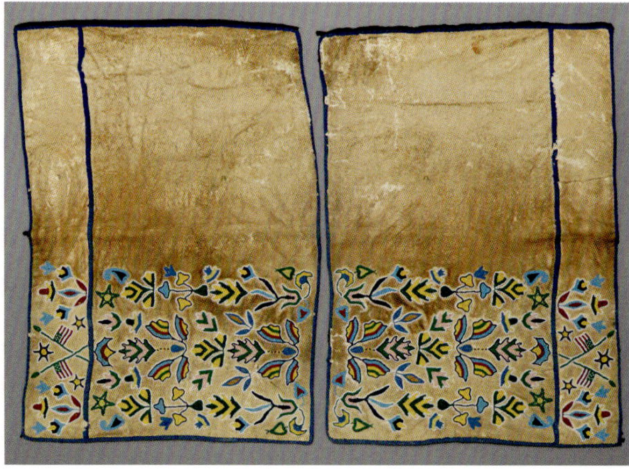

91

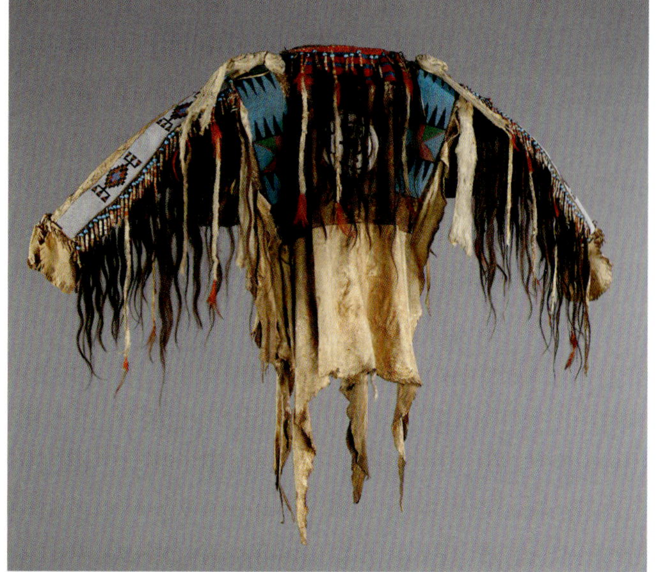

93

90. Artist unknown, Northern Inunaina (Arapaho) or Northern Tsistsistas / Suhtai (Cheyenne)

Tobacco bag, about 1860

Native-tanned hide, glass beads, and sinew
72.4 x 12.1 x 5.1 cm
Purchased through the Mrs. Harvey P. Hood W'18 Fund and the Julia L. Whittier Fund; 2009.66

91. Artist unknown, Sioux-Métis

Half leggings, about 1890

Native-tanned hide, glass beads, cotton cloth, cotton binding, metal, and thread
45 x 64 cm
Gift of Edward W. Bush Jr., Class of 1945, Tuck 1947; 47.12.10803

92. Artist unknown, Red River Métis

Saddle, about 1880

Native-tanned hide, glass beads, wool cloth, cotton cloth, cotton binding, porcupine quills, dye, rawhide, paint; leather, metal, and thread
48 x 58 cm (including tab pendants); 100 cm girth/cinch strap; 36 cm girth/cinch strap (opposite side)
Gift of Newton Buckner; 46.10.10783

93. Artist unknown, Siksika (Blackfeet)

Beaded and fringed hide man's shirt, about 1880

Native-tanned hide, glass beads, porcupine quills, human hair, wool cloth, cotton cloth, ermine, downy feathers, paint, and dye
111 x 165 cm (cuff to cuff over shoulders)
Purchased through the Mrs. Harvey P. Hood W'18 Fund; 2009.14

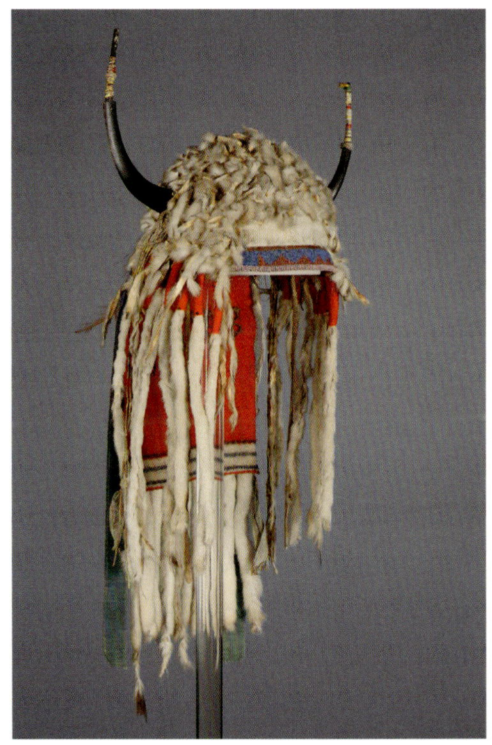

94

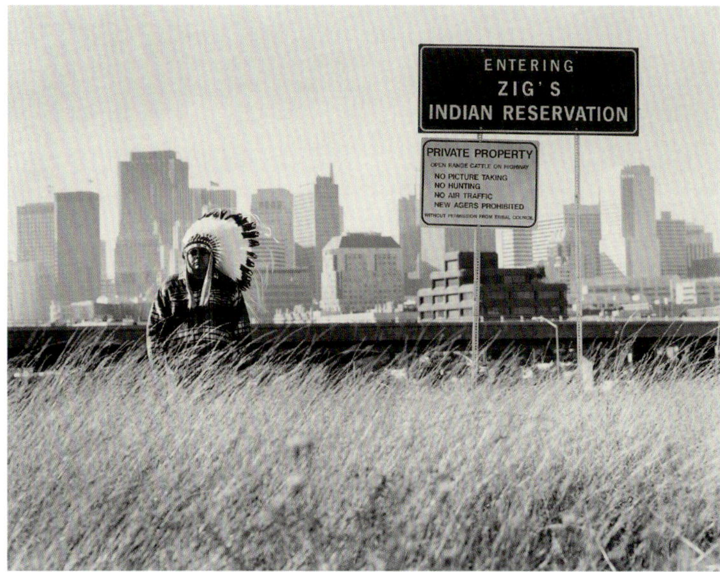

96

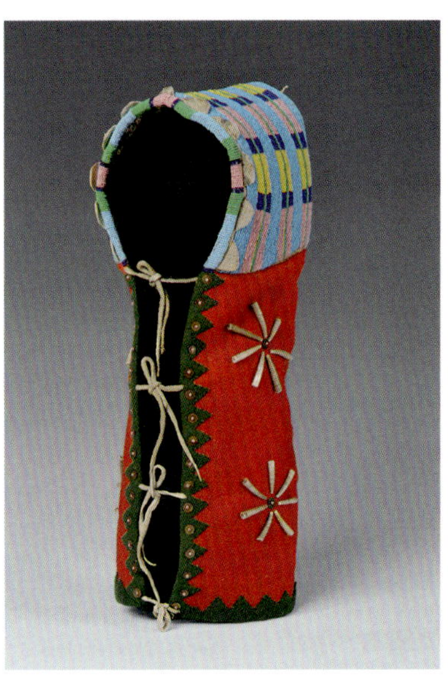

95

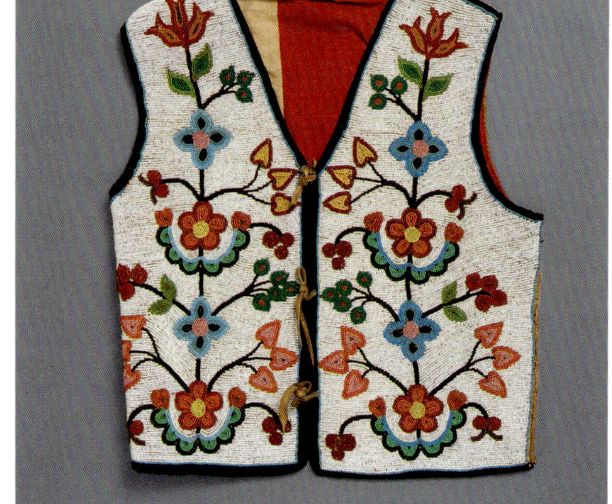

97

94. Artist unknown, Northern Plains

Split horn bonnet, late 19th–early 20th centuries

Felt, commercial leather, Native-tanned hide, bison horn, weasel fur, wool cloth, glass beads, quills, feathers, sinew, thread, and lazy stitch beading
74 cm
Gift of Guido R. Rahr Sr., Class of 1951P; 985.47.26647

95. Artist unknown, Northern Plains

Toy cradle, about 1890

Wool, cotton cloth, canvas, Native-tanned hide, rawhide, glass beads, metal sequins, dentalium shell, and thread
12 x 13.5 x 39.5 cm
Purchased through the Mrs. Harvey P. Hood W'18 Fund; 2008.86

96. Zig Jackson, Numakiki (Mandan) / Minitari (Hidatsa) / Sahnish (Arikara), born 1957

China Basin District, number 2 of 4, from the series *Entering Zig's Indian Reservation,* negative: 1997, print: 1997–98

Gelatin silver print
36 x 45 cm
Purchased through the Harry Shafer Fisher 1966 Memorial Fund; 2007.37.1

97. Artist unknown, Néhiyawak (Plains Cree)

Man's vest, about 1890

Hide, glass beads, metal beads, cotton cloth, cotton binding tape, and thread
50 x 41.5 cm
Gift of Guido R. Rahr Sr., Class of 1951P; 985.47.26596

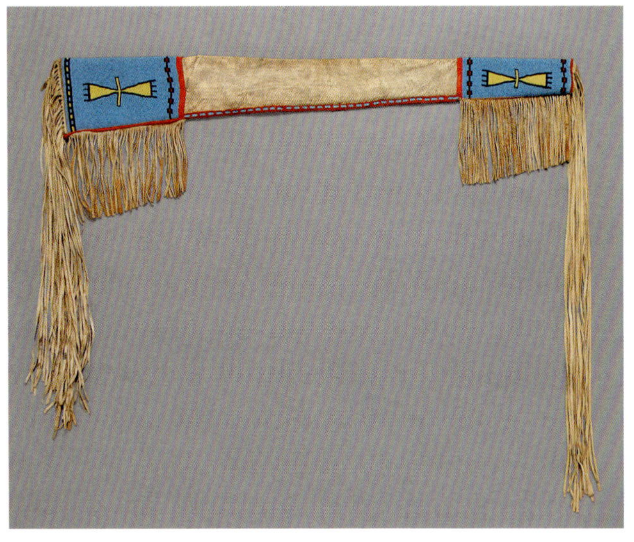

98

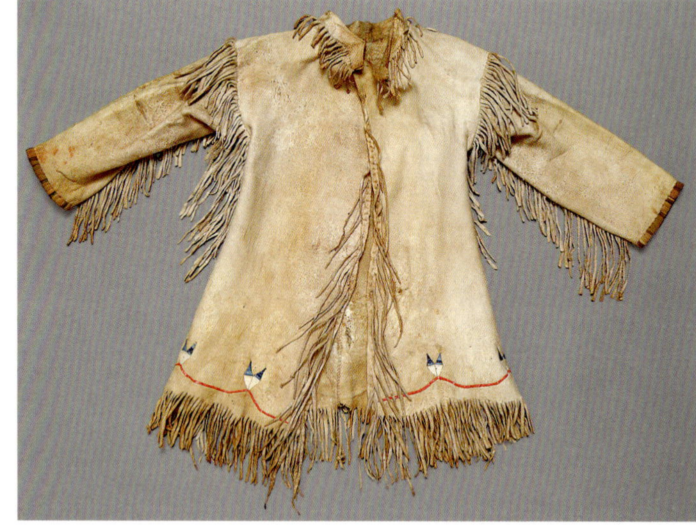

100

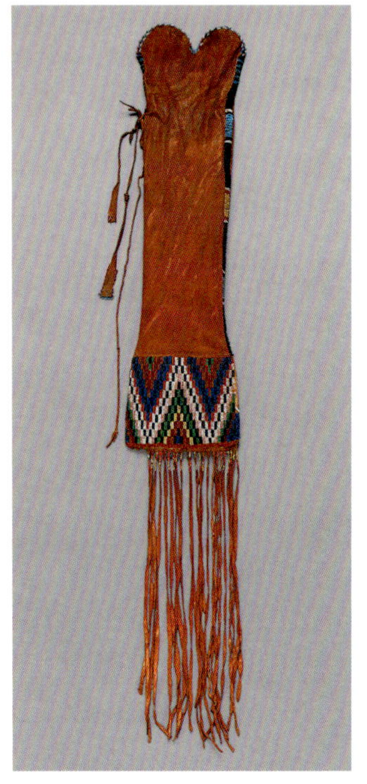

99

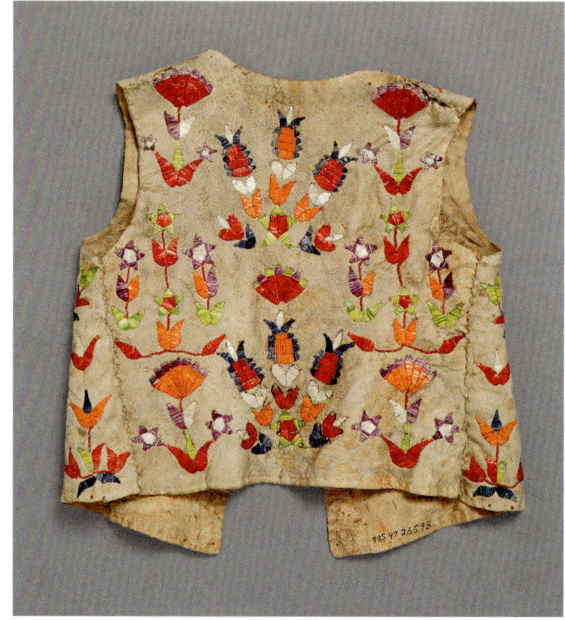

101

98. Artist unknown, Siksika (Blackfoot) or Assiniboine (Nakota [Yankton Sioux])

Gun case, about 1890

Native-tanned hide, glass beads, wool cloth, clay wash (possibly), and thread
108 x 16 cm; 95 cm (long fringe at terminal end); 78 cm (long fringe at opening)
Gift of Guido R. Rahr Sr., Class of 1951P; 985.47.26569

99. Artist unknown, Siksika (Blackfoot), Assiniboine (Nakota [Yankton Sioux]), Néhiyawak (Plains Cree) or Tsuu T'ina (Sarcee)

Pipe bag, about 1890

Native-tanned hide, glass beads, porcupine quills, ochre, dye, sinew, and thread
97.5 x 15.3 x 3 cm (including fringe)
Gift of Guido R. Rahr Sr., Class of 1951P; 985.47.26560

Central Plains

100. Artist unknown, Dakota (Eastern Sioux)

Boy's coat, early 20th century

Native-tanned hide, porcupine quills, cotton cloth, aniline dye, sinew, and thread
60 x 65.5 cm
Gift of Guido R. Rahr Sr., Class of 1951P; 985.47.26604

101. Artist unknown, Dakota (Eastern Sioux)

Boy's vest, about 1880

Native-tanned hide, porcupine quills, dye, ink, sinew, and thread
39 x 38 cm
Gift of Guido R. Rahr Sr., Class of 1951P; 985.47.26598

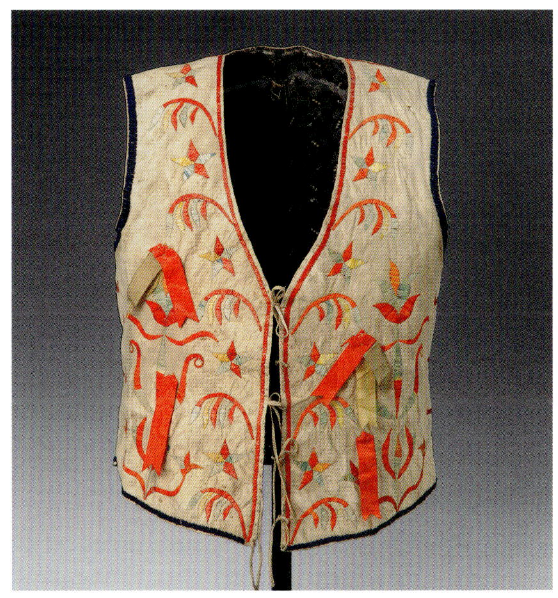

102

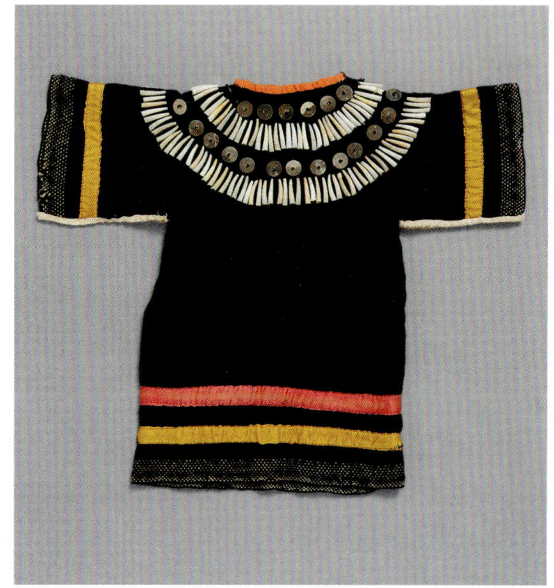

104

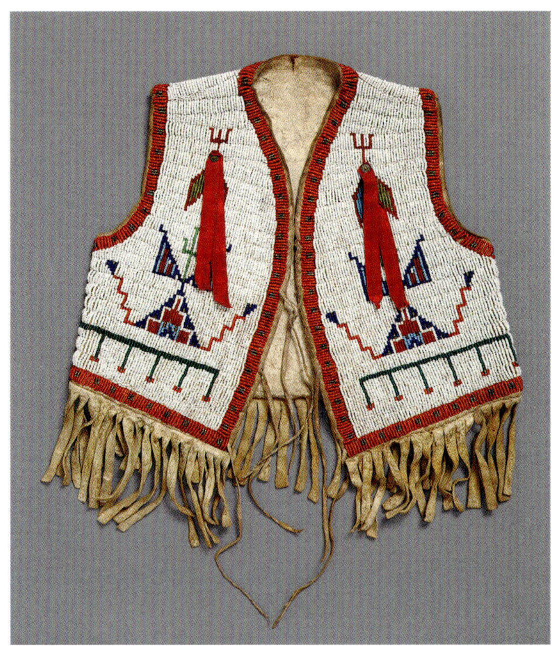

103

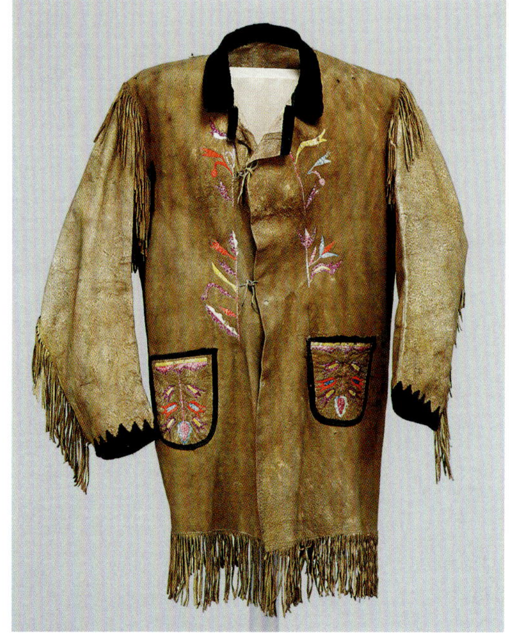

105

102. Artist unknown, Dakota (Eastern Sioux)

Vest, about 1880

Native-tanned hide, cotton fabric, porcupine quills, ribbon, glass beads, aniline dye, ink, sinew, and thread
56 x 34 cm
Gift of Stephen A. Lister, Class of 1963; 2008.82

103. Artist unknown, Lakota (Teton / Western Sioux)

Boy's vest, about 1890

Native-tanned deer hide, glass beads, metal beads, metal sequins, ribbon, ochre, sinew, and thread
39 x 35.5 cm
Gift of Guido R. Rahr Sr., Class of 1951P; 985.47.26593

104. Artist unknown, Lakota (Teton / Western Sioux)

Child's dress, about 1890

Wool cloth, ribbon, dentalium shell, metal sequins, cotton cloth, and thread
32.4 x 38.5 cm
Gift of Glover Street Hastings III; 181.2.26089

105. Artist unknown, Lakota (Teton / Western Sioux)

Coat, about 1880

Native-tanned hide, velvet, porcupine quills, cotton cloth, dye, ochre, paint, sinew, and thread
92 (with fringe) x 148 cm (cuff to cuff)
Bequest of Frank C. and Clara G. Churchill; 46.17.9817

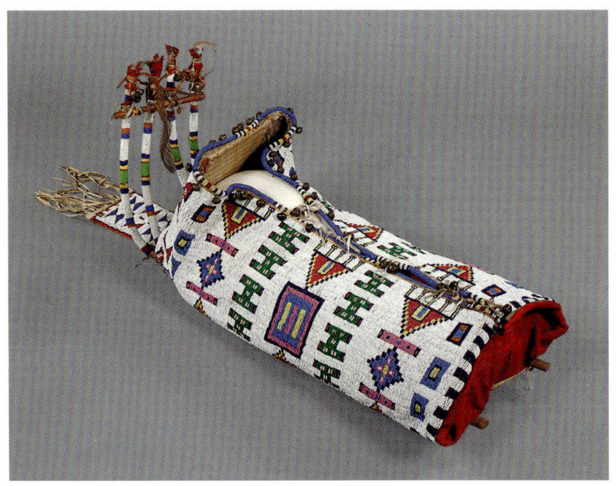

106

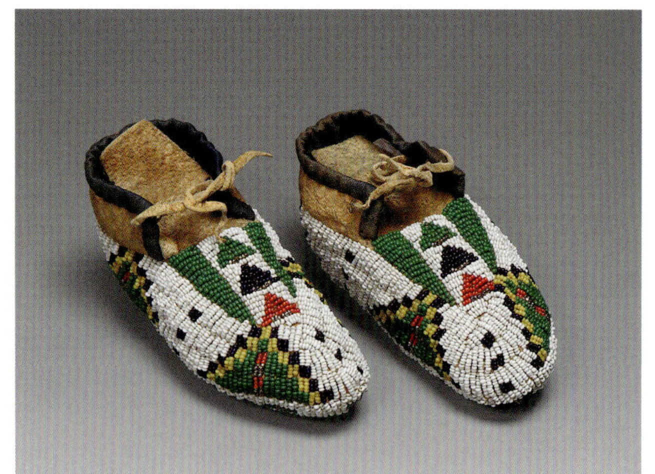

108

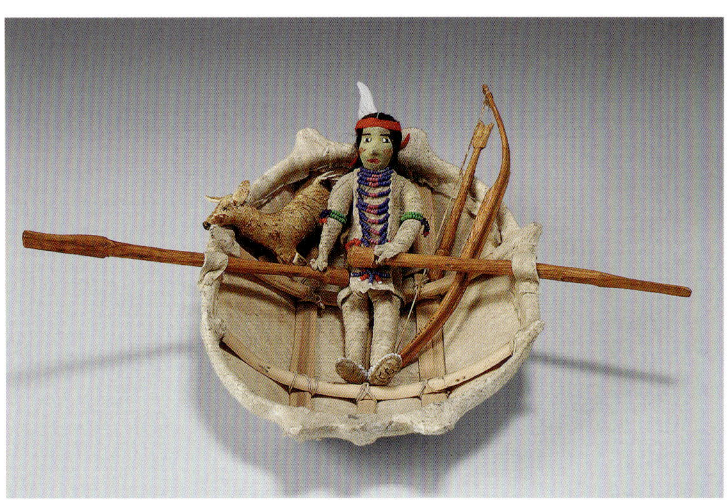

107

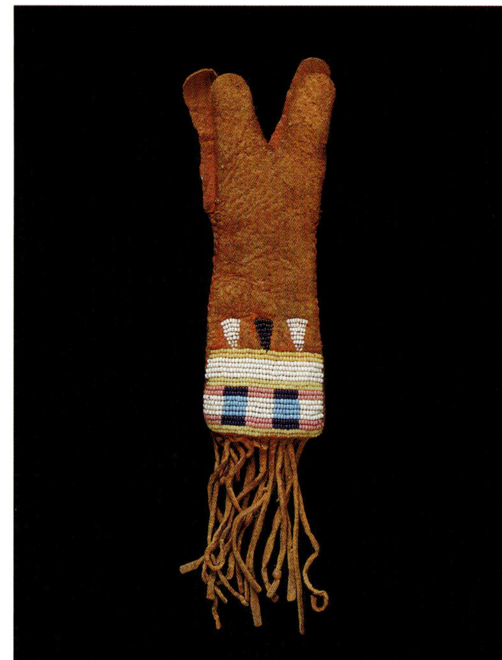

109

106. Pretty Eagle (Mrs. Lone Dog), Lakota (Teton / Western Sioux), Fort Peck, Montana, late 19th–early 20th centuries

Cradle, about 1890

Glass beads, Native-tanned hide, wood, cotton cloth, wool cloth, brass bells, horse hair, downy feathers, dye, ochre, cord, and thread
84 x 35 x 27 cm
Bequest of Frank C. and Clara G. Churchill; 46.17.9831

107. Artist unknown, Lakota (Teton / Western Sioux), Standing Rock, North Dakota

Figure of man and boat, 1957

Native-tanned hide, glass beads, wool, cotton batting, human hair, wood, feather, string, thread, sinew, ochre, paint, and ink
9 x 22.5 x 17 cm
The Wellington Indian Doll Collection: Gift of Barbara Wellington Wells; 987.35.26829A–B

108. Artist unknown, Lakota (Teton / Western Sioux)

Child's moccasins with beaded soles, about 1900

Native-tanned hide, glass beads, metal beads, ribbon, and thread
6 x 14 x 6.2 cm
Bequest of Frank C. and Clara G. Churchill; 46.17.9961

109. Artist unknown, Lakota (Teton / Western Sioux)

Paint pouch, about 1890

Hide, glass beads, red hematite, and sinew
23.5 x 5 x 1.4 cm (includes fringe); 14.5 cm (pouch only)
Gift of the Fairbanks Museum and Planetarium; 172.12.25346

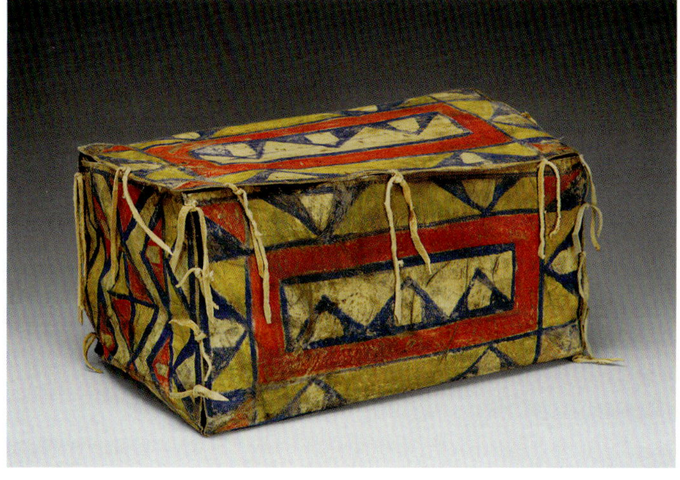

110

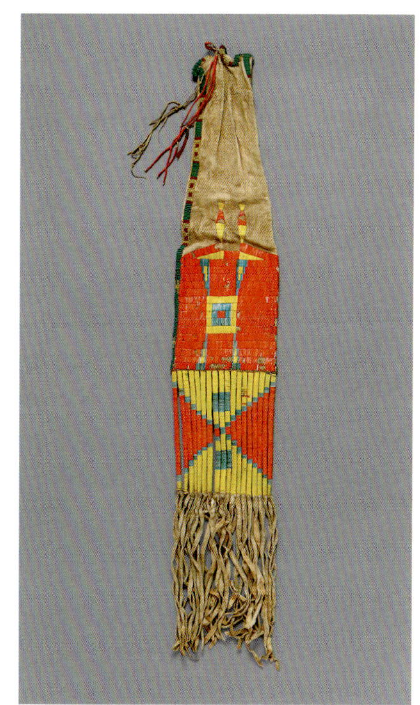

112

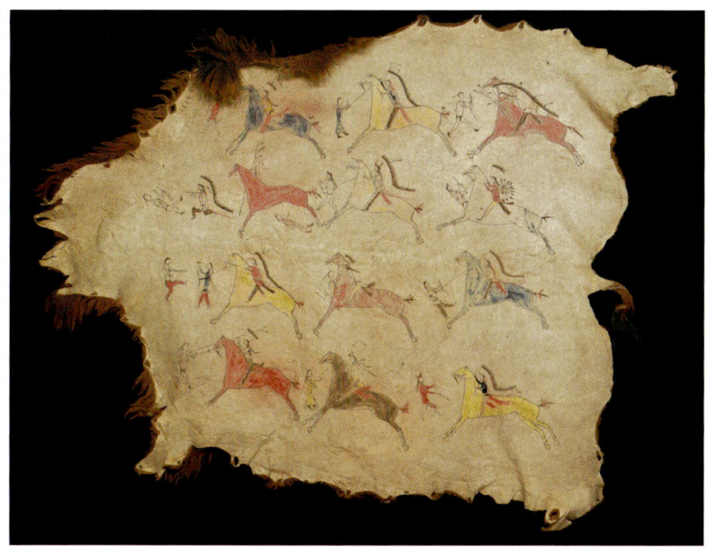

111

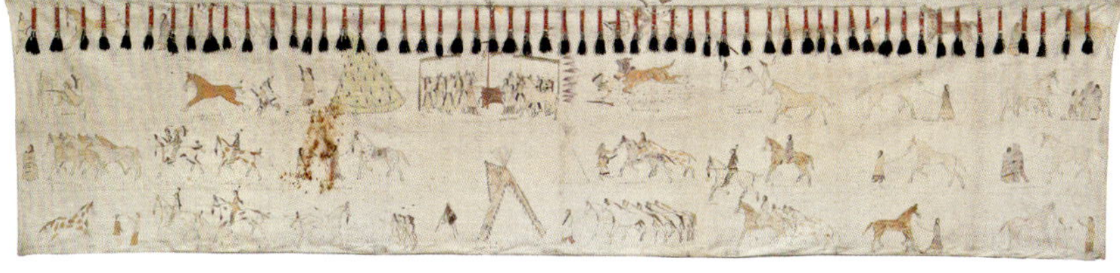

113

110. Artist unknown, Lakota (Teton / Western Sioux)

Parfleche storage container, about 1900

Cow rawhide, Native-tanned leather, and paint
21 x 41.5 x 21 cm
Gift of Guido R. Rahr Sr., Class of 1951P; 985.47.26523

111. Artist unknown, Lakota (Teton / Western Sioux)

Pictorial buffalo robe, about 1870

Buffalo hide, paint, ink, and sinew
218.5 x 260 cm; 300 cm (including tail)
Purchased through the Florence and Lansing Porter Moore 1937 Fund; 2009.13

112. Artist unknown, Lakota (Teton / Western Sioux)

Pipe bag, about 1880

Native-tanned hide, rawhide, porcupine quills, glass beads, horse hair, paint, dye, tin, sinew, and thread
89 cm h. (including quill-wrapped rawhide and hide fringe) x 15 cm w.
Gift of Mrs. Ida Farr Miller; 44.18.8800

113. Artist unknown, Lakota (Teton / Western Sioux), Standing Rock Agency, Fort Yates, North Dakota

Tipi liner, about 1910

Muslin, paint, porcupine quills, rawhide, Native-tanned hide, cotton cloth, tin cones, dye, wool yarn, ink, string, and thread
88.5 x 374 cm
Purchased through the Mrs. Harvey P. Hood W'18 Fund; 2009.10

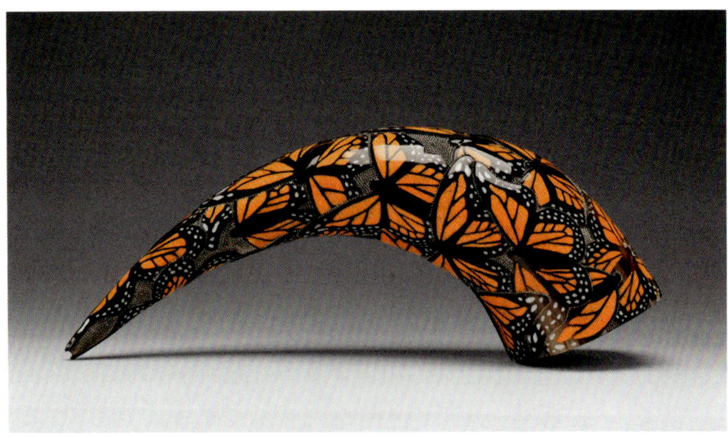

114

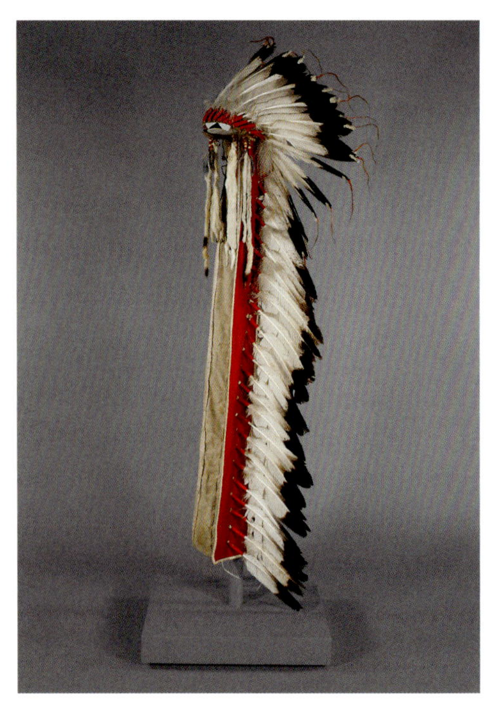

116

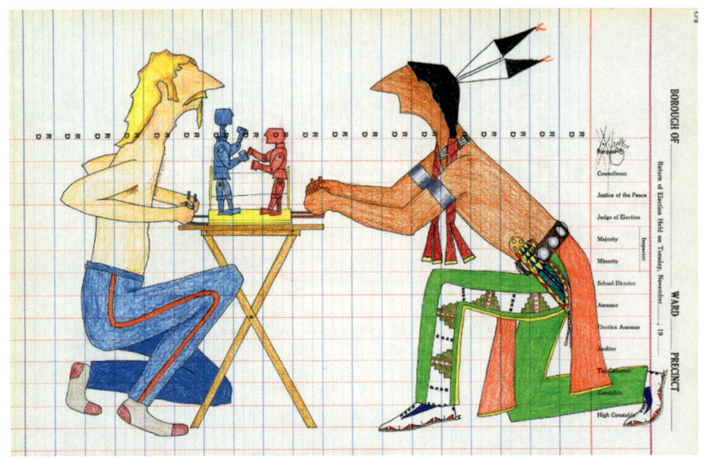

115

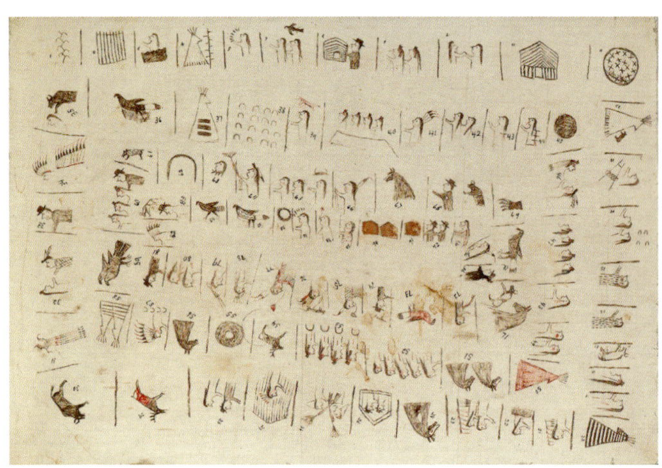

117

114. Kevin Pourier, Oglala Lakota, born 1959

Monarch Buffalo Horn Cup, 2009

Buffalo horn, sandstone, and mother of pearl
8.9 x 29.5 x 15.9 cm
Purchased through gifts from the Lathrop Fellows; 2009.59

115. Dwayne Wilcox, Oglala Lakota, born 1957

Best Two Outa Three, 2008

Crayon, graphite, colored pencil, and felt-tipped pen on ledger paper
29 x 45 cm
Purchased through the Guernsey Center Moore 1904 Fund; 2008.59.7

116. Artist unknown, Nakota (Yankton Sioux)

Headdress, about 1900

Native-tanned hide, golden eagle feathers, wool cloth, glass beads, weasel fur, yarn, thread, and overlay stitch beading
164 cm
Gift of Mrs. Guido Rahr Sr., Class of 1951P; 986.45.26658

117. Artist unknown, Nakota (Yankton Sioux)

Winter count, recording the years 1823–1917, about 1917

Colored pencil and crayon on muslin
76.5 x 110.8 cm
Purchased through the William S. Rubin Fund, the Guernsey Center Moore 1904 Memorial Fund, the William B. and Evelyn F. Jaffe (58, 60, & 63) Fund, the William B. and Evelyn A. Jaffe Hall Fund; 2009.65

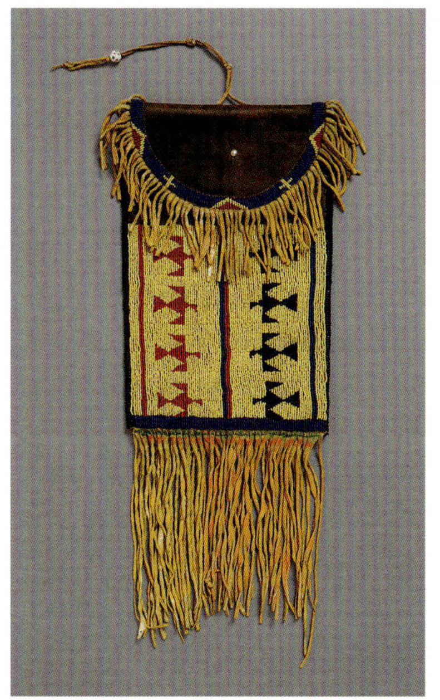

118

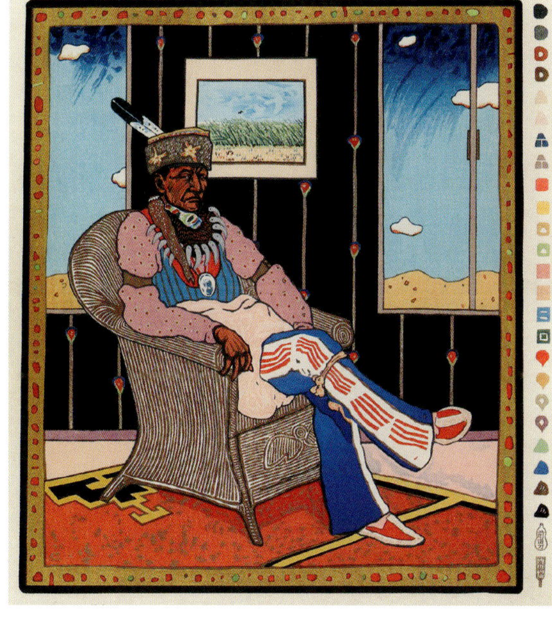

120

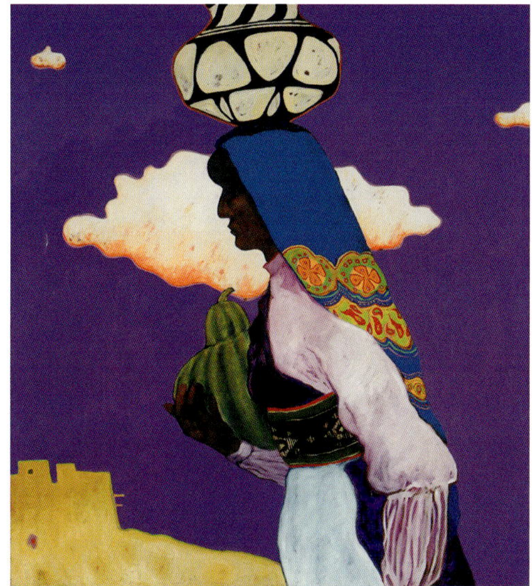

119

121

Southern Plains

118. Artist unknown, Inunaina (Arapaho)

Dispatch case with thunderbird design, about 1875

Leather, glass beads, metal button, ochre, paint, and sinew
46 x 17 cm (including fringe); 65.3 cm (including suspension loop)
Gift of Newton Buckner; 46.10.10791

119. T. C. Cannon, Gaigwa (Kiowa) / Caddo / Choctaw, 1946–1978

Cloud Madonna, 1975

Acrylic on canvas
152.4 x 137.16 cm
Promised gift of Charles E. Nearburg, Class of 1972; EL.2010.86

120. T. C. Cannon, Gaigwa (Kiowa) / Caddo / Choctaw, 1946–1978, with Kentaro Maeda (woodblock carver) and Matashiro Uchikawa (printer)

Collector No. 5, about 1977

Color woodblock print
48.3 x 41.6 cm
Purchased through the Stephen and Constance Spahn '63 Acquisition Fund and the Hood Museum of Art Acquisition Fund in honor of Barbara Thompson, Curator of African, Oceanic, and Native American Collections, Hood Museum of Art, 2002–2008; 2008.57

121. Artist unknown, Gaigwa (Kiowa), Oklahoma

Boy's shirt, about 1880

Native-tanned hide, tin, brass, glass beads, ochre, paint, and thread
89.5 cm h. (from shoulder to longest fringe) x 122 cm w. (cuff to cuff); 33 cm w. (waist)
Bequest of Frank C. and Clara G. Churchill; 46.17.9856

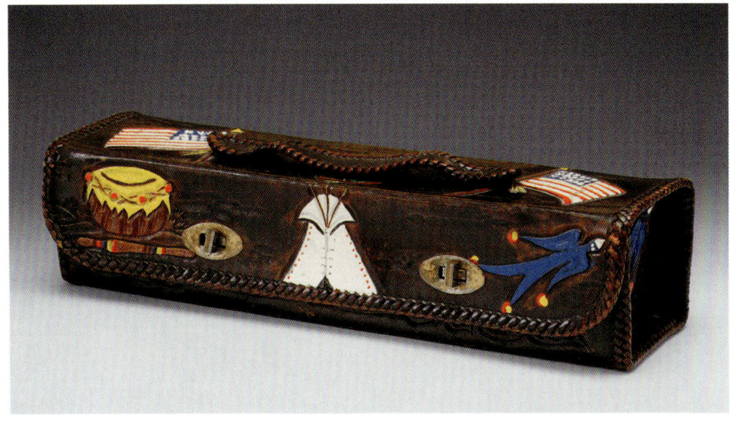

122

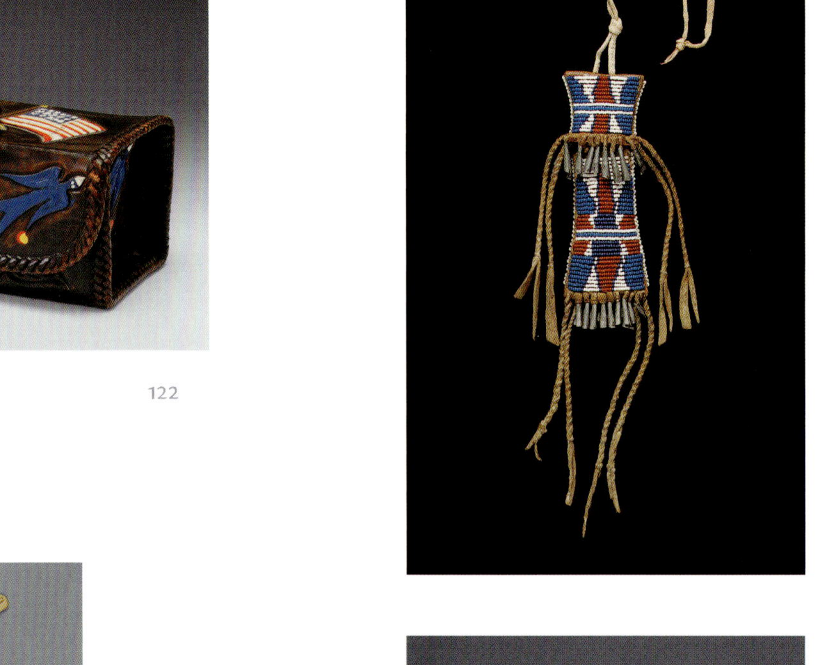

124

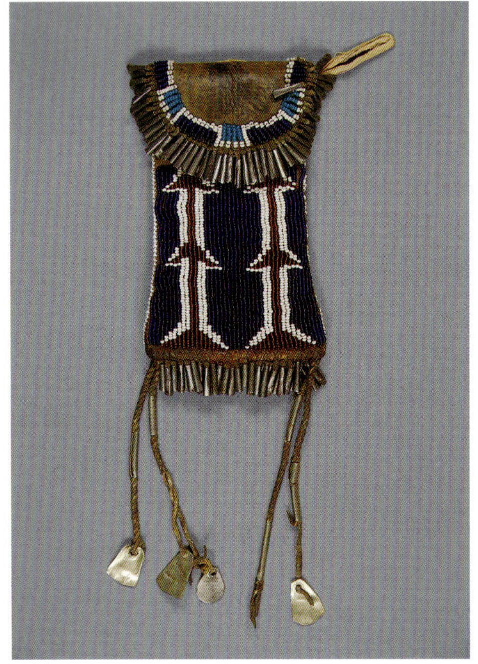

123

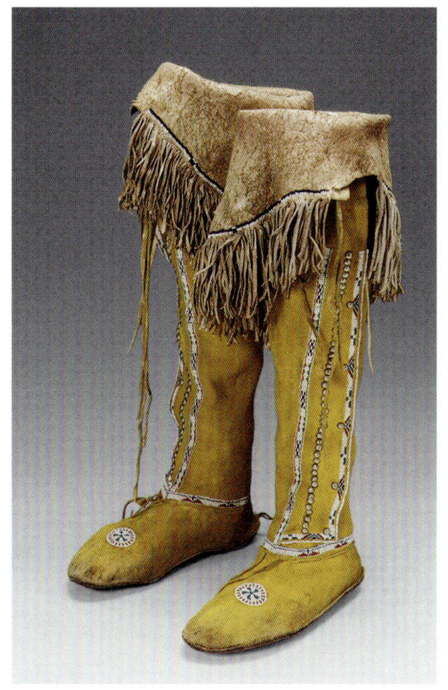

125

122. Artist unknown, Gaigwa (Kiowa) or Niuam (Comanche)

Peyote box, about 1940

Leather, paint, brass, metal, and thread
11 (including handle) x 40.7 x 12 cm
Purchased through the Endowment Fund for the Acquisition and Preservation of Native American Art and the Hood Museum of Art Acquisitions Fund; 2009.32

123. Artist unknown, Gaigwa (Kiowa)

Strike-a-Light pouch, about 1870

Leather, hide, glass beads, tin cones, metal, cotton cloth, ochre, and thread
Overall: 25.7 cm; with tin cone fringe: 15.2 x 8.3 cm
Gift of Mrs. William M. Leeds; 13.13.742

124. Artist unknown, Gaigwa (Kiowa)

Whetstone case, about 1870

Leather, hide, glass beads, tin cones, and sinew
Overall: 41.5 cm; including fringe: 14 x 4.7 x 2.5 cm
Gift of Mrs. William M. Leeds; 13.13.744

125. Artist unknown, Gaigwa (Kiowa)

Woman's boots, about 1880

Native-tanned hide, rawhide, glass beads, tin, ochre, and thread
66 cm x 26 (full extension including fringe); foot: 24 x 8.5 cm
Bequest of Frank C. and Clara G. Churchill; 46.17.9859

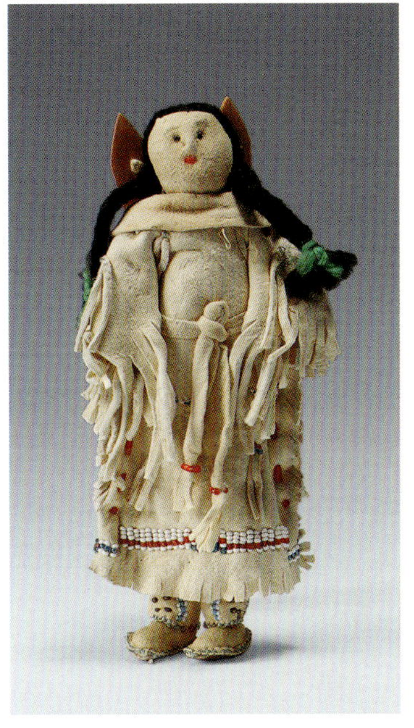
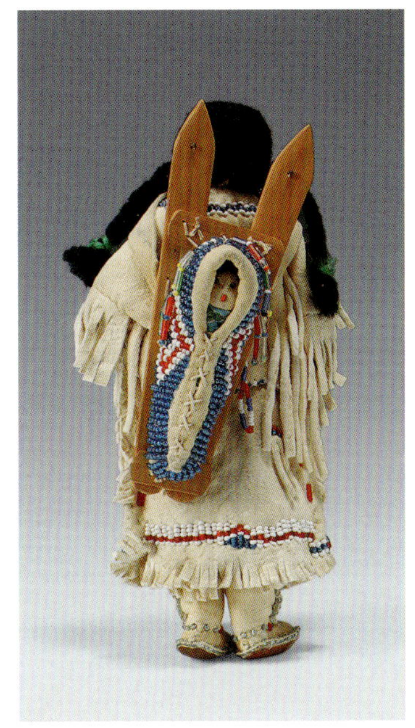

126

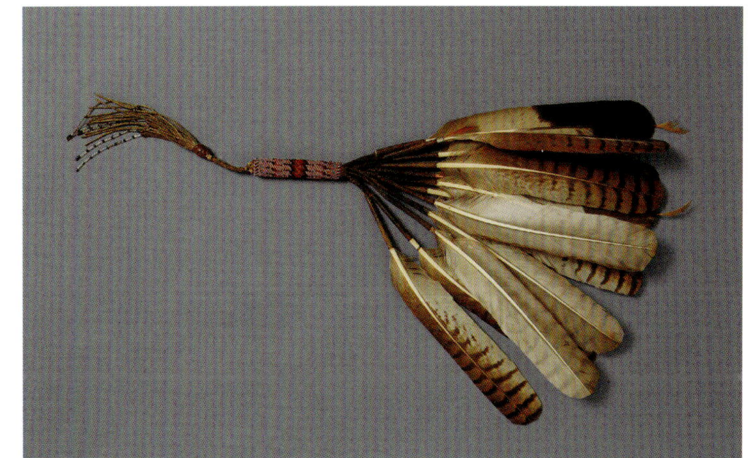

128

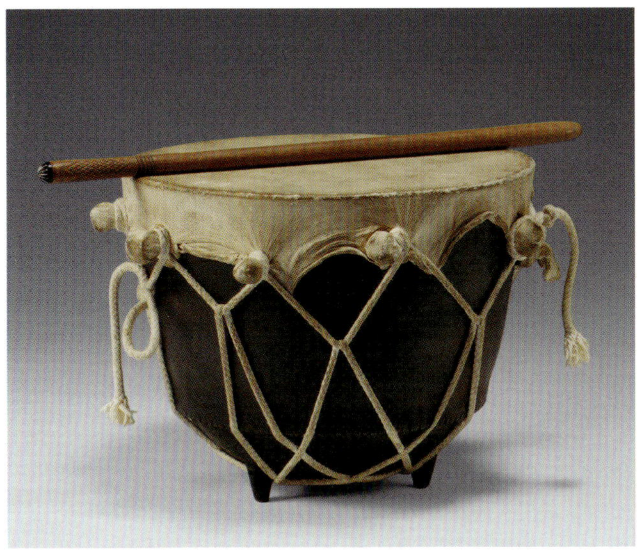

127

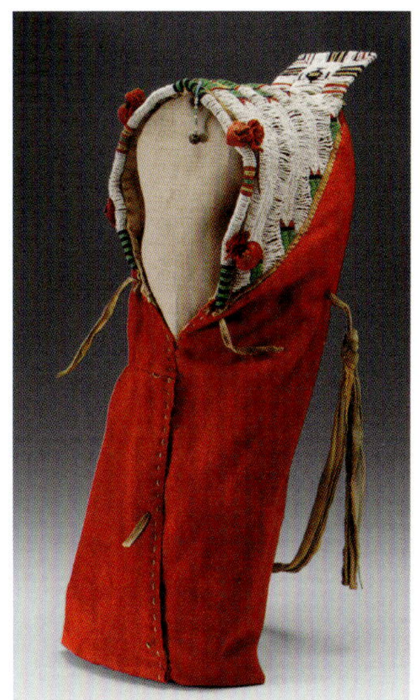

129

126. May Wanqua (Wauqua), Niuam (Comanche), active 20th century, Fort Sill Indian School

Niuam (Comanche) woman and child, 1946

Native-tanned hide, glass beads, metal beads, yarn, cotton cloth, wood, canvas, commercial leather, thread, and ink
19.8 x 9.5 x 6 cm
The Wellington Indian Doll Collection: Gift of Barbara Wellington Wells; 987.35.26791

127. Artist unknown, Southern Plains

Drum and drum beater, about 1930

Drum: iron, Native-tanned hide, cord, and stones; drum beater: wood and paint
Drum: 17.7 x 25.5 cm; drum beater: 32.4 x 1 cm
Museum purchase; 158.28.14245

128. Artist unknown, Southern Plains

Peyote fan, about 1900

Hawk feathers, eagle feathers, downy feathers, Native-tanned hide, rawhide, commercial leather, glass beads, metal, dye, and thread
53 (including fringe) x 35 cm; 35.5 cm (without fringe)
Gift of Guido R. Rahr Sr., Class of 1951P; 985.47.26474

129. Artist unknown, Tsistsistas / Suhtai (Cheyenne)

Cradle, about 1870

Glass beads, stroud, Native-tanned bison hide, rawhide, wood, cotton cloth, brass bell, string, sinew, and thread
110 x 37 cm
Gift of Guido R. Rahr Sr., Class of 1951P; 985.47.26531

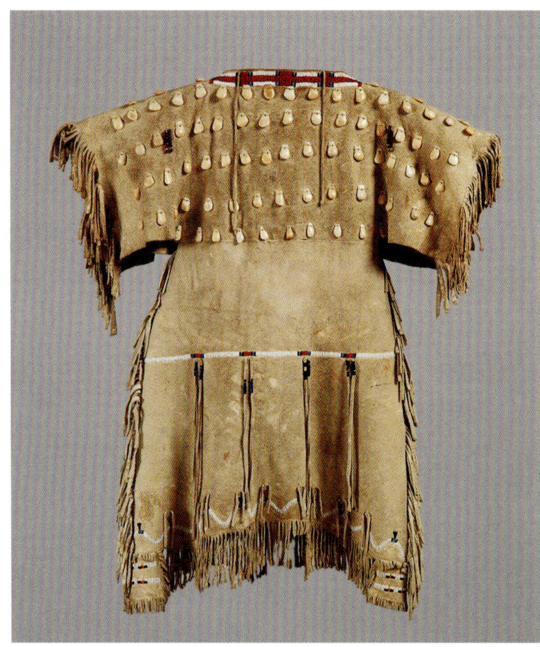

130

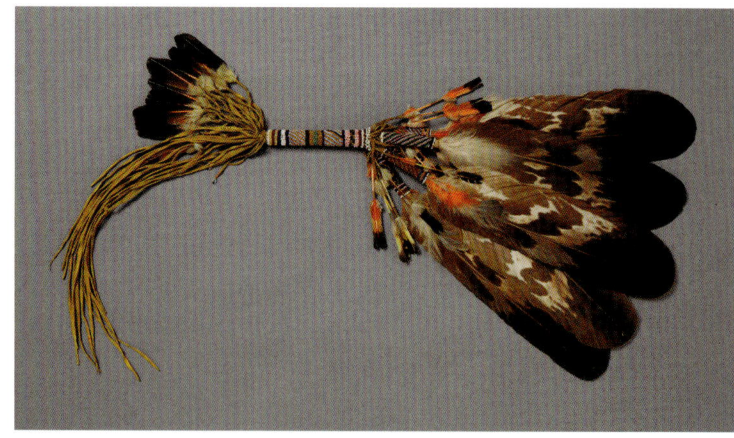

132

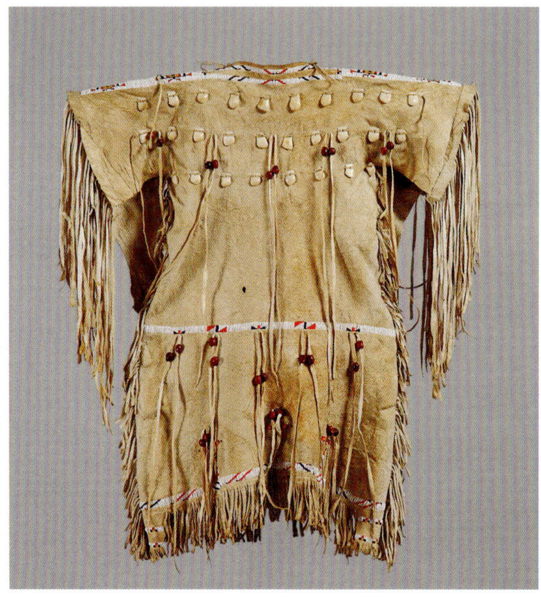

131

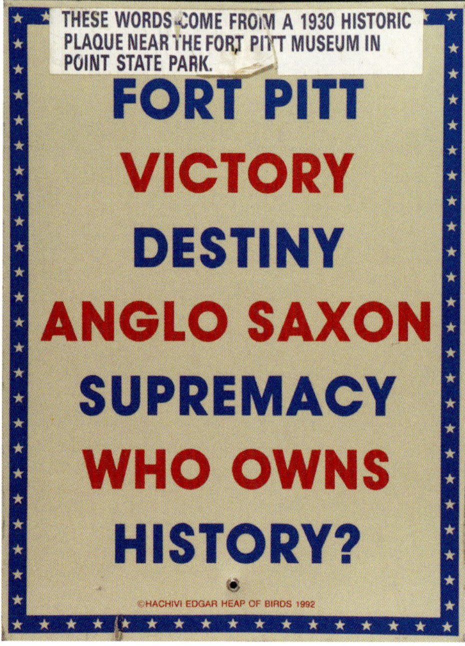

133

130. Artist unknown, Tsistsistas / Suhtai (Cheyenne)

Girl's dress, about 1930

Native-tanned hide, glass beads, bone, string, sinew, and thread
94.5 x 95 cm (across shoulders including fringe extended); 77 cm (across shoulder without fringe); 66 cm (across bottom edge)
Gift of Newton Buckner; 46.10.10795

131. Louisa Littlechief (Mrs. Victor Little Chief), Northern Tsistsistas / Suhtai (Cheyenne), 1875–1937

Girl's dress, about 1900

Native-tanned elk or deer hide, glass beads, bone, sophoro beans, sinew, and thread
77 x 63.3 cm (without fringe); 121.5 cm (with fringe extended)
Gift of Guido R. Rahr Sr., Class of 1951P; 985.47.26603

132. Artist unknown, Tsistsistas / Suhtai (Cheyenne), Oklahoma

Peyote fan, about 1900

Eagle feathers, flicker feathers, downy feathers, hide, glass beads, ochre, sinew, dye, and thread
78 x 26 x 2.5 cm
Bequest of Frank C. and Clara G. Churchill; 46.17.9852

133. Hachivi Edgar Heap of Birds, Tsistsistas / Suhtai (Cheyenne) / Inunaina (Arapaho), born 1954

Who Owns History?, 1992

Metal sign
61.2 x 43.9 cm
Gift of Monroe A. Denton Jr., Class of 1968; MIS.2003.25.1

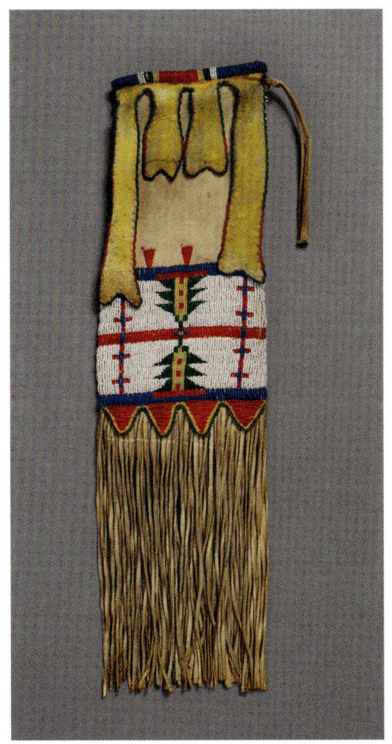

134

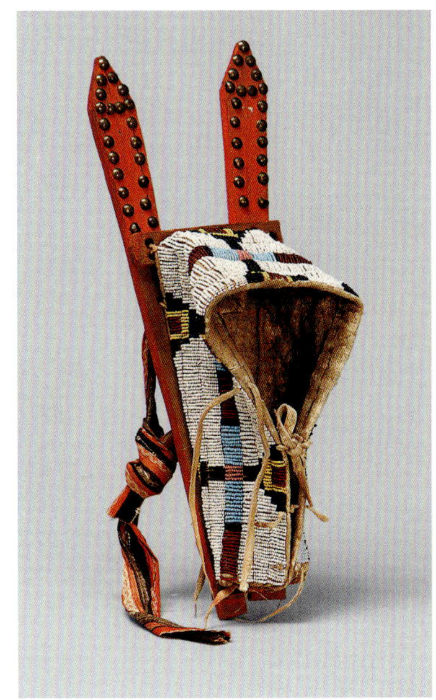

135

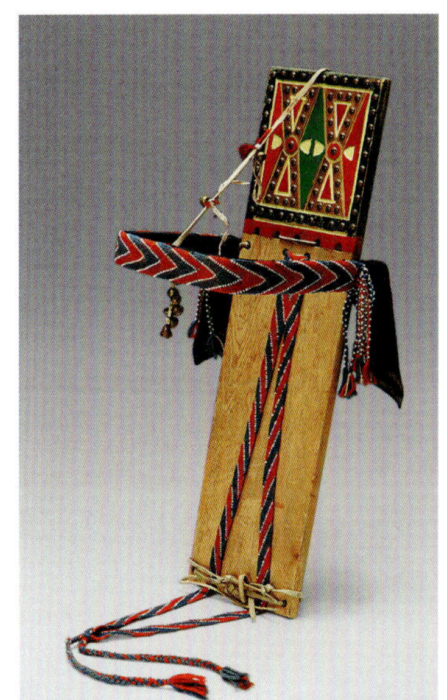

136

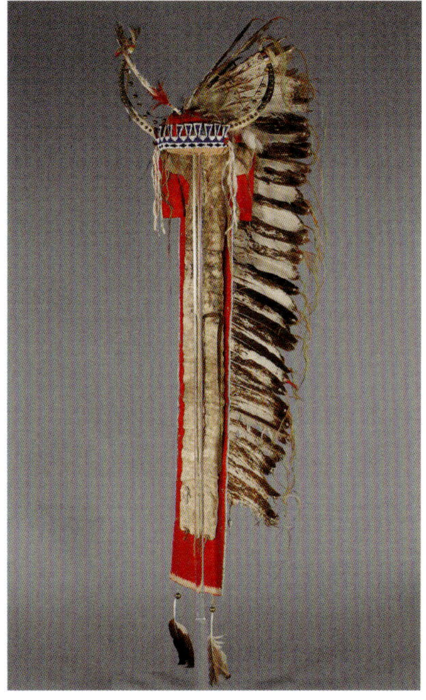

137

134. Artist unknown, Tsistsistas / Suhtai (Cheyenne)

Pipe bag, about 1890

Native-tanned hide, glass beads, sinew, and ochre
49 x 13.4 x 4 cm
Gift of Guido R. Rahr Sr., Class of 1951P; 985.47.26556

135. Artist unknown, Tsistsistas / Suhtai (Cheyenne)

Toy cradle, about 1870

Wood, glass beads, hide, brass, cotton cloth, paint, sinew, and thread
12 x 41.3 x 14 cm; cotton tie attached to back: 30 cm
Gift of Mrs. William M. Leeds; 13.13.760

Prairie

136. Artist unknown, Osage, Oklahoma

Cradleboard, about 1900

Wood, brass tacks, brass bells, glass beads, yarn, paint, wool cloth, cotton cloth, Native-tanned hide, ribbon, cord, string, and metal
61.4 x 21.8 x 23 cm (with bow)
Purchased through the Hood Museum of Art Acquisitions Fund in honor of Mary Kean Raynolds and David R. W. Raynolds, Class of 1949; 2008.66

137. Artist unknown, possibly Osage or Chaticks Si Chaticks (Pawnee), Oklahoma

War bonnet, about 1870

Hide, rawhide, bald eagle feathers, downy feathers, toned turkey feathers, cow horn, glass beads, metal beads, brass hawk bells, brass tacks, wool cloth, ermine, thimbles, ribbon, horse hair, lead weight, dye, sinew, string, and thread
167 x 42 cm
Gift of Mrs. William M. Leeds; 13.137.4094C

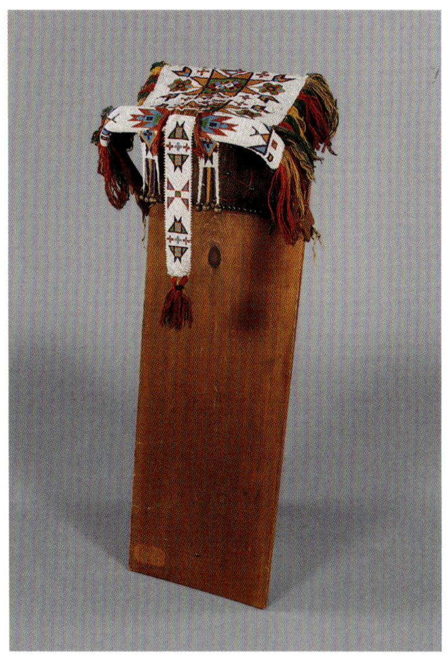

138

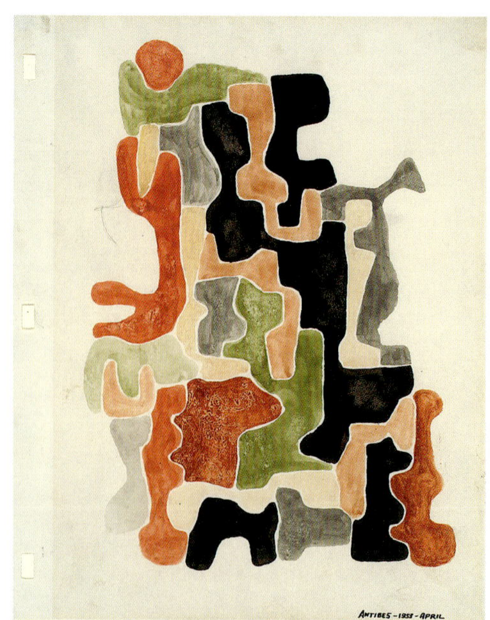

140

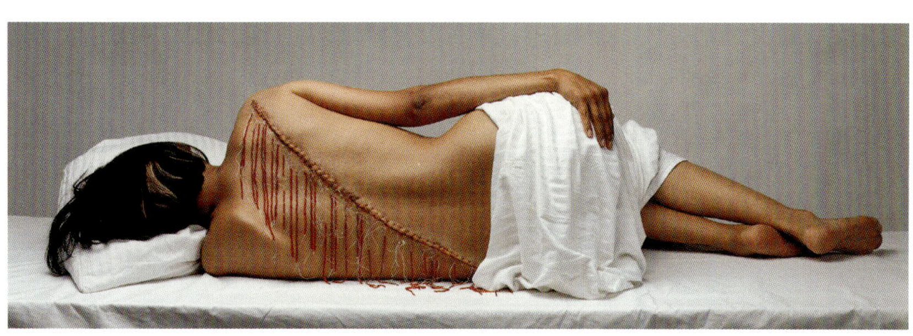

139

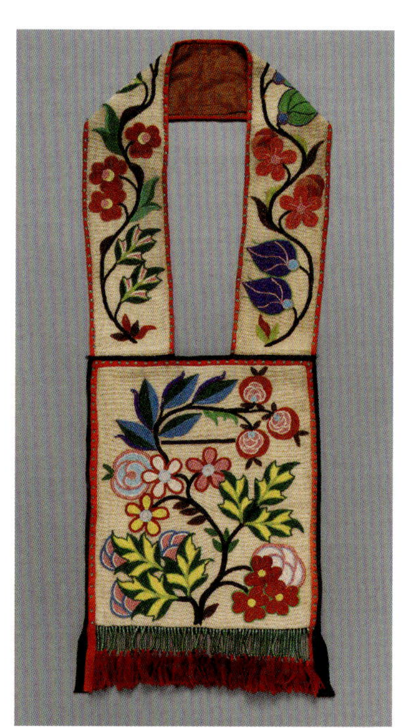

141

138. Artist unknown, Ponca, White Eagle, Oklahoma

Cradle, about 1900

Wood, glass beads, hide, brass tacks, yarn, cotton cloth, paint, and thread
100 x 31 x 25.5 cm
Bequest of Frank C. and Clara G. Churchill; 46.17.9855

Woodlands

Great Lakes

139. Rebecca Belmore, Anishinaabe (Chippewa / Ojibwa), born 1960

Fringe, 2007

Digital print on archival paper
53.3 x 160 cm (border: 6.4 cm)
Purchased through the Elizabeth and David Lowenstein and the Olivia H. Parker and John O. Parker '58 Acquisitions Fund; 2010.65

140. George Morrison, Anishinaabeg (Chippewa / Ojibwa), 1919–2000

Abstraction, April 1953

Watercolor on paper
Sheet: 27.9 x 19.4 cm; frame: 38.4 x 30.8 cm
Gift of Evelyn A. and William B. Jaffe, Class of 1964H, through the Friends of Dartmouth Library; W.956.37.1

141. Artist unknown, Anishinaabeg (Chippewa / Ojibwa), White Earth Reservation, Minnesota

Bandolier bag, about 1900

Glass beads, cotton cloth, wool yarn, wool binding, and thread
106 x 36.5 cm (including strap); 53.2 cm (strap only)
Bequest of Frank C. and Clara G. Churchill; 46.17.9874

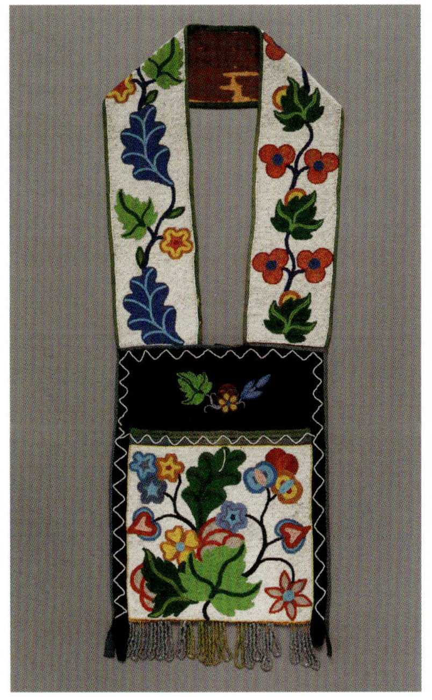

142

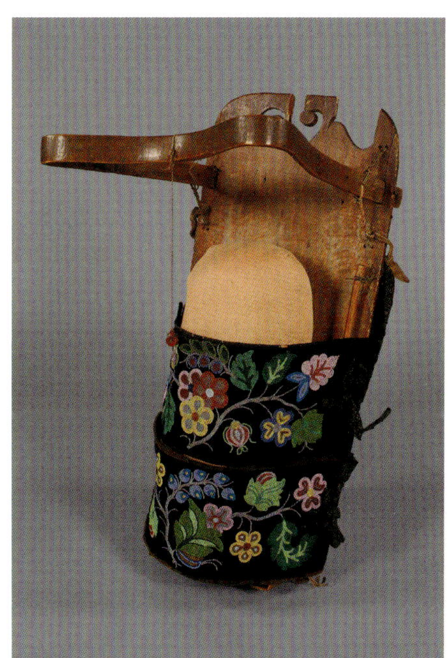

144

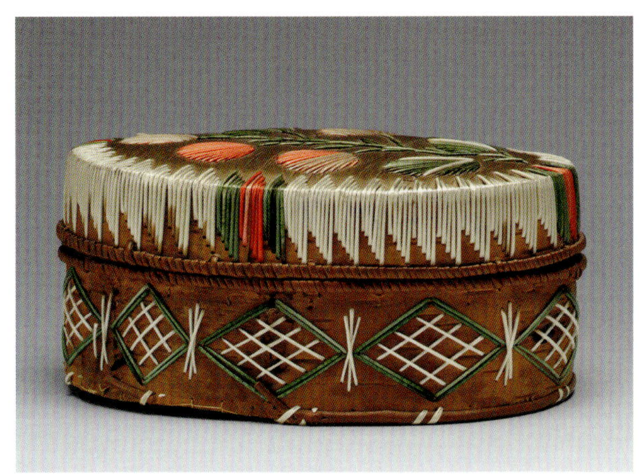

143

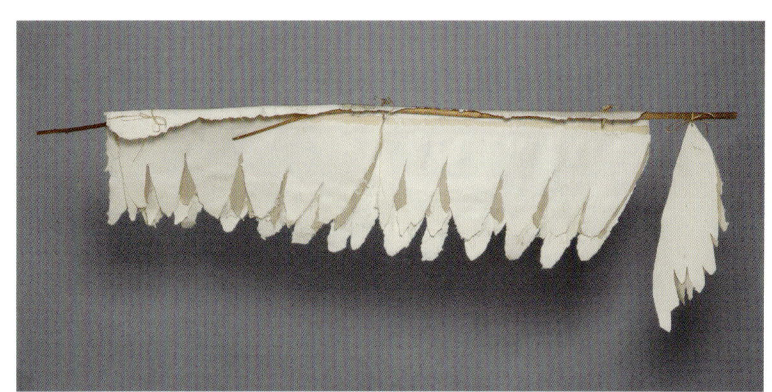

145

142. Artist unknown, Anishinaabeg (Chippewa / Ojibwa), White Earth Reservation, Minnesota

Bandolier bag, about 1890

Glass beads, cotton cloth, velveteen, wool binding tape, string, and thread
95 x 32.5 cm
Gift of Glover Street Hastings III; 181.2.26046

143. Artist unknown, Anishinaabeg (Chippewa / Ojibwa)

Basket, about 1900

Birch bark, spruce root, wood, porcupine quills, thread, and dye
6.2 x 16.4 x 10.5 cm (container only); 4 x 16.6 x 10.5 cm (lid only); 8 cm (container and lid together)
Bequest of Frank C. and Clara G. Churchill; 46.17.9562

144. Artist unknown, Anishinaabeg (Chippewa / Ojibwa)

Cradle, about 1890

Wood, birch bark, velveteen, cotton cloth, glass beads, hide, rawhide, metal, catlinite, lead, twine, and thread
74 x 31 x 40 cm
Gift of Guido R. Rahr Sr., Class of 1951P; 985.47.26533

145. Truman Lowe, Ho-Chunk (Winnebago), born 1944

Wing, 1995

Corkscrew willow branch, handmade paper with watermarks, cotton fibre abaca, sisal, and flax
Size variable
Purchased through the Class of 1935 Memorial Fund; 2008.41.3

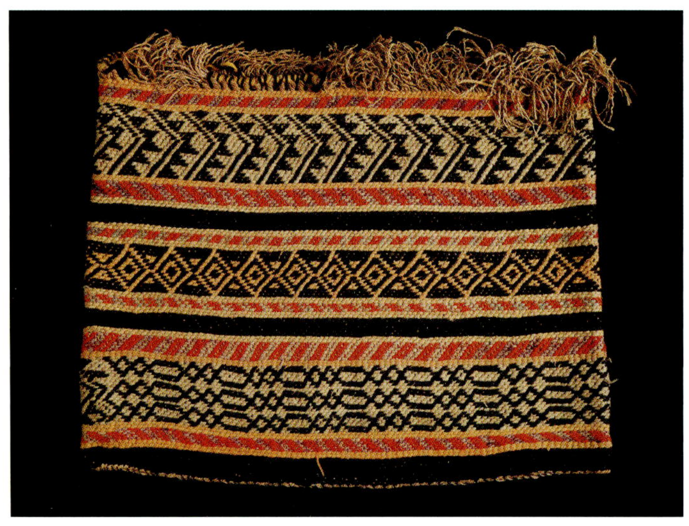

146

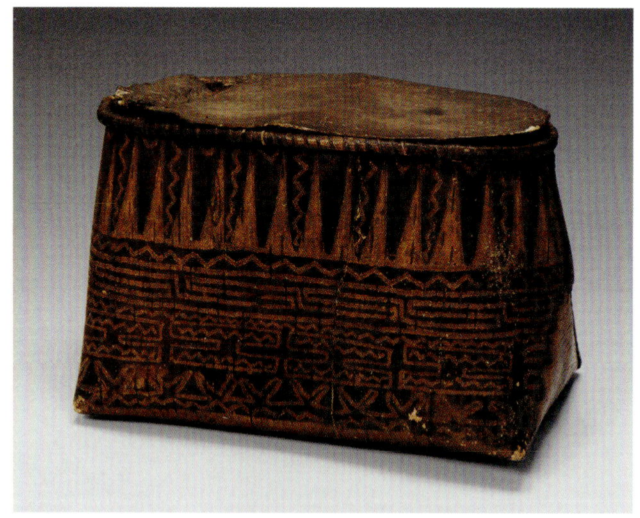

148

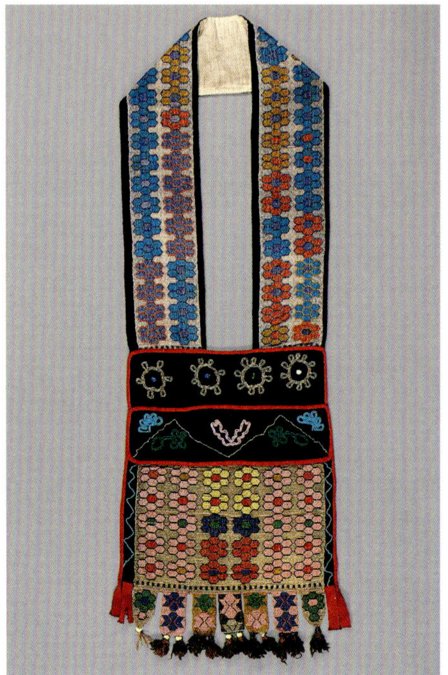

147

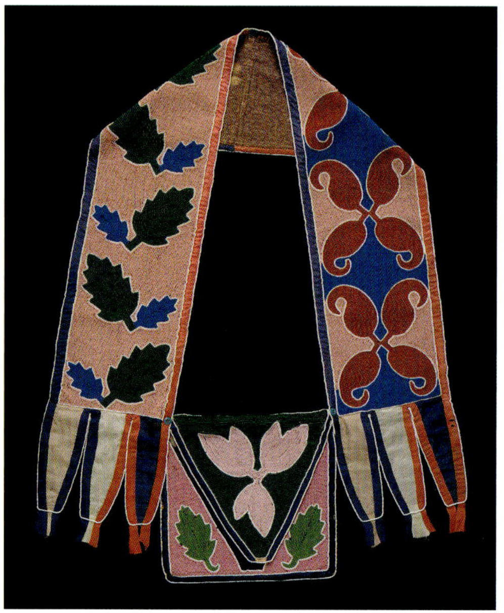

149

146. Unknown, artist, Potawatomi or Menominee (Menomini), Wittenberg, Wisconsin

Bag, about 1890

Yarn, fibre, aniline dye, and thread
44.5 x 55.5
Acquired by exchange from the Cranbrook Institute of Science; 55.4.13245

147. Artist unknown, Potawatomi, Wisconsin

Bandolier bag, about 1880

Glass beads, velvet, muslin, wool yarn, cotton binding, and thread
97 x 32.5 cm (including strap); strap: 51 cm
Bequest of Frank C. and Clara G. Churchill; 46.17.9893

148. Artist unknown, Woodlands, Great Lakes, Wisconsin area

Container depicting the cosmological universe and, on the underside, two Thunderbirds, about 1800

Birch bark, wood, spruce root, and twine (added later)
21 x 30.4 x 15.5 cm (container only); 4.2 x 28.5 x 14 cm (lid only); 22 cm (container and lid together)
Museum purchase; 163.66.15194

Mid-Atlantic

149. Artist unknown, Lenape (Delaware)

Bandolier bag, about 1850

Collected Wichita Falls, Texas, near the former Caddo-Wichita-Delaware Reservation
Glass beads, cotton cloth, ribbon, wool cloth, buttons, and thread
76 x 58 cm
Purchased through the Miriam and Sidney Stoneman Acquisitions Fund; 2008.93

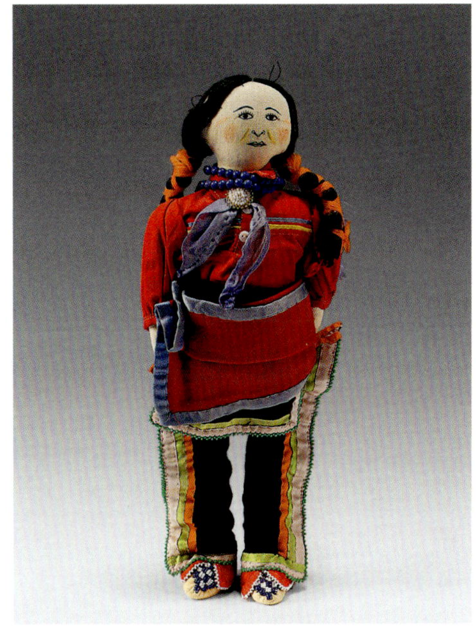

150

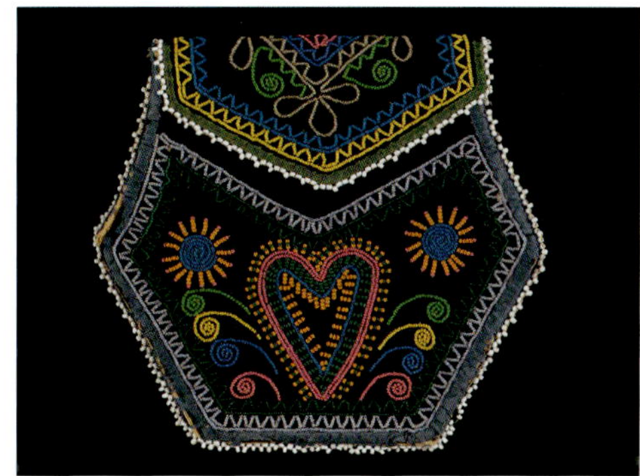

152

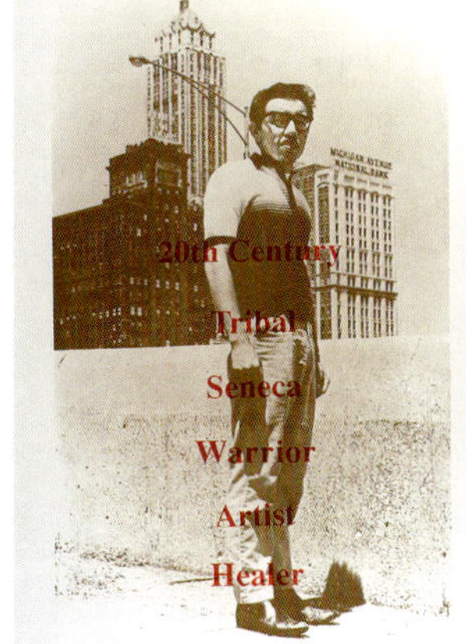

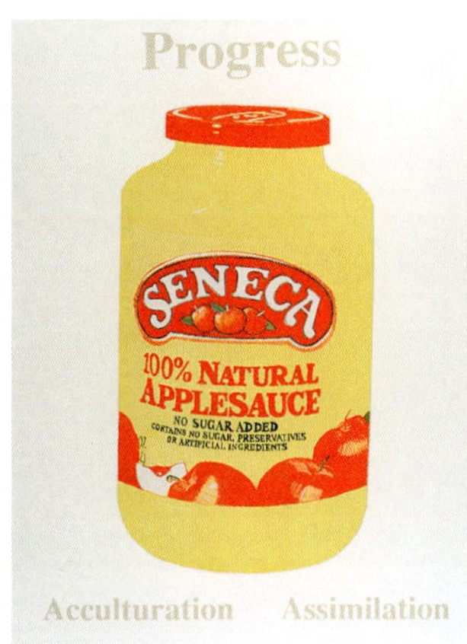

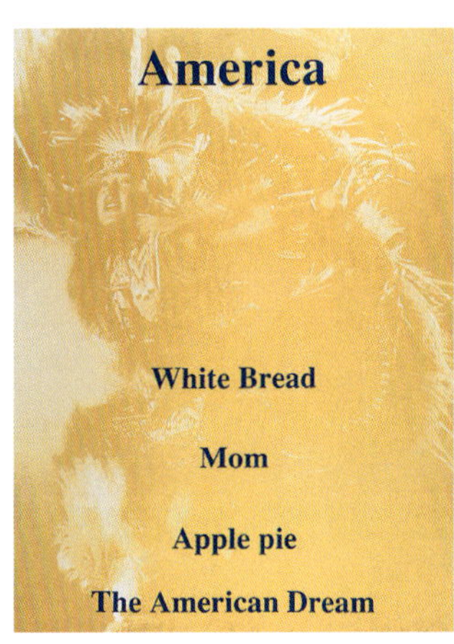

151

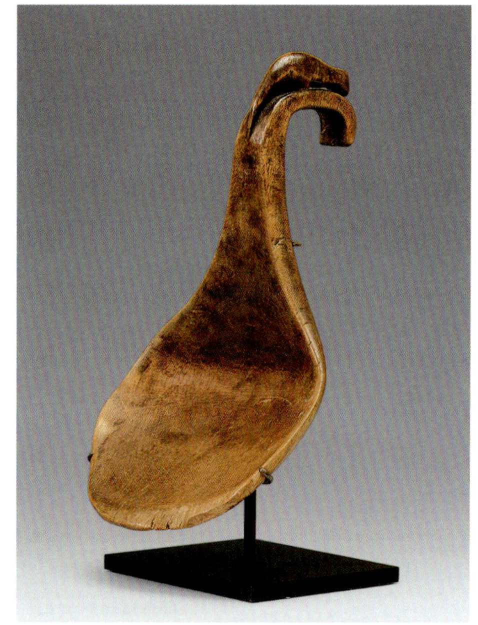

153

150. Maye Redbird, Lenape (Delaware), active 20th century

Figure of a Lenape (Delaware) man, 1946

Collected Wichita, Oklahoma, near the former Caddo-Wichita-Delaware Reservation
Cotton cloth, wool cloth, yarn, ribbon, hide, glass beads, plastic beads, bell, tobacco, plastic sequin, buttons, thread, and ink
30.5 x 12.5 x 6 cm
The Wellington Indian Doll Collection: Gift of Barbara Wellington Wells; 987.35.26737

Northeast

151. George C. Longfish, Seneca / Tuscarora; Haudenosaunee (Iroquois), born 1942

Modern Times, 1994

Triptych: color lithograph on Arches 88 paper
Each panel: 105.4 x 76.2 cm
Purchased through the Class of 1935 Memorial Fund; 2008.41.5

152. Artist unknown, Seneca; Haudenosaunee (Iroquois), New York

Bag, about 1830

Glass beads, velvet, cotton cloth, ribbon, and thread
15.5 x 17 cm
Purchased through the Mrs. Harvey P. Hood W'18 Fund and the Hood Museum of Art Acquisitions Fund; 2009.4

153. Artist unknown, Haudenosaunee (Iroquois)

Effigy feast ladle, about 1860

Wood
21 x 11.4 x 11.4 cm
Purchased through the William S. Rubin Fund; 2009.58

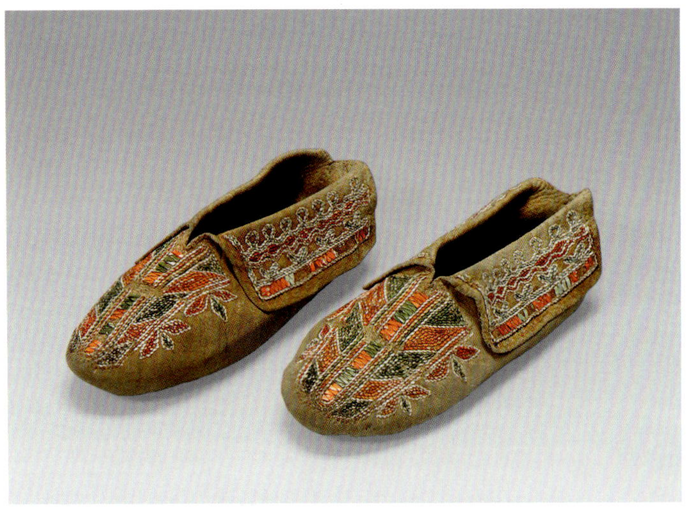

154

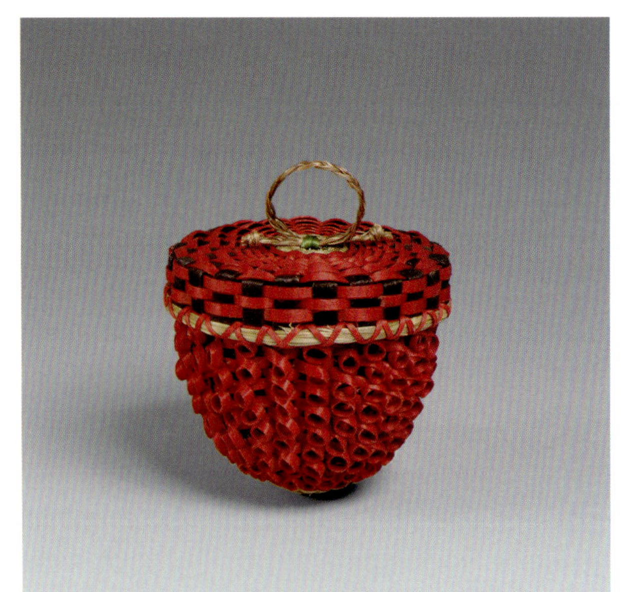

156

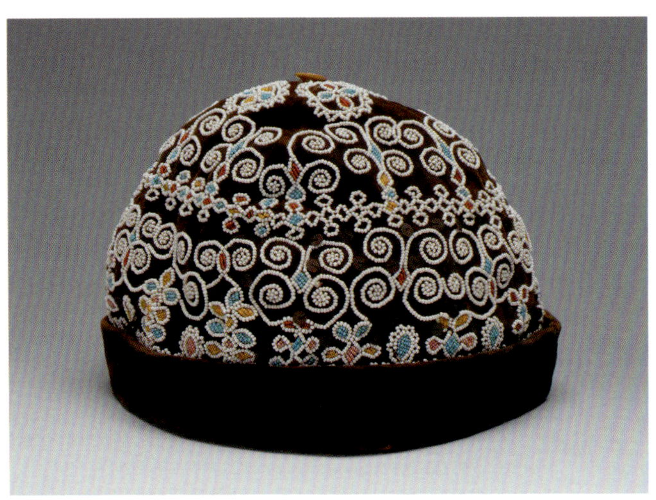

155

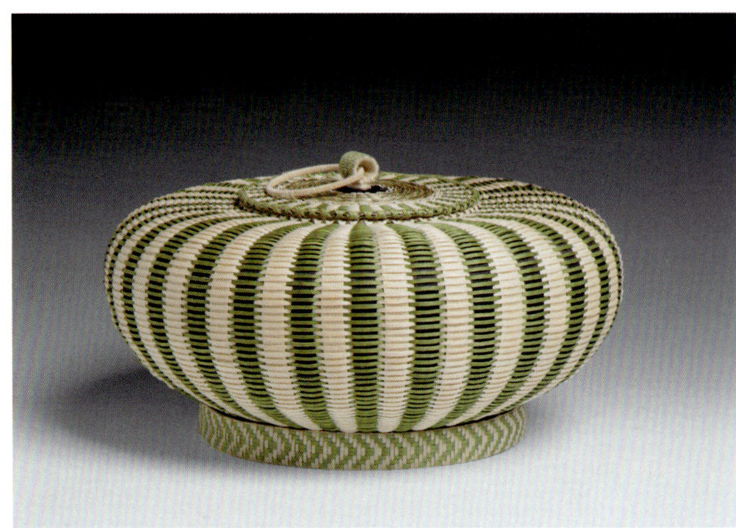

157

154. Artist unknown, Seneca; Haudenosaunee (Iroquois), New York

Moccasins, about 1820

Deer hide, porcupine quills, dye, sinew, ribbon, and thread
24 x 10 x 6 cm
Gift of Robert G. Chaffee, Class of 1936; 159.14.14400

155. Artist unknown, Mi'kmaq (Micmac); Wabanaki or Haudenosaunee (Iroquois), Nova Scotia, New Brunswick, or New York

Man's cap, about 1860

Velvet, cotton cloth, glass beads, sequins, ivory, and thread
14.5 x 15.5 cm
Purchased in memory of Stacey Coverdale, Class of 1988, made possible by an anonymous gift; 988.29.26943

156. Matthew Dana, Passamaquoddy; Wabanaki, born 1979

Strawberry basket, 2008

Brown ash, sweet grass, and dye
10.2 x 7.6 cm
Purchased through the Alvin and Mary Bert Gutman '40 Acquisitions Fund; 2008.47

157. Jeremy Frey, Passamaquoddy; Wabanaki, born 1978

Green urchin basket, 2008

Brown ash, sweetgrass, dye
15 x 23.5 cm; circular hoop on lid: 5 cm; bottom support ring: 2 cm
Purchased through the Phyllis and Bertram Geller 1937 Memorial Fund; 2008.51

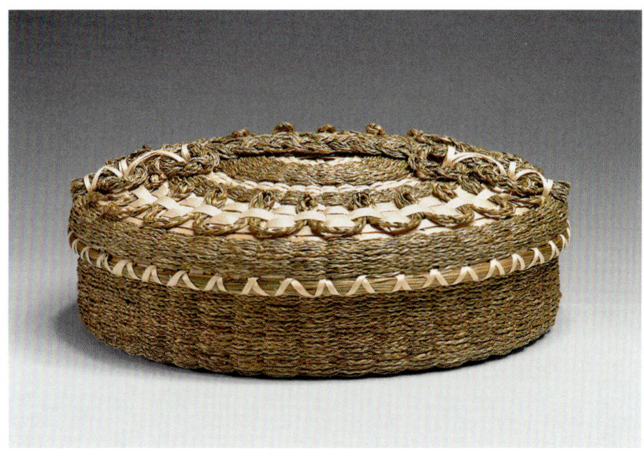

158

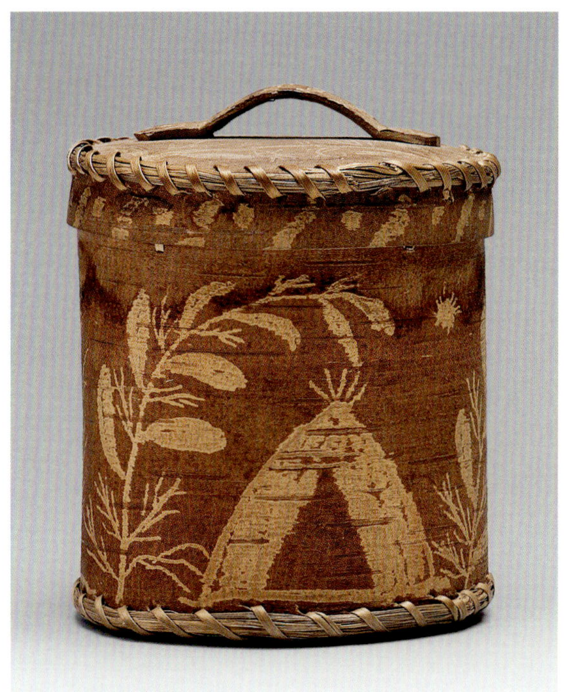

159

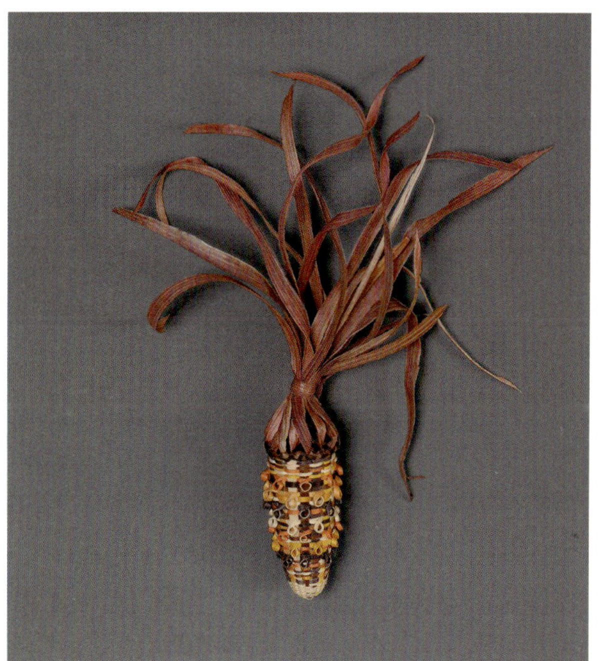

160

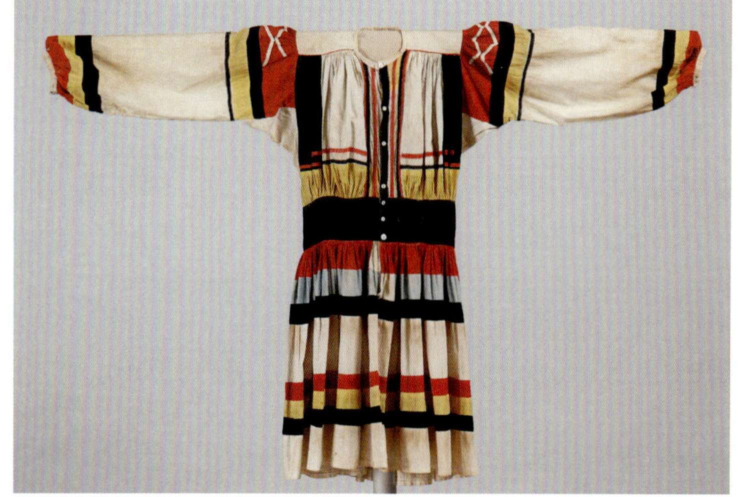

161

158. Clara Neptune Keezer, Passamaquoddy; Wabanaki, born 1930

Fancy sweetgrass flat basket, 2007

Brown ash and sweet grass
10.1 x 27.3 cm
Purchased through the Alvin and Mary Bert Gutman '40 Acquisitions Fund; 2007.40.1

159. Artist unknown, Passamaquoddy; Wabanaki

Container, about 1890

Birch bark, spruce root, grass
7.8 x 7.5 cm (container only); 2.2 x 8 cm (lid including handle); 9.5 cm (container and lid together)
Gift of Mr. and Mrs. George H. Browne; 42.12.8512

160. Sarah Sockbeson, Penobscot; Wabanaki, born 1983

Miniature corn basket, 2008

Brown ash, sweet grass, cornhusk, and dye
21 x 17.2 cm (cornhusk); 3 cm (basket proper)
Purchased through the Alvin and Mary Bert Gutman '40 Acquisitions Fund; 2008.48.3

Southeast

Florida

161. Artist unknown, Seminole, New River, Florida

Man's shirt tunic, about 1900

Cotton cloth, dye, buttons, and thread
101.5 x 31.5 cm (at waist); 149 cm (cuff to cuff along top of shoulders)
Bequest of Frank C. and Clara G. Churchill; 46.17.9956

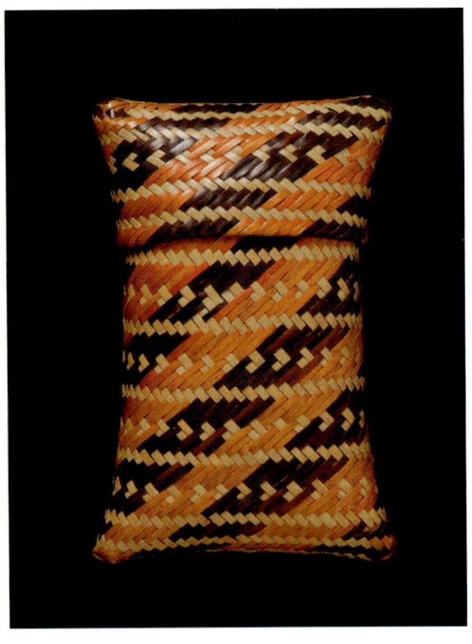

162

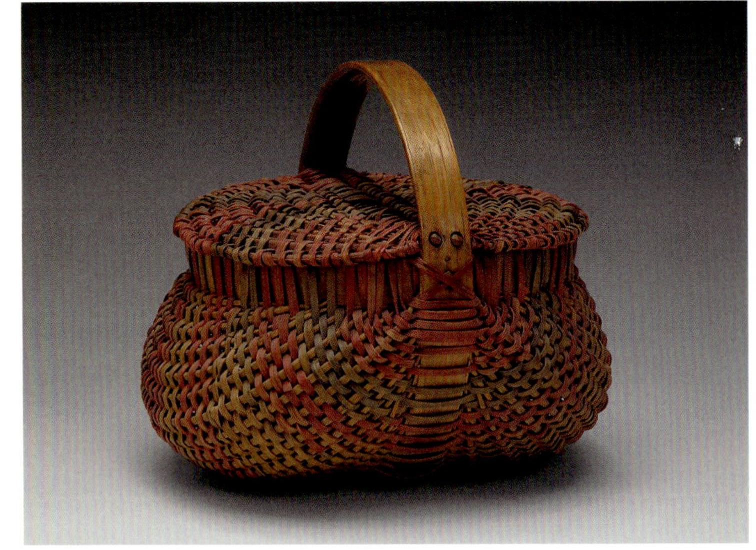

164

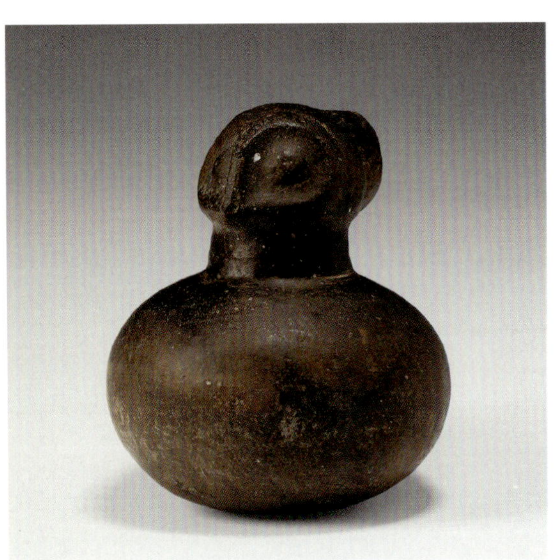

163

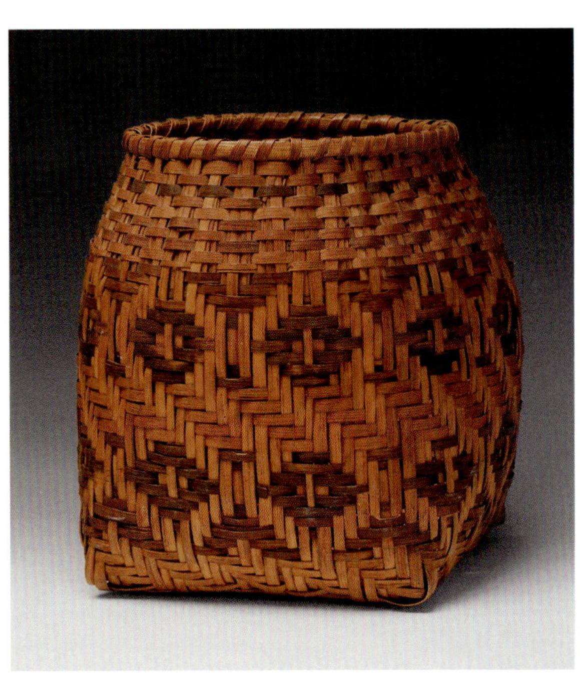

165

Gulf and Southeastern Uplands

162. Artist unknown, Chitimacha, Louisiana

Cigar case or wallet, about 1900

River cane, butternut root dye, and bloodroot dye
13.5 x 9 x 4 cm
Bequest of Frank C. and Clara G. Churchill; 46.17.9533

163. Artist unknown, Mississippian Tradition

Owl effigy bottle, Mississippian Period, about 1450 CE

Grey earthenware
12.6 x 9 cm
Gift of Alexis Chapman Proctor, Class of 1918; 167.38.24228

164. Artist unknown, Cherokee, North Carolina

Melon basket, about 1900

Oak and dye
12.5 x 13 x 12.2 cm
Bequest of Frank C. and Clara G. Churchill; 46.17.9555

165. Artist unknown, Cherokee

Storage basket, about 1915

River cane, butternut root dye, and bloodroot dye
27.5 x 24 x 24 cm
Gift of Mary Louis Warden Stewart; 996.42.30331

Related Exhibitions

The following exhibitions are given in reverse order, from the present back to 1961.

Native American Ledger Drawings from the Hood Museum of Art: The Mark Lansburgh Collection (Joe Horse Capture, guest curator), October 1–December 19, 2010

Contemporary Native American Ledger Art: Drawing on Tradition, August 14, 2010–December 19, 2010

Spirit of the Basket Tree: Wabanaki Ash Baskets from Maine (Jennifer Sapiel Neptune, guest curator), December 20, 2008–June 28, 2009

Hulleah Tsinhnajinne: Photographic Memoirs of an Aboriginal Savant (Living on Occupied Land), February 9–May 4, 2008

Our Land: Contemporary Art from the Arctic, organized by the Peabody Essex Museum, Salem, Massachusetts, the Governments of Canada and Nunavut, and the Department of Culture, Language, Elders, and Youth, March 27–May 20, 2007

Thin Ice: Inuit Traditions within a Changing Environment (Nicole Stuckenberger, guest curator), January 27–May 13, 2007

Myth of the Noble Savage, A Space for Dialogue: Fresh Perspectives on the Permanent Collection by Dartmouth's Students 31 (Meghan Rice, Class of 2006, student curator), April 4–May 21, 2006

Picturing Change: The Impact of Ledger Drawing on Native American Art, December 11, 2004–May 15, 2005

The Land of the Totem Poles: Native Peoples of the Northwest Coast, Anthropology 49: The Art of the Northwest Coast, Harrington Gallery teaching exhibition, March 25–May 18, 2003

Reservation X: The Power of Place; Seven Native Artists, Seven Installations, organized by the Canadian Museum of Civilization, Gatineau, Quebec, October 6–December 16, 2001

Cultural Survival: Chiricahua–Fort Sill Apache Identity Explored through Wearable Art (Lisa LeFlore, Class of 2001, student curator), Harrington Gallery teaching exhibition, May 19–June 24, 2001

Survival/Art/History: American Indian Collections from the Hood Museum of Art (Rayna Green, guest curator), November 19, 2000–April 7, 2002

Pueblo Pottery from New Mexico: A Selection from the Museum's Collection, September 16, 1997–September 1998

Tribal Identity: An Installation by James Luna, October 11–December 24, 1995

Contemporary Native American Paintings and Sculpture, September 27–November 26, 1995

Image and Self in Contemporary Native American Photoart: Works by Carm Little Turtle, Shelly Niro, Jolene Rickard, Hulleah Tsinhnahjinnie, and Richard Ray Whitman (Jennifer Skoda, August Lopez, and Ronald Martinez, student curators), September 9–November 26, 1995

Native American Designs of the Northern Woodlands, February 20, 1995–February 9, 1997

To Image and to See: Crow Indian Photographs by Edward S. Curtis and Richard Throssel, 1905–1910 (Wendi-Starr Brown, student curator], July 1–September 5, 1993

Peoples and Cultures of the Plains, Northwest Coast, Arctic Region, NAS 21 and Anthropology 40, Harrington Gallery teaching exhibition, October 31–December 20, 1992

Ancient Native Americans, Anthropology 32, Harrington Gallery teaching exhibition, January 7–February 9, 1992

Peoples and Cultures of the Northwest Coast and Arctic Regions, NAS 21 and Anthropology 40, Harrington Gallery teaching exhibition, September 22–October 14, 1990

Northern Native American Baskets from the Permanent Collection (Davina Begaye, student curator), May 4, 1990–October 20, 1991

Plains Indian Arts: Continuity and Change, organized by the National Museum of Natural History, Smithsonian Institution Traveling Exhibitions Service, Washington, D.C., September 23–December 10, 1989

Objects of Bright Pride: Northwest Coast Indian Art from the American Museum of Natural History, organized by the American Federation of Arts, New York, July 8–August 27, 1989

Patterns of Life, Patterns of Art: The Rahr Collection of Native American Art, May 2–July 19, 1987

Native American Art, September 28, 1985–January 12, 1986

The following exhibitions were installed in either the Hopkins Center or Wilson Hall.

Pottery Vessels from Acoma Pueblo, September 16–November 20, 1983

Native American Studio Art/Ames Awards, May 11–June 3, 1979

Allan Houser (Spring Artist-in-Residence), April 20–May 20, 1979

Traditional Art of the American Indian, March 23–May 20, 1979

Native American Art and Artifacts, March 16–September 30, 1979

The Arts of Native America: Clothing, March 9–May 13, 1979

The Eastern Woodland: Algonkian and Iroquois, March 6–November 11, 1979

Northwest Coast Indian Art (Children of the Raven), December 9–April 23, 1978

Native American Clothing, fall 1978

The Search for an Ancient Arctic Past, May 27–December 31, 1977

Southwest Indian Pottery and Basketry, May 28, 1976–February 4, 1977

Southwestern Pottery and Basketry, January 1975

T. C. Cannon (Summer Artist-in-Residence), July 18–August 31, 1975

Navajo Rugs, 1974

Native American Art and Artifacts, March 7–April 13, 1974

North American and African Beadwork, October 8–December 15, 1974

Fritz Scholder (Fall Artist-in-Residence), September 28–October 21, 1973

Arizona Indians, fall 1973

Native American Arts and Crafts, May–October 1972

Hopi Exhibition, December 15, 1970–January 20, 1971

The Kachina Paintings of Edwin Earle, April 1–May 20, 1970

Braves and Dolls, November 1969–March 1970

Menominee Indian Headdress, December 20, 1967–January 13, 1968

Eskimo Prints from the Beekman Pool Collection, March 29–April 20, 1967

Cape Dorset: The Art of an Eskimo, December 20, 1966–January 13, 1967

Eskimo Graphic Arts, organized by the Smithsonian Institution, Washington, D.C., December 17, 1966–January 1967

Indians of the Southwest, May 1965

Navajo Weaving, May 1961

There were twenty-four Native American–themed exhibitions by students in Wilson Hall during the 1960s and 1970s.

Selected Chronology of the Native American Collection at Dartmouth College

Deborah T. Haynes

This chronology does not include the extensive archaeological collections of the museum.

1772

A mastodon molar is the first recorded object in the college's "cabinet." It is not known where the college's collection was housed from 1772 to 1790. (The molar is in the collection today.)

1783

The first "curiosities" are obtained by President John Wheelock (1754–1817), Class of 1771, second president of Dartmouth College, 1779–1815. This date is recognized as the date of the founding of the museum's ethnology collection.[1]

1791–1811

The collection is housed in Dartmouth Hall.

1796

Elias Hasket Derby (1739–1799), Esquire, of Salem, Massachusetts, donates a collection of curiosities from Asia, Africa, and the Northwest Coast of the Americas. The "1810 Catalogue" (see below) lists "An Indian's Spear from the N. West Coast, by Mr. Derby, Salem." Derby was a wealthy Salem merchant and the son of the sea captain Richard Derby (1712–1783). There are several early spears in the collection; however, a secure identification is not possible.[2]

1810

A partial inventory, known as the "1810 Catalogue," documents the objects given to the college before that date. The only Native American objects listed that are extant are two "Indian Axes found in Lebanon, Connecticut," given by William H. Woodward, Esquire (1774–1818), Class of 1792. The "1810 Catalogue" provides a view into the lives of prominent New England men whose professions as sea captains, missionaries, and military men brought them into contact with Native Americans. Unfortunately, the current disposition of these objects is unknown: "Cherokee pipe," donated by Moses Fisk (1759–1843), Class of 1783, missionary to the Cherokee in 1799; "Horn Comb from Nootka Sound," given by A. Holden; "Squaw's fan," given by Captain John Kendrick (about 1740–1800), who explored the Northwest coast in 1781; "Indian bow and quiver of arrows," given by Dr. Lemuel Hedge (1765–1801), Class of 1788h; "Various Indian specimens from the Chippewas, Sioux and Winnibagos," given by Captain Josiah Dunham (1769–1844), Class of 1789, who was stationed at Fort Detroit in 1805.[3]

1811–96

The college's collection is housed in the Medical Building or in Dartmouth Hall, 1811–28; Dartmouth Hall, 1829–40; Reed Hall, 1840–71; Culver Hall, 1871–96.

1881

A collection of Mississippian culture pottery, excavated from the Missouri Mounds, is donated to Samuel Colcord Bartlett (1817–1898), Class of 1836 and the eighth president of Dartmouth College (1877–1892), by Horatio Nelson Rust (1826–1898). Rust was an antiquarian and amateur archaeologist. He sold collections of archaeology to the Peabody Museum, Harvard University, the Smithsonian Institution, and the Logan Museum, Beloit College. Rust designed an installation at the 1893 World Columbian Exposition that received an award for the best archaeology exhibit.[4]

About 1886

William M. Leeds (1829–1886) was a chief clerk of the Bureau of Indian Affairs, Washington, D.C., from 1878 until 1879 (when he resigned). In the aftermath of the Nimi'ipuu (Nez Perce) war against the federal government, the warrior Hinmaton Yalakit (Chief Joseph) made a diplomatic visit to Washington in 1879, where he was hosted by Leeds. It is assumed that during this time Leeds collected the Native American objects his wife later gave to the museum, including a photograph taken by Charles Milton Bell of Hinmaton Yalakit and about forty other objects from the Nimi'piuu (Nez Perce), the Osage, and the Tsistsistas (Cheyenne). It is believed that the collection was donated to Dartmouth because Leeds's brother, the Reverend Samuel Penniman Leeds (1824–1910), was the pastor at the Church of Christ at Dartmouth College from 1860 to 1900. The exact date of the donation is unknown; however, it was probably donated between 1886, when William B. Leeds died, and 1891, when the collection was inventoried.[5]

1889

A collection of objects from China and the Arctic is donated by Mary E. Hall Hubbard of Croyden, New Hampshire. The objects were collected by her father, Captain Worthen Hall (1802–1887). Hall sailed on a whaling vessel from 1827 to 1855. The collection includes a "skin waterproof suit of Eskimaux." A large collection of Arctic objects catalogued in 1913 are believed to be part of the Hall collection.[6]

1896
The collection moves to the new Butterfield Hall, where it remains until 1928.

1904
Porter Tremain and Charles Tremain of Fayetteville, New York, donate a collection of late-nineteenth-century Eastern Woodlands objects. Some of them were acquired by the missionary Marilla Baker Ingalls (1828–1900) in "Burma"; however, it is unclear whether Ingalls also collected the Woodlands objects. The relationship between Ingalls, the Tremains, and Dartmouth College is unknown.

1913
The museum's collection is inventoried and recatalogued by Charles Henry Hawes (1867–1943), professor of anthropology and curator of the anthropological collections from 1911 to 1917. All of the early donations to the museum start with the number 13; this indicates that the objects were accessioned (not donated) in the year 1913.[7]

1914
David Hogan Markham (1891–1978), Class of 1915, a member of the Cherokee Nation from Tahlequah, Oklahoma, donates a small collection of Cherokee objects during his senior year. The gift includes the book *Constitution and Laws of the Cherokee Nation,* published in Cherokee syllabary in 1892; an arrow used to hunt deer; a blunt (cartridge tip) for hunting small game; and a photograph of "cornstalk shooting" (a game that entails shooting an iron-tipped arrow at corn stalks, each side counting the number of stalks the arrow pierces).

1922
Margaret R. Kimberly of West Newton, Massachusetts, donates a collection of eighty-five objects from the Northwest Coast, in addition to a total of 2,032 objects from around the world. These objects are reported to have been collected by a "sea captain" who traveled in the Pacific from about 1820 to 1860. The collector was a friend of Mrs. Kimberly's uncle, General John Hewston of San Francisco. The collection includes a group of early Haida figures depicting stern-faced missionaries.

1928
The Dartmouth College Museum moves to Wilson Hall, where it remain until 1983.

1929
The Carpenter Hall galleries are founded.

1930
Professor Robert Addison McKennan (1903–1982), Class of 1925, taught in the Sociology Department (1930–66) and then in the newly founded Anthropology Department (1967–69). McKennan collected 170 objects for the museum during his fieldwork. The collection includes sixty-three Dena'ina (Tanaina) objects from Alaska.

1931
Ronald Burnett Sundown (1901–1982), Class of 1932, a member of the Tonawanda Band of Seneca in Akron, New York, gives a snow snake to the museum. In the May 1929 *Dartmouth Alumni Magazine,* Sundown supplied the article "Throwing the Snake (An Iroquois Winter Sport) by R. B. Sundown, '32, an Iroquois Indian." The game involves seeing who can throw the snow snake (a wood and metal stick) the farthest.

1934–61
Wilfred Wedgwood Bowen (1899–1987) was a professor of zoology as well as curator (1934–45) and then director of the Dartmouth College Museum (1946–61). In 1939, Bowen donated a archaeological collection from the Northwest Coast. During his tenure at the museum, he donated over 119 objects from Africa, Asia, and the Americas. In 1958, Bowen wrote the volume *A Pioneer Museum in the Wilderness,* an invaluable resource.

1934
William Patten (1861–1932), Class of 1908H (honorary master's degree), was a professor of zoology from 1893 to 1931 and curator of the zoological collections; he both studied and collected fossil fish. In 1934, Bradley Merrill Patten (1889–1971) donates his father's collection of over 280 objects. The collection is predominantly objects from Papua New Guinea; however, it does include ten Native American objects from the Plains and Southwest.

1935
Mrs. Winston Fearn Garth of Huntsville, Alabama, purchased a collection of forty-seven Mississippian Culture jars from the Alabama Museum of Natural History specifically to be given to the Dartmouth College Museum. Mrs. Garth, trustee of the Alabama museum, was involved in dispersing duplicate Mississippian culture material to other institutions. These objects were presented to Dartmouth during the senior year of her grandson Winston Fearn Garth II (1913–1980), Class of 1935.

1935
Abby Aldrich Rockefeller (1874–1948), mother of Nelson A. Rockefeller, Class of 1930, donates a collection of twenty-two watercolors by the Kiowa Five and the Santa Fe Studio School artists to the Carpenter Hall galleries under the leadership of Churchill "Jerry" P. Lathrop (1900–1995), professor in the Department of Art and

director of the Carpenter Hall galleries (1935–62) and the Hopkins Center Art Galleries (1962–69 and 1972–74). (See the introduction to the collection by Karen Miller for more about this gift.)[8]

1940
Robert L. Ripley (1890–1949), Class of 1939H, the creator of the newspaper series, radio show, and television show called "Ripley's Believe It or Not," lends and then donates about one hundred objects to the Dartmouth College Museum. This collection of "exotica" is displayed in the museum's "Robert L. Ripley Room" in Wilson Hall. Most of the Ripley objects are from Africa and Asia; however, one of the finest objects in the Ripley collection is a Chilkat Tlingit robe. Ripley's promoter, Douglas Storer (1899–1985), Class of 1921, orchestrated Ripley's relationship with Dartmouth in order to help Ripley establish himself as a scholarly collector.

1942
George Henry Browne (1857–1931) was the founder and headmaster of Browne and Nichols School, Cambridge, Massachusetts, from 1883 to 1928. Browne wrote several books on education, was a lifelong friend of the poet Robert Frost, and was instrumental in the development of U.S. figure skating. Browne and his wife, Emily Robbins Webster Browne (died 1941), collected over five hundred objects during their extensive travels in the Southwest. When Emily Browne died, her sister Miss Ellen A. Webster of Webster Farm, Bridgewater, New Hampshire, donated the Browne collection to Dartmouth, because it was her sister's wish that the collection be kept in her native state.

1942
Alfred T. Clifton Jr. (1906–1996), Class of 1927, arranges the donation of his father's collection of sixty-six objects. Lieutenant Colonel Alfred T. Clifton (1875–?) was a member of the U.S. Army Signal Corp for over thirty years. He was stationed in the Philippines in 1901 and in Alaska in 1903–4, when he began to collect. The sixteen Arctic objects in his collection include Yup'ik masks and model kayaks.

1943
Captain Herbert L. Shuttleworth II (1913–2010), Class of 1935, donates a collection of 105 Native American objects. Shuttleworth was the president and chief executive officer of Mohasco Corp. (formerly Mohawk Carpet Mills, Inc.) of Amsterdam, New York, until he retired in 1980. The provenance of the collection is unknown. Some of the objects are noted as being collected by the missionary Stephen Earl Taylor (1873–?). The objects in the collection represent many cultures and date from the late nineteenth century.

1944
Ida Farr Miller (1863–1953) donates ninety-six Native American baskets that were collected by her mother, Ellen Frances Burpee Farr (1840–1907). Ellen was the widow of Evarts Worcester Farr (1840–1880), Class of 1863, from Littleton, New Hampshire. After her husband died, she pursued her career as an artist, first in Boston (1883–87) and then in Pasadena, California (1887–1907). She was a still-life painter who was known for her paintings of Native American baskets; her work was exhibited in the California Building at the World's Columbian Exposition in Chicago in 1893. Almost half of the Farr baskets are from California, and some were purchased from Farr's friend, the Pasadena dealer and collector Grace Nicholson (1822–1951).[9]

1946
Mortimer Norton Buckner (1873–1942) was president and chairman of the board of the New York Trust Company. Before 1926, Buckner traveled extensively in the West and was involved with the expansion of the railroads. In 1942, his art collection was bequeathed to his son Newton Buckner (1913–2005) of Greenwich, Connecticut. At the suggestion of his father-in-law, John Carleton Sterling (1888–1964), Class of 1911, Buckner donates the collection to Dartmouth.

1946
Colonel Frank C. Churchill (1850–1912) was a special inspector in the U.S. Indian Service. Churchill and his wife, Clara G. Churchill (1851–1945), visited over one hundred tribes between 1899 and 1909. For three years, the Churchills were stationed at Muskogee, Oklahoma, in the Indian territory of the "Five Civilized Tribes." The Churchills traveled widely through the Southwest and greatly augmented their collections with almost four hundred objects that were representative of the pueblo dwellers and other tribes of the area. These include a series of over forty Navajo blankets as well as large *ollas* from Acoma, New Mexico. They also collected beaded work from Lakota (Sioux), Gaigwa (Kiowa), Siksika (Blackfoot), Tsistsistas (Cheyenne), and other Plains groups. In the summer of 1905, President Teddy Roosevelt appointed Churchill a special emissary to Alaska to investigate "Eskimo" schools and the progress of the government-sponsored program for the domestication of reindeer. For three months the Churchills voyaged more than ten thousand miles, mostly aboard the U.S. Revenue cutter *Bear*. The couple went ashore at Point Barrow, the northernmost settlement on this continent. During this time they collected almost two hundred Arctic objects, along with numerous other Northwest Coast items. In 1909, the Churchills returned to Lebanon, New Hampshire, where Clara opened the "Churchill Museum." Clara Churchill bequeathed her Native American collection and the contents of her house, tallying 1,600 objects, to the museum in 1946.

1947
Edward W. Bush Jr. (1923–2006), Class of 1945, Tuck 1947, donates a group of eight Lakota (Sioux) objects he inherited from his granduncle, Captain Charles Akers Johnson (1840–1893). Captain C. A. Johnson was assigned to the Red Cloud Agency and Fort Robinson, Nebraska, between 1877 and 1879, and he was responsible for gathering a large section of the "Crazy Horse Surrender Ledger." The ledger is a census of Crazy Horse's band, compiled by the U.S. Army on May 6, 1877, the day Crazy Horse and his nearly nine hundred followers surrendered at Fort Robinson, Nebraska.[10]

1948–74
Robert Gibson Chaffee (1914–1986), Class of 1936, was the Dartmouth College Museum's curator of geology (1948–69) and director (1969–74). During Chaffee's tenure, he donated over 185 objects, including some Haudenosaunee (Iroquois) objects.

1950–1960s
Between 1914 and 1974 (and especially in the 1950s), the Dartmouth College Museum participated in exchanges with other museums interested in diversifying their collections. The museum acquired many early Native American objects through exchanges with the Museum of the American Indian, New York; Bates College, Lewiston, Maine; Colorado College, Colorado Springs, Colorado; Cranbrook Institute of Science, Bloomfield Hills, Michigan; Ralph C. Altman, Los Angeles, California; Peabody Museum, Salem, Massachusetts; The Rushford Collection, Salem, Massachusetts; Fairbanks Museum, St. Johnsbury, Vermont; Milton Babcock, Milton, Massachusetts; and Robert T. Emery, Lebanon, New Hampshire. Some of these objects were originally acquired by the collector Milford G. Chandler (1889–1981); painter and theorist Wolfgang Paalen (1905–1959); and ethnographer George T. Emmons (1852–1945). Unfortunately, the museum also "exchanged-out" some important objects that were perceived at the time as duplicate material but are now seen as important to the original context of each collection.

1950
Louisa G. Sheldon of Woodstock, Vermont, donates twenty-seven objects collected by her husband, Charles Sheldon (1867–1928). Sheldon was a hunter, author, and early environmentalist who took part in the effort to create Denali National Park. During Sheldon's work in the Arctic with the U.S. Biological Survey (1903–19), he collected many fine Arctic and Northwest Coast objects. In 1920, Sheldon continued his survey work in the Southwest, where he collected some early Pueblo objects as well.[11]

1953
An exhibition is held in Carpenter Hall galleries featuring the work of the Creek/Potawatomi artist Woodrow "Woody" Wilson Crumbo (1912–1989). At the close of the exhibition, the Carpenter Hall galleries purchases four of Crumbo's prints, marking the first purchase of art from a contemporary Native American artist. Stylistically, Crumbo's prints form a foundation for the development of modern Native American art.

1954
Donald Cahoon McIntire (1884–1961), Class of 1906, donated six Hupa, Karuk (Karok), and Yurok baskets acquired by his great aunt, who was a missionary on the Hoopa Valley Reservation in Eureka, California, about 1908–10.

1955–75
Alfred Frank Whiting (1912–1978) was the curator of anthropology and an assistant professor of anthropology from 1955 to 1975. During his tenure, Whiting held his classes in the museum and encouraged his students to "curate" some of the museum's collections. Whiting had a strong interest in collecting objects made by contemporary Hopi artists. Many of his donations were purchased at the Hopi Craftsman Exhibition, held at the Museum of Northern Arizona in Flagstaff. Whiting invited Edmund Nequatewa (about 1880–1969), a Hopi teacher, to discuss Hopi life ways with the students. In 1958, Whiting acquired a print by the contemporary Navajo artist Beatien Yazz (Jimmy Toddy; born 1928).

1957
Victor Justice Evans (1866–1931) was a patent attorney, founder of the firm Victor J. Evans and Co., real estate developer, and counsel for numerous tribal cases, including the Lakota (Sioux) tribe in the Black Hills Case. Evans was a collector of Native American art and of rare animals, which he kept on his estate, named "Acclimation Park." At the time of his death in 1931, his animals were given to the National Zoological Park, and his collection of five thousand Native American objects was given to the Smithsonian Institution. However, his wife, Karen Gram Evans, retained sixty objects. Mrs. Evans remarried in 1940 to the philosopher James Foster Scott (1852–1953). In 1957, Mrs. Evans was living in Meriden, New Hampshire, and gave her late first husband's collection to the museum in his honor.

1959–69
The museum's largest collection of Northwest Coast objects (numbering 206) was a partial gift and partial purchase from Doris Meltzer and the Meltzer Gallery. The collection was assembled in the 1920s and 1930s by Axel Rasmussen (ca. 1887–1945), the superintendent of schools in southern Alaska, who lived in Wrangell and then in Sitka. Los Angeles dealer Earl L. Stendahl (1887–1966) reassembled his collection of approximately eight hundred objects after Rasmussen's death, and Robert Tyler Davis, director of the Portland Art Museum, raised funds through a public subscription campaign to acquire it from Stenhadl.[12] The objects that were not acquired by the Portland Art Museum were sold to the New York dealer Doris

Meltzer, and Dartmouth College Museum Director Elmer Harp Jr. (1913–2009) worked with Meltzer to place those objects at the college.

1960–61
In 1960 and 1961, Vilhjalmur Stefansson (1879–1962) and his wife, Evelyn Stefansson Nef (1913–2009), founders of Dartmouth's Arctic Studies Program (now the Institute of Arctic Studies), were responsible for bringing two exhibitions featuring contemporary Inuit art to Dartmouth. The Dartmouth College Museum purchased carvings by the Inuit artists Lucassie Amm and Levi Komaluk from an exhibition of art by the Sculptors Society of Povungnetuk, Quebec, founded in 1958. The next year, the Carpenter Hall galleries purchased a collection of prints from an exhibition sponsored by the Canadian Department of Northern Affairs and the Canadian Consulate. The prints are from the 1960 edition produced by West Baffin Eskimo Co-operative, Cape Dorset, founded in 1959.

1961
Seth Towse (1934–2010), Class of 1957, of Loudonville, New York, donates a pair of Tsistsistas (Cheyenne) moccasins. The moccasins were collected by an "elderly friend of the Towse family in Indian Territory," about 1885–90.

1962
The Hopkins Center Art Galleries open.

1969–79
Elmer Harp Jr. (1913–2009) was cofounder, with Professor Robert A. McKennan, of the Department of Anthropology. He was curator of anthropology (1946–52) and then director of the museum (1961–69), responsible for overseeing a very rich period of Arctic material collection. Harp himself donated over 125 Inuit objects from the Northwest Territories.

1969
Corey Ford (1902–1969), Class of 1921H, donates 203 objects he collected during his travels around the world, approximately 75 of which are from the Arctic. Corey Ford was a humorist, author, outdoorsman, and screenwriter. He traveled extensively in Alaska and Canada from 1934 to 1940. In 1952, Ford moved to Hanover, New Hampshire, where he became an honorary member of the Dartmouth College Class of 1921. Ford was an advisor to the Delta Kappa Epsilon fraternity and to several student publications. He helped organize the Dartmouth College Rugby Football Club and opened a gym in his home near campus for students interested in boxing. When he died in 1969, he left his property and the contents of his house to the college.[13]

1972
Mary Perley donates a collection of thirty Native American objects that she had inherited from her father-in-law, Henry Gabriel Perley (Maliseet-Passamaquoddy; 1885–1972), also known as Chief Henry Red Eagle, of Greenville, Maine. He collected the objects during his life as a professional stage Indian with the Kickapoo Indian Company Troupe, the Barnum and Bailey Circus, Buffalo Bill's Wild West Show, and Coney Island's Dreamland, among other productions; he also acted in fifty silent films. Later in life, Perley became a writer, lecturer, Maine guide, and trapper.[14] Some of the objects were made by Perley's wife, Wanna R. Eagle (1897–1967), who was also engaged in show business. The stage clothing is an inventive mix of pan–Native American cultural attributes. Perley's son was Henry Gabriel Perley Jr. (1921–1972), Class of 1943. Perley Jr. died in April 1927 (just seven months before his father), and it was in his memory that his widow, Mary, donated this unique collection.

1974
Under economic pressure, the college decides to divest the museum's natural history collection and bring the art collection (Hopkins Center Art Galleries) and the anthropology collection (Dartmouth College Museum) under one administrative unit called the Dartmouth College Museum and Galleries. The Director of the Dartmouth College Museum, Robert G. Chaffee, founds the Montshire Museum of Science in 1974 with Dartmouth's natural history collection. In 1976, Chaffee retires from Dartmouth and the Montshire opens to the public.[15]

1976–99
Tamara Northern, curator of ethnographic art from 1975 to 1999, was responsible for the acquisition of three major donations of Native American art—the Hastings (1981), Rahr (1985), and Wellington (1987) collections. During her tenure she also oversaw several purchases, including a Mimbres bowl; a Tlingit box; *Apache Pull-Toy,* by Bob Haozous; and a Mi'kmaq (Micmac) cap. The cap was purchased in memory of Stacey Coverdale, Class of 1988, who died in a car accident just hours after her graduation on June 12, 1988. Coverdale was a member of the Shinnecock tribe of Long Island and an anthropology major who was active in the Native American Studies Program. Northern also organized Native American exhibitions in the new Hood Museum of Art and worked closely with Native American student interns.

1978–81
The college recognizes the need to centralize the Dartmouth College Museum and Galleries collections. This goal is realized with the generous bequest of Harvey P. Hood in 1978. On February 24, 1979, the Trustees of Dartmouth College vote "to name the proposed new fine arts center in honor of Harvey P. Hood of the Class of 1918, a distinguished Trustee of the College from 1941 to 1967."

Toward the end of 1981, all museum publications are using the name Hood Museum of Art.

1980
In the 1980s, generous donors and museum supporters Jane and Raphael Bernstein give two paintings by Fritz Scholder, and Heidi and Arthur Lewis Wood, Class of 1934, give a large Zuni *olla*.

1981
Glover Street Hastings III of West Newton, Massachusetts, and Bridgeton, Maine, became interested in Dartmouth College's Native American collection through his friendship with W. W. Bowen, a former director of the Dartmouth College Museum, and Victor M. Cutter, Class of 1903 (donor of six hundred Mesoamerican objects). When Hastings died in 1949, he bequeathed his collection of 1,750 objects to Dartmouth, with the provision that his collection be retained by his daughter, Carlena Hastings Redfield (1888–1981), during her lifetime. The collection is comprised of 1,600 archaeological objects, representing a range of prehistoric cultures, and 150 ethnographic objects, strong in Plains and Northeastern cultures.

1983
The Dartmouth College Museum galleries in Wilson Hall close to the public.

1985
The new Hood Museum of Art building is dedicated. A longtime trustee of Dartmouth College and a friend and advisor to three Dartmouth presidents, Harvey P. Hood, Class of 1918, endorsed the view that an education must include exposure to the full breadth of human knowledge and experience for the fullness of human potential to be realized. The generous gifts of Harvey P. Hood and his wife, Barbara C. Hood, along with gifts from the Hood family and from other friends of the arts at Dartmouth, make the museum a reality.

1985
Guido Reinhardt Rahr Sr. (1902–1985) of Manitowoc, Wisconsin, gives the museum a collection of 224 Native American objects, made predominantly by Plains and Northern Woodlands peoples of the late nineteenth and early twentieth centuries. The Rahr collection is given to the college because the donor's son, Guido R. Rahr Jr. (1928–2005), is a member of the Dartmouth Class of 1951 and a generous lifelong college benefactor. Gregory C. Schwarz, assistant curator and associate registrar (1974–88), catalogues the collection and works on the 1987 exhibition and publication entitled *Patterns of Life, Patterns of Art: The Rahr Collection of Native American Art*.

1987
Barbara Joan Wellington Wells of Barre, Vermont, gives the college a collection of 188 Native American dolls. The dolls were commissioned by her father, J. W. "Duke" Wellington (1896–1987), between 1943 and 1960. Wellington worked for the Bureau of Indian Affairs in various capacities in Montana, Nevada, and North Dakota. Through his agency contacts, Wellington wrote letters to about forty-five officials to commission the dolls, all wearing tradition clothing, for his daughter's collection. Many of the letters indicate that the agency officials sought out tribal elders who were still working with traditional materials and who had the skills and knowledge to complete this task. This collection provides a unique perspective upon Native artists working during the mid-twentieth century.[16]

1989
Between 1989 and 2002, longtime museum supporter and donor Virginia Williamson, Class of 1962W, donates three works of contemporary Native American art: *Coyote Woman in the City*, by Harry Fonseca; *Afternoon Rest*, by Allan C. Houser; and a storage jar by Lonnie Vigil.

1990
The Native American Graves Protection and Repatriation Act (NAGPRA) is signed into law. In response, Kellen G. Haak, Hood Museum of Art NAGPRA coordinator (and registrar and collections manager from 1990 to 2009), inventories, reviews and reports on the college's holdings of Native American art to over five hundred federally recognized tribes (see the report that follows this chronology).

1993
Varujan Boghosian, studio art professor from 1968 to 1996 and presently professor emeritus, has given the museum over 139 objects, including a collection of art by artists-in-residence at Dartmouth. In 1993, Boghosian donates three works by Fritz Scholder: the painting *Dancers and Dogs* and two prints, *Fritz Scholder: The Dartmouth Portraits* and *Untitled (Screaming Indian).*

1995
Timothy Rub, museum director from 1991 to 2000, had a strong interest in acquiring contemporary prints for the collection. In 1995, he purchased nine prints by James Lavadour from the Rutgers Center for Innovative Print and Paper, New Brunswick, New Jersey. Lavadour (Walla Walla) is a master printmaker and the cofounder of the Crow's Shadow Institute of the Arts, Umatilla Reservation.[17]

1998
The museum and the Dartmouth community receive several gifts from the Estate of Michael A. Dorris (1945–1997). Dorris was the founder of Dartmouth College's Native American Studies Program in 1972 and served as its chair from 1972 to 1984. Tragically, Dorris passed away in April 1997, on the eve of the twenty-fifth anniversary of the program. A year after Dorris's death, his widow, the writer

Louise Erdrich, Class of 1976, holds a giveaway ceremony at the college. During the ceremony, the college is given a Modoc beaded ceremonial vest, made and worn by Dorris's paternal great-grandmother, and a headdress, made by Erdrich and presented to Dorris at his Modoc Naming Ceremony.[18]

2001

Susan R. Malloy donates a collection of seven Pueblo pots by Steven Lucas, Nona Naha, Nampeyo, and Maria Martinez in memory of her husband, Edwin A. Malloy (1926–1998), Class of 1983P. Their son, Timon J. Malloy, is a member of the Class of 1983.

2002–8

Barbara Thompson, curator of African, Oceanic, and Native American collections from 2002 to 2008, was responsible for the acquisition of about 260 works of Native American art. Thompson worked with Mark Lansburgh, Class of 1949, to bring his collection of Plains ledger drawing to Dartmouth; it was acquired through a partial gift and partial purchase in 2007. Thompson built the museum's collection of contemporary Native American photography, new media, and sculpture, in addition to building a collection of twenty-six contemporary Wabanaki baskets. Mary Alice Kean Raynolds and David R. W. Raynolds, Class of 1949, donated funds for the purchase of the important sculpture *Peaceful Serenity* by Allan C. Houser, which is located near the Sherman House on campus. Donations by Frieda and Prentiss Carnell, Class of 1956; Ann H. and Harte C. Crow; Putnam W. Blodgett, Class of 1953, Tuck 1961; Monroe Denton Jr., Class of 1968; and Joel M. Halpern are made during this time. (See the introduction to the collection by Karen Miller in this volume for a more complete history of this phase of acquisitions.)

2008–10

In 2008, guest curators George Horse Capture, Joe Horse Capture, and Joseph Sanchez visit the museum to begin planning for the exhibition *Native American Art at Dartmouth*. At this time, through generous donations from museum supporters, the museum purchases important objects from the Northwest Coast, Woodlands, Plains, Plateau, and Southwest regions. Works are also donated by Stephen A. Lister, Class of 1963; Harry T. Lewis, Class of 1955, Tuck 1956; Marsha J. and Joel D. Ash, Class of 1956, Thayer 1958; Robert G. Sands, Class of 1959, Tuck 1960; Charles Nearburg, Class of 1972; and Kendal Currier. (See the introduction to the collection by Karen Miller in this volume for a more complete history of this phase of acquisitions.)

NOTES

1. W. Wedgwood Bowen, *A Pioneer Museum in the Wilderness* (Hanover, N.H.: Dartmouth College Museum, 1958), 6.
2. Ibid., 11.
3. T. Morgan, *A Shovel of Stars: The Making of the American West, 1800 to the Present* (New York: Touchstone, 1995), 105.
4. Logan Museum of Anthropology, Beloit College, available at http://www.beloit.edu/logan/collections/collectors/.
5. *Senate Report No. 708*, 46th Congress, 2nd Session Serial, 1899, p. 159.
6. *Biographies of Croydon, Sullivan County, New Hampshire* (Chicago: The Lewis Publishing Co., 1918).
7. Bowen, *A Pioneer Museum in the Wilderness,* 40.
8. See also Barbara MacAdam, *Marks of Distinction: Two Hundred Years of American Drawings and Watercolors from the Hood Museum of Art* (Hanover, N.H.: Hood Museum of Art, Dartmouth College, 2005), 44.
9. See www.whitemountainart.com, 2009.
10. Nebraska State Historical Society, Papers of Charles Akers Johnson (RG1652.AM).
11. See http://www.charlessheldon.org/.
12. Center for Native American Art at the Portland Art Museum: http://www.tfaoi.com/newsm1/n1m206.htm.
13. See ML-30, The Papers of Corey Ford in the Dartmouth College Library, January 1983.
14. E. R. Williamson, J. D. Perley, M. F. Burnham (editors), *Aboriginally Yours, Chief Henry Red Eagle* (Greenville, Maine: Moosehead Communications, 1997), xvii–xviii.
15. *Treasures of the Hood Museum of Art* (Hanover, N.H.: Trustees of Dartmouth College, 1985), 18–19
16. See Montana State University Libraries, Collection 2029, J. W. "Duke" Wellington Papers.
17. See Crow's Shadow Institute of Art, http://www.crowsshadow.org/artists/show/7.
18. The Native American Studies Program, Dartmouth College, Michael Dorris, http://www.dartmouth.edu/~nas/history/Dorris.html.

The Hood Museum of Art's Compliance with the Native American Graves Protection and Repatriation Act (NAGPRA)

Kellen G. Haak

On November 16, 1990, the Native American Graves Protection and Repatriation Act (NAGPRA) was signed into law. The act provides a legal framework within which federally recognized Indian tribes and Native Hawaiian organizations can request the return, from federal agencies, museums, and other collection-holding organizations that have received federal funds, of ancestral human remains and certain cultural items—funerary objects, sacred objects, and objects of cultural patrimony. Once a tribe has initiated a request to repatriate, there is a formal process of consultation, a review of the object's history, and a clear determination of cultural affiliation. Finally, the institution that has custody of the object or remains works with the Nation Park Service to publish a "Notice of Intent to Repatriate" in the Federal Register. If the claim is not contested for thirty days after the notice is published, the repatriation can go forward. For more information about this federal law, see the National Park Service NAGPRA Program website at http://www.nps.gov/nagpra/.

As stipulated in the law, collection-holding institutions were required to meet two reporting deadlines. In 1993, in full compliance with NAGPRA, the Hood Museum of Art at Dartmouth College sent written summaries of culturally affiliated holdings to more than five hundred federally recognized tribes. In 1995, an inventory of human remains and associated funerary objects was completed, and in 1996 the associated "Notices of Intent to Repatriate" were published in the Federal Register. Between 1990 and 2009, Kellen G. Haak, as collections manager and registrar, also served as the NAGPRA coordinator for the museum and facilitated five repatriations. Summaries of those repatriations follow are described below.

1994: Hui Malama I Na Kupuna 'O Hawai'i Nei

In 1994 the Hood Museum of Art began consultations with Native Hawaiian organizations as part of the process of preparing inventories of human remains for the 1995 NAGPRA deadline. In December 1994, Hui Malama I Na Kupuna 'O Hawai'i Nei (Hui Malama) submitted a formal request for the repatriation of three partial sets of ancestral human remains identified as being Native Hawaiian in origin. On June 26, 1995, three members of Hui Malama came to the museum and were provided with a private space in which they could ceremonially prepare the remains for their return to Hawaii. The delegation expressed their gratitude for the concern expressed for their cultural ways in a thank-you letter: "Hui Malama I Na Kupuna 'O Hawai'i Nei believes that in restoring that which belongs to Hawai'i, we restore the mana [energy] of this very special place. It is the strengthening of mana that helps restore life to Hawai'i and its native people, and enhances our view towards the future." All of the Hawaiian remains were collected by Frederick Chaffee around the turn of the century, possibly at Kaena Point, on the island of Oahu. In 1939, Chaffee's son Robert, professor of biology and curator of the Dartmouth College Museum, gave the remains to the museum. See http://www.nps.gov/history/nagpra/fed_notices/nagpradir/nic0032.html.

1995: Pueblo of Zuni

In 1995, the governor of the Pueblo of Zuni requested the repatriation of two items identified by the elders and religious leaders of Zuni Pueblo as both "sacred objects" and "objects of cultural patrimony" under NAGPRA (25 U.S.C. 3001). The two prayer sticks in question had been listed in the summary that was sent to the Zuni in 1993. The prayer sticks were further identified as having been used in ceremonial practices associated with the Ahayu:da or Twin Gods in Zuni cultural ideology. They were originally removed from their shrine on the Zuni reservation in 1903 and collected in situ by Frank C. and Clara G. Churchill at Zuni Pueblo; they were subsequently donated to Dartmouth College in 1946.

The Hood Museum of Art acknowledged the importance of the two prayer sticks to the ongoing religious practices of the Zuni, and noted that both were well documented as being culturally affiliated with the Zuni. The two prayer sticks were repatriated back to the Pueblo of Zuni on August 22, 1995. See http://www.nps.gov/nagpra/fed_notices/nagpradir/nir0020.htm.

1996: Abenaki Nation of Missisquoi

Pursuant to Section 5 of the law, the NAGPRA, the repatriation coordinator was contacted by the Missisquois Band of the Abenaki Nation on August 2, 1995, about a set of ancestral human remains in the custody of the Hood Museum of Art. The remains in question were discovered on June 10, 1945, in Tuftonboro, New Hampshire, where they had washed out of a bank on the shore of Lake Winnipesaukee. They were recovered by the New Hampshire State Police and brought to Dartmouth College for forensic examination by doctors at the medical school and anthropologists at the Dartmouth College Museum. The remains were subsequently identified as those of a ten- to twelve-year-old Native American child that had been interred for a long period of time. The remains were donated to the Dartmouth College Museum (now Hood Museum of Art), where they were held for the next fifty years.

Although, under NAGPRA, these remains were technically considered to be "culturally unidentifiable" because the Abenaki are not a federally recognized tribe, the NAGPRA Review Committee was charged with determining the final disposition of "unidentifiable" remains. The Hood's NAGPRA coordinator offered to pursue the matter with the committee, if the Abenaki were interested in doing so. The offer was embraced and the consultation process began.

The NAGPRA Review Committee was petitioned on September 27, 1995, for a recommendation on the disposition of the remains in question. The request was considered at the committee's October meeting, and on December 11, 1995, the departmental consulting archaeologist of the National Park Service wrote with the committee's recommendations and a protocol for proceeding with the repatriation process. The committee asked that the Abenaki's request to repatriate be publicized in local newspapers with circulation in both New Hampshire and Vermont. Then, if no other claimants came forward after a period of thirty days, a "Notice of Inventory Completion" could be created and published in the Federal Register for thirty days.

Classified legal notices and/or feature articles describing the repatriation request were published between January 31 and March 24, 1996. Since no counterclaims were received for thirty days after the last publication, the Hood's NAGPRA coordinator submitted a detailed progress report and a draft "Notice of Inventory Completion" to the park service consulting archaeologist on April 23, 1996. On May 17, 1996, the notice was published in the Federal Register and ran its thirty days without comment or dispute.

On September 9, 1996, delegates of the Abenaki Nation of Missisquois took possession of the remains. With the permission of the current landowner, the remains were interred near the original location of their burial on the shore of Lake Winnipesaukee. See http://www.nps.gov/nagpra/fed_notices/nagpradir/nic0075.html.

2002: Deisheetaan Clan, Kootznoowoo Tribe of Tlingit Indians

In 1995 the Hood Museum of Art was awarded a National Park Service NAGPRA Grant to bring a delegation of Tlingit Indians from various Native communities in southeastern Alaska to the Hood and to Harvard's Peabody Museum. During the site visit, Matthew J. Fred Sr., the delegate representing the Kootznoowoo tribe of Angoon, Alaska, identified a Chilkat tunic in the Hood's collection as belonging to the Deisheetan Clan. The pre-1882 tunic was created when a Chilkat robe was cut into four panels that were then sewn into two tunics. Mr. Fred related the story of how two brothers, Kanaalku and Kichnaalx, of the Yeil Hit (Raven House) of the Deisheetaan Clan inherited a Chilkat robe that, in order to allow both to use it, was cut up and made into the two tunics.

On December 31, 1997, the Kootznoowoo Cultural and Education Foundation (KCEF) submitted a formal request on behalf of the Deisheetaan Clan for the repatriation of the tunic. Subsequently, as part of the consultation process, the Hood's director wrote a letter requesting further clarification on a number of points related to the evidence being offered in support of the request to repatriate. Before a response to this letter was completed, the KCEF lost its funding, and the request lay dormant until February 21, 2002, when the cultural resource specialist for the Central Council of Tlingit and Haida Indian Tribes of Juneau, Alaska, responded to the questions and explained that the council had been authorized by the KCEF to pursue the repatriation on their behalf.

Following an internal review of the evidence as presented by the council, the acquisitions committee of the Hood Museum of Art authorized the repatriation of the tunic on June 12, 2002. A draft "Notice of Intent to Repatriate" was written by the Hood's NAGPRA coordinator and submitted to the National Park Service on June 20, 2002. The notice was published in the Federal Register on August 29, 2002, and ran through September 30 without comment or dispute.

The Central Council of Tlingit and Haida Indian Tribes of Juneau, Alaska, lacking funds to retrieve the tunic, asked that the Hood's NAGPRA coordinator hand-carry the tunic to Angoon so that it could be presented to the Deisheetaan Clan on the occasion of a *Koo.èex'* (memorial potlatch) for Matthew J. Fred Sr. (1924–1999). The clan was particularly interested in having this old and important ceremonial object on hand for the potlatch, because Mr. Fred was an important clan leader and had been instrumental in starting the consultation process that ultimately led to the successful repatriation of the tunic.

The tunic was returned to Deisheetaan Clan leaders on November 16, 2002, about an hour before the ceremony began. It was immediately returned to its ceremonial function and placed on a table used for the formal display of the clan's *at.óow,* or regalia. One of the most striking aspects of the following thirty-hour potlatch was the presentation and donning of the regalia by the deceased's clan. During this part of the ceremony, Matthew Fred's niece, a member of both his clan and his house, was dressed in the tunic that her uncle had helped to repatriate. See http://www.nps.gov/nagpra/fed_notices/nagpradir/nir0227.html.

2003: Seneca Nation of Indians

A cultural item in the Hood Museum of Art's 1993 summary was described as a ball-headed wooden war club with a carved and painted diamond pattern on the handle. The club was subsequently identified by the Seneca Nation of New York and the Tonowanda Band of

Seneca Indians as an unassociated funerary object, as defined under NAGPRA, and was requested for repatriation. The Seneca based their claim of cultural affiliation on an analysis of the club's stylistic patterns, which are consistent with other known Seneca war clubs. They also provided evidence that placing such an item with an individual's remains was a common practice historically. The Seneca further explained that clubs of this type were highly respected individual objects of power, and as such, they would have been placed in close proximity to their owner's remains. The club was donated to Dartmouth College in 1937 by Charles W. Bethune, Dartmouth Class of 1940 and a resident of Buffalo, New York.

The object was repatriated on December 3, 2003, to the Haudenosaunee Standing Committee on Burial Rules and Regulations on behalf of the Seneca Nation of New York and the Tonowanda Band of Seneca Indians of New York. See http://www.nps.gov/nagpra/fed_notices/nagpradir/nir0228.html.

In addition to the repatriations described above, the Hood Museum of Art's participation in NAGPRA also involved a number of site visits by tribal delegations interested in viewing and consulting on objects and remains in the museum's collection.

Formal Consultations

Hopi Tribal Council, Arizona, April 7, 1995. Also visited the Peabody Museum at Harvard and the American Museum of Natural History as part of a collaborative National Park Service NAGPRA grant awarded to Harvard.

Central Council of Tlingit and Haida Indian Tribes of Alaska, Juneau, Alaska, May 22, 1995. Also visited the Peabody Museum at Harvard as part of a collaborative National Park Service NAGPRA Grant awarded to Dartmouth.

Hui Malama I Na Kupuna 'O Hawai'i Nei, June 26, 1995. This consultation was conducted as part of the site visit associated with the repatriation of three sets of ancestral human remains (see above).

Winnebago Tribe of Nebraska, Winnebago, Nebraska, July 12, 1999.

Standing Rock Sioux Tribe, Fort Peck, Montana, March 15, 2002.

Seneca Nation of Indians, Salamanca, New York, December 3, 2003. This consultation was conducted as part of the site visit associated with the repatriation of an unassociated funerary object (see above).

Selected Bibliography

Exhibition Catalogues

All Roads Are Good: Native Voices on Life and Culture. Washington, D.C.: Smithsonian Institution Press, in association with the National Museum of the American Indian, 1994.

American Kaleidoscope: Themes and Perspectives in Recent Art. Washington, D.C.: National Museum of American Art, Smithsonian Institution, 1996.

Art of the Great Lakes Indians. Flint, Mich.: Flint Institute of Arts, 1973.

The Decade Show: Frameworks of Identity in the 1980s. New York: MoCHA, The New Museum, The Studio Museum of Harlem, 1990.

Dimensions of Native America: The Contact Zone. Tallahassee: Museum of Fine Arts, Florida State University, 1998.

Documents Northwest: The PONCHO Series; Crossed Cultures. Seattle: Seattle Art Museum, 1989.

Gifts of the Spirit: Works by Nineteenth Century and Contemporary Native American Artists. Salem, Mass.: Peabody Essex Museum, 1996.

Image and Self in Contemporary Native American Photoart. Hanover, N.H.: Hood Museum of Art, Dartmouth College, 1995.

Our Land/Ourselves: American Indian Contemporary Artists. Albany: University Art Gallery, SUNY Albany, 1990.

Patterns of Life, Patterns of Art: The Rahr Collection of Native American Art. Hanover, N.H.: Hood Museum of Art, Dartmouth College, 1987.

Picturing Change: The Impact of Ledger Drawing on Native American Art. Hanover, N.H.: Hood Museum of Art, Dartmouth College, 2004.

Shared Visions: Native American Painters and Sculptors in the Twentieth Century. Phoenix: The Heard Museum, 1991.

Spirit of the Basket Tree: Wabanaki Ash Splint Baskets from Maine. Hanover, N.H.: Hood Museum of Art, Dartmouth College, 2008.

Thin Ice: Inuit Traditions within a Changing Environment. Hanover, N.H.: Hood Museum of Art, Dartmouth College, 2007.

Treasures of the Hood Museum of Art, Dartmouth College. Hanover, N.H.: Hood Museum of Art, Dartmouth College, 1985.

Tribal Identity: An Installation by James Luna. Hanover, N.H.: Hood Museum of Art, Dartmouth College, 1995.

Will/Power: New Works by Papo Colo, Jimmie Durham, David Hammons, Hachivi Edgar Heap of Birds, Adrian Piper, Amenah Brenda, Lynn Robinson. Columbus: Wexner Center for the Arts, The Ohio State University, 1993.

Secondary Sources

Abbott, Lawrence, ed. *I Stand in the Center of the Good: Interviews with Contemporary Native American Artists.* Lincoln: University of Nebraska Press, 1994.

Abel-Vidor, Suzanne, Dot Brovarney, and Susan Billy. *Remember Your Relations: The Elsie Allen Baskets, Family and Friends.* Ukiah, Cal.: Grace Hudson Museum, 1996.

Adams, David Wallace. *Education for Extinction: American Indians and the Boarding School Experience, 1875–1928.* Lawrence: University Press of Kansas, 1995.

Anthes, Bill. "Postscript: Making Modern Native American Artists." In *Native Moderns: American Indian Painting, 1940–1960.* Durham: Duke University Press, 2006.

Archambault, JoAllyn. *Plains Indian Art: Continuity and Change.* Washington, D.C.: National Museum of Natural History, Smithsonian Institution, 1989.

Archuleta, Margaret, and Rennard Strickland. *Shared Visions: Native American Painters and Sculptors in the Twentieth Century.* Phoenix: The Heard Museum, 1991.

Axtell, James. *The European and the Indian: Essays in the Ethnohistory of Colonial North America.* New York: Oxford University Press, 1981.

Berkhofer, Robert F. Jr. *The White Man's Indian: Images of the American Indian from Columbus to the Present.* New York: Vintage, 1978.

Berlo, Janet C. "Nineteenth-Century Plains Indian Drawings." *The Magazine Antiques* 150 (1971): 686–95.

———. *Plains Indian Drawings, 1865–1935: Pages from Visual History.* New York: Harry N. Abrams, 1996.

Berlo, Janet C., ed. *The Early Years of Native American Art History.* Seattle: University of Washington Press, 1992.

Berlo, Janet C., and Ruth B. Phillips. *Native North American Art.* Oxford: Oxford University Press, 1998.

Biron, Gerry, and Jo-Anne Biron. *Made of Thunder, Made of Glass: American Indian Beadwork of the Northeast.* Published by Gerry Biron, 2006.

Bowen, W. Wedgewood. *A Pioneer in the Wilderness.* Hanover, N.H.: Dartmouth College Museum, 1958.

Brasser, Ted J. *"Bo'jou, Neejee!": Profiles of Canadian Indian Art.* Ottawa: National Museum of Man, 1976.

———. "By the Power of their Dreams." In *The Spirit Sings: Artistic Traditions of Canada's First Peoples*, ed. Julia D. Harrison, 93–131. Toronto: McClelland and Stewart, 1987.

Breeskin, Adelyn D. *Two American Painters: Fritz Scholder and T. C. Cannon.* Washington, D.C.: Smithsonian Institution Press, 1972.

Brooks, Joanna, ed. *The Collected Writings of Samson Occom, Mohegan: Leadership and Literature in Eighteenth-Century Native America*. New York: Oxford University Press, 2006.

Burke, Christina E. "Wani Yetu Wowapi: An Introduction to Lakota Winter Counts." In *Year the Stars Fell: Lakota Winter Counts at the Smithsonian,* ed. Candace S. Greene and Russell Thornton, 1–11. Washington, D.C.: Smithsonian National Museum of Natural History, Smithsonian National Museum of the American Indian, in association with the University of Nebraska Press, 2007.

Calloway, Colin G. *The Indian History of an American Institution: Native Americans and Dartmouth*. Hanover, N.H.: University Press of New England, 2010.

Chancey, Jill R., ed. *By Native Hands: Woven Treasures from the Lauren Rogers Museum of Art*. Laurel, Missouri: Lauren Rogers Museum of Art, 2005.

Clifford, James. *The Predicament of Culture: Twentieth Century Ethnography, Literature, and Art.* Cambridge, Mass.: Harvard University Press, 1988.

Conn, Richard. *Native American Art in the Denver Art Museum*. Seattle: University of Washington Press, 1979.

Daniell, Jere R. "Eleazar Wheelock and the Dartmouth College Charter." *Historical New Hampshire* 24 (Winter 1969): 3–44.

Dauenhauer, Nora Marks, Richard Dauenhauer, and Lydia T. Black, eds. *Anóoshi Lingít Aaní Ká: Russians in Tlingit America*. Seattle: University of Washington Press, 2008.

De Laguna, Frederica. *Under Mount Saint Elias: The History and Culture of the Yakutat Tlingit*. Washington, D.C.: Smithsonian Institution Press, 1972.

Deloria, Vine Jr. *God Is Red: A Native View of Religion.* Golden, Colo.: Fulcrum Publishing, 1992.

Donnelley, Robert G. *Transforming Images: The Art of Silver Horn and His Successors.* Chicago: David and Alfred Smart Museum of Art, in association with the University of Chicago Press, 2000.

Dorris, Michael. *The Broken Cord.* New York: Harper and Row, 1989.

Dubin, Margaret D. "Collecting Native America: The Culture of An Art World." Ph.D. dissertation, University of California, Berkeley, 1998.

Dunn, Dorothy. *American Indian Painting of the Southwest and Plains Area.* Albuquerque: University of New Mexico Press, 1968.

———. *1877: Plains Indian Sketch Books of Zo-Tom and Howling Wolf.* Flagstaff: Northland Press, 1969.

Dye, David H. "Art, Ritual, and Chiefly Warfare in the Mississippian." In *Hero, Hawk, and Open Hand: American Indian Art of the Ancient Midwest and South,* ed. Richard F. Townsend, 191–205. Chicago: Art Institute of Chicago, in association with Yale University Press, 2004.

Ewing, Douglas. *Pleasing the Spirits: A Catalogue of a Collection of American Indian Art*. New York: Ghylen Press, 1982.

Fair, Susan W. *Alaska Native Art: Tradition, Innovation, Continuity.* Fairbanks: University of Alaska Press, 2006.

Ferguson, Russell, et al., eds. *Discourses: Conversations in Postmodern Art and Culture.* Cambridge, Mass.: MIT Press, 1990.

———. *Out There: Marginalization and Contemporary Cultures.* New York: The New Museum of Contemporary Art, in association with MIT Press, 1990.

Foster, Michael K., and William Cowan, eds. *In Search of New England's Native Past: Selected Essays by Gordon M. Day*. Amherst: University of Massachusetts Press, 1998.

Frascina, Francis, and Jonathan Harris, eds. *Art in Modern Culture: An Anthology of Critical Texts.* New York: Harper Collins, 1992.

Frederick, Joan. *T. C. Cannon: He Stood in the Sun.* Flagstaff: Northland Publishing, 1995.

Graburn, Nelson H. H., ed. *Ethnic and Tourist Arts: Cultural Expressions from the Fourth World.* Berkeley: University of California Press, 1976.

Hall, Judy, Leslie Tepper, and Judy Thompson. *Threads of the Land: Clothing Traditions from Three Indigenous Cultures.* Hull, Quebec: Canadian Museum of Civilization, 1994.

Harris, Moira F. *Between Two Cultures: Kiowa Art from Fort Marion.* St. Paul: Pogo Press, 1989.

Her Many Horses, Emil. "Afterward: Tasunka Ota Win Waniyetu Wowapi (Her Many Horses Winter Count)." In *Year the Stars Fell: Lakota Winter Counts at the Smithsonian*, ed. Candace S. Green and Russell Thornton, 312–22. Washington, D.C.: Smithsonian National Museum of Natural History, Smithsonian National Museum of the American Indian, in association with the University of Nebraska Press, 2007.

Highwater, Jamake. *The Sweet Grass Lives On: Fifty Contemporary North American Indian Artists.* New York: Lippincott and Crowell, 1980.

———. *The Primal Mind: Vision and Reality in Indian America.* New York: Meridian, 1981.

Hill, Tom, and Richard W. Hill Sr., eds. *Creation's Journey: Native American Identity and Belief.* Washington, D.C.: Smithsonian Institution Press, in association with the National Museum of the American Indian, 1994.

Holmes, Leilani. "Heart Knowledge, Blood Memory, and the Voice of the Land: Implications of Research among Hawaiian Elders." In *Indigenous Knowledges in Global Contexts: Multiple Readings of Our World.* Sefa Dei, Hall, Rosenberg, OISE/UT, University of Toronto, 2000.

Hudson, Charles. *The Southeastern Indians.* Knoxville: University of Tennessee Press, 1976.

Karp, Ivan, and Steven D. Lavine, eds. *Exhibiting Cultures: The Poetics and Politics of Museum Display.* Washington, D.C.: Smithsonian Institution Press, 1991.

Karp, Ivan, Christine Mullen Kreamer, and Steven D. Lavine, eds. *Museums and Communities: The Politics of Public Culture.* Washington, D.C.: Smithsonian Institution Press, 1992.

Katz, Jane B., ed. *This Song Remembers: Self-Portraits of Native American in the Arts.* Boston: Houghton Mifflin, 1980.

Kershner, Charles Jay. "Eleazar Is Outdone." *Dartmouth Alumni Magazine* 63 (Oct. 1970): 32.

King, Jonathan. *Thunderbird and Lightning: Indian Life in Northeastern North America*. London: Trustees of the British Museum by British Museum Publications, 1982.

Lankford, George E. "World on a String: Some Cosmological Components of the Southeastern Ceremonial Complex." In *Hero, Hawk, and Open Hand: American Indian Art of the Ancient Midwest and South*, ed. Richard F. Townsend, 206–17. Chicago: Art Institute of Chicago, in association with Yale University Press, 2004.

Lippard, Lucy. *Mixed Blessings.* New York: Pantheon, 1990.

———. *Overlay: Contemporary Art and the Art of Prehistory.* New York: The New Press, 1995.

———. *The Lure of the Local: Senses of Place in a Multicentered Society.* New York: The New Press, 1997.

Love, W. DeLoss. *Samson Occom and the Christian Indians of New England* (1899). Reprint. Syracuse: Syracuse University Press, 2000.

Lowie, Robert H. *Crow Indian Art.* Anthropological Papers of the American Museum of Natural History 21. New York: American Museum Press, 1924.

Marcus, George, and Fred Myers, eds. *The Traffic in Culture: Refiguring Art and Anthropology.* Berkeley: University of California Press, 1995.

McEvilley, Thomas. *Art and Otherness: Crisis in Cultural Identity.* Kingston, N.Y.: McPherson and Company, 1992.

Maurer, Evan. *Visions of the People: A Pictorial History of Plains Indian Life*. Minneapolis: Minneapolis Institute of Art, 1992.

McCallum, James Dow, ed. *The Letters of Eleazar Wheelock's Indians*. Hanover, N.H.: Dartmouth College Publications, 1932.

McMaster, Gerald, ed. *Reservation X: The Power of Place in Aboriginal Contemporary Art.* Seattle: University of Washington Press, in association with the Canadian Museum of Civilization, 1998.

McNutt, Jennifer Complo. "Contemporary Native Art Offers Two Levels of Experience." *Native Peoples* 13, no. 1 (1999): 18–20.

Miller, Miles R. "*This Place Called Home:* A Columbia Plateau Arts & Culture Exhibit & Study Guide." Master's thesis, University of Washington, 2008.

Murray, Laura J., ed. *To Do Good to My Indian Brethren: The Writings of Joseph Johnson, 1751–1776*. Amherst: University of Massachusetts Press, 1998.

Paul, Frances. *Spruce Root Basketry of the Alaska Tlingit*. 2nd ed. Sitka: Sheldon Jackson Museum, 1991.

Petersen, Karen Daniels. *Plains Indian Art from Fort Marion.* Norman: University of Oklahoma Press, 1971.

———. *American Pictographic Images: Historical Works on Paper by the Plains Indians.* New York: Alexander Gallery, 1988.

Peyer, Bernd. "The Betrayal of Samson Occom." *Dartmouth Alumni Magazine* 91 (Nov. 1998).

Phillips, Ruth B. *Patterns of Power: The Jasper Grant Collection and Great Lakes Indian Art of the Early Nineteenth Century*. Kleinburg, Ontario: McMichael Canadian Collection, 1984.

———. "Northern Woodlands" and "Like a Star I Shine: Northern Woodlands Artistic Traditions." In *The Spirit Sings: Artistic Traditions of Canada's First Peoples: A Catalogue of the Exhibition*, ed. Julia D. Harrison. Toronto: McClelland and Stewart, 1987.

———. "Dreams and Designs: Iconographic Problems in Great Lakes Twined Bags." In *Great Lakes Indian Art*, ed. David W. Penney, 52–69. Detroit: Wayne State University Press, 1989.

———. *Trading Identities: The Souvenir in Native North American Art from the Northeast, 1700–1900*. Seattle: University of Washington Press, 1998.

Pratt, Richard Henry. *Battlefield and Classroom: Four Decades with the American Indian, 1867–1904*. New Haven: Yale University Press, 1964.

Ray, Dorothy Jean. *A Legacy of Arctic Art.* Toronto: Douglas and MacIntyre, 1996.

———. *Eskimo Masks: Art and Ceremony.* Seattle: University of Washington Press, 1967.

Reilly, F. Kent III. "People of Earth, People of Sky: Visualizing the Sacred in Native American Art of the Mississippian Period." In *Hero, Hawk, and Open Hand: American Indian Art of the Ancient Midwest and South*, ed. Richard F. Townsend, 124–37. Chicago: Art Institute of Chicago, in association with Yale University Press, 2004.

Rushing, W. Jackson III. *Allan Houser: An American Master (Chiricahua Apache, 1914–1994).* New York: Harry N. Abrams, 2004.

———. *Native American Art and the New York Avant-Garde: A History of Cultural Primitivism.* Austin: University of Texas Press, 1995.

Szabo, Joyce M. *Howling Wolf and the History of Ledger Art.* Albuquerque: University of New Mexico Press, 1994.

———. "Chief Killer and a New Reality: Narration and Description in Fort Marion Art." *American Indian Art Magazine* 19 (Spring 1994): 50–57.

Thompson, Barbara. "Collecting 'Africa' at the Hood Museum of Art, Dartmouth College." *Collections: A Journal for Museum and Archives Professionals* 3, no. 4; 4, no. 1 (Spring 2008).

Thompson, Judy. *From the Land: Two Hundred Years of Dene Clothing.* Hull, Quebec: Canadian Museum of Civilization, 1994.

Thornton, Russell. "A Rosebud Reservation Winter Count, Circa 1751–1752 to 1886–1887." *Ethnohistory* 49, no. 4 (2002).

Townsend, Richard F., ed. *Hero, Hawk, and Open Hand: American Indian Art of the Ancient Midwest and South*. Chicago: Art Institute of Chicago, in association with Yale University Press, 2004.

Vickers, Scott B. *Native American Identities: From Stereotype to Archetype in Art and Literature.* Albuquerque: University of New Mexico Press, 1998.

Vigorelli, Leonardo. *Gli Oggetti Indiani Raccolti Da G. Constantino Beltrami*. Bergamo, Italy: Civico Museo E. Caffi, 1987.

Vincent, Gilbert, et al. *Art of the North American Indians: The Thaw Collection*. Cooperstown: New York State Historical Association, in association with the University of Washington Press, 2000.

Wade, Edwin L., ed. *The Arts of the North American Indian: Native Traditions in Evolution.* New York: Hudson Hills Press, in association with Philbrook Art Center, 1986.

Wade, Mason, ed. *The Journals of Francis Parkman*. New York: Harper and Bros., 1947.

Walker, Deward E. Jr., and Virginia Beavert. *"T'at'aliya": The Way It Was (Anaku Iwacha Yakima Indian Legends).* The Consortium of Johnson O'Malley Committees, Region IV, State of Washington, 1974.

Wallo, William, and John Pickard. *T. C. Native American: A New View of the West.* Oklahoma City: Persimmon Hill Publication, 1990.

West, W. Richard. *The Changing Presentation of the American Indian: Museums and Native Cultures*. Seattle: University of Washington Press, 1999.

Wildschut, William, and John Ewers. *Crow Indian Beadwork: A Descriptive and Historical Study*. New York: Museum of the American Indian, Heye Foundation, 1959.

Contributors

Leah Bowe, Seminole, has been part of the curatorial research staff at several American museums, including the Burke Museum of Natural History and Culture in Seattle and the Art Institute of Chicago. She currently lives and teaches in Saint Paul, Minnesota.

Sherry Brydon, independent scholar, is the former curator of the Eugene and Clare Thaw Collection of American Indian Art, Fenimore Art Museum, New York State Historical Association, Cooperstown, New York.

Colin G. Calloway is John Kimball Jr. 1943 Professor of History and Professor of Native American Studies at Dartmouth College. He received his PhD from the University of Leeds in England in 1978. His books include *The Indian History of an American Institution: Native Americans and Dartmouth* (2010); *White People, Indians, and Highlanders: Tribal Peoples and Colonial Encounters in Scotland and America* (2008); *The Shawnees and the War for America* (2007); *The Scratch of a Pen: 1763 and the Transformation of North America* (2007); *One Vast Winter Count: The Native American West before Lewis and Clark* (2003); *First Peoples: A Documentary Survey of American Indian History* (1999); *and New Worlds for All: Indians, Europeans, and the Remaking of Early America* (1997).

George P. Horse Capture Sr., A'aninin (Gros Ventre), is an anthropologist/writer/lecturer/curator who served as assistant professor of American Indian studies at Montana State University. He was hired as the first curator of the Plains Indian Museum at the Buffalo Bill Historical Center in Cody, Wyoming. At the National Museum of the American Indian, beginning in 1993, he was active in the establishment of the museum, retiring in 2005 as the senior counselor to the director.

Joe D. Horse Capture, A'aninin (Gros Ventre), is associate curator of Native American art at the Minneapolis Institute of Arts. His most recent exhibition, *From Our Ancestors: Art of the White Clay People*, chronicles the art and culture of his people as the first exhibition/catalogue to focus on the A'aninin. His publications include *Beauty, Honor and Tradition: The Legacy of Plains Indian Shirts* (2003), *Sacred Legacy: Edward S. Curtis and the American Indian* (contributor, 2000), and *Warrior Artists* (co-author, 2000). He has been a guest curator and consultant for numerous exhibitions and projects involving Native American art and culture.

Heather Igloliorte is an Inuk curator and art historian from the Nunatsiavut Territory of Labrador. She is currently a PhD candidate in Cultural Mediations at Carleton University in Ottawa, Ontario.

Karen S. Miller, assistant curator for special projects at the Hood Museum of Art at Dartmouth College, curated *Contemporary Native American Ledger Art: Drawing on Tradition,* August 14, 2010–January 16, 2011, and coordinated *Native American Ledger Drawings from the Hood Museum of Art: The Mark Lansburgh Collection*, October 2–December 19, 2010, as well as *Native American Art at Dartmouth: Highlights from the Hood Museum of Art*. Karen spent fifteen years in Alaska and wrote her MA thesis on the work of contemporary Inupiaq sculptor Susie Qimmiqsak Bevins.

Miles R. Miller, Yakama/Nez Perce, is an independent scholar and beadwork artist. He studied at the Institute of American Indian Art, Evergreen State College, and the University of Washington, and has been awarded several national and international collection management internships.

Jennifer Sapiel Neptune is a member of the Penobscot Nation. She is a brown ash and sweetgrass basketmaker, beadworker, and independent scholar. She is also an employee of the Maine Indian Basketmakers Alliance and has represented her community at indigenous basketmakers' gatherings across North America.

Joseph M. Sanchez, who is of Spanish, German, and Pueblo descent, was formerly deputy director and chief curator at the Institute of American Indian Arts in Santa Fe, New Mexico. Since 1970, he has worked with many artists and art professionals around the world, developing artist organizations, curating exhibitions, directing museums, and sharing his experiences with school children. These experiences are informed by a full cultural and ceremonial life and the guidance and wisdom of many elders.

Megan A. Smetzer, independent art historian, was born and raised in Fairbanks, Alaska. She earned her BA from Smith College, her MA from Williams College, and her PhD from the Department of Art History, Visual Art, and Theory at the University of British Columbia in Vancouver.

Joyce M. Szabo, Regents Professor of Art History at the University of New Mexico, was the William H. Morton Distinguished Fellow at Dartmouth in the fall of 2010. A specialist in Native American art and museum studies, Professor Szabo obtained her undergraduate degree in art and English from Wittenberg University, her MA in art history from Vanderbilt University, and her PhD in art history from the University of New Mexico. Her area of particular focus is Plains drawing and painting from the late nineteenth and early twentieth centuries. Her publications include *Imprisoned Art, Complex Patronage: Plains Drawings by Howling Wolf and Zotom at the Autry National Center* (2011); *Fort Marion Art: The Arthur and Shifra Silberman Collection* (2007); *and A Life in Balance: The Art of Conrad House* (2006).

Jenny Tone-Pah-Hote (Kiowa) is currently a postdoctoral research associate in American Studies at the University of North Carolina, where she is working on a book manuscript based on her dissertation titled "Envisioning Nationhood: Kiowa Expressive Culture, 1875–1939." Jenny received her PhD in American Indian and modern U.S. history from the University of Minnesota in 2009.